Dictionary of 19th Century Antiques

and later objets d'art

George Savage

Dictionary of 19th Century Antiques

and later objets d'art

G. P. PUTNAM'S SONS, NEW YORK

Published in the United States in 1979
by G. P. Putnam's Sons, New York

FOR YVONNE

Library of Congress Catalog Card Number: 78-53435
SBN: 399-12209-5

Printed in Great Britain

Contents

List of Colour Plates

Acknowledgements

I desire to record my gratitude to the several Museums and their Curators, to the Antique Collectors' Club and to Sotheby & Co., and Mr. A. J. B. Kiddell for the use of photographs, the source of which is acknowledged beneath the picture in question.

I am also grateful to the Wedgwood Museum for illustrations of Wedgwood wares, to Henry Sandon of the Dyson Perrins Museum for photographs of Royal Worcester, to the Pilkington Glass Museum of Saint Helens, and to all those of my friends who have contributed photographs of objects in their collections.

Among the friends who have helped me also in other directions, especially with research and the location of specimens, I owe so much to Mrs. Constance Chiswell and Miss Yvonne Willsmore that the old *cliché*, 'without whom this book could not have been completed', is in the present instance amply justified.

Many of the photographs and transparencies have been taken by my friends, Colin Stubbley and the late Wilfrid Walter, as well as by myself. I have included as many photographs as possible of objects of a kind which the collector of modest means will not find too difficult to acquire.

G.S.

Preface

Today, when antiques in good condition of periods earlier than the 19th century are becoming increasingly scarce, those of the period from 1800 onwards are enjoying unprecedented popularity. This is due to a variety of causes. Depreciation of currency and the search for objects of permanent value to offset it affects antiques of all periods, but it bears most heavily on those of the 19th century because they are still the most easily obtained. Antiques of all kinds have been aptly termed the 'new currency', and they are the only form of investment which has suffered no major setback since the Second World War. Some antiques have shown an appreciation in value amounting to thousands percent.

Until recently the 19th century was a neglected study. To some extent this was because it was so close to us in time that everyone assumed that they knew much more about it than they really did. Partly, the neglect was due to prevailing theories of art which not only damned excessive ornament, but even ornament at all. Minor Victorian clutter in antique shops tended to reinforce the judgement, which started with Gilbert and Sullivan in the 1870s—

> Art stopped short
> At the cultivated Court
> Of the Empress Josephine

Also responsible for the neglect was the complexity of the subject. The vast quantity of material available to the art historian, largely unsorted and unclassified, almost defied analysis. For the first time a period existed which had no real style of its own, and which had drawn its decorative elements from almost every period and place, as witness some of the popular contemporary books of ornament.

A few books have been written on well-defined aspects of the subject, where research material existed in, for example, the form of factory archives. The furniture of William Morris and the Arts and Crafts Movement, for instance, are sufficiently important to have already warranted close study. The Empire, Regency, and *art nouveau* styles were popular enough among collectors to provoke examination in detail,

and subjects such as porcelain 'fairings' and *Animalier* bronzes became the subject of monographs. For the rest, most of what has been written about the 19th century in the 20th is to be found in the pages of magazines, studies by collectors researching in a limited field.

It is not only that the 19th-century attitude to questions of style was unprecedented, but that the social climate was completely new. Fashion, formerly set by a very limited circle steeped in tradition now took its cue from the middle classes and the manufacturers. And the development of machinery, and of new processes and techniques, profoundly affected the manufacture of many decorative objects which had formerly been made by hand.

In the pages that follow the emphasis is on 19th century England, because this is where the Industrial Revolution started and where its impact was greatest. France had its own very sound traditions, made fashionable throughout Europe by Louis XIV and Louis XV. Change proceeded at a much slower pace and such styles as the Neo-Gothic were never taken very seriously.

The United States, with a predominantly European population, inevitably followed European and, in particular, English styles, but the genius of the people for machine manufacture and mass-production began to show itself at a comparatively early stage. Towards the end of the century America produced some of the most important pioneers of the modern movement.

The information in this Dictionary is listed alphabetically with cross-references to related entries, usually indicated by an asterisk. It includes discussion of styles, materials, processes, manufacturers, designers and artists, and deals with those subjects most likely to be of interest to the collector. Its purpose is to help him attribute and date the objects discussed, and to form some notion of their rarity and desirability. In these days of economic uncertainty there would be little point in attempting to estimate either prices or price-levels. Every sale-room report lists new record prices.

ABRAHAM, ROBERT FREDERICK (1827–1895)
Porcelain painter who studied art in Paris and Antwerp, painting somewhat in the manner of Etty. He exhibited at the Royal Academy between 1846 and 1853, and his porcelain painting for Coalport* in the manner of Sèvres* occurred on vases exhibited at the London Exhibition of 1862. He became Art Director to Copeland* in 1865, where he painted landscapes and portraits. His son, Robert John Abraham (1850–1925), modelled architectural *faïence* for Copeland's.

ABRASIVES
Hard substances, such as emery, employed to cut and fashion materials which are not generally suitable for working with metal tools. Hardstones, like jade and agate, are worked in this way, and cut and engraved glasses are decorated with the aid of revolving copper wheels charged with abrasives of one kind or another. Particles of the abrasive are embedded in the metal surface giving it a cutting edge.

ACANTHUS
The leaf of the acanthus, or bear's breech, has been widely used for ornamental purposes in European decorative art for upwards of 2,000 years as part of the various classical* styles. In the 19th century it

ACANTHUS. Part of a textile of c. 1860 decorated with typical acanthus foliage.

was most often seen during the Regency* period, when it appeared in carved form on furniture, on silver, and on porcelain in classical and semi-classical styles. Later in the century it was used as a textile pattern. In profile it is usually termed a *scrolling acanthus*.

ACID GILDING
Method of gilding developed by Minton* in the 1860s for decorating porcelain with matt and burnished gilding on the same piece. It was probably inspired by the matt gilding of metal devised by the 18th-century French goldsmith, Pierre Gouthière*. The glaze under the parts of the gilt pattern to be left matt was lightly etched with hydrofluoric acid* to remove the surface polish and then gilded. The rest of the pattern was burnished in the usual way.

ADAMS, NEHEMIAH (1769–1840)
Cabinet-maker of Salem, Mass., to whom is attributed tables, chairs, etc. of good workmanship. Adams supplied furniture to the Southern States.

ADAMS, WILLIAM (1748–1832)
Adams founded a factory at Cliff Bank, Stoke-on-Trent, in 1804, where he made blue printed earthenware and figures. Adams took his sons into partnership and the business soon became extremely large, making almost every type of ware current in Staffordshire. The firm finally closed in 1863.

Adams's earthenware printed in dark blue was extensively exported to America. A series of American Views* was popular and included the Niagara Falls; the 'Columbus Views' depicted the landing of Columbus. There was a companion 'English Views' series and one of 'London Views'. The firm also produced fine quality bone-china (see *Porcelain*), well painted and gilded, lustre wares, ironstone china*, and Egyptian black*.

The mark was *ADAMS* impressed, except for the printed wares which bore a printed mark, usually *ADAMS WARRANTED STAFFORDSHIRE* in circular form in conjunction with a crown or an American eagle.

AEROGRAPH

Apparatus for spraying earthenware and porcelain with colour to form coloured grounds—a type of airbrush. The aerograph has been increasingly used since its introduction in the 1890s as a replacement for previous methods of ground-laying*, but since the technique has the mechanically precise appearance associated with mass-production and poor quality it is not generally employed for the finer decorative wares.

AESTHETIC MOVEMENT

Movement in the late 1860s representing an extreme development of the Arts and Crafts Movement*, which had few followers outside fashionable *avant garde* circles. It succeeded the pre-Raphaelites* and displayed an 'intense' interest in the arts. The movement was satirized in *Punch* and by Gilbert and Sullivan with a character in *Patience* who 'walked down Piccadilly/with a poppy or a lily/in his medieval hand'. The women wore Renaissance style gowns with long amber necklaces and the sunflower* and the peacock* were adopted as decorative *motifs* (see *Peacock Room*).

Primarily the movement was a reaction against the notions of John Ruskin*, Augustus Pugin*, William Morris* and others. Its guiding principle was *Art for art's sake* (*L'art pour l'art*), a quotation from a lecture by Victor Cousin (1792–1867) given at the Sorbonne, which was adopted by James McNeill Whistler (1834–1903). From Morris the Aesthetics took their

AESTHETIC MOVEMENT. Glass dish, the border moulded with peacocks and sunflowers, the centre with peacock's feather ornament in relief. English. 1879. *Victoria & Albert Museum, London*

preference for craftsmanship. The movement became less fashionable in the early 1890s, with the advent of more recognizably *art nouveau** styles. Among the most industrious promoters of the style was the poet and playwright, Oscar Wilde (1854–1900), especially in America, where he made successful lecture tours.

AFFENKAPELLE (German)   See *Monkey Band*

AGATA GLASS

Type of art glass made by the New England Glass Company* of Cambridge (Mass.). It somewhat resembles peachblow* with some added mottling.

ALCOCK & CO., SAMUEL

Samuel Alcock commenced business at Burslem, Staffordshire, in 1830 as a manufacturer of porcelain,

ALCOCK, SAMUEL. Two theatrical figures*, the famous ballet-dancers, Elssner and Taglioni. Two very rare biscuit figures of superb quality by Samuel Alcock*. c. 1855. *Constance Chiswell*

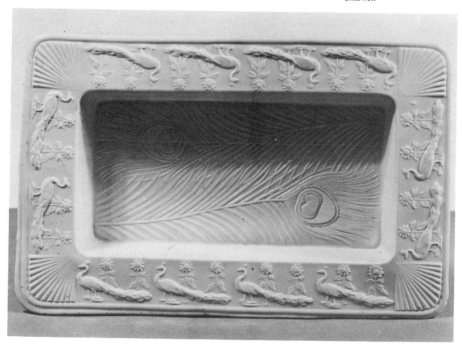

ALCOCK, SAMUEL. A pair of vases by Samuel Alcock*, the basic form registered in 1843. *Antique Collectors' Club*

biscuit figures, and later Parian* figures and vases. The French sculptor, Hugues Protât*, contributed models to Alcock, who produced some very distinguished figure models. The transfer-printed* wares include a portrait of William III made for the Northern Irish Orange Society of which the Duke of Cumberland was Grand Master. The factory closed in 1859.

The mark is either SAM^L ALCOCK & CO
BURSLEM
or S.A.& CO. or S.ALCOCK & CO. Sometimes the Royal Arms with Alcock's name beneath is used.

ALEXANDRA PORCELAIN WORKS
Name of porcelain factory operated by Ernst Wahliss* after 1905. The mark employed bears the name.

ALEXANDRITE
A type of art glass made by T. Webb & Sons* of Stourbridge and Stevens & Williams* of Wordsley. The Webb version, patented in 1903, shades from blue, through rose, to yellow, the effects being obtained by variations of heat. Stevens & Williams achieved somewhat similar effects by using a glass of transparent yellow cased with rose and blue, and then cut through the upper layers where required.

ALHAMBRESQUE
Nineteenth-century designs based largely on Hispano-Moresque ornament, especially that found in the Alhambra; a particular type of amphora-shaped vase with large wing handles, partly of classical and partly of Moorish origin, was excavated in the precincts of the palace, and termed the Alhambra vase. The form was sometimes employed in the 19th century by contemporary potters. A jug made by Ridgway* about 1845 with pseudo-Moorish ornament, and called the 'Alhambra' jug, was based on illustrations in Murphy's *Alhambra*.

ALLEN, ROBERT (1744–1835)
The manager of the Lowestoft porcelain factory in Suffolk in the 18th century. After 1802 he became an independent porcelain enameller with a studio in Lowestoft. A teapot of Chinese export porcelain with the 'Jesuit' decoration of the Crucifixion has added

flowers by his hand (Victoria & Albert Museum, London). He signed *'Allen Lowestoft'*.

ALLEN, THOMAS (1831–1915)
Painter and designer, educated at Stoke School of Design, he began to work for Minton* as a painter of figure-subjects, and a vase by him was included in Minton's exhibits in 1851. In 1852 he went to the newly-established South Kensington School of Design to study, remaining until 1854. From 1854 until 1875 he continued as a figure-painter with Minton's and in the latter year he transferred to Wedgwood* at Etruria, where he remained until 1906. Until 1900 he was art-director and chief designer, and he continued to provide Wedgwood with figure subjects of pre-Raphaelite inspiration. Perhaps his most notable work is a decoration based on Scott's *Ivanhoe*, the original drawings for which survive in the Wedgwood Museum at Barlaston, Staffordshire. His diary for the year 1852–1853 is also preserved in the archives there.

ALLISON, MICHAEL (fl. 1800–1845)
New York cabinet-maker. A neighbour and contemporary of Duncan Phyfe*.

ALUMINIA FAÏENCE COMPANY (Denmark) See *Royal Copenhagen Porcelain Factory*

ALUMINIUM
This metal was not discovered until the 19th century and at the Court of Napoleon III it was regarded as a precious metal from which spoons and forks were made as a valuable novelty. It has rarely been employed for decorative metalwork, except architecturally, but there are a few examples of its use for casting sculpture, notably *Eros* in Piccadilly Circus, London. The moonlight effects on *papier mâché* furniture made in Wolverhampton in the 1860s were achieved by using powdered aluminium.

AMATEUR CRAFTWORKERS
The 19th century, especially in England, was notable for the number of amateur practitioners in the arts and crafts. They were usually young women who were allowed very little freedom by the customs of the time to follow their own inclination. Most of them learned one or more arts or crafts to occupy their time, and some of them achieved a degree of skill to a point where it is now difficult to distinguish their work from that of the professional.

In some crafts, like wax fruit and flowers, shellwork*, hairwork pictures*, etc., very little genuine professional work was done, and practically all the specimens one sees were made by amateurs. A good deal of porcelain and glass painting was also done by amateurs at home and put out for firing in a small professional kiln. Studios were opened to employ young women at these and other crafts before the introduction of the typewriter and the telephone lured them to other ways of earning a living.

Despite the vast amount of work by recorded artists and craftsmen in the 19th century, therefore, there is also an enormous amount of competent anonymous work, especially in the categories already mentioned. Factory-made objects during the period under review usually bear some kind of identification mark, and porcelain factories in particular were inclined to allow the work of their more important artists to be identified by a signature, a monogram, or some kind of device. Therefore, except in the case of furniture, metalwork, or glass, all of which obviously needed workshop facilities, anything that bears no mark of identification could possibly be the work of an amateur. Only on very rare occasions can these works be traced to a named craftworker.

AMBERINA

A lead art glass of a lustrous pale amber colour with ruby tinges, introduced by the New England Glass Co.*, Cambridge (Mass.), and by their successors, the Libbey Glass Company*. A similar glass was also made elsewhere among American glass-makers.

AMERICAN CHINA MANUFACTORY (Philadelphia, Pa.)

This factory was established in 1831 by William Ellis Tucker and Joseph Hemphill for the manufacture of fine quality porcelain. Artists were imported from France, England and Germany, and the influence of Sèvres* is especially noticeable, Tucker porcelain having been sold as French. Tucker died soon after the business had been started, however, and it was closed in 1838. The wares of this factory (usually called 'Tucker porcelain') are among the best and most sought of American porcelains.

AMERICAN ENCAUSTIC TILING COMPANY (Zanesville, Ohio)

Company founded in 1880 which made unglazed floor-tiles known as *Alhambra*. Glazed tiles were also produced, either decorated with relief or in imitation of mosaic.

AMERICAN FLINT GLASS WORKS (South Boston, Mass.)

There were several glass works on this site before the American Glass Works was successfully established by Patrick Slane about 1850. It made pressed and cut-glass until about 1870.

AMERICAN VIEWS

Staffordshire earthenware, the early examples transfer-printed* in blue, decorated with American subjects for export to that country. Most frequent are plates and platters decorated with views of buildings or well-known places, usually named, but portrait, genre scenes and historical incidents also occur quite commonly. After 1840 other colours—green, red and black—became popular.

Staffordshire potters, Wedgwood* especially, had been exporting to America since the 1770s, and the Potteries generally were sympathetic to the cause of the Colonists during the War of Independence. The wares discussed here, however, did not begin to arrive in the States until after 1810, and were not made in large quantities until after 1817, when J. & R. Clews* of Cobridge began to export blue printed ware.

By this time considerable improvements had been made in the art of transfer-printing, principally in the engraving of the copper-plates from which the designs were transferred. Detail was sharper, but by varying the depth to which the engraved lines were cut, effects of light and shade became possible. These effects were further enhanced by combining line-and-stipple engraving of the type introduced by Bartolozzi late in the 18th century. At the same time tissue paper, which took up a clearer impression from the plate than the old, coarse paper used by the 18th-century transfer-printers, permitted further improvements. By this time the 18th-century creamware* had been mostly abandoned for this kind of work, and Wedgwood's pearl ware, invented in 1789, had been developed into something much harder and lighter by adding fusible feldspathic rock (Cornish stone). This body was known by a variety of names—semi-china, stone-china, ironstone china*—and it provided a much more efficient ground for the improvements in transfer-printing. The effect was still further enhanced by an improved glaze which was not so prone to scratching as the earlier, softer glazes.

The subject matter of the transfer-prints was, for the most part, taken from topographical engravings imported from the United States. The source is sometimes recorded in the wording of some back-stamps although it usually goes unacknowledged. Many of these sources, however, have now been traced, like W. G. Wall's *Hudson River Portfolio* of 1818. The views were topical as well as topographical. For instance, one depicts the *Landing of Lafayette* on the occasion of his return visit to the United States in 1824. It is probable that American Views enjoyed a limited sale on the home market, and reproductions of early wares with American subjects have appeared in English shops during the past few years.

The best-known makers of this kind of pottery include James and Ralph Clews of Cobridge (1817–1832), Joseph Stubbs* of Longport (1818–1834), Enoch Wood & Sons*, Burslem (who made American Views from 1819 until 1846), Adams of Tunstall, Job Meigh* of Hanley, John and William Ridgway* of Hanley, T. Rogers of Longport and Stevens & Williams* of Cobridge. All these names may be found impressed. Enoch Wood also employed the American eagle and the words *E pluribus unum* added as part of the mark on some wares of this kind, usually in conjunction with their name. The same eagle has also been observed without further addition on a tureen and its stand, the manufacture of which could only doubtfully be assigned to Wood, and which may be more correctly attributable to another Staffordshire manufacturer.

ANGLO-JAPANESE FURNITURE

Furniture inspired by the Japanese exhibit in the International Exhibition of 1862, and principally designed by E. W. Godwin* and Thomas Jeckyll*. In general the designs are notable for Japanese ornamental *motifs* grafted on to European furniture since, unlike China, Japan did not make furniture suitable for normal European interiors. Some examples termed Anglo-Japanese are strongly suggestive of Chinese designs, and this is probably the source from which they were taken, since Chinese furniture* was fairly well-known in England and there has always been a tendency among the less well-informed to confuse Chinese and Japanese objects.

ANGLO-MOORISH STYLE

Also sometimes called the *Anglo-Arab* style. Hotel and club lounges and smoking rooms were sometimes decorated with imported Near-Eastern furniture, tables inlaid with mother of pearl, etc., at a time when Turkish baths enjoyed popularity. Little or nothing appears to have been made in the West for interiors of this kind. Most of them were merely pieces of theatrical nonsense but the Arab Hall*, in Lord Leighton's house in London, is an important and noteworthy example of the fashion at its best. A Moorish smoking-room from John D. Rockefeller's house in New York is now in the Brooklyn Museum, and Moorish decorations were popular in fashionable Boston.

ANIMALIERS, LES

A group of sculptors headed by Antoine-Louis Barye (1796–1875)* who took animals, both wild and domestic, as their subject. This was a Romantic* reaction to neo-classicism*. The subject had already been explored by such painters as George Stubbs in England, and by Delacroix and Géricault in France. The work of the Victorian animal painter, Landseer, was also extremely popular in France. The *Animalier* bronzes popular both in the 19th century and today were small enough to stand in a cabinet or on an

ANIMALIERS, LES. *Equestrian Group* by *Animalier* Count Stanislas Grimaldi. Signed. Dated 1886. *Antique Collectors' Club*

ANIMALIERS, LES. *Lion with a serpent*. A characteristic bronze by the founder of the *Animalier* school, Antoine Louis Barye*. Third quarter of the 19th century. *Antique Collectors' Club*

occasional table, and some were reductions of larger work executed with the aid of a technique invented by Achille Collas* in 1839 and used in conjunction with the *fondeurs*, Barbedienne et Cie* and Susse Frères*. Most small works of this kind were published in limited editions, but there were sometimes reissues using fresh moulds, or, as in the case of Barye, early *cire perdue* casts were followed by inferior sand-casts.

The style of the *Animaliers* was naturalistic and realistic, even if the subject was romantic and treated romantically. They were generally full of life. Barye,

ANIMALIERS, LES. *Lion and lioness*, group by Jules Moigniez*. Third quarter of the 19th century. Signed. *Antique Collectors' Club*

5

for instance, produced a superb *Jaguar devouring an alligator*, and other groups of the same kind are sometimes reminiscent of the best of the 18th-century porcelain hunting groups, such as those of Auliczek at Nymphenburg. The *Animaliers* took great interest in the actual casting of their work. Cain*, for example, shared a foundry with his father-in-law, P. J. Mêne*. Many of them specialized in particular types of animals, without necessarily limiting themselves entirely to one kind. Jules Moigniez*, for instance, more or less confined himself to accurate depictions of birds in a style influenced by painting.

The output of some of the *Animaliers* was considerable. Susse Frères, for instance, listed 217 models by P. J. Mêne, and variants on individual models

ANIMALIERS, LES. Figure of a camel in cast-iron from the Coalbrookdale Ironworks*. Second quarter of the 19th century. *Ironbridge Gorge Museum Trust*

exist from several of the better-known and more prolific artists. The patination on the surface also varies in some cases from one artist to another: Moigniez, for example, preferred a light golden-brown.

Most *Animalier* bronzes are signed by the sculptor in one way or another, and details of the signature have been given whenever possible under the appropriate heading. Founders' stamps also occur on some. Unsigned bronzes, however, are also found, and their value must be judged by quality of modelling and casting.

The artificial patination of bronzes was extensively practised during the 19th century, and no bronze should ever be cleaned with more than a little good soap and water, followed by drying and polishing the surface with a trace of sweet oil on a soft cloth.

ANTIMACASSAR
A crocheted or embroidered mat made to be placed on the upholstery of chairs and settees to protect the covering from oily hairdressings such as bear's grease or macassar oil. Its name derived from the latter.

ANTIQUE COLLECTING IN THE 19TH CENTURY
The practice of antique collecting considerably influenced the course of the decorative arts in the 19th century. Collecting as it developed in the 1830s hardly existed in earlier times, when furniture, silver, porcelain and paintings were employed for their proper purpose of decorating the interiors of houses. Collecting in the 18th century was largely confined to such natural curiosities as mineral specimens, dried plants, stuffed mermaids for the gullible, and prints, which were gathered together in portfolios. Porcelain and silver were used on the dining table, and the porcelain figures, which the 19th century entombed in glazed cabinets, were part of a table decoration.

Collecting porcelain began in the closing years of the 17th century, but was limited to Chinese and Japanese objects, many of which had no practical use. There is, however, one well-known instance of a 17th-century collection of Italian *maiolica**, sold by auction at Christie's in the 19th century. Horace Walpole (1717–1797), whose collection was sold by the auctioneer, Robins, in 1842, was not a specialized collector in the 19th-century sense. He was a man of taste who collected by whim, and his possessions ranged from Cardinal Wolsey's hat to the scrying stone of the Elizabethan magician, Dr John Dee. Antiques, at that time, were usually termed 'curios'—a term of many meanings.

The first hints of collecting in the modern manner are to be found in the 1830s. Ten years later Balzac published his novel, *Cousin Pons*, largely concerned with antique collecting, and in 1850 Frederick Marryat published his *History of Pottery and Porcelain, a handbook for collectors*. Contemporary with Marryat's *Handbook* was Jules Labarte's *Handbook of the Arts of the Middle Ages*, which undoubtedly influenced design in medieval styles, as well as the collecting of medieval objects. About the same time a large and important collection of pottery and porcelain belonging to Ralph Bernal, Esq., was dispersed at Christie's in a sale lasting several days. William Chaffer's *Marks and Monograms on Pottery and Porcelain* was first published in 1863.

The modern movement in antique collecting strictly began with the French Revolution, when the possessions of the king and the aristocrats were looted, and found their way into the clutches of second-hand dealers during the years that followed, or were sold by the Revolutionary Government in a series of auction sales at which the Prince Regent and the Marquis of Hertford bought heavily.

Marryat includes in the 1857 edition of his *Handbook* a list of collectors of old pottery and porcelain of his day. By far the greater number devoted themselves to Sèvres porcelain* and Italian *maiolica*. There were, at this time, few collectors of English porcelain, and they limited themselves to Chelsea. Only one collector of Meissen porcelain* was listed. By 1870, Lady Charlotte Schreiber, whose remarkable collection of English porcelain is now in the Victoria and Albert Museum, London, was hunting for her speciality widely in England and Holland; she bought a Chelsea rabbit tureen for £4 in Holland, and recorded the purchase in her diary as 'very dear'. It would now realize £2,000 or more.

By the last quarter of the century, Meissen* porcelain was being increasingly collected, particularly the Baroque 'crinoline' groups of Kändler, and this period is notable for reproductions of all kinds from a variety of sources—Samson* of Paris and Carl Thieme* of Potschappel, to name only two.

That 18th-century English furniture was being sought by 1870 is evident from the reproductions of Adam furniture then in demand, but throughout the second half of the century the furniture sought by the wealthy was Parisian made between the Régence and the Revolution (1716–1789), for which vast sums in gold were sometimes paid. For instance, Baron Edmond de Rothschild paid £80,000 for Mme du Barry's commode—more than a million pounds today.

Italian furniture of the High Renaissance was bought by the new millionaire class, not necessarily because it was rare and expensive, but often, as in the case of Pierpoint Morgan, from a genuine antiquarian interest. These men laid the foundations of the great American public art-collections. It should also be remembered that the Americans were among the first patrons of the French Impressionists, and often paid substantial prices at a time when their work was either unknown in England, or likely to induce a fit of apoplexy in those whose proud boast was that they knew nothing of art, but knew what they liked. When, in later years, the English art-patron slowly began to realize by how much he had missed the boat, the pendulum swung the other way, and induced him uncritically to accept a great deal of rubbish in case it had an esoteric or aesthetic significance he was unable to comprehend.

Until the 1880s, in England especially, the discriminating buyer had few opportunities for exercising his critical abilities in the field of contemporary work, most of which was in execrable taste, and wealthier patrons primarily bought antiques. For almost the whole of the century, from about 1830 onwards, taste was strongly influenced by the demands of the antique market. This may be seen from the way in which such specific wares in the field of pottery as those of Bernard Palissy*, the faïence d'Oiron (Henri Deux ware*), and 16th-century Italian maiolica, or porcelain like the 18th-century work of Sèvres, and to a lesser extent that of Chelsea and Meissen, continued to supply factories with inspiration. Furniture was less closely copied, and such decorative furniture as that of the 18th-century Paris ébénistes was repeated in much more ornate versions, like the Jackson & Graham* cabinet of 1855. These 19th-century pieces are to this day confused by the uninitiated with the genuine furniture of the Louis XV and Louis XVI periods. A few ébénistes, like Pierre Dasson*, pro-

duced fine-quality replicas for people of taste, and these cost almost as much as genuine 18th-century examples, proof that people were paying for quality rather than age. Today quality still commands prices comparable with those paid for the best of antique work. This may be seen, for instance, in the £17,500 paid for a pair of quail designed by the late Dorothy Doughty* in 1932, and made by the Worcester Royal Porcelain Company*. It is also instructive to compare 19th-century sale-room prices for certain kinds of antique objets d'art, and then to trace how soon commercial reproductions appeared on the market after the antique examples had reached a figure sufficiently high to give them an unassailable position in the esteem of the buying public.

Gerald Reitlinger has pointed out that the market in works of art began early in the 19th century with the emphasis on fine craftsmanship, and then gradually turned away from this aspect to emphasize something entirely new, something often called genius. Renoir* was under no illusions about the necessity for craftsmanship. The difference was not so much the negation of craftsmanship as its adaptation to the expression of new and more subjective ideas, and its subordination to the total effect. Ghiberti's Gates of Paradise gave place to Rodin's* Gates of Hell. The two are not strictly comparable. So, at the end of the century, we have the superb craftsmanship of Fabergé*, reminiscent of that of the goldsmiths of Louis XVI, and the comparative crudity of some art nouveau metalwork. Craftsmanship like that of Fabergé fought a losing battle because fewer people could afford to pay for it.

Throughout most of the 19th century the primary inspiration was French. In 1848 and 1870 French artists fled from troubles at home to seek work in England, especially in the ceramic industries, and they proved to be a salutary influence in some branches of the decorative arts in England which were suffering from an excess of Pugin's* Gothic.

The strength of Pugin's influence during his lifetime to some extent was due to the English Royal Family, German in origin, which received powerful reinforcement for its Teutonic outlook by the marriage of Queen Victoria to Prince Albert of Saxe-Coburg-Gotha. The medieval tradition in the German States was much stronger than in France, where the course of art had been redirected by Louis XIV who detested Gothic. The balance really began to change in favour of France after Queen Victoria's successful visit to Paris in 1855, the year of the Exposition, when she experienced the glitter and luxury of French Court life and the charm of Napoleon III.

The 19th-century English preoccupation with the Orient was partly because of Empire-building, but was due much more to a relatively small number of Romantic scholars like Sir Richard Burton and Edward Lane-Poole. Since the days of Elizabeth I there had always been some tenuous connections between England and the Islamic world. Elizabeth presented the Sultan of Turkey with an organ; 18th-century clockmakers produced elaborate examples of their art for the Turkish market; England, France, and Turkey joined together to defeat Russia during the Crimean war. The influence of Isnik pottery* designs on the work of William de Morgan*, however, had nothing to do with Turkey. At the time these wares were thought to have been made in Rhodes, and were called 'Rhodian'. Their origin in Anatolia remained undiscovered almost until the 20th century. Some of the Isnik patterns came at second-hand from 16th-century Italian *maiolica*, on which they were also popular. Many of the so-called Persian designs used by de Morgan and others were really inspired by the pottery of Damascus. A certain amount of interest was taken in Hispano-Moresque—the golden lustred pottery of Malaga and Valencia—and copies were made of an amphora-shaped vase unearthed in the palace of the Alhambra at Granada. High prices were paid by collectors for fine quality dishes, and Hispano-Moresque ornament was popularized by the work of Owen Jones*.

Most of the Chinese designs employed during the 19th century were either of European origin, and are strictly *chinoiseries*, or were derivations from wares which had already been copied in the 18th century. Wares not hitherto influential, which the technical progress of the century made it possible to reproduce, include the celadon* and *sang-de-boeuf** glazes. The fashion for Chinese porcelain among collectors which began late in the 1860s was, at this time, mainly for 18th-century blue-and-white in England and to a smaller extent for some of the coloured wares. Throughout the century ignorance of Chinese art and civilization was profound, and the Ming dynasty was, for the most part, as far back as even the most devoted sinologist was prepared to go.

It is surprising how little influence the possession of an Indian Empire had on the decorative arts. At the beginning of the century the pavilion at Brighton had an exterior influenced by Indian architecture, but it was Chinese inside. Vast quantities of Indian bric-à-brac were imported throughout the 19th century, as contemporary advertisements testify, and such objects as Benares* brass trays may, in some cases, have been made in Birmingham and exported to India for sale to tourists. Some Staffordshire blue transfer-printed pottery was decorated with Indian scenes. For the most part, however, imports from India were tawdry, and evidently they did not offer a chance of profit to those who might otherwise have copied them. Few serious collections of Indian art seem to have been made at the time, although early Indian sculpture was sought by a limited number of buyers in Germany.

The difference between genius and craftsmanship could not have been exemplified more plainly than in the difference between Japanese *raku* ware, which attracted such French collectors as Edmond de Goncourt, and the delicately carved ivories and lacquers which appealed to English taste. Several collections of the second kind were dispersed in the early years of the 20th century, notably the Behrens collection. *Raku* wares had some influence in France towards the end of the 19th century. Worcester*, Wedgwood* and other English porcelain makers produced wares influenced by Japan, but these were based on ivories. Worcester referred to their porcelain as their 'ivory' body. Nevertheless, the influence of China and the Near-East proved to be transitory, but that of Japan exerted tremendous influence on the decorative themes of *art nouveau**. Collecting Oriental works of art became an increasingly scholarly pursuit in the 20th century, and its influence on Western decorative arts diminished.

With the advent of the Arts and Craft Movement* and the growth of the *art nouveau* style, the influence of antique collecting generally began to diminish until recent times, when the obvious advantages of antiques and works of art as an anti-inflation hedge were realized. This has started a new cycle of reproductions, many of them objects not previously copied in this way, although few of them are really deceptive. The dealer who specializes in selling works of this kind as genuine, however, now has to contend with the Trade Descriptions Act, which is not calculated to make his life any easier.

APOSTLE JUG
A jug modelled with figures of the Apostles in niches formed by an arcade, made by Charles Meigh*, and based on 16th-century Rhineland stoneware*.

ARAB HALL, THE
The Arab Hall now forms part of a house in West London originally built in 1866 to the designs of architect, George Aitchison (1825–1910), for Frederic Leighton (1830–1896), later Lord Leighton and President of the Royal Academy. It is, perhaps, the most impressive survival of a fashion for Near Eastern decoration which was to flourish in the 1870s. Leighton toured the Near East in 1868 and 1873 and acquired a large number of antique tiles, mainly from Isnik (Turkey), Persia and Damascus, some of which had been found for him by the explorer, Sir Richard Burton. These, with some additions by William de Morgan*, and wooden lattices from Damascus, were incorporated into a large room added to the house in about 1880, with tiled walls in the Near Eastern manner, the design of which was apparently based on a Saracen palace at Palermo. It is now open to the public.

ARABESQUES
From the Italian *arabeschi*. Ornament consisting of interlaced lines, bands and strapwork, and abstract ornament of one kind or another adapted by Islamic artists and craftsmen from Roman sources. It is sometimes confused with grotesques* but representation of living figures is rare and then only in stylized

form. Arabesques were often referred to as Moresques in the 19th century when they were a popular form of decoration on some kinds of pottery. Moresques were derived from sources originating in Spain and Sicily, both of which were at one time under Saracen domination.

See *Grotesques*

ARABIA OSAKEYHTIO
Finnish subsidiary of the Swedish Rörstrand* factory established in 1874 for the manufacture of glass and china. Since the First World War production of wares of all kinds has greatly increased. The factory has pursued an enlightened policy in the employment of artists as designers, and in the provision of studio facilities. It also maintains a museum.

ARGY-ROUSSEAU, GABRIEL (b. 1885)
French artist in glass who worked mainly in *pâte-de-verre*. He made a large number of decorative objects, ranging from pendants to vases, and usually employed the mark *GA-R* impressed.

ARGY-ROUSSEAU, GABRIEL. *Pâte-de-verre* vase by Gabriel Argy-Rousseau. Signed. c. 1925. *Sotheby & Co*

ARMORY SHOW, THE (1913)
The Exhibition held at the Armory of the 69th Regiment in New York which opened on February 17th, 1913, and later moved to Chicago, was the most controversial event to hit America up till that date, and it strongly influenced the course of art thereafter. The project began as an exhibition of contemporary American art arranged by a group of people among whom were Arthur B. Davies, Walt Kuhn, and the collector, John Quinn. Up to this point it could hardly be regarded as either spectacular or controversial, but it was apparently Davies who suggested including *avant garde* work from Europe. He and Kuhn went to Paris, where they joined with art-critic Walter Pach and Gertrude Stein to select objects for inclusion. Their selection included work which had hardly been seen in America up till that time. Paintings included works by Matisse and the Fauves*, early Cubist* paintings by Picasso and Braque, and work by Léger, Picabia, Marcel Duchamp, and many more. Sculpture

included work by the German, Lehmbruck, and Brancusi. These works were grouped in the middle of the exhibition, with native works on the periphery, and it exploded on New York like a bombshell. Sales of American artists suffered from the juxtaposition. More than 120,000 people came to see the show, which broke all records. Some came to be converted, and others to jeer. President Theodore Roosevelt, who disliked the new art, came nevertheless, and was given a guided tour of the exhibits by John Quinn. Probably from a sense of duty the Metropolitan Museum bought a Cézanne, but did their best to keep the purchase secret. In the press the works were attacked, defended, derided, and praised, but in the end everyone agreed that nothing would ever be the same again. Commercial exploitation began almost at once, and within a year six small New York galleries were exhibiting work of the same kind. The exhibition was subsequently transferred to Chicago, where the reaction was similar. Since the Armory show American taste favours the post-Impressionists and the post-Fauve paintings of Matisse, although its attitude to Cubist works is still somewhat more conservative. The event undoubtedly helped to produce a favourable climate for the *art déco** and Bauhaus* styles after the 1914–18 War.

ARNOUX, JOSEPH-LÉON-FRANÇOIS (1816–1902)
French ceramist who studied at the École des Arts et Manufactures, and then, after making the acquaintance of Brongniart*, studied aspects of pottery at the Paris depôt of the Sèvres* factory in the rue de Rivoli. Until 1848 he managed a family firm of *faïence** potters, Fouqué, Arnoux et Cie, of Toulouse, and in 1848 he came to England and met Herbert Minton*. He was appointed art-director of Minton's, a position which he held until 1892. He was responsible for producing some of the old Sèvres ground-colours, especially an approximation of Chrouet's *rose Pompadour* which was termed *rose du Barry**, he worked on the development of 'Majolica'* and Henri Deux ware*, a crackled glaze in imitation of Chinese porcelain, and other projects.

In 1878 he was awarded the Austro-Hungarian Order of Franz Joseph, and became a *Chevalier* of the *Légion d'Honneur*. Arnoux was to a considerable extent responsible for French influence in 19th-century English ceramic design.

ARSON, ALPHONSE-ALEXANDRE (1822–1880)
French *Animalier* sculptor who specialized in birds, either singly or in groups which sometimes include small mammals. Arson began to exhibit in the *Salon* in 1859, and continued to do so until his death. He signed *ARSON*.

See *Animaliers, les*

9

ART DÉCO FIGURES. A gilt-bronze and ivory group, *Toujours les amis*, by Demêtre Chiparus. c. 1925. *Antique Collectors' Club*

ART DÉCO

Art déco is sometimes known as the nineteen twenties style, but this limitation depends on how strictly it is defined. It had its origins before the First World War and extended until 1939. Certainly an important influence on *art déco** was the Exhibition of the Wiener Werkstätte* of 1908 in the Kunstschau, which in 1910 was transferred to Paris. This showed the designs of the *Jugendstil** already evolving into recognizably Cubist* forms. The year before, in 1909, the *Ballets Russes* of Diaghilev had exploded on the Paris scene and was received with wild enthusiasm. These early years of the 20th century were among the most fertile periods in the history of art, and from 1905 to 1914 one innovation followed another, in a sense accumulating capital which art has been living on ever since. Fauvism and Expressionism* started in 1905, Cubism in 1908, and Futurism in 1909. The

most significant part in the development of what was to become *art déco* in the years before the 1914-18 War was painting. The Fauves used pure colour to paint two-dimensional patterns.

The French refer to *art déco* as the '25 style', which came from the Paris Exposition Internationale des Arts Décoratifs et Industriels Modernes, originally projected for 1915 and finally held in 1925. This Exposition was by no means fully representative of the modern movement and it was predominantly French. It would be not unreasonable to contend that the German Bauhaus* in particular had a greater and more lasting effect on the modern style, yet this was not even represented. Germany, in French opinion, was still an enemy.

The increasing cost of labour was putting individually designed, and made, decoration out of reach of all but the wealthiest; but industrial manufacturers were becoming more enlightened and so, for that matter, was the new generation of consumers. Artists were employed to design objects of interior decoration in the modern idiom, and although Paris was still playing a leading part in setting fashionable trends, it was no longer the acknowledged leader. Academic art had fallen from its position of influence during the last twenty years or so of the 19th century, and historicism* was dead. Instead of Chinese and Japanese art, which were now objects of serious study by a limited group of scholars, the arts of primitive peoples were in demand as decoration, especially African sculpture and the arts of pre-Columbian America. 'Airport art' and 'mission school art' had yet to make their appearance among African carvings. Negro carving influenced Picasso and Braque, who broke with Fauvism, and started to represent objects reduced to simple geometrical forms—a movement

ART DÉCO FIGURES. Painted cast metal *art déco** figure on an onyx marble base. Signed *T. H. ULLMANN.* c. 1925. *Private collection*

ART DÉCO. *Art déco** glass cosmetic box faceted and painted in silhouette with a girl fishing. Probably French, c. 1925. *Private collection*

of Chinese pottery which, until late in the 19th century, were almost unknown in Europe. This particularly applies to the coloured-glaze stonewares of the Sung dynasty (960–1280). Some of these monochrome glazes—celadons* and *flambés** especially—were being made in Europe by 1900. The most important wares of the 1920s were individually made pots with monochrome glazes inspired by the Far East, but characteristic of the decorated industrial pottery of the period are some of the Clarice Cliff* designs, such as *Bizarre* and *Fantasque*.

In France a number of *faïence** factories produced painted wares with the aid of noted artists, and the Sèvres factory* made a special contribution to the 1925 Exposition. In glassware René Lalique* led the way by accepting a certain amount of machine-production by which he both increased his output

termed Cubism. The painter whose influence on the 1920s movement was probably greater than that of any other single artist was Piet Mondrian. He was attracted to Cubism before the First World War, and then developed a purely abstract style based on right-angles, using the 'colours' black, white and grey.

The futurism of the Italian poet, Marinetti, arrived in Paris in 1909. 'Speed', he proclaimed, 'is our god . . . a racing-car is more beautiful than the Victory of Samothrace.' These three movements—Fauvism, Cubism and Futurism—had great influence on the style of the 1920s. Less influential was Dada, the movement with its basis in irrationality, which was to become Surrealism.

The period between the decline of *art nouveau* and the First World War was one of confusion. The *avant garde* designers produced plain furniture which could be made cheaply with the aid of machines, but its reception by a public accustomed to equating ornament with value was not favourable, and there was a reversion to 18th-century styles for conventional purposes. Brightly painted and lacquered furniture or furniture decorated in black and silver, inspired by the success of the *Ballets Russes* in 1909, had become fashionable by 1925. The 1920s style in the decorative arts is probably best seen in furniture much of which was designed by architects and artists. Much of it, too, was an attempt to adapt traditional styles to modern designs.

The last part of the 19th century and the early years of the 20th saw the increasing influence of the studio-potter. Painted pottery and porcelain was becoming less fashionable, partly because of the cost of skilled labour and partly because of the increasing Oriental influence. It is often said that this was from Japan, and to some extent this is correct, but it was also in great part due to the increasing accessibility of types

11

and was able to reduce prices. Maurice Marinot*, on the other hand, regarded glass as a handcraft. Metalwork followed the general style of the period.

ART DÉCO FIGURES

Small sculpture was a popular form of decoration during the currency of *art déco**. The most desirable figures are of bronze, a combination of bronze and ivory, or porcelain of good quality from a reputable factory. Ivory used for jewellery and carving during the *art nouveau** and *art déco* periods came from the African elephant and is whiter than Oriental ivory. Its popularity was due to the strenuous efforts made by the Belgian government to market large stocks which had accumulated in the Belgian Congo.

Some animal figures belong to this period, but by far the greater number are girls who are nude, or almost so, and usually in a dancing pose. The figure is of the contemporary fashionable variety which hardly existed outside the artist's imagination. The arms and legs are long and slim, the breasts slight, the belly flat, and the buttocks small. Its period is unmistakable, since nothing quite like it had ever occurred before. It remained standard in works of decorative art from the early 1920s almost until the outbreak of the Second World War.

These figures were produced in very large numbers, and it is rare to find anything at this period issued in limited editions, except for the work of such serious sculptors as Jacob Epstein.* Paris was the centre of manufacture, and unless there is a signature it is difficult to attribute works to a known artist. The signed work of F. D. Preis and D. H. Chiparus is among the best. The signature of Lorenzl, about whom almost nothing appears to be known, also occurs. In collecting work of this kind quality of materials and workmanship are the best guide. There are plenty of inferior examples available—spelter imitates bronze, plastics imitate ivory, and porcelain figures can be cheap slip-casts* especially designed for mass-production. Spelter (zinc*) is a white metal underneath, even when the surface has been bronzed, and it is lighter and much softer than bronze. Plastics are moulded, not carved, and traces of mould-seams are often present. They are lighter than ivory, and the surface lacks the perceptible grain.

ARTE DELLA CERAMICA (Florence)

Ceramic workshop which flourished from 1896 to 1906. After 1906 it became Chini & Co. The principal production was porcelain painted in lustre* with floral and animal designs. The moving spirits were two brothers, Galileo Chini (1876–1956), art-director, designer and flower-painter, and Chino Chini, technical director from 1901 to 1906.

ARTE VETRARIA MURANESE

Venetian glasshouse founded by Giulio Radi in Murano, and chiefly noted for decorative glass.

Vittorio Zecchin (1878–1947), the Venetian glass-designer in the *art déco** style, and art-director of P. Venini*, worked with the Arte Vetraria Muranese.

ART FURNITURE

In the 1860s, and the decade which followed, a notion grew up that 'art' was something which could be applied to furniture to make it more desirable. For the most part this consisted of applying Gothic and early Renaissance ornament, and it was felt that the more ornament (or 'art') of this kind which could be added, the more aesthetically important a piece became. In the hands of a designer like William Burges*, who was prominent in the art-furniture movement, the result was often interesting, even if it was difficult to take seriously. By the 1870s art furniture manufacturers were placed in a special category, apart from such ordinary mortals as cabinet-makers, and the attitude at the time is very neatly expressed in a remark attributed to William Morris*, 'I wouldn't mind a lad being a cabinet-maker if he only made art furniture'. Towards the end of the 1870s 'art glass'* and 'art metalwork' had come into existence, and interiors were decorated in 'art' colours.

Even though the situation had its lighter side, which by no means escaped everyone (particularly *Punch*) at the time, the purpose behind the movement was reasonable enough. Increasingly during the 18th century and the early decades of the 19th there had been a movement to divide the arts into a superior kind known as the fine arts, which included painting, sculpture, and architecture, and what had come to be known as the industrial, applied, or decorative arts, which were regarded as inferior. The reason is fairly obvious. It was thought that superior imaginative faculties were required to practise the fine arts and, in the 19th century, with the increasing use of the machine in the making of ornament, this was to a certain degree true. In former times however, especially during the Renaissance, the two art forms had not been divorced. Artists maintained studios in which they employed assistants and pupils and these masters often signed cooperative work. They were often equipped and prepared to make furniture, metalwork, and all kinds of decoration. Cellini* was at least as famous as a goldsmith as he was as a sculptor. Many 18th-century portrait painters executed head and hands and then passed the work over to a drapery hand. Even from artists such as Boucher, patrons ordered paintings by subject, size, and final position.

The Romantic* movement, which began at the end of the 18th century, considerably altered the status of the artist, who selected his own subjects and painted them in a manner to suit himself, taking the chance of finding a patron who was attracted to his work. Painting began to take on an almost religious significance and as it did so, mere craftsmanship, now assisted by the machine and seeking inspiration

ART GLASS. Beaker decorated in *Schwarzlot* (black linear drawing) in the manner of the late 17th-century *Hausmaler**. German, third quarter of the 19th century. *Sotheby & Co*

from design-books, produced dull and lifeless ornament which was often a jumble of period and provenance. In these circumstances, William Morris* and others revolted against the machine, and endeavoured to restructure relationships between the fine and applied arts. The 'art' movement was the first, albeit unsuccessful, attempt to break out of the vicious circle which had been created. The first style of importance emerged later in the form of *art nouveau**.

ART GLASS

A late 19th-century term not now in general use for decorative glass, especially that in the making of which new techniques and processes had been employed. The term includes Agata*, Amberina*, Burmese*, Peachblow*, Satin* and Tiffany's iridized 'Favrile'* glass.

ART NOUVEAU

Art nouveau, which grew out of the Arts and Crafts Movement* in the last decade of the 19th century, was, perhaps, the only movement worth calling a style to emerge since French Empire became unfashionable. *Art nouveau* began to surface early in the 1880s, although some of its elements can be noted at least ten years earlier. When it first began to separate from the current fashionable style early in the 1890s it received a variety of names—the 'Modern' style, the 'Quaint' style*, the *style anglaise*, the *style moderne*, the *Jugendstil**, the *stile liberté* etc. The term *art nouveau* only came later, and was taken from the name of Samuel Bing's* Paris gallery, La Maison de l'Art Nouveau. A magazine called *Le Style Moderne* was founded in Paris in 1881.

The style was short-lived in England, where it had its beginnings, although it survived longer in Scotland, where the work of Charles Rennie Mackintosh*, who abandoned curves for straight lines, was very influential, especially in Austria and Germany. In England it was apt to be known as the 'Spook'* style in reference to its attenuated vertical lines and general appearance.

In England A. H. Mackmurdo* is regarded as one of its earliest exponents. His typical swirling plantforms in the embryo *art nouveau* style are seen particularly well in part of the title-page of *Wren's City Churches*, published in 1883. A study of the *motifs* of the style suggests that the principal sources of inspiration were neo-Gothic and Japanese. The general asymmetry in the disposition of the ornament is Japanese; so are the swirling plant forms. The popularity of the tulip is, perhaps, Near Eastern in origin, and the ivy-leaf had earlier been used by William de Morgan*. Whiplash tendrils are Gothic rather than Japanese; so is the emphasis in many objects on vertical rather than horizontal lines.

The social climate of the time was responsible for the popularity of the female nude, and the generally feminine nature (in distinct contrast to the masculine art of the mid-century) of much of the decoration of

ART GLASS. Vase of purple frosted glass shading to clear glass at the base, overlaid with a silver mount in the form of clover leaves and flowers. c. 1900. *Sotheby & Co*

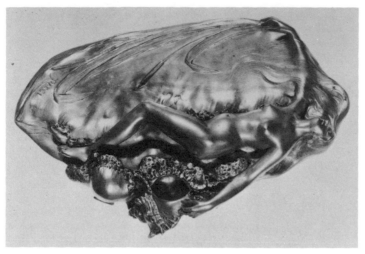

ART NOUVEAU. Gilt-bronze *art nouveau** inkstand in the form of a reclining nude, by Rossi. Signed. c. 1900. *Sotheby & Co*

art nouveau. The style reflects the increasing influence of women, not so much those who moved in rigidly conventional spheres, but more those who moved in the circles of the stage and demi-monde. Inspiration came not from Mrs Pankhurst, but from Loïe Fuller*, Cleo De Merode and the stars of the Moulin Rouge immortalized by Toulouse-Lautrec.

The Studio* magazine founded in London in 1896 devoted its efforts to promoting the *art nouveau* style, but it had greater influence on the Continent than in England. To some extent it may have suffered in England from its association with the Aesthetic Movement*, which was never taken very seriously by any but a comparatively small circle.

'Art for art's sake' was, in any case, antipathetic to the English social conscience, inherited from the Puritans, and it was difficult to justify the existence of *art nouveau* on any but frivolous grounds. This was especially so when, as the movement advanced, ornament became so profuse that it tended to conceal construction. The less-favoured Continental nations were under no such handicaps, and first in Belgium and then in France the new style began to make headway. By the end of the century it was firmly established by the Paris Exposition of 1900 (not entirely successful at the time), the efforts of Samuel Bing, the Vienna *Sezession**, the work of designers, artists, and craftsmen, like Émile Gallé*, and Hector Guimard*, and many more, and there was a revival of enamelling* of fine quality by Alexander Fisher* and others. Jewellery was an especial feature of the style, much of it based on ancient Celtic designs. Figures in *ormolu* and bronze designed as table-lamps were of fine quality, and there was also a fashion for bronze figures with ivory faces and hands (see *Chryselephantine work*).

In America L. C. Tiffany* made substantial contributions to the development of the style, and in Spain Antoni Gaudi* was providing his own highly individual designs in furniture and architecture.

Among the most characteristic works of the period are the wrought-iron gates of Paris Métro stations designed by Hector Guimard, also noted for his furniture. Metalwork generally, large and small, is an important aspect of the style. Equally important is

ART NOUVEAU. Chair of oak designed by Charles Rennie Mackintosh* for the Glasgow School of Art*. 1897. *Glasgow School of Art*

ART NOUVEAU. Goblet of coloured glass on a stem decorated with fruit and flowers. English *art nouveau*, early 20th century. *Victoria & Albert Museum, London*

sculpture were in any way of superior value to the decorative arts, and Toulouse-Lautrec did posters* and Gauguin made pottery. One of the most important and influential of *art nouveau* artists, Émile Gallé, concentrated on glass.

After 1900 commercial manufacturers increasingly

ART NOUVEAU. Armchair in the *art nouveau* style, the back inlaid with floral *motifs*. English, c. 1890. *Antique Collectors' Club*

ART NOUVEAU. Title-page of *Wren's City Churches* by A. H. Mackmurdo*, the earliest design definitely to be regarded as belonging to the *art nouveau** style. 1883. *William Morris Gallery, Waltham Forest*

glass. The technical resources of the craft, and the nature of the material itself, made glass especially suitable to the demands of the style. Glass in one form or another was particularly useful for making decorative shades for electric lights, then coming into fairly general use, and Tiffany table-lamps* are now especially sought. Less in evidence are pottery and porcelain. Few factories employed the style to any great extent, and most *art nouveau* work in this medium came from studio-potters. Among the great porcelain factories, Sèvres* was one of the few to take the style seriously, making a contribution to the Paris Exposition of 1900. Comparatively little painting in a recognizably *art nouveau* style exists, although a number of artists of the time were influenced by it. The *art nouveau* artists denied that painting and

began to adapt the style's *motifs* to quantity production. This was disastrous, and the original impetus was soon lost. The early years of the 20th century in England saw a return to the reliance on former styles. The Ritz Hotel in Piccadilly, London, for instance, is a superb example of interior decoration in Edwardian *rococo*.

Despite its relatively short life *art nouveau* played an important part in preparing the ground for 20th-century developments. Other aspects are discussed under the headings of *Art déco, Japanese influence*, and *Les Symbolistes*.

ART-POTTERY (United States)
The term is synonymous with studio-pottery, since in the 19th century even an enterprise like Rookwood* produced individual pots, and did not repeat its designs exactly. 'Art' pottery began to appear on the market after the Philadelphia Centennial Exhibition of 1876 (to which the Japanese Government contributed a representative collection of their pottery) and continued into the early years of the 20th century. The principal makers were Rookwood and the Chelsea Keramic Art Works* at Chelsea, Mass. Pottery basically similar in intent was made in England during the currency of the Aesthetic movement*.

ART UNION, THE
A society founded in 1836 devoted to the encouragement of the arts which produced its first journal, also called *Art Union*, in 1839. On payment of an annual

ARTS AND CRAFTS MOVEMENT. Cabinet of satinwood designed by A. H. Mackmurdo* and made by E. Goodall & Co., Manchester. Exhibited Manchester, 1887, and Arts and Crafts Exhibition*, 1888. It is 7ft 3in. high, 8ft 6in. wide and the painted design on the upper doors includes a quotation from Shelley which reads: 'Nor heed, nor see/What things they be/But of these create he can/Forms more real than living man'. c. 1886. *William Morris Gallery, Waltham Forest*

subscription each member became entitled to participate in a lottery with works of art as prizes, often those which had previously been shown at Royal Academy exhibitions. Later the Union began to commission figures in Parian porcelain* (from Minton*) and bronzes (a reduction of Bell's* *Eagle Slayer* is an example), as well as lithographs and engravings, all of which were inscribed with the origin. The Art Union became both popular and fashionable among the middle classes, and, encouraged by the Prince Consort, other art unions were started, such as the Crystal Palace Art Union of 1858.

ARTS AND CRAFTS EXHIBITION SOCIETY
An offshoot of the Art Workers' Guild* founded in 1888. Its first chairman was Walter Crane*, and William Morris* and Edward Burne-Jones* were members of the committee. Well-known members included C. R. Ashbee*, Ernest Gimson*, Reginald Bloomfield the architect, George Jack*, A. H. Mackmurdo* and C. F. A. Voysey*. The Society held exhibitions annually, with some exceptions, from its foundation until the beginning of the 20th century. Its designs were usually ahead of their time and in particular included furniture and metalwork.

ARTS AND CRAFTS MOVEMENT
The term which describes an extremely influential movement in the last quarter of the 19th century that stemmed largely from the ideas of Morris* and Ruskin*, and includes such men as Crane*, Ashbee*, Mackmurdo*, Lethaby*, Norman Shaw*, Voysey*, etc. They were united by a detestation of commercial manufacturing standards and laid special emphasis on hand-craftsmanship. Most of them subscribed to Morris's dictum that the true root and basis of all art lies in handicrafts, but this introduced a difficult problem, because careful handcraft was time-consuming and expensive, and objects made in this way could only be brought within reach of the great mass of the people by paying the craftsmen low wages. Both Ruskin and Morris believed that the creation of beauty was a duty owed to society, and they were determined to bridge the gulf between what were termed the 'fine' and the 'applied' arts, which had become much wider with the growth of manufacture by machine.

To the manufacturer using machines questions of art were incidental. He needed neither skill as a designer (designs could be taken from the many books on the subject which were proliferating in the 1850s), nor skill as a craftsman beyond that needed to design and make the machines which did the work. The result was that many industrialists were largely devoid of taste, or possessed it only to a rudimentary degree. The *penchant* of the time was for an excess of ornament, since this was taken to be an indication of the costliness of the object and the affluence of the owner, and many objects of utility were decorated with ill-chosen, irrelevant and meaningless devices selected largely for their suitability for machine repetition. C. R. Ashbee was, perhaps, the first among the movement to realize that the machine had come to stay, and that it was more important to devise means of making its products aesthetically acceptable than to replace it by handwork which was no longer economically viable.

A variety of societies and guilds were formed within the arts and crafts movement with the same, or similar, objects. Notable among them were the Century Guild* of Mackmurdo and Image* in 1882, the St. George's Art Society, founded by some of Norman Shaw's pupils, which later gave rise to the Art Workers Guild* of 1884, the Home and Arts Industries of the same year devoted mainly to rural crafts, and Ashbee's Guild of Handicrafts*. The Arts and Crafts Exhibition Society* held exhibitions in 1888, 1889, 1893, 1896 and 1899.

The movement also had considerable influence on the Continent and in the United States, but it was largely superseded by *art nouveau** outside England. True *art nouveau*, as demonstrated by the designs of Charles Rennie Mackintosh*, grew out of the Arts and Crafts movement, but owed relatively little to it in its developed form. The movement survived into the 20th century in the styles adopted by such manufacturers as Heal & Son*.

See *Aesthetic movement*

ART WORKERS' GUILD
English association of artists, architects, and craftsmen founded in London in 1884. Walter Crane* and Lewis F. Day* both took a prominent part in establishing it. Among those connected with it may be numbered William Morris*, C. R. Ashbee*, Ambrose Heal*, George Jack*, C. F. A. Voysey*, W. R. Lethaby*, and W. A. S. Benson*. Its intention was to bring artists and craftsmen of all kinds into closer association; its principal aim was a renaissance of the decorative arts, then generally known as the industrial arts, and more tolerable conditions for those who had to work in factories. Guilds on similar lines were also established in Birmingham and Liverpool. The London association ceased to exist in 1889 and its place and function were taken over by the Arts and Crafts Exhibition Society*.

ART WORKERS' GUILD OF AMERICA
A society with somewhat similar aims to those of its English counterpart. It was founded by the artist, Sydney Burleigh (1853–1931), about 1885 at Providence, R.I. A founder-member was Charles Stetson (1858–1911), who settled in Italy from 1897.

ASHBEE, CHARLES ROBERT (1863–1942)
English architect and designer who came under the influence of William Morris* and founded the Guild of Handicrafts* in 1888. As a designer he was mainly influenced by the neo-Gothic style and interested himself principally in silver and jewellery. Among his

ASHBEE, C. R. Textured gilt-metal sporting cup attributed to the Guild of Handicrafts* and designed by C. R. Ashbee*. c. 1900. *Sotheby & Co*

numerous writings is a translation of Cellini's* *Treatise on the Art of the Goldsmith*. He used the initials CRA as his maker's mark on silver. Many of his designs were made by the Guild, who were actuated by Ashbee's insistence that useful things should be made well and made to be beautiful. His rare furniture-designs used carving, metalwork and tooled leather as ornament. He was a member of the Art Workers' Guild* (Master in 1929) and of the Arts and Crafts Exhibition Society*, and exhibited at the Vienna *Sezession**, where his work was influential.

To a considerable extent Ashbee modified the ideas of Morris and his friends by trying to adapt artistic expression to the requirements of the machine. His designs attracted the attention of a number of London's manufacturers and Liberty's* in particular adopted both his furniture and silver designs. Their 'Cymric'* silver especially owes a lot to Ashbee's influence. The furniture designs of Ambrose Heal* and Ernest Gimson* were both influenced by his work.

ASHSTEAD POTTERIES
A small pottery established after the First World War to give employment to disabled ex-service men with the assistance of pottery manufacturers. It manufactured simply-painted earthenware, and figures, usually in white with touches of colour. These were modelled by Joan Pyman in 1930–1931, and are excellent in quality. The mark is a tree and the name *Ashstead Potteries*. It appears to have closed in 1936.

ASHWORTH & BROTHERS, GEORGE L.
In 1857 Francis Morley*, who bought Mason's* moulds, engravings etc, was joined by the youngest son of George L. Ashworth, Taylor Ashworth (1837–1910). Morley retired in 1862, and George Ashworth bought the business for his sons. The eldest son, George Leach Ashworth, was the head of this firm, but the day-to-day running was in the hands of Taylor Ashworth.

The firm built up a considerable trade in domestic and utility ware, including hotel china, but in 1883 financial difficulties forced the Ashworth brothers to sell the factory to John Goddard, who wanted it for his son, also called John (1857–1939).

Since then the firm have made service-ware and decorative wares of the kind designed by C. J. Mason. For these, executed in a good-quality white earthenware, the firm made use of Mason's moulds, engravings, and backstamps, which they inherited from Francis Morley by way of the Ashworth brothers.

The usual mark employed is the word *MASON'S* over a crown with *PATENT IRONSTONE CHINA* below. Another mark sometimes used states *ASHWORTHS REAL IRONSTONE CHINA*, or a crown above A BROS and the words *REAL IRONSTONE CHINA*. The factory has a collection of old wares.

ASYMMETRY IN ORNAMENT

Classical ornament is symmetrical: if it is bisected by a line drawn vertically down the middle, everything which falls on one side of the line will be balanced by what falls on the other. This is one of the important features of the classical style, and it has always figured prominently in Western decorative art; for instance, vases and porcelain figures have been made in pairs, mantel-clocks have had a vase on either side, and so on.

Although some early Gothic ornament abandoned the rigid symmetry of classicism, true asymmetry was first seen in Europe in the second half of the 17th century with the import of Japanese lacquer panels and the porcelain decorated by Sakaida Kakiemon. These were especially notable for a very effective asymmetry, in which perhaps one third of a plate was employed for decoration and the painted area balanced with two-thirds white porcelain surface. This is a technique which neither the Chinese nor the Europeans ever learned to handle with complete success, although Kakiemon's work was wildly successful in Europe, and copied by many factories, including Meissen* and Chelsea.

Asymmetry in European art does not occur until some of the designs of Jean Bérain *père*, at the beginning of the 18th century, where elements on one side of a design differ in minor ways from those on the other. No doubt the delay was due to Louis XIV's passion for symmetry, because the picture begins to change very soon after his death in 1714.

One of the earliest instances of asymmetry is to be seen on the drawer-fronts of a commode of about 1720 by Charles Cressent, where the bronze mounts differ noticeably on either side. This asymmetry is one of the key features of the following rococo style. The carved ornament at the top of a chair-back or a mirror-frame, for example, was twisted to one side, and naturally represented flowers mingled with entwining C- and S-scrolls* were employed for many purposes. Japanese lacquer panels were especially fashionable in Paris, where they were made up into furniture, by far the greater number being in gold on a black background with an asymmetrical design of figures in pavilions or a landscape. The influence of Japanese asymmetric art is less noticeable in England. Kakiemon decorations were probably copied at Chelsea from Meissen, because the Japanese trade had been almost wholly in the hands of the Dutch on the Continent, while the English East India Company traded particularly with South Chinese ports. Asymmetry came to England at second-hand, and in furniture was first seen in the 1750s with the designs of Chippendale.

Classical symmetry reasserted itself in the 1760s and lasted from then until the reopening of Japanese trade. In the first half of the 19th century it continued to prevail, except for the rococo revival of the period between about 1825 and about 1850, when asymmetry was revived in the design of porcelain, and to a lesser extent, of some kinds of silver.

Generally, the 19th century until the 1880s preserved a classical symmetry even in most of its neo-Gothic designs, but *art nouveau** absorbed Japanese influence to a point where asymmetry became one of its principal features. One of the most outstanding contributions of Japanese art to that of the West has been the demonstration that the arts of design are not wholly dependent on the principle of symmetry.

See *Japanese influence*

AUDUBON, JEAN JACQUES FOUGERE (1785–1851)

Audubon was born in Haiti, the natural son of a French mercantile agent and a Creole woman. During his school-days in France, where he was legally adopted in 1794, he developed a talent for drawing the local wildlife and became a naturalist of considerable ability. He is reputed to have had lessons in drawing from Jacques-Louis David.

AUDUBON, J. J. F. The Great American Cock (Wild Turkey) from *The Birds of America. Christie, Manson & Woods*

In 1803 he settled in America and in 1819, after business failures, he decided to devote himself to depicting the birds of America, the product to be sold by subscription, and he spent much of his time in Louisiana. Failing to find sufficient support in America he travelled to England in 1826. Here he successfully showed his drawings at the Royal Institution in London, where his novel depictions of birds in their natural surroundings of trees and flowers were much acclaimed. The *Birds of America* (1827–1838) was produced in 87 parts, with 435 plates showing more than a thousand birds with accompanying plants and insects; expensive at the time, the work sold slowly. The earlier plates were engraved by W. Home Lizars, but from 1827 they were executed in aquatint by Robert Havell (1793–1878), then almost unknown. The work was finally completed in 1838 with a text by William MacGillivray, the Scottish ornithologist.

Audubon's last work, unfinished at his death, was

The *Viviparous Quadrupeds of North America*, in which he was assisted by his sons. Audubon has, from time to time, influenced artists in other media, the most recent instance being the American Birds in Royal Worcester* porcelain by Dorothy Doughty*. Audubon prints are now much sought after.

AUGARTEN PORZELLANFABRIK (Vienna)
Porcelain factory established in 1922. Its designs were influenced by the Wiener Werkstätte*, and Josef Hoffmann designed one of its table-services about 1928. Figures include those of Lippizaner horses from the Spanish Riding School. Usual mark, a crown above a shield and *Wien*.

AULT, WILLIAM (1841–?)
English potter originally in partnership with Henry Tooth (see *Bretby Art Pottery*), who founded his own pottery at Swadlincote, near Burton-on-Trent, in 1887. Here he produced wares designed by Christopher Dresser*. His daughter, Clarissa, painted vases with flowers and butterflies, and he introduced an aventurine* glaze, that is a glaze with small spangles of copper suspended in it. From 1923 to 1937 the style was Ault & Tunnicliffe Ltd, and from 1937, Ault Potteries Ltd. It employs the mark of a tall vase and the word *Ault*.

AURENE GLASS
The trade name for a kind of iridized glass devised by Frederick Carder*, manager of the Steuben Glass Works*, New York, and first marketed about 1905. Aurene glass was probably inspired in the first instance by Tiffany's* 'Favrile'* glass, but was made in far greater variety. Although Carder was remarkable for his high command of techniques, Aurene was probably his most widely known and successful product and is now collected. An exhibition including Aurene was held at the Pilkington Glass Museum, St Helens, Lancashire, and subsequently at the Victoria and Albert Museum, London, in the autumn of 1972.

AUGARTEN. Porcelain figure, *Malaize*, modelled for the Porzellanfabrik Augarten*, Vienna, by Matilde Jaksch-Brandis. c. 1925. *Victoria & Albert Museum, London*

AUSTIN, FELIX
Austin bought the moulds belonging to Van Spangen, Powell & Co.*, in 1828, and he made decorative objects of all kinds from artificial stone and terracotta, many of them designed by contemporary architects, until 1850.

See *Coade & Sealy*

AUTOMATA
Automatic devices of one kind or another go back to times long before the present era. The Romans had a device which opened temple doors when a fire was lit on an altar in the forecourt. They were popular at the Mongol court in the 13th century—and at the medieval court of Burgundy. Clock-makers of the 16th and 17th centuries often specialized in such devices, which usually operated when the hours were struck. Records from the 18th century of such objects are numerous and some of them have survived.

AULT, WILLIAM. A *jardinière* with swept wing handles in the Egyptian taste designed by Christopher Dresser*. Swadlincote, Burton-on-Trent. c. 1892–1896. *Sotheby & Co*

Those of the 18th and 19th centuries were usually provided with movements similar to those of the musical box* which played as the figures moved. The largest number of survivals date from the 19th century, but the craftsmanship deteriorated progressively. Birds in cages date from about 1790, and the musical accompaniment to their movement was produced by air forced through a whistle by miniature

AUTOMATA. Mantel-clock by Joseph Schwer of Vienna, the pierced face with striking automata of a grinder and a smith. Early 19th century. *Antique Collectors' Club*

bellows, with a mechanism for varying the pitch and volume of the sound. By the 1830s Japanese bird-cages were being made at Wolverhampton with a recess in the base for the fitting of a mechanical movement imported from France by makers such as Charles Bontemps, or from Switzerland. Some of the more delicate and complicated mechanisms, which involved several birds apparently flitting from branch to branch, were placed under glass shades.

The musical-box movement, in which the teeth of a steel comb were vibrated by being struck with steel pins projecting from a revolving brass cylinder, dates from 1820, and was invented by David le Coultre. It was a development from a slightly earlier device used by English clockmakers, in which the projecting pins were used to raise hammers to strike bells. In the case of automata, the clockwork mechanism which turns the cylinder of the musical movement also turns a shaft fitted with cams which lift the activating rods of the figures at predetermined intervals.

It is perhaps not surprising that the best of these automata were designed in conjunction with a clock, the mechanism of which supplied some of the motive power.

Dolls capable of performing a number of actions automatically, and perhaps, at the same time, of speaking or singing, were usually made by those specializing in mechanisms of this kind—makers of clockwork, musical boxes, etc.—and mechanical dolls with a head by someone like Jumeau are not unknown. The greater number of mechanical dolls belong to the second half of the 19th century. A walking doll rejoicing in the name of Autoperipatetikon (the kind of pompous Greek neologism of which the Victorians were inordinately fond, and which merely means self-propelling) was produced about 1862. Excellent dolls of this kind, which are on wheels under their skirts, were made by Jules Steiner of Paris in the 1860s and 1870s. Steiner, who described himself as a *mécanicien*, took out a number of patents later in the century for improved clockwork mechanisms for walking dolls. Alexandre-Nicolas Théroude et Cie of Paris specialized in mechanical dolls around 1865. One specimen turns its *papier mâché* head from side to side as it moves. The American firm of E.R. Ives (founded 1866) of Bridgeport, Conn., later Ives & Blakeslee, made mechanical dolls, probably under licence from the patentee, Arthur Hotchkiss, on the evidence of a mark on one of a series, which includes *Uncle Tom* and a *Heathen Chinee* inspired by Bret Harte. Most mechanisms are key-wound clockwork, but some German dolls, usually those playing a violin or mandoline, and including a musical-box of some kind, are actuated by squeezing the sides, which operates both the movements and the sound. Musical dolls include the American Webber singing doll and the Edison Phonograph doll. High prices are often paid for rare specimens in good condition, but valuation is difficult. Most specimens fail to be valued both as dolls and as mechanisms. If either part is defective, or poor in quality, value is reduced accordingly. Damage to mechanism should be seriously considered; most repairs are now very difficult to get done, and very expensive.

See *Dolls and doll-houses*; *Musical boxes*

AUTOMATA. An automaton in carved bone made by French prisoners of war. c. 1810. *Antique Collectors' Club*

AUTOMOBILE MASCOTS

This is one of the most recent additions to the collector's range. The fitting of radiator cap mascots dates from the early years of the present century until the outbreak of the Second World War when, except for a very few marques such as Rolls-Royce, the practice was abandoned. No one seems to know the origin of the custom; perhaps it is looking too far afield to recall that both the ancient Chinese and the nomadic Scythians decorated their chariots with bronzes which may have had ritual significance, or merely acted as charms to ensure success in hunting.

The most important trophy to the present-day collector is the mascot introduced by Rolls-Royce in 1911. This, modelled by Charles Sykes in an *art nouveau** style, was a female nude (an ever-popular subject) leaning forward into the wind. Called the *Spirit of Ecstasy* by the makers, she is usually irreverently referred to as 'Emily' by owners of vintage and veteran cars. In 1936 she assumed a kneeling posture but has since regained her original stance. Like all the earlier mascots she is mounted on the radiator cap, and if offered without it, has probably been illegally acquired by the adept use of a hack-saw.

The hey-day of the mascot was in the 1920s, when they were to be found in great variety on all but the cheapest automobiles. They also tended to be designed in a more abstract style related to *art déco** *motifs* of the period. Mascots to individual choice often replaced those supplied by the factory to add a touch of individuality to the vehicle, and they range from those which are works of small sculpture to poor-quality casts. One of the latter, a red painted devil with long tail, horns, and fingers outspread and held to his nose, was very popular, and H. V. Morton records seeing one preserved in a glass case in a Near-Eastern museum labelled 'The god, Baal, c. 900 B.C.'.

About the middle of the 1930s the radiator cap began to be placed under the hood in many cars, so a new mounting had to be designed for the mascot. The eponymous jaguar mounted on the radiator shell dates from this time.

The material of which mascots were made varied with the metal used for the radiator shell, for example, the Rolls-Royce 'Emily' was made of German silver. Others were made of nickel-plated brass, but perhaps the rarest and most sought are the glass mascots of Lalique*. Prices now range from a few pounds to £500 or more, the latter sum being paid for Lalique mascots.

AVENTURINE

Glass in which small flakes of copper or gold have been suspended. This is a very ancient technique, which was revived during the 19th century in Europe and America for decorative glass, and made by a number of factories.

AVISSEAU, CHARLES

Avisseau established a factory at Tours (Indre et Loire) in 1842. Here he reproduced the work of the 16th-century potter, Bernard Palissy*, which was then in great demand among collectors, and the so-called Henri Deux ware (*Saint-Porchaire faïence**), also from the 16th century, the rare surviving specimens of which were much sought at the time. After his death in 1861 he was succeeded by his son, M. E. Avisseau. The firm was awarded a medal at the London Exhibition of 1862 for work in the Henri Deux and Palissy styles.

AYNSLEY, JOHN (1752–1829)

Manufacturer of porcelain and cream-coloured earthenware, the latter often decorated with black transfer-prints of moral and improving subjects, such as 'Keep within Compass', signed *Aynsley, Lane End*. Traditionally he was one of the first to make porcelain in Staffordshire, and the first to use lustre*. In about 1860 his descendant founded the firm of John Aynsley & Son, porcelain makers of Longton, whose mark was *Aynsley, England,* beneath a crown.

B

BACCARAT GLASS FACTORY (Lorraine)

Although this undertaking grew from a small factory founded by the Archbishop of Metz in 1765, it did not assume importance until the early decades of the 19th century. It then incorporated three undertakings—the crystal glass factory at Vareche, a town originally French which became Belgian after the Congress of Vienna in 1813, the factory of Sainte-Anne at Baccarat, and another at Trelon (Nord) acquired in 1828.

Baccarat began to make lead crystal in the English manner in 1819, and from then onwards it supplied cut crystal glass of fine quality for which it became famous. Opaline* glass was made from an early date, but the exact year of its introduction is uncertain. The word 'opaline' for glass of this kind was coined at Baccarat about 1823, when the Saint-Louis factory was calling it *pâte-de-riz*. Production of opaline at Baccarat was at its best between 1850 and 1870, after which it declined. Baccarat was also noted in the 1840s for the quality of its paperweights*.

From 1822 to 1858 the factory was directed by Jean-Baptist Toussaint to whom much of the technical and artistic success of the factory was due. A joint merchandising arrangement with the Saint-Louis* undertaking was concluded about 1828, with showrooms in the rue de Paradis, Paris, where they still remain.

BACCHUS & SONS, GEORGE (Birmingham, Warwickshire)

At first known as Bacchus & Green, the style above was adopted in 1840. Bacchus probably introduced the manufacture of press-moulded* glass into England, especially wares imitating cut-glass*, around 1840. Opal (opaline*) glass was first made around 1850 and exhibited at the Great Exhibition in the following year. Vases especially were decorated with hand-coloured transfer-prints*, and 'Etruscan' subjects were popular. Their products also included ice glass* and *millefiori* glass, especially paperweights*. Some of their mid-century glass was influenced by popular Bohemian* work, including cased glass* with engraved decoration.

BAG-TABLE

Small English or American table, usually with turned legs and a drawer or drawers in the frieze. Where there is more than one drawer the lower of the two has, instead of the normal wooden floor, a dependent cloth bag for the storage of sewing materials. Sewing-tables somewhat similar in design, the storage compartment with tapering wooden sides covered with cloth, belong to the same period (from about 1780 to 1840).

BAGULEY, ISAAC (fl. 1820–1850)

Foreman china painter at the Rockingham* factory who continued after the factory closure by buying white porcelain in Staffordshire. He marked his work 'Baguley, Rockingham Works', and sometimes added the griffin mark.

BAILEY & CO. (1864–1889)

C. J. C. Bailey was a London potter who, in 1864, bought and enlarged the Fulham pottery formerly occupied by John Dwight at the end of the 17th century. Here the firm made stoneware*, terracotta* and, about 1873, a limited amount of porcelain. In addition to domestic wares they produced vases and

BACCARAT GLASS FACTORY. Crystal tumbler decorated with an inset medallion. Cristallerie de Baccarat*. France. *Pilkington Glass Museum*

BAILEY & CO. Oval stoneware *jardinière* (seen from one end) decorated with majolica-type coloured glazes and pseudo-Renaissance *motifs*. Probably J. C. Bailey, Fulham. c. 1880. *Constance Chiswell*

BACCHUS & SONS, GEORGE. White glass vase decorated in enamel colours with the subject of Bellerophon, mounted on Pegasus, slaying the Chimera. Bacchus & Sons, Birmingham. c. 1855. *Victoria & Albert Museum, London*

figures in terracotta, stoneware, and incised or impressed decoration, or with foliage, birds, and animals. J. P. Seddon* designed stoneware *jardinières* with incised decoration.

The marks employed were BAILEY or C. J. C. BAILEY and either FULHAM or FULHAM POTTERY.

BAILY, E. H. (1788–1867)
English sculptor who executed the statue of Nelson in Trafalgar Square. He was also chief modeller to Rundell, Bridge & Rundell, silversmiths to the Prince Regent.

BAKEWELL, PEARS & COMPANY (Philadelphia, Pa.)
This glass factory was founded in 1808 by two Englishmen who are reputed to have been the first to make flint glass* in America. They are also said to have made the first crystal chandelier* in the United States. They made table-ware of almost every kind and enjoyed a large export trade with South America.

BALDOCK (London)
China-dealer in the early years of the 19th century who employed Robins, Randall* and others to decorate white porcelain for sale. He bought extensively at the sales of white porcelain held at Sèvres* by Brongniart soon after 1800, and had it decorated in the more sumptuous '*vieux Sèvres*'* styles. He also bought slightly decorated wares, removed the painting with hydrofluoric acid* and then had it re-enamelled with more expensive decorations. London-decorated Nantgarw* porcelain is in some instances the work of Baldock who was always searching for suitable white porcelain for painting. The trade in redecorated porcelain had largely disappeared by the early 1820s when the newer factories, such as those of John Rose*, Minton*, and Spode* were imitating Sèvres styles fairly extensively.

BALLOON-BACK
A very common type of back for drawing-room and dining-room chairs until at least 1875, so-called because the shape of the back somewhat resembles the outline of a hot-air balloon of the type introduced by the Montgolfier brothers towards the end of the 18th century. Drawing-room chairs were usually of walnut, less often of rosewood and, especially after 1850, often had a serpentine seat-rail, cabriole legs, and a certain amount of carved ornament. Dining-chairs, also with carved ornament, had a straight front seat-rail and turned legs.

The balloon-back in a modified form first appeared in the 1830s, but in its commonest form it dates from the 1840s. It also occurs in a lighter form in birch or maple as a bedroom chair. It has no exact equivalent on the Continent, the French and Biedermeier* chairs made for these purposes having backs of a more elaborate contour. The type of balloon-back in which a transverse rail, sometimes with carved ornament, joins the sides of the curved back-rail, is often termed a buckle-back.

BALLOON-BACK. The curves of the back have been slightly modified, and it is carved in what is essentially a revived rococo style. The front legs are turned. c. 1850. *Author*

BALLOON CLOCKS
Type of clock made in England from the last quarter of the 18th century until about 1810 and reproduced later in the 19th century. The case is circular at the top, curving inwards and then outwards, near the bottom, to the base. The type is based on French clocks of about the same period with cases of gilt-bronze.

BAMBOO
The use of simulated bamboo in the making of decorative furniture is to be found in the 18th century, when it was known as 'bamboo turning'. Decorative furniture of this kind was supplied for the Prince Regent's Royal Pavilion (Brighton)*, where the cast-iron stair-rails were made in similar form. In the 1880s there was a fashion for inexpensive furniture made from bamboo and woven rattan* cane, or from bamboo simulated by turned wood painted in natural colours.

BANJO CLOCKS
American wall-clock made from 1801 to 1860 with circular face, a straight trunk to accommodate the pendulum rod, and a rectangular or almost square compartment at the bottom to house the pendulum bob, usually with decorative glass panels. The best were made by the inventor, Simon Willard*, and his family. The movement was of brass, and it had the dead-beat escapement* invented by the English clockmaker George Graham. Simon Willard intended the banjo clock to replace the grandfather clock, but it more nearly resembles contemporary French lyre clocks, and it is sometimes thus called. Simon Willard's clocks are the most sought, but those made by Aaron Willard*, Lemuel Curtis* and others are also highly regarded.

BARBEDIENNE ET CIE, FERDINAND (Paris)
Celebrated bronze-founders established in 1839 in association with Achille Collas*. Also decorative metalworkers, Barbedienne's London agent in the mid century was Mungo, Jackson & Graham* of Oxford Street, and at this time the foundry was producing reductions of large sculpture in bronze using a technique invented by Collas known as *appareil réducteur*, a mechanical device for reducing precisely any piece of sculpture to a chosen scale. Among the subjects thus reproduced were the works of Ghiberti and Michelangelo.

Ferdinand Barbedienne (1810–1892) was among the most important of 19th-century bronze-founders, and he cast for the *Animalier** sculptor Barye*. After the latter's death Barbedienne bought some of his models and reissued them. Founder's signatures recorded include *F. Barbedienne*, *FB*, and a circular gilt medallion, *Collections Barbedienne*. He exhibited in London in 1851 and 1862, and in Paris in 1855, with considerable success. The first of these exhibitions included a bookcase of ebony with bronze mounts by the sculptor, Clesinger. Barbedienne later did excellent enamel work, a specially fine example of which was included in the 1862 International Exhibition and is now displayed in the Bethnal Green Museum, London. The firm closed in 1953.

BARBOTINE (French)
Technique of decorating ware with the aid of liquid slip of various colours, either laid on the surface by trailing or applied by painting. The process was developed in France by Ernest Chaplet*, but it presented certain difficulties, inasmuch as disagreements in the shrinkage rate between slip and body during firing could cause it to flake off. For this reason the process was abandoned after 1900. The term is also sometimes loosely and inaccurately employed for other types of slip decoration.

BARGE WARE
Also known as Long-Boat ware, or Meascham ware. Heavy brown glazed earthenware with applied white clay decoration of flowers, or bunches of flowers, in primary colours which tend to flow into one another, often with a commemorative or presentation impressed inscription in a curved panel of white glazed clay e.g. 'To Joe & Lil, with love from Ma 1885'. Typical articles include large teapots, some with an extra hold on the front of the spout, with the lid of the pot a teapot in miniature, sets of jugs, bowls etc.;

BARGE WARE. A very large brown glazed barge ware* teapot, the cover surmounted by a miniature teapot. The inscription, *A present to a friend*, is impressed with printers' type, a not unusual technique in the case of small potteries. Last quarter of the 19th century. *Constance Chiswell*

period late 19th, early 20th century. Modern reproductions bear little resemblance to the originals.

BARLACH, ERNST (1870–1938)
German Expressionist sculptor who visited Russia in 1906 and who subsequently drew a great deal of inspiration from Russian peasants. During the years before the First World War he designed figures of this kind for the Thuringian porcelain factory of the Schwarzburger Werkstätten für Porzellankunst at Unterweissbach. Much of his sculpture was in carved wood with similar subjects.

BARLOW, FLORENCE (d. 1909)
Sister of Hannah Barlow*. She joined Doulton's* factory in 1873 decorating stoneware* with birds in the manner of her sister. She also painted '*faïence*'*, and decorated stoneware with birds and foliage painted in slip (see *Barbotine*). She marked her ware *FEB*.

BARLOW, HANNAH (1851–1916)
Pottery decorator who studied at Lambeth Art School and joined the staff of Doulton* in 1871. Her decoration of animals (horses, dogs, sheep, etc.) were incised into the surface of stoneware* vessels in a free and spirited manner, and her work is now much sought. Her later work is 'tighter' and more detailed. Hannah Barlow also painted '*faïence*'*, and marked her work, *HBB*.

BARNES, B. (1769–1842)
One of the most prolific makers of pewter in America, Barnes worked in Philadelphia from 1812 to 1817.

BARNSLEY, SIDNEY (1865–1926)
Furniture designer of the Cotswold School, partner, with Gimson*, in Kenton & Co.* His London furniture styles were fairly ornate, but his work

developed in the direction of simplicity when he moved to Cirencester, Gloucestershire, in 1893.

BAROVIER, ERCOLE (b. 1899)
Italian glass-maker, descendant of a 15th-century family. Founded Barovier & Toso of Murano, Venice. Barovier has been largely responsible for the modern Venetian style in glass-making. He has introduced new varieties of glass, and has especially sought novel surface effects, such as *vetro gemmato*—opaque glass with an irregular, matt surface in several colours.

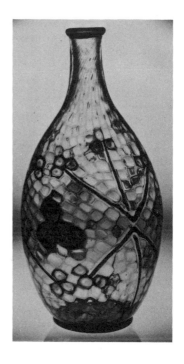

BAROVIER, ERCOLE. Bottle-shaped *millefiori** vase by E. Barovier* of Murano, Italy. *Pilkington Glass Museum*

BARTLETT, WILLIAM HENRY (1809–1854)
Engraver whose two-volume work, *Canadian Scenery*, was published early in the 1840s. These volumes were used in Staffordshire in the 1840s and 1880s for decorating Staffordshire transfer-printed* earthenware. Much of it was made by Padmore, Walker & Co., Francis Morley & Co.* and Morley's successors George L. Ashworth & Bros.* Marked pieces are comparatively rare.

BARUM WARE See *Brannam, Charles H.*

BARWIG, FRANZ (1868–1931)
Modeller and woodcarver, who modelled animals for Augarten* and the Wienberger Werkstättenschule für Keramik. His mark was an incised signature or initials.

BARYE, ANTOINE-LOUIS. *Lion*, bronze by Antoine-Louis Barye*. Third quarter of the 19th century. *Antique Collectors' Club*

BARYE, ALFRED

Son of Antoine-Louis Barye*, and also an *Animalier* sculptor who exhibited studies of racehorses in the *Salons* of 1864, 1865 and 1866. His work is competent, but without his father's inspiration. He signed *A. BARYE FILS*.

BARYE, ANTOINE-LOUIS (1796–1875)

French *Animalier* sculptor who is regarded as the founder of the School, and one of Rodin's* sources of inspiration. Barye was a very influential figure in the field of French Romantic sculpture of the 19th century.

He was apprenticed to a goldsmith and had begun to model small animals while still thus employed. He frequented zoological gardens and horse-fairs, and whenever he had the opportunity he dissected dead animals to study their anatomy. He met with a complete lack of recognition among Academic circles and to overcome this he established his own foundry for making such decorative objects as clock cases, candelabra, and furniture mounts, and also cast his own models in the *cire perdue* technique. His clock cases, designed by himself, were often decorated with animal subjects. He was also skilled in the colouring and patination of bronze. Bronzes cast before 1848 by Barye, and by his assistants, Gonon* and his sons, are very fine in quality.

Despite his efforts, Barye was no business man and by 1848 he became bankrupt. At this point Émile Martin stepped in, took charge of his models and casts, and proceeded to have them cast by a cheaper and inferior sand-casting process. The exact relationship between Barye and Martin is uncertain, but it seems he was something more than a creditor, and was perhaps some kind of man of business who undertook to help Barye straighten his affairs, which had been achieved by 1857. Already known in England, by 1858 he had attracted attention in the United States, and he soon became popular in American art-circles.

Barye stands far above the other *Animaliers* in the artistic quality of his work, both large and small. His numerous small bronzes are characterized by a lively

movement which is rarely incongruous. His human figures are less successful. His talent in the handling of difficult subjects may be seen in the small model of an elephant charging. His groups include a large number of animal combats of one kind or another—a stag attacked by hounds or a jaguar devouring an alligator, for instance. Two ambitious groups of a lion hunt and a bull hunt were originally commissioned as table centrepieces by the Duc d'Orléans, but were less successful than his simpler compositions.

Barye usually incised his name BARYE in small capitals. *A-L. BARYE* occurs occasionally. *A. BARYE* is the signature of his son, Alfred*. Work is known unsigned, and a stamp, *BARYE*, was sometimes used. A signature *Barye* is probably spurious. Barye's bronzes are much sought and highly valued.

BASALTES WARE. Two small vases of black basaltes* stoneware in the neo-classical* style. The example on the right is engine-turned. Made by Josiah Wedgwood & Sons Ltd. *Mrs F. H. Stubbley*

BASALTES WARE. Black basaltes* covered sugar-bowl with engine-turned decoration, inspired by Wedgwood's basaltes ware. Mark: *Creil* impressed. Early 19th century. *Victoria & Albert Museum, London*

BASALTES WARE

This is the name given to a black fine-grained, hard-fired, unglazed stoneware by Josiah Wedgwood*, who developed it from an existing Staffordshire ware known as 'Egyptian black'. The spelling *basalt* often employed today is not strictly accurate.

Basaltes has much of the hardness of the natural stone. It will take a high polish, and can act as a touchstone for gold. It has been used almost continuously since the 18th century for high-quality ornamental wares. Like jasper*, it was copied by other Staffordshire firms, and by a number of Continental factories, especially Königsberg and Ulfsunda.

BASKET-FURNITURE   See *Wicker furniture*

BASSE-TAILLE
Technique in which a transparent enamel is employed to cover metal which has previously been engraved or engine-turned*.

See *Champlevé enamelling*; *Cloisonné enamel*; *Enamels, painted*; *Plique-à-jour enamel*.

BASTIANINI, GIOVANNI (fl. 1860–1870)
Italian sculptor from Fiesole who achieved notoriety as a deceptive and highly-skilled copyist of *quattrocento* terracotta* and marble. No claim was ever made by Bastianini, or the dealer who negotiated the sale of one of his most important works, that these sculptures were genuinely old. Buyers were simply allowed to deceive themselves, and when Bastianini's portrait of the Florentine philosopher, Bienvieni (1453–1542), was bought at auction by the Louvre, attributions to Verrocchio and Donatello were canvassed. An example of his work is in the Victoria and Albert Museum, London, but its 19th-century date has, with the passing of time, become more obvious.

BATES, ELLIOT & COMPANY (Dalehall, Longport, Staffordshire)
Large manufacturers of pottery from the early decades of the 19th century. They made domestic wares (dinner-, dessert-, tea-, and toilet-services), as well as the popular blue printed ware. In the 1870s they acquired the moulds of Turner's jasper* and used them to make reproductions of earlier wares. Excellent terracotta* figures of classical subjects were produced, some of them modelled by William Beattie*. The firm later became Bates, Walker & Co. and used the name impressed as a mark, or the initial *B. W. & Co.*

BAT-PRINTING   See *Transfer-printing*

BATTAM, THOMAS (1810–1864)
Art-director of W. T. Copeland* in London and Stoke-on-Trent from 1835 to 1856. Battam has been credited with the invention of the Parian* body, and is said to have made copies of oil paintings on porcelain plaques. He specialized in the reproduction of ancient Greek and Etruscan pottery, at first the black-figure and then the red-figure type, which he copied from specimens in the British Museum. Huge reproductions of classical vases by Battam were shown at the Great Exhibition of 1851.

BAUDISCHE-WITTKE, GUDRUN (b. 1907)
Austrian studio-potter who worked as a ceramic designer from 1926 to 1930 in the Wiener Werkstätten* under Josef Hoffmann. She worked in Berlin from 1936 to 1942, and in 1943 established her own pottery at Hallstadt. Marks: signs *G. BAUDISCH* or monogram, incised or printed.

BAUDOINE, CHARLES A (fl. 1845–1900)
New York furniture-maker at 325 Broadway who employed 200 men. Baudoine manufactured furniture in revived rococo* and Renaissance styles, and like John Belter*, with whom he was in competition, he employed laminated wood. Generally he used rosewood* for much of his production, except for dining-room furniture, which was in oak.

BAUER, LEOPOLD (1872–1938)
Designer of glass for Lötz*, and also of ceramics, mainly in the *Jugendstil*. A pupil of Otto Wagner's, he worked in Vienna with Josef Olbrich and Josef Hoffmann.

BAUHAUS, THE
German School of Design founded in Weimar by the architect Walter Gropius in 1919. Associated with him were Paul Klee, Wassily Kandinsky, Laszlo Moholy-Nagy, Marcel Breuer*, and others. The new School occupied the buildings of the former School of Arts and Crafts which had been directed, until its closure in 1915 by the Belgian architect and designer Henri van der Velde*. The new School attempted to relate construction to function, and to design according to the needs of machine-production. They also aimed to combine the teaching of art with that of craft. The product of this thinking came to be known as the International Style, and it was notable for box-like forms, straight lines, glossy surfaces, metal tubing (usually chromium plated) and plywood. Decoration, rarely added at all, was strictly geometrical in design. Its effect was to eliminate non-essentials, but the designs of the Bauhaus were severely criticized at the time by traditionalists. In 1933 it was closed down by the Nazis, and Gropius, Breuer and Moholy-Nagy fled to the United States, where Gropius joined the Harvard Graduate School of Design, to be followed by Mies van der Rohe* in 1937. Here they continued their work with a marked success which has profoundly influenced the course of interior decoration in the modern manner since that time.

See *Art déco*; *Functionalism*

BAXTER PRINTS
Colour-prints produced by a process invented by George Baxter (1804–1867) and patented in 1836. These prints were produced with the aid of oil-based inks and wood-blocks, one for each colour. Baxter prints were produced in large quantities, and with a great variety of subjects—topographical views, portraits of Royalty, and *genre* scenes. Particularly

BAXTER, THOMAS. Circular plaque of porcelain decorated with exotic shells by Thomas Baxter*. Worcester, Chamberlain's* factory. c. 1820. *Private collection*

popular were his prints of the Great Exhibition. Baxter sold licences to use his process to a number of other printers. After his death about 70 of his plates were purchased by Abraham Le Blond who used them to produce inferior reproductions, as well as issuing new subjects of his own.

BAXTER, THOMAS (b. 1782)
Porcelain painter. At first an independent decorator in London, he removed to Worcester* in 1814 where he continued in the same capacity and also taught apprentices. In 1816 he went to Swansea* to work for Dillwyn, but returned to Worcester in 1818. His status as a painter is considerable. He was very versatile, painting landscapes, figures, and flowers in meticulous detail, but he specialized in the very fashionable subjects of feathers and shells.

BAYEUX (Calvados)
The porcelain factory of Vologues was moved here by Joachim Langlois in 1810, and by 1820 it employed about 80 workmen. Much of the best painting and gilding was done by M. Langlois, his wife, and two daughters. After his death in 1830 the enterprise was continued by his wife and son, Frédéric, and the factory was sold to M. Gosse in 1849. Gosse greatly enlarged the works, but made a considerable quantity of industrial porcelain. The best production was during the lifetime of Joachim Langlois, when 'Japan' patterns were produced in great variety. A small group of a Chinese spice merchant surrounded by jars has the name Langlois in pseudo-Chinese lettering on one of them, but much Bayeux porcelain of this period is otherwise unmarked. It was given an extremely hard firing, and was highly regarded by Alexandre Brongniart* at Sèvres*, where the Museum has specimens. There are also examples in the museum at Bayeux.

BEARDSLEY, AUBREY VINCENT (1872–1898)
English draughtsman whose black and white drawings were at first much influenced by the pre-Raphaelites*, and later by Japanese prints and French rococo designs. Beardsley began to draw for *The Studio** in 1893, and in the following year did a series of drawings illustrating Wilde's *Salome*. In 1894 he became the art-editor of the *Yellow Book* and illustrated *Lysistrata*. He contracted tuberculosis in 1897 and died at Mentone in the following year. Beardsley's work was a distinct factor in the development of the *art nouveau** style, especially in Germany and Austria.

BEATTIE, WILLIAM (fl. 1829–1864)
English sculptor who first exhibited at the Royal Academy in 1829. He showed a solid silver statuette of the Prince Consort at the Great Exhibition of 1851. He exhibited with the Birmingham Society of Artists in 1855, and about the same time he was employed by Wedgwood*, for whom he modelled *The Finding of Moses*, *The Flute Player*, and figures emblematic of England, Scotland, Ireland, and America. He also modelled terracotta* figures for Bates, Elliot & Co.*

BEAUVAIS (Oise)
Beauvais has always been a pottery-making area, and there were important potteries here in the 16th century. In the 19th century (about 1840), there was a manufacturer of decorative stoneware* (*grès*), the designer for whom was Jules-Claude Ziegler (1804–1856) working in Beauvais from about 1839 to 1843. His stoneware was decorated with natural flowers and climbing plants in relief which are to be found on such objects as brown stoneware jugs and tobacco and pickle jars. A specimen of Ziegler's work originally exhibited at the Paris Exposition of Industrial Art in 1844 is in the Victoria and Albert Museum, London. Ziegler published a book of ceramic designs in 1850.

BEAUVAIS STONEWARE. Brown stoneware* wine jug decorated with vine-leaves and grapes modelled in high relief. France, Beauvais. c. 1830. *Constance Chiswell*

BEAUX-ARTS STYLE

Name given to a style of the last quarter of the 19th century, especially in the United States, which was based largely on French decorative art of the Renaissance* and the period of Louis XIV, Louis XV, and Louis XVI. These *motifs* were very freely adapted, one piece of furniture being described at the time as being in the manner of 'all the Louis's'. The time was one in which wealthy collectors were paying high prices for French art of the royal period, housing their possessions in imitations of *châteaux*. Lower down the social scale Beaux-Arts furniture and accessories were employed to decorate smaller houses in the same *château* style. The style, of course, is far from dead, and reproductions of 18th-century French furniture and metalwork, especially the Louis XVI style, are much in demand.

BEAVER FALLS ART TILE COMPANY (Beaver Falls, Pa.)

Factory founded in 1886 which specialized in the manufacture of ornamental tiles mainly decorated in relief or in *intaglio*, especially for such sites as the interior walls of public buildings.

BECKERT, ADOLF (1884–1929)

Art-director at the Lötz glass factory, Vienna, from 1909 to 1911. He studied at the Prague Kunstgewerbeschule, and the Fachschule at Haida in Bohemia. During his period with Lötz, Beckert produced glass with etched floral ornament in the French manner. From 1911 to 1926 he taught at the Fachschule in Steinschönau.

BECKFORD, WILLIAM. View of the Great Western Hall of Beckford's* Fonthill Abbey. c. 1825. After Rutter's *Delineations of Fonthill*

BECKFORD, WILLIAM (1789–1844)

English author, traveller, art-collector, and arbiter of taste. Beckford's influence was, perhaps, at its greatest so far as matters of taste are concerned with his employment of the architect, James Wyatt, to build a Wiltshire country-house called Fonthill Abbey*, with a design based on Salisbury Cathedral. Largely due to the machinations of a fraudulent contractor the tower fell down in a gale, and the rest of the house has since been demolished. It is, however, very well known from contemporary descriptions, and a volume of engravings by Owen Rutter called *Delineations of Fonthill*. Beckford, who referred to Walpole's Strawberry Hill as 'a Gothic mousetrap', distinctly influenced the Victorian neo-Gothic* style. It was probably with Fonthill and Pugin* especially in mind that Osbert Lancaster referred to the large, humourless moth of Victorian Gothic blundering out of Walpole's charming 18th-century chrysalis.

Beckford was among the earliest collectors of Chinese art to exercise a scholarly discrimination in his purchases instead of forming an assemblage of curiosities. He is, perhaps, still known today for his Eastern tale of the *Caliph Vathek*, originally written in French.

BEDS, FIELD

American portable beds in use during the greater part of the 19th century and sometimes in England. Four turned posts support a light framework with curved laths between, over which is stretched a covering of some light material such as cotton. They replaced the four-poster with its heavy tester. Sometimes called a tent bed.

BEDS, SLEIGH

Beds with a rolling curved head- and foot-board giving them the appearance of a sleigh. They belong to the period of the Empire style* and are usually French.

BELL, JOHN (1812–1895)

English sculptor born in Hopton, Suffolk, educated at the village school in Catfield, Norfolk and at the Royal Academy Schools. In 1833 he won the Silver Medal of the Society of Arts for a bust. The Art Union* said of his work, 'It is deeply imbued with poetic feeling, he is one of the few artists who attempts higher efforts than mere busts.'

His *Una and the Lion* was reproduced in Parian porcelain* by Copeland* and sold in large numbers. In 1845 he designed a table for the Coalbrookdale Pottery Company* to be cast in iron, 'The deer-hound hall table'*. It consisted of four life-size stag-hounds seated on their haunches supporting a table decorated with emblems of the chase, vine-leaves, and grapes, which was commended by the Art Union, and exhibited in Paris in 1845. It was highly successful. He contributed statues in bronze and *ormolu* of Queen Victoria and the Prince Consort to the Exhibition of

BELL, JOHN. *Andromeda*. Bronze figure by John Bell* cast by the Coalbrookdale Ironworks* and exhibited at the Great Exhibition* of 1851. *Ironbridge Gorge Museum Trust*

1851. His bronze group, *The Eagle Slayer*, now exhibited at the Bethnal Green Museum, London, was issued to subscribers in a bronze reduction by the Art Union. Perhaps his most popular Parian* figure is a reduction of *Dorothea* (a character from *Don Quixote*) done for Minton*, which had originally been a statue executed in 1844 for Lord Lansdowne.

Most of his later work was in execrable taste, marred by the kind of sickly sentimentality which was enjoyed by most of the mid-Victorians, although the *Art Journal* especially made many acid comments on Bell's work at the time.

BELL, JOHN & MATTHEW (Glasgow)

Although this Glasgow pottery was founded early in the 19th century it did not begin to make ornamental wares until after 1840. It then produced blue printed earthenware, Parian* figures, and vases in the Etruscan style. The factory used the mark of a bell sometimes with the initials JB, and sometimes surmounted by a crown and surrounded by a laurel wreath. It closed towards the end of the 19th century.

BELLEEK PORCELAIN FACTORY (County Fermanagh, N. Ireland)

Porcelain factory established in 1857 on an island in the river Erne by David McBirney with Robert Armstrong as art-director. They used Cornish clay and Irish feldspar from a nearby site, materials that had already been tested at Worcester*, which imported supplies from Ireland. The factory is best known for its version of Parian* ware covered with an iridescent glaze. Highly modelled porcelain services were produced, based on shells and other marine subjects, sometimes with glazed and unglazed areas. They also made ironstone* and earthenware with painted or printed decoration, and workmanship is in general extremely good.

The characteristic glaze was made under licence to the patent of M. Brianchon*, and, when the patent expired in 1872, Armstrong's son emigrated to America and worked making iridescent glazed porcelain at Trenton, N. J. Belleek ware had become much admired and copied in the United States by then.

The usual mark was BELLEEK CO. FERMANAGH or a mark which combines a seated greyhound, a tower, a shamrock and an Irish harp. The addition of IRELAND to the mark denotes manufacture after 1891.

'BELLEEK' PORCELAIN, AMERICAN

A porcelain inspired by the wares of the Irish Belleek* factory and made at a number of American factories between 1880 and 1900. The version made by Knowles* of East Liverpool, Ohio, was termed 'Lotus' ware.

BELLE VUE POTTERY (Hull, Yorkshire)

A factory manufacturing creamware* printed and painted in blue was established here in the first half of the 19th century with a depot at Hamburg, and they did a considerable export trade with Germany. The mark records the name of the pottery and the town. A pair of bells included refers to the proprietor, William Bell.

BELTER, JOHN HENRY (1804–1863)

German furniture manufacturer of New York, originally Johann Heinrich Belter. He served an apprenticeship as a woodworker in Württemberg and emigrated to the United States some time before 1844, in which year he was working as a cabinet maker in New York. By 1858 he had a factory on Third Avenue where he employed many assistants. Most of his furniture was in a revived rococo* style. He made considerable use of serpentine marble tops and cabriole legs reminiscent of the style of Louis XV.

Much of the furniture is lightly carved in rosewood*, which is hardly suitable for the purpose. To overcome this difficulty, Belter invented a method of laminating the wood with the grain of each thin sheet at right angles to the next, the sheets were then glued and consolidated in a press, yielding a material resembling the modern plywood. Flat laminated sheets were moulded into curves with the aid of steam heat and then carved. Belter's production was in competition with imported French furniture in the South, and after his death, probably as a result of the Civil War, his firm became bankrupt. Much of Belter's production consisted of chairs, sofas, and tables which he shipped to all parts of the country. His work is represented in the Metropolitan Museum, New York.

BENARES BRASSWORK
Brassware, especially large trays, decorated with intricately engraved and *repoussé* work, much of it by machine. Although it was sold as being of Indian workmanship, much of it was made in Birmingham and exported to India for sale to tourists. Trays were usually provided with a light wooden stand and used as coffee-tables.

BENHAM & FROUD (London)
Manufacturers of copper and brassware during the second half of the 19th century. Christopher Dresser* designed a copper kettle for them.

BENNETT, EDWIN (b. 1818)
English potter who emigrated to America in 1841 and worked at East Liverpool, Ohio. He founded his own factory at Baltimore, Maryland, in 1846, which was the first to be established south of the Mason-Dixon line. He produced ware of good quality. The enterprise became the Edwin Bennett Pottery Company* in 1890.

BENNETT, JAMES
Brother of Edwin*, who arrived in America in 1834. After working in Jersey City and Troy, Ind., he started the first pottery in East Liverpool, Ohio, in 1839.

BENNETT POTTERY COMPANY (Baltimore, Maryland)
A factory established in 1846 by Edwin Bennett*, who had previously worked for his brother in East Liverpool, Ohio. The products of the Baltimore factory were the Rockingham type brown-glazed ware and yellow, sage-green, and blue ware. White ware was made from 1869, at which date decorating studios were added, and porcelain was first made in 1890. The 'REBEKAH' teapot is among their best-known products.

BENNINGTON POTTERY (Vt)
A pottery was established at Bennington in 1793 by Captain John Norton, who was succeeded by his son. The factory made redware and stoneware until 1894. A grandson, Julius Norton, introduced the Rockingham* brown glazed ware about 1830. Large

quantities of utility wares were manufactured with glazes of this type, as well as decorative items such as candlesticks, lamps, vases, and figures. Among the best of the Bennington decorative wares are large dogs, deer, and lions. The chief modeller, Daniel Greatbach*, came from Staffordshire, arriving in 1851. Julius Norton formed a partnership in 1844 with Christopher Fenton, and in 1853 they founded the United States Pottery. Fenton developed a porcelain body by 1847 which is usually termed 'Bennington Parian'.

A good deal of Bennington ware was unmarked, and much pottery in its style was made elsewhere, which often makes attributions hazardous. Fenton's factory closed in 1857, and the main Bennington factory in 1894.

BENSON, WILLIAM ARTHUR SMITH (1854–1924)
Architect and designer of furniture and metalwork. Benson was a friend of William Morris* and one of the founders of the Art Workers' Guild* (1884) and the Arts and Crafts Exhibition Society* (1887). He became director of the furniture department of Morris & Co.* in 1896. From 1883 Benson owned a factory in Hammersmith where he made well-designed domestic metalwork, and he also opened a showroom in Bond Street. Furniture designed by Benson is usually of rosewood* inlaid with other woods, and often has elaborate metal mounts.

BENSON, W. A. S. Cabinet of rosewood* inlaid with purplewood, tulipwood and ebony, with glazed doors and 'old silver' mounts, designed by Benson, one of the founders of the Arts and Crafts Exhibition Society*. Made by Morris & Co.* c. 1899. *Victoria & Albert Museum, London*

BENTHALL AND POSENHALL POTTERIES (Shropshire)
The potteries here were founded early in the 18th

century, and were occupied by a succession of producers of earthenware until 1862. The Benthall Pottery works came into existence under the direction of William Allen. It produced Salopian Art pottery from 1882 to 1920.

BENTWOOD FURNITURE
Bending wet wood into the parts of chairs and appropriate kinds of furniture has been practised from very early times, and it is commonly employed today for some types of mass-produced furniture. The most important manufacturer of bentwood furniture, however, beginning in the 1840s, was Michael Thonet*. Bentwood should not be confused with curved laminated wood of the kind produced by John Belter* of New York.

BERGER, HENRI (d. 1920)
Sculptor and glass-designer who worked for Daum Frères* from about 1897 to 1914. From about 1908 he made models which were cast in *pâte-de-verre*.

BERLIN PORCELAIN FACTORY
This factory was started privately and acquired by Frederick the Great in 1763. It was one of the principal 18th-century factories. From 1763 until 1918 it was known as the Königliche Porzellan-manufaktur (KPM) and from 1918 as the Staatliche Porzellanmanufaktur. *KPM* occurs as a mark not only on Berlin porcelain, but on that from elsewhere. It simply means 'Royal Porcelain Factory'. *SPM* means 'State Porcelain Factory', but the letters do not appear as a mark. Other factories, such as Nymphen-burg*, have become a state factory since 1918, when royal patrons were dispossessed.

BERLIN PORCELAIN. One of a pair of vases and covers, the fluted ovoid body after an 18th-century model, painted with flowers and panels of lovers within a moulded wreath border, the cover surmounted by an eagle. (The eagle formed part of the Hohenzollern Arms.) Mark: the sceptre in underglaze blue. c. 1900. Königliche Porzellanmanufaktur, Berlin

BERLIN PORCELAIN. Plaque enamelled with Pharaoh's daughter finding Moses in the bullrushes. Königliche Porzellanmanufaktur, Berlin. Mid-19th century. *Antique Collectors' Club*

BERLIN PORCELAIN. Ice-pail from the Prussian Service presented to the Duke of Wellington about 1818, and now in Apsley House. Modelling was by Gottfried Schadow, and the complete service cost 29,000 thalers. *Author*

Berlin produced a good deal of good quality porcelain in its own characteristic style, and its finely painted plaques are especially sought. The factory also produced large vases in the Empire* and Biedermeier* styles. Generally their wares are much more restrained than those of Meissen. About 1830 the factory began to produce lithophanes*, and, like other major European factories, they produced a 'Majolika'*, specimens of which were shown at the Paris Exposition Universelle of 1867.

In the 20th century distinguished figure modelling was done by Josef Wackerle from Nymphenburg* and Paul Scheurich, who was later to do important work for Meissen. After 1918 the factory produced services to designs supplied by the Bauhaus. It was destroyed during the Second World War, but re-opened in West Berlin afterwards, and still specializes in services decorated with fine quality floral painting. It makes an excellent model of the Berlin bear as a tourist souvenir.

From 1800 to 1823 the mark was a sceptre in blue or red. From 1832 the mark of the orb and the letters *KPM* came into use. From 1837 the sceptre and *KPM* was impressed on plaques and lithophanes. This was disused in 1844. From 1823 a mark based on the Prussian crowned eagle within a double circle was employed in a number of variations.

BERLIN WOOLWORK
A kind of embroidery carried out in coloured wools on a canvas foundation, using a pattern printed on squared paper and transferred to the canvas. The first patterns were made by a Berlin print-seller named Philipson for his wife in 1805, and another Berlin print-seller named Wittich began to produce the patterns on a large scale about five years later. Wittich became the largest producer and exporter of patterns, which were popular in England from the first.

The coloured wools were spun in Gotha and dyed in Berlin. The earliest patterns were floral or pictorial, and used for cushion covers or inclusion in the frames of firescreens. By about 1830 well-known paintings were being copied and framed for hanging, as well as religious subjects and such exotic birds as parrots. New ways of using the canvas panels were devised, and from about 1840 onwards it is not unusual to find Berlin woolwork used to cover the seats of stools, for the seats and backs of easy chairs, and even to cover small sofas. Quality began to decline about 1860, when some of the wools were coloured with aniline dyes. The quality of the needlework also deteriorated. By 1880 the fashion had run its course. The pastime was also very popular in the United States from about 1820, and specimens are not uncommon either there or in England, although those of exceptional quality are rare.

BETJEMAN & SONS, G.
Furniture manufacturers who produced, mainly, writing-desks, dressing-cases and book-slides (see *Book-trough*) which they exhibited in the International Exhibition of 1862.

Betjeman patented hinges with spring-loaded catches stamped with their name.

BIBLIOTHÈQUE TOURNANT (French)
Small revolving bookcase usually of ebony, ebonized wood, or rosewood*, and often with a marble top, popular during the Second Empire* period.

BIEDERMEIER GLASS See *Bohemian and Austrian glass*

BIEDERMEIER STYLE
The style principally current in Austria and the German states from about 1814 to the political disturbances of 1848. It developed from the Empire style* under the influence of Schinkel* and others.

The beginning of the style first became noticeable immediately after the Battle of Waterloo which ended the Napoleonic Wars. It was essentially a *bourgeois* style. The *bourgeoisie* had been rising to power and a modest affluence during the preceding half century, and a *Biedermann* in German is an honest, upright citizen, a pillar of society, usually pompous and self-righteous. The term 'Biedermeier' was first applied to the style in the 1890s, the period of the *Sezession**, and was then intended to be derogatory and patronizing. There are two explanations of the term usually

BIEDERMEIER STYLE. Provincial furniture in a late version of the Empire style, termed Biedermeier*. c. 1820. *Historisches Museum, Basel*

advanced. The first is that it was taken from two cartoon characters, *Biedermann* and *Bummelmeier*, who appeared in a Berlin satirical journal of the 1850s, and the second, that it was taken from the pseudonym of a poet who satirized the middle-classes under the name of 'Biedermeier'. The term is generally used for furniture and schemes of interior decoration but it is also applied to Bohemian glass* and porcelain of the period. Elsewhere, 'Biedermeier' would be an appropriate description of some furniture of William IV and the first years of the reign of Victoria in England and of Louis-Philippe* in France.

Biedermeier furniture is based on the Empire style, although forms are simplified. A few examples occur about 1830 with neo-Gothic* decorative *motifs* which are classifiable as Biedermeier and, especially in the south, some early examples are decidedly baroque. Towards the 1840s there are some examples with Renaissance* influence and brass inlays reminiscent of those of Boulle*. Variants of this kind, however, are comparatively infrequent. Up until 1830 much use was made of pattern-books based on the designs of Percier and Fontaine*, the architects of the Empire style.

Most Biedermeier furniture was made by handcraft methods; sophisticated woodworking machines were not generally available in Germany until after 1850, although both timber and veneers were cut with the aid of steam-power. Two keynotes of the style are the use of walnut and of light coloured fruitwoods, such as pear and cherry, and the use of geometric forms. There was limited use of painted ornament, and the occasional employment of metal mounts. Biedermeier furniture, in fact, is sometimes an odd mixture of variety of technique and proportion with sophisticated *motifs*.

BIGOT, ALEXANDRE (1862–1927)
Studio-potter and chemist who specialized in *flambé* glazes*, as well as a distinctive greenish-yellow. Some of his stoneware was mounted in silver by Edward (Eugène) Colonna*.

BILBAO MIRRORS
Mirrors in a frame of marble with gilt ornament and a scroll cresting imported in the early years of the 19th century into New England ports from Bilbao in Spain, but perhaps of Italian origin.

'BILLIES AND CHARLIES'
Name given to certain spurious medieval objects made by two London workmen, William Smith and Charles Eaton, who found a genuine object in the Thames mud soon after 1825. They sold it for a relatively large sum, and their success excited their cupidity. They began to make medallions, daggers, figures, and other small objects of cock-metal, an alloy of copper and lead. The medallions in particular must have been made in considerable numbers when the number still surviving is considered. They bear nonsense inscriptions and the gross error of a date in Arabic numerals, usually 1000, 1001, or 1002, where a genuine medallion would have had a date in Roman numerals. They were also modelled with the figures of knights in an unrecognizable kind of armour, which bears no relation to any type in use around the end of the first millennium. These things succeeded in deceiving a large number of inexpert collectors and some have even been excavated, suggesting that certain places were 'salted'.

BILLINGSLEY, WILLIAM (1760–1828)
Porcelain maker and decorator, who was responsible for introducing a distinctive style of flower-painting fashionable during the first half of the 19th century.

Billingsley was apprenticed as a painter at the Old Derby* factory at the age of 14. Here he met Zachariah Boreman who had been a painter at the Chelsea factory and from him it appears Billingsley acquired a porcelain formula which he later used at a number of commercially unsuccessful factories he helped to found. His style in flower-painting dates from about 1784. It was immediately successful, and a complete breakaway from tradition. The modelling of the flowers, especially roses, was achieved by painting the petals in full colour, followed by wiping out the highlights with a dry brush. He was also fond of white flowers, and of long single sprays which emerged from the central grouping. This style was extensively copied in the 19th century, especially at Coalport*, but Billingsley himself was more interested in establishing the manufacture of his porcelain formula. He left Derby in 1796 for Pinxton, near Mansfield, where he started a factory in association with John Coke. This venture failed, and it is thought by some that he made porcelain at Torksey and Wirksworth, but this is very unlikely, and it is probable that he supported himself by painting porcelain bought in white from elsewhere. In 1808, in company with his son-in-law, Samuel Walker, he obtained employment at Worcester*, where they stayed until 1813. In this year they arrived at Nantgarw*, in South Wales, and established a factory there in collaboration with William Weston Young.

BILLINGSLEY, WILLIAM. Large mug painted in the manner of William Billingsley*, and probably by his hand. Porcelain, probably Worcester c. 1810. *Private collection*

Here Billingsley once again began to manufacture his soft-paste porcelain, which was superb in quality but very wasteful in manufacture. He enjoyed a measure of success because circumstances were propitious. To rehabilitate the Royal Sèvres* factory after the French Revolution the director, Alexandre Brongniart*, started to sell stocks of slightly defective soft-paste porcelain (the so-called 'vieux Sèvres'*) which had accumulated since the 1750s, and this had been eagerly bought by Paris and London decorators, painted in Sèvres styles and put on to the market. This was the start of the fashion for copying 'vieux Sèvres' porcelain which persisted through much of the 19th century. When London decorating studios found that the source of Sèvres porcelain dried up they began to search for something comparable and Billingsley's soft-paste was closest to 18th century pâte-tendre*.

Billingsley petitioned the Board of Trade for help and a member of the Board, Sir Joseph Banks, President of the Royal Society, asked Lewis Dillwyn of the Cambrian Pottery, Swansea, for a report on prospects at Nantgarw. Dillwyn reported favourably, and as a result Billingsley and Walker moved to Swansea in 1814 and production was placed on a larger scale. There, also, much was sent to London for decoration, but kiln-wastage (which at times reached nine-tenths) could not be overcome. Dillwyn received a letter from Worcester pointing out that Billingsley and Walker had broken their contract with them, and Dillwyn and Billingsley disagreed on the question of modifications to be made to the porcelain body to reduce kiln-wastage. It seems that Billingsley's agreement with Worcester provided for him to manufacture porcelain on his own account, but not to divulge the secret to others. In 1817 Billingsley and Walker returned to Nantgarw, and in 1819 they accepted an offer of employment from John Rose* of Coalport*, who bought the moulds and employed some of the Nantgarw workmen. Rose seems to have experimented with Billingsley's porcelain formula, and occasional specimens of obvious Coalport manufacture resemble Welsh production. Much Coalport flower-painting of the period is obviously inspired by Billingsley's style.

No signed examples of his painting exist, but patterns numbered 56, 135, 144, 172, 174, 176, 180, 246, 326, and 351 in the old Derby pattern book are listed as being done by him, and therefore form a basis for comparison. (See Coalport Porcelain Factory; Nantgarw; Swansea pottery and porcelain)

BILLINGTON, DORA MAY
Studio-potter and teacher who studied at Hanley, Staffordshire and South Kensington. She worked for Bernard Moore* until 1912, and decorated industrial pottery made by Meakin's. She also made and decorated her own pottery, which was influenced by the contemporary Continental movement. Mark: painted or incised monogram, DB or DMB.

'BILLY WATERS'
A London character of about 1815. A negro fiddler with a wooden leg who is the subject of both earthenware and porcelain figures. Those of porcelain came from Derby*, and were modelled by Edward Keys*.

BIMANN, DOMINIK (1800–1837)
Glass engraver, who specialized in portraits and figure subjects. Bimann studied at the Prague Academy, beginning in 1826 and his first dated work was executed in this year. After spending some years in Prague as a glass engraver he removed to Franzenbad, a well known spa, where he engraved portraits of visitors on crystal glass in his shop on the Kirchengasse. These were executed on drinking glasses, or on flat medallions. His signature is variable—Biman, Rimann, or Biemann. The last version is the latest, and appears on work done after 1830.

BING, SAMUEL
Wealthy art-dealer and patron of German origin, who was an authority on Japanese art, and an impresario of the art nouveau* movement in the 1890s. Even the term, art nouveau, given to the style was suggested by the name of the gallery (La Maison de l'Art Nouveau) which he opened in 1895. In 1897, in company with Julius Meier-Graefe, he commissioned Henri van der Velde* to design four rooms for the Dresden Exhibition. During the Paris Exposition of 1900 he encountered a great deal of criticism from orthodox French circles, and he was compelled to show the more avant garde of the works he offered in a private pavilion. He sold furniture, textiles, ceramics, glass, jewellery, and interior decoration generally—the principal vehicles for the new style—and as an Orientalist he was to a considerable extent responsible for the Japanese influence which pervaded it.

In his gallery he exhibited work from Beardsley*, Rodin*, Gallé*, Tiffany*, Crane*, Mackintosh*, Lalique*, and Toulouse-Lautrec. He also displayed the work of Eugène Colonna*, Georges de Feure*, and Eugène Gaillard*, then almost unknown.

BING & GRONDAHL (Copenhagen)
Factory for the manufacture of porcelain*, stoneware*, and earthenware* founded in 1853. Although they often derived styles from the Royal Copenhagen Porcelain Factory*, a good deal of their work is original. Excellent figures were made in porcelain and stoneware by modellers such as J. Nielsen (1885–1961), the Danish sculptor who began to design figures and service-ware in 1921, and Jean-René Gauguin*, son of the painter, who modelled animals. The art-director, Pieter Krohn (1840–1905) designed the well-known heron service which combined painted decoration with low relief in 1888. A type of blue painting in which the pigment combines with the glaze during firing was introduced about 1910 and proved very popular on porcelain and stoneware.

BINNS, CHARLES FERGUS (1857–1934)

Member of the English family connected with porcelain manufacture who, before he emigrated to America, held a supervisory post at the Worcester* factory. Shortly before 1900 he became principal of the New York State College of Ceramics at Alfred University, and in 1922 published a book entitled *The Potter's Craft*. His own work was inspired by the more austere Chinese wares of the Ch'ing dynasty.

BISEGLIA, MARIO (fl. early 20th century)

Bronze-founder working in Paris who used an impressed mark: *CIRE PERDU BISCEGUE*.

BLACK, STARR & FROST (New York)

Jewellers and silversmiths with premises on Broadway since 1810. They were principally jewellers, and dealt in diamonds on a large scale, so that at one time their shop was known as the Diamond Palace of Broadway.

BLACK, STARR & FROST. A set of three *tazze* with applied borders of embossed and pierced flowers and leaves, on pedestals similarly decorated. Makers' mark. New York. Early 20th century. *Sotheby & Co*

BINNS, R. W.

Partner from 1852 with W. H. Kerr in the Worcester porcelain factory. Art-director from 1862, when the firm became the Worcester Royal Porcelain Company*. Much of the firm's success at this time was due to his innovations.

BIRD'S-EYE MAPLE

A light golden-yellow wood with small brown marks thought to resemble birds' eyes. Much used in Victorian times for framing prints and engravings.

BIRKS, ALBOIN (1861–1941)

Pupil of M. L. Solon*, from whom he learned the art of *pâte-sur-pâte*. He was employed by Minton* from 1876 to 1937. Some pieces by him are signed *A. Birks*.

BISCUIT PORCELAIN

Unglazed porcelain. Biscuit porcelain was first employed for figure modelling at the Sèvres* factory about 1753, its introduction being assigned to the art-director, J-J. Bachelier. It continued to be employed with varying popularity for figures and groups throughout the remainder of the 18th century, and ever since, some very effective work being done in the 19th century. Most of the 18th-century factories who specialized in figure-work also employed biscuit porcelain for the purpose. In England the Derby* factory made many figures of this material from 1770 until well into the 19th century, when it was superseded by a modified body which came to be known as Parian*. Biscuit figures were more expensive than glazed and painted figures, since minor blemishes could not be tolerated and figures less than perfect were covered with glaze, enamelled, and sold more cheaply. Wedgwood's* jasper* was imitated in biscuit porcelain early in the 19th century, principally at Sèvres.

BLACKAMOOR

The figure usually of a crouching negro used as a table-support. These first occurred in the early years of the 18th century, but were used again during the period from 1850 to 1870 in both England and the United States.

BLACKAMOOR. A large pair of Blackamoor figures carrying *jardinières* on their heads, decorated in brilliantly coloured majolica glazes, and mounted on Renaissance-style pedestals. Minton's. 1865. *Sotheby & Co*

BLAKE, WILLIAM (1757–1827)

English poet, mystic, and artist. Blake engraved illustrations for the 1815–1816 catalogue of Wedgwood's* creamware*.

BLASHFIELD, JOHN M. (Stamford, Lincolnshire)

Blashfield was at first located at Southwark as a manufacturer of terracotta* and artificial stone. About 1850 he bought Coade's moulds (See *Croggan*,

William), and he removed to Stamford in 1858, where he made statuary and architectural ornament. He exhibited at the 1862 International Exhibition.

BLOOMER, MRS AMELIA
In 1849 Mrs Bloomer, a member of the American Women's Rights Movement, invented a costume consisting of a short jacket and a skirt reaching to the knees which covered a pair of turkish-style trousers. The trousers later became known as 'Bloomers', after the inventor. Mrs Bloomer was celebrated in song, and appears on music-covers of the period. She also occurs in the form of Staffordshire pottery figures* derived from the music-covers.

BOCH FRÈRES
Belgian associates of Villeroy and Boch*, established in 1841 at La Louvière and Tournai in Hainault, and Septfontaines in Luxembourg. Large quantities of table-ware decorated with transfer-printing* were made, and art-pottery formed part of the production. The firm also made wares inspired by the tin-enamelled pottery of Delft and the Middle East. A. W. Finch* and Marcel Goupy* were among the designers. *Grès-Keramis* and *Keramis* are among its trade-marks.

BOCK, JOSEF
Viennese porcelain manufacturer who succeeded his father in 1887. He built decorating studios in 1893, and commissioned designs in the *art nouveau*** style of the *Sezession**. Artists include D. Peche*, Koloman Moser*, and J. Sika. In 1898 the firm became known as the Wiener Porzellanmanufaktur Josef Bock. Mark: Impressed or printed with initials *WPM* or the name *JOSEF BOCK*.

BODLEY, EDWIN J. D. (Burslem, Staffordshire)
E. J. D. Bodley became proprietor of the existing firm of Bodley & Diggory in 1878. In the 1880s they specialized in elaborately decorated vases for lamps and chandeliers in the current Aesthetic* style.

BOEHM BIRDS
Figures of birds naturalistically modelled and coloured made by Edward Marshall Boehm at Trenton, N. J. from 1955 to 1969.

BOHEMIAN AND AUSTRIAN GLASS
During the last decades of the 18th century Bohemia had produced little of consequence, but at the beginning of the 19th century it began once more to demonstrate its capacity for producing decorative glass of fine quality, and of setting the pace for others. From about 1800 until 1840, when the French took over, Bohemia dominated the field.

Facet-cutting in the English manner, using coloured and cased glass*, had begun in Bohemia before 1800, and in the years which followed the Romantic* movement in art revived an interest in glass staining.

Romanticism was also responsible for the subject-matter used by glass-engravers and decorators and, indeed, by artists who worked on porcelain and in other media. Ruins, and mountain scenery were wheel-engraved into facet-cut glass, usually through a coloured flashing into clear glass beneath. Romantic and topographical landscapes had been popular as engravings for some time and now came into vogue as subjects for porcelain. It was not long before they were being enamelled on to glass. This kind of work was carried out by Samuel Mohn* (1762–1815) and his son Gottlob (1789–1825). Gottlob Mohn was also influenced by the porcelain painter and gilder, Anton Kothgasser* whom he met in Vienna.

By this time very little entirely colourless glass was being produced in Bohemia. Most of it was either coloured throughout, cased, or overlaid with another colour, or flashed* (i.e. lightly stained). Ruby red was the most popular colour, but opaque white, amber, topaz, blue, green, and a greenish-yellow from uranium oxide* can all be noted. There were also new varieties, such as the Hyalith* glass from factories owned by Count von Buquoy, which was made in sealing-wax red and dense black, the latter colour often inspired by Wedgwood's basaltes* stoneware. 'Lithyalin'* was a marbled glass first made in 1829 by Friedrich Egermann* (1777–1864) of Blottendorf. Until about 1840 the general style of Bohemian glass was either Empire* or Biedermeier*.

The second half of the 19th century was characterized in Bohemia principally by revived styles and a continuation of techniques popularized during the first half. After 1864 the initiative passed to Austria, where the firm of J. & L. Lobmeyr* of Vienna, founded in the 1820s, gathered notable Bohemian and Austrian designers and craftsmen together to produce fine quality work in *tiefschnitt** and *hochschnitt**.

BOHEMIAN AND AUSTRIAN GLASS. Ink-bottle of ruby glass cut and engraved with gilt and enamel enrichment. The decoration is characteristic of mid-19th century production, and is of the type which *The Times* recommended English manufacturers to copy. Probably Bohemian. c. 1850. *The Corporation of Dudley*

Lobmeyr also produced iridescent glass* by 1879, and included it among its exports to America. A Bohemian glass-house contemporary with Lobmeyr which did some distinguished work was that of Johann Lötz*, founded in 1836. After his death it operated under the style of J. Lötz Witwe ('Witwe' meaning 'widow'). This factory also made iridescent glass soon after 1870, at the same time as Lobmeyr. Tiffany* patented his process for iridizing glass in 1880, so it would seem that Lobmeyr preceded him by some years and that Lötz, who made glass inspired by Tiffany's 'Favrile'* glass, succeeded in producing an iridized surface about the same time. Both Lobmeyr and Lötz Witwe became noted for glass in the *art nouveau** style.

BOHM, AUGUST (1812–1890)

Bohemian glass engraver, born at Meistersdorf, Steinsschönau. After 1830 Bohm travelled to Stourbridge, Worcestershire, and the United States, where he spent his active working life. Signed examples exist.

BOIS DURCI (French)

Literally, hardened wood. *Bois durci* was a wood-based plastic consisting of fine sawdust bound with albuminoid and glutinous substances, coloured with vegetable pigments and moulded under pressure with the aid of heat. It was introduced about 1850 and employed for the manufacture of numerous small ornamental objects, of which portrait medallions are the most frequent survivals.

The process was patented in London and Paris in 1855 by the inventor, Charles Lepage. The medallions, probably inspired by the jasper* medallions of Wedgwood*, are principally portraits of European royalty, of which Napoleon III and the Empress Eugénie are among the most frequent survivals. Notable personages range from the Duke of Wellington to Molière and Abd-el-Kader, the Algerian patriot who was captured by the French in 1843 and released by Napoleon III in 1862 with a pension.

Apart from medallions, objects made of *bois durci* include small boxes and picture frames, brooches, and other articles of jewellery, chessmen, ornament for application to furniture such as rosettes, and umbrella handles. There were a number of other plastic materials used for similar purposes about the same time, some of which closely resemble *bois durci*.

See *Xylonite*

BONE CHINA See *Porcelain*

BONHEUR, ISIDORE-JULES (1827–1901)

Brother of Rosa Bonheur*, who studied painting at the École des Beaux-Arts and then turned to sculpture, using predominantly *Animalier** subjects. He was a regular exhibitor in the *Salon* from 1848 onwards, and was awarded a Gold Medal at the Paris Exposition of 1889. His studies of horses are particularly successful, and equestrian bronzes include a

BONHEUR, ISIDORE-JULES. Bronze equestrian portrait of the Prince of Wales, later Edward VII, by Isidore-Jules Bonheur*. Late 19th century. *Antique Collectors' Club*

portrait of the Prince of Wales (later Edward VII). He also produced well observed studies of cattle and a variety of other animals. His uncle Hippolyte Peyrol was a bronze-founder who exhibited at the London International Exhibition of 1862, and cast the work of both Rosa and Isidore. His signature as *fondeur* appears on some of the bronzes. Isidore usually signed I. BONHEUR incised in small capitals, and occasionally the name in full. His large sculpture includes the two lions flanking the steps of the Palais de Justice, Paris.

BONHEUR, ROSA (1822–1890)

Painter of animals and rustic scenes who achieved great fame during the 19th century. She had the Emperor and the Court as a patron in France and in England she was known as the 'Landseer of France' and was patronized by Queen Victoria. She was much influenced by George Sand, and followed the latter's example in some of her extravagances. She studied animal anatomy in the slaughter-house, as Stubbs had done before her, disguised in workman's clothing. As a sculptor she was responsible for a few *Animalier** subjects—sheep and domestic cattle—which bear an obvious relationship to her painting.

BONTEMPS, GEORGES (1799–1884)

Bontemps was one of the most important names in the making of decorative glass in the 19th century. He became director of the glasshouse at Choisy-le-Roi* in 1823, remaining until the Revolution of 1848, when he emigrated to England and found employment with Chance Brothers of Birmingham. During his time at Choisy, Bontemps devoted himself to the production of new types of decorative glass and to the rediscovery of old ones. The production of opaline* began in 1827, of *latticinio** glass in the old Venetian manner in 1839, and of *millefiori** glass, much used in the making of paperweights*, in 1844. He also installed a stained glass studio. His very influential handbook, *Guide du Verrier,* published in Paris in

1868, became a standard work which was not superseded until recent times.

After the Paris Exhibition of 1855 he produced a long report on the state of French and English glass manufacture which was among those presented to both Houses of Parliament in 1856. At this time he was a Chevalier of the Legion d'Honneur.

BOOK-TROUGH

The book-trough was made for library use. Generally, it stood on the desk-top and contained reference books. The commonest type was made with a v section which held the books at an angle. The adjustable trough (also known as a book-slide) is usually more ornamental, and sometimes made its appearance in the drawing-room.

BOOK-TROUGH. Book-trough* (or book-slide) by Betjeman of London, decorated at either end with cut brass sheet surrounding a portrait painted on an oval porcelain medallion in the manner of Callowhill* of Worcester. c. 1865. *Constance Chiswell*

BOOTE, T. & R. (Burslem, Staffordshire)

Manufacturers of Parian* figures and ornamental wares, founded 1842. They later made 'Granite' ware and tiles.

BOOZE BOTTLES

Whisky bottles, but especially those made in the 1860s for Edmund G. Booz of Philadelphia by the Whitney Glass Works.

BORNE (French)

A type of circular padded bench, with a similar back, in the interior of which is a well with provision for a potted plant, such as a palm. Introduced in France during the 1850s.

BOSTON AND SANDWICH GLASS COMPANY (Sandwich, Mass.)

The factory was founded by Deming Jarves* near to a convenient and plentiful source of wood fuel. It made large quantities of lead glass of good quality, and the pressed glass* technique was introduced about 1828. Much of the production was of lacy glass*, cup-plates* being especially popular. Coloured and opaline* glass was made from 1830, the ruby glass being in great demand. Cut and etched glass was produced during the later years, and paper-weights* made by a glassworker from Saint-Louis*, Nicholas Lutz*, are much sought. The factory also specialized in glass lamps, and made a variety of other ornamental wares. In the 1860s the factory employed about 500 workmen and enjoyed a large export trade. It closed in 1888, probably due to a combination of expensive fuel and the competition of lime glass*.

Usually termed 'Sandwich glass' by collectors, the factory's products are now much sought.

BOSTON ROCKER

A type of rocking-chair based on the Windsor chair which first appeared in New England about 1825. It has a seat with an upward curve and a wide scrolled top-rail joined to the back of the seat by delicate spindles. It was usually of maple and pine, painted black and decorated with stencilled ornament. It was very popular, and widely manufactured by many firms, including Hitchcock*.

BOTT & CO. (Lane End, Staffordshire)

Potters in the early decades of the 19th century. They made earthenware busts and figures, blue printed wares, and silver lustre. An example of their work is in the Victoria and Albert Museum, London. They marked their products *BOTT & CO* impressed.

BOTT, THOMAS (1829–1870)

Glass and porcelain painter who first worked for Richardson* of Wordsley, joining the firm in 1846. Some of his glass was shown by Richardson at the 1851 Exhibition. Bott joined the Worcester* porcelain factory in 1853 and helped to decorate the Shakespeare Service*. In 1854 he was entrusted with the new decoration in white enamel on a dark blue ground that imitated Limoges enamel*, work which was much praised by the Prince Consort. Specimens of this work were bought for the Royal collections by Queen Victoria. One of his most important works, the decoration of scenes from the Norman Conquest

BOTT, THOMAS. A stand, the form based on the Greek *Kylix*, the centre painted in Limoges enamel style in white on a royal blue ground with a woman riding a centaur, the stem and the foot painted with acanthus* leaves. By Thomas Bott. Gold borders. c. 1855. *Worcester Royal Porcelain Company*

after Daniel Maclise on a pair of vases, was also his last, since he died soon after completing it.

BOTT, THOMAS. Ewer and stand, the decoration by Thomas Bott* influenced by Limoges enamel*. Worcester*, Kerr & Binns period. c. 1855. *Antique Collectors' Club*

BOTT, THOMAS JOHN (1854–1932)
Son of Thomas Bott*, apprenticed at Worcester*, 1870, where he worked until 1885. His work includes Limoges enamel*-type porcelain similar to that of his father, from whom he probably learned the art. The work of the two men is sometimes confused. In 1889 Bott was working in the London studio of Brown, Westhead, Moore & Co.*, becoming art-director at Coalport* in the following year, where he remained until his death.

BOTTLES AND FLASKS
Large quantities of flat-moulded glass bottles decorated in relief with portraits of national heroes, presidential candidates, patriotic symbols such as the flag and the eagle, visiting celebrities like Jenny Lind, and subjects such as 'Success to the Railroad', were made by many American glass works between 1820 and 1870. The earliest appear to have been made about 1808, and they range in size from a half-pint to a quart. They were made in clear and coloured glass and several hundred different patterns have been recorded.

Decorative bottles, principally wine and liqueur bottles, of a somewhat similar kind, were also made in large quantities in France after 1830. Subjects include historical personages, monks, nuns, well-known buildings, all kinds of subjects in fact likely to attract the consumer of the time. Many of these were made at Trelon, Nord, which was a branch of the Baccarat* factory. Some of the more exotic liqueurs are still supplied in decorative bottles, and old bottles of this kind, as in the United States, have become a very popular collectors' item.

These bottles were factory-made of the cheaper grades of glass, some of the latest American bottles being made of lime glass*, introduced in 1864 as a cheap substitute for lead glass. Scent-bottles, the best made in France and at Stourbridge in England, were of much better design and quality and are separately discussed.

See *Perfume-bottles*

BOULLE MARQUETRY
André-Charles Boulle, *ébéniste** to Louis XIV, devised a technique of covering furniture with a marquetry of brass and tortoiseshell. Thin sheets of brass and tortoiseshell were clamped together, and the design to be attached to the surface of the furniture was cut out in one operation. This gave two kinds of design, one in which brass was most important and another in which tortoiseshell predominated. These were employed on different pieces of furniture. Gilt-bronze mounts were used almost invariably. Both silver and pewter sometimes occur as part of the marquetry at all periods. Mother-of-pearl and lapis lazuli are occasional 19th-century additions.

This way of decorating furniture proved very popular and continued to be fashionable throughout the 18th century, not only for furniture but also for rococo clock cases. Boulle's marquetry continued in vogue during most of the 19th century and excellent work in this style was done by Louis le Gaigneur of West London, who was an *emigré* French craftsman. The Prince Regent bought furniture from him in 1815, and a table bearing his stamp, *Le Gaigneur*, is in Windsor Castle. Later in the century a good deal of inferior furniture of this kind was made, at a time

BOULLE MARQUETRY. Clock in a Boulle* case in the Régence style (1715–1725) with an eight-day striking movement by F. Bautoir le jeune, Epinal, France. Second half of the 19th century. *Antique Collectors' Club*

41

when it was commonly called Buhl-work for some reason unknown. Some small works of excellent quality were made about the middle of the 19th century.

See *Buhl-work*

BOULLE MARQUETRY. Portable stationery-case of ebonized* wood, the exterior with the brass and tortoise-shell ornament characteristic of boulle work*, the interior with inlaid ornament. Probably French, c. 1860. *Leslie Curtis*

BOULLEMIER, ANTOINE (1840–1900)
Porcelain painter at Sèvres*, and at Minton* from 1872. He also worked for Brown, Westhead, Moore & Co.* His sons, Lucien and Henri, worked for Minton. Boullemier specialized in cupids after François Boucher of the kind fashionable at Sèvres during the 1750s and 1760s.

BOURGEOISIE (French)
A word now commonly used in Anglo-Saxon countries as a term of opprobrium or contempt. Actually it means no more than the middle or commercial classes, and in this sense it is used here. During the latter part of the 18th century and the early part of the 19th a great deal of wealth created by the industrial revolution found its way into the hands of the *bourgeoisie*, who consequently replaced the aristocracy as arbiters of taste in matters of design.

BOYER, VICTOR (Paris, fl. mid 19th century)
Boyer was a manufacturer of *objets d'art* in silver, bronze, enamels etc., whose London agents were Lightly & Simon of Fenchurch Street. He was successor to Feuillet* in Paris.

BOYLE, JOHN (d. 1846)
Boyle was in business in Hanley, Staffordshire, as an earthenware manufacturer in the 1820s. From 1836 to 1841 he was in partnership with Herbert Minton* and from 1843 to his death with Wedgwood*.

BRACE, RODNEY (fl. early 19th century)
Clock-maker at North Bridgewater, Brockton, Mass., who made small shelf-clocks* which were very popular.

BRACQUEMOND, FÉLIX (1833–1914)
French painter and ceramic designer who contributed greatly to the spread of Japanese influence in the second half of the 19th century. Many of his decorative *motifs* were based on those of Japan and sometimes appear on creamware* from Creil* of 18th-century form. In the 1860s Bracquemond worked in the studio of Théodore Deck*, and for a short time in the Sèvres* factory. From 1872 to 1880 he was art-director to the Auteuil (Paris) studio of C. F. Haviland*. Bracquemond was also an etcher noted for his prints after Gustav Moreau.

BRADBURY & SONS, T. (Sheffield, Yorkshire)
Silversmiths, makers of Sheffield plate* and, after 1840, electro-plated* ware under licence from Elkington*. The firm was established as Matthew Fenton & Co. in the 18th century. After 1795 it became Watson & Bradbury, and then, about 1832, Thomas Bradbury & Sons. Most of their 19th-century work was purely commercial and they employed Alfred Stevens* as a designer.

BRADLEY & CO (London)
China decorators and dealers. Among the wares enamelled by Bradley are basaltes*, creamware*, and porcelain*, especially the porcelain of Coalport*. They were still working in 1828.

BRADLEY, WALTER (fl. 1795–1800)
Proprietor of the Coalport Pottery (also called the Shropshire Delft works), which made imitations of Wedgwood's basaltes ware* and creamware*, and probably blue-and-white delft (i.e. tin-enamel glazed ware).

BRAIN & CO., E. (Fenton, Staffordshire)
Edward Brain acquired the Foley China Works about 1880. The wares are of no special interest until 1934 when the firm was associated with A. J. Wilkinson Ltd*, in an exhibition of table-ware of contemporary design by distinguished living artists held at Harrods. Marks include the words *PEACOCK POTTERY* and the initials *E. B. & CO*. The Foley Pottery (mark *EKB*) made blue transfer-printed* ware between 1822 and 1830.

BRAMPTON (Derbyshire)
There were several potteries here making brown stoneware* during the 19th century. Brampton was the source of stoneware puzzle-jugs*, Toby jugs, posset-pots, and loving-cups, jugs decorated in relief (including those with a handle in the form of a greyhound), spirit-casks, and similar decorative wares. Only Oldfield & Co. at nearby Chesterfield, who made similar wares of excellent quality, marked their products. They used the impressed mark, *J. OLDFIELD* or *OLDFIELD & CO*, which is sometimes found on gin-flasks*. Their products were sometimes called 'New Brampton'.

BRAMPTON, DERBYSHIRE. Stoneware*
puzzle jug* of traditional form. The
liquid may be sucked through one of
the spouts when the correct air-vents
have been closed by the finger-tips
Brampton, Derbyshire. Mark: *J.
OLDFIELD*, impressed. Second half of
the 19th century. *Constance Chiswell*

BRANGWYN, R. A., SIR FRANK. Glass-fronted cabinet by Sir
Frank Brangwyn* containing a Doulton* dinner-service
also designed by him. *William Morris Gallery, Waltham
Forest*

BRANGWYN, R.A., SIR FRANK (1867–1956)

English painter and designer, assistant to William
Morris*, and later designer of textiles and stained
glass for Samuel Bing*. He went to sea and travelled
in the East, which is reflected in some of his painting.
He enjoyed great success as a mural painter and
produced an enormous volume of work, not only as a
painter, but as a designer of furniture, interior
schemes, and pottery for Royal Doulton* about 1926,
one design being known as 'Brangwyn' ware. He was
knighted in 1941.

After the Second World War his painting declined
in popularity, but it has been more in demand in
recent years.

BRANNAM, CHARLES H. (Barnstaple, Devon)

Thomas Brannam took over the Litchdon Pottery
early enough in the 19th century to exhibit at the
Great Exhibition of 1851. From 1879 it passed to his
son. The early marks were *C. H. BRANNAM
BARUM* incised in script letters, or *C. H. BRANNAM*
impressed. LTD. was added about 1913. The arms of
Barnstaple were also employed in printed form.

A variety of wares was produced, some with trade
names such as 'Castle Ware' and 'Royal Barum
Ware'. The firm made a certain amount of Motto
ware*, now a popular collectors' item.

BRANGWYN, R. A., SIR FRANK. *Hollyhocks* by Sir Frank
Brangwyn*, marquetry panel. c. 1900. *William Morris
Gallery, Waltham Forest*

BRANNAM, CHARLES H. Terracotta* jug
in the form of an owl. Incised mark.
Barnstaple, Devon. c. 1890. *Constance
Chiswell*

43

BRATEAU, JULES-PAUL (1844–1923)
French sculptor and *art nouveau* designer who studied at the Ecole Nationale des Arts Décoratifs, Paris, and made objects in *pâte-de-verre** from about 1908.

BRETBY ART POTTERY (Woodville, near Burton-on-Trent, Staffordshire)
Pottery for the manufacture of decorative wares established by Henry Tooth in 1883. Until this year he was in partnership with W. Ault*. Manufacture was continued until 1920. The wares were described by G. W. Rhead as 'extremely quaint and artistic', and the most distinctive are those imitating hammered copper or bronze with jewelled ornament in the *art nouveau** style. Early wares were covered with *sang-de-boeuf** and other coloured glazes. A matt black glaze dates from 1912. The mark is BRETBY with the rays of the rising sun above it.

BRETBY ART POTTERY. Two small vases decorated with coloured glazes, and exhibiting signs of Japanese influence. Mark: *BRETBY* impressed. *Constance Chiswell*

BREUER, MARCEL (b. 1902)
Architect and designer of Hungarian origin who joined the Bauhaus* in 1920. He taught there in 1926–1928 and collaborated closely with Gropius. The most widely known of his designs is a chair of cantilevered form in chromium plated steel tubing. This was made by Thonet* of Vienna with bentwood and curved seat-frame and back. In a modified version with slung

BREUER, MARCEL. Day-bed designed by Marcel Breuer* for the Isokon Furniture Company*. c. 1935. *Sotheby & Co*

canvas seat and back they were made in quantity and very widely distributed, especially because of the facility with which they could be stacked for storage. In 1930 he went to Berlin and designed plywood tables and *chaises-longues** for the firm of Isokon*. From about 1937 he was in America.

BREWER, ROBERT AND JOHN (fl. early 19th century)
Landscape painters in water colour, and in enamels on Derby* porcelain. The elder, John, also painted hunting subjects, and was a drawing-master in Derby. He died in 1815, aged 51. Robert was a pupil of Paul Sandby. He left the Derby factory in 1817, perhaps to take over his brother's connections as drawing-master. He later painted landscapes for Coalport* and Worcester*.

BREWSTER, ELISHA (1791–1880)
Clock-maker of Bristol, Conn., from 1833 to 1862. He was the first to make spring-driven clocks in America and exported them to England, where he had a London show-room.

BŘEZOVÁ (Czechoslovakia)
Formerly Pirkenhammer, Bohemia. Porcelain factory founded in 1803 by Friedrich Holke with the help of Thuringian workmen. The Empire style*, current in Vienna, was introduced about 1806, but lack of success caused the factory to be sold to Fischer and Reichenbach in 1811. Painting was of very good quality and included views of Prague after Morstadt, mythological scenes, and landscapes. Figures were made after 1840, but Březová did not specialize in them to the same extent as the other Bohemian factories. From 1857 it was operated by Fischer and Mieg.

BRIANCHON, JULES See *Belleek Porcelain Factory*; *Lustre, nacreous*

BRIGHTON PAVILION See *Royal Pavilion*

BRIQUET (French)
A lighter. A mechanism consisting of a wick immersed in inflammable spirit, ignited by sparks generated by rotating a wheel with a roughened surface against a flint. Modern lighters employ butane gas instead of spirit.

Collecting lighters probably began in France after the Second World War, and they were to be found in the shops of some *antiquaires* and *brocanteurs* from the 1950s onwards. The earliest are in the form of table-lighters for cigars, and appeared in the 1830s. Table-lighters are found in many decorative guises, of which a favourite is the knight in armour. The wick and striking-wheel are housed in the head and are reached by opening the upper part of the helmet. The cigarette and cigar lighter of pocketable size existed in the 1890s, but their use did not become

BRIQUET. A metal cigar-cutter, 1½″ high, and a bronze gas cigar-lighter. Late 19th century. *Antique Collectors' Club*

really general until the First World War, when a certain amount of time in factories and engineering shops was used for the clandestine making of lighters from brass lawfully intended for munitions. Cartridge cases were very popularly employed for the purpose. A similar phenomenon was observable during the Second World War.

These early lighters, which used petrol (gasoline) as fuel, were generally inefficient, but the better quality commercially-produced lighters made after 1918, especially when fuelled by high-quality petrol, gave little trouble. A type of cigar-lighter for continuous illumination was connected to the coal-gas supply, and employed mainly in tobacconists and cigar-divans during the 19th century.

BRITANNIA METAL
An alloy invented during the 18th century which is almost indistinguishable from hard solder. The constituents are tin and antimony with a small amount of either copper or bismuth. This produces a metal melting at a relatively low temperature. **Britannia metal teapots can be melted by an ordinary hot-plate or gas flame.**

When newly manufactured the metal is white with a bluish cast, but it soon becomes dark grey in colour, when it resembles pewter. It was often electro-plated*, and some specimens are marked EPBM (Electro-plate on Britannia metal). Most of the domestic wares normally made in pewter are also to be found in Britannia metal, and much the same techniques were employed to make it, including spinning on the lathe. Seams were soldered and feet, knobs to covers, etc. were cast and soldered into position. Britannia metal was especially popular from about 1820 onwards until 1850, when it began to be replaced by nickel-silver (German silver)*.

BRITISH PLATE
An alloy somewhat similar to German silver* much used for imitations of silver between 1830 and 1855. It was finished by plating with silver. Its principal danger lies in the very close and deceptive imitations

of hall-marks with which it was provided. Sometimes the only difference is that the punches used have minor variations from genuine punches and are used in impossible combinations. For instance, the sovereign's head has a reversed profile. The crowned leopard's head, obsolete as a silver mark, was also employed. No specimen of British plate, however, bears an exact replica of a hall-mark, which would be a criminal offence, so the remedy is to examine any marks carefully. To the experienced eye objects of British plate also differ from silver in form, colour, ornament, and general appearance.

BRITISH SILVERWARE LTD
A company which now includes Elkington & Sons* and Mappin & Webb.

BROAD GLASS PROCESS
Term describing the making of window-glass by blowing a bubble of glass which is swung at the end of the blowpipe until it becomes elongated. It is then rolled on a table into a cylinder with domed ends. The hemispherical ends are cut off, and the resulting cylinder split up the side and opened out into a flat sheet. The simple cylindrical glass shade* was made in the same way by cutting off only one of the ends. Oval shades were produced by reheating cylindrical shades and reworking them into shape while the glass was soft. This type was naturally more expensive.

BROCARD, JOSEPH (fl. 1870–1895)
Glass-worker in Paris who specialized in reproductions of early enamelled glass, especially such objects as the very rare 11th-century Islamic mosque lamps, some of which can be deceptive to anyone not acquainted with genuine examples. Objects such as *tazze* and goblets made by Brocard, which do not occur among surviving Islamic specimens, were inspired by Venetian glass enamelled in the Islamic style. Brocard later turned his attention to decorative glass painted with stylized flowers. Some of his work is signed. He exhibited at the Paris Exposition of 1878.

BROCARD, JOSEPH. Copy of an 11th-century Islamic enamelled glass mosque lamp with a Kufic inscription, by Joseph Brocard*. c. 1875. *Sotheby & Co*

BROCARD, JOSEPH. Two enamelled drinking-glasses by Joseph Brocard* inspired by early Venetian types. One (right) is enamelled in white and gilt, and the other (left) with a scale pattern in shades of blue and gilt. Signed *Brocard* and shown at the Exposition Universelle, Paris, 1878. *Victoria & Albert Museum, London*

BRONGNIART, ALEXANDRE (1770–1847)

Geologist who was appointed director of the Sèvres national porcelain factory in 1800 at a time when it was virtually bankrupt. He directed the sale of remaining stocks of white ware and 'seconds' to help to raise money, and discontinued finally the manufacture of even the small amount of soft paste made since 1770, when hard paste was introduced. His *Traité des arts céramiques* (1844) was very influential. See *Porcelain*

BRONZED-ZINC CASTS See *Geiss, M.*

BRONZES D'AMEUBLEMENT (French)

French term meaning 'furnishing bronzes'. The term includes not only things like bronze mounts for furniture, clock cases, and similar types of ornamental metalwork, but also decorative figures and groups which were popular throughout the 19th and into the 20th century. The best of these, were issued in limited editions. The introduction of electrotyping* in 1840

made it possible to reproduce bronzes fairly cheaply, and most middle-class interiors had their quota of bronze ornaments, either reductions of large sculpture, or reproductions of Renaissance and 18th-century small bronzes. Clodion terracottas were popular for turning into bronzes, and some have what purports to be a signature.

French and Italian bronze-casters were expert moulders, and they continued to use traditional methods. Generally, the *cire perdue** or 'lost wax' method was employed for the best casts, and founders' sand for cheap bronzes. The Italians, in particular, made excellent copies of ancient bronzes on a fairly large scale. The *Dancing Faun*, excavated in Herculaneum, is a not uncommon ornament in English gardens. Copies of small Roman bronzes from the Naples Museum, the surface suitably corroded, also occur occasionally. They were made within the last century or so, and belong to the same category as copies of Roman glass, too thick and clumsy, with a surface proclaiming recent manufacture, which were made either in Italy or Germany.

Society in the 19th century had changed radically. Those who would formerly have been the patrons of the sculptor belonged to a disappearing class. The sculptor was forced to adapt, and to find another method of earning a living to add to the diminishing number of public and monumental commissions available. He did this by providing a model for the foundry, which produced it in signed, limited editions. Two founders who specialized in this kind of work were Barbedienne* and Susse Frères* of Paris. Both published the work of some of the *Animaliers**.

See *'Editing' of bronzes*

BRONZES D'AMEUBLEMENT. Red Indian Chiefs in coloured bronze by G. Kauba. Late 19th/early 20th century. *Antique Collectors' Club*

BRONZES D'AMEUBLEMENT. *Stag attacked by hounds*. Bronze by Antoine-Louis Barye*. *Antique Collectors' Club*

These founders were notable exhibitors in London at the Great Exhibition* of 1851, and, in Paris at about this time, in the region of 6,000 men were kept in continual employment on work of this kind, which obviously represented a relatively large annual output.

These founders were skilled in the colouring of bronze, and objects were produced with a variety of artificial patinations. The composition of the metal varied little. It was about 80% copper, 17% zinc, and 3% tin and lead. This is virtually brass, except for the modification provided by the small quantity of lead which improved the casting qualities of the metal.

Commercial studios, like that of Carrier de Belleuse*, provided models for furnishing bronzes in large numbers, inspired by a variety of sources. Many were no more than reductions of large sculpture; some were *pastiches* based on a number of existing works; some were free adaptations of earlier works. For instance, the pair of knights illustrated under the **Eglinton Tournament*** will seem not unfamiliar to anyone who has seen the tomb of the Emperor Maximilian in the Hofkirche at Innsbruck. Few 19th-century bronzes can be regarded as entirely original work.

Nevertheless, the 19th century produced some sculptors of importance who made small bronzes. Antoine-Louis Barye*, and the rest of the *Animaliers*, did excellent original work in small size, much of it issued in limited editions. The work of men like Fremiet*, Cain*, and Mêne* was freely exported. Jules Dalou* who, as a political refugee, held a professorship at the South Kensington School of Art in 1871, started a fashion for figures of peasants, suggested by the popularity of Millet's sentimental paintings of the subject. Rodin*, who worked in his youth for Carrier de Belleuse, also produced small bronzes of considerable interest based on figures and groups from his unfinished *La Porte d'Enfer* (The Gate of Hell). Daumier modelled a number of bronzes, cast by Valsuani*, which were political

lampoons. These are now very rare. Much sought are the bronzes of the painter Dégas, which were originally done in wax as an aid to figure-drawing. They were cast by A.-A. Hébrard after the artist's death. Renoir's small bronzes, modelled under his supervision in the last years of his life, are entirely characteristic and very rare. The *art nouveau** style inspired a certain amount of small bronze sculpture. The dancer, Loïe Fuller*, was a favourite subject. Apart from bronzes she also featured in *biscuit* porcelain from Sèvres and glass from Daum* of Nancy. The bronzes are usually adapted to act as a table-lamp. In the 20th century small bronzes of distinction have come from artists like Georges Braque and Henri Matisse.

The cost of furnishing bronzes had been greatly reduced in the 19th century by good workshop

BRONZES D'AMEUBLEMENT. *Knights in Combat* by Jean-François-Théodore Gechter. Signed. Second quarter of the 19th century. *Antique Collectors' Club*

BRONZES D'AMEUBLEMENT. Bronze nude study, *The Sluggard*, 21″ in height, signed. Frederick, Lord Leighton.
Antique Collectors' Club

BRONZES D'AMEUBLEMENT. Bronze figure, *Charity*, by Jules Dalou*. 1880.
William Morris Gallery, Waltham Forest

organization and marketing, but the demand grew to a point where it was greater than could be supplied. Zinc* (spelter) casts could be made more quickly and cheaply than bronze, and the surface could be bronzed to give it a somewhat similar colour. These casts were in no way comparable with good quality bronzes to the discriminating buyer, but they were not intended for this market. The early zinc casts were of good quality, but the demand for cheap metal ornaments became so great that quality declined, and the cheapest examples were very crudely finished. The effect of this flood of spelter ornaments was to depress the market for good quality bronzes, in the same way that cheap imitations of '*vieux Sèvres*' or Palissy's* rustic pottery ultimately depressed the value of the genuine object.

Recent years have seen a revival in the popularity of 19th century bronzes, particularly those of the *Animaliers*, which are much in demand. Small bronzes by Daumier and Dégas have sold for extremely large sums.

BRONZITE

Type of decoration on glass dating from about 1910 designed by Josef Hoffman of the Vienna *Sezession** for J. & L. Lobmeyr*. Stylized figures, animals, and flowers are painted on the surface in matt black enamel.

BROWN, ALFRED

English silver designer who worked principally for Hunt & Roskell* on presentation plate, race-cups and hunting trophies. He specialized in modelled ornament which was liberally applied to much of his work. He was fond of hunting-dogs, stags, deerstalkers, and similar subjects.

BROWN, WESTHEAD, MOORE & CO. (Cauldon Place, Hanley, Staffordshire)

This firm succeeded Ridgway* in 1859, and made porcelain, earthenware, ironstone, and Parian* of excellent quality, a good deal of it inspired by contemporary wares from Minton*. They specialized in polychrome colour-printing, and produced excellent figures. The company continued until 1920.

BROWNFIELD, WILLIAM (Cobridge, Staffordshire)

English potter; partner in the firm of Robinson Wood & Brownfield, makers of good quality earthenware, to which he succeeded in 1850. He took his son, W. E. Brownfield, into partnership in 1871, when the firm traded as W. Brownfield & Son. Porcelain and Parian* figures were added in the same year. Louis Jahn* from Minton* was art-director from 1872 to 1895. W. E. Brownfield retired about 1890, and the business was reorganized by Arthur Brownfield as a cooperative enterprise. It failed shortly afterwards.

Marks WB within a Staffordshire knot; name and town in full.

BROWN, ALFRED. Centrepiece representing the business duties of the Goldsmith's Company designed by Alfred Brown*, made by Hunt & Roskell*. London hall-mark for 1855–1856. *The Worshipful Company of Goldsmiths*

BUGATTI, CARLO. Cabinet of wood covered with vellum and inlaid with ebony, pewter, and brass. Designed by Carlo Bugatti*. c. 1905. *Sotheby & Co*

BROUWER, THEOPHILUS A. (1864–1932)

Artist-potter who founded the East Hampton Pottery, Long Island, in 1893, where, with the aid of two assistants, he experimented with lustre glazes and gold leaf underglaze. Later, he depended entirely on glaze effects. He moved to the Brouwer Pottery, Westhampton, New York, and finally abandoned pottery for sculpture. Mark: *Brouwer* incised.

BUGATTI, CARLO (1855–1940)

Italian furniture designer born in Milan, the father of car-designer Ettore, and the *Animalier** sculptor, Rembrandt. From about 1890 Carlo Bugatti became noted for highly original designs in which he employed such novel materials as vellum covered wood. His interest in the art of Japan led him on at least one occasion to decorate the arms of a chair with Japanese characters inlaid in pewter. This is now in Brighton Museum, Sussex. Some of his designs are also asymmetrical, and in some of his later work he employed Egyptian and Etruscan *motifs*. He exhibited at Turin in 1902.

BUGATTI, REMBRANDT (1885–1916)

Son of Carlo Bugatti* and brother of Ettore. Studied under his father, moved to Paris in 1902, and then settled in Antwerp (1906–1916). Awarded the Legion d'Honneur in 1911. Specialized in bronzes of wild animals and birds, and became widely known as an *Animalier** sculptor in both France and Holland.

BUGATTI, CARLO. Chair by Carlo Bugatti*, upholstered in leather, the arms inlaid with Japanese characters in pewter. Signed. c. 1910. *Brighton Museum & Art Gallery, Sussex*

BUGATTI, REMBRANDT. A rare *Animalier** figure of a lion on an irregularly shaped base, with a rock at the back, by Rembrandt Bugatti. Bronzes by Bugatti are less uncommon. Signed: *R. Bugatti.* 1906–1916. *Sotheby & Co*

BUHL-WORK
An erroneous form of the name Boulle* employed during the 19th century. It may have arisen from the fact that A. C. Boulle was said to be of Swiss origin.

BULLARD, CHARLES (1794–1871)
Painted glass fronts and dials for clocks by Simon Willard*.

BULL-BAITING GROUPS
These pottery groups, depicting a bull attacked by dogs were made in Staffordshire about 1830, for the most part by Obadiah Sherratt*. Good specimens are very rare.

BULLERS LTD (Milton, Staffordshire)
A firm of industrial porcelain manufacturers who produced figures and ornamental wares in the Staffordshire tradition from 1937 to 1955. Their work is represented in the Hanley Museum.

BURGES, WILLIAM (1827–1881)
English architect and designer of furniture and metalwork. Burges worked in a medieval style and he was responsible, with W. Slater, for the Medieval Court at the London International Exhibition of 1862. His furniture was designed either for a client or for his own use, and it does not appear to have been made commercially. A cabinet made by Harland & Fisher in 1858 and exhibited in 1862 strongly resembles a medieval bronze *chasse* in its upper part. It is decorated with paintings by E. J. Poynter. Most of Burges's furniture was painted.

He was employed to design metalwork by the Ecclesiological Society in the 1860s. His metalwork was notable for glass vessels mounted with metal (often gold and silver) strapwork inset with semi-precious stones and decorated with enamel in a medieval style, made by Barkentin & Krall, silversmiths of London, who specialized in ecclesiastical plate.

See *Art furniture*

BURMANTOFTS POTTERY CO. (Leeds, Yorkshire)
Makers from 1880 until about 1904, of high quality 'art' pottery, including coloured wares, *sang-de-boeuf** and terracotta*. Mark: Burmantoft's Faience.

BURMESE GLASS
Art glass of pale greenish-yellow shading to a delicate pink introduced about 1885 by the Mount Washington Glass Company* of New Bedford (Mass.). It was used for both domestic and decorative purposes, and was made in England under licence by Thomas Webb & Sons* of Stourbridge.

See *Fairy lamps*

BURNAYS, DANIEL (1760–1838)
Clock-maker, at first at East Windsor, Conn., and after 1800 at Andover, Conn. He is noted for long-case clocks with brass movements, engraved silvered dials with spandrels, and often phases of the moon, calendar work, and striking and chiming trains. His clocks are sought after.

BURNE-JONES, SIR EDWARD COLEY, BART (1833–1898)
Painter and designer, born in Birmingham, entered Exeter College, Oxford, in 1852 where he met William Morris*. Both he and Morris joined the pre-Raphaelite* movement under the influence of Rossetti*. In 1860 he married Georgiana Macdonald, and in the following year became a founder member of Morris, Marshall, Faulkner & Co.*, whom he continued to provide with designs for a variety of objects until his death. Italian influence predominated in his work after 1862, when he travelled there in company with his wife and John Ruskin*. He was elected ARA in 1885, but resigned in 1893. His baronetcy dates from the following year.

BURGES, WILLIAM. Two chairs designed by William Burges*, upholstered in red Morris Utrecht velvet. Decoration is in red enamel and gilding, the backs painted with a merman and a mermaid by Edward Burne-Jones*. *William Morris Gallery, Waltham Forest*

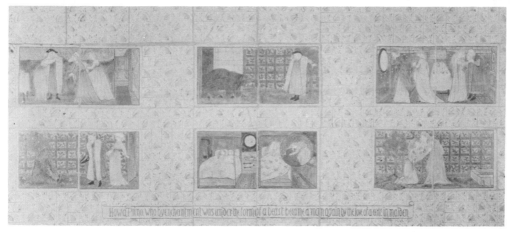

BURNE-JONES, SIR EDWARD. *Beauty and the Beast*, a tile-panel of six pictorial tiles with a blue and white surround. Designed as an overmantel for Birket Foster's house at Witley, Surrey. This was one of the first tile designs to be produced by Morris, Marshall, Faulkner & Co*. *William Morris Gallery, Waltham Forest*

BURNISHED GOLD

When gold is first applied to porcelain it is brown and dull in appearance and needs to be burnished, or rubbed by hand with a burnishing tool, to make it bright and smooth. Burnishers are made of various materials, such as hard smooth stones or a dog's tooth.

BURSLEY WARE   See *Rhead, Charlotte*

BUSTS, PORTRAIT

The portrait bust in marble, plaster, or terracotta* was a well-established adjunct to the gentleman's library in the 18th and 19th centuries. At the beginning of the 19th century Enoch Wood*, who was himself a talented sculptor, produced earthenware busts suitable for library decorations in a

selection to suit all tastes, secular and ecclesiastical. Among those not uncommonly to be found are the blind Homer, Plato, the Czar Alexander, the philosopher Locke, Shakespeare, Washington, the Madonna, the preachers Wesley and Whitefield, and a bust of Britannia which could equally serve for Minerva.

Portrait busts from almost every section of society—royalty (including the Bonaparte family), politics, the armed services, literature, science and philosophy, religion and mythology were made in earthenware, biscuit porcelain*, and Parian*. They were made in various sizes, ranging from about 5 inches in height to a foot or more. In the case of the larger busts the head is inclined downwards. Many bookcases in the classical style were surmounted by a broken pediment, between the two sides of which was placed a circular stand intended for a portrait bust, the pose of the head being adapted to this elevated position. At mid-century busts of glass became popular, but soon afterwards portraits of this kind started to decline in popularity, no doubt due to the fashion for portrait photography.

After 1945 the firm of William Kent* reproduced a number of the Enoch Wood busts which can be recognized by poor quality enamelling, the use of 'bright gold' (where gilding is present), and the painting on of such details as medals and epaulettes which, in the case of old specimens, would be part of the modelling afterwards coloured.

BUSTS, PORTRAIT, GLASS

Small solid glass portrait busts, frosted on the exterior, were made in Birmingham by Follett & Clarkson Osler* and Lloyd & Summerfield, the latter also making portrait medallions. Queen Victoria was the most popular subject, and specimens are still not uncommon. Many other notabilities of the time were

BURSLEY WARE. Dish designed by Charlotte Rhead*, c. 1925. *Mrs F. H. Stubbley*

made, but these are more difficult to find. Portrait busts of Queen Victoria and Prince Albert in the Victoria and Albert Museum, London, are marked F. & C. Osler, and dated 1 May 1845.

BUTTERFIELD, WILLIAM (1814–1900)

English architect and designer who specialized in revived Gothic*. He also restored Gothic churches, and was appointed chief designer of Church plate and interior fittings to the Camden Society of Cambridge. The Victoria and Albert Museum, London, exhibits a Bishop's Throne designed by Butterfield for All Saints' Church, Margaret Street, West London. He also designed some simple domestic furniture, usually in walnut with inlays of sycamore and ebony, somewhat in the manner of Philip Webb*.

BUTTONED UPHOLSTERY

The practice of sewing buttons deeply into upholstery seems to have started in the 1830s, both in England and France, as a result of the demand for greater comfort and thicker and softer padding for easy chairs, settees, etc. Its purpose was to prevent the padding from shifting as a result of wear and tear, and it led later in the century to the production of overstuffed chairs and sofas. It remains the only practical way of dealing with the problem today when traditional padding materials are employed.

See *Capitonné, capitonnage*; *Overstuffed*

ARAB HALL, THE. Interior in the Anglo-Moorish style,
Leighton House, Holland Park. *Photo: Author*

NORTHWOOD, JOHN. Cameo glass copy of the Portland Vase signed by John Northwood I and dated 1876. From the Northwood-Pargeter collection. *Sotheby & Co*

THE PORTLAND VASE. One of fifteen copies of the Portland Vase made in 1878 and lapidary-polished by John Northwood. Offered for sale by Philips of London, but the names of the subscribers are unknown. The only perceptible difference between this and the 1790 version is the initials of Northwood *JN*, incised among the decoration. *Trustees of the Wedgwood Museum, Barlaston*

C

C AND S SCROLLS

Scrolls of this form, usually asymmetrically disposed, are one of the key features of the rococo style of the 18th century and the revived rococo* style of the 1830s and later.

CABINET

The cabinet is a piece of furniture of many different shapes intended for a diversity of purposes. It may be defined as a decorative enclosed cupboard or cupboards, or a series of shelves or drawers usually enclosed by doors. It usually (but not invariably) comprises a separate upper and lower part, as with the French *buffet à deux corps*. In form it varies between the wardrobe on the one hand and the sideboard on the other. The cabinet as a piece of luxury furniture dates from the early years of the 16th century when the elaborately carved *buffet à deux corps* first made its appearance in France. It was at its most decorative and luxurious in the 17th century, when inventories of Cardinals Richelieu and Mazarin, and Louis XIV describe specimens made of materials like lapis lazuli, ebony, and gilt bronze. In England especially, Japanese and Chinese lacquer panels were employed to make colourful cabinets on gilt or silvered carved wood stands.

The decorative cabinet was less fashionable during the 18th century, but it became popular once more as

CABINET. A glass-fronted china cabinet in the *art nouveau** style characteristically decorated. English. c. 1900. *Sotheby & Co*

a *tour-de-force* of the makers of fine quality furniture, like Jackson & Graham*, in the middle of the 19th century. It was in vogue from about 1850 to 1880, and many such pieces were exhibited at one or other of the International Exhibitions of the period. Most of them were in a pseudo-Renaissance style*, but some were in a mixed 17th- and 18th-century style based on the design of royal French furniture of the period. A number of them still exist, and are to be found in such museums as the Victoria and Albert Museum, London, and the Musée des Arts Décoratifs, Paris.

CABRIOLE LEGS

Outwardly curving legs in the revived rococo* style of Louis XV which were popular for drawing-room chairs from about 1830 to at least 1880, usually in combination with a balloon-back*. Chairs with straight front legs in the manner of the Louis XVI style are usually dining-room chairs.

CADINEN KÖNIGLICHE MAJOLIKA WERK-STÄTTE

Factory for the manufacture of pottery privately owned by Kaiser Wilhelm II (1859–1941). Plaques in

CABINET. English walnut cabinet decorated with floral marquetry and mounted with ormolu* in the French style. c. 1865. *Sotheby & Co*

low-relief were designed by the sculptor, Ludwig Manzel (1858–1936), who signed with his initials, *LM*, incised. The mark is *CADINEN*, impressed.

CADOGAN TEAPOT

Teapot based on the Chinese peach-shaped wine-pot which was filled through a hole in the bottom. It had no lid. It received its name from the fact that the Hon. Mrs Cadogan was reputed to have brought a pot of this type to England about 1790. The earliest examples were made at Swinton, Yorkshire, and covered with the rich brown Rockingham* glaze. They were popularized by the china-dealers, Mortlock* of Oxford Street, London, who ordered them in porcelain from such factories as Copeland* and Davenport*. They had become fashionable by 1840.

CAIN, AUGUST-NICOLAS (1821–1894)

French *Animalier** sculptor who married the daughter of P. J. Mêne*. Cain was a pupil of François Rude. He exhibited consistently in the *Salon* between 1846 and 1888. He shared his father-in-law's bronze foundry, which he continued to run after the latter's death, casting his own small sculpture. Some of his larger work was cast by Barbedienne*. Cain's small work was sold by Susse Frères*. His large work includes a monumental equestrian sculpture of the Herzog Karl von Braunschweig at Geneva completed in 1879. His style was strongly influenced by that of Mêne, and his best and livelier works are usually those depicting struggles between animals. He signed *Cain* or *A. Cain*.

CALLOWHILL, JAMES & THOMAS (fl. 1855–1885)

Porcelain painters at Worcester*, among the most noted artists of their time. Thomas worked on the Countess of Dudley service and a nautilus shell cup painted by him was exhibited in Paris in 1878.

CAMBRIAN POTTERY   See *Swansea pottery and porcelain*

CAMEO

Small plaque, usually oval or circular, carved with a variety of *motifs* from some form of hardstone, such as agate or sardonyx, using abrasives and small diamond-pointed chisels. Cameos which belong to classical times are carved from materials of two or more differently coloured layers, the design being formed by carving through the upper layer (or layers) to reveal those beneath. By extension the term is employed for work in other materials. Ancient glass (of which the Portland Vase* is an example) was carved in this way, and the technique was revived in the 19th century (see *Cameo glass*). Wedgwood* introduced jasper* cameos inspired by those of ancient times in the 18th century and continued to produce them in the 19th century. The helmet and conch shells (which exhibit white on brown or white on pink respectively) were employed in Italy during

CADOGAN TEAPOT. Peach-shaped teapot covered with a mottled glaze, and filled through the bottom. A Chinese wine-pot which became fashionable as an extremely impractical teapot in the early decades of the 19th century. English. c. 1810. *Author*

the 19th century to carve cameo-like reliefs usually mounted as brooches which were very popular during the second half of the 19th century and are fashionable today. The best were mounted in gold; the coarser qualities in pinchbeck.

Recently reproductions of shell cameos have been imported from Italy. Most of the subjects employed for 19th century cameos were classical, but Gothic or medieval subjects occur occasionally.

See *Shells, cameo-carved*

CAMEO GLASS

Glass of one colour cased with another (see *Cased glass**) the decoration of which is carved through the top layer with the aid of small chisels. Usually, in the case of 19th-century cameo glass, abrasives and hydrofluoric acid* have also been employed for part of the work. Glass decorated only with the aid of revolving wheels and abrasives is usually termed 'cut' or 'engraved'. Perhaps the most elaborate example of cameo glass to be made in the 19th century was John

CAMEO GLASS. Cameo-engraved bowl by George Woodall for T. Webb & Sons*, Stourbridge, Worcestershire. c. 1895. *Pilkington Glass Museum*

CAMEO GLASS. A silver mounted claret-jug* decorated with sprays of poppies, by Daum Frères*, France, Nancy. c. 1900. *Antique Collectors' Club*

CAMEO GLASS. A sea-nymph, or Nereid, on a circular plaque of cameo glass, white on blue, executed by George Woodall, pupil of John Northwood*, Stourbridge. c. 1890. *The Corporation of Dudley*

Northwood's* copy of the Portland Vase*, but the technique was also employed by his pupils, and by such Continental glassworkers as Gallé* and Daum*.

CAMPAIGN DESK OR CHEST See *Military chest*; *Military desk*

CAMPAÑA VASE
Bell-shaped vase. A neo-classical* vase shape of the early years of the 19th century based on the ancient Greek bell krater. Fine examples from Derby* and Worcester* are decorated with topographical painting.

CANARSAC, LAFON DE (1821–1905)
Manufacturer of porcelain who invented a process for using photography in its decoration in 1854. He was awarded a medal for his exhibit at the London International Exhibition of 1862.

CANARY GLASS
A greenish-yellow art glass* coloured with uranium oxide* introduced by the Boston & Sandwich Glass Company*. The French version is termed *verre canari*.

CANDELABRA
A decorative lighting appliance made for table use which has several branches arising from a central pillar, each with nozzle and drip pan. With only one candle nozzle it is a table candlestick. Candelabra are usually in pairs but sometimes in multiples of a pair when intended for very large tables. They usually carry from three to five candles. Large multi-branched candelabra, usually very ornate, were made with special stands and placed in the room for general lighting. The candelabrum in its present form dates from the 18th century and is still in use. It is sometimes termed a girandole*.

The best candelabra are of silver. A great deal of workmanship was lavished on some. Others were made from pre-fabricated parts The best ormolu or gilt-bronze candelabra equal silver for workmanship, the ornament being carefully chiselled after casting.

CANARSAC, LAFON DE. Cup and saucer decorated with medallions enclosing photographs in the process invented by Lafon de Canarsac*. c. 1862. *Victoria & Albert Museum, London*

CANDELABRA. Candelabrum of ormolu and Sèvres porcelain* with a lilac ground. French, mid-19th century.
Antique Collectors' Club

The poorer qualities are relatively coarse, only surface blemishes being removed. Porcelain candelabra are much sought. They come principally from Meissen* and the German factories, and are usually decorated with figures. The best, *en suite* with the service, come from Meissen. Spelter and electro-plate on base metal are the cheapest, and the latter are being made today. Quality of these is extremely variable.

CANDLE-EXTINGUISHER

These were made of metal or porcelain in the 19th century in a variety of fanciful shapes. Among the most sought are the extinguishers made by the Worcester Royal Porcelain Company* in the form of figures from the trial of the Tichborne Claimant*.

CANEWARE

A buff, unglazed stoneware* developed in 1770 by Josiah Wedgwood* and made almost continuously ever since. Early in the 19th century it was popular for casseroles made in a variety of decorative forms, the top of which was intended to represent the pastry of a pie. Caneware was also decorated with coloured enamels, and Minton* used a body of this nature as the foundation for their 'Majolica'*. Caneware was also used to make vases in the form of a section of the bamboo, and for this reason is sometimes known as bamboo-ware. Later caneware tends to be more distinctly yellow in colour than the buff of the earlier specimens.

CANING

The use of split cane from the rattan* palm interwoven to make seats and backs for chairs was introduced from the Far East in the 17th century. It remains popular in both France and England for informal and easy chairs, especially those which need to be moved frequently. It was especially fashionable in England during the second half of the 19th century.

CANOVA, ANTONIO (1757–1822)

Neo-classical* sculptor who lived in Rome from 1781. In consequence of the French invasion of Italy he left for Vienna in 1797, but in 1802 he accepted Napoleon's invitation to Paris, where he became an admirer of the Emperor, and modelled and carved a number of portraits of all kinds. An heroic statue in marble, 'liberated' by Wellington and now in Apsley House, is pictured here. In 1807 Canova carved a figure of Napoleon's sister Pauline Borghese as Venus, which is now in the Borghese Gallery, Rome, and in 1815 he played a leading part in securing the return to Italy of numerous art-treasures looted by Napoleon's armies. For this he was ennobled by the Pope. Canova's work greatly influenced the classical style

CANDELABRA. Porcelain candelabrum in the style of Sèvres*. Minton*. c. 1870.
Victoria & Albert Museum, London

CANDELABRA. Pair of three-light candelabra in the form of figures on tripod bases. Made by E. J. Barnard. London hall-mark for 1858. *Antique Collectors' Club*

CANOVA, ANTONIO. Heroic statue of the Emperor Napoleon I, carved by Antonio Canova* from a solid block of marble ten feet high, and weighing ten tons. It was sold by Louis XVIII after Napoleon's exile to Elba to the only bidder, the British government, apparently for the cost of the marble—66,000 francs. The cost of packing and carriage was borne by the French government. *Apsley House, London*

during his lifetime, and throughout the first half of the 19th century.

See *Flaxman, John; Gibson, John; Thorwaldsen, Bertel; Volpato Porcelain Factory*

CANTAGALLI, ULISSE (fl. 1878–1901)

Italian potter at Doccia, near Florence, who specialized in copies of 16th-century Italian *maiolica** from Urbino, Faenza and Deruta. He also produced work in the style of the Della Robbias. The factory's work is usually marked with a crowing cock, the meaning of 'Cantagalli'. Included among their reproductions

CANTAGALLI, ULISSE. A roundel in high relief covered with tin-enamel (*maiolica*) glazes inspired by the della Robbia workshop, representing May (*Maggio*) from a set of the *Months*. Mark: A crowing cock, incised. c. 1885. *Constance Chiswell*

are some examples of Isnik* styles, then called 'Rhodian', and Near Eastern wares generally. The factory executed some designs for William de Morgan* during his visits to Italy after 1892. Towards the end of the century Cantagalli produced wares in an *art nouveau** style.

CANTERBURY

Originally a holder for plate and cutlery, designed in the 18th century for supper parties. Sheraton attributed the name to the fact that the first one was ordered by a Bishop of the See of Canterbury. In the 19th century the name became attached to a stand for sheet-music or magazines. The canterbury of this kind is a low piece of furniture having several vertical partitions on a base which usually contains a small drawer. It is mounted on casters.

CAPE COD GLASS COMPANY (Sandwich, Mass.)

Factory started by Deming Jarves* in 1858 after his resignation from the Boston & Sandwich Glass Company*. The glass produced was similar, but the Cape Cod works closed in 1869 when Jarves died.

CAPITONNÉ, CAPITONNAGE (French)

Stuffed, padded, quilted, or deep-buttoned. Capitonnage is the material employed for these purposes. The *siège capitonné* (a well-stuffed, deep-buttoned chair)

57

became very popular in France shortly before the middle of the 19th century, and occurs in a wide variety of forms.

See *Borne*; *Buttoned upholstery*; *Confident*

'CAPO-DI-MONTE'
This is a very confused subject. Originally, a factory of this name was established in 1743 by Charles, King of Naples. It made some distinguished figures in soft-paste porcelain (now very rare) and table-ware in the styles of the period. It closed in 1759.

The still-existing factory of Doccia*, Florence, was started by the Marchese Carlo Ginori about 1739. Probably in the 1760s the factory, under the director-ship of Lorenzo Ginori, introduced a type of decoration consisting of classical figure-subjects in relief picked out with enamel colours. The subjects, for the most part, seem to have been taken from Renaissance bronze plaquettes. During the 19th century, by some curious chance, these relief wares were assigned to Capo-di-Monte. Marryat in his *Handbook* of 1859 is evidently uncertain, because he illustrates a vase decorated in this style which he captions 'Capo-di-Monte or Doccia'. Eventually Doccia gained the reputation for copying wares of this kind from Capo-di-Monte and imitations were made elsewhere by Edmé Samson* of Paris and Ernst Böhme of Rudolstadt, for instance. Some carry the crowned N mark of the later Naples factory and a few of the later versions even bear the *fleur-de-lys* of the original Capo-di-Monte factory. Many copies from South German factories are poor in quality. Wares of this kind are usually cups and saucers, bowls, vases, and, occasionally, caskets. Modern figures and groups of figures on sale at present under the name of 'Capo-di-Monte' bear no resemblance whatever to any ware termed 'Capo-di-Monte' in discussions of antique porcelain.

To summarize this complex subject—no relief wares were made at Capo-di-Monte; they were first made at Doccia, and continued to be made there during the 19th century; the greater number surviving are imitations made in either France or Germany, especially those marked with a crowned N or a *fleur-de-lys*. A specimen marked with a red star probably came from Doccia, and was made before 1850. Examples thus marked are very rare, and differ in paste, glaze and enamelling from the French and German copies.

CARAFE
A wide-mouthed bottle intended for either wine or water. It has no stopper since it was intended to have a tumbler inverted over the short neck. Until about 1800 the carafe was an item of table glassware in England. Throughout the 19th century, however, it was relegated to the bedroom to hold water. More recently it has returned to popularity in English restaurants for the service of *vin en carafe*. The English 19th-century carafe is not often decorated, but simple engraving sometimes occurs and ice glass* was employed for some examples.

CARAMANIAN PATTERN
Views on blue transfer-printed* earthenware made by Spode* from about 1810 onwards. The views were principally of a part of Asia Minor then called Caramania and they were taken from *Views in Egypt, Palestine, and the Ottoman Empire* published 1801–1804.

CARDER, FREDERICK (1864–1963)
Glass designer with Stevens & Williams* from 1881 until 1900, where he was associated with John Northwood*. In 1903 he founded the Steuben Glass Company*, Corning, N.Y., where he produced Aurene* and other types of art glass*, and experimented with the application of the bronze *cire perdue* casting technique to the making of glass.

CARDEW, MICHAEL (b. 1901)
Studio-potter; pupil of Bernard Leach*. From 1926 to 1939 he produced slipware at the Winchcombe Pottery, Gloucestershire, and from 1939 to 1942 he made stoneware* at Wenford Bridge in Cornwall. In 1942 he left for the African Gold Coast, where he established a pottery.

An example of his work is in the Victoria and Albert Museum, London.

CARDHEILAC FAMILY
Paris manufacturing silversmiths founded by Vital-Antoine Cardheilac in 1802. They rapidly became important producers of silver and wares in substitute alloys. Ernest Cardheilac joined the firm in 1860.

CARDEW, MICHAEL. Cider-jar of earthenware covered with a black glaze through which the decoration has been incised, a technique perhaps inspired by certain wares of Tz'u Chou (Chihli Province) of the Sung dynasty (960–1280). Michael Cardew, Winchcombe Pottery, Gloucestershire. 1926–1930.

Under his direction some excellent work in a fairly plain *art nouveau** style was produced, most of the designs being by Bonvallet. Ernest Cardheilac died in 1904 and the firm was continued by his sons, Jacques and Pierre. It merged with Christofié* in 1951.

CAREY, THOMAS & JOHN (Lane End, Staffordshire)
This firm of potters was in existence in 1818 and closed by 1842. In his *19th-century English Porcelain* Geoffrey Bemrose refers to their production of chimney-piece ornaments in a glassy porcelain not unlike that of the 18th-century Longton Hall factory.

CARLILE, JOHN (1762–1832)
Cabinet-maker of Providence, R.I., who worked mainly in the Sheraton and Hepplewhite styles with simple inlaid decoration.

CARLTON WARE LTD (Stoke-on-Trent, Staffordshire) See *Wiltshaw & Robinson Ltd*

CARLTON WARE LTD. Dish decorated in the Chinese manner, by Wiltshaw & Robinson Ltd*, Carlton Works, Stoke-on-Trent. c. 1925. *Constance Chiswell*

CARNIVAL GLASS
Cheap pressed glass made after the First World War and commonly used as fair-ground prizes, hence the name. It principally consists of fruit-bowls, sugar bowls and similar objects with profusely moulded decoration in coloured glass with an iridescent* surface. The colours include red, blue, green, mauve, silver, and gold, the latter sometimes termed 'Marigold'. As its use implies this glass was made in fairly large quantities in Europe and America but it is no longer produced and is now collected.

CARPEAUX, JEAN-BAPTISTE (1827–1875)
French sculptor, born in Valenciennes, who was responsible among other important works for the fountain called *The Four Quarters of the World* in the

Luxembourg Gardens. He provided a number of designs for biscuit porcelain* for the Sèvres* factory, including a pair of the dog and bitch belonging to the Duchesse d'Orléans, and made in the 1850s.

CARRARA
The name of a variety of Italian marble, so called from the district where it was quarried, as Parian* was derived from the marble quarries of the Island of Paros. 'Carrara' was the name given by Josiah Wedgwood & Sons* to their version of 'Parian' porcelain.

CARRARA STONEWARE
A white stoneware, usually covered with a thin, matt glaze, made by Doulton of Lambeth about 1885. Specimens were further decorated with enamels, sometimes lustre pigments,* and gilding. The mark is 'Carrara', in addition to *Doulton, Lambeth*. This ware should not be confused with the earlier 'Carrara'* Parian ware of Wedgwood*.

CARRIAGE CLOCKS
Small brass clocks of rectangular form varying between three and eight inches in height, expecially made to be portable. The small carriage clocks were usually supplied *en suite* with dressing-sets. The larger examples were less frequently employed for actual travelling, but were carried from room to room as required.

Most have four brass corner pillars and glass sides through which the movement is visible. Some of the more decorative French clocks have coloured enamel on metal or porcelain dials. Enamelled side panels are painted and sometimes pierced. Gold is occasionally substituted as a form of decoration for the dial. The top has a carrying handle, and a glass panel let in

CARRIAGE CLOCKS. Carriage clock with repeating and alarm mechanisms. 6in. high. Last quarter of the 19th century. *Antique Collectors' Club*

CARRIAGE CLOCKS. A miniature brass carriage clock, 2⅜in. high, by Chaude of Paris. *Antique Collectors' Club*

through which the moving escapement can be inspected. The movements are spring-driven and of excellent quality, the best either of French or English make.

The better-quality carriage clocks are made to strike the hours and the quarters, and sometimes to repeat even the minutes. The repeater mechanism actuated by a push button is for the purpose of telling the time in the dark. Most clocks with a striking mechanism also have an alarm mechanism. The most complex striking mechanisms are to be found on French clocks. English and American specimens rarely do more than strike the hour and half-hour.

Clocks were made in parts (cases, dials, movements, escapements, etc.) and assembled in special factories. The name on the dial is not that of the maker or the assembler, but of the vendor. The earliest carriage clocks were produced in France about 1850, and they were at their best, decoratively, about 20 years later. Good quality clocks of this type were made in England. They were also manufactured in the United States, but these are not generally of much interest to collectors. The carriage clock continued to be made until the early years of the 20th century, and reproductions of earlier types have become fairly common since.

CARRIER DE BELLEUSE, ALBERT ERNEST (1824–1887)

French sculptor who established a very successful studio in Paris for the production of decorative sculpture in terracotta*, marble, and bronze. He also supplied models to a number of porcelain factories, including Minton*, Sèvres*, Wedgwood*, Brownfield*, and Copeland*. He spent about three years in

Staffordshire at Minton's factory, and became art-director at Sèvres in 1870. Rodin* was employed by the Carrier-Belleuse studio in his youth.

The studio specialized in reductions of 18th- and early 19th-century sculpture in bronze for interior decoration, not all of which were signed by them, and consequently have sometimes been mistaken for original work. The use of bronze in conjunction with an ivory face and hands has been noted in the case of a small, signed figure in a revived medieval style, a technique more often employed towards the end of the century. The Carrier-Belleuse studio exhibited in London at the Great Exhibition of 1851. Work is usually signed *Carrier-Belleuse* or *A. Carrier*.

CARRIER DE BELLEUSE, ALBERT ERNEST. Tazza of Algerian onyx marble and gilt metal made by A. Pallu et cie. (Compagnie des Marbres Onyx d'Algerie), and designed and modelled by Albert Carrier de Belleuse*. Signed *A. Carrier*. From the London International Exhibition, 1862. *Victoria & Albert Museum, London*

CARRIÈRE, ERNEST (1858–1908)

Painter and modeller who worked for Théodore Deck* from about 1890. Appointed art-director at Sèvres*, c. 1906. Signature: *Ernest Carrière* incised.

CARRIÉS, JEAN (1856–1894)

Studio-potter, born at Lyon, who established himself at Montriveau, near the old *faïence** town of Nevers. His work includes grotesque* figures and stoneware* vases inspired by fruit and vegetable shapes covered with a variety of ingenious glazes.

CARTER, STABLER & ADAMS (Poole, Dorset)

A company founded in 1921 to take over the Poole Pottery owned by Owen Carter. This had been founded in 1873 and at one time supplied blank tiles to William de Morgan*. The firm made good quality tableware and decorative wares. The marks employed were *Carter Poole* in script, *Carter, Stabler, Adams,*

CARTER, STABLER & ADAMS. Vase covered with a tin-enamel glaze over a buff stoneware* body with formal floral decoration in green, mauve, yellow, blue, black and buff. Rectangular mark impressed: *CARTER, STABLER & ADAMS, POOLE, ENGLAND*. No. *116* incised. *16x* fired on. *Constance Chiswell*

Poole, England impressed, and *Poole, England* with a dolphin in black underglaze.

CARTON-PIERRE (French)

A type of *papier mâché* employed during the 1880s, usually to imitate carved wood or moulded plaster. It differs from ordinary *papier mâché* in having the addition of whiting to the paper pulp and size.

CASE-BOTTLES

Four-sided bottles made to fit into a case or tantalus. They are well known in ancient Roman glass, when they are termed 'common squares'.

CASED GLASS

Cased glass is glass of one colour covered with one or more layers of differently coloured glass, the decoration being engraved through the upper layer or layers to reveal those underneath. This type of glass was extensively manufactured by Bohemian factories in the early years of the 19th century, but it did not become very popular with English glass makers until the repeal of the Glass Excise Act in 1845 which had levied duty on manufactured glass based on the weight of the raw material. Soon after 1845 English glasshouses were making a variety of colour combinations, although the quality of their products was adversely criticized by English newspapers in comparison with those of Bohemia shown at the Great Exhibition of 1851, *The Times* suggesting that English manufacturers should buy Bohemian cased glass to copy. Quality rapidly improved, especially at Stourbridge, and cased glass continued to be popular for the next 25 years. The earlier types which employed only transparent coloured glasses were developed into those with layers of opaque glass. White opaque glass

layers were often additionally decorated with enamelling and gilding. Most of the wares of this kind were decanters, spirit bottles, and bottles for scent and for sal volatile. They are generally of two layers, usually red cased over clear glass, but three layers incorporated into the engraved design occur occasionally.

It is not always easy to determine whether a glass is English or Bohemian, but Bohemian glass is usually of the potash variety whereas English glass is a lead glass, and is therefore heavier. After the repeal of the Glass Excise Act there was no longer much incentive for the English manufacturer to make his glass lighter in weight, so most are of thicker glass more heavily cut, with deeper engraving than Bohemian specimens. There are also differences in the decorative *motifs* and the forms employed, which are generally best recognized from an acquaintance with both varieties. Usually, Bohemian decoration is more sophisticated as befits an industry which had inherited the German glass-engraving tradition of the 17th and 18th centuries. Czechoslovakia has produced some copies of Bohemian cased glass in the 20th century, but the wheel-engraving is rarely of the same high quality as old work, and this is probably the best guide. Apart from the cased glass of David Greathead & Green of Stourbridge, excellent and important work was done in the middle years of the 19th century by George Bacchus & Sons* and Price, Harris & Sons, both of Birmingham. Their vases are especially sought and are rare.

See *Flashed glass*

CASTELLANI, FORTUNATO PIO AND SONS (Rome)

Italian jeweller and art-dealer who started business in 1814. He was later joined by his sons Augusto and Alessandro. Fortunato died in 1865 and the business was continued by Augusto. Alessandro established himself as a dealer in works of art and antique jewellery, one of his customers in 1872 being the British Museum. The Victoria and Albert Museum, London, also made large purchases of Italian *maiolica* and Medici porcelain at a sale held after Alessandro's death in 1883.

One of the Castellani specialities was the production of jewellery decorated with gold granules soldered to the surface in the Etruscan manner, a process thought to be a lost art. This was initiated by Fortunato and developed by his sons. These reproductions of Etruscan jewellery have occasionally been passed off as ancient. The Castellani had two followers in the imitation of ancient jewellery—Carlo Giuliano, who had a London establishment, and Mellilo of Naples.

CAST GLASS

Glass cast in a mould in a manner similar to the casting of metal. Objects of this kind are usually solid. Frederick Carder* and others have occasionally made use of the *cire perdue** (lost wax) process in the casting of glass. This is more commonly employed in the casting of bronze.

CASTING

The use of moulds in the formation of objects was a technique much employed during the 19th century, especially for such metals as iron and bronze. A model is first made in plaster or wood of the object to be cast, and from this model moulds are made. The metal in molten form is poured into the mould, and takes up the shape of the original model. There are many refinements and variants of this process. For example, a core approximately the shape of the model but slightly smaller is used as the foundation for the model itself, which is modelled in wax over its surface. Moulds are then formed over the wax, and moulds and core carefully secured together with metal pins. The wax is then melted out, and the molten metal poured into the space it occupied. This technique yields a thin, hollow cast, light in weight, and more economical of metal than a solid cast. It is termed the *cire perdue* or 'lost wax' process, and was much employed for the best 19th-century French furnishing bronzes. There are several variations on this basic method. Cast-iron was often cast in founder's sand, a soft, clinging substance which will take a fairly sharp impression of anything pressed into it. A model, usually of wood, is pressed into the surface, and the impression filled with molten iron. This technique was mainly employed for such flat objects as fire-backs and door-porters* and for the parts of machines afterwards cleaned up on the lathe. More elaborate cast-iron objects were formed in moulds of fireclay—a refractory clay with a fusion point well above that of the metal. Bronze is also cast in moulds of fireclay or of plaster of Paris mixed with brick dust.

Casting in plaster of Paris moulds was extensively employed in the pottery industry, and is still so used. The moulds are of plaster of Paris, and the casting material is clay mixed to a fluid, creamy consistency with water. The mould is filled with this fluid (known as slip) and the porous plaster rapidly takes up water from the slip in contact with it until there is a layer of firm clay adherent to the walls. The surplus slip is then poured off, and the mould put aside to dry. As the water evaporates the clay adherent to the mould shrinks slightly and pulls away from the walls, facilitating the removal of the mould which is then ready to be used again. The more elaborate examples of moulded porcelain require a technique known as piece-moulding. The mould is made in a number of pieces each so constructed so that it will 'draw' from the surface of the cast without injuring it, the pieces being contained, and held in position by a simple outer case. Piece-moulding, which is used for repetitive work of all kinds, demands a high degree of skill. The best modern porcelain figures are often made by using this technique, in whole or part.

Small works of art in metal, especially the precious metals, are often a mixture of techniques, with the addition of cast ornament although, where possible, cast ornament was often replaced from the latter part of the 18th century onwards with ornament stamped in the hydraulic press for common work. Ornament of this kind, of course, was still made by hand with hammer, chisels, files, drills, and punches in the finest work, but this became very rare during the 19th century and, in the end, came only from such Houses as that of Fabergé*.

CAST-IRON   See *Ironwork*

CASTLEFORD (Yorkshire)

There were a number of factories making earthenware and stoneware* at Castleford in the 19th century. The most important is that of David Dunderdale, who established a manufactory of creamware*, basaltes* and fine stoneware in 1790. It closed in 1820. The most characteristic product was an unglazed fine stoneware (teapots, cream-jugs, etc.), the decoration moulded in low relief in panels which are surrounded by a blue line. Teapot-lids have a stoneware hinge, and many teapots are octagonal in

CASTING. Working on the cast of a medallion in Morris Singer's foundry. A plaster mould shown on the left and a cast from it on the right. *Morris Singer*

CASTLEFORD (YORKSHIRE). Castleford* pottery teapot with a swan finial painted with a landscape. The Gothic* arcade round the gallery at the top helps to date it to about 1820. *Hove Art Gallery & Museum, Sussex*

shape, inspired by contemporary silver models. The stoneware used was obviously intended to resemble Wedgwood's jasper*, and can, perhaps, best be described as like a kind of opaque Parian*. Marks used include D. D. & CO and Castleford Pottery.

CASTLE HEDINGHAM POTTERY (Essex)
Pottery decorated with coloured glazes made at Castle Hedingham by Edward Bingham (b. 1821) in the middle decades of the 19th century. The wares themselves consisted of dishes, mugs and the like based, for the most part, on prototypes from the 16th and 17th centuries and earlier. Among the wares more or less directly copied may be numbered a dish by Bernard Palissy* and a *situla* (bucket) taken from an excavated Roman bronze. Although some of the medieval wares were sold to collectors at the time as ancient, it is doubtful whether Bingham ever intended this to happen. Many of his productions have the name of the pottery incised into the base, and none are deceptive to anyone acquainted with the wares he was copying.

The mark is a castle in relief on the base with BINGHAM below or E. BINGHAM, CASTLE HEDINGHAM, ESSEX.

CATHEDRAL STYLE, THE
French neo-Gothic style; the Troubadour style* current from about 1825 to 1848.

'CAUDLE' FLASKS
Stoneware* gin-flasks made by Doulton* of Lambeth about 1846 inspired by Douglas Jerrold's *Mrs Caudle's Curtain Lectures* which first appeared in *Punch*.

CAUGHLEY (near Broseley, Shropshire)
Porcelain factory founded in 1772 by Thomas Turner which made a soaprock porcelain decorated, for the most part, in Worcester* styles. It was bought in 1799 by John Rose of Coalport*, and until it closed in 1814 it made biscuit* porcelain which was glazed and painted at Coalport.

CAULDON PLACE WORKS See *Brown, Westhead, Moore & Co.*; *Ridgway & Sons, Job*

'CAVALLO'S WORCESTER'
Sparsely decorated 18th-century Worcester* porcelain from which the original painting has been removed or covered by an opaque ground-colour and to which (usually) fruit or flower painting has been added. Much work of this kind was done in the 1870s by the former *chef* of the Italian Minister in London, a man named Cavallo, and the term 'Cavallo's Worcester' was applied to it by contemporary collectors and dealers. Its quality is poor, and the glaze show signs of the re-firing to which it has been subjected.

A sale of old Worcester white ware took place in 1841, when the Flight and Chamberlain* factories

amalgamated, and it is probable that some 'blanks' already partially decorated with scale-blue found their way on to the market at this time. Undecorated specimens can be found occasionally, but they must have been bought for decoration originally.

CAZIN, JEAN-CLAUDE (1841–1901)
Potter, director of the École des Beaux-Arts and curator of the Museum at Tours. In 1871 he taught at Lambeth Art School, London. He made stoneware influenced by Japanese wares at the pottery of H. J. C. Bailey, Fulham, and was adviser to the young Martin Brothers*. He exhibited as a painter in the Paris Salon of 1895. His son, J. M. Michel Cazin (1869–1917), exhibited stoneware decorated with flowers and fruit in relief from 1897 onwards. Marks: père, *CAZIN*, incised; fils, *J. M. Michel Cazin*, incised.

CELADON GLAZE
Chinese glaze employed on stoneware* and porcelain*. In its early and classic form it was the result of covering the unfired vessel with a thin coat of ferruginous slip before glazing, followed by firing in a reducing atmosphere. True celadon glazes vary from a putty colour to olive-green, but the most sought shade in Europe was a sea-green, much treasured from the 16th to the 18th century. The colour, however, was very difficult for European potters to attain, although one or two specimens which approached it fairly closely were made at Meissen* in the 1740s. With the greater chemical knowledge of the 19th century, however, celadon greens became more common, and celadons were produced at several factories, including Sèvres*, Copenhagen* and Rookwood*, although they were only an approximation to the Chinese version.

CELLINI, BENVENUTO (1500–1571)
A Florentine sculptor and goldsmith widely known for his *Autobiography*. His *Treatise on the Art of the Goldsmith* was translated towards the end of the 19th century by C. R. Ashbee*. Very much influenced by Michelangelo, who considered Cellini the greatest sculptor in the world, his best-known surviving works are the *Perseus* at Florence and the *Nymph of Fontainebleau* in the Louvre. Of his goldsmith's work, only a gold salt made for François I survives, in the Kunsthistorisches Museum, Vienna. Other small works are sometimes claimed for Cellini from time to time, but, at best, such attributions are uncertain. Nevertheless during the 19th century a good deal of metalwork in the revived Renaissance style* was said, without very much reason, to be in the manner of Cellini. Most such descriptions may be taken as examples of Victorian 'name-dropping'.

CELLULOID See *Xylonite*

CELTIC DESIGNS

Designs copied from, or inspired by, the Celts, who arrived in Britain before the present era, and were forced by the Romans and succeeding invaders to occupy Ireland, Wales, Cornwall, and lands to the north and west. The Celts were skilled bronzeworkers and enamellers, and examples of their work, particularly jewellery, have been excavated in Britain and Ireland, as well as at numerous sites on the Continent. Celtic ornament was based on circles, spirals and curving tendrils. This feature was especially incorporated into many *art nouveau** designs including the pewter and silver wares sold under the trade names of 'Tudric'* and 'Cymric'*.

CENTURY GUILD, THE

The Century Guild of Artists, to give it its full title, was founded in 1882 by a group of artist-craftsmen of whom A. H. Mackmurdo* was the leading spirit. It was a time when the line of demarcation between the fine and the applied arts was being drawn increasingly heavily, and one of the aims of the Century Guild was to restore the relationship between the two which had existed in early Renaissance times, when an artist had been equally prepared to paint an altarpiece or a

CENTURY GUILD, THE. Dining-chair designed by A. H. Mackmurdo* for the Century Guild*. Mahogany, with fretwork back and painted decoration. Made by Collinson & Lock*. c. 1882. *William Morris Gallery, Waltham Forest*

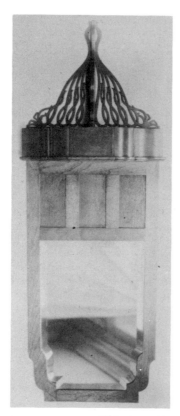

CENTURY GUILD, THE. Wall-mirror with a fretwork bracket designed by A. H. Mackmurdo* for the Century Guild*. c. 1890. *William Morris Gallery, Waltham Forest*

CENTURY GUILD, THE. Bronze hanging-lamp, probably by George Eshing and/or Kellock Brown of the Century Guild*. c. 1890. *William Morris Gallery, Waltham Forest*

cassone. This necessarily implied raising the level of industrial design to that of painting and sculpture. Mackmurdo was the principal designer, particularly of textiles and wallpapers. The Guild's work was retailed by Goodall of Manchester and Wilkinson* of Bond Street, London. Its designs were also displayed at Exhibitions in London and the provinces. A quarterly magazine, *The Hobby Horse*, began publication in 1884. Despite a small circulation it was very influential until it ceased publication in 1892.

In the work of the Century Guild is to be found the beginning of English *art nouveau**, especially, perhaps, in the sinuousness of the plant-forms decorating the metalwork of George Eshing and Kellock Brown. The Guild was short-lived, disbanding formally in 1888, although its members continued, for the most part, to work in cooperation with each other.

CERAMIC ART COMPANY (Trenton, N.J.)
A factory established in 1889 which produced a porcelain closely resembling that of Belleek*, in Ireland. They made a ware in the Belleek body with decoration in relief left unglazed, a technique probably inspired by a Chinese prototype.

CERAMIC PASTRY
During the Napoleonic Wars, when flour was both scarce and dear, Wedgwood* made game-pie dishes in cane-coloured stoneware* to imitate pie-crust, the interior being filled with meat.

CHAISE-LONGUE (French)
A long chair on which the occupant reclined, leaning against the carved end, with the feet up in the intimate surroundings of the *boudoir*. It was derived partly from the Jacobean day-bed and partly from the French *duchesse brisée* of the 18th century. Popular during the Regency*, it became fashionable again in the 1860s with the vogue for French furniture styles. Mrs Patrick Campbell referred to marriage as the 'deep, deep peace of the double-bed after the hurly-burly of the *chaise-longue*', which indicates the part it played in some sections of Victorian society. It can be found either caned in traditional styles or upholstered.

CHALKWARE
Term employed in America for chimney-piece figures made of plaster of Paris which were fashionable as substitutes for figures of pottery and porcelain from about 1860 to the early years of the present century. Figures of this kind were first imported from Europe, and then manufactured throughout America, especially by John Rogers* of New York. Figures made by Rogers were large, often 20 inches or more in height, and coloured with oil-paint. Chalkware figures generally were hand-painted or tinted in oil or watercolour and afterwards sized or varnished. Rogers' subjects were taken from American life and bear his name and patent number. Other chalkware subjects include a variety of animals, as well as fruit pyramids in urns.

CHALON, LOUIS (fl. late 19th century)
French sculptor who provided models for E. Colin & Cie.* His signature, *L. CHALON*, is incised.

CHAMBERLAIN, ROBERT (fl. late 18th and early 19th century)
Robert Chamberlain, a painter at Worcester*, left the factory in 1783, when it was bought by Thomas Flight, and opened a factory of his own. At first this was no more than a decorating studio painting porcelain made at Caughley*, but the manufacture of porcelain was started in 1792. The body at this time was dense, hard, greyish and inferior to the porcelain of Flight's factory, but it was continually improved, and in 1811 Chamberlain introduced the 'Regent' body, the quality of which was exceptional. Chamberlain was in partnership with his son, Humphrey, and Richard Nash. For this reason the mark *H. Chamberlain* is not unknown. The amalgamation of the Chamberlain and Flight factories took place in 1840, and in 1847 the combined enterprise was removed to Chamberlain's Diglis site, where it still remains.

Most of the factory's work before 1840 consisted of elaborately painted and gilded service-ware and vases, often with coloured grounds. Japan patterns, similar to those of Derby*, were also popular. Most painting was of exceptional quality. The mark employed was usually *Chamberlains Worcester* in script.

See *Worcester Royal Porcelain Company*

CHAMBER POTS
The upper part of the Victorian house was plentifully supplied with chamber pots. The water-closet at this time was accommodated on the lower floor, or even, in the case of artisans' houses, in the yard, and every bedside-table included a cupboard for the chamber pot (which the Victorians euphemistically called a 'po', shortening the French *pot de chambre*. The best pots were made by the porcelain factory for the *bourgeoisie* and were often handsomely decorated with enamel painting and gilding, although cheaper varieties less elaborately decorated were also available. In the early decades of the 19th century, the labouring classes showed a robust and lively sense of humour, and earthenware pots, from Sunderland especially, were decorated with ribald verses and such *motifs* as a portrait of Napoleon in the bottom, or a large eye. Both varieties are now eagerly sought, the former principally as flower-vases, the latter as collectors' 'conversation pieces'. The porcelain chamber pot was made *en suite* with a water-jug and basin and a covered slop-pail for the wash-stand. The *bourdaloue,* a more portable pot shaped rather like a large sauceboat without a pouring lip and intended for female use, was still being made in the early decades of the century as a coach-pot, but the fashionable feminine delicacy of the Victorian era, which became almost pathological, led to its discontinuance. They also are now a much sought collectors' item.

About 1965 questions asked in Parliament revealed the fact that Admirals of the Fleet were still being supplied with chamber pots bearing the Royal Arms—a worthwhile acquisition for any collector.

CHAMELEON GLASS
Literally chameleon-like, an opaque glass of several colours introduced by Egermann* in 1835.

CHAMPLEVÉ ENAMELLING

An enamelling technique in which the pattern is formed by scooping depressions in the metal surface to be decorated, each of which is intended to confine a single colour in powder form in preparation for firing. Often employed in conjunction with *cloisonné* enamel.

CHANDELIERS

Chandeliers made to be suspended from the ceiling, intended for a large number of candles, and hung with faceted glass drops to multiply the reflection of the candle-flames were popular during the 18th

CHANDELIERS. One of the arms of an English cut-glass* chandelier showing the method of cutting, disposition of drops, etc. c. 1815. *Victoria & Albert Museum, London*

century. They became even more elaborate in the early years of the 19th, when the Prince Regent indulged his passion for this form of lighting at the Royal Pavilion (Brighton)*. The crystal chandelier continued in popularity for many years, Perry & Co. supplying the great chandelier of the Throne Room in Buckingham Palace in 1835. Small modern versions of this type of lighting appliance are still being made in Czechoslovakia and some so-called antique examples have been made up from drops salvaged from the break-up of damaged earlier specimens.

In America chandeliers were made in the 19th century by Bakewell, Pears & Company* of Pittsburgh, the New England Glass Works*, and the Boston and Sandwich Glass Company* among others.

Gas chandeliers of metal were introduced in England by 1850. Models especially constructed for electric lighting were available towards the end of the century, but the adaption of old candle chandeliers for electric lighting only took place later when suitable bulbs were developed.

CHAPLET, ERNEST (1836–1909)

French artist-potter apprenticed at the Sèvres* factory. In the 1870s Chaplet experimented with decoration in coloured clay slips (*barbotine**) using the *faïence** of the Bourg-la-Reine factory. In 1886 he was joined by Paul Gauguin*, who made stoneware* in Chaplet's studio which had been started four years previously to make stoneware for Haviland*. Later Chaplet turned his attention to Chinese glazes and succeeded in reproducing the *flambé**. He also devised turquoise and mauve glazes. His work for Haviland*

CHANDELIERS. A forty-light ormolu chandelier (one of a pair) in the revived rococo* style, adapted for electric light. English. Early 20th century. *Antique Collectors' Club*

CHAPLET, ERNEST. Porcelain vase with a streaked green and purple glaze—a type of *flambé*. Ernest Chaplet*. French. Late 19th century. *Victoria & Albert Museum, London*

& Co. was marked *H & CO* within a chaplet (i.e. a wreath of flowers or leaves for encircling the head).

CHAPUS, HENRI MICHELLE (1833–1891)
Pupil of Duret's who modelled biscuit* figures for Sèvres, including a bust of President Carnot.

CHARPENTIER, ALEXANDRE (1856–1909)
French sculptor and designer in the *art nouveau* * style, and a member of the École de Nancy. Charpentier designed furniture which is highly characteristic of the *art nouveau* style with heavy mouldings and harmonious curves. He is represented in the Musée des Arts Décoratifs, Paris.

CHAUVIGNÉ, AUGUSTE (1829–1904)
Potter who studied under Charles Avisseau* and established his own workshop for the imitation of Bernard Palissy*. Mark: monogram *AC*, painted.

CHELSEA KERAMIC ART WORKS (Chelsea, near Boston, Mass.)
Factory founded in 1866 by A. W. Robertson, who was joined in 1867 by his brother, Hugh C. Robertson (1845–1908). They were joined in 1872 by their father, James Robertson, an experienced potter, who died in 1880. In 1875 the factory produced excellent pottery, especially flasks, in a body closely resembling that of ancient Greek red-ware. Chelsea '*faïence*', with floral decoration and a soft, brilliant glaze, dates from 1877.

Hugh Robertson took over the direction of the factory in 1884, when his brother retired. Under him the factory produced many notable wares of an experimental nature based on Chinese techniques. He succeeded in reproducing both the *sang-de-boeuf* * glaze, and the crackle effects employed by the Chinese as a form of decoration. These things were somewhat in advance of their time, however, and sold slowly. The factory closed in 1889. It reopened soon afterwards with new finance, but it was transferred to Dedham, Mass., where it became the Dedham Pottery* Company.

CHERET, JOSEPH (1838–1894)
Sculptor. The son-in-law of Albert Carrier de Belleuse*, Cheret designed furniture and glass and, from 1887, modelled for the Sèvres* factory. Signed, *Joseph Cheret*, incised.

CHESAPEAKE POTTERY (Baltimore, Md.)
Factory founded in 1881 by D. F. Haynes & Co. which achieved a reputation for wares of high quality, including 'Severn' ware which dates from 1885 and has an olive-grey body. Semi porcelain* and Parian* ware were introduced at about the same time. Medallions, plaques and portrait busts were made in the latter body. A majolica was termed 'Clifton' ware. The factory employed the monogram *DFH* as a mark.

CHESTERFIELD
A large sofa with overstuffed back and ends and deep buttoned upholstery, looking (in the words of one 19th-century writer) like a gigantic pin-cushion, and named after the 19th Earl of Chesterfield. The type was introduced about 1880, but after 1900 it became smaller and more elegant.

CHESTNUT-ROASTER
A circular brass box, about ten inches in diameter and three inches deep, with a pierced cover and a handle about 18 inches long, used for roasting chestnuts over an open fire. Old examples are comparatively rare; reproductions fairly common. Sheet-iron versions also exist.

CHESTS OF DRAWERS
The 19th-century chest of drawers was a much less elaborate piece of furniture than its 18th-century counterpart. From about 1800 to 1860 it was generally fitted with wooden knobs instead of brass furniture. The cheaper were of painted deal; a better quality was veneered with mahogany and French-polished. Few were of solid mahogany. The most sought are bow-fronted. Serpentine-fronted chests are very rare in the 19th century, except as reproductions of 18th-century types.

CHEVERTON, BENJAMIN (1794–1876)
English sculptor. In 1828, in association with a Mr Hawkins, he invented a machine for reproducing in ivory large works of sculpture and reliefs in miniature.

CHIFFONIERS (French)
In France the chiffonier is a small decorative chest of narrow, shallow drawers, either six or seven. With seven drawers it is sometimes termed a *semainier*. It derives its name from its purpose as storage for *chiffons*, silks, muslins, and articles of dress and toilet.

In England the piece of furniture known as a chiffonier does not occur before 1800, and rarely in anything like its original form after the death of George IV in 1830. Caricatures of it occur, however, almost as late as the 1860s. Essentially, the English chiffonier is a kind of sideboard with cupboards below and book-shelves above. The wood employed was nearly always rosewood* and low, pierced ormolu* galleries, mouldings and mounts, or brass stringing, occur on typical specimens. Ormolu mouldings, however, have sometimes been added later to plain specimens to make them more expensive. The chiffonier was also made of stained and grained deal, and in painted deal. Painted examples, which are sought after, are rare. Metal *grilles* in the door panels are not uncommon. The top is often of marble, as were the tops of 18th century Paris prototypes.

CHINESE EXPORT PORCELAIN AND THE AMERICAN TRADE
The United States began to compete with the English

East India Company directly independence had been gained, the first boat to sail to Canton being the 360-ton *Empress of China*, which left New York in 1784. This voyage was highly successful, and by 1800 the trade with China was well established on a large and growing scale. It was carried on by fast, small ships which were a great deal speedier than the 1500-ton East Indiamen plying between London and the East. From 1800 to 1850 the trade reached its greatest extent, and the merchants and sailors brought home not only the staples of the trade, like porcelain, lacquer, tea, silks, spices and so forth, but many curiosities of one kind or another, which led to the formation of collections. Like the European merchants, the Americans were compelled to use the port of Canton, where lived the Chinese merchants appointed to deal with foreigners. The foreigners had their *hongs*, or warehouses, on the waterfront. Porcelain bowls with a view of these Canton warehouses, each with its national flag, date from the final years of the 18th century, and good specimens are much prized.

The amount of porcelain imported into the United States from 1800 to about 1850 can be measured in tons. Much of it was painted in Canton to the customer's order. The largest centre of manufacture then existing in China was at Ching-tê Chên. For the export trade white ware was sent to Canton. Ware decorated in undeglaze blue, which was a factory operation, was sent to Nanking, another port of shipment, or to Canton itself, especially if additional enamelling was called for. Hence blue and white export services are still sometimes called 'Nanking', and the decoration is usually more Chinese in style than the enamel painting of Canton, where the

painters were copying a pattern or design provided by their foreign customer.

Porcelain made for the American market is less varied than that made earlier for Europe. The fashionable style was neo-classical, and no porcelain factory, Chinese or European, succeeded in making its forms pleasing. The Canton enamelling shops were no longer as prepared as they had been in the past to paint to special order, but relied on stock patterns. The Chinese invented the production-line towards the end of the 17th century, and this had now been developed to the point where the elements of a pattern were broken down and the separate parts painted by a different person.

Much sought by collectors are those wares decorated with the American eagle, or such *motifs* as a portrait of George Washington after a contemporary American engraving. Large bowls painted with ships engaged in the China trade are highly valued. Vases decorated profusely at Canton in the *rose-verte* palette (see *Famille verte*) were popular, and are generally termed 'Mandarin' vases. The subject of decoration was mainly figures of the Chinese 'official' class painted in panels surrounded by elaborate diaper borders. Service ware excessively decorated in a similar palette in conjunction with underglaze blue, and a glaze having an irregular or slightly undulating surface, was popular from the last quarter of the 18th century until the early decades of the 19th. The forms are western, but the decoration is Chinese.

After 1800 Chinese porcelain, and many other export commodities, declined markedly in qualities of design and workmanship. There was a general tendency to copy 18th-century styles. Around 1790 porcelain with the coat of arms in a spade-shaped shield was introduced and employed on otherwise slightly decorated pieces of neo-classical form. A little later a decoration of butterflies and flowers on a celadon* green ground became popular. This is often called the 'Canton' style.

The Metropolitan Museum, New York, has an important collection of Chinese export porcelain, the McCann Collection. The Victoria and Albert Museum, London, also houses a significant collection.

CHINI & CO. (Florence)   See *Arte della Ceramica*

CHIPARUS, D. H.   See *Art déco figures*

'CHIPPLEWHITE STYLE'
Term derived from a combination of Chippendale and Hepplewhite, 18th-century cabinet-makers, to describe furniture in a mixture of their respective styles made in the 1870s and later.

CHOISY-LE-ROI (Seine)
Manufacturers of porcelain* and *faïence-fine* from 1804, founded by Paillart. Table-services were painted with topographical scenes and classical subjects. They also made use of transfer-printing* on

CHINESE EXPORT PORCELAIN. Covered jug painted with a portrait of George Washington. Chinese, decorated for the American market. Early 19th century. *Author*

'CHIPPLEWHITE' STYLE. Mahogany armchair of good quality designed with a Hepplewhite shield back and Chippendale legs and proportions—an example of 'chipplewhite'*, a hybrid so unsuccessful as to be almost comic. c. 1880. *Leslie Curtis*

both porcelain and *faïence-fine*. Amusing decorative objects like plates for oysters or asparagus were made in the 1850s as well as copies of Henri Deux* ware. In 1885 the factory was joined by Ernest Chaplet* who experimented with the reproduction of *flambé*￼and other Chinese glazes on a stoneware* body.

From 1824 to 1836 the mark was *P & H CHOISY* and from 1836 *H B & CO CHOISY LE ROI* (the first for Paillart & Hautin and the second for Hautin & Boulanger). Chaplet's mark was a chaplet (or necklace) with a cross attached and the monogram *HB*.

CHOISY-LE-ROI GLASS WORKS (Seine)

Glasshouse founded by Georges Bontemps* at Choisy-le-Roi, a suburb of Paris, in 1821. Here was produced both ordinary and crystal glass of fine quality, and they soon achieved a good reputation. Nevertheless, the enterprise was seriously affected by the political troubles of 1848, when Bontemps left Paris to work in Birmingham with Chance Brothers on the making of optical glass. Choisy produced overlay glass* in the style of Bohemia. It also made opaline* and *millefiori*￼glass, the latter from 1844. *Latticinio*￼glass from Choisy was included in the Paris Exposition of 1839. Although it is obvious from surviving records that glass of excellent quality and in a diversity of techniques was made, attributions are not always easy or certain.

CHOPIN, F. (fl. mid-19th century)

A French *fondeur*￼who worked in Saint Petersburg during the second half of the 19th century. He exhibited at the Paris Exposition of 1878.

CHRISTIAN, DESIRÉ (1846–1907)

Glassmaker who established a glasshouse in Meisenthal, Lorraine, about 1896 where he produced *art nouveau*￼glass, including iridescent* vases, lamps, etc. Printed mark.

CHRISTOFLÉ ET CIE (Paris)

Sometimes called 'the Elkington* of Paris'. A firm of goldsmiths, silversmiths and jewellers founded in Paris in 1829 in the rue de Bondy and still in existence today. In 1842 they bought a plating process from a French chemist, but were compelled to negotiate with Elkington, whose earlier patent it infringed, before they could use it. Christoflé enjoyed the patronage of Napoleon III for whom they made a dinner-service in a revived Empire·style*, mainly derived from Greek sources, which they exhibited at the Paris Exposition of 1855. They made centrepieces, tureens, casseroles, tea-urns, wine-coolers and candlesticks of electroplated* metal and specialized in reproducing *ciselure* by electrotyping. Much of their work was decorated by enamelling* in the form of bands and borders. A centrepiece of this period, made for Napoleon III, is in the Musée des Arts Décoratifs, Paris. Among the designers employed by them may be included Carrier-Belleuse*, and some of their metalwork in the 1870s shows traces of Japanese influence. Towards the end of the century they made tentative use of *art nouveau*￼forms, but after the First World War they became much more progressive, and produced a good deal of well-designed *art déco*￼metalwork.

They now operate factories in Switzerland, Milan, New York and Buenos Aires.

Among the Christoflé innovations of the 1930s were a series of plates decorated by Jean Cocteau and the Vicomtesse Marie-Laure de Noailles (Marie-Laure) in a Surrealist style.

CHROMOLITHOGRAPHY

Lithographs* in the early decades of the 19th century were coloured by hand, but polychrome lithographs began to be produced in the 1850s. The invention of the process which made this possible has been attributed to Charles Joseph Hullmandel (1789–1850). By this method pictures could be printed in oil-based inks directly from a series of stones each carrying a different colour, cheaply and in large quantities. About the same time the excise duty on sheet-glass needed for picture-framing was removed, and chromolithographs (also known as oleolithographs) became an extremely popular item of household decoration in Europe and America. Popular Royal Academy pictures were bought by print-makers and owners of magazines. In the latter case, they were often given away by the hundred thousand as free supplements inside the periodical. They are nevertheless inclined to be scarce today because large numbers of the poorer quality specimens were destroyed as valueless earlier in this century.

See *Baxter prints*; *Currier & Ives*

CHRYSELEPHANTINE WORK

Originally 'chryselephantine' referred to statues of ivory and gold in ancient times. The most famous example of the technique was the 45-foot high seated statue of Zeus by Pheidias, which stood in a temple at Olympia. It was constructed of plates of ivory and gold attached to a wooden foundation and a reproduction, taken from ancient coins on which the statue appeared, was displayed at the Paris Exhibition of 1855. A seated statue of Abraham Lincoln in the pose of Zeus is in Washington, D.C.

In the 1855 Exhibition Mme Meurice exhibited statues in ivory and silver by Pradier and Feuchère, but the combination was not much admired. Bronze figures with faces and hands of ivory are not uncommon during the currency of the *art nouveau** style, no doubt inspired by the earlier work, but were at their most popular during the 1930s.

See *Art déco figures*

CHRYSELEPHANTINE WORK. *The Bathers.* Group by Fritz Preis* in bronze and ivory in the *art déco** style. c. 1925. *Antique Collectors' Club*

CIGAR-CASES

Decorative cigar-cases are often collected. The cigar reached Western Europe from Spain and South America about 1790, and manufacture was started in France in 1823. Cigars had become popular in England by 1827, when there was a Cigar Divan in King Street, Covent Garden, where men could foregather to smoke a cigar and drink coffee. This was decorated in an oriental (probably Moorish) style which was popular for this kind of masculine establishment.

Cigar-cases date from about 1820, and are to be found in a wide variety of materials; the best of them can be classified as *objets d'art*. Even before 1860 decorative cigar-cases were luxurious enough to attract the attention of the contemporary moralizer, who stigmatized them as effeminate and recommended the use of cases of plain Russian leather. The leather cases were probably commonest at the time and continued to be popular among the conservative. Those of moulded hide are not uncommon, and cases of the better kind include those of tortoiseshell with gold mounts, some of which, shown at the Paris

Exposition of 1867, were decorated in the Japanese* manner. Horn cases imitated those of tortoiseshell. *Papier mâché** was very popular, especially before 1860, the best examples coming from Jennens & Bettridge* of Birmingham. Spiers* of Oxford sold *papier mâché* cases decorated with views of the colleges. Cases decorated with woven straw on a thin wood foundation, or even cardboard, date from the 1860s, and have nothing to do with earlier straw-work by French prisoners of war*. Cases ornamented with beadwork date from about the same period. Unusual today, although popular in some English circles in the 1850s, is the case painted with a *grivoiserie**. The finest 19th century cigar-cases were undoubtedly those made by Fabergé* towards the end of the century. One of gold made for Kaiser Wilhelm II has the royal monogram in *plique-à-jour* enamel. Cigar-cases continued to be made until the outbreak of the Second World War, but rarely thereafter.

CIGAR-STORE INDIANS

The life-size wooden figure of an Indian which once stood outside tobacconists' shops as a sign appears to have been introduced into New York about 1850. All kinds of wooden figures were made as shop signs, but these inscrutable, carved Indians were the most numerous. They were made by men who had at one time carved figure-heads for ships, but who found themselves in the mid-19th century supplying a diminishing demand. The output seems to have been in the region of 300 a year, but of course old figures were also repaired and repainted. They vary from the figure in profile sawn out of a flat board to the fully modelled figure carved in the round. Generally, there was not a great deal of variety in the poses, which are few and characteristic, but occasional examples of better quality occur. Carvers are, for the most part, anonymous, but Thomas Brooks of New York was a known figurehead carver who turned to making cigar-store Indians.

CINCINNATI ART POTTERY COMPANY (Cincinnati, Ohio)

Founded in 1880 by T. J. Wheatley & Company. Its products were excellent in quality, the most notable being ivory-coloured *faïence** decorated with natural flowers and gold scroll-work.

CINCINNATI POTTERY CLUB (Cincinnati, Ohio)

Group of women pottery decorators organized by Mary Louise McLaughlin (1847–1939). They bought undecorated ware, principally from the Rookwood Pottery*, painted and glazed it, and returned it to Rookwood for firing. After 1883 Rookwood were no longer able to give facilities for firing underglaze decoration, and the Club employed enamel colours instead. Work was marked *Cin. Pottery Club*, with the initials of the artist and the date.

CIRE PERDUE (French)

Literally, 'lost wax'; a very ancient method of casting ornamental bronzes which was commonly employed by French *fondeurs* in the 19th century. The model to be cast is made in wax, and a mould of refractory (i.e. largely fireproof) material formed over it. The wax is then melted out, and the liquid bronze run in.

See also *Casting*

'CLANTHA' WARE

Trade name for a type of pottery with a black matt glaze and angular patterns, introduced about 1912 by the Bretby Art Pottery*.

CLARET-JUGS

Silver or silver-mounted glass jugs with a pouring lip and handle for the purpose of serving wine at table. Most had provision for a stopper or cork. A popular Victorian type was a straight-sided glass vessel

CLARET-JUG. Engraved glass claret-jug* with silver mounts by Elkington* of Birmingham. Hall-mark for 1879.
Antique Collectors' Club

tapering towards the top, with a silver pouring lip. Wine-jugs in a variety of forms were made on the Continent. Gallé* of Nancy, for instance, made some characteristic examples,

CLARK, DANIEL (1760–1830)

Cabinet-maker who established himself in Salem, Mass., in 1796. He made tables, chairs, chests, etc. decorated with carving.

CLASSICAL

A term meaning, strictly, of the highest excellence, and applied by general consent to the art and architecture of Greece and Rome, and to later work in this style. Neo-classical* (i.e. the *new* classical style) implies an interregnum, in this case the asymmetrical rococo style, classical design being noted for symmetry.

CLEWS, JAMES AND RALPH (Cobridge, Staffordshire)

Manufacturers of blue printed earthenware from 1817 to 1835. Much of their production, excellent in quality, was made for the American market.

The usual mark was *Clews, Warranted Staffordshire,* underneath a crown. Among the subjects employed were American Views* within several different borders: English Views similarly treated; scenes from *Dr Syntax** and *Don Quixote* and domestic scenes after Wilkie.

CLICHY (Paris)

This factory, which eventually rivalled Baccarat* and Saint-Louis* for the quality of its decorative glass, began in 1837 as an enterprise founded by Ronyer & Maes for the large-scale production of cheap glass. It was at first situated at Billancourt, near the Pont de Sèvres, and it was eventually taken over by the Verrerie de Sèvres about 1885. Its name is derived from the fact that the factory was moved to Clichy-la-Garenne in 1844, when cased glass* was being produced. The production of *millefiori* paperweights* was on a fairly large scale before 1849, and the factory exhibited at the Great Exhibition in London in 1851. At the London International Exhibition of 1862 an engraved glass *tazza* of superb quality was purchased and later placed in the British Museum collection. The factory's work is now difficult to identify with certainty.

CLIFF, CLARICE (b. 1900)

Ceramic designer and decorator who studied at Burslem School of Art and became art-director of A. J. Wilkinson Ltd* until 1939. Clarice Cliff designs of the kind now sought are mainly *art déco** in style and painted in bright colours, her palette including orange, purple, and red. Vases are often lavishly gilded. Two well-known and sought-after patterns are *Bizarre* and *Fantasque*. Her work bears the signature *Clarice Cliff*.

CLIFTON ART POTTERY (Newark, N.J.)

A pottery established in 1905 by W. A. Long which imitated the forms and decorations of American Indian pottery.

CLOCK CASES, CARVED OAK

Towards the turn of the century when furniture and interior decoration in the Jacobean style were fashionable, carved oak clock cases were produced with the intention of fitting Georgian long-case movements into them, the original walnut or mahogany case doubtless being destroyed. These oak cases were highly carved with floral and foliate *motifs* from cresting to base.

CLOCK-JACKS

A cylindrical clockwork device for rotating joints of meat hung for roasting before an open fire. Excellent clock-jacks were made in Roxbury, Conn., by Simon Willard*. Most specimens in both England and America belong to the 19th century.

CLOCKS, AMERICAN

Up to about 1800 the long-case clock was the most popular type to be made by American clockmakers, often from imported movements. American movements were excellent in quality and the cases were not dissimilar from those popular in England, except that they tended to be wider. By the end of the 18th century a clock of this general type only four feet high, and often referred to as a grandmother clock, became popular and continued to be made in the early decades of the 19th century.

Clocks with a short pendulum driven by a spring, and intended to be set on a wall-bracket (bracket-clocks), were made in England throughout the 18th century, and these had been imported into America. In America, wall- and shelf-clocks* (mantel-clocks) equipped with the short pendulum were made from about 1800 onwards. The cheapest of these were made with movements of wood. Brass movements only became cheap enough to be within reach of most people later in the century. It is probable that the idea of wooden movements came from imported German Black Forest clocks, where the type had been made since the 17th century, and had become a popular export in the 19th.

The popularly priced shelf-clock was largely the product of Eli Terry*, whose pillar and scroll cases still owed much to the form of the long-case clock. The form of the clock was rectangular, enclosed by a glazed door, at the bottom of which a landscape was often painted or transferred. This type was especially popular in the 1840s.

The banjo clock* of Simon Willard* was not only very popular and widely copied, but it formed the basis in the 1840s for numerous variations, such as the lyre clock, the hour-glass case and the acorn case. Cases also began to be made with materials other than wood, like *papier mâché**, marble, ormolu and

CLOCKS, ENGLISH. An English long-case clock in an elaborately carved case, the movement with temperature-compensated pendulum showing phases of the moon. Westminster chimes. J. Stockall, London. Second half of the 19th century. *Sotheby & Co*

even cast-iron, although porcelain* cases do not seem to have been made in America.

The wooden movement was outmoded by Chauncey Jerome* and his inexpensive one-day clocks with brass movements. For the remainder of the century, the American clock industry concentrated on improvements in methods of quantity production, mechanical efficiency and increasingly large-scale organization. A considerable export trade grew up with Europe; American wall- and shelf-clocks of the

CLOCKS, ENGLISH. An English long-case
clock in carved mahogany case.
Westminster Chimes. London, Maple
& Co. c. 1900. *Sotheby & Co*

CLOCKS, ENGLISH. Combined clock and
barograph by J. L. Cassartelli. The
barograph, for automatically recording
pressure changes, was introduced into
London in the 1860s by Negretti and
Zambra. *Antique Collectors' Club*

first 60 years or so of the 19th century are not
uncommon in England, where they are rarely highly
valued.

CLOCKS, ENGLISH

During the Regency* period the production of long-
case, bracket-, and mantel-clocks followed traditional
paths. For most of the 19th century clock styles were

largely imitative of the highly successful 18th-century
types, although there were innovations: the neo-
Gothic* style inspired the lancet-shaped mantel
clock-case in rosewood*, but the style otherwise had
little effect at this time; dials were now enamelled on
better quality clocks, and painted on the cheaper
clocks, especially for the long-case variety which were
of the 30-hour type in an oak case instead of
mahogany or rosewood. Chimes on a gong or gongs

CLOCKS, ENGLISH. Walnut basket-topped mantel-clock in the style of an 18th century bracket-clock. Third quarter of the 19th century. *Sotheby & Co*

CLOCKS, ENGLISH. English mantel-clock in a case of cast brass, the decoration a mixture of styles in which revived rococo* perhaps predominates. Third quarter of the 19th century. *Sotheby & Co*

CLOCKS, ENGLISH. Mid-19th century clock with a brass two-train movement in the form of a 17th-century brass lantern clock. Inscribed G. *WOODE, GUILDFORD. Sotheby & Co*

CLOCKS, ENGLISH. Clock with a case of pottery and hardstone mounted in copper and brass, with a cut-brass Gothic revival* pediment. The inner, upper, pair of articulated columns are of malachite*, the outer, lower, columns of serpentine. The two heads represent *Night* and *Morning* respectively. Mid-19th century. *Sotheby & Co*

formed from rods or spirals of spring steel instead of tuned bells were introduced about 1850.

As the century advanced cases became more elaborate, with carving, inlays and massive proportions at variance with 18th-century elegance. The Victorians called the long-case a 'grandfather' clock, and a small version was introduced, little more than half the height and width, which was sometimes called a 'grandmother' clock. At this time few cheap clocks other than long-case clocks were made. These had a simple weight-driven movement, whereas bracket- and mantel-clocks were necessarily fitted with much more expensive and complex spring-driven movements. Many of the cheaper oak-case clocks have a provincial maker's name on the dial, but quite often these men were not makers in the

CLOCKS, ENGLISH. Clock in a gilt-bronze case, the floral ornament in a kind of revived rococo* style. French, third quarter of the 19th century. *Sotheby & Co*

CLOCKS, ENGLISH. Bracket-clock with white enamelled dial and engraved back-plate. Regency style, by Leach of London. c. 1820. *Antique Collectors' Club*

ormolu cases. At the same time clock cases made from marble and usually fitted with French or French-type movements (at one time in demand as parting gifts for retiring long-service employees) also found their way to the mantel-shelf of the dining-room chimney piece.

The market for cheap wall-clocks was supplied from the 1840s onwards from American mass-produced clocks. These, glass-fronted, were colourfully decorated with painted scenes or the transferred type known as decalcomania*. These have not uncommonly survived.

CLOCKS, FRENCH

To the French the decorative qualities of the clock case had always been of greater importance than the movement. Even in the 18th century, the movement had been more or less standardized and was excellent in quality, but the designing and making of cases had been in the hands of sculptors and designers of note and represented an important art-form. Empire* clocks in the early decades of the 19th century were as lavishly luxurious as their predecessors, and it was not until the reign of Charles X and Louis-Philippe that any notable divergences from this style began to be apparent.

After about 1825 repetitions of earlier 18th-century styles grow fairly common. The Boulle marquetry* case of about 1700 was popular for fine quality specimens and paralleled the contemporary fashion for Boulle furniture. Technical difficulties led to the early 18th-century practice of putting each numeral on a separately affixed enamel-painted plaque. These had been overcome by about 1745, but the fashion occurs on much later clocks in the earlier styles, and

strict sense of the word, but assemblers of parts bought from manufacturers. The most desirable clocks during this period remain those made by London members of the Clockmakers' Company in mahogany or rosewood cases.

The extension of travelling and the development of small clock movements able to withstand jolting, led to the development of the carriage clock*. These were a French innovation, but they proved very popular in England, where they were both manufactured and assembled from imported parts. Clocks with decorative painted porcelain dials, with vases *en suite*, were imported from France in the 1880s, and then made in England. These dials were fitted into rectangular cast

CLOCKS, FRENCH. Mantel-clock in an ormolu* case decorated with *cloisonné enamels*, the pendulum temperature compensated. French. Second half of the 19th century. *Antique Collectors' Club*

75

CLOCKS, FRENCH. Mantel-clock, the case decorated with porcelain plaques. French, mid-19th century. *Antique Collectors' Club*

is not necessarily a reliable guide to dating. The Troubadour style*, dating from about 1825, was employed for clock cases of architectural design in the form of a Gothic tower. These are often called 'Cathedral' clocks, and occur both in bronze and porcelain, the latter usually from the factory of Jacob Petit*. Clock cases in the Louis XVI style are notable for the combination of marble and gilt-bronze which became fashionable during that period, bases usually being bronze-mounted.

Contemporary descriptions of decorative metal-work are very imprecise because the term 'ormolu' became current for gilt-metal regardless of its composition. French 18th-century work of this kind was made from gilded bronze and a good deal of the best 19th-century work was of the same kind. This was

described in the 18th century as *dorure d'or moulu* (gilding with gold paste). Similar work was done in England in a light yellow metal which received the name first of *or moulu*, and by the 19th century had become 'ormolu'. This was a kind of brass, and was basically a copper-zinc alloy which did not require gilding. Most work in the alloy termed ormolu is of reasonably good quality, but most spelter (zinc*), except the earliest, is poor. Casting in zinc alone was undertaken before mid-century and the resulting casts bronzed and gilded. Zinc (known to the trade as spelter) is a soft white metal revealed by a scrape with a penknife blade in an inconspicuous place when it has been bronzed or gilded.

Cases of good quality were also made by electro-typing*, but the French were expert casters, and made less use of this process than either the English or the Germans, who both developed it. Porcelain clock cases are usually of fine quality, and the best are very decorative. Exceptionally fine cases with figure-subjects handsomely painted were made by the factory of Jacob and Mardochée Petit*, and Sèvres*

CLOCKS, FRENCH. Calendar mantel-clock in a black marble case, the movement by Bally à Paris. No. 1565. Third quarter of the 19th century. *Sotheby & Co*

provided urn-shaped vases for clocks like those made by the factory during the reign of Louis XVI.

The clock in the French style became very popular, usually associated with vases *en suite* and those for the mass-market were designed to be stamped out and put together with screws and nuts, or the metal was drilled and tapped for screws. These stamped parts rarely registered accurately, and cases of this kind are very poor in quality.

The French movement from about 1800 onwards was circular, and extremely well designed, the mechanism being packed into a very small space. Many improvements were made over the years without making any very obvious alterations. Achille Brocot (1817–1878) devised a 'dead-beat' escape-ment* for small clocks, and a modification for the pendulum which allowed timekeeping to be adjusted

CLOCKS, FRENCH. Clock in gilt-bronze and porcelain, the base painted with *putti*, and the top surmounted by two *putti* in a chariot drawn by goats, the wheel of the car acting as the clock-dial. Revived Louis Seize or neo-classical* style. Signed: *E. WHITE, PARIS*. Third quarter of the 19th century. *Sotheby & Co*

CLOCKS, FRENCH. Mantel-clock in an ormolu case surmounted by an urn, the dial and side panels of enamelled porcelain. The style of the numerals was introduced early in the 18th century. The urn and the top-shaped feet vaguely suggest the Louis Seize style. The flanking vases owe something to 18th-century porcelain. A typical 19th-century *mélange. Leslie Curtis*

from the front. This was introduced soon after 1850 but did not become popular for fine quality clocks until after 1870. Movements of good quality were fitted into fairly plain marble cases after 1870, and these continued to be popular until the early years of the 20th century, but few of them are important.

It was the practice throughout most of the 19th century, except for special instances, to make cases and movements in separate establishments, and to marry them at, or near, the point of sale, either at home or abroad. The best cases were gilt-bronze in the old style, and figures and often accessories were separately cast and assembled with the aid of screws and nuts. This was repeating 18th-century practice,

CLOCKS, FRENCH. Porcelain clock in the revived rococo style surmounted by an Algerian horseman, the base painted with a battle-scene. The struggle of the Algerians under Abd el Kader against the French lasted from 1832 to 1847. Jacob Petit. Fontainebleau. c. 1840. *Constance Chiswell*

when clock cases consisting of several figures were only rarely cast integrally. Records tell us that when an 18th-century owner tired of the figures on his clock he sometimes changed them for new ones. This may also have been done occasionally in the 19th century

CLOCKS, GERMAN
A clock-making industry using movements made from wood had been located in the Black Forest, Bavaria, since the 17th century. Their most popular and widely known product, the 'cuckoo' clock, is still being made there. This, however, is only one example of Black Forest ingenuity, and the picture-frame clock was very popular in the 1840s and later. This, a novelty in 18th-century France, usually took the form in Germany of a painted moonlit scene with a church-tower, the small clock-dial being mounted in the tower to represent the church clock. Occasionally small musical-box movements were also fitted.

CLOCK, GERMAN. Meissen* porcelain clock-case of architectural form, encrusted with flowers, and flanked by a *putto*. Late 19th century. *Antique Collectors' Club*

The wooden movement began to be superseded by brass movements about 1850, and factory production became more general. Nevertheless, the wooden movement has persisted among small makers for clocks made as curiosities in the traditional manner. American shelf-clocks were imitated in the Black Forest region.

CLODION, CLAUDE MICHEL (1738–1814)
French sculptor who worked mainly in terracotta*. He spent the years from 1762 to 1771 in Rome. Clodion specialized in small figures and groups for interior decoration, usually with a pastoral subject and of a more erotic character than the products of his contemporaries. After the Revolution he turned to a more strongly marked classical style. Clodion modelled figures for reproduction in biscuit porcelain* at Sèvres* and was in trouble on one occasion when he modelled Marie-Antoinette almost completely nude to commemorate the birth of the Dauphin. He may have provided models for the Niderviller

porcelain factory in 1795, although these could have been pirated.

Clodion was extremely popular in the 19th century, when copies, forgeries, and adaptions of his terracottas were frequently made, many of which purport to bear his signature. Small bronzes based on his terracottas, some bearing a signature, were made at the same time. The greatest care should be exercised in acquiring anything signed by Clodion, or attributed to him, from any but a reliable source.

CLOISONNÉ ENAMEL

An enamelling technique in which the pattern is formed by wires soldered to the surface of a metal (usually copper) object to be decorated, to form cells or *cloisons,* each of which is intended to confine a single colour in powder form or as an enamel paste to prevent them from intermingling during firing. *Cloisonné* enamelling is often employed in conjunction with *champlevé**.

See *Basse-taille*; *Champlevé enamelling*; *Enamels, painted*; *Plique-à-jour enamel*.

CLOSE PLATE

Small objects of flat-ware (knife-handles, forks, spoons, fish-slices, various kinds of serving-tongs, etc.) made of iron or steel and covered with silver-foil are referred to as close plate. This silver substitute was made from about 1809 until 1840; in the latter year it was superseded by the newly-invented process of electro-plating*. Some examples made after about 1830 were plated on German silver* (nickel-silver) instead of on iron or steel, but these are few. In cases of doubt, a magnet is an excellent method of making certain of the nature of the metal underlying the silver as it is only attractive to the ferrous metals.

The object to be plated was first dipped into a sal ammoniac flux and then into molten solder. Silver-foil, more or less cut to shape, was then pressed on to the surface, and the object again heated to remelt the solder. It was finished by burnishing. The process is a simpler form of French plating, although objects of this kind, usually marked *Argent*, belong to the 18th century, and are rare in England. They are, moreover, plated on copper. French plating was sometimes employed to repair defective pieces of Sheffield plate*.

The silver-foil on close plate sometimes blisters, and since it is covering ferrous metal, where the silver wears away rusting is quite likely to occur. An object of close plate is distinctly heavier than a comparable object of silver or electro-plate owing to the nature of the base-metal.

Decoration is always simple. Piercing is not uncommon. Slight relief mouldings as in the case of King's pattern cutlery handles, or light chasing, may be noticed. Crests occur on fork and spoon handles. These made cutlery of close plate readily identifiable, and, unlike silver, it was valueless for melting. It

therefore offered small temptation to dishonest servants.

Makers' marks are common. One mark, *SILK*, for Robert Silk, was registered in 1809. Another, *PS*, has been taken to mean Paul Storr, but it actually means plated steel. These were punch-marks, and, like all silver substitutes, the maker endeavoured to make the marks look like hall-marks, usually by repeating them several times.

'CLUTHA' GLASS

Glass designed by Christopher Dresser* and made during the 1880s and 1890s by James Couper* of Glasgow. 'Clutha' glass was inspired by old Roman glass, and its forms often resemble those of ancient vessels. The metal is streaked and bubbled, giving an effect somewhat similar to that of early specimens.

'CLUTHA' GLASS. Flask of 'Clutha'* glass made by J. Couper & Sons*, Glasgow. The shape and the appearance of the metal is characteristic. c. 1895. *Victoria & Albert Museum, London*

COADE & SEALY (Lambeth, London)

19th-century successors to Mrs Eleanor Coade of the long-established Artificial Stone Manufactory at Lambeth. This partnership between Mrs Coade's daughter and John Sealy lasted from 1796 to the latter's death in 1813, when Miss Coade took William Croggan as her partner. He eventually purchased the business in 1821, and continued it until 1836, when he retired. The works closed soon afterwards, having been successfully operated for almost 70 years.

Throughout this period statuary and architectural ornament in artificial stone and terracotta* were produced in large quantities at relatively modest prices. De Vaere and Flaxman* were among the many sculptors to work for them, and the output ranged from statues made by repetitive casting to friezes, capitals, chimney-pieces, urns and ornamental detail of all kinds. Mrs Coade made the gate-piers for Strawberry Hill in 1772; the tympanum of the pediment of Greenwich Palace designed by Benjamin West was made by Coade's in 1810. Their work, commonly decorating the exterior of country houses or the gardens, has not uncommonly survived.

COALBROOKDALE IRONWORKS. Seated hound, almost life-size, in cast-iron, from the Coalbrookdale* iron foundry. Second quarter of the 19th century. *Ironbridge Gorge Museum Trust*

COALBROOKDALE

District in Shropshire; location of the famous ironworks (see below).

'Coalbrookdale' is also a name given to certain kinds of Coalport porcelain, principally flower-encrusted vases. The mark *CBD* occurs on some porcelain from this factory. The area which centres around Ironbridge is well known to antique collectors. Apart from Coalbrookdale and Coalport not far away, Randall's 19th-century porcelain factory was situated at Madeley, and in the 18th century Maurice Thursfield made pottery at Jackfield. The old Caughley* factory was also nearby in the district of Broseley, which gave its name to the Caughley dragon pattern. The Ironbridge Gorge Museum Trust is active in preserving the historical buildings and records of the area.

COALBROOKDALE IRONWORKS. *Stag*, small cast-iron figure in the *Animalier** style, from the Coalbrookdale* iron foundry. *Ironbridge Gorge Museum Trust*

COALBROOKDALE IRONWORKS (Shropshire)

An enterprise founded by Abraham Darby early in the 18th century. He invented a method of smelting iron with the aid of coke. The foundry was very successful and towards the end of the 18th century it made a speciality of casting ironwork for works in architecture and civil engineering.

Soon after 1830, Abraham's sons Francis and Alfred established the business of art casting in iron for which the company was to become famous. Among their larger works were ornamental gates which stood at the entrance to the transept of the Great Exhibition of 1851, and now divide Kensington Gardens from Hyde Park. A fountain, *Cupid and the Swan*, designed by John Bell*, was placed in front of the gates. This has now been removed to the Coalbrookdale Museum together with Bell's *Andromeda*, which was also in the Exhibition. The foundry's

COALBROOKDALE IRONWORKS. Cast-iron* garden-seat probably designed by Christopher Dresser* and made at the Coalbrookdale* Foundry. Mark: *C-B-Dale*. Registration mark for 1862. *Sotheby & Co*

exhibit in 1851 comprised garden furniture and ornaments, such interior furniture as hat- and umbrella-stands, chairs, tables and plant-stands, such ornamental fixtures as mantelpieces and grates, and minor items like door-knockers and door-porters.

The foundry also made decorative items such as elaborately pierced dishes, or a cast-iron version in low relief of Leonardo's *Last Supper*. Some art castings, such as the pierced plates mentioned were bronzed on the surface, a process which may have been derived from Berlin, where Geiss* was bronzing zinc casts.

See *Deer-hound table*; *Eagle-slayer, The*

COALBROOKDALE POTTERY COMPANY (Ironbridge, Shropshire)

A small amount of earthenware was produced here, in addition to metal castings, between about 1861 and 1895. Production was principally of garden ornaments, the larger in terracotta*, but some smaller objects decorated by painting were also made.

COALPORT PORCELAIN FACTORY (Coalbrookdale, Shropshire)

In 1796 there were three porcelain factories in this area—the Caughley factory of Thomas Turner, the Coalport factory of John Rose on the opposite bank of the river Severn, and the nearby factory of Thomas Rose* and his partners. John Rose bought Caughley in 1799, and used it to make biscuit porcelain to be glazed and decorated at Coalport. In 1814, when he acquired his brother's factory, the whole enterprise was brought under one roof. When Rose acquired the Cambrian Pottery in 1820 the moulds and stock of the Swansea and Nantgarw porcelain factories were transferred to Coalport, together with Billingsley* and Walker, and it was intended that the manufacture of their porcelain should be continued. John Rose died in 1842, and his place was taken by his nephew, William F. Rose. The latter retired in 1862, his place being taken by William Pugh, who was not a success as an administrator, and second-grade wares were produced and much early defective 'white ware' sold to decorators. The factory was rescued in 1885 by Peter Bruff, and his son Charles Bruff, who became managing director in 1890, began a new period of prosperity, when a large export business developed with Canada. The firm was acquired by Cauldon Potteries Ltd, and two years later it was moved to Staffordshire. Production is continued by Coalport China Ltd at Stoke-on-Trent.

Undoubtedly there has been a great deal of confusion between the early wares of John Rose's Coalport and those of Caughley, Worcester, and probably also with the Coalport of Thomas Rose, and it is not until 1820 that a greater degree of certainty begins to be possible. A certain amount of confusion must also arise from the factory's habit of selling white porcelain to independent decorators in the first twenty years or so of its existence, a practice already

COALPORT. Porcelain bowl commissioned by Liberty & Co.* from Coalport*, and issued in a limited edition of 250 copies in 1975 to commemorate the firm's centenary. *Coalport*

established at Caughley before John Rose acquired it. To this period belongs the origin of the popular 'Indian Tree' pattern. The acquisition of the Swansea and Nantgarw moulds and recipes led to a finer quality and a more translucent paste. The moulded decoration of some of the plates suggests a Swansea origin. The flower-painting obviously owes its inspiration to Billingsley, even though his hand cannot certainly be identified. Wares of this kind were produced up to about 1850. During this period close imitations of old Sèvres porcelain, especially vases, and to a lesser extent imitations of Meissen and Chelsea, were produced for the London market, and one of the marks employed was a simulation of the Royal Sèvres double *L* monogram. Imitations of the prized *rose Pompadour* of Sèvres were called *rose du Barry*, and paintings in reserved panels were framed in chased relief gilding in the 18th-century French manner. Imitations of this kind were displayed with great success at the Great Exhibition of 1851. Coalport has also been credited with forgeries of Chelsea 'Goat and Bee' jugs of the 1745–50 period, and small tureens in the form of a cabbage purporting to be Chelsea of about 1755. This, however, is not proven, and these things may have come from some other factory. Wares of this kind formed part of the production in the revived rococo style; vases, and small objects decorated with applied modelled flowers, were commonly produced, and form a category often referred to among collectors as 'Coalbrookdale'. Painted plaques by Aston, Rouse, and others are also much sought. These were a fashion probably derived from Sèvres where they were a speciality.

With the advent of Peter Bruff the factory again sought a quality market, and T. J. Bott* was appointed art-director in 1890, when emphasis was placed on fine enamelling, including services decorated with landscapes and flowers. The Parian body was also combined with glazed ware in the making of decorative centrepieces and comports. In more recent times porcelain figures of excellent quality have been produced. Marks are numerous, and include *C.Dale*

COALPORT. Three pieces from the Angerstein Service decorated with silhouettes of children at play. Coalport. *Christie, Manson & Woods*

and *Coalport* in script, the initials *CD.* also in script, several marks giving the name in full, an imitation of the Sèvres monogram, and a combination of the letter *C* and the Chelsea anchor. A deceptive mark adopted after 1875 is *Coalport A.D.1750* which refers to the date of the founding of a factory for the manufacture of earthenware on the Caughley site.

COALPORT POTTERY See *Bradley, Walter*

COFFEE TABLE
Low, long table in a variety of materials now usually placed in front of a sofa or couch. It is a late 19th-century introduction. Examples in the *art nouveau** style are known.

COLCUTT, T. E. (1840–1924)
Architect and furniture designer who worked for Gillow*, Maples, Collinson & Lock* and others. Colcutt was one of the first to design ebonized cabinets* with painted panels in the simple art furniture* style, but he also, when required, designed ornate pseudo-Renaissance* furniture.

COLE, SIR HENRY (1808–1883)
Civil servant educated at Christ's Hospital, who became the founder and first director of what is now the Victoria and Albert Museum, London, from 1853 to 1873. As Felix Summerly, a pseudonym under which he wrote some 20 children's books, he won a Society of Arts award in 1847 for the design of a tea-service, and then founded Summerly's* Art Manufacturers which commissioned design for utilitarian wares in a variety of materials. In this he was associated with the architects Owen Jones* and Matthew Digby Wyatt*. Cole became a member of the Society of Arts in 1846, and he enjoyed considerable influence almost at once. He was associated with the Prince Consort in the organization of the Exhibition of 1851, and suggested the site in Hyde Park. Later, with Wyatt, he strongly defended Paxton's* Crystal Palace against the criticisms of Ruskin* and Pugin*.

COLE, THOMAS (1800–1864)
English horologist whose clocks were made for prominent firms of retailers and usually bear their name. He exhibited at the London Exhibitions of 1851 and 1862.

COLIN, E. ET CIE (Paris)
Manufacturers of ornamental metalwork using mass-production methods. They employed models by such sculptors as Louis Chalon*. They used the impressed mark: *E. COLIN & CIE PARIS*.

COLLAGE (French)
Pictures made by gluing various substances to a background, usually of wood or canvas. Historically, the technique has principally been a ladies' amusement and dates from the 17th century. Most of such work, however, was done during the first half of the 19th century.

COLLAS, ACHILLE
Associate of Barbedienne* who invented a process

COLCUTT, T. E. Ebonized mahogany cabinet designed by T. E. Colcutt* and made by Collinson & Lock* in 1871. Painted decoration by Albert Moore*. An early example of art furniture*, this piece was shown in the London International Exhibition of 1871. *Victoria & Albert Museum, London*

for reducing large sculpture to small size for use as *bronzes d'ameublement**.

See *Cheverton, Benjamin*; *Pointing machine*

COLEMAN, WILLIAM STEPHEN (1829–1904)
Designer and painter, art-director at Minton*, 1871–1873, and director of Minton's Art Pottery Studio*, South Kensington, at the same time. Coleman began by working for Copeland*, but moved to Minton's in 1869. As a naturalist he specialized in these subjects, and also in nude children. After 1873 he worked as a freelance.

COLLINOT, E. (Boulogne-sur-Seine)
Maker of earthenware during the second half of the 19th century who specialized in a kind of relief enamel decoration outlined in black inspired by the *cloisonné* enamel* technique. Some of his decorations

COLLINOT, E. Bottle of red earthenware by E. Collinot* decorated with coloured relief enamels outlined in black in imitation of *cloisonné* enamel. The ornament is based on Venetian arabesques* of about 1600. France, Boulogne-sur-Seine, third quarter of the 19th century. *Victoria & Albert Museum, London*

based on a 17th-century type of grotesque* ornament popular in Venice are fairly typical of the designs which Collinot (who published a collection of designs for art and industry in 1867) regarded as 'Persian'.

COLLINSON & LOCK (London)
Cabinet-makers who made good quality art furniture*. They merged with Jackson & Graham* in 1885, and the combined firm was absorbed by Gillow* in 1897. Their furniture is often stamped with their name. Collinson & Lock employed a number of talented designers, including Bruce Talbert*, T. E. Colcutt*, E. W. Godwin*, and J. Moyr Smith*, and most of their production was large, solid, and of excellent craftsmanship.

COLONNA, EUGÈNE (EDWARD) (fl. 1862 until after 1908)
Designer of German origin who studied architecture in Brussels. He emigrated to America where he designed furniture and railroad-car interiors, and then joined Tiffany's* interior decorating branch. He returned to Paris in the 1890s and began to design furniture, metalwork, and jewellery for Samuel Bing*, including complete rooms for the Paris Exposition of 1900. He was also represented at the Munich *Sezession** (1899) and Turin Exhibition (1902). He returned to America in 1908.

COLONNA, EUGÈNE (EDWARD). Table in the *art nouveau** style designed by Edward Colonna.* French. c. 1900. *Sotheby & Co*

COLOTTE, ARISTIDE (1885–1959)
Colotte opened an engraving workshop at Nancy in 1927 where he specialized in crystal glass with deeply cut geometric designs in the *art déco** style. Signature: *COLOTTE NANCY* incised.

'COMFORTER' DOGS
Large earthenware figures of spaniels made in Staffordshire and used as fireplace ornaments. They were supposed to be companionable to lonely people and were probably a variation of the board figures of the 18th century which stood in the same position for a similar purpose. These also were known as 'comforters' at the time.

COMMEMORATIVE GLASS (ROYAL SOUVENIRS)
English glass which, in its decoration, commemorates royal occasions has a history of production extending back to the 17th century. Before 1800 the decoration was engraved, very rarely enamelled, but subsequently engraving, etching, and press-moulding* were all employed. The first 19th-century coronation to be commemorated was that of the Prince Regent, who became George IV in 1820 and was crowned in July in the year following. Engraved rummers are comparatively scarce. More frequent, and more varied, are glasses commemorating the coronation of William IV in 1831, and crystallo-ceramie* items by Apsley Pellatt* exist.

The next coronation was that of Victoria in 1837,

but examples of this date are rare. Very much more common is glassware of all kinds relating to the Golden Jubilee year of 1887, the inscriptions giving both dates 1837–1887. Especially common are pressed glass* plates with the wording 'Victoria' on the top and 'Jubilee' at the bottom, with the dates on either side, which were made in immense quantities and widely distributed. Even larger were the quantities of glass souvenirs made to commemorate the Diamond Jubilee of 1897, although objects of good quality are not easy to find.

For the coronation of Edward VII in 1902 souvenirs which revived the old technique of enclosing a coin in the glass were made. Examples relating to the coronation of George V in June, 1911, are comparatively scarce and the 1936 Jubilee souvenirs were made principally by the potteries. A large number of souvenir productions of all kinds, including some engraved glass of excellent quality, was made for the coronation of Edward VIII and dated 1937. These were never placed on general sale, but some of them found their way into circulation and are sought today. In the same year the coronation of George VI was commemorated by the glass-makers. A certain amount of glass enclosing coins was made, as was the case with the coronation of the present Queen in 1953. Some of the drinking-glasses were decorated with fine quality engraved work.

COMMEMORATIVE WARE
Apart from ware commemorating royal occasions like jubilees and coronations, the glass-makers and

COMMEMORATIVE WARE. A Doulton* stoneware* jug commemorating Queen Victoria's Diamond Jubilee in 1897. *Constance Chiswell*

the potters have produced all kinds of ware commemorating special occasions. For example, Wedgwood made a bust of Shakespeare in 1864 for the tercentenary of his birth, and later made a creamware jug to mark the death of Thomas Carlyle. More recently Coalport marked the bicentenary of Turner's birth with the vase here illustrated. Many other events of all kinds have been commemorated like the opening of the Saint Lawrence Seaway or the centenary of Brooklyn Bridge, and usually wares of this kind are issued in limited editions. In recent years several of the principal factories have produced Christmas plates in limited editions which are issued annually. Many of the 19th-century Staffordshire figures, of course, commemorate a person or event. Wares of this kind were also made in cast-iron by the Coalbrookdale Ironworks*, and they can be found in pewter, brass, and copper.

See *Staffordshire portrait figures*

COMMEMORATIVE WARE. A Coalport porcelain vase painted by Malcolm Harnett with the 'Old Chain Pier, Brighton' after Turner, issued in a limited edition of 100 copies in 1975 to celebrate the Bicentenary of Turner's birth on 23 April 1775. The cover has a gold eagle finial. *Coalport*

COMMEMORATIVE WARE. Creamware* jug, transfer-printed* with a portrait of Thomas Carlyle, who died in 1881. It bears the back-stamp of the distributor, John Mortlock*, and the impressed mark of Wedgwood*. Josiah Wedgwood & Sons Ltd. *Private collection*

COMOLERA, PAUL (1818–1897)
French *Animalier**, pupil of Rude, who specialized in birds. He first exhibited at the Salon of 1847, and in 1850 he worked for Minton*, where he modelled a life-size peacock, of which about five copies were made. He returned to France about 1853. Most of his work was cast by Susse Frères*.

COMPAGNIE DES ARTS FRANÇAIS See *Suë et Marc*

COMTOISE CLOCKS
Comtois refers to the former eastern French province of Franche-Comté and *Comtoise* clocks were a provincial type made from the 17th century onwards in this region. By about 1800 the area was almost the sole source of relatively simple, inexpensive clocks, spring- or weight-driven and fitted with a large decorative pendulum of thin embossed gilt metal, usually with a violin-shaped outline. The pendulum occasionally has a kind of grid-iron suspension which imitates the appearance of the temperature-compensating suspension of the more expensive regulator clocks made by Paris horologists. When a striking mechanism is present, the clock usually repeats the hour a minute or so afterwards. The name which appears on some dials is usually that of the retailer and not the maker.

Production continued at least until 1914, and clocks of this type may have been reproduced since. Cases of the long-case type were made in the province where the clocks were sold and usually followed the local furniture style.

Both long-case and wall-clocks were made, although the latter are the more often seen outside France. One type of wall-clock from this region has been sold recently under the name of 'Vineyard' clocks.

CONFIDENT (French)
Two or three padded easy chairs joined together in opposing directions. In this way occupants of different sexes could sit more closely together than convention would have permitted had they been seated on a sofa, and they could converse in low tones without risk of being overheard. The double-chair is the more common of the two, but the *confident* for three occupants is sometimes to be found. Introduced in France during the 1850s, it hardly survived the Second Empire*.

CONTA & BÖHME, PÖSSNECK
Porcelain manufacturers.
See *Fairings*; *Pössneck*

COOKE, WILLIAM (fl. 1850s)
Notable woodcarver of the Warwick School*. His best-known work is the *Kenilworth Buffet*, decorated with pictorial carvings of scenes from Walter Scott's *Kenilworth*. Much of it was carved from a fallen oak from Kenilworth. This sideboard was exhibited at the Great Exhibition of 1851. Cooke also made chairs, fire-screens, mirror-frames and other items of domestic furniture.

COOPER, SUSIE (b. 1903)
Designer and manufacturer of pottery in the contemporary styles of the 1930s. Originally a student of Burslem Art School, Susan Cooper R.D.I. founded potteries at Burslem and Longton in the early 1930s, and her wares enjoyed considerable popularity in the markets she sought. Crayons made from ceramic colours, first introduced about 1865, were employed in decorating some of her work.

COPELAND, WILLIAM TAYLOR, M.P. (1797–1868)
The son of William Copeland, the partner of Josiah Spode II*, William Taylor Copeland became the sole owner of the Spode factory in 1833. Two years later he was Lord Mayor of London, and from 1837 to 1863 he was Conservative M.P. for Stoke-on-Trent. He dissolved his partnership with Thomas Garrett in 1847, and took his son into partnership in 1867. Marks associated with him include *Copeland & Garrett* (1833–1847) and *Copeland, late Spode* (1847–1867).

Under Copeland the factory specialized in rich ground colours, fine quality painting, and highly modelled forms, with lavish gilding. They were, at this time, strongly influenced by Sèvres, but they carried the more flamboyant of that factory's styles to excess. In general it is fair to say that the Copeland-Spode decorative wares are what most people have in

COPELAND, W. T. *Emily and the white doe of Rylston*. Parian figure inspired by Wordsworth. Copeland. c. 1850.

BAYEUX. Figure of a Chinese spice-seller. The pseudo-
Chinese mark 'Langlois' reading vertically downwards
occurs on one of the jars. France, Bayeux, Langlois factory.
c. 1835. *Private Collection*

FLASHED GLASS. Scent-bottle in the form of an obelisk. Cut-glass flashed with ruby and decorated with wheel-engraving. Bohemia. c. 1830. *Private Collection*

ART DECO. A console table of wrought iron and marble surmounted by a mirror. Paris. c. 1925. *Brighton Art Gallery & Museum*

COPELAND, WILLIAM TAYLOR. *Innocence*, figure in Parian porcelain from William Copeland*. c. 1860. *Author*

COPELAND, WILLIAM TAYLOR. Cabinet cup and saucer finely painted with flowers on a pale yellow ground, with claret borders covered with gilt scale ornament. The form of the cup belongs to the early Victorian period. c. 1840. *Private collection*

mind when they stigmatize Victorian porcelain as fussily vulgar and over-decorated. Vases and other ornamental wares of this kind were shown at the Great Exhibition of 1851.

According to the journal of the *Art Union* in 1848 Thomas Battam*, Copeland's art-director, was actively engaged in the development of Parian* ware in 1845, although there are other claimants, and the formula was soon widely known throughout Staffordshire. Among the artists working for the factory were Daniel Lucas (fl. 2nd half of the 19th century), son of the Derby painter, who painted landscapes; C. F.

COPELAND, WILLIAM TAYLOR. The Victorian passion for moral tales is illustrated by this allegorical plate from William Copeland* entitled *The Peasant's Integrity*, or *The Lost Lamb Restored*. c. 1860. *Private collection*

Hürten*, German flower-painter noted for working directly from nature, with Copeland's from 1859 to 1898; the designer and painter of figure-subjects, George Eyre, art-director in 1864–1865; R. F. Abraham*, who followed him; and Samuel Alcock who painted allegorical figures on vases and dessert-services in the 1880s. It is evident, however, that the factory found it necessary to reduce prices to meet competition, because in the 1870s and 1880s outline transfer-printing, which could be used in conjunction with semi-skilled labour, was introduced.

Japanese patterns were also employed, probably to meet competition from Worcester*. The factory, like other contemporary porcelain factories, also made earthenware and 'Majolica'*.

The Copeland family remained in charge of the enterprise's fortunes until very recent times, and the factory maintains an excellent museum.

COPENHAGEN PORCELAIN   See *Royal Copenhagen Porcelain Factory*

COPIER, ANDRIES DIRK (b. 1901)
Designer who joined the Royal Dutch Glass Works* at Leerdam in 1917, and worked on the creation of the *Serica* and *Unica* types of glass-ware with Chris Lebeau*. Copier was head of the *Unica* studios from 1923, and subsequently became art-director. His mark includes his own name and the trade name of the glass, thus: *Serica-Copier*, engraved.

'COPPERETTE' WARE
Trade name for a type of pottery imitating hammered copper first made about 1890 by the Bretby Art Pottery*.

85

'CORALENE' GLASS

Type of art glass* introduced by the Mount Washington Glass Works*, but popular also in Europe. It is ornamented with raised coral-like branches formed from enamels to which were applied minute drops of clear or opalescent glass.

CORK PICTURES

Making pictures in relief from carved cork was largely an amateur pastime of the 1850s and 1860s. Most of them depict either castles or classical ruins, inspired by the popularity of Walter Scott's novels or tours in Italy. It was usual to provide the picture with a background of black velvet and a maplewood frame. Trees and shrubbery were made from dried moss. Good specimens are now scarce.

CORNING GLASS WORKS (Corning, N.Y.)

Successors to the South Ferry Glass Works, founded in 1875. It is now one of the leading American glass factories, making every variety of glass. It merged with the Steuben Glass Works* of Frederick Carder* in 1918, and it maintains an extremely important glass museum.

COSY CORNER

These were a feature of interior decoration in the 1860s, and the earliest took the form of cushioned, draped, built-in alcoves which were the product of contemporary interest in the Near East. These were later made by commercial manufacturers as a kind of hooded settee and sold extensively in England and America during the 1880s.

COTTAGES, POTTERY AND PORCELAIN

The vogue for the cottage in porcelain dates from about 1820, and the earliest examples appear to have been made by the Coalport* and Rockingham* factories. Marked specimens of both types are known.

COTTAGES. Pastille-burner* in the form of a cottage in a romantic Gothic revival* style. Staffordshire. c. 1830.
Author

Buildings in pottery and porcelain had of course existed long before this date, like the salt glaze 'house' teapot of the 1750s, but there had been nothing of the kind discussed here.

Porcelain cottages are usually about five inches in height, but occasionally Coalport, Rockingham and Spode made larger versions. Some seem to be based on an existing house, or an architect's drawing. Those from Coalport and Rockingham especially are often decorated fairly liberally with applied flowers.

Cottages of Staffordshire earthenware either take the form of pastille-burners or money-boxes. Some of them depict buildings which had gained notoriety in their day, like the Red Barn of Polstead, Suffolk, where William Corder murdered and buried Maria Marten in 1827, or Potash Farm, the house of the murderer James Rush. The Red Barn exists in two versions, with and without miniature figures of Maria Marten and Corder. In the case of the latter version two separate figures exist which were intended to be stood on either side. Most of the other earthenware buildings are not so readily identifiable.

Small pastille-burners in the form of castles reflect the influence of Walter Scott. Italianate cottages recall a fairly short-lived architectural fashion of the years before mid-century. The pointed arches of revived Gothic are not uncommon. A collection of porcelain and earthenware cottages related to the designs of architects of the period before 1850 for the small house could easily be made.

Stoneware tobacco jars in the form of the cottage, the lid being the roof, have a flat, removable, slab inside to keep the tobacco compressed and moist.

Forgeries of porcelain cottages, usually in a Continental hard paste body, are not at all uncommon, and unmarked examples need care.

COTTERILL, EDMUND (1795–1858)

English silver designer of the mid-19th century who worked for Garrard & Co.* and Hunt & Roskell*. He employed a naturalistic style in conjunction with meticulous detail. Some of his work is in the Royal collections.

COUPER, JAMES & SONS (Glasgow)

Scottish glass-makers who developed 'Clutha'* glass about 1885. Basically 'Clutha' glass was green with bubbles and striations in forms reminiscent of Roman domestic glassware, well known from excavated specimens.

Designs were principally by Christopher Dresser* and George Walton*. 'Clutha' glass was sold by Liberty & Co.* Mark: Clutha/Designed by *CD*.

COVENTRY GLASS WORKS (Coventry, Conn.)

Glass works founded in 1813 by Thomas Stebbins which closed in 1848 due to the shortage of fuel. The works are principally noted among collectors for being among the earliest producers of historic flasks, notably one bearing a portrait of General Lafayette.

The flasks, in green and amber glass, are excellent in quality.

COWAN, R. GRAY (1884–1957)
Artist-potter, studied under Charles F. Binns* at Alfred University. He began as a studio-potter in Cleveland, Ohio, in 1912 and moved to Rocky River, Ohio, in 1920. He employed several assistants and made a wide variety of decorative ware, including figures. The pottery closed in 1931. Mark: *COWAN*. Impressed or incised.

CRACE, J. G. & SONS (London)
Interior decorators who also made furniture. The firm survived until 1899, and were fashionable in their day. In the 19th century they helped to decorate the Royal Pavilion*. They specialized in the 'Elizabethan' style, and made elaborately carved neo-Gothic* furniture to the designs of Pugin*. The firm became closely associated with the latter in 1849, and he and John S. Crace decorated the Medieval Court of the Great Exhibition in 1851. The firm also made furniture for Chatsworth among other great houses.

CRANBERRY GLASS
Decorative glass, light red in colour, produced in large quantities at Stourbridge and elsewhere from about 1840 until the start of the First World War. For the most part cranberry glass is table-glass—wine-glasses, tankards, decanters (large and small), jugs, carafes* and tumblers, cruets, honey-jars, and comports. Perfume-bottles* and other decorative objects also occur. Cranberry glass was never press moulded*, and it is not often cut and engraved. Some of the best, however, is decorated with a 'threading' of glass of a contrasting colour applied by a machine patented by Richardson* of Stourbridge in the 1870s.

Most of the more important specimens of cranberry glass are in conjunction with glass of some other colour, like vases and table-centres which are partly of clear yellow glass. Cranberry bowls and flower-holders are decorated with trailed ornament of yellow glass in the form of flowers and leaves. Cranberry glass made after 1900 is inclined to be a much deeper colour than early specimens and is more often decorated by cutting. Table-glass of the mid-Victorian type, especially plain wine-glasses, are also found in green glass, but they are rarer than those of cranberry glass, and were probably not so popular at the time.

CRANE, WALTER (1845–1915)
English artist, designer and writer on art subjects, associated with William Morris* and a leading figure in the Arts and Crafts Movement*. President of the Art Workers' Guild*, 1884; President of the Arts & Crafts Exhibition Society* 1888–1890 and 1895–1915; Principal of the Royal College of Art, 1898. In the field of ceramics, Walter Crane supplied Wedgwood* with designs from 1867 to 1877, and Minton* about 1870. He also designed lustre* decorated vases and tiles for Maw & Co.* and later provided the Pilkington Tile & Pottery Co.* with designs for similarly decorated wares. He also designed a certain amount of furniture and some tapestries and became

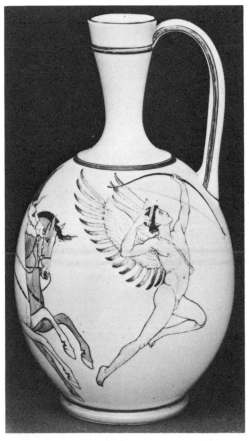

CRANE, WALTER. Jug by Wedgwood* decorated with a subject designed by Walter Crane and entitled *Imagination*. c. 1890. *Josiah Wedgwood & Sons Ltd*

CRANBERRY GLASS. A basket of cranberry glass*, made in the Stourbridge area. Late 19th century. *Antique collectors' Club*

CRANE, WALTER. Plate decorated with a
design taken from *Flora's Feast* by
Walter Crane. c. 1890. *Minton Museum,
Royal Doulton Tableware Ltd*

CREIL. Bowl of creamware* (*faïence-fine**) transfer-printed*
with a view of Heveningham Hall, Suffolk. France, Creil.
c. 1820. *Victoria & Albert Museum, London*

noted for book illustration. His writings were directed
against the debasement of standards as a result of
manufacture by machine, and with William Morris
he did much to promote a revival of craftsmanship.
Crane had considerable influence on the style of
ceramics in the early years of the 20th century, and he
employed the mark of a crane within a letter *C*.

CRAZING
Minute cracks covering the glazed surface of pottery
and some kinds of porcelain as a result of a
disagreement in the shrinkage rates of body and glaze
during cooling. The Chinese induced crazing of this
sort in porcelain glazes as a kind of decoration
(crackled ware). Particularly in the case of earthenware, crazing can develop as a result of reheating in
an oven.

Crazing of the glaze is a feature of some Staffordshire earthenware figures, and forgeries of the more
valuable types sometimes have an imitation of crazing
painted on to the glaze with a fine brush. This can be
detected with a reasonably powerful magnifier.
Among the figures thus treated have been noted a
pair of cricketers cast in the old moulds.

CREAMWARE
Earthenware of fine quality, light buff in colour and
covered with a transparent glaze, developed by Josiah
Wedgwood* and named 'Queensware' by him in the
mid-1760s. Manufacture was taken up very widely in
Staffordshire and elsewhere, especially at Leeds,
Yorkshire. It has continued to enjoy a considerable
share of the market in one form or another until the
present day.

CREIL (Oise)
A factory was founded here in 1794 to make *faïence-
fine** and other English-type wares. It merged with
Montereau* early in the 19th century, and closed
finally in 1895. A good deal of creamware* decorated
with transfer-printing* was made here, and among
the most interesting subjects are topographical prints
of English country-houses, titled in French. Towards

mid-century a kind of ironstone china* was produced,
as well as a type of black basaltes* ware. From about
1819 to 1824 soft-paste porcelain in the English
manner was made at Creil by a pottery chemist,
Saint-Amans. The mark is *CREIL* impressed.

CRISTALLERIE DAUM See *Daum Frères*

CROGGAN, WILLIAM (fl. 1813–1840)
Croggan became the partner of his cousin, Miss
Eleanor Coade, owner of the famous artificial stone
works at Lambeth, in 1813. When she died in 1821,
he bought the business and continued it until about
1836. Coade's supplied cast statuary and architectural
ornament in artificial stone and terracotta*. Flaxman* was among the sculptors who provided Croggan
with designs and in the 1820s the manufactory
supplied a good deal of decorative work for the
gardens and exterior of Buckingham Palace.

See *Coade & Sealy*

CROS, HENRI (1840–1907)
Modeller at the Sèvres* porcelain factory in the last
quarter of the 19th century who was the first to
experiment with *pâte-de-verre**. A large piece of
sculpture in low relief in this medium, *L'Histoire de
feu*, formed an important part of the Sèvres factory's
exhibit at the Paris Exposition of 1900.

CROSS-BANDING
Bands of veneer of varying width in which the grain
of the wood runs across the band. They are usually
found at the edge of a table. Common in the 18th
century, it is also often to be noted on early 19th-
century tables.

'CROWN DEVON' See *Fielding & Co. Ltd*

CROWN DERBY See *Derby Porcelain Factory*;
Royal Crown Derby Porcelain Company

CROWN DUCAL WARE See *Rhead, Charlotte*

CROSS-BANDING. A Regency* breakfast-table of rosewood, cross-banded with amboyna. The well-marked figuring in the wood has been used as decoration. English, first quarter of the 19th century. *Antique Collectors' Club*

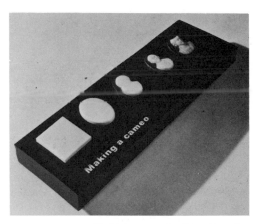

CRYSTALLO-CERAMIE. Model demonstrating the making of a cameo used in sulphides* and incrustations. *Pilkington Glass Museum*

CRYSTAL FOUNTAIN, THE   See *Osler, F. & C.*

CRYSTAL GLASS
Clear glass of fine quality especially suitable for facet-cutting and the making of prismatically cut drops for lustres and chandeliers. So called from the Italian *cristallo*, glass of this kind first being made in Venice early in the 16th century where it was thought to resemble the hardstone known as rock-crystal, then highly valued for carving into small *bibelots*.

CRYSTALLINE GLAZES
Glazes with added mineral salts which develop crystals when cooled slowly. The effects obtained were entirely fortuitous. Crystalline glazes were employed by Meissen* in the 1880s, and exhibited by them at the Paris Exposition of 1900. The Royal Copenhagen Porcelain Factory* and the Rookwood Pottery* in the United States both used crystalline glazes about the same time, and Pilkington* adopted the technique in the early years of the 20th century.

CRYSTALLO-CERAMIE
The practice of enclosing a cameo of porcelain or some other heat-resistant material in a ball of glass began in Bohemia about the middle of the 18th century, but little was done with it until the technique was developed in Paris by Barthélemy Desprez. It was further improved in England by Apsley Pellatt*, who patented his process in 1819. In France work of this kind was done at Baccarat*, Saint-Louis*, and Clichy*, and in America at several glasshouses in New England and the Pittsburgh region. The crystallo-ceramie process was employed in the decoration of a variety of wares, principally paperweights, but

CRYSTALLO-CERAMIE. Glass paperweight enclosing a ceramic head of Queen Victoria. Apsley Pellat*. c. 1840. *Victoria & Albert Museum, London*

quite commonly tumblers, vases, and any other suitable objects. The cameos were nearly always portraits, and anything else is distinctly rare.

These things are also known (especially in America) as sulphides*, incrustations, and (rarely) cameo incrustations. They have been made more or less continuously since the early decades of the 19th century and are still being produced in the old styles.

CUBISM
A movement in art which strongly influenced the *art déco* style in the 1920s. It started with Cézanne, who remarked that 'everything in nature is based on the sphere, the cone and the cylinder', by which he meant that geometric forms were the essential reality which underlies all representations of natural forms. The use of the cube in a new approach to painting began about 1906, when Georges Braque started to super-impose several different views of an object on one another in an attempt to represent it as a whole, rather than its appearance from a single viewpoint. In this he was followed by Picasso, whom he had met in 1907, and together they proceeded to develop the movement, turning it into an extremely influential one. Cubism became one of the principal styles of the

89

1920s and by 1925, the year of the Paris Exposition des Arts Décoratifs, it had affected the design of much of the most fashionable industrial art, its influence being especially obvious in sculpture and poster-design.

See *Art déco*

'CUCKOO' CLOCKS

Weight-driven wall-clocks in which the hour is indicated by a 'cuckoo' which emerges from a trap at the top of the dial. They have been made more or less continuously in the Black Forest area of Germany since the early years of the 19th century, and to a lesser extent in the area of Lake Neuchâtel in Switzerland. Swiss examples, however, are not very common outside their country of origin.

CUP-PLATES

Plates of either porcelain or glass, about four inches in diameter, on which the teacup was stood while tea was consumed from the saucer. Its purpose was to prevent the tea-table from being marked by a hot cup. Cup-plates seem to have been made from about 1815, but the custom of drinking tea from the saucer was much earlier. Towards the end of the 18th century tea-bowls in the Chinese manner were provided with deep saucers from which to drink. By 1860 cup-plates were becoming unfashionable and the custom of drinking from the saucer survived only among the working class.

CURRIER & IVES (New York)

'Printmakers to the American people' who provided pictures of almost everything. The firm was founded by Nathaniel Currier in 1834 and he took James Merritt Ives into partnership in 1857. They retired from business in 1880, the firm being continued by their sons. It closed finally in 1907. Up until about 1880 Currier & Ives prints are basically monochrome lithographs* hand-coloured. After 1880 they were chromolithographs*. They range from postcard size to about 18 inches by 27 inches and include sheet music covers. Subjects are diverse, perhaps the most sought being views of the Mississippi River, railroad prints, sporting subjects, horses, views of towns and cities, houses, hunting and fishing subjects, and contemporary events and portraits.

Although the prints of Currier & Ives are the most sought, many other American firms issued prints of much the same kind which enjoyed wide circulation in the 19th century. Currier & Ives's prints have been reproduced in modern times with varying degrees of persuasiveness, the best being very deceptive.

See *Lithography*

CURTIS, LEMUEL (1790–1857)

Clock-maker, in business at Concord, Mass., and later at Burlingham, Vt. Originally apprenticed to Simon Willard*, he made an improvement to the Willard movement which he patented in 1816. He produced shelf- and wall-clocks only.

CUSHMAN SISTERS, THE

Charlotte (1816–1878) and Susan (1822–1859) were American actresses who came to London in 1845 and were very popular as Romeo and Juliet. They returned to America in 1849, but were back in England in 1852, staying until 1857. They were the subject of much-sought groups of Staffordshire figures* of the 'Tallis'* type, which occur in a version largely decorated in gold on white and another more profusely enamelled. Reproductions exist, but the enamelling and gilding is crude and the base is titled *Romeo and Juliet*.

CUT-GLASS

Glass decorated with facets in the form of geometric patterns with the aid of the grinding wheel. English and Irish lead glass and Bohemian potash glass were particularly suitable for this kind of work, which depended for its effectiveness on the refraction of light from the polished facets into which the surface was cut.

Cut-glass became fashionable during the last quarter of the 18th century, but it was at its most popular during the early decades of the 19th. Its decline dates from the invention of pressed glass* which, before mid-century, made it possible to produce glass closely resembling cut-glass at a fraction of the cost.

The effect of the Glass Excise Act, levied on the weight of the metal and not repealed until 1845, tended to concentrate the art of facet-cutting in Ireland, where the duty, payable on the contents of

CUT-GLASS. Oval cut-glass preserve-bowl and stand. Irish. c. 1825.
Pilkington Glass Museum

the crucible, was not in operation. Not only was a great deal of cut-glass of fine quality exported to England from such centres as Waterford, Cork, Dublin, and Belfast, but the American market was also supplied from the same sources. The industry, largely supplied with workmen and capital by the tax-oppressed English glass-makers, lost its advantages with the repeal of the Act and the growth of moulded glass*.

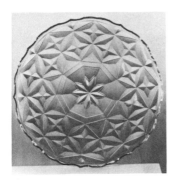

CUT-GLASS. Circular cut-glass tray showing the principles of good facet-cutting and its general appearance. English or French. c. 1800. *Victoria & Albert Museum, London*

The fashion perhaps received its coup-de-grâce from Ruskin*, who considered that to treat glass as though it were a hardstone, and to carve it with abrasives, was a distortion of the material, which more properly should be blown in the manner of Venetian soda-glass. He entirely disregarded the fact that English and Bohemian types of glass were as unsuitable for blowing as was Venetian glass for cutting and engraving. As an arbiter of taste, however, he undoubtedly did the industry a great deal of harm from which it has never really recovered.

French factories made small quantities of cut-glass in the English manner early in the 19th century, but turned increasingly to fine quality moulded glass, the detail of which was sharpened on the grinding wheel by hand. These French copies, of greyish glass, are sometimes very deceptive.

In the case of a genuine cut-glass object the edges of the facets are quite sharp; moulded edges are blunt unless the wheel has been used to sharpen them. In the first case *all* the edges are sharp; in the second, only selected edges, where the pattern is most easily seen, are thus treated. Moulded patterns are always perfectly symmetrical. In the case of hand-work the patterns are often very slightly askew or disjointed, even though this may not at first be obvious.

Glass with a greyish or bluish tinge is often erroneously associated with Waterford. Where the specimen is genuinely of this colour it is much more to be associated with early English cut-glass, but moulded specimens deliberately made as forgeries of early cut-glass are usually of greyish or bluish toned

glass. Usually the colour (deliberately added) is too intense. Cut-glass in the old style is now, once again, being manufactured in Waterford and Galway, but is not particularly deceptive.

CUT-PAPER WORK
The best cut-paper work belongs to the 18th century and is associated with Mrs Delany (1700–1785) who invented flower-mosaic. From 1800 until well into the 1860s, however, a good deal of elaborate cut-paper work was produced—Valentines, memorial cards, flowers and landscapes, as well as a form of paper sculpture in which figures were cut out and bent into shape. Cut-paper work of all kinds was especially popular among amateurs, whose work has rarely survived.

CUTTS, JAMES (fl. 1835–1870)
Designer and engraver of transfer-prints for earthenware. He worked in an individual style for Wedgwood*, Davenport*, and others, and his signature '*J. Cutts Desn*' occurs in conjunction with the Davenport mark on some wares designed by him.

CUTTS, JOHN (1772–1851)
Porcelain painter at the Pinxton factory which he bought in 1804. It closed finally in 1813. From 1812 to 1816 Cutts painted porcelain for Wedgwood*, but could not achieve the quality required. He then opened an independent business as an enameller and gilder in Hanley, later becoming a manufacturer of earthenware figures on a fairly large scale. Those of his sons who were engaged in the business predeceased him. His son James* worked independently.

'CYMRIC'
Trade name for silver marketed by Liberty & Co.*

'CYMRIC'. Frame in the *art nouveau* style decorated with enamels. Mark: *L&Co*. Birmingham hall-mark for 1902, and the stamp 'Cymric'*. *Victoria & Albert Museum, London*

from about 1900. Basically of Celtic inspiration (as the name implies) its forms were those of the Arts and Crafts Movement*. Surfaces on which the hammer marks were allowed to remain, strapwork with rivet heads, enamelling and semi-precious stones are fairly typical of early designs. 'Cymric' designs were manufactured for Liberty's by W. H. Haseler & Co.* of Birmingham under an agreement which ended in 1926. The same firm also made jewellery under the same trade name, as well as 'Tudric'* pewter.

See *Knox, Archibald*

CYPRUS GLASS
Type of glass made by Fritz Heckert* in Petersdorf from 1889 onwards. The glass was made in shades of green reminiscent of the medieval *Waldglas*, one variety being described as *Princessgrüncypern*, which was further embellished by enamelling. The Berlin graphic artist, Fritz Sütterlin (1875–1917), designed for Heckert.

DALLAS POTTERY

Pottery at Cincinnati, Ohio, acquired by Frederick Dallas in 1865, which, after 1879, produced *faïence* to be painted by members of the Cincinnati Pottery Club*. Dallas died in 1881, and the factory closed in the following year. Mark: *Dallas* impressed.

DALOU, JULES (1838–1902)

French sculptor, who studied under Carpeaux*. He held office under the Paris Commune in 1871, and was forced to make a hurried retreat to London. He was given a professorship at the South Kensington Museum in 1878, but returned to France in the following year. While in London he exerted a profound influence on English sculpture, then almost moribund. He produced, in addition to his more formal work, a series of small bronzes and terracottas* of peasants in naturalistic style inspired by the painting of Millet.

DALPAYRAT, ADRIEN-PIERRE (b. 1844)

French studio-potter whose stoneware* and porcelain, often inspired by Japanese sources, was mainly

DAMMOUSE, ALBERT. Porcelain vase with a rough surface covered with light blue and red glazes, the former streaked with green. Albert Dammouse* of Sèvres*. 1896. *Victoria & Albert Museum, London*

DALOU, JULES. *A Woman Sewing.* Terracotta by Jules Dalou*. c. 1870. *Victoria & Albert Museum, London*

in the *art nouveau* style. He devised excellent blue, yellow and reduced copper-red glazes which sometimes occur on asymmetrical forms. He was associated with Ernest Chaplet*.

DAMM (Aschaffenburg, Germany)

Factory making *Steingut** which acquired the moulds of the Höchst porcelain factory when it closed in 1798. These were subsequently used to make copies of figures and groups originally by the Modellmeister, Johann Peter Melchior, which were given the wheel-mark. These are superficially quite deceptive. The moulds later passed to the Nymphenburg* Porcelain Factory.

DAMMOUSE, ALBERT (1848–1926)

French potter who began his career at Sèvres* where he was engaged in *pâte-sur-pâte** decoration. Later he worked for Haviland* where his decorations were mainly in the Japanese* style. In the 1890s he turned to glass in the *art nouveau* style, using chiefly the *pâte-de-verre** technique with floral decoration. He employed the mark AD or A. DAMMOUSE, the latter sometimes surrounding the letter *S* for Sèvres.

93

DAMON, LOUIS (d. 1947)
An independent decorator who worked on glass bought from Daum Frères*. His mark was *L. DAMON PARIS*, incised.

DANIEL, H. & R. (Shelton and Stoke-on-Trent, Staffordshire)
Henry Daniel (1765–1841) was chief enameller to Spode* and is reputed to have introduced a technique of decoration with raised gilding. The exact date when the firm of H. & R. Daniel came into existence is unknown, but 1826 is probable, in which year Daniel introduced a new ground-laying* process which was employed to make decorative wares of fine quality. In 1840 the firm received orders for services from the Prince and Princess Borghese. The factory was continued for about ten years after Henry Daniel's death by his son.

DANIELL, LONDON
Circular mark on porcelain of good quality made by Coalport* and others. Daniell was a London china-dealer of the period.

DANTESQUE STYLE
The revival of 15th- and 16th-century Renaissance furniture styles in Italy during the 1850s was thus termed.

DARLING, GRACE HORSLEY (1815–1842)
English heroine, daughter of William Darling, keeper of Longstone Lighthouse on one of the Farne Islands off the Northumberland coast. She and her father rescued nine people from the wreck of the *Forfarshire* in 1838 in tempestuous seas with the aid of a small boat. This became widely known and subscription lists were opened for the gallant rescuers, but Grace Darling probably acquired immortality by dying in 1842 of consumption, a disease which had romantic and sentimental connotations for the Victorians. Grace Darling is commemorated as the subject of Staffordshire figures*, music-covers, and other forms of popular art.

DARMSTADT See *Grossherzogliche . . .*

DASSON, PIERRE (fl. mid-19th cent.)
Ébéniste in Paris who specialized in the making of fine quality reproductions of 18th-century Paris furniture by the *maîtres ébénistes*. The quality of his work is usually fully equal to that of the originals he copied. An example of his work, a copy of the *bureau du roi Louis XV* by Oeben and Riesener is in the Wallace Collection, London.

DAUM FRÉRES (Nancy, Lorraine)
French glass-makers, Auguste (1853–1909) and Antonin (1864–1930) Daum, were members of the École de Nancy, and followers of Émile Gallé*, working mainly in his style, and using his methods.

Their factory produced a good deal of *art nouveau** glass, cameo carved and enamelled, and later, *pâte-de-verre**. More recently they have produced glass in the style of Marinot*. Examples are marked *Daum* or *Daum, Nancy*, and the Cross of Lorraine also occurs from time to time. The firm is now the Cristallerie Daum.

DAVENPORT (American)
A large upholstered sofa. Hence, davenport-table—a sofa-table*.

DAVENPORT FACTORY, THE (Longport, Staffordshire)
Earthenware, stone-china, and porcelain manufacturers founded towards the end of the 18th century by John Davenport who retired about 1830, when the business was continued by his sons, William and Henry Davenport. They enlarged and extended the business, which continued until 1882. Tea-, dessert- and dinner-services decorated in colours with Oriental patterns were commonly made, as well as vases, some of which, when unmarked, might well be confused with similar products from Langlois of Bayeux*. They also made a good deal of very well painted ware in the Derby* style. Thomas Steele*, the Derby fruit-painter, worked here. So, too, did James Rouse*, who painted landscapes on plaques of Davenport porcelain. Other painters included Edwin Steele, who painted flowers in the Rockingham* style, Jesse

DAVENPORT FACTORY. Vase for pot-pourri in a semi-classical style decorated with slightly raised flowers in gold on a dark underglaze blue ground. Staffordshire. c. 1840. *Private collection*

94

Mountford, a landscape painter, and W. Fletcher, a figure-painter. James Cutts* was an independent engraver who worked for the factory. Unmarked rococo vases of excellent quality, sometimes misattributed to Coalport* or Rockingham*, probably came from here. The firm made blue printed wares from its inception, but its best work was done by 1830, although this type of ware was never discontinued. Most of the early examples were of *chinoiserie* patterns more or less closely related to the so-called 'Willow' pattern*. European subjects, on the whole, are somewhat later (post-1815), and the factory does not seem to have made any special designs for the American market, although undoubtedly they exported some of their wares.

Until 1820 the mark was an anchor and Davenport impressed. About 1820 the mark began to be transfer-printed, and in 1835 the factory started to put numbers on either side of the anchor which are the last two figures of the year of manufacture.

DAVIDSON & COMPANY, GEORGE (Gateshead, Co. Durham)

Glasshouse founded in 1867 to produce utility domestic glassware, but it later became one of the largest producers of pressed* and slag glass*. The greater part of their production was tableware, and they developed a large export trade, especially with Australia. Towards the end of the century they patented two forms of art glass—Pearline* and Primrose*. They employed the mark of the lion *rampant* on pressed glass.

DAVIS, HARRY (fl. 1898–1965)

Porcelain painter at Worcester* who executed many of the factory's most important 20th-century commissions, and helped to develop the painting of the Doughty* birds.

DAVIS, GREATHEAD & GREEN (Stourbridge, Worcestershire)

Glass-makers who exhibited copies of Greek vases in painted glass at the Great Exhibition of 1851. Similar vases were also made by Bacchus* of Birmingham, probably imitating Wedgwood's* earlier copies, but the type does not seem to have been very popular. Davis, Greathead & Green were also among the earliest British glasshouses to make pressed glass*, including lacy glass*.

DAY, LEWIS F. (1845–1910)

Artist and designer; Master of the Art Workers' Guild*; examiner for the royal Society of Arts. Day started life as a glass-designer and established his own business in 1870, where he produced designs for textiles, wallpapers, pottery, glass and furniture, although most of his furniture designing was confined to exhibition pieces. He designed clocks for Howell & James* of Regent Street, London, which were provided with a ceramic face decorated with a

sunflower* that give more than a hint of the coming *art nouveau*.

DAY DREAMER, THE

A *papier mâché* armchair which aroused considerable interest at the Great Exhibition of 1851. Designed by H. Fitz Cook, it was notable for a profusion of symbolism which is described in the catalogue as follows: it is decorated at the top with two winged thoughts—the one with bird-like pinions and crowned with roses representing happy and joyous dreams; the other with leathern and bat-like wings—unpleasant and troublesome ones; behind is displayed Hope under the figure of a rising sun; the twisted supports of the back are ornamented with poppy, heart's ease, convolvulus and snowdrop, all emblematic of the subject; in front of the seat is a shell containing the head of a Cherub and on either side of it, pleasant and troubled dreams are represented by figures; at the side is seen a figure of Puck, lying asleep in a labyrinth of foliage and holding a bunch of poppies in his hand.

Although Fitz Cook's enthusiasm for symbolism was perhaps excessive, the chair represents an aspect of mid-19th-century art which was very fashionable, and symbolism of this kind may be found in many other of the exhibits.

'DEATH OF MUNROW (MONROW), THE'
See *Monroe, The Death of*

DE BAY (Paris)

Makers of statuary and ornaments, particularly of the garden variety, in artificial stone and a patent fired clay capable of resisting all kinds of weather. They exhibited in London in 1851.

DAY DREAMER, THE. A *papier mâché* chair, called the Day Dreamer*, which aptly illustrates the Victorian love of allegory. Great Exhibition, 1851. *Illustrated Exhibitor*

DECALCOMANIA

From the French, *decalquer,* to transfer, trace or copy. Once known as 'transfers' among the young. Pictures applied in reverse to a paper backing which could then be applied to furniture and other materials. When the paper was removed the picture adhered to the surface to be decorated. The technique was commonly employed in the United States to decorate furniture, some Hitchcock* chairs being ornamented in this way instead of by stencilling. Glass panels which formed part of American clock cases were commonly decorated with these transfers. They were first employed towards the end of the 18th century.

DECANTERS

During the opening years of the 19th century the cylindrical decanter with sloping shoulders decorated with facet-cutting was the most popular. Square section decanters, usually in fitted cases with glasses *en suite,* intended for spirits and liqueurs, date from the closing years of the 18th century, and were continued into the 19th. These, too, were largely decorated by cutting. The early examples were usually intended for travelling, but those cases of the 19th century fitted with locks were intended to preserve the contents from the depredations of the domestic staff. One such case, made so that the decanters were visible but could not be removed when locked, was termed a *tantalus,* after the mythical personage of this name who was immersed in the river Styx up to his chin but unable to drink. The cylindrical shapes, well adapted to cutting as a means of decoration, began in the 19th century to give place to bulbous and pear-shaped forms with engraved decoration.

The glass had been considerably improved. It was whiter than glass used during the 18th century and there were fewer flaws. By 1850 the globular decanter with a long neck and spherical stopper, decorated with engraved or sometimes etched patterns, was the most fashionable type. Decanters were now supplied in matching sets with wine-glasses. The popularity of Bohemian glass at the Great Exhibition led to the production of decanters and glasses in cased glass*, but these, expensive at the time, are relatively rare today. Coloured glasses such as cranberry glass* were also employed for decanters and glasses in sets and in the 1860s trailing leaves (popular at Stourbridge), and other types of applied decoration, were seen fairly frequently. A few rare decanters were decorated with *millefiori** work in the manner of the paperweight* of the day.

Towards the end of the century cutting once more became popular for decanters, although it was of a much less elaborate type than the earlier varieties of cut-glass*.

For the most part America imported its decanters, and they rarely occur in catalogues of glassware of the time. The New England Glass Company* made a few decanters, but generally it must be supposed that there were technical difficulties in the way of efficient manufacture by automatic means and they preferred to import supplies.

DECK, THÉODORE (1823–1891)

French artist-potter, art-director at Sèvres* from 1887 until 1891. Deck's early work was much influenced by the Near East, and he exhibited decoration of this style at the Paris Exposition of 1861. In the 1870s he experimented with a medieval technique in which threads of clay formed *cloisons* which kept differently

DECK, THÉODORE. Tile by Théodore Deck* painted with a subject representing *Autumn*, from a set of the *Seasons.* Mark: Deck's monogram, *THD*, within a circle. Exhibited at the Paris Exposition of 1855. *Private collection*

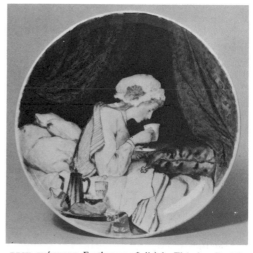

DECK, THÉODORE. Earthenware* dish by Théodore Deck*, the enamel painting by Albert Ankers. Signed. 1866. *Victoria & Albert Museum, London*

coloured glazes from mingling with each other. He also produced tin-enamelled ware (*faïence**) about the same time. In the 1880s he turned his attention to high-fired wares—stoneware* and porcelain*, the former employed for architectural ceramics. He experimented with underglaze colours on porcelain,

DECOEUR, ÉMILE. Porcelain vase with cream and brown crackled glaze, a type inspired by 18th century Chinese glazes with decorative crazing (*craquelure*). French. c. 1910. *Victoria & Albert Museum, London*

DECOEUR, ÉMILE. Tall Chinese-inspired stoneware vase covered in reduced crimson and grey glazes. c. 1920. *Victoria & Albert Museum, London*

especially *flambé* glazes* and probably inspired Bernard Moore*. He also promoted the revival of a type of soft-paste porcelain at Sèvres used to reproduce some 18th-century styles, usually those with a turquoise ground.

DECOEUR, ÉMILE (1876–1953)
French studio-potter. He started by making *faïence**, but turned to high-temperature wares about 1905, making first stoneware* and then, about two years later, porcelain*. His early work was decorated in a variety of techniques, but in the 1920s his shapes became simpler and his typical product became the stoneware vase with a matt, monochrome glaze in yellow, green, pink, blues or white. Painted decoration was largely determined by the shape on which it was painted. His work is marked *E. Decoeur* or the surname alone.

DÉCORCHEMENT, FRANÇOIS ÉMILE (1880–1971)
French artist in glass working mainly at the small town of Conches, Normandy, in the *art nouveau** and *art déco** styles. He specialized in decorative objects in *pâte-de-verre** or *pâte-de-cristal* and marked his work with his name.

DEDHAM POTTERY (Dedham, Mass.)
The Chelsea Keramic Art Works* were revived and transferred here in 1895, when they were renamed. Hugh Robertson, the leading spirit, has been regarded as fifty years in advance of his time and he produced Chinese 'crackled' glazes. Monochrome vases, coloured red, green, yellow, and slate, were given a high-temperature firing, and sometimes have streaked or iridescent effects. An interesting type of serviceware was given (rather surprisingly) a crackled glaze, and was decorated in blue underglaze with animals and foliate motifs. After Hugh Robertson's death in 1908 the factory came under the direction of his son William, and closed in 1943.

The mark is *Dedham Pottery*, incised or painted.

DEER-HOUND TABLE
Hall table designed and modelled by John Bell* in 1845 and cast in iron at Coalbrookdale*. It was

DEER-HOUND TABLE. John Bell. *Ironbridge Gorge Museum Trust*

DE FEURE, GEORGES. Cast silver fittings based on plant-forms in the *art nouveau* style for a *suite* of bedroom furniture. Made for Samuel Bing's* Maison de l'Art Nouveau, Paris. c. 1900. *Victoria & Albert Museum, London*

DELABRIÈRE, E. *Senegalese lion and antelope*, bronze by Paul Edward (Edouard) Delabrière*. Shown at the Paris Exposition, 1866. *Antique Collectors' Club*

included in the Paris Exposition of that year with great success. Described by one authority as a 'fearsome thing', it comprised four life-size deer- or stag-hounds seated on their haunches, turned outwards and supporting a circular table on their backs. It was additionally ornamented by emblems of the chase and vine-leaves and grapes. It weighed in the region of three tons, and its manufacture was a masterpiece of the Coalbrookdale Ironworks*. It reappeared on the market in a West-of-England saleroom in 1975.

DE FEURE, GEORGES (1868–1928)

Designer of furniture and ceramics born in France, who spent his early life in Holland and was brought back to France by Samuel Bing*. His furniture is light and elegant, veneered in pale woods. His ceramics, decorated with curving plant forms, were usually made at Limoges* to the order of Bing. He also helped to design Bing's Pavilion at the 1900 Paris Exposition.

DEGAS, EDGAR (1834–1917)

French Impressionist painter who modelled dancers and horses in wax or clay to help with his painting. These were found in his studio after his death and cast by the founder A. Hébrard* under the direction of the dealer, Durand-Ruel. Out of almost 150 survivals only about 70 were fit to cast and most were cast as found between 1919 and 1921, except for a few which were repaired by the sculptor Bartholomé. Seventy-three were cast in editions of 22. The 20 for sale were marked with the letters A to T, one unlettered copy was retained by Hébrard and one marked *HER* went to the artist's heirs. Each model was numbered from 1 to 72, the seventy-third (cast later) being unnumbered. Each had the incised signature of Degas and the stamp of the founder, A.-A. Hébrard. These bronzes are much sought and highly valued.

DELABRIÈRE, PAUL EDOUARD (1829–1912)

French *Animalier** sculptor who produced animals singly and in groups in plaster or terracotta*, which were converted into bronze. His style owes more than a little to Barye*. He signed *E. DELABRIÈRE*.

DELAHERCHE, AUGUSTE (1857–1940)

French stoneware potter, originally from the Beauvais area, who succeeded Chaplet* in Haviland's* Paris workshop. In 1894 he removed to Armentières and later to La Chapelle-aux-Pots. He had a depot in the rue Halévy, Paris, and used a circular mark with his name in full, or the initials *ADLH* on small wares. His forms were simple, his decoration, sometimes in low relief, usually floral, or an intermingling combination of coloured glazes, usually green, brown and purple, which were also sometimes iridescent. Much of his production was as a designer rather than as a working potter.

DELFT (Dutch)

Earthenware covered with a glaze opacified with tin oxide made at Delft in Holland, or in England, from the 17th century onwards. The manufacture of *delft*

DELAHERCHE, AUGUSTE. Stoneware* plate glazed over grey slip, with sunken floral ornament. Auguste Delaherche*. 1889. *Victoria & Albert Museum, London*

DELLA ROBBIA WARE. Lustre dish by Charles Collins decorated in green and yellow with sunflowers. English. Della Robbia Pottery. c. 1900. *Sotheby & Co*

in England had been more or less discontinued before 1800, and it has since enjoyed only limited revivals by artist-potters.

Old Dutch delft was particularly popular among collectors at the end of the 19th century, and reproductions were made in considerable quantities by Edmé Samson* of Paris and in Holland. This trade still continues, and more recently figures of animals have been offered to the public by small dealers in bric-à-brac which are modern and unlikely to deceive

anyone but a novice. There seem to be no deceptive reproductions or forgeries of English delft at the time of writing, but this state of affairs will not necessarily continue.

DELLA ROBBIA, LUCA (1399–1482) AND HIS NEPHEW ANDREAS (1435–1525)

Italian sculptors who were fond of making terracotta* portrait roundels within a border of modelled flowers, leaves and fruit, the whole covered with tin-enamel glazes of several colours. Most of their work was done for architectural settings. Many copies and derivations of della Robbia ceramic sculptures were made during the 19th century, notably by the Italian Doccia* factory and by Minton* in England.

DELLA ROBBIA WARE

Art-pottery made between 1894 and 1906 at Birkenhead, Cheshire, by Harold Rathbone, a painter, and sculptor Conrad Dressler. The primary inspiration was Italian 15th-century *sgraffito* decoration, but *maiolica* painting also influenced the factory's work. They made some architectural pottery modelled in relief. The mark impressed incised or painted is *Della Robbia* in full, or the initials DR and a ship. Sometimes the initials of the workman responsible for the decoration also appear.

DEMIDOFF (St Petersburg [now Leningrad] Russia)

At mid-century Demidoff specialized in ornamental objects of malachite* which were often of very large size. They exhibited pieces both large and small in the 1851 Exhibition, including furniture, vases, busts, and small objects like paperweights*. They owned the mines from which the malachite was procured.

DE MORGAN, WILLIAM See *Morgan, William de*

DE MORGAN, WILLIAM. One of a pair of de Morgan* tile panels in the so-called 'Persian' style, painted in typical colours with a rampant lion. c. 1890. *William Morris Gallery, Waltham Forest*

DE MORGAN, WILLIAM. 'Flower-pot and flies', dish painted in lustre by Jim Hersey for William de Morgan*. Mark: *JH* incised, *20* impressed. c. 1900. *William Morris Gallery, Waltham Forest*

DE MORGAN, WILLIAM. An oak cabinet designed by Philip Webb*, the cupboard doors painted by William de Morgan*. 1870. *William Morris Gallery, Waltham Forest*

DE MORGAN, WILLIAM. Bowl in the so-called 'Persian' colours painted by Fred Passenger for William de Morgan*. Late 19th century. *Victoria & Albert Museum, London*

DENBY POTTERY (Derbyshire)

This pottery manufacturing common brown stoneware* was taken over in 1812 by Joseph Bourne, whose father owned the Belper pottery nearby. The two factories were operated in conjunction until 1834, when the Belper pottery was closed and removed to Denby. Denby specialized in stoneware gin-flasks*, mostly those in which the head, neck, and shoulders formed the upper part, the lower part being a plain oval bottle shape. Most of their productions seem to have been concerned with the Reform Bill and the large John Barleycorn flask is also attributed to them.

A stoneware inkwell in the form of a small hollow head, an open mouth and protruding lower lip forming the hole in which the pen was dipped, was probably made here. The mark was *Bourne's Potteries Denby and Belper Derbyshire* impressed and variously arranged.

DENVER CHINA & POTTERY COMPANY

Founded in Denver, Colorado, by William A. Long of the Lonhuda Pottery*. Here he made art pottery, mainly in the *art nouveau*ics* style decorated with local flora. The style is often similar to that of the Lonhuda Pottery. Mark: *DENVER* or *DENAURA DENVER,* impressed.

DERBY PORCELAIN FACTORY

This important English porcelain factory located at Nottingham Road, Derby, was founded by William Duesbury in 1756. He acquired the Chelsea factory in 1770, and ran it largely as a decorating studio. When its lease expired in 1784 many of the workmen and the moulds were removed to Derby which had already acquired a reputation for fine enamel-painting and for figures in biscuit porcelain*, the latter a fashion inspired by the popularity of biscuit figures at Sèvres*. William Duesbury died in 1786, and the business was inherited by his son, also William, then aged 23. Trade became more difficult, because the trade treaty negotiated with France, which opened the way to exports of Wedgwood's specialities, also brought competition into the fine porcelain market from French factories, the designs of which were more sophisticated. Derby met this competition by an emphasis on fine quality enamelling which was carried over into the early years of the 19th century. Duesbury took Micheal Kean into partnership in 1795, but died in the following year. Kean continued to run the factory until 1811, but business remained difficult owing to the Napoleonic wars and the Continental blockades.

Kean abandoned the business in 1811 and it was taken over by the head clerk, Robert Bloor, who had to raise the money to pay for it. He adopted a method sometimes employed elsewhere to raise money—he set the painters to work decorating sub-standard white ware which had accumulated over the years. Among the characteristics to be noticed, Bloor porcelain often exhibits a crazed glaze and enamels are inclined to flake off, due to experiments with pastes and glazes in an attempt to lower the cost of production. Bloor aimed at the new *bourgeoisie,* who wanted bright colours and lavish gilding. Among the most popular of the new patterns were those derived from Japanese Imari patterns* which had been introduced towards the end of the 18th century. These have long remained fashionable, and those manufactured by the later Royal Crown Derby Porcelain Company are much sought by gypsies, some of whom have large and valuable collections. The adaptation of mercuric gilding to porcelain decoration at Derby towards the end of the 18th century, which replaced the old honey gold, made gilding cheaper and easier.

Fine painting, however, was not abandoned. John and Robert Brewer*, the latter a pupil of the water-colourist Paul Sandby, did landscapes and hunting scenes from 1795 until about 1811. After 1811 Thomas Steele* painted fruit, birds were done by Richard Dodson*, George Robertson painted landscapes and shipping scenes, Leonard Lead, flowers, and Cuthbert Lawton, hunting scenes. These are rare today. James Rouse* bridges most of the period under review, being apprenticed to the 18th-century painter 'Quaker' Pegg*, and still working, at the time of his death in 1888, for the Royal Crown Derby factory.

Many of the figures of the period were repetitions of 18th-century models and styles, sometimes in biscuit porcelain (which undoubtedly inspired the development of Parian*). Sometimes figures are painted in dark, thick colours, including maroon (unknown to the 18th century), which have a distinct tendency to flake off. Among the modellers are numbered Edward Keys* (who left to go to Minton in 1826) and Samuel Keys*. The first made a set of the Monkey Band* inspired by the 18th-century Meissen* series, and portrait figures of George IV and Napoleon. Samuel Keys was inspired by the theatre, and modelled Liston, Mme Vestris and Miss Foote in character. He made two figures of *Hebe* and *Innocence* 28 inches in height, decorated with flowers by Leonard Lead, but only one pair was finished. By the same hand are a number of amusing figures illustrating the adventures of Dr Syntax*.

Bloor died in 1848 and the factory closed. Some of the workmen, led by William Locker*, moved with equipment and moulds to a small factory in King Street, Derby. Locker died in 1859, and the firm came successively under the control of Stevenson and Sharp, Stevenson and Hancock, and then Sampson Hancock alone.

See *Hancock, Sampson*; *Locker, William*; *Royal Crown Derby Porcelain Company, The*; *Stevenson & Hancock*.

DERBYSHIRE, JOHN (fl. c. 1870-1880)
Manchester glass-maker who employed a mark *JD* followed by an anchor. Among his products are a press-moulded lion paperweight* which has a Patent Office Design Registry Number for 1874, and figures of Punch and Judy made in 1875.

DERBYSHIRE MARBLE WORK
Decorative marble work made from stone quarried near Ashford-in-the-Water was most popular during the 1840s and 1850s. Samuel Birley, an Ashford furniture-maker, exhibited a table with a black circular top inlaid with flowers, foliage and birds at the International Exhibition in 1862. The industry began to flourish when the Duke of Devonshire gave local workers access to his collection of Florentine mosaics. Coloured marbles and other stones were

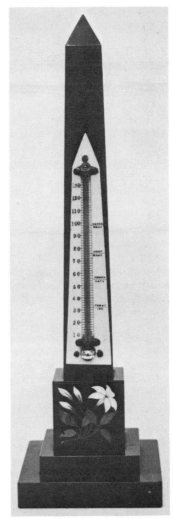

DERBYSHIRE MARBLE WORK. Table thermometer in the form of an obelisk of black Derbyshire marble, decorated with painted flowers. c. 1860. *Constance Chiswell*

embedded in a cement matrix in a variety of more or less elaborate patterns. For a time the industry was so successful that firms engaged in it sprang up not only in Ashford but also in Buxton, Derby, Matlock and Bakewell. However, the expense of the work was too great for continued large-scale production. After 1860 it declined rapidly, but did not die out until 1900.

See *Pietra Dura*; *Scagliola*

DE SAINT-MARCEAUX, RENÉ (1845–1915)
Sculptor who modelled figures for reproduction in porcelain by Sèvres. Signature: *Marceau*.

DESPRET, GEORGES
Owner of a glasshouse at Jeumont (Nord) founded in 1859 by his uncle, Hector Despret. He began to experiment with *pâte-de-verre* in 1890, and exhibited

DESSERT SERVICES. Part of a Paris dessert service (small sauce tureen, ice-pail, and shaped dishes) decorated with naturally painted birds. c. 1830.
Christie, Manson & Woods

at the Paris Exposition of 1900. Painted mark; *Despret*. The glasshouse closed in 1937.

DESPREZ (Paris)

A manufacture of porcelain and cameos was founded about 1790 by Desprez who had formerly been a modeller at Sèvres*. His portrait cameos were competitive with the 18th-century glass pastes of Tassie and the portrait medallions of Wedgwood*. In 1808 Desprez exhibited cameos consisting of white reliefs on a blue background and by 1819 he had devised a technique for embedding his reliefs in crystal glass, which probably inspired the crystallo-ceramie* of Apsley Pellatt*. Some late examples of this work are signed *Desprez fils et Lamarre*. In 1812 the son of Desprez took out a patent for a new porcelain body and for enamel colours to decorate it.

DESSERT SERVICES

These decorative services were introduced in the 18th century, and were very popular during the 19th. Usually of porcelain, some were made in fine quality earthenware, such as Wedgwood's 'Queensware'*. Painting is generally of excellent quality, and the comports of the service are often upheld by figures, to be seen from both Meissen* and Minton*. Dishes are in a variety of shapes, and the service is provided with ice-pails and small sauce-tureens and stands.

DE STIJL (Dutch)

Association of Dutch artists founded in 1917 at Leiden, Holland, by Theo van Doesburg. The aims of the group were expounded in a magazine, *De Stijl*, which was published from 1917 to 1930. These were similar to the ideas of the Bauhaus* and the *art déco* style. Ornament was rejected, the palette was limited to the primary colours, and rectangular forms were popular. The association was disbanded in 1931.

DEUTSCHES WERKBUND

Association, founded by Hermann Muthesius in 1907, of manufacturers, architects, artists, craftsmen and writers in Munich. Among those associated with it from the first were Henri van der Velde*, Richard Riemerschmid* and Josef Hoffmann*, and after the First World War, Mies van der Rohe*, Le Corbusier*

and Walter Gropius. The Werkbund aimed at co-ordinating the efforts of designers and craftsmen with the exigencies of machine-production. Functional designs were produced which were made of simple materials uncomplicated by extraneous ornament.
See *Functionalism*

DEUTSCHES WERKSTÄTTEN

Workshops established in Dresden in 1898 by Karl Schmidt to design furniture especially for machine production. They exhibited at the Dresden Exhibition of Industrial Art in 1899 and again in 1905. Richard Riemerschmid*, brother-in-law of Karl Schmidt, designed furniture for these workshops.

DEVARANNE & SON, S. P. (Berlin)

Devaranne exhibited zinc* (spelter) casts at the Great Exhibition of 1851.

DE VARREUX, CAMILLE (fl. 1910)

Art-director of the Pantin* glasshouse, which produced mainly etched and deeply cut glass. De Varreux used the pseudonym, *DE VEZ*.

DE VILLE, JAMES (1776–1846)

Plaster-figure maker and phrenologist of London. De Ville made plaster figures of all kinds, many taken from moulds of original works by sculptors of note, and he possessed the moulds of the busts of Napoleon which he purchased at the latter's death. He also specialized in casts and busts illustrating the pseudo-science of phrenology* which was then extremely popular.

DEWSBURY, DAVID (fl. 1889–1918)

Flower painter at Doulton* specializing in orchids.

DIAPHANIE (French)

The imitation of stained glass windows by means of sheets of specially prepared paper applied to clear glass and varnished.

DICKENSWARE

Art-pottery decorated with characters and scenes from the novels of Charles Dickens introduced at a pottery owned by Samuel A. Weller of Zanesville (Ohio) at the turn of the century. It proved very popular.

DILLWYN, LEWIS WESTON   See *Swansea pottery and porcelain*

DISTIN FAMILY, THE

The Distin family formed a brass quintet playing the saxhorn, an instrument which appeared in London at a series of promenade concerts under the baton of the conductor, Jullien. They were a sensation at the time, and their collective portrait occurs in relief, holding the saxhorns made for them in Paris by Adolphe Saxe, on a Parian* jug with a rustic handle made by Samuel Alcock* of Burslem. The figures, white against a pale mauve ground, were probably modelled by Hugues Protât*. The family were also the subject of a lithograph* portrait in 1844.

'DISTRESSED MOTHER, THE'

Parian* figure made for Felix Summerly's* Art Manufactures by Minton*. This was taken from a monument to Mrs Warren in Westminster Abbey made in 1816 by the sculptor, Sir Richard Westmacott, who repeated the subject of 'The Distressed Mother' in 1822 for Lord Lansdowne.

DIXON & SONS, JAMES (Sheffield, Yorkshire)

Manufacturers of Britannia metal* and Sheffield plate*, founded about 1805. In 1829 they registered their first silver mark, *D & S*, which was changed to *J D & S* in 1867. The words *Sterling silver* occur on pieces intended for export to America. In 1848 they began electro-plating* under licence from Elkington*, and they succeeded in applying the process to Britannia metal, increasing its resemblance to silver. They also supplied both silver and plated ware to Felix Summerly's* Art Manufactures.

DOAT, TAXILE. Porcelain vase by Taxile Doat*. *Manufacture nationale de Sèvres.* 1900. *Victoria & Albert Museum, London*

DIXON, AUSTIN & CO. (North Hilton Pottery, Sunderland)

The firm also owned the Garrison Pottery in the same district. Principally they produced earthenware decorated with crudely coloured transfer-prints, often in conjunction with pink lustre. Sentimental inscriptions are not uncommon and the Wear Bridge a favourite subject. Chamber pots* and toad mugs* formed part of the output, although these are now rare. Figures, and such objects as watchstands*, were made here and are sometimes marked, but they are rare. Marks are *Dixon & Co.* or *Dixon, Austin & Co. Sunderland* impressed. A good deal of unmarked ware of this kind was probably made here.

DOAT, TAXILE (1851–after 1909)

French potter who worked at the Sèvres* factory from 1875 to 1905, when he emigrated to America and worked at the University City Pottery. He specialized in high-temperature firing and wrote a book on the subject. His work at Sèvres includes vases in the *art nouveau** style, and small plaques.

DOCCIA (near Florence, Italy)

Porcelain factory founded by the Marchese Ginori in 1735 some of whose products have been confused with those of Capo-di-Monte*.

In the 19th century, apart from decorative porce-

DOCCIA. A porcelain urn and cover moulded with mythological scenes in relief in characteristic style. Doccia. This type of decoration is sometimes wrongly attributed to Capo-di-Monte*. Crowned *N* mark. Last quarter of the 19th century. *Sotheby & Co*

lain, the factory produced reproductions of 16th-century *maiolica**, and pottery influenced in form or decoration, or both, by the Near East. The merging of the company with the Società Ceramica Richard was followed by the production of ware in the *art nouveau** style, and in the 1930s some well-designed *art déco** wares were made. The firm still makes high quality porcelain, which has been its speciality since its inception.

DODSON, RICHARD (fl. after 1810)
Bird painter on Derby* porcelain, said to have employed heavy colouring. Identification of his work is generally uncertain.

DOGETT, JOHN (fl. early 19th century)
Cabinet-maker, carver and gilder of Roxbury, Mass., who also made clock cases for Simon Willard*.

DOGS AS CHIMNEY ORNAMENTS
Seated dogs of the spaniel type were made as chimney-ornaments by Sampson Smith*, Kent* and others in Staffordshire from about 1840 until the beginning of the First World War. Dogs of other types and sizes were also made both in Staffordshire and Yorkshire; some of the moulds of all kinds have survived and are being employed today to make reproductions.

See '*Comforter*' dogs

DOLLS AND DOLL-HOUSES
Dolls are very ancient, and examples are as old as the beginnings of civilization. Survivals from the 17th and 18th centuries are not excessively rare, and many of them once formed part of nativity scenes. The male adult doll is more frequent at this period than it is in the 19th century, and wooden dolls are not uncommon from the early periods. This article, however, is mainly concerned with the 19th century, and wooden dolls made at Grödnertal in Germany were imported into England during the Regency period, and are now much sought. They vary in size from half an inch to 45 inches, and are usually dressed in costumes which are Regency or Empire in style if they are original. The bodies are articulated and a carved comb decorates the hair. The quality of wooden dolls later in the century becomes variable, but few can be regarded as outstanding in this respect. Wooden dolls of the folk type have, of course, been made at all periods, but they are rarely of much interest to the doll collector. Excellent examples of the wooden doll were produced in America by the Vermont Novelty Works at Springfield at the end of the 19th century, basing their productions on designs by Joel Ellis, and the Schoenhut Company made good quality wooden dolls with patent wire spring joints.

Papier mâché dolls are rare, probably because the heads are fragile and easily damaged. Most seem to have been made in Germany, and there does not appear record of their manufacture by any of the established English firms. The early ones dating from

c. 1835 represent women, with children predominating after 1860. Bodies are of leather or fabric, and the hair was painted on, although wigs may have been added later. Ludwig Greiner patented a doll head of *papier mâché* in America in 1858, and specimens are now much sought.

Dolls with heads of wax have a fairly long history. Wax, of course, was a popular medium for portrait sculpture from Renaissance times. It had the disadvantage of melting easily if exposed to even a comparatively low degree of heat, but portraitists made various additions to the wax which made it less liable to accidents of this kind, and no doubt the makers of dolls had their own favourite recipes also. Dolls of poured wax are the most fragile; usually they are the best quality, and the most sought. Others are made from a thin coating of wax over a composition foundation. Most dolls of these types seem to have been made in Germany or England, although specimens marked with the names of Pierotti or Montanari suggest Italians working in England. A doll of c. 1870 marked 'Meech. Maker to the Royal Family. 50. Kensington Road, London', is recorded by Constance King. Another of c. 1910 made by Mrs Lucy Peek is marked 'The Dolls Home or Dolls House, 131, Regent Street, London, W.' Both are of poured wax. Dolls of this type are, for the most part, children, and those representing adults are rarer. Both types were made throughout the 19th century and into the 20th.

Heads of glazed porcelain seem to have been introduced in the 1840s, probably at the Berlin* factory. Manufacture was soon taken up by other German factories, notably those of Thuringia. Porcelain factories, of course, were well equipped to make things of this kind, using slip-casting*. To the head was attached a shoulder-plate pierced so that it could be sewn to the body, or so made that it could be attached to a jointed wooden body by small wooden pegs. In general, porcelain heads were of good quality, well modelled and painted, as one might expect from factories accustomed to figure-modelling and intricate casting. Heads which are painted with strong colour seem to coincide in date, more or less, with a fashion for strong colouring on decorative figures. Dolls about 4 inches in height (about the size of some figure models) were made for doll-houses.

The type of head known to the doll-collector as 'bisque' or 'Parian*' dates from about 1855. It is doubtful whether a true Parian was used, but probable that all are biscuit (ie. unglazed) porcelain* delicately tinted. In this respect the doll's head seems to have preceded the use of tinted biscuit or Parian for other decorative purposes, and may even have suggested the development. Most sought among the 'bisque' dolls are those with swivelling necks and glass eyes.

Fine quality dolls with French 'bisque' heads and dressed in the manner of fashionable Parisiennes, sometimes accompanied by many miniature accessories, were popular in Paris in the best shops, and some were exported. A good deal of the value today depends on the clothes, and how stylish they are. These dolls are usually termed 'Parisiennes', and the work of several makers is especially sought, notably that of Mme Marie Rohmer of Paris, whose factory was called 'Aux Enfants Sages'. She took out a number of patents between 1857 and 1886. Bodies are usually of leather, although wooden bodies with articulated limbs are sought, and the swivelling head is a desirable feature. German 'bisque' dolls of this type belong to the 20th century.

The French *bébé* doll appeared about 1870. Until this time dolls had more often than not represented adults, but the French decided that children would prefer an effigy of themselves, and began to make a kind of idealized child's head. Some of the earliest and best were made by the firm of Bru, and those made by Steiner of Paris founded in 1855, who won a gold medal at the 1889 Exposition, were often provided with mechanisms by which they could move their limbs and cry 'Mama'. Rabery & Delphieu of Paris were another old-established firm going back to 1856, and much sought today are the products of the Jumeau factory, which was working from 1842 to 1899. They then amalgamated with others to form the Societé Française de Fabrication des Bébés et Jouets. The quality of Jumeau dolls is variable, and they are generally marked *Tête Jumeau*. The mark *FD* is attributed to Fernand Gaultier, who was awarded a silver medal at the Paris Exposition of 1878. This firm became Gaultier Frères in 1889. Rabery & Delphieu who, with Jumeau, Bru, and others, joined the syndicate in 1899, were working in 1880 producing good quality dolls with the mark *RD*. Paris, of course, was one of the important traditional French centres for the manufacture of porcelain, including biscuit porcelain. The other is Limoges, near the Saint-Yrieix clay-beds, and dolls were made at Limoges by the firm of A. Lanternier et Cie (founded 1855). Quality is not usually very good, and specimens seem to belong to the 20th century.

German bisque-headed dolls are relatively numerous. The Thuringian factories were the traditional source of inexpensive porcelain, and they made heads in great variety. The earliest date from the 1870s, and most of them belong to the 20th century. Perhaps the largest makers were Ernst Heubach and Armand Marseille of Köppelsdorf who operated as the Vereinigte Köppelsdorfer Porzellanfabriken, and were established as makers of hard-paste porcelain in 1887. Th. Recknagel of Alexandrinenthal founded his factory in 1886, and Schoenau and Hoffmeister of the Porzellanfabrik Burggrub in Bavaria not until 1901. Simon & Halbig made 'bisque' heads for Kammer & Reinhardt who introduced the 'character headed' doll, especially popular in America, about 1910. The term 'character head' refers to one based on a real child instead of an idealized one. They were given names, like Hans, Gretchen or Else. Dolls were designed in America by such designers as Grace Storey Putnam (fl. 1920s) for the Borgfeldt Company,

New York; Mme Georgène Averill, who designed character-headed dolls for the Averill Manufacturing Company operated by her husband; or Joseph Kallus, of whose work large quantities were sold by the Cameo Doll Company. These designs were executed by a number of German factories, such as Kestner & Co. (from 1907) and C. F. Kling & Co. (founded 1836), both of Ohrdruf (Thuringia), a town in which Baehr & Proeschild (founded 1871) also made dolls' heads. Some of the factories known to have made dolls' heads and limbs may have more or less confined themselves to this work, because they do not appear in the usual lists of factories making domestic and decorative wares, but this seems quite feasible when we take into account that 50,000 specimens of one popular doll were sold on the American market alone.

Allied to bisque-headed dolls are those which are made entirely of biscuit porcelain, head, body and limbs, or with 'bisque' head and limbs and a composition body. Those which are made in one piece, and not articulated, are often termed 'Frozen Charlottes' by collectors, and do, in fact, come very near to the porcelain figure. Half-figures, or head and bust only, were made in glazed or biscuit porcelain before the 1914–1918 War for turning into pincushions, and during the 1920s to surmount a cover for the old-fashioned pillar-telephone, an instrument of incredible ugliness. They were made by the German factories. These figures are pierced with holes at the lower edge for sewing. The fashionable *boudoir* dolls of the 1920s often disguised something utilitarian, like a night-dress case.

Fabric dolls are not so widely popular. Many were home-made, and only exceptional specimens are likely to have been preserved. For the home-maker during much of the 19th century 'bisque' or porcelain heads could be bought separately, so there was not a great deal of inducement to lavish craftsmanship on a rag doll. In America, however, the Arnold Print Works introduced designs printed on fabrics which could be made up at home, and Dean's Rag Book Company did the same in England. Both companies were followed by others. Popular in the 19th century, and produced since, were lithographed sheets of card printed with a basic doll and a variety of clothes which could be cut out and attached. These, related to the 'penny plain, twopence coloured*' sheets of stage-figures, are now collected. Many of the *boudoir* dolls of the 1920s were made of fabric.

There are other kinds of dolls which are difficult to categorize but which are nevertheless related to the subject. These include Oriental figures made for tourists—Indian, Chinese, or Japanese—usually made of some kind of composition and clothed with such fabrics as cotton, or even silk. Indian figures modelled in lightly fired terracotta and brightly painted, instead of clothed in fabric, belong to the same group. Puppets may be classified as dolls, and some are of fine quality and of exceptional interest. Unusual, and often belonging to the early years of the

19th century, or even earlier, are fine quality figures of wax. Folk-dolls made of wood and rag are of interest to some doll-collectors, as well as to the ethnographist. There are dolls which, like Janus, have a face on either side, and a modern head with three faces, each showing a different mood, has been recorded. The variety leaves plenty of scope for the collector in search of novelty.

As with most things, value depends on quality, rarity, condition, and age, more or less in this order of consideration, although either rarity or age may sometimes take precedence. Most value is likely to be attached to quality allied to fine condition—undamaged head, sound limbs and body, original clothes, etc., and a head which bears the mark of a well-known maker stamped on the shoulder-plate will add to the interest. Facial expression should be pleasing although this is a matter of taste, and many people will prefer character to insipid idealization. A poor quality head will not only be made without much expression or detail, but colouring will be indifferent, with badly chosen colours that are often crude and too strong. A swivelling head is probably later than a fixed head, and the more elaborate limb-articulations are also comparatively late introductions, but fixed-position heads and the simpler articulations, were not abandoned just because more elaborate types were available. If a head is of exceptional quality, the substitution of another tolerably well-matching body is not a disaster. If the doll has been taken apart, the head is the most important part, and heads are often sold separately. The replacement of worn-out clothing by well-made and well-designed substitutes in the right period style does not seriously affect value. Much will depend on circumstances.

Since the collecting of dolls began to be popular, and prices started to rise, reproductions of heads which are sought after have been made. A number of the Thuringian factories are still in existence, and porcelain factories usually keep master-moulds from which fresh working-moulds can be made. Usually when using early moulds at a later date factories adopt a special mark, but in its absence only colouring is likely to provide a guide to the difference between old and new. Generally, heads which are recognizably the same as those made in the 19th century, but about one-sixth smaller in size should be viewed with suspicion, unless it is known that more than one size was made at a time. They may be modern remoulds from an old head. Porcelain always shrinks by this amount during firing. (See *Casting*). As in the case of other antiques and *objets d'art*, expensive dolls should be carefully examined for signs of restoration. Some repair is probably inevitable to what has been, after all, a child's plaything, and both porcelain and wax can be repaired almost invisibly by professional china restorers, who use paint and varnish to cover their work. In the case of a highly valued doll where restoration is suspected it would certainly be worth examining the head by ultra-violet light, in the same way as valuable porcelain is examined. Any considerable variation in the colour exhibited by the surface should be investigated. Paints and varnishes fluoresce in a different way from a porcelain or wax surface. The Hanovia Inspectolite is a suitable apparatus for the purposes, and many dealers and auction-rooms have them. Even the best heads sometimes have replacement wigs and it is rare for the maker to add a poor quality wig to a good head. If a wig is a replacement there is no reason why it should not be replaced, in its turn, by something better, and nearer to the original if this can be done. Doll-collecting is a field where the collector can hardly know too much, and experience is important.

Small dolls suitable for doll-houses have always been made, and houses and furniture have also been made commercially at all periods. The greater number, however, and especially the finest, have been made by amateurs. The cost in time and labour necessary to produce fine quality models would have been too great. It has been possible since the early part of the 19th century to buy paper especially printed with brick- or stone-work, &c. for covering external and interior walls, but interior furniture and fittings, especially when handmade by someone accustomed to the styles of the period represented, and even more importantly when they have been copied from a well-known house, have caused the best model houses to realize large sums of money at auction, in one recent case, more than £100,000.

See *Automata*; *Casting*; *Porcelain figure-making*

DON POTTERY (Swinton, Yorkshire)
This factory was founded by John Green at the end of the 18th century. It belonged to a number of owners during the 19th century, and closed finally in 1893. The factory made creamware*, green-glazed ware, painted and transfer-printed* ware, Egyptian black* and stoneware* generally. A great deal of earthenware was produced transfer-printed in blue, much of it unmarked, the most desirable of which is a series of named views of Italy. The best work of this kind was done before the factory was purchased by Samuel Barker in 1834. The pottery also made amusing earthenware figures.

The mark, impressed or printed, always includes the name DON or DON POTTERY. After about 1820 the device of a lion holding a flag was adopted.

DOOR-KNOCKERS
Ornamental door-knockers were made by Renaissance bronzeworkers in the 16th century. They were fashionable during much of the 19th century, until they were replaced by electric bells, both in Victorian England and on the Continent. They were usually of brass or cast-iron in England and of bronze on the Continent, where, especially in parts of France, a popular form of knocker is the clenched fist. The dolphin was a favourite subject during the Regency period* in England, no doubt dating from Nelson's

victory at Trafalgar. Classical *motifs* include a Medusa head.

DOOR-PORTERS
Door-stops, usually of cast-iron, less often of brass. These were familiar objects in the Victorian home and took a variety of forms—celebrities of the time, like the Duke of Wellington and Lord Nelson, animals such as cats, dogs, Jumbo the elephant and swans, Mr Punch and his Judy dating from the inception of the magazine, and such inanimate objects as Stephenson's *Rocket*. Some door-porters can be dated with a fair amount of certainty. For instance, a knight under a Gothic canopy was made by the Coalbrookdale Ironworks* to a design which, according to the mark, was first registered in 1841. Mr Punch cannot be earlier than the 1840s; Jumbo the elephant belongs to the 1860s.

The best of the door-porters were cast by the Coalbrookdale Company, who often marked their products. Some examples of their manufacture were bronzed. The exact date of the introduction of this process is undetermined. The records of the Great Exhibition attribute the invention of bronzed-zinc to Geiss* of Berlin some time in the 1840s, so this date may be inferred for a similar surface treatment of cast-iron. Cast-iron door-porters have been reproduced in recent years, principally from old specimens pressed into founder's sand. Usually copies made in this way are slightly smaller than the originals and lack some of the sharpness of detail.

Door-porters were also made of glass in a variety of forms. Those of glass were made at Bristol, Nailsea* and Birmingham, usually of green bottle-glass, and these have recently been reproduced. Generally, the reproductions look shiny and new. Door-porters of a poor quality lead-glass are rare and date from the repeal of the Glass Excise Act in 1845. Some are crudely decorated with embedded flowers in a manner similar to the paperweights* of the period.

DORÉ, LOUIS AUGUST GUSTAVE (1833–1883)
Doré is principally remembered for his book illustration, but he was also a talented painter and sculptor. His statue of Dumas is in the Place Malesherbes, Paris.

The 19th-century development of book illustration, printing, and the making of books generally, made illustrated books widely available to an increasingly literate public, and Doré, who was a prolific worker, enjoyed wide popularity. He became a regular contributor to the *Journal pour Rire*, Paris, at the age of 16, and at 22 he illustrated the *Gargantua and Pantagruel* of Rabelais. These, with his illustrations to Dante's *Inferno* and Cervantes's *Don Quixote*, are still the best known. Doré was as popular in England as in his native France, and in 1869 he rented a large gallery in New Bond Street, London, as a place where he could permanently display his work; this is now the auction-rooms of Sotheby & Co.

He had ambitions to gain a reputation as a serious artist and to this end he exhibited in London a series of enormous religious paintings, of which the best known is, perhaps, *Christ Leaving the Praetorium*, 20 feet in height and 30 feet wide, which took nearly five years to paint. It was rapturously greeted by the press, the *Morning Post* writing 'The grandeur and versatility of M. Gustave Doré's genius have never been displayed to such striking effect as in his new picture'. Some of these paintings were widely distributed in the form of steel-engravings, which were framed and hung in many Victorian homes.

Doré's last work, an illustrated edition of Coleridge's *Ancient Mariner*, was a commercial failure, although the plates are among his best. His drawings of London slums and docks are still well-known and he executed a similar series of drawings of Paris low-life. Much of his work is fantastic, such as the illustrations to the *Gargantua*, and a distinct morbidity underlies a good deal of his other work, like the illustrations to the *Inferno* and the *Ancient Mariner*, which often have a nightmarish quality. Of a painting of the deserted amphitheatre by moonlight showing a few lions finishing a leisurely meal of Christian martyrs, a contemporary comment was, 'We confess that we took more pleasure in that one picture at the Doré Gallery than in all the pictures of the Royal Academy put together'.

DORFLEIN, PHILIP (1816–1896)
American maker of metal moulds for pressed glass*. He was responsible for many bottle designs with portraits of historical personages and began working in Philadelphia soon after 1840.

DOUGHTY, (SUSAN) DOROTHY (1892–1962)
Porcelain designer, daughter of Charles M. Doughty, the Arabian explorer. Her work was almost entirely confined to models of birds and flowers for the Worcester Royal Porcelain Company*, starting in

DOUGHTY, DOROTHY. From Dorothy Doughty's* American Bird Series, a blue-grey gnat-catcher on dog-wood. *Worcester Royal Porcelain Company*

DOUGHTY, DOROTHY. *Moorhen chick on water-lily*, from the 'British Birds' series by Dorothy Doughty*. *Worcester Royal Porcelain Company*

1935 with the *Redstart on Hemlock* inspired by one of Audubon's* engravings. This was the beginning of a series of American birds issued in strictly limited editions, some of which were modelled from stuffed specimens or from birds kept in aviaries. Later she visited America to study the birds in their natural surroundings, and many of her finest models date from this time.

By 1960 she had completed the American bird series, and began work in earnest on a project which she had been considering for several years—a series of British birds. Those she was able to complete before the unfortunate accident which led to her death in 1962 are now being issued by the factory, also in limited editions.

The Doughty birds, which, for quality, rank with the best of figures and floral decorations produced in the past, have been collected almost from the first, and some very high prices are paid for models from editions now exhausted. The Dyson Perrins Museum at the factory has a representative collection.

DOULTON (Lambeth, London)

Important firm of stoneware* potters founded by John Doulton (1793–1873). He served an apprenticeship at the Fulham stoneware pottery and, in 1815, formed a partnership with John Watts. As Doulton and Watts they began to make jugs, mugs and bottles (including gin-bottles) relief-decorated at a factory in Lambeth. The business grew very rapidly. London was fast expanding and greatly in need of effective drainage and the best and cheapest material for drainpipes and other sanitary ware was salt-glazed stoneware. Water-filters were also much in demand, and later in the century the infant electrical industry demanded insulators. To keep pace with all these demands Doulton built factories and were soon a large and flourishing concern, specializing in salt-glazed stoneware and terracotta*. Of the latter material they produced figures, vases, and ornamental chimney-pots and other architectural work. John Watts retired in 1854, the firm thereafter being known as Doulton & Company. Until 1854, and possibly for a year or two after, the firm used an impressed mark

DOULTON & WATTS, usually with *LAMBETH POTTERY, LONDON* added, on stoneware and terracotta.

Until the 1860s the production of ornamental wares was more or less limited to mugs, jugs and flasks, especially gin-flasks* commemorating the Reform Bill of 1832. At the beginning of the 1860s Henry Doulton, son of John Doulton, influenced by his acquaintance with John Sparkes, principal of the Lambeth School of Art, started an art department at the pottery for the manufacture of ornamental wares. Students from the School were employed and permitted to sign or mark their work.

The factory also introduced new bodies for the ornamental wares. 'Lambeth faience', from its composition, was a kind of fine white stoneware decorated with underglaze painting. It was introduced in 1873. 'Silicon' ware, another fine stoneware, was employed from 1880 to 1912, and on one or two occasions since for limited editions. 'Chiné' ware introduced in 1886, was the name of a ware which was given a novel surface texture by pressing lace and coarse textiles into the surface of the raw clay. The mark DOULTON AND SLATER'S PATENT occurring on special wares refers to John Slater, Burslem art-director and member of a well-known family of Staffordshire potters. He helped to develop 'Chiné' ware, and experimented with photographic methods of decoration, patenting a technique of transfer-printing* in 1889. He also introduced lustre* decoration at Doulton's and his printed designs include birds and marine subjects.

In 1877 Doulton's acquired the factory of Pinder, Bourne & Company which produced good quality domestic earthenware. The manufacture of bone china was added in 1882. For the most part this

DOULTON. A Royal Doulton* Sung vase decorated by E. Eaton, and signed by C. Noke. Marks: *NOKE* and *SUNG No. 2140*. 1930. *Sotheby & Co*

DOULTON. A rare Doulton* Carrara*
vase by Hannah and Florence Barlow*.
Initialled *HHB* painted and *FEB*
incised. Lambeth. 1882–1890. *Sotheby
& Co*

From 1955 the style of the firm was changed to Doulton's Fine China Ltd. Marks used always include the name DOULTON. The marks of Doulton & Co., Burslem, nearly always have 'Burslem' added; those on wares made at Lambeth nearly always have 'Lambeth' added. Many of the early marks also provide a way of ascertaining the date, and those with 'ENGLAND' in the mark were made after 1891. Wares bearing the mark of a lion over a coronet with ROYAL DOULTON beneath are correctly dated 1902 or after. In this year, the firm was granted the Royal Warrant. Wares signed by the artist or marked with a monogram, are especially numerous, and make

DOULTON. Jug decorated in coloured
transfer-printing* with an early
motoring scene. Royal Doulton*.
c. 1910. *Constance Chiswell*

factory produced wares with painted decoration. One of the principal artists was Charles John Noke (1858–1914) who became art-director in 1914. He was responsible about 1895 for the introduction of 'Holbein' ware—portraits executed in contrasting inlaid clays, and 'Rembrandt' ware in 1898. The latter was decorated in relief, sometimes with figures of animals. He was also responsible, with the chemist Charles Bailey, for the development of the brilliant red *flambé* glaze*, animals thus decorated now being much sought. Noke developed two wares, 'Sung' and 'Chang' noted for decorative glazes, but the names do not imply any resemblance to Chinese wares of the Sung dynasty. His son, Cecil John Noke, joined the firm after the First World War, and became head of the engraving department, and then, in 1936, art-director in succession to his father. He died in 1954.

DOULTON. An elephant modelled by C. Noke, and coloured
orange *flambé*, blue and green by W. Allen. Royal
Doulton*. First quarter of the 20th century. *Sotheby & Co*

DOULTON. Doulton* stoneware* bottle
with handle decorated with coloured
glazes, its form and the disposition of
the relief decoration inspired by
Chinese Ming dynasty ware. *Constance
Chiswell*

109

Doulton's early wares especially attractive to collectors. The name of a particular type of ware also occurs as part of the mark. The marks are too numerous to list here in detail, and should be consulted in Geoffrey Godden's *Encyclopædia of Marks on British Pottery and Porcelain*. Generally, Doulton ornamental ware is very well documented.

The list of artists of note employed by Doulton's is very long, beginning with the Barlows* (Arthur, Hannah, and Florence) early in the 1870s. Others include Mark Marshall, George Tinworth*, Frank Brangwyn R.A.* (Brangwyn ware), Vera Huggins*, and many more.

DRAGON LUSTRE
A decoration by Daisy Makeig-Jones on Wedgwood* porcelain of a Chinese dragon chasing the flaming pearl under an iridescent glaze.

See *Fairyland lustre*

'DRESDEN' PORCELAIN
Porcelain, usually made or decorated in imitation of Meissen*, in and around the City of Dresden during the 19th century. Meissen porcelain of the period is sometimes erroneously thus called. The most notorious factory copying Meissen was that of Carl Thieme* of Potschappel which produced, among other things, reproductions of the 'Crinoline' groups by the 18th-century sculptor, Kändler. Thieme used the crossed swords mark with the addition of the letter *T*. Helena Wolfsohn* of Dresden employed the *AR* (Augustus Rex) mark of the 1730s on porcelain quite unlike anything made at Meissen at this time.

DRESSER, CHRISTOPHER. Glass claret-jug with silver mounts, designed by Christopher Dresser*. Hall-mark for 1879–1880. *Victoria & Albert Museum, London*

DRESSED PRINTS
Prints where the figures have been 'dressed' by applying a modicum of padding which was then covered by dresses made from fragments of cloth. Gold-leaf and real hair were often added, as well as imitations of jewellery. The earliest date from about 1820, and dressed prints were sometimes called 'Amelias' after the originator. There is a detailed description in *The Young Ladies' Book* of 1829.

DRESSEL, KISTER AND COMPANY (Passau, Bavaria)
Porcelain manufacturers who produced deceptive copies of Meissen, Ludwigsburg, Frankenthal, and Höchst figures in the latter part of the 19th century. These figures were given copies of the old marks.

DRESSER (American)
A low chest of drawers in which clothing was stored, with a mirror to enable it to be used as a dressing-table.

DRESSER (English)
From the French, *dressoir*, a kind of sideboard, with open shelves behind for china.

DRESSER, CHRISTOPHER (1834–1904)
English designer who travelled in Japan in 1867 and was a noted collector of Japanese art. He started a warehouse for the sale of Japanese decoration of all kinds in 1879, but it did not survive. Dresser's Art Furniture Alliance had a showroom in New Bond Street, where most of the articles sold had been designed by him. While in Japan, Dresser collected old silver for Tiffany* of New York, whose own productions were much influenced by the Japanese style.

Dresser designed 'Clutha' glass*, made by James Couper & Sons of Glasgow, and Ault *faïence** (marked *Chr Dresser* in script) for William Ault* of Swadlincote (Burton-on-Trent) which gained a gold medal at the Chicago World's Fair of 1893. He also provided designs for pottery for the Linthorpe factory, Yorkshire, which bears the impressed mark *Chr Dresser LINTHORPE*. This factory closed in 1889.

Dresser's designs are noted for a simplicity and freedom from extraneous ornament which made him one of the precursors of the modern movement. His work is among the best of the period, and is becoming increasingly valuable.

DRESSING MIRRORS
Swing mirrors between twin posts on a solid base, used on the top of a chest of drawers or a draped dressing table. These mirrors were popular throughout most of the 19th century, but, unlike 18th-century examples, drawers were no longer provided in the base. Barley-twist supports, distantly echoing William and Mary twists, were popular about 1860. Victorian dressing mirrors are a fairly common survival.

DRESSLER, CONRAD (1856–1940)
Sculptor, designer of ceramics for architectural purposes, friend of William de Morgan* and designer of the first tunnel-kiln (1910).
See *Della Robbia ware*

DRESSLER, CONRAD (1856–1940)
Sculptor, designer of ceramics for architectural purposes, friend of William de Morgan* and designer of the first tunnel-kiln (1910). See *Della Rabbia ware*.

'DRY' BODIES
Stonewares originally developed in the last quarter of the 18th century by Josiah Wedgwood*, such as caneware*, jasper*, basaltes* and rosso antico*, which were impermeable and did not require a glaze, although those intended for holding liquids were often glazed inside. A 'dry' body developed during the 19th century was Parian*, called 'Carrara' by Wedgwood.

DUBUCAND, Alfred (b.1828)
French *Animalier* who exhibited at the *Salon* from 1867 to 1883. His work, not well known, includes horses and game birds.

DUFRÊNE, MAURICE (1876–1955)
French designer, especially of furniture, and director of La Maîtrise workshop of the Galeries Lafayette, Paris. He specialized in the interior decoration of bedrooms, boudoirs and drawing-rooms in the current fashionable taste.

DUKE & NEPHEWS, SIR JAMES (Burslem, Staffordshire)
Successors to Samuel Alcock & Co.*, manufacturers of good quality porcelain services, Parian* figures, transfer-printed* earthenware, and decorative stoneware*. They exhibited at the London Exhibition of 1862.

DUNAND, JEAN (1877–1942)
Swiss sculptor and metalworker working in Paris, a master of numerous metalworking techniques, including patination, gold and silver inlay, enamelling and lacquer, often employing several methods in the same piece. Before 1918 his *motifs* were naturalistic; afterwards they were mainly geometric. He used eggshell lacquer (i.e. lacquer with a matt, satiny surface) on furniture and metal. In the 1920s he became noted for lacquer furniture and screens. He exhibited at the 1925 Exposition, and in the 1930s designed furniture and decorative panels for the liner *Normandie*.

DURAND, FRANÇOIS (fl. mid-19th cent.)
Paris goldsmith who exhibited some extravagantly elaborate ornamental pieces in London in 1851 which were much praised. They included a large silver centrepiece.

DUXER PORZELLANMANUFAKTUR (Dux, Bohemia)
This factory, making Royal Dux porcelain, was established in 1860 by E. Eichler. It produced a wide range of ornamental wares, including portrait busts* and ornate vases. The wares were extensively exported to America, and they are not uncommon in England, but most of them are artistically negligible. Marks: *Royal Dux. Bohemia*.
Dux is now Duchov, Czechoslovakia.

DYOTT, THOMAS W. (1771–1861)
Self-styled doctor and pedlar of patent medicines who emigrated to America in 1796. He bought the Kennington Glass Works in 1831, presumably to supply his need for glass bottles for patent medicines. He became bankrupt in 1838, but the factory continued in operation as the Dyottville Glass Works. It has been especially noted for bottles and flasks.

DYSART WARE
A monochrome glazed ware developed by Wedgwood* at the request of Lord Dysart about 1870. The glaze was yellow, due to vanadium.

E

EAGLE
A common ornamental motif of the Empire style* due to its connection with Napoleon 1. It surmounts Regency mirrors, and often occurs as a decorative *motif* in the United States where it is the national emblem. The double-headed eagle is part of the arms of Austria, Prussia and Tsarist Russia.

EAGLE SLAYER, THE   See *Bell, John*

EARTHENWARE
A generic term for objects made of clay fired at a relatively low temperature which, when unglazed, remains porous. Earthenware is usually white or cream (creamware*) in colour, and it is always opaque when held to the light. During the 19th century much earthenware was decorated with transfer-printing*, generally in blue but sometimes in other monochromes, such as lilac or brick-red.

Earthenware was also extensively employed for the making of chimney-piece ornaments in the form of figures, of which the Staffordshire 'flat-backs'* are the most numerous. White or cream-coloured earthenware was also widely manufactured on the Continent under the name of *faïence-fine** in France, *Steingut** in Germany, and *terra inglese* in Italy.

EASTLAKE, CHARLES LOCK (1836–1906)
Nephew of Sir Charles Lock Eastlake (1793–1865), president of the Royal Academy and director of the National Gallery from 1855. The younger man was an architect and a designer of furniture who had considerable influence on design in Britain and America. His book, *Hints on Household Taste,* ran into many editions after its first publication in 1868. He deplored competition which led to shoddy finish, and he disliked machine manufacture, especially the facility with which designs could be altered to give rise to artificial fashion changes. Nevertheless in his furniture designs he not only drew freely on Gothic and even Japanese ornament but adapted them to machine production. He exerted his influence in favour of simplicity of design and construction, and produced largely rectilinear designs rather than the curves which had hitherto predominated. He also exerted considerable influence on the Arts and Crafts Movement*.

EASY CHAIR
The easy chair with sprung or well-padded upholstery was a product of the *bourgeois** culture of the 19th century. Nevertheless many were still based on 18th-century chairs, such as the English wing chair or the French *bergère*. The overstuffed chair or sofa with buttoned upholstery is purely a product of the 19th century, and it gave rise to many different varieties.

See *Capitonné, Capitonnage*; *Chesterfield*; *Davenport*

ÉBÉNISTE (French)
When ebony (*ébène*) was first imported into France in the 16th century it was a rare and precious wood, and only the finest craftsmen were allowed to handle it. They became known as *ébénistes,* and their work as *ébénisterie*. Later, when ebony was no longer so fashionable, the *ébéniste* made case-furniture, marquetry, and those tables decorated with such techniques as Boulle* inlay.

EASY CHAIR. Overstuffed desk chair with turned legs. English. c. 1860. *Antique Collectors' Club*

113

EASY CHAIR. An easy chair with cabriole legs. English. c. 1860. *Antique Collectors' Club*

EBONIZED FURNITURE

French, *bois noirci*. The fashion for ebonized baywood or black walnut lasted in England from about 1870 to 1885 for art furniture*, the best of which was sometimes painted. Collinson & Owen, among the foremost producers of art furniture, exhibited an ebonized cabinet at the London Exhibition of 1871. On the Continent ebonized furniture usually took the form of cabinets, and was often decorated with porcelain panels from Sèvres* or Meissen* instead of painting.

ECLECTICISM

A term frequently met in discussions of 19th-century art. Eclecticism is a philosophical principle which may be defined thus: every system which is not false is incomplete; by uniting them we shall have a complete system adequate to the totality of consciousness. When this notion was applied to the arts it provided an excuse for mixing classical and Gothic styles, and even Gothic and Oriental. 'Japanese-Gothic' was a short-lived style of the 1860s, while Minton* produced a vase of classical urn-shape on a pedestal decorated with Gothic arcades. This notion had been derided in the 18th century by Horace Walpole who, when he wanted an example of an absurdity, referred to a garden-seat 'Gothic at one end and Chinese at the other', but the eclecticists of the 19th century would have found nothing strange about it. With the 19th-century publication of books of ornament in former styles for the use of manufacturers and others, some very curious hybrids were produced by those who sought novelties for the mass-market.

See *'Chipplewhite Style'*

ÉCOLE DE PARIS

There are two meanings of this term: 1) School of modern painting by artists resident in and around Paris. André Metthey* produced a series of tin-glazed earthenware vases, plates etc. decorated by artists of this school, including Pierre Bonnard, André Derain, Odilon Redon, Georges Rouault, Kees van Dongen and Maurice Vlaminck, shown in the Salon d'Automne in 1909; 2) Style of *art nouveau* furniture from such designers as Gaillard*, Colonna* and de Feure*, who were associated with Samuel Bing*.

'EDITING' OF BRONZES

An *éditeur* in France is a publisher; an editor (as in England) is a *rédacteur*. References in some English works to the 'editing' of bronzes are usually a too literal translation from the French, and refer to the 'publishing' of limited editions. They do not necessarily mean that the founders altered or adapted the original models in any way. This misunderstanding serves to emphasize how essential it is not to assume that, because the spelling of a French word is similar to that of an English one, its meaning is also the same.

EDWARDS, ABRAHAM (1761–1840)

Clock-maker of Ashby, Mass., from about 1790 to 1820, in partnership with his younger brother, Calvin, until 1796. Edwards produced long-case clock movements which, during his brother's lifetime, were numbered, the highest number being about 600. After this date Abraham Edwards appears to have made far fewer movements, which were not numbered. The

ECLECTICISM. Oriental eclecticism in Minton's bone china. A vase in the form of an ancient Chinese jade astronomical instrument known as a *tsung*, the carved Eight Trigrams on the corners being suggested by painting, the remaining decoration inspired by Japanese *cloisonné* enamel. (The *tsung* is a cylinder, squared on the exterior, formerly used as a sighting tube.) c. 1875. *Minton Museum, Royal Doulton Tableware*

early Edwards clocks had wooden movements, but these were superseded by the use of brass.

EDWARDS, EMILY J. AND LOUISA E. (fl. 1870–1890)

Emily was a pottery artist working at Doulton's* Lambeth factory from 1872 to 1879. Her designs are incised foliate *motifs,* including acanthus* leaves, on a diapered ground. She was also responsible for training other artists. Louisa E. Edwards, at Doulton from 1873 to 1890, was responsible for floral designs in a Near Eastern manner.

EGERMANN, FRIEDRICH (1777–1864)

Egermann, whose *atelier* was in Blottendorf, near Haida, Northern Bohemia, decorated glass with enamelling somewhat in the manner of Kothgasser* in the 1830s. In 1828 he invented an opaque glass which he called Lithyalin*. This resembled a semi-precious stone in appearance with marbling or agate-like veining, and often with painting, gilding, cutting and other forms of decoration in addition. These opaque glasses were later much imitated elsewhere in Bohemia and Silesia, and influenced the making of coloured glass in France. Egermann introduced a yellow and red flashed glass* in 1820 and 1840 respectively. His business was very large and he enjoyed royal patronage.

EGGSHELL PORCELAIN

Exceptionally thin porcelain, hardly more than two layers of glaze with a paper-thin layer of porcelain between them, made in imitation of Chinese wares by Minton* and at Belleek* as well as in Japan.

EGLINTON TOURNAMENT

A revival of a medieval tournament held in 1839 in the grounds of Eglinton Castle, the seat of the Earl of Eglinton, one of the oldest English families. At a time when medieval styles and Scott's novels were fashionable the tournament proved to be a well-attended social event. The contestants, among whom was Prince Louis Napoleon, were clad in plate armour, and the whole affair was arranged with colourful

EGLINTON TOURNAMENT. A pair of figures of knights studded with semi-precious stones. The figures are reminiscent of those executed by Peter Visscher for the tomb of Maximilian in the Hofkirche, Innsbruck. German, first half of the 19th century. *Antique Collectors' Club*

medieval panoplies. Unfortunately the occasion was ruined by bad weather, the horses found the going difficult and muddy, and the sport had to be abandoned. Disraeli described it in his novel, *Endymion.* Attempts have been made to revive the medieval tournament in England in recent years.

EGYPTIAN BLACK

Staffordshire term for the type of black stoneware called basaltes* by Wedgwood*.

EGYPTIAN SERVICE

Two services with this name were made at Sèvres* in 1808. The first was presented by Napoleon to Czar Alexander I of Russia. The second was intended for the Empress Josephine but declined by her after the divorce. It later came into the possession of Louis XVIII who gave it to the Duke of Wellington. The edges of the plates are painted with Egyptian *motifs,* and the centres with scenes from the campaign of 1798. The biscuit porcelain* table-decoration in the form of sphinxes, etc., is very elaborate.

EGYPTIAN SERVICE. Two plates and a *sucrier* from the Egyptian service made by Sèvres* to the order of Napoleon I. France. c. 1812. *Christie, Manson & Woods*

EGYPTIAN STYLES

There were several periods during the 19th century when Egyptian decorative *motifs* were fashionable. The first was after Napoleon's Egyptian Campaign of 1798, when *motifs* mainly derived from the Baron Vivant Denon's sketch-book form part of the decoration of French Empire* and English Regency* furniture and interior decoration.

EHRENFELDER GLASHÜTTE See *Zitzmann, F.*

ELECTRO-PLATING

The method of covering one metal with a thin layer of another by electrical deposition, usually a copper alloy with silver. The process is similar to that employed in electrotyping*. The metal to be plated is suspended by a wire in an electrolytic solution. At the opposite pole a piece of the plating metal is immersed, and an electric current is passed between this and the object to be plated. As it does so particles of metal are detached from the plating metal, carried across to the object to be plated, and deposited on the surface. Electro-plating was discovered by George Elking-

ton*, who took out three patents in 1836, 1838, and 1840. This invention marked the beginning of the end of Sheffield plate*.

ELECTROTYPING

A process similar in principle to electro-plating* by which metal is deposited electrically on the prepared surface of a mould. An exact copy of the mould-surface is thus obtained, down to the smallest detail, and the deposit varies in thickness according to the length of time the current is allowed to flow. Usually electrotyping is employed for making comparatively small works, but specialist firms in Berlin in the middle of the 19th century—Winckelmann, Sussmann, and Möhring—all possessed troughs to contain electrolyte which were twelve feet long and proportionately wide. The process has been employed for making exact copies of *objets d'art*, i.e. as exact as the mould taken from the originals.

The process has also been used for fraudulent purposes, to take copies of such things as small bronzes. The fact that the metal has been deposited particle by particle rather than poured in liquid form is usually perceptible.

ELKINGTON & SONS (Birmingham, Warwickshire)

Firm of silversmiths founded in the 1830s by George Edward Elkington (1801–1865) and his cousin, Henry Elkington (c. 1810–1852). The firm developed the process of electro-plating* with gold and silver soon after 1840, and in 1842 Josiah Mason became a partner, which he remained until his death in 1859. The firm's registered makers' mark at this time was *EM & Co.* and this it remained until 1864. Towards 1850 the factory began to introduce an increasing amount of machine-production, including steam-presses for forming objects of nickel-silver which were then electro-plated (EPNS). During the same period the firm maintained an electro-plating workshop in Moorgate, London, which until 1849 was under the direction of Benjamin West, Jr. About the same time they began to develop the technique of electrotyping* as an alternative to the casting method of Coalbrookdale* and the Continent. In the early 1840s they had sold licences to use the patented technique of electro-plating to a number of firms abroad and in the Great Exhibition of 1851 Berlin manufacturers also exhibited examples of electrotyping on an impressive scale. Contemporary records speak of troughs 12 feet long which contained electrolyte.

By this time business had expanded considerably and during the 1850s Elkington's followed the example of the porcelain manufacturers and began to employ French artists and designers. When George Elkington died in 1865 the firm employed over 1,000 workmen. In the 1860s they began to experiment with Japanese styles, including both *champlevé* and *cloisonné* enamels*, and in the 1880s they procured

Above:
DAUM FRÈRES. Bowl with a high foot decorated with a
landscape in relief by Auguste and Antonin Daum. Signed.
France, Nancy. c. 1900. *Private Collection*

Below:
FAIRYLAND LUSTRE. Bowl on a high foot designed by Daisy
Makeig-Jones and made by Josiah Wedgwood & Sons Ltd.
Trustees of the Wedgwood Museum

COALPORT PORCELAIN. An enamelled porcelain candlestick figure in 18th-century style. c. 1830. Coalport Porcelain Factory. *Private Collection*

WORCESTER ROYAL PORCELAIN COMPANY. Nautilus shell in ivory porcelain. Worcester Royal Porcelain Company. c. 1880. *Constance Chiswell*

designs from Christopher Dresser*, who had visited Japan and who also supplied designs to Hukin & Heath* of Birmingham and Tiffany* of New York. In 1881 the factory sent technicians to Russia to make electrotyped copies of some of the important English silver in the Imperial collections in Saint Petersburg.

Since 1963 the firm has been a part of British Silverware Ltd.

ELTON, SIR EDMUND (d. 1920)

Studio-potter of Clevedon Court, Somerset, maker of art-pottery from 1880. The ware was lead-glazed, made from local clay, and decorated with coloured slips. Jugs and vases, often decorated with modelled flowers, are sometimes bizarre in shape. From 1900 glazes with a metallic appearance and a crinkled surface were produced. Mark: *ELTON* incised.

ÉMAIL OMBRANT (French)

Porcelain or pottery impressed with a design in *intaglio,* which is then covered with a coloured glaze in such a way that the surface is level. The varying depths of the design, and therefore the thickness of the glaze, yields a monochrome effect of light and shade. In principle, plaques of this kind are analogous to the lithophane*. The process was said to have been

ELTON, SIR EDMUND. Terracotta* vase by Sir Edmund Elton decorated with floral and foliate *motifs* in variously coloured slips. Mark: *ELTON* incised. *Constance Chiswell*

invented by Baron A. du Tremblay of Rubelles*, near Melun, France. In England very limited use of the Baron's patent was made by Wedgwood* among others.

EMPIRE STYLE, THE

The Empire style was a version of neo-classicism* which became popular with the installation of Napoleon 1 as Emperor of France. It was largely fostered by him, and by designers and craftsmen he employed and patronized, notably Percier and Fontaine who, in most respects, may be regarded as the real originators of the style.

In the early years of the revived classical style in the 1770s one of the principal sources of inspiration had been the newly discovered cities of Pompeii and Herculaneum. The Empire style drew its inspiration from Imperial Rome, and to a lesser extent from Greece. Colours became rich but darker, and design was rigidly symmetrical. Forms of furniture were massive and the lines straight. Gilt-bronze was not so lavishly employed as in the 18th century, but its intentions were often different, a bas-relief of classical figures, for instance, ornamenting a frieze or a cabinet door. The Roman curule chair was copied, and a chair with a low back which curves round to join the arms, known in France as '*en gondole*'. Stools were of the X-stretcher type. Bureaux and commodes were much more massive than in the 18th century and usually of a dark wood like mahogany. Beds were boat-shaped (*en bateau*), and the table was circular on a central massive pedestal. Feet were quite commonly shaped like those of animals, either the lion's paw or the deer's hoof.

Motifs of decoration were for the most part Græco-Roman or Egyptian, the latter arising not only from Napoleon's Egyptian Campaign of 1798, but from the general interest in Egypt to be noted throughout the 18th century. Predominating are pilasters, caryatids and sphinxes, but most of the ornamental *motifs* fashionable in the Rome of the Caesars, and even later, can be found from time to time. Trophies, especially trophies of arms, were very commonly

employed. So too were emblems associated with
Napoleon himself—the letter N, the eagle, the palm,
and the crowned Victory. The Empire style became
very widely popular in Europe generally, and continued to be influential until the early 1840s. One variant

became known in Germany as the Biedermeier style*,
and the English Regency style* follows it very closely.

ENAMELS AND ENAMELLING

The Gothic revival* of the 19th century favoured an
antiquarian taste which included a minor fashion for
enamels, especially that employing the *champlevé*
technique. In the 1840s the archaeologist Albert Way
contributed papers on recently excavated enamels to
the Archaeological Society, and the *De Diversis
Artibus* of Theophilus, which discusses the various
techniques of medieval art, was translated in 1847.
From 1839 onwards a number of discoveries of Celtic
and Anglo-Saxon enamel work of importance took
place at several sites. The Prince Consort, who
collected the painted enamels of Limoges*, inspired
the Worcester Royal Porcelain Company* to produce
porcelain in the Limoges style. This was done by
Thomas Bott* in greyish-white on a cobalt blue
ground. He painted female nudes in an Ettyish style
which was very popular around mid-century.

Although much of the interest was antiquarian,
and devoted to the formation of collections, contemporary artists and craftsmen turned to the medium
around mid-century, and the *Art Journal* remarked in
1851 that it had been left to modern times to produce
enamel paintings with every possible excellence.
They went on to say that the rich depths of Rembrandt
and Rubens could be perfectly rendered, together
with all their peculiarities of handling and texture.
These were painted enamels and imitated oil-paintings. They were similar to enamel painting on
porcelain except that the glaze of porcelain was
replaced by an enamel ground laid on a copper base.
Similar work was done on porcelain at Sèvres* and a
number of other factories, and probably inspired
enamelling of this kind. In 1862 Barbedienne* sent
enamel-work to the Exhibition in London, and in
1886 M. Dalpayrat of Paris began to give lessons in

painted enamels to students of the Royal College of Art where the manner of Limoges was imitated.

Towards 1900 enamelling of all kinds became popular for decorating metalwork in the *art nouveau** style. René Lalique* exhibited at the Paris Exhibition of 1900, especially flowers, butterflies, and figures in enamel, using *champlevé, cloisonné*, basse taille** and *plique-à-jour** techniques. Other Paris enamellers whose work is to be found in England are M. Thesmar and M. Gaillard, the former being noted for *plique-à-jour* work. Carl Fabergé* employed enamelling techniques frequently in much of his work. In England a flourishing school of enamellers existed in Birmingham, and the work of Alexander Fisher* is to be found in the Victoria and Albert Museum, London. He contributed several articles on the subject to *The Studio* in 1901 and 1902. At the same time a good deal of work was done for the mass-market, where cheap enamels were fused in sunken spaces obtained by stamping the metal with a steel die. A retrospective exhibition of enamels was held in Paris in 1900.

See *Enamels, Japanese*; *Jeypore enamels*; *Enamels, painted*

ENAMELS, JAPANESE

Japanese enamel-work (*Shippō*) was very popular in the West during the closing decades of the 19th century and it is not uncommon today. Despite the fact that the craft had reached China before the Ming dynasty by way of the Arabs, it was rarely practised in Japan until comparatively late in the 19th century. The old techniques were then revived, and some new ones developed, notably enamels resembling decoration in the *cloisonné** technique, but without the wires which form the *cloisons* (*mutai*). Vases of the true *cloisonné* type inspired by 18th-century Chinese work of this kind are usually coarser than those from China, and the colours are dull and opaque. This technique is termed *moriagé*. Japanese enamels had a certain amount of influence on the fashion for enamelling in the West at the end of the century.

See *Enamels and enamelling*; *Enamels, painted*.

ENAMELS, PAINTED

The metal object to be enamelled, usually of copper, is first covered with a ground of opaque white or coloured enamel of a sensible thickness. The decoration is afterwards painted with brushes, using colours which are very similar to those employed to decorate porcelain glazes, with which the work has much in common. If the painted work is subsequently covered with a layer of transparent enamel, sometimes employed on objects like gold-boxes inset with painted decoration, this addition is known as *en plein*, a technique sometimes employed by Fabergé*.

See *Basse-taille*; *Champlevé enamelling*; *Cloisonné enamels*; *Plique-à-jour enamel*

'END OF DAY' GLASS See *Friggers*

ENGINE-TURNING LATHE

A lathe which is given an eccentric motion by means of a cam so that the cutting tool is brought into contact with the surface of the rotating object only at predetermined intervals. In this way geometric patterns are cut into metal or pottery. By equipping the lathe with a guide, known as a rosette, curved and circular repetitive patterns may be cut. This lathe had been introduced into England from France by 1760, and was in use at Matthew Boulton's Soho factory. By 1764 Wedgwood had bought one for decorating vases, and this lathe is still in occasional use. During the latter part of the 19th century patterns incised into gold and silver by this lathe were covered with clear enamel in the *basse-taille** technique.

ENGRAVED GLASS

Engraving on glass is a very ancient type of decoration. It is executed with the aid of a diamond point, which gives a very fluent line similar to that of a pen on paper, or with small revolving copper wheels charged with sand or powdered emery.

ÉPERGNES (French)

A centrepiece for the dining-table sometimes with branches from which baskets or a vase of flowers can be suspended. Épergnes are to be found in silver*, Sheffield plate*, porcelain*, creamware* and glass. First made in the 18th century, they became popular in the 19th century.

EPGS

An occasional alternative to EPNS, principally employed in the early days of electro-plating. It means 'electro-plate on German silver', this term being an alternative to 'nickel silver', with the same meaning.

ENGRAVED GLASS. Glass decanter finely engraved on the wheel with *putti* amid vine-leaves and grapes. French or English. *Victoria & Albert Museum, London*

119

EPSTEIN, SIR JACOB. Bronze head entitled *Kitty* by Sir Jacob Epstein*, one of the greatest of 20th-century portrait sculptors. He freely acknowledged his debt to Rodin*. *Author*

EPNS
Electro-plating on nickel silver.

EPSTEIN, SIR JACOB (1880–1959)
Sculptor, especially of portraits. Born in Brooklyn, he did not come to England until 1905 and for many years he had little cause for gratitude to his adopted country. His work was the subject of a barrage of ignorant jeers and libellous misrepresentation, some of which may have had its origin in the anti-Semitism then current in some quarters. Nevertheless, he enjoyed considerable esteem in more informed or better-disposed circles, and he is noted for a remarkable series of portrait heads and busts in bronze. His technique was undoubtedly influenced by Rodin*, whose influence Epstein freely acknowledged, and he took great interest in certain kinds of ancient and primitive sculpture. He must undoubtedly be numbered among the leading sculptors of modern times. Several replicas of most of his bronze portraits exist.

ESCALIER, ÉLÉONORE (1827–1888)
French ceramic decorator who worked for Théodore Deck*, and from 1874 to 1888 at the Sèvres* factory. She was greatly under Japanese influence, and produced asymmetrical decorations of birds and plants. She signed in full, or with a monogram.

ESCAPEMENT, DEAD-BEAT
Type of escapement for clock movements designed to eliminate the recoil to be observed in the simpler forms of escapement, and thus to increase the accuracy of the time-keeping. It was first applied to long-case clocks in England about 1715 by George Graham and later employed in the United States by Simon Willard* of Roxbury, Mass., and others. A type of dead-beat escapement mounted in the centre of the dial was invented for small movements about 1840 by the Paris horologist, Achille Brocot. This later became popular for good quality clock-movements.

See *Clocks, French*

ÉTAGÈRE (French)
Tiers of open shelves supported on turned columns, The *étagère* takes a variety of forms; the backs of the shelves are sometimes filled in and occasionally a small enclosed cupboard forms part. They are ornamental pieces of furniture dating from the reign of Louis XVI, and are usually decorated with carving, ormolu mounts, etc. They were popular throughout the 19th century till the end of the Second Empire*.

See *Whatnot*

ETCHED GLASS
Process employed to decorate glass during the 19th century using hydrofluoric acid*. First, those parts of the surface that were to remain plain were protected with an acid-resistant varnish. The acid was then applied and the pattern etched, the depth of etching depending on the strength of the acid and the amount of time it was left in contact with the glass. The object was then washed to remove the acid, and the varnish dissolved with a solvent.

ETRURIA POTTERY (Trenton, N.J.)
Pottery operated by the Ott & Brewer Company. They made a variety of Belleek* from American materials which for lightness of body and brilliance of the glaze was extremely close to that of Ireland. The factory also produced semi-porcelain* and granite ware*, both transfer-printed* and hand-painted. An excellent Parian* ware was also made.

ETRUSCAN MAJOLICA
Name for a type of earthenware decorated with coloured glazes produced in the last decades of the 19th century at Phoenixville, Pa., by Griffen, Smith & Hill.

ÉTAGÈRE. Mahogany *étagère* with two drawers in the frieze, two lower shelves on slender turned supports, and turned feet. Louis-Philippe style*. c. 1835. *Sotheby & Co*

EVANS, DAVID (d. 1814)

Cabinet-maker of Philadelphia whose account-books are preserved by the Pennsylvania Historical Society. He made a great variety of furniture between 1774 and 1811.

EXHIBITION, INTERNATIONAL, LONDON, 1862

At the time of the Great Exhibition of 1851 it had been intended to hold major exhibitions in London at ten-year intervals. For a variety of reasons, one of which was internal trouble in Italy (the Italians being one of the exhibitors), the second Exhibition was postponed for a year, during which period the Prince Consort, who had played a major part in promoting the first Exhibition, died.

The second Exhibition was held on what are now the sites of the Natural History Museum, the Geological Museum and the Science Museum in South Kensington, and it was considerably larger than the first Exhibition of 1851. It was, however, organized on largely similar lines, and contained both manufactured goods and works of art. Many of the exhibits, intended to impress, were of an unusually large size. The changes in style which had taken place since 1851 were considerable. Morris, Marshall, Faulkner & Co.* here exhibited for the first time, and a feature of the Exhibition was a cabinet designed by William Burges* and painted by E. J. Poynter, now in the Victoria and Albert Museum, London. It also included such objects as glass designed by Philip Webb* which pointed the way towards the new styles which were to emerge with the Arts and Crafts Movement*.

Many of the objects exhibited are now in the Victoria and Albert Museum collections (then the South Kensington Museum), either acquired at the time or presented later.

EXHIBITIONS

Elsewhere in this book many references are made to the inclusion of objects and manufactures in exhibitions of one kind or another. The exhibition is of considerable value in charting the history of 19th-century decorative arts and styles, and many pieces were especially made for display, some bearing an appropriate mark. Porcelain figures have been observed with underglaze marks recording the fact that they were made for the purpose. Manufacturers attempted to outdo each other, if not in artistic value, at least in sheer size, and most exhibition pieces until 1870 and sometimes after are much larger than anything made for ordinary commercial purposes. An excellent example is the Crystal Fountain made by Osler* for the Great Exhibition of 1851.

The great international exhibitions noted below, as well as some smaller events, such as the Glasgow Exhibitions of 1901 and 1911, and that held in Brussels in 1897, profoundly affected the course of style in the arts and crafts during the second half of the century and later, and the Exposition des Arts Décoratifs et Industriels Modernes of 1925 gave its name to a style—*art déco**.

There was nothing new about trade exhibitions in the 19th century, but they became larger, international in scope, and more influential. In medieval times annual fairs were held at centres like Leipzig where merchandise of all kinds was exhibited and sold. When the first Meissen* porcelain was put on sale to the public in 1711, Leipzig fair was selected for the purpose. During the 18th century exhibitions of art became both fashionable and popular as a method of attracting clients to the artist, especially in France. Napoleon I organized an exhibition in Paris for the purpose of helping to regenerate French industry, which had declined as a consequence of the Revolution, and this was followed by others at intervals of a few years.

The idea of a great international exhibition in 1851 was suggested by the success of smaller exhibitions in France and England, and this, held in Hyde Park between May and October 1851, was by far the largest to be organized up to that time. The building which housed it, the Crystal Palace (removed after the Exhibition to a site near Sydenham in South London), was prefabricated from iron and glass, and it housed examples of the industrial arts (pottery, glass, textiles, metalwork etc.), raw materials, and machinery from almost every civilized country. The leading spirits were Prince Albert and Henry Cole* and the intention was not only to promote trade, but to elevate popular

EXHIBITIONS. Ornate cabinet in a pseudo-Louis XIV style (a kind of baroque) made by Jackson & Graham* for the Great Exhibition of 1851. It is typical of the excessively large and over-decorated contributions which manufacturers felt necessary to make at exhibitions for prestige purposes. *Illustrated Exhibitor*

taste in the arts which, by general agreement, was very poor. The Great Exhibition was followed by an exhibition (Exposition Universelle) held in the Champs Elysées, Paris, in 1855 which was the first of two such events during the reign of Napoleon III, the second held in 1867.

A second International exhibition was projected for London in 1861, but the death of the Prince Consort caused it to be postponed until 1862, when it was opened on a site now occupied by the Natural History Museum. This Exhibition, the subject of a commemorative exhibition at the Victoria and Albert Museum in 1962, revealed marked changes in fashionable taste during the preceding eleven years.

The Worcester Royal Porcelain Company* was specially commended for its Japanese-inspired porcelain at Vienna in 1873, and in 1876 the Philadelphia Centennial Exposition commemorated the signing of the Declaration of Independence in 1776. This attracted special exhibits from Japan, the pottery and porcelain section eventually finding its way to London's Victoria and Albert Museum.

In 1878 an exposition in Paris advertised France's recovery from the Franco-Prussian War of 1870 to the world. Here Worcester gained a Gold Medal for its porcelain, and its director, R. W. Binns, was awarded the Cross of the Legion of Honour. The most important of the Paris Expositions was that of 1889, celebrated by the erection of Gustave Eiffel's 1,000-ft tower. This exhibition marked the emergence of the influences which led to the modern movement, and Japanese influence was strong.

In 1893 America celebrated the passage of four centuries since its discovery by Christopher Columbus. This immense International Exposition was located in Chicago's Jackson Park, its buildings, much criticized by the architect Louis Sullivan, mainly in the neo-classical* style. Despite its international scope, the glass, china and furniture, with some notable exceptions, were in a late Victorian style which had not then been very seriously influenced by the Paris Exposition four years previously.

For sheer size in almost every aspect the largest exposition held up to that time was the Paris Exposition Universelle of 1900 where *art nouveau** (sometimes called *le style 1900*) was introduced to a larger public by Samuel Bing*. This Exposition, held on the Champ de Mars, was visited by about 50 million people—more than the entire population of France. Almost equally important was the 1902 Exposition at Turin, where the *art nouveau* styles were much in evidence, but, unlike the earlier Paris Exposition, the newer styles of the 20th century were beginning to emerge.

In 1904 the centenary of the Louisiana Purchase was commemorated by the St Louis International Exposition, and there were a number of other small fairs held in various places in the United States between this and the American entry into the First World War. After the war the most influential Exposition was held in Paris in 1925. This, the Exposition des Arts Décoratifs et Industriels Modernes, saw the crystallization of the *art déco* style.

The year 1933 saw the Chicago Fair devoted to the

EXHIBITIONS. Two pot-lids* decorated with views of the Great Exhibition, 1851, and one showing the Philadelphia Centennial Exhibition. Staffordshire. Second half of the 19th century. *Antique Collectors' Club*

EXHIBITIONS. The Belgian Section of the Great Exhibition of 1851 showing some details of the building's construction. Also shown are examples of the large quantity of sculpture for which the Exhibition was noted. After the *Illustrated Exhibitor*

EXHIBITIONS. Italian carved walnut cabinet made by A. Barbetti of Siena and shown at the Great Exhibition of 1851. *Victoria & Albert Museum, London*

theme 'A Century of Progress', but the New York World's Fair of 1939 was overshadowed by the Second World War.

Catalogues and contemporary descriptions and criticisms of these exhibitions still exist, although many are difficult to find. They give, however, a great deal of useful information about the arts and crafts of the period.

EXPRESSIONISM (German)
A contributing style to *art déco*. A form of art in which the artist endeavours to express his emotions by distorting form, or by emphasis on, or choice of, colour. The style is largely a modern phenomenon, more specifically German, although one of the best known Expressionist artists, Edvard Munch, was Norwegian, and Vincent Van Gogh was Dutch. In the early years of the 20th century the German Expressionist School divided into two streams—Die Brücke (The Bridge) and Der Blaue Reiter (The Blue Rider). The first was to some extent influenced by the fashion for negro and primitive art, and included such artists as Kirchner, Nolde, Pechstein, Schmidt-Rottluff and Heckel. The Blaue Reiter group was founded in 1911, and it took its name from the title of one of Kandinsky's paintings. Kandinsky founded the group in association with Franz Marc and August Macke, and it was later joined by Paul Klee and some of the French Cubists. The Blaue Reiter School is the more abstract of the two.

See *Sezession*; *Jugendstil, der*

EYLES, HENRY (fl. 1850–1860)
English furniture designer and manufacturer of Bath, Somerset, who exhibited in the Great Exhibition of 1851. He specialized in highly carved and over-decorated work. Chairs inset with portraits of the Queen and the Prince Consort, shown in the Exhibition, are now in the Victoria and Albert Museum, London.

F

FABERGÉ, PETER CARL (1848–1920)

Russian Court jeweller, goldsmith, and designer. Of Huguenot descent, Fabergé's family settled in Saint Petersburg early in the 19th century, and his father, Gustave, became a noted jeweller and dealer in *objets d'art* of fine quality, establishing his business in 1842. This his son, Peter Carl, inherited. By 1870 the latter was already manufacturing works of the kind now associated with his name, and he successfully exhibited in the Pan-Russian Exhibition in Moscow of 1882. Not only was he patronized by the Russian royal house, but he became noted internationally for his work, which was sought by princes and wealthy aristocrats and industrialists in an age when expensive trifles were lavished on the courtesans of the time.

Fabergé was especially noted for the taste and skill with which he combined a variety of precious and semi-precious materials. He rarely or never made anything himself, but acted as designer, his designs being carried out in a number of workshops by talented craftsmen supervised by workmasters. His own workshop, where he was later assisted by his sons, was overseen by a Swiss, François Birbaum. Of the independent workshops, the best known is that supervised by the workmaster Michael Perchin

FABERGÉ, PETER CARL. Pair of Fabergé* glass flasks engraved in the revived rococo* style, the necks silver-mounted, and the stoppers mounted with strapwork. Probably Bohemian glass* mounted in Moscow. c. 1900. *Constance Chiswell*

(1860–1903). The marks used by these workmasters are listed in the standard work on this subject, A. Kenneth Snowman's *The Art of Carl Fabergé*. There were a number of branch establishments—Moscow, Kiev, Odessa, and from 1903 to 1915, London. The output of the various workshops until the Revolution in 1917 was considerable, and only the more important objects can be regarded as excessively rare.

Until 1893 the principal influence on Fabergé's work was French. Much of it is in the rococo style of Louis XV, although the richer neo-classical* *motifs* of Louis XVI also occur. The workmanship is comparable to that of 18th-century French work. The Far East also provided inspiration, not only in the designs employed, but in the use of such materials as jade (nephrite and jadeite, as well as chloromelanite not ordinarily used there). Many works, such as the small hardstone figures of Moujiks and other peasant types, are entirely Russian in inspiration. They may have been suggested by peasant figures made by the Moscow porcelain factories.

Among his products which owe little or nothing to outside influence are such novelties as objects in miniature, like sedan-chairs, pieces of furniture, and flowers of hardstone in rock-crystal vases. Belonging to this category are the Easter Eggs which also seem to have been suggested by those produced by Russian and Polish porcelain factories. Fabergé made his first egg in 1884 for the Czar Alexander III to present to the Czarina. The custom was continued by Nicholas II when he acceded in 1894. The earliest examples are realistic eggs; the later specimens are increasingly elaborate variations on an ovoid theme.

Fabergé was the last of the Court goldsmiths in the tradition of those of France, or of Dinglinger in Saxony. He made not only *objets d'art* but a great deal of jewellery which was fashionable at the time, and has enjoyed considerable esteem since.

FACTORIES AND MASS PRODUCTION

There is a common belief that the factory—Blake's 'dark Satanic mill'—only antedates the 19th century by one or two decades, and that the Industrial Revolution started with Wedgwood*, Matthew Boulton, and the invention of the power-loom. Actually

FACTORIES AND MASS PRODUCTION.
Rocking-chair made from prefabricated
turned and machine-cut parts. English,
c. 1865. *Antique Collectors' Club*

factories for large-scale production were a feature of
Roman economic life, especially in the pottery
industry and although concrete evidence is lacunary,
no doubt in the metalworking industries also. Pottery
marked with the name of the factory, and bronze
saucepans with the trade-mark of a swan are both
known, and the arming of the Legions with standard
equipment suggests a fairly advanced factory
organization.

Factories for the making of works of art were
founded by Colbert for Louis XIV in the 17th century
which firmly established the position of France as the
arbiter of artistic fashion in Europe for the next three
centuries. Nevertheless, until the end of the 18th
century the practice of breaking down the manufacture of objects into a large number of separate
operations carried out by a different operative was
largely unknown in Europe, although it already
existed in the Chinese porcelain industry. In general
the reason for this was the difficulty of making a large
number of parts separately which could be brought
together to fit accurately. Towards the end of the 18th
century we see Sheffield plate* and silver made by
Boulton and some of the major silversmiths produced
in a few simple parts, some by casting and stamping,
which were accurate enough to be put together
without much trouble. However, true mass-production was to a far greater extent a product of the pottery
industry, especially the factory of Wedgwood, where
operations tended to multiply and objects were put
together from a series of simple parts. It is interesting
to remember that a very similar sequence of operations was employed at the Chinese Imperial factory
of Ching-tê Chên which had been described in detail
by some of the Jesuit missionaries, among them Père
du Halde, whose book in English translation was in
Josiah Wedgwood's library.

Throughout the 18th century all kinds of machinery
were invented to manufacture the parts of objects,
rather than complete objects. The establishment of
factories for assembling the parts followed inevitably.
A further step, which had taken place by the time the
century was half completed, was the buying of
manufactured parts from several outside sources.
These were then put together into a complete object,
in much the same way as the automobile is produced
today. In the 19th century, clocks were often made in
this way, and Singer mass-produced sewing machines.

The effect of this system of manufacture was to
produce workpeople who were able to put things
together from manufactured parts, even to make
minor adjustments necessary to make the parts fit
accurately, but most of them were incapable of
making the parts in the absence of a machine to do
the work for them, and therefore quite unable to
produce the complete object. The pottery industry
has retained a far larger number of skilled operations,
and therefore more skilled craftsmen, than the
metalworking industries. Woodworking also has
always needed a nucleus of skilled operatives, but in
general the system has led to the creation of a large
class of unskilled and semi-skilled workpeople when
compared with the craftsmen of former times, many
of whom could produce objects of fine quality from
the raw materials.

This has presented some difficult problems on a
number of levels, not least the unsatisfactory nature
of semi-skilled work of this kind to many people, and
the problem was debated in the 19th century by
William Morris* and others. The difference in artistic
value between an object made in a factory and
designed to be mass-produced and one made entirely
by hand was also recognized, as the demand for the
work of the craftsman and studio potter will witness.
Various attempts have been made to provide a
satisfactory solution, especially since 1920 (see *Functionalism*), but the emphasis of informed taste today
is still on the products of the individual craftsman.

FAÏENCE (French)
A type of earthenware covered with a glaze opacified
with tin oxide, thus concealing the colour of the body
underneath, which can be seen on any unglazed part.
This type of ware was introduced from Italy (where
these wares are known as *maiolica*) during the 16th
century, and employed during the 19th century partly
for close copies of early work. The glaze is being used
today in France for reproductions of much-sought
earlier wares, such as those of the Veuve Perrin at
Marseille and of Montpellier which, when genuinely
old, sell for very high prices.

FAÏENCE-FINE (French)
Creamware* in the English manner; white or cream-
coloured earthenware covered with a transparent
glaze. Also known in France as *faïence anglaise* and in
Germany as *Steingut*.

FAÏENCE-FINE. Square dish of creamware* (*faïence-fine*) decorated with a transfer-print* representing 'Southill, Angleterre, Residence of the Comte de Bedford'. Creil*. Early 19th century. *Victoria & Albert Museum, London*

FAIRINGS

The name given to small, brightly-coloured porcelain groups, or small boxes for keeping pins (see *Pin-boxes*), made in Germany of hard paste porcelain by Conta & Böhme*. Fairings, so called because they could either be bought for a few pence at fairs or were given away at sideshows as prizes, were made in large quantities and given painted captions in black or gilt. Most of them were comparatively poor in quality in comparison with the ordinary commercial production of many factories, but occasional specimens are of much better quality, and these are often titled in French, as though made for that market.

The subjects of these small groups are usually slightly indelicate, at least by Victorian standards. Most of them deal with courtship, marriage and domestic life. Typical of the titles are 'The last in bed to put out the light' which depicts a couple scrambling into bed; 'Shall we sleep first, or how?' of a couple about to get into bed; 'Coming home from the seaside', a family of bears in human dress; and many more in the same vein. There are others in which the maid is to be seen, partially undressed, in compromising situations. Many of the titles strongly suggest that someone whose first language was German was responsible. Some of the subjects have been traced back to English comic papers of the 1860s and '70s, and it is assumed that the English importers supplied the manufacturers with inspiration.

Fairings have been much sought by collectors in recent years, and high prices paid for rare models. Reproductions have appeared on the market, and the novice collector would be well advised to deal with a reliable source.

FAIRY LAMPS

Samuel Clarke was a maker of night-lights and took out his first patent in 1857 for a candle or night-light inserted into a metal or glass base, the flame of which was protected by a dome-shaped glass or porcelain shade. These early lamps, like the 'Cricklite' with clear glass shades mounted on a column which he patented in the early 1860s, were comparatively plain and of good quality. The fairy lamps were more decorative, and Clarke obtained his shades from such makers as Webb of Stourbridge*, Osler* of Birmingham, and the Worcester Royal Porcelain Company*. From illuminating the bedroom or darkened passageway, by 1886 the new Fairy lamps became a very popular type of decoration for the dinner table, being placed at intervals between the appointments. They consisted of an ornamental glass base with a night-light in the centre, covered by a decorative glass shade, with flowers and ferns occupying the space between the outer rim of the stand and the central shade. The shades were of art glass*, including 'Queen's Burmese', now very rare. These, made by Thomas Webb of Stourbridge about 1887 utilized the American 'Burmese' glass patent. Fairy lamps soon became more widely popular than merely for table decoration, and they were successfully used to decorate garden fêtes held in the evening. They were also adapted to chandeliers* and the decoration of wall mirrors. Clarke's various trade names for his products, and the trade mark of a fairy with a wand, were moulded on to the box. Webb's name sometimes occurs on the 'Burmese' glass shades. Despite its enormous popularity the fairy lamp was doomed before its career was far advanced by electric lighting, and as decoration it hardly survived the 19th century.

FAIRY LAMPS. Very rare 'Fairy Pyramid' night-light stand with moulded clear glass drip-pans by Samuel Clarke. The shades of Queen's Burmese glass are by Thomas Webb & Sons*. They are of pink shading to pale yellow, painted with berries and blue flowers. The central flower-holder, and the two additional holders are similarly painted. Marks: *Thos. Webb & Sons, Queen's Burmese ware patented* and *S. Clarke's Fairy patent Trade Mark*. c. 1887. *Sotheby & Co*

FAIRYLAND LUSTRE

A decorative kind of bone-china designed for Wedgwood by Daisy Makeig-Jones* between October 1914 and 1931. The ware is so called from the nature of the subject-matter of the decoration, which consists of fairies, goblins, elves, and the appurtenances of fairyland. A type of ware, also by her, depicting dragons in a Chinese style, is usually referred to as dragon lustre. The predominant features of the ware are an irregular blue ground, which also imitates the effect of Chinese 'powder-blue', or 'bleu soufflé', and a markedly iridescent glaze. These characteristics were copied by other manufacturers in Staffordshire at the time, in conjunction with other subjects of decoration, such as flowers (see *Carlton Ware Ltd*).

The turn of the century saw a fashion for children's books about fairies and elves of a kind which, to Daisy Makeig-Jones, must have formed a considerable part of her childhood literature, and her own designs are perceptibly influenced by earlier illustrations to this kind of book. The best known of these illustrators, Edmund Dulac, seems undoubtedly one such source of inspiration. The output of Fairyland lustre was not great at the time, and it has since become a much sought collector's item.

FALCON GLASS WORKS   See *Pellatt, Apsley*

FAMILLE VERTE, FAMILLE ROSE ETC.

Terms first applied to the overglaze decoration of Chinese porcelain in the middle of the 19th century by Jacquemart. He grouped the wares into 'families' characterized by the predominant colour—*verte* (green), *rose* (a colour varying from pink to mauve), *jaune* (yellow), and *noire* (black). On some early 19th-century export wares the first two palettes are combined, when they are termed *rose-verte*. True *famille verte* and *famille rose* palettes do not occur on 19th-century porcelain unless it copies earlier wares. *Famille jaune* and *famille noire* are both very rare, although the latter has been forged.

FANCY GLASS

Alternative term for art glass*

FAULKNER, CHARLES J., KATE AND LUCY
(fl. 1855–1898)

Charles Faulkner was an Oxford friend of William Morris* and Burne-Jones* who became one of the founding partners of Morris, Marshall, Faulkner & Co.* The partnership continued until 1875, when Morris went on alone. Kate Faulkner (d. 1898), Charles's sister, painted tiles, worked in *gesso* and designed wallpaper. Lucy, another sister, painted tiles and published *The Drawing Room, its decoration and furniture* in 1878.

FAUTEUIL VOLTAIRE

An easy chair of polished wood with open arms introduced during the reign of Louis-Philippe (1830-

1848). It bore little resemblance to the preceding style, and can properly be classified as French Biedermeier*.

FAUVISM

Movement in art which originated in Paris in the early years of the present century. The group, which included Matisse, Marquet, Vlaminck, Rouault, and Dérain, exhibited in the Salon d'Automne of 1905, when the art-critic, Louis Vauxcelles, referred to their work collectively as a *cage aux fauves* (a den of wild beasts). The name 'Fauves' was adopted by the group. It only held together for three years, but it was extremely influential, especially on German Expressionism* and some pre-Revolutionary Russian painting. The strong, flat colours of Fauvist painting had considerable effect on modern art generally.

See *Armory Show, The (1913)*

'FAVRILE'

A trade name used for products marketed by L. C. Tiffany*. Best known, and most sought, is a type of iridescent glass, usually in a well-marked *art nouveaue* style, developed by Tiffany in 1893. Both colours and appearance are variable. Iridescence alone was not a novelty at the time of its introduction. Austrian glass, and some porcelain glazes, had both been made in iridescent forms since the 1870s in the case of glass, and even earlier for porcelain. What appears to be unique in the case of 'Favrile' glass is the method adopted for inducing iridescence.

FEATHER PICTURES

Pictures formed from feathers glued to a paper background. The usual subjects are birds, especially ducks, or flowers, the birds with a background indicated in water-colour or *gouache*. As amateur productions feather pictures date from about 1820. After 1850 some were made professionally.

FEDERAL STYLE

American style in the arts current from about 1780 to 1830. It largely corresponds to the neo-classical* and Empire* periods in Europe. The basis of the Federal style is classical, and its modifications reflect the influence of Adam, Hepplewhite, Sheraton, and Regency* in England, and Louis XVI, Directoire, Empire* and possibly Restoration in France. Furniture in the Federal style is predominantly mahogany in its early phases and rosewood later. Satinwood was replaced by woods like curly maple, and fruit wood was not uncommonly employed for less expensive work. Veneering was used very commonly, as in Europe, and brass and ormulu mounts and fittings followed European practice. Ornamental *motifs* include the characteristic classical vocabulary of the period—lion paws, acanthus* leaves, lyres, swags and festoons*, scrolls at the ends of couches and beds. The eagle also occurs more commonly than in Europe. Modifications to European fashions and styles were made by such fine craftsmen as Duncan Phyfe*, and the style is also reflected in contemporary silver designs.

See *Biedermeier style*

FELIX SUMMERLY'S ART MANUFACTURE   See *Summerly, Felix*

FELL, THOMAS & CO. (Newcastle-on-Tyne, Northumberland)

Makers of earthenware at St Peter's Pottery founded about 1817. The mark until 1830 is *FELL*, after which it becomes *FELL & CO,* sometimes in conjunction with an anchor and cable, or the Arms of Newcastle. The collectable wares are principally blue and white transfer-printed* wares, of which the 'Tomb' pattern, based on Charlotte weeping over the tomb of Werther, and the 'Woodman' pattern pirated from an earlier Spode* pattern, are the most sought.

FELSPAR PORCELAIN

Type of porcelain devised by Josiah Spode* about 1820 which included a proportion of feldspathic rock (Cornish stone). It was marked with the name 'Spode' and the words 'Felspar Porcelain' transfer-printed*.

FENTON, CHRISTOPHER WEBBER (1806–1865)

American potter who was responsible for much of the output of the Bennington, Vermont, factory between 1846 and 1858. Fenton had marked ability as a promoter and administrator, as well as being a practical potter.

FESTOONS

Series of pendant loops of drapery or flowers painted, carved, or applied in the form of a metal mount, to be found decorating neo-classical*, Empire*, Regency*, and Federal* furniture. They are also employed decoratively on works in other media. The origin is in Greek and Roman art.

FEUILLÂTRE, EUGÈNE (1870–1916)

French sculptor, goldsmith, and enameller. First employed by René Lalique*, he later set up on his own account and specialized in *plique-à-jour* work, i.e. translucent enamels from which the metal background has been removed. He also experimented successfully with the application of enamels to silver and platinum. He was awarded prizes at the Paris Exposition of 1900 and the Turin Exposition of 1902.

FEUILLET (Paris)

Porcelain in imitation of '*vieux Sèvres*'* and marked *FEUILLET*, or the letter F within the opposed *L*'s monogram of Sèvres*, have been observed without any definite information about the maker. The probability is that the porcelain was purchased 'in white' from Limoges* and painted in a decorating studio of this name about the first quarter of the 19th century.

See *Paris decorating studios*

FIELDING & CO. LTD., S. (Stoke-on-Trent, Staffordshire)

Earthenware manufacturers of Devon Pottery since 1879. Their early productions include 'Majolica' of good quality, but from 1913 they have been noted for decorative earthenware marketed under the name of 'Crown Devon'. They also produced a lustre ware in the *art déco** style.

FINCH, ALFRED WILLIAM (1854–1930)

Painter and potter of English origin, born in Brussels. He studied at the Brussels Academy from 1878 to 1880. In 1884 he founded *Le Vingt* group of artist-craftsmen. He made *art nouveau** earthenware in the *Keramis* studio of Boch Frères*, and in 1897 he went to Finland to run the Borga workshops. His products were sold in Paris at La Maison Moderne*. In 1902 he became a teacher of ceramics at the Central School of Arts and Crafts, Helsinki. Incised marks, *IRIS* and *AWF*.

FINE ARTS

The term 'fine arts' is usually employed to denote painting, sculpture and architecture. The remaining arts are usually termed 'decorative' or 'applied'. In the 19th century the term 'industrial arts' was commonly used, a handbook with this title discussing pottery, enamels, metalwork etc. being published by the South Kensington Museum, London. This schism between the two categories was something which had grown up slowly over the preceding two or three centuries. Renaissance artists kept studios with pupils and assistants where they executed commissions for paintings, made decorated furniture, produced bronzes and other kinds of sculpture, and generally were prepared to provide most kinds of decoration.

The division between the two was well-marked in England by the 18th century, at a time when in France painters like Boucher and sculptors like Falconet were happy to provide material for the Sèvres* porcelain factory, and the great 18th-century furniture craftsmen like Boulle*, Riesener, or Benemann ranked with fashionable painters of the day.

By the time Victoria came to the throne, the fact that Britain was ahead of the Continent in industrializing the making of objects formerly the province of the craftsman accentuated the division to a point where it was almost complete. In these days only the better quality products of the 19th century have survived, so the picture is incomplete, but the decline in public taste had already become apparent to certain sections of contemporary thought before 1851. The Great Exhibition of that year, which marks the low-water mark of European taste, was actually an attempt by the Prince Consort, aided by Henry Cole* and others, to raise taste by providing suitable models for manufacture. This led to the establishment of the South Kensington Museum, which was intended to assist designers and manufacturers.

William Morris*, his friends and the Arts and Crafts Movement*, were all concerned to reunite the fine and applied arts, which is one reason why Morris, Burges*, and others designed furniture to be decorated by painting. An increasing understanding of Oriental art, especially that of Japan, brought the West into contact with civilizations where painting, pottery, lacquer and such crafts as jade-carving, enjoyed equal status, where every piece of porcelain was unique, and where accidental effects in pottery glazes were esteemed. Although Oriental art had been imported into Europe for centuries, it was only in the last decades of the 19th century and the early years of the 20th that any serious attempt was made to understand it.

To a public accustomed to the meticulously detailed naturalistic painting of the middle decades of the 19th century, to the series of carefully controlled replicas produced by the porcelain factories, and the exactness and precision of machine production generally, this new aesthetic was a distinct and salutary shock. The growth of photography, especially of portraiture, seemed to some to spell the end of painting, and some miniaturists abandoned their profession to colour portrait photographs. Eadweard Muybridge (1830–1904) published a detailed series of photographs of the horse in motion in 1878 which proved conclusively that no artist had ever succeeded in capturing the exact sequence of movements, and their depiction of race-horses was positively ludicrous. This kind of development increasingly turned the artist from the kind of painting popular 30 years earlier. In France the Impressionists, partly inspired by Turner and partly by the Japanese wood-block print, began to represent new aspects of nature, and the public grew increasingly confused. The artists of the *art nouveau** style simply denied that any kind of distinction between the fine and applied arts existed, and awarded them equal rank.

The line of demarcation today between the so-called 'fine' arts and the decorative arts is growing faint. It is now a period when a Chinese vase can fetch as much at auction as an important Old Master painting, or where a pair of figures by a modern porcelain factory can realize more than the cost of a work by some fashionable modern painter. Nevertheless, the division played an important part in thinking about art in the 19th century, and was part of the motivating force behind the thinking of Morris and his friends.

FIRE-GILDING

Also known as 'mercuric gilding'. Powdered gold is mixed with mercury to form an amalgam, or pasty mass, which can be applied with a brush to a metal or porcelain surface. This is followed by heating to about 360° centigrade to volatilize the mercury which leaves the gold adherent. The fumes are exceedingly poisonous, and the process is not suitable for amateur use. It was superseded for metals by electro-gilding in the 1840s.

FISHER, ALEXANDER (1864–1936)

English painter, sculptor and silversmith, who studied at the South Kensington Schools. About 1880 he was asked by a friend to repair a valuable antique enamel box, and this turned his attention to the problems of enamelling*. He subsequently journeyed to Italy and Paris to study this ancient craft more closely. In 1885 he was a member of the first small class established in South Kensington to study enamelling. He later taught at the Finsbury and Regent Street Art Schools, also accepting pupils at a studio which he set up in London. At this time the old craft of enamelling on metal had become almost a lost art, and a great deal of research had to be undertaken to trace information in old books which were mainly French, since Limoges* had been one of the most important enamelling centres in Europe. When Fisher started to enamel metalwork suitable enamels were unprocurable, and those employed to decorate pottery glazes required considerable modification. He therefore had to make and grind his own.

By the 1890s Fisher was specializing in enamels. He exhibited with the Arts and Crafts Society*, and, yielding to the persuasion of friends, he sent enamels to the Royal Academy in 1893, one of which was exhibited, despite the fact that nothing in this medium had previously been accepted. He also wrote extensively on the craft.

In the ancient world the Celts were highly skilled enamellers on bronze and copper, and Celtic *motifs* may be traced in *art nouveau**. The trade name 'Cymric'*, employed by Liberty & Co.*, was derived from a word of Celtic origin, and the style seems to some extent to have derived inspiration from Fisher's use of old interlacing Celtic *motifs*, principally based on the circle, known as *entrelacs*, which were popular for some Arts and Crafts jewellery. This, too, affected the *art nouveau* style generally.

The most difficult metal technically to enamel was silver, because the legal alloy in England contained too small a quantity of base metal. This was a difficulty experienced by Fabergé* in making enamelled silver for the English market, which he later overcame. The most suitable metals are copper and bronze. Fisher employed all these metals. He also employed layers of foil underneath transparent enamels which not only gave an illusion of depth but also enhanced the colour. This was an ancient technique for improving colour and appearance of 'paste' jewels first employed by the Romans in glass mosaics. Fisher's enamels are represented in the Victoria and Albert Museum, London.

FLAMBÉ GLAZES

Chinese glazes dating from the 11th century for which

the colouring agent was copper oxide fired in a reducing atmosphere, i.e. one in which the kiln atmosphere is largely carbon monoxide instead of oxygen. In these circumstances copper oxide yields red, instead of the more usual green or blue which results from interaction with oxygen. The Chinese employed the technique during the 18th century for covering vases and bowls with a colour termed ox-blood (sang-de-boeuf*) the glaze of which was often slightly streaked or suffused with blue. These glazes were termed *flambés* in France, and much prized among collectors during the 19th century. European potters were unable to master the secret until the technique was discovered by Bernard Moore*, and the glaze was later employed by Doulton* under the name of 'Sung'.

FLASHED GLASS

Like cased glass* the flashed variety was first made in Bohemia early in the 19th century. Not unlike cased glass in appearance, the coloured layer is no more than a film and only very light engraving was necessary or possible. The usual colour was a ruby red, although green and yellow occur occasionally. Table-glass of this kind was introduced into England from Bohemia in the 1840s, and the process was being employed by the glass-engraver, Thomas Wood of Stourbridge, by 1850. The colouring oxide was applied to the surface of the vessel and developed in a muffle

FLASHED GLASS. Crystal glass goblet, the bowl ground with circular medallions flashed with ruby glass, each medallion engraved with a miniature subject, the incisions passing through the flashing to the clear glass below. Bohemian. c. 1830. *Private collection*

kiln, being almost indistinguishable from a transparent or translucent enamel. This technique was also employed for flashing, or staining, press-moulded* or mould-blown glass, and was one of the factors which led to the neglect of cased glass in the 1870s. It is a typical example of the way in which technical progress was used to produce cheap substitutes for high quality work of craftsmanship, which, in consequence, fell out of fashion.

See *Cased glass*; *Reproductions and copies*

'FLAT-BACKS'

Name given to earthenware figures principally made in Staffordshire during the 19th century which are very summarily finished at the back. The finest porcelain figures of the 18th century were those modelled in the round by men like J. J. Kändler (see *Meissen*); deterioration in quality set in later when subjects began to be closely copied from engravings, since the modeller had to imagine what he could not see, and modelling was sketchy at the back in consequence. Most of the better quality 19th-century earthenware figures were also modelled 'in the round', even if sometimes crudely, but a vast number of those manufactured after about 1850 by firms like Sampson Smith* were only slightly modelled at the back.

Most of these figures were taken from a published source of some kind, and many of the best and most sought were derived from music-covers. Nearly all of them were produced in three-piece moulds, one fairly deep piece for the front, one nearly flat shallow piece for the back, and one convex mould to close the base. These were squeeze moulds into which a bat (a thin slab of soft clay) was pressed and removed when firm enough. The pieces were luted together with an adhesive made of clay diluted with water (slip), and then sponged with underglaze blue (where appropriate), covered with raw glaze, and fired, leaving the final touches of colour to be added overglaze. Additional parts not included in the principal mould were moulded separately and attached before firing.

Figures in the round were either hand-modelled throughout (a tedious and fairly expensive process unless the modelling was extremely crude) or the method adopted by the porcelain factories was used, by which the parts of the figure (arms, legs, torso, head, attributes, etc.) were moulded separately and joined together before firing. This was a highly-skilled process, and only the best figures were made in this way. Inspection will always show which method was employed.

FLAT-CHASING

The decoration of metal surfaces with linear ornament by indenting the lines with a punch and a light hammer. Especially employed for Sheffield plate* where engraving was impossible.

FLAXMAN, JOHN (1755–1826)

English neo-classical* sculptor and designer whose

father was a maker of plaster casts. He studied at the Academy Schools and was employed from 1775 onwards by Josiah Wedgwood* especially as a designer of jasper* ware, and was responsible for some of the most important examples of the period. In 1787 he left for Rome, where he remained until 1794. During this time he continued to provide Wedgwood with designs and to oversee other modellers working in Rome for the factory. He was elected to the Royal Academy in 1790, and in the 19th century he began to design silver for Rundell, Bridge & Rundell*. His most important work was the Trafalgar vase of 1805, replicas of which were given to the admirals and captains serving in the battle by Lloyd's Patriotic Fund. As a lecturer Flaxman had considerable influence on his students at the Academy Schools, and his lectures on sculpture were published.

FLINT GLASS
Glass in the composition of which the silica content is derived from calcined flint, and the flux is lead oxide. It is therefore a type of lead glass.

'FLINT JACK' (EDWARD SIMPSON) (b. 1815)
Forger of prehistoric and Roman antiquities, born in Whitby, Yorkshire. As a boy he was employed by a geologist, Dr Young, and accompanied his master on fossil-hunting expeditions. Later he collected fossils and sold them to dealers, and began to develop skill in the faking of flints, starting with simple things like arrow-heads and becoming more ambitious. With growing skill he turned his attention to pottery, and made crude urns which passed as 'prehistoric' among uninformed collectors. He made a Roman breast-plate from an old tea-tray and fabricated a Roman milestone. Eventually he formed an association with a Colchester dealer, and together they supplied the London trade. 'Jack' always claimed that some of his work had been sold to the British Museum, and he demonstrated his skill in the art of making flint tools and weapons before the Geologists' Association in 1862, making arrow-heads on the spot and selling them to his audience at sixpence apiece.

FLIP-TOP TABLE
A card-table or breakfast-table with a single leaf which folds back and rests on a leg pulled out from the back.

FLORENTINE MOSAIC
Small pieces of variously coloured stones embedded in a cement matrix so as to form pictorial subjects of one kind or another—usually floral and plant forms, birds, figures, etc. Quality is variable, but the best specimens are made from the smallest stones. The English Derbyshire marble* mosaics, while similar in technique, are much coarser in quality. Mosaics of this kind were usually employed for table-tops, but also for such objects of *vertu* as decorative boxes.

FLOWERS, PORCELAIN
The application of flowers to porcelain vases, dessert-baskets and other decorative items continued to be popular during the 19th century, especially at Coalport* and Meissen*. A number of smaller factories, like Grainger's Worcester*, also employed modelled flowers decoratively. For the most part these were of an indeterminate species, although Coalport seems to have made a speciality of more accurately modelled flowers in the 1830s and 1840s. In modern times flower-modelling was revived by the late Dorothy Doughty*, both as a decorative adjunct to her birds and as separate models. The Dorothy Doughty flowers are exact botanical specimens arranged in the form of sprays. The flowers themselves are made petal by petal in plaster press-moulds and then assembled in rest-moulds before being built up into sprays for attachment to the bases. Some of the flowers and plants, such as the hogweed to which the chiff chaff is clinging, are a very considerable technical achievement of a kind which has only been attempted within recent years.

FOLEY CHINA WORKS   See *E. Brain & Co.*

FOLEY POTTERY (Fenton, Staffordshire)
Founded in 1820 by the firm of Elkin, Knight and Bridgwood to make earthenware, to act as china-dealers and to manufacture ceramic colours to the trade. The pottery made a great deal of blue printed earthenware. A series of 'Irish Scenery' is sought after. The Etruscan series of 1827–40 depicts classical subjects. They also produced the 'Willow'* and 'Broseley' pattern. The usual mark was *E.K.B.*

FOLLOT, PAUL (1877–1941)
French interior decorator and furniture designer who worked in both the *art nouveau*￼* and *art déco*￼* styles. In 1923 he took over the Pomone workshop in the Bon Marché store, and was responsible for the Pomone stand at the 1925 Exposition. He was co-director (with S. Chermayeff) of Waring & Gillow's* French furniture department. Follot's designs were noted for the use of fine materials and expensive techniques. His furniture was decorated with marquetry, lacquer surfaces and bronzework. He was influenced by *art nouveau*, neo-rococo, and Cubism,* and specialized in luxury furniture produced mainly by hand.

FONDEURS (French)
Bronze-founders. Producers of small and large sculpture, clock cases, furniture-mounts etc. by means of casting, either in the *cire perdue*￼* (lost wax) (see *Casting*) technique, or by sand-casting. In general, the sculptor did little more than furnish the model and, on the more important objects, they did some of the cleaning up of the cast where necessary, and perhaps some of the chiselling of detail. On furniture-mounts and clock cases, chiselling was undertaken

by craftsmen termed *ciseleurs*. The *fondeurs* of Paris were especially skilled in the colouring (patination) of bronzes, either by modifying the alloy itself or by treating the surface. A common 19th-century alloy contained 80 per cent copper, 17 per cent zinc and 3 per cent of tin and lead. This is almost indistinguishable from brass. The Parisians were highly skilled casters, and they made little use of the process of electrotyping introduced in the 1840s. This was developed in Birmingham by Elkington*, and in Berlin by Geiss*. For many years they resisted using zinc* (spelter), which had also been developed in Berlin as a casting material. This was both cheaper and easier to handle, but it also provided a strong temptation to produce inferior work. France had a long tradition of bronze-casting going back to the 16th century, when their skill even surprised Cellini into words of unusual praise, and they have succeeded in sustaining this reputation ever since. In England casting of excellent quality, both small and large, was done by the Coalbrookdale* foundry during the middle decades of the 19th century. In modern times distinguished casting of art objects has been done by the firm of Morris Singer.

See *Barbedienne, F*; *Casting*; *Susse Frères*

FONTAINEBLEAU (Seine-et-Marne)
A factory for the manufacture of hard-paste porcelain* was founded here in 1795, and in 1832 it was owned by Baruch Weil, with a decorating studio in Paris. What may have been an offshoot of this factory was bought by Jacob and Mardochée Petit* in 1830. Noted for decorative porcelain, it became extremely popular.

FONTHILL ABBEY   See *Beckford, William*

FOOTBATHS
A popular item in the Victorian household, the footbath was usually made in Staffordshire of ironstone china* and decorated with underglaze blue transfer-printing*. Today they are sought as *jardinières*.

FOREST FOLK
A popular printed decoration (including such animals as squirrels), for 'Queensware'* plates, which was designed for Josiah Wedgwood & Sons* by Victor Skellern in 1934. It marked the reintroduction of transfer-printing.

FORGERIES
Beginning about 1840 the 19th century saw the rise to popularity of antique collecting. As prices began to escalate at the sales of the day so forgeries started increasingly to trouble the market. Forged paintings largely date from the 18th century, when Englishmen made the Grand Tour, and bought 'classical' antiquities and Italian 'Renaissance' paintings especially produced for them. In the 19th century forgers turned

their attention to works of craftsmanship, and some of the larger porcelain factories did work which was almost indistinguishable in intent from forgery. It is said of John Rose of Coalport* that he called his factory manager into the office and showed him a vase, Rose told him that being dissatisfied with the accuracy of the factory's reproductions, he had bought a Sèvres vase at a London sale for them to copy. The manager turned up the base, looking for secret marks, and then said, 'We made this one about a year ago'. Actually no English reproduction of '*vieux Sèvres*' made in the 19th century is deceptive to those acquainted with genuine work, but obviously it was at the time. It is always much more difficult to detect a forgery made in one's own time because although the forger has been unable to free himself from the contemporary artistic idiom, this inability is shared by the person examining the object. With the lapse of 50 or 100 years this idiom becomes obvious, often startlingly so. It is nearly always easy to detect 19th-century forgeries and reproductions of 16th-century Italian *maiolica* from the characteristics of the drawing, especially figure-drawing, which patently belongs to the later period. It must be remembered that standards of scholarship in the 19th century were not high. Books were inadequately and sparsely illustrated, and there were few museum collections in the modern sense to act as a source of comparison. The forger's task, therefore, was relatively easy, and his work did not even have to be very accurate. The Tiara of Saitaphernes, a gold crown made by Isaac Rouchomowsky* of Odessa, was decorated with ornament drawn from actual examples which were several centuries apart; yet it deceived a famous Continental museum. Mistakes of this kind were common, and although most 19th-century forgeries have long since been detected, some of them still occasionally emerge from hiding from time to time in the hope of fooling more of the people for some of the time. So many 19th-century *objets d'art* were closely based on those of former times that it is sometimes a little difficult to be sure whether a particular object was intended as a forgery or not. Further information about specific forgeries is included under appropriate headings.

See *Reproductions and copies*

FOUNDER'S SAND   See *Casting*

FOURDINOIS, ALEXANDRE GEORGES (fl. from 1850)
Maker of luxury furniture in Paris. He specialized in highly decorative cabinets in a 17th-century style similar to those described in the inventories of Mazarin, Louis XIV etc. An example is in the collections of the Bethnal Green Museum, London. Fourdinois displayed an enormous chimney-piece of oak with gilt-bronze mounts and carving in the manner of Donatello at the Paris Exposition of 1855, as well as a cabinet in the style of Jean Goujon, and another made of ebony inset with painted enamel.

FRAKTURSCHRIFTEN (German)

The Germans who emigrated to Pennsylvania brought with them the custom of framed and elaborately decorated certificates of birth, baptism, and marriage to hang on the wall. The certificates were called *Taufscheine*. They were decorated with similar *motifs* to those to be found on the painted chests (see *Pennsylvania-German*) somewhat in the manner of medieval illuminated manuscripts. The language is German, and the lettering Gothic, the alphabet customary in Germany until recent years. After 1800 certificates were obtainable in printed form with blanks for filling in the necessary information, although the decoration was still painted by hand. In addition to these certificates, certain pictures, such as portraits of national heroes in the same style, are also referred to as Fraktur.

FRATIN, CHRISTOPHER (1800–1864)

French *Animalier** sculptor, the son of a taxidermist, who studied under Géricault, and exhibited in the *Salon* from 1831. He was awarded a medal at the Great Exhibition of 1851. Fratin published his own bronzes which he sent to be cast in the form of plaster models to a number of *fondeurs**, including the small Paris foundry of E. Quesnol, and especially to Susse Frères*. A small number were cast by Alfred Daubré after 1855, who also published some of Fratin's work. Fratin enjoyed considerable success both at home and abroad. His style is romantic, and the surface treatment of his subjects owes some of its features to the influence of his master, Géricault. His most impressive models are those of horses, but his deer, cattle and game are also lively models, well-observed and of excellent quality. Of his large sculpture, *The Two Eagles Guarding Prey* of 1850 is in Central Park, New York. The only signature known is FRATIN incised in small capitals, or an impressed stamp in lieu.

FREMIET, EMMANUEL (1824–1910)

French *Animalier** sculptor who studied under his uncle François Rude (1784–1855). His animal sculpture dates from 1843, and he began with studies of cats and dogs, going on to horses, both individual and in groups. His equestrian sculpture includes a mounted portrait of Napoleon III. Among his later work may be found some very pleasant models of domestic animals with their young. No doubt introduced into influential circles by his uncle, one of the greatest sculptors in France, Fremiet eventually became, like A. L. Barye*, a Professor of Drawing at the Natural History Museum, a Grand Officer of the Légion d'Honneur, and an Associate of the British Royal Academy.

Among his monumental sculptures may be numbered the well-known Jeanne d'Arc just off the rue de Rivoli, Paris. His signature is E. FREMIET incised in large capitals. Sometimes an impressed stamp is also found on a few examples.

FRENCH STYLE, THE

Term used during the 19th century to include furniture in the Renaissance, Louis XIV and Louis XV styles, which were commonly confused then, and are often confused today. Although all these styles influenced English furniture designs at the time when they were current, there are no exact equivalents. Some Charles II and William-and-Mary chairs are closely based on Louis XIV prototypes and the most characteristic furniture of Chippendale was derived from the styles of Louis XV.

Generally, however, French traditions are very different from those of England, particularly in cabinet-work, and the large expensively decorated 17th-century French cabinet has no English counterpart. Some American cabinets which feature a curved broken pediment come nearer to their source of inspiration, but they are still a long way from it. The Louis XV style is more or less synonymous with rococo (see *Rococo, revived*), and its principal and most obvious feature is asymmetry of ornament. This was current from soon after 1725 almost to the death of Louis in 1774, but the ornament of some examples of 19th-century furniture said to be in this style are symmetrical, and much more obviously in the following neo-classical style of Louis XVI. The 19th-century revived rococo style in any medium is usually a long way from its source of inspiration unless it is a direct copy, but perhaps porcelain comes closer to the spirit of the 18th century than anything else.

In the case of furniture the French style of the 18th

FREMIET, EMMANUEL. Two studies of cats in bronze by Emmanuel Fremiet*. Third quarter of the 19th century. *Antique Collectors' Club*

FREMIET, EMMANUEL. Bronze hound by
Emmanuel Fremiet*, showing
signature on the base. Third quarter of
the 19th century. *Author*

century, which was the best known and most sought
by wealthy collectors in the 19th, principally employed
veneers of exotic woods, marquetry, and gilt-bronze
mounts. The fashion for solid wood was not imported
from England until comparatively late in the century.
Chairs and settees were made of carved wood, painted
and gilt.

The use of porcelain plaques for table-tops and the
decoration of furniture generally began in the 1760s
and continued until the Revolution, but the plaques
were small and not excessively numerous. The use of
painted plaques in the 19th century, when not
employed for the decoration of replicas, or near-
replicas, of 18th-century pieces, tended to be exces-

FRENCH STYLE, THE. Small *bureau à
cylindre* in mahogany with ormolu*
mounts, in the revived rococo* or Louis
Quinze style. Painted decoration signed
by J. Hausse. Late 19th century.
Sotheby & Co

sively painted and were often inset in cabinets of
ebonized wood. Eighteenth-century plaques were
largely of floral subjects, and were made at Sèvres*.
Nineteenth-century plaques commonly depicted figure-subjects, and often came from Germany.

The Louis XVI style was revived in France in the
1850s, and it became very popular in America from
about 1860 to 1900. It never became very popular in
England, where neo-Gothic* was firmly entrenched.

FRENCH STYLE, THE. A low easy chair,
the back with carved cresting, the
fluted, turned legs deriving from Louis
XVI chairs, although the proportions
are far from being those of the 18th
century. English. c. 1855. *Antique
Collectors' Club*

FRENCH STYLE, THE. Large French *bureau-plat* with gilt-
bronze mounts in the neo-classical* or revived Louis Seize
style. Mid-19th century. *Sotheby & Co*

135

FRENCH STYLE, THE. Victorian *fauteuil* (chair with open arms) in the revived rococo style of c. 1850. Its Gallic appearance would have been even stronger had the front legs been of the cabriole type instead of turned, as may sometimes be found. *Antique Collectors' Club*

FRIGGERS. A group of birds of glass wrought at the lamp, and spun glass simulating a fountain. Probably West of England. Mid-19th century. *Victoria & Albert Museum, London*

The Louis XVI style was originally the product of the revived interest in classical styles which stemmed from the attention widely given to the excavations at Pompeii and Herculaneum in the 1750s. Therefore symmetry returned to favour. Instead of the cabriole leg the straight, tapering leg is to be found on chairs and tables. The curved top to tables and commodes popular with rococo designers disappeared, to be replaced by straight lines. 19th-century furniture follows these general principles.

FRIGGERS

Glass-makers' term for such novelties as walking-sticks, pipes, small animals, shoes etc. made 'at the lamp', i.e. by manipulating glass softened in the flame of a bunsen burner or some similar source of heat. These friggers could either be made as part of the man's job, or for himself from glass left over in the crucible at the end of the day. In the latter case objects of this kind are often termed 'end of day'* glass, and were the workman's perquisites. The American equivalent term is 'off-hand'* glass.

FRITSCHE, WILHELM (fl. 1870–1880)

Bohemian glass engraver who settled at Stourbridge and worked for Thomas Webb & Sons*. He engraved floral and figure subjects in the *Hochschnitt*＊ technique.

FRODSHAM & COMPANY, CHARLES (London)

English makers of fine quality clocks, watches, and barometers, who took over the business of Vulliamy* & Son, clock-makers to the Royal family since the days of George III, in 1854. The firm is still in existence.

FRIGGERS. Friggers, otherwise known as 'end of day glass' or, in the U.S.A., 'off-hand' glass. English, factory unknown. Late 19th, early 20th century. *Antique Collectors' Club*

FRIGGERS. Glass ship of clear and blue glass. Bristol. First quarter of the 19th century. *Victoria & Albert Museum, London*

FROMENT-MEURICE, F. D. (1802–1855)

Maker of decorative silver and other metalwork, often ornamented with precious and semi-precious stones and enamels. Froment-Meurice was among the most notable of French silversmiths in the middle years of the century, and he was especially in demand for the execution of presentation pieces, of which he displayed a number at the Great Exhibition of 1851. An unusual exhibit here was a casket of cast-iron with chiselled foliate decoration made for the Comte de Paris, and a toilet-table for the Duchess of Parma. His workshops in Paris also produced jewellery, especially diamond and enamel brooches in the form of bouquets of flowers, as well as objects of carved ivory. The styles employed included Moorish, Byzantine, Renaissance, and Gothic.

FROSTED GLASS

Glass with a matt, more or less opaque outer surface made by exposing the surface to the vapour of hydrofluoric acid* or, after 1870, by sand-blasting*.

FRUIT, GLASS

Glass fruit for decorative purposes was first made in Venice in the 18th century by Guiseppe Briati, and revived in the 19th century at Stourbridge and elsewhere. It was usually arranged in a basket accompanied by glass leaves as a sideboard or table decoration.

FULLER, LOÏE

Veil dancer of American origin who lived and worked in Paris at the turn of the century. It has been said that she profoundly revolutionized the technique of the dance, and Paul Roche designed a theatre for her in the *art nouveau** style for the Paris Exposition of 1900, which has since been destroyed. The exterior walls were made to simulate in plaster the veils which she swirled and draped around herself. No dancer of the time inspired as many artists as Loïe Fuller. Bronze statuettes, drawings, and posters all testify to this. Raoul Larche produced a bronze statuette with swirling veil that recalls a series of biscuit porcelain* figures, called *Le Jeu d'Echarpe* modelled for Sèvres by Léonard*. These were probably intended to represent Loïe Fuller.

FUMED OAK

Oak which has been exposed to the fumes of ammonia in an enclosed chamber. When freshly-cut its colour is a greyish-brown which fades to a yellow-brown. A popular furniture wood since the 1890s.

See *Heal, Sir Ambrose*; *Limed oak*

FUNCTIONALISM

Even during the most florid days of revived historic styles in the 19th century there were signs that a reaction was gathering strength. Both Morris* and Eastlake* were firmly opposed to an excess of ornament, especially ornament which had the effect

FULLER, LOÏE. Gilt-bronze figure of Loïe Fuller* wrapped in the draperies for which she became famous. This model was also made in *pâte-de-verre** by the brothers Daum* of Nancy. c. 1900. *Sotheby & Co*

of concealing the basic lines of an object. The notion of honest simplification existed in Europe in the furniture of Michael Thonet* and the silver of Christopher Dresser*, and in America, in the furniture of the Shakers*. It could also be seen in America in the 1880s with the increasing popularity of Mission* style furniture, and in 1896 Eugene Klapp and Herbert Stone of Chicago began the publication of a magazine called *The House Beautiful* which exhorted its readers to end vulgar display. The Paris-trained Chicago architect Louis Sullivan, who greatly influenced Frank Lloyd Wright, brought similar ideas of clean, uncluttered lines to contemporary architecture, and inspired a certain amount of contemporary furniture design. The movement, as it developed in Europe, became based on such dicta as 'form follows function' and 'less is more'. It centred on the Bauhaus*, a school of design at Weimar started by Van der Velde* but taken over in 1919 by Walter Gropius, the painters Paul Klee, Wassily Kandinsky, Laszlo Moholy-Nagy, and the architect and furniture designer, Marcel Breuer*, among others, with the object of combining the teaching of art with that of craft. The school was widely influential, and it founded what came to be called the International Style.

The style is noted for an absence of bright colours, severe geometric ornament, glossy, highly polished surfaces, straight lines and box-like forms, plywood and metal tubing, and the occasional use of silver and chromium plated metal as an addition to furniture. Typical of the period is a chair of cane and chromium-plated tubing designed by Marcel Breuer, and the 'Barcelona' chair of Mies van der Rohe*.

The Bauhaus was closed by the Nazis in 1933, and several of its guiding lights, including Gropius, Moholy-Nagy, and Breuer, emigrated to America.

See *Art déco*; *Bauhaus*

FURNITURE, CAST-IRON

Cast-iron furniture was principally made for use outdoors, and it became especially popular in the United States. A cast-iron chair was illustrated by J. C. Loudon in his *Encyclopedia of Cottage, Farm, and Villa Architecture and Furniture* (London, 1833), who stated that it could be produced more cheaply than a comparable wooden chair. Cast-iron furniture made in England was displayed at the Great Exhibition, 1851, and the same Exhibition showed furniture made of twisted wire which included a table and plant-stands. The popularity of cast-iron in the United States dated from the 1850s either in a rustic style, imitating untrimmed tree-branches, or in a mixture of revived rococo* and neo-Gothic* styles.

See *Coalbrookdale Ironworks*

FURNITURE, CHINESE

Chinese furniture and furniture made in China for the Western market (the two things are not quite the same), were imported into Europe throughout the 19th century, but especially during the second half of that period. In many ways social conditions in China were not unlike those in Europe. The 19th century was essentially a period during which the *bourgeoisie* became increasingly influential, and, like the *bourgeoisie* of Europe, they demanded an excess of ornament as an outward and visible sign of their wealth and influence. This is perceptible not only in furniture, where carving tends to be excessive in comparison with earlier periods, but also in such fields as porcelain, where over-decoration is common. The best of 19th-century furniture, like the best porcelain, copied the work of earlier periods more or less faithfully, but examples are not often seen in Europe because they did not appeal to merchants responsible for the trade. A 19th-century feature is the setting of marble panels in the backs and arms of chairs and in the tops of stands intended for flower-pots. Stands were made with the Western market in mind, so the low stand is much more likely to belong to the middle of the century and the high stand to the last decades, since they would then have blended best with the fashionable interior style. Much of the exported furniture was produced in and around Shanghai where, towards the end of the century, elaborate inlays of mother-of-pearl became a speciality. This was a period, in fact, when demand in Europe for Chinese furniture was at its greatest and most examples are either heavily carved, decorated with jade mounts, or otherwise exotically contrived to appeal to Western demand, but much at variance with classic Chinese taste. Many examples of this period are based, either in form or decoration, on European furniture.

The most numerous imports from China seem to have been plant-stands; these are a common survival. Chairs, also, are fairly common, usually in pairs. Like the stands, they vary in quality. Tables are of several kinds: the low *K'ang* table (a table used by persons reclining on the platform termed a *K'ang*) often does duty as a coffee-table; the altar table (higher than the average European table) has scrolled ends, the scroll-table (for unrolling pictorial scrolls) is roughly the same shape and height, but its ends are plain. Display

FURNITURE, CAST-IRON. Table and two chairs of painted cast-iron from the Coalbrookdale Ironworks*, Ironbridge, Shropshire. *Ironbridge Gorge Museum Trust*

tables and cabinets were especially made for the European market, and therefore are strongly influenced by Western forms. The Chinese wardrobe, and similar furniture, while rarely exported to the West, seems to have been a more likely source of inspiration for Godwin's* Anglo-Japanese furniture* than any-thing imported from Japan. The true explanation of confusions of this kind is that, at this time, Japanese art was not only regarded as more important than Chinese, but that most people could not see any essential difference between the two.

See *Japanese furniture*

G

GAILLARD, EUGÈNE (1862–1933)
French furniture designer who worked for Samuel
Bing* and helped to design his Pavilion at the
Exposition of 1900. He specialized in bedroom and
dining-room *suites* with abstract decoration.

GAJ, PIETRO (fl. mid 19th century)
Gaj, who described himself as a sculptor, came to
England in 1862 to see the Exhibition, and visited
Wedgwood*, offering the secret of the early 16th-
century Gubbio ruby lustre*. He was thought to be
responsible for the red and yellow lustres employed
by the Carocci Company, but despite extensive trials
his formulae could not be made to work, and for this
reason Wedgwood refused to pay the final instalment
of the sum agreed. There is a reproduction Gubbio
plate made about this time in the Wedgwood
Museum.

GALLÉ, ÉMILE (1846–1904)
Gallé was born at Nancy in Lorraine, the son of
Charles Gallé, a retailer of glassware and *faïence*
who also designed some of the wares he sold. Charles
Gallé obtained his glass from a factory at Miesanthal
and his *faïence* from Saint-Clément, where the
tradition of manufacture dated back to the middle of
the 18th century. Émile studied for several years at
the Weimar Art School and in 1874 he was given
control of the family business. Early in life Émile had
developed a passion for botany, which emerges in his
later work as a manufacturer and designer. He
devoted himself primarily to glass and furniture, his
faïence being comparatively rare. The latter can be
identified from a Lorraine cross lightly incised into
the tin-enamel glaze, and his initial is also impressed
or incised.

Among the earliest examples of Gallé glass are a
series of vessels termed *verreries parlantes* which were
inspired by *Symbolistes** like Verlaine and Mallarmé.
Gallé took quotations from the *Symbolistes* as a source
of inspiration which suggested the form and decoration of the glass, and the quotation was engraved on
it. A good deal of his early work was enamelled,
influenced by Venetian and Islamic work rather than
German. Some examples were included in the Paris

Exposition of 1878, about the same time as Brocard*
was producing his imitations of medieval Islamic
glass. Later Gallé produced enamelled glass commercially, and turned for his more important work to
moulded or blown glass, usually vases, cased in one or
more layers of differently coloured glass which were
cut through to form the design (cameo glass*). These
were shown at the Paris Exposition of 1889. The best
were carved mostly by hand, but they were also
produced commercially by removing some of the
unwanted glass with the aid of hydrofluoric acid*.
These are coarser in quality.

The rapid rise to popularity of Japanese art* during
the second half of the 19th century influenced Gallé
from the 1880s onwards. He was also one of the
precursors of *art nouveau**, and his contribution to the
Paris Exposition of 1900 was almost entirely in this
style. He exerted considerable influence on other
makers of decorative glass, notably the Daum*
brothers, and he was one of the founders of the École
de Nancy in 1903. This was an association of
craftsmen and designers who shared similar ideas.

Glass made by Gallé bears his signature in relief;
that made in his factory to his designs is marked
'*cristallerie d'Émile Gallé*'. A collection of the work of
those included in the École de Nancy is preserved in
the Museum there.

GALLIA WARE
Type of plated ware introduced by Charles Christoflé*
at the Paris Exposition of 1900. Georges de Feure*
and Eugene Colonna* designed objects in the *art
nouveau** style to be carried out in Gallia plate.

GALUSHA, ELIJAH (1804–1871)
Furniture-maker of Troy, N.Y., in the revived
rococo* and Renaissance styles. He used mahogany
and rosewood principally, and much of his work was
noted for finely carved details.

GALVANOPLASTIC
A mid-century term for electrotyping.

**GAMBART, JEAN JOSEPH ERNEST THÉO-
DORE (1814–1902)**
'Prince' of the Victorian art world, Gambart was born

at Courtrai, in Belgium, to a French-speaking, cultured, Jewish family whose livelihood came from printing and book-selling.

Ernest Gambart, as he was known, came to England in 1840 to sell French engravings for the firm of Goupil.

His next job was colouring English sporting prints, then in great demand, for the firm of McLean, and by 1842 he was in a firm dealing in imported and English prints. Very soon he became a print publisher, and by 1847 was issuing prints after J. R. Herbert, Ansdell, Etty, Landseer, and others, and his first print after Frith.

In a changing art world, where the dealer was taking the place of the patron, and modern art taking the place of the old masters, Gambart became a dealer in the works of contemporary painters, and put on various exhibitions of their work, although his first exhibition, in 1849, was of *Animalier* bronzes by Pierre Jules Mène.

By 1851, the year of the Great Exhibition, Gambart was acting as catalyst to sell modern art to the new rich from the Midlands. Dealing in the works of Holman Hunt, the Rossettis, Madox Brown, Millais etc., he became friend and *confidant* of many of the artists. Artists now also sold the reproduction copyrights of their pictures and, until the camera ruined their trade, made extra money by this means.

Gambart himself prospered and acquired a very large collection of contemporary works and became an almost legendary figure, living in style and giving luxurious parties on his estates at Spa and Nice, to which latter he had retired.

From his collection here he lent works of art to hang on the walls of Queen Victoria's rooms during her visits to Nice. His friends were the leading artists, writers, and musicians of the day, among them being Rosa Bonheur and Alma Tadema. Heaped with honour, he became Spanish Vice-Consul at Nice.

GARDEN ORNAMENTS

Ornaments in the form of figures, urns on pedestals, tubs for shrubs and small trees, bird-baths, feeding-tables, fountains, and sun-dials, were made of artificial stone by Coade & Sealy* and their successors, of terracotta* and stoneware* by Doulton*, Minton*, and several other factories, and of Parian* porcelain by Minton and others.

The tendency for garden ornaments to be neo-classical* in style probably reflects the Victorian love of the nude* female figure more than the persistence of the style, since the makers employed Greek and Roman models and most of these garden ornaments were goddesses or mythological personages such as Andromeda. A child with a dog, however, was a popular subject in some gardens, usually a pair, one a boy and the other a girl. These are sometimes to be found cast in lead, although most lead figures are either earlier, or more recent copies. Parian figures of

this kind were employed to decorate the conservatory rather than the garden.

Other garden ornaments include the amphora, usually antique and excavated either in Italy or Spain and imported for the purpose. The Iberian amphora (a large pointed wine-jar of terracotta) was not an uncommon survival in either Italy or Spain. The base and part of a fluted column as a garden ornament was inherited from the 18th century, when it was made in miniature in jasper* by Wedgwood*. These things continued to be made until the end of the century, but the vogue declined thereafter.

GARDET, GEORGES (1863–1939)

French *Animalier*, who studied under Fremiet* at the École des Beaux-Arts and began to exhibit in the *Salon* in 1883. He supplied a number of designs for porcelain figures to Sèvres*, and specialized in such wild animals as tigers, lions, and panthers.

GARIBALDI, GIUSEPPE (1807–1882)

Italian patriot, liberator, and guerrilla leader. He spent most of his life fighting for the freedom and unity of Italy against Austria and the power of the Papal States. He became dictator of Sicily and, crossing to the mainland, expelled Francis II from Naples, joining his army to that of Victor Emmanuel, King of Sardinia and Italy, when the latter invaded the kingdom of Naples. A hero to the Italian people, Garibaldi was very popular in England, and a number of portrait figures were made in Staffordshire, usually titled with the name 'Garibaldi'. At least 16 models were issued in 1864, the year in which he visited England.

GARRARD & CO.

Noted London firm of silversmiths. The business was inherited by Robert Garrard in 1802, and when he died in 1818, he was succeeded by his son, also Robert (1793–1887), and two other sons, James and Sebastian. The firm succeeded Rundell, Bridge & Rundell*

GARRARD & CO. Combined centrepiece and four-division inkstand. Made by Robert Garrard. London hall-mark for 1878. *Antique Collectors' Club*

GARRARD & CO. Centrepiece in silver-gilt designed by Prince Albert, made by Robert Garrard and exhibited at the Annual Exhibition of British Manufactures, 1849. It bears the Arms of Queen Victoria and Prince Albert, and there are models of the Queen's four favourite dogs on the base. *By gracious permission of Her Majesty the Queen*

as Royal Goldsmiths in 1830. Garrard's were extensively patronized by European royalty, and the Prince Consort provided them with some designs. They specialized in centrepieces, race-cups, and presentation silver. Their chief designer until 1858 was Edmund Cotterill* (1790–1858) whose style was extremely naturalistic. Garrard's opened a factory and showrooms in Albemarle Street, W. London, in 1911. The factory was closed in 1952.

GAUDI, ANTONI (1852–1926)
Spanish architect and designer, the son of a coppersmith, Gaudi was trained as an architect in Barcelona where virtually all of his work is to be found. His early work was in a revived Gothic style of an extremely individual kind, but the Guell residence, built in 1885–1889 for his patron Eusebio Guell, a wealthy industrialist, was an early example of *art nouveau**; as important, in its way, as a key work as Mackmurdo's* title page for *Wren's City Churches*. Much of Gaudi's architecture with its wavy outlines has a nightmarish quality, and he carried over its violent asymmetry to furniture designed for Guell.

GAUGUIN, JEAN-RENÉ (1881–1961)
Son of Paul Gauguin. He became a modeller and chief designer to the Danish porcelain factory of Bing & Grondahl*, where he was noted for his figures of animals.

GAUGUIN, PAUL (1848–1903)
Painter and potter, who studied under Chaplet*. Gauguin's pottery, of which fewer than a hundred pieces are known, takes the form of vases and jugs, unglazed, decorated with moulded figures, or vases thrown on the wheel and glazed and decorated with landscapes and figures in coloured glazes. Some later examples are decorated with designs in painted slips and *sgraffito** techniques. This work is sometimes signed *P. Gauguin*, and some also bears the mark of Chaplet or Haviland*.

GAUL, AUGUST (1869–1921)
German *Animalier** sculptor whose models were made in metal and pottery. Pottery models were produced by the Teplitz Fachschule, Bohemia. Incised signature, *A. Gaul*.

GEISS, M.
A *fondeur** in Berlin, Geiss may have been the first to use zinc (spelter*) for the production of decorative statuary, figurines and architectural metalwork. He also invented a process of bronzing the casts to imitate the much more expensive objects of bronze. Bronzed-zinc casts could be produced cheaply. Manufacture later became widespread, and enabled the makers to supply a much larger market with decorative metalwork. Geiss exhibited in London in 1851, and in the same exhibition a large group of an *Amazon On Horseback Attacked By A Tiger*, a sculpture of 1839 by Professor A. Kiss, was copied in zinc by the sculptor and bronzed by Geiss.

GELATINE MOULDING
Method of making plaster-casts from a mould lined with gelatine.
See *Vincent, Hippolyte*

GÉLY, LÉONARD
Decorator at the Sèvres* factory who used the *pâte-sur-pâte** technique. A specimen of his work exhibited at the Paris Exposition of 1855 is now in the Bethnal Green Museum, London.

GERMAN SILVER
Nickel-silver; an alloy of copper, zinc, and nickel first produced in 1849. Chinese *paktong* is a natural alloy of these metals imported during the 19th century. This alloy was much used as a base for electro-plating, and objects thus treated are usually stamped EPNS or EPGS.

GIBSON, JOHN, R. A. (1790–1866)
English neo-classical* sculptor, Gibson was apprenticed to a firm of cabinet-makers, but was brought to the attention of Francey's, the Liverpool statuaries and makers of architectural ornament in marble and stucco. Offered an apprenticeship in their studios, he submitted work to the Royal Academy in 1816 which was accepted. In the following year he travelled to

London with introductions to Lord Brougham and the auctioneer, Christie. There is evidence that he entered the studio of Nollekens for a short time. He arrived in Rome in 1817, where he was befriended by Canova* who took him as a pupil, and later by Thorwaldsen*, who was then in Rome. Although his growing success strongly suggested a return to London, he nevertheless preferred to live in Rome, continuing to send work for exhibition to the Academy, which elected him an Associate in 1833 and an Academician in 1838. He returned to London in 1844 and executed a statue of Queen Victoria, one of the first statues to which he added touches of colour, a departure which some critics found to be shocking. He was once more in England in 1850 to execute another statue of Queen Victoria for the rebuilt Houses of Parliament, and between this year and 1857 he completed the *Tinted Venus**. He died in Rome in 1866. The *Tinted Venus* was sold at Christie's in 1890 realizing £1,837.

GIEN (Loiret, Orléans)

Manufacturers of *faïence** and *faïence-fine** established in 1822. The *faïence-fine* with transparent lead glaze is often transfer-printed*. Table-services including large tureens, and inkstands, are a frequent survival. From about the middle of the 19th century when 18th-century Rouen *faïence* began to be keenly sought by collectors, Gien was one of the factories producing a tin-enamel glazed ware painted in the so-called *style rayonnant*. This comprises a central medallion from which radiates the *lambrequin* ornament popular in the 1730s. To a lesser extent tin-enamelled ware in the styles of Italian *maiolica** was also produced.

From 1864 marked wares bear a castle and the word *Gien* under it.

GILDING ON POTTERY AND PORCELAIN

The standard 19th-century method of gilding good quality wares was to apply an amalgam of mercury and powdered gold. This could be painted on. When fired at the appropriate temperature the mercury was driven off as a gas, leaving the gold behind to be burnished. Acid gilding*, introduced in 1863, was a technique of decorating porcelain with matt gilding by etching a pattern lightly into the glaze with hydrofluoric acid* followed by gilding over the roughened area. It was usually combined with burnished gilding. Relief gilding, done in imitation of the old honey gold of 18th-century Sèvres* porcelain, is often found on later copies of these wares. In the 19th century it was the product of first applying enamel in relief where the gilding was required, and then covering it with gold.

'Bright gold', introduced about 1860, did not require burnishing, and could be applied with greater facility than by earlier techniques, but it easily wore off and was generally unsatisfactory for good quality wares. Both transfers and rubber-stamps have been employed to gild pottery and porcelain.

GILLERLAND, JOHN (fl. 1815–1850)

Glass-maker noted for the quality of his work. His decanters and wine glasses were said to be fully equal in quality to those of Ireland. Until 1823 he was with the New England Glass Company* of Cambridge, Mass. In this year he left to join the South Ferry Glass Works, Brooklyn, which produced some of the best American cut-glass in the 1840s and 1850s.

GILLINDER, WILLIAM T. (1823– ?)

Born at Gateshead-on-Tyne, first worked in a glasshouse at the age of eight. He migrated to the Birmingham-Stourbridge area, and in 1851 was secretary to the National Flint Glass Makers' Society of Great Britain and Ireland. In 1853 he emigrated to America to take a position of considerable technical responsibility with the New England Glass Company of Cambridge (Mass.). He did not stay at Cambridge for long, but began to move about the country, going to Pittsburgh, St Louis, Baltimore, and Philadelphia, making a brief stay in each place until finally, in 1861, he bought a small factory in Philadelphia, the Franklin Flint Glass Works. In 1863 he took into partnership a potter, Edwin Bennett. The factory made principally utility wares and moulded and cut-glass. They acquired another factory, the Philadelphia Flint Glass Works, where they made fancy coloured glass, silvered glass, door-knobs and table-glass. They also acquired showrooms in New York. Gillinder bought out Bennett in 1867, and in 1871 his two sons took over the business.

In 1876 the Company created a sensation by erecting their own building at the Centennial Exhibition containing a complete factory which sold its products as souvenirs. Paperweights moulded of clear glass in such forms as Lincoln and Washington were part of the production. Some time after 1890 the pressed ware department merged with the U.S. Glass Company. In 1912 the three sons of William T. Gillinder withdrew from the firm to found Gillinder Brothers Inc. at Port Jervis, New York. The Philadelphia company closed in 1930; the latter firm still exists.

Perhaps the most sought objects made during the lifetime of William T. Gillinder were *millefiori** paperweights which are much sought.

GILLOT, F. (Paris)

Manufacturers of gilt clock cases and matching candelabra of good quality during the Second Empire*. They also made figures and groups of figures.

GILLOW (Lancaster and London)

Firm of furniture-makers founded by Robert Gillow in Lancaster in 1695. It was transferred to London in 1761. Many of the more prominent Victorian designers worked for Gillow, including Pugin*, Talbert*,

GILLOW. Marquetry cabinet made by
Gillow* and shown in the 1867 London
Exhibition. *Victoria & Albert Museum,
London*

and Colcutt*. They also worked in a variety of styles,
and many of the better quality reproductions of 18th-
century furniture, especially Chippendale, came from
here. In the 1880s they were attracted to the Arts and
Crafts Movement*, and produced furniture in the
new styles. Gillow also enjoyed considerable success
at the Paris Exposition of 1900. Their furniture was
always of good materials and workmanship, but
design rarely broke new ground of importance. They
enjoyed an excellent reputation among the prosperous
bourgeoisie which they possessed enough commercial
wisdom not to disturb by provoking the strong
prejudices against change that characterized the class
and the time.

After about 1820 much of their production was
stamped *Gillow* and a serial number. The firm bought
Collinson & Lock* in 1897, and amalgamated with S.
J. Waring to become Waring & Gillow* in 1900.

GIMSON, ERNEST (1864–1920)
English architect and furniture designer associated
with the Arts and Crafts Movement*. He later
became one of the most noted of the artist craftsmen
of the time. Gimson was a member of the Arts and
Crafts Exhibition Society* and a partner in the firm
of Kenton & Co.* until it was wound up, when he
joined Sidney and Ernest Barnsley (the former also a
partner in Kenton & Co.) in setting up a workshop in
Cirencester, Gloucestershire. Gimson's furniture depended largely on the natural beauty of the wood.
Ornament was very restrained, with the occasional
use of inlays of ebony, mother-of-pearl and bone.

GIN-FLASKS, STONEWARE
These have become a popular collector's item during
the last twenty years or so. Stoneware* was a pottery

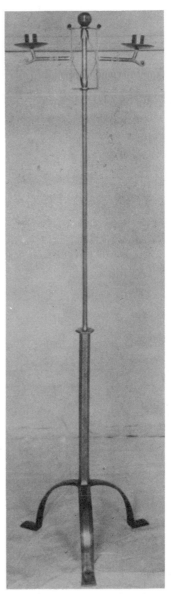

GIMSON, ERNEST. Steel candle-stand
designed by Ernest Gimson*, perhaps
for Kenton & Co.* c. 1891. *William
Morris Gallery, Waltham Forest*

body first made in the 16th century in the Rhineland
and imitated in England towards the end of the 17th
century by John Dwight of Fulham. A brown and
drab stoneware, usually employed for mugs and jugs
decorated with applied reliefs, continued to be made
during the 18th century. In the early years of the 19th
century John Doulton*, in partnership with John
Watts, started a factory for the production of
stoneware at Vauxhall, later removed to Lambeth.
Stephen Green* & Co, of the Imperial Potteries,
Lambeth, also made flasks in addition to utilitarian
stonewares. A pottery for the manufacture of stone-

145

GIMSON, ERNEST. Cabinet on stand of ebony and mother-of-pearl. Designed by Ernest Gimson* c. 1910.
Leicestershire Museums & Art Galleries

GIN-FLASKS, STONEWARE. Gin-flask* in the form of a barrel in light and dark brown stoneware*. Impressed mark of Stephen Green*, c. 1820. *Constance Chiswell*

wares was set up near Derby by William Bourne. This later passed to his son, Joseph, and became the Belper and Denby Pottery*, their flasks usually being referred to as 'Denby' stoneware.

Gin-flasks, brown above and drab below, like the 18th-century mugs, were made in great variety, from about 1820 onwards. Manufacturers' impressed marks are not uncommon, usually DOULTON & WATTS or STEPHEN GREEN, the BELPER and DENBY mark being comparatively rare. The flasks were made in a variety of forms, from those bearing a portrait relief on either side to those (like one representing Queen Caroline) in the form of a hollow figure, or those (like some representing Lord Brougham and Vaux) in the form of a bust above and a bottle below. There were also flasks in such forms as casks, pistols, fish and mermaids, the latter (which also occur in pottery with a Rockingham* type glaze) have a face uncommonly like that of the young Queen Victoria. It will soon be obvious to the collector that the greater number of these flasks have a political connotation and many are concerned in their subject and inscription with the Reform Bill of 1832.

The most common type has Lord Brougham as its subject. He was both concerned with the Reform Bill, and with the defence of Queen Caroline at her trial. A comparatively rare flask is a figure of Caroline bearing a scroll impressed with the words 'My hope is in my people'. Other flasks depict William IV, Queen Adelaide, Queen Victoria (who acceded in 1837), the Duke of York, the Duke of Wellington, Sir Robert Peel etc. Many are impressed on the base or the back with the name and address of a tavern. They were all small and fairly uniform in size and only one large storage flask appears to be recorded, apart from stoneware casks which date from the 18th century. This is an almost life-size head of John Barleycorn, from which the smaller flasks were filled.

During the 20th century Doulton has produced similar flasks in the shape of such recent notabilities as Lloyd George, Balfour, Asquith, Austen Chamberlain, and Lord Kitchener. Reproductions of early flasks have also appeared on the market. These are not difficult to detect to those acquainted with old ones. There is a marked difference in the glaze and body, and the finish is much more precise. It should also be remembered that the old flasks were made primarily for use, not decoration, and that they were closed with a cork. The hole at the top was therefore cylindrical. Reproductions often have a slight ridge just inside the top which would have made the insertion of a tight-fitting cork impossible.

GIRAFFE, THE
Some rare Staffordshire figures* in this form were modelled as vases. The earliest models were made about 1840. The first giraffe arrived in England in 1827.

GIRANDOLE (French)
From the Italian, *girandola*. In the 19th century this term came to mean a candelabrum of glass, porcelain or metal with several branches hung with faceted glass drops, made to be stood on the mantelshelf or a side-table. The term is also applied to certain lyre-shaped clocks made about 1820 by Lemuel Curtis*, a Massachusetts clock-maker. Less accurately, candlesticks hung with prismatic drops, made in pairs, are sometimes called girandoles, and are sometimes *en suite* with the vases known as lustres* as a mantelshelf garniture.

The term has always been used very loosely.

GLASGOW SCHOOL OF ART AND DESIGN
In 1885 Francis H. Newberry became the principal of the School. He immediately began to widen its activities in the direction of furniture and metalwork

GLASGOW SCHOOL OF ART AND DESIGN. Table of oak designed by Charles Rennie Mackintosh* for the Glasgow School of Art* in 1892. *Glasgow School of Art*

design which was of a distinctive character and became known as the 'Glasgow Style', or more irreverently from its elongated and attenuated lines, as the Spook School*. The latter term especially applied to the designs inspired by Charles Rennie Mackintosh*. Lectures delivered by Francis Newberry in 1893 on the art of design contributed to the development of *art nouveau**.

GLASS, AMERICAN

Although glass was made in the American colonies from the earliest times very little decorative glass was made before 1800, and in the early decades of the 19th century the glass factories were principally engaged in developing the mass-production of moulded glass. Henry William Stiegel at Manheim, Pa., produced a certain amount of mould-blown glass between 1765 and 1774. Manufacture was taken up again by the Baltimore Glass Works in Maryland, founded in 1790 with the aid of some of Stiegel's workmen. The Glassboro' Glass Works* of Glassboro', N.J., founded in 1781 and purchased by the Whitney Brothers in 1840, also produced moulded glass and, under its new direction, a long-necked flask with a moulded portrait of Jenny Lind to celebrate that singer's American tours of 1850–1852.

Despite the war of 1812, most of America's requirements for good quality glass continued to be supplied from England so far as the eastern seaboard was concerned, and the industry tended to concentrate in the Middle West, where it supplied the flourishing liquor trade with bottles. There were, however, a number of factories in and around Pittsburgh supplying the need for bottles and these made press-moulded glass of good quality, the designs largely based on cut-glass*.

Bakewell, Pears & Company* (1808–1882) specialized in cut-glass in great variety and were the first commercial producers of this type in the United States. Somewhat later was the New England Glass Company* (founded in 1818) which employed workmen from Ireland. It closed in 1888 when cut-glass began to become unfashionable. The first reference to press-moulded glass in the United States is a patent awarded to John Robinson of the Stourbridge Glass Works, Pittsburgh, for pressed glass door-knobs. The earliest presses were hand-operated, the steam-operated press coming into use in 1864 and the revolving block, which contained several moulds injected in turn with molten glass, in 1871. Soon after 1870 glass-cutting as a form of decoration began to fall out of favour, and the kind of pressed glass which imitated cut-glass also became unfashionable. The decline in popularity of cut-glass in the United States was probably influenced by an earlier decline in England and Ireland, whence much of the better quality glass of this kind has been obtained. The reasons for this are noted under the heading of cut-glass.

About 1870 new kinds of glass for decorative purposes were becoming popular. These were the product of advances in the science of glass-making, and were inspired, to begin with, by glass from France and from Stourbridge in England. These new types of American glass may be grouped under a general heading of 'art glass'*, and its varieties were given various trade names, such as Amberina*, Peachblow*, Burmese*, Pomona*, and, early in the 20th century, the Aurene of Frederick Carder*, all of which are now sought by collectors. Carder founded the Steuben Glass Works* at Corning, N.Y., in 1903 which merged with the Corning Glass Company in 1918. From 1933 Sydney Waugh, the sculptor, was engaged, and produced many distinguished designs.

GLASSBORO' GLASS WORKS (N.J.)

This factory was purchased by the Whitney Brothers in 1840, and became the Whitney Glass Works. They produced the 'Jenny Lind' portrait flask in 1850 which was very popular.

See *Glass, American*

GLASS, FRENCH

Despite the fact that the French were the first to devise an efficient process for making plate and mirror-glass towards the end of the 17th century, until the end of the 18th century they were content to import their table and decorative glass from Bohemia and England. The French decorative glass industry did not really assume importance until the 19th century when, due to the work of a series of distinguished glass chemists and craftsmen such as Bontemps*, Rousseau* and Gallé*, it attained a leading position internationally. The Cristallerie de Baccarat* and the Cristallerie de Saint-Louis* became famous for the quality of their table-glass, and produced many decorative varieties, like opaline*,

GLASS, FRENCH. Glass bowl with the engraved decoration of a Harlequin. Mark: *E. Gallé* etched, and *EG* engraved. 1888. *Victoria & Albert Museum, London*

and paperweights* of all kinds. Artists in glass, especially Émile Gallé, contributed enormously to the development of the *art nouveau** style, and in the 20th century such designers as Lalique* found many new ways of utilizing glass for decorative purposes.

Elsewhere, in England, Bohemia and the United States, great ingenuity was displayed in using this technical knowledge to produce large quantities of decorative glass of good quality for expanding markets, but it was left to France to supply the artistic inspiration that influenced such designers as Tiffany* and the 20th-century Scandinavians.

See *Art nouveau*

GLASS IN THE 19TH CENTURY

The art of glass exhibited much greater variety and originality in the 19th century than at any other time during the previous 2,000 years or so. This was due to the many discoveries in both chemistry and physics which inspired new colours and techniques, and to historicism* which was responsible for the revival and development of several ancient techniques.

Since the days of Imperial Rome glass working had been divided into two principal categories—the work of the *vitrearius* and that of the *diatretarius*. The *vitrearii* were glass-blowers and they manufactured their wares either by free-blowing in which a vessel starts as a bubble on the end of a blowpipe and is subsequently manipulated into any desired shape, or by blowing into a mould. The latter process was the earlier of the two, and it formed the principle of glass-blowing machines of the 19th century. The *diatretarii* were cutters of cameos in hardstones, for which purpose they used such abrasives as emery (brought from Cape Emeri on the Island of Naxos) and chisels formed from diamonds from India. They turned their attention to glass as a substitute for hardstones and carved such remarkable works as the Portland Vase* and the Lycurgus Cup, both in the British Museum, London, and the fine cage-cup in Cologne.

Cutting decorative facets in the surface of glass with the aid of rotating wheels charged with abrasives began with the Romans, although specimens are very

GLASS IN THE 19TH CENTURY. Vase of blown and cased glass, with acid-etched decoration. Emile Gallé*. France, Nancy. c. 1890. *Corning Museum of Glass, N.Y.*

rare; but by the end of the 18th century the technique of cutting facets had become the chief method of decorating good quality glass in England and Ireland, as well as being commonly employed in Bohemia. English and Irish glasshouses used the type of lead glass developed by Ravenscroft in the 17th century. The Bohemians used a potash glass of the kind they had employed for distinguished engraved work for more than a century. Cut-glass* remained popular in England until the mid-19th century, but it was gradually superseded by press-moulded glass*, a mechanical process by which the appearance of cut-glass could be reproduced cheaply.

It was probably the cheapness of these reproductions which made hand-cutting unfashionable. Pliny remarks, in his *Natural History*, that since serving-maids had taken to wearing gold shoe-buckles, their mistresses had reverted to those of silver, which serves to explain the falling out of fashion in the 19th century of objects like cut-glass for which cheap machine-made substitutes became available. Cutting was also condemned by Ruskin*, who, thinking only of Venetian soda-glass, considered that blowing, and manipulation while hot, were the only true methods of making objects of glass. The techniques of the *diatretarius* were revived in the 1870s by John Northwood* who, in 1873, completed a copy in cased glass* of the Portland Vase.* The task took him three years. He had one important advantage which the

CLOCKS, ENGLISH. Clockcase inset with Minton *pâte-sur-pâte*
panels decorated by Marc-Louis Solon. c. 1890. *Minton
Museum, Royal Doulton Tableware Ltd*

DERBY PORCELAIN. A very rare pair of Crown Derby
Porcelain Company vases, finely painted with flower panels
by James Rouse Senior, signed. The reverse panels are
painted with still-life subjects. Date c. 1882. 10 in. high
George Woods Collection

GLASS IN THE 19TH CENTURY. Bottle of green glass with a handle of clear glass decorated with radial gilt ornament. English. Mid-19th century. *Victoria & Albert Museum, London*

Roman craftsman did not possess—he used hydro-fluoric acid* to clear away large areas of unwanted glass. For the remainder, the technique was probably the same—diamond-pointed chisels (or hardened steel chisels) struck with a small mallet. Northwood founded a school of workers in this technique at Stourbridge which flourished until the end of the century, but the work was excessively time-consuming and therefore expensive.

English glass-makers had been grossly handi-capped for many years by the infamous Glass Excise Act by which duty was levied on the weight of the materials going into the crucible. In England this led to the manufacture of an inferior glass, lighter in weight than Irish glass which had been exempt from duty, and cutting was generally much shallower, since duty was, in effect, levied on the glass which was cut away. The industry was freed from this handicap in 1845 with the repeal of the tax, but by this time the press-moulding machines were affecting the sales of cut-glass, and English manufacturers in search of novelties turned to coloured glass and Bohemian styles. The English exhibits at the Great Exhibition in 1851 leaned heavily on Bohemia, but their products were noticeably inferior, and *The Times* led the way in suggesting that the lesson of quality should be more closely studied. Nevertheless, in certain technical aspects the English manufacturers had nothing to learn from the Bohemians. Especially notable at the Great Exhibition was the enormous Crystal Foun-

tain*, 27 feet high and several tons in weight, which dominated the Transept and formed the focus for the Royal party during the opening ceremony.

The collection of 19th-century glass in the Muni-cipal Offices at Stourbridge, Worcestershire, gives an excellent notion of the variety of decorative glass made in the town during the second half of the century. This clearly reveals the inspiration of Bohemia in the early years following the Great Exhibition, and the very experimental nature of some later glass, indicating the workers' acquaintance with Gallé and the French School.

Bohemia (now Czechoslovakia) had a very long tradition of fine quality decorative glass going back to the 16th century, but towards the end of the 18th century the industry had fallen into decline. The first decades of the 19th century, however, were notable for a revival of the industry, and the introduction of new processes and techniques. Especially sought is the work of studio-painters (*Hausamaler**) like Samuel and Gottlob Mohn* and Anton Kothgasser*. The glasshouses specialized in coloured glass (especially a fine ruby), and in cased* and flashed glass*. Cased glass is glass of one colour covered with that of another, usually decorated by cutting through the upper layer into the one beneath. Flashed glass is glass which has a much thinner coating of colour, hardly more than a stain, over either clear or coloured glass. Also from Bohemia were glasses like Hyalith* and 'Lithyalin'* which were opaque, or virtually so, and coloured throughout. The Bohemians were skilled glass-cutters, but they rarely employed facet-cutting alone in the English manner—it was usually employed in conjunction with coloured and cased glass and enamel painting. The firm of Lobmeyr* in Vienna, founded in the 1820s, continued the Bohemian tradition of high quality engraving, both *Hochschnitt** (high relief) and *Tiefschnitt** (low relief). In the 20th century distinguished engraving had been done in Vienna by Wilhelm von Eiff (1890–1945), who worked mainly in *Hochschnitt*.

The Bohemians made little use of manipulative techniques, largely because potash glass, the charac-teristic Middle European type, is much more suitable for cutting. It passes from the plastic to the rigid state fairly quickly, and, unlike Venetian soda-glass, is not very tolerant of reheating. Nevertheless in the 1830s experiments were made with *millefiori** techniques employed for paperweights* and similar small deco-rative items. In South Germany, particularly by Fleischmann of Nuremberg, reproductions of 16th- and 17th-century Bohemian and German enamelled glass were made. These are not very deceptive, although quality of painting is excellent. No one acquainted with old work is likely to be deceived about their age or provenance. Not uncommon is the large and imposing *Reichsadlerhumpen* (Imperial eagle tankards). These bear the arms of the Holy Roman Emperors flanked by those of the Electors. The recent appearance in English antique shops of glasses bearing a superficial resemblance to the old ones suggests that enamelled glasses inspired by the 17th century are still being made in Germany for decoration and tourist souvenirs.

By the end of the 18th century the manufacture of glass in Venice had virtually ceased. It was not until the middle of the 19th century that the industry showed signs of revival, but Venice sent nothing to the Great Exhibition in 1851. In the second half of the century the Venetian glasshouses began to revive early styles, sometimes deceptively, and it was not until the 20th century that Barovier*, Venini* and others developed a distinctive modern style. Also from 19th-century Italy are copies of Roman domestic glass vessels of the kind found at Pompeii and Herculaneum apparently copied from originals in the Naples Museum. The glass is thicker than ancient glass, excessively green with superficial and hardly deceptive attempts to imitate some of the signs of age. The iridescent surface of excavated Roman glass, of course, suggested the practice of iridizing glass as a form of decoration in Austria, England and America (see *Iridescent glass*).

France saw the greatest number of important innovations. The development of opaline glass*, the decorative paperweight (especially the *millefiori* type), and the individual work of such men as Leveillé*, Gallé, and Daum*, as well as the productions of factories like Baccarat and Saint-Louis, contributed to France's dominant position in the world of artistic glass. Men like Georges Bontemps* were responsible for technical developments and the researches of Bontemps in particular were widely known outside France.

The United States was principally responsible for the introduction of mass-production methods of making glass, such as press-moulding and automatic blowing. All these methods were also employed in Britain and France, but not to the same extent. Press-moulding, which began as an inexpensive method of producing glass with the fashionable facet-cutting, was soon adapted to other patterns entirely unrelated to cut-glass, and bottles were produced by machines in which glass was blown into moulds decorated with a great variety of subjects. All these objects are now collected, and have been reproduced in recent years.

Virtually every kind of decorative glass made in Europe was also made in the United States by such factories as that of the Boston & Sandwich Glass Company*.

Towards the end of the century Louis Comfort Tiffany* produced his 'Favrile' glass*, with an iridescent surface in a variety of colours, employed for highly decorative objects in the *art nouveau* style. Like Gallé, Tiffany also made lamp-shades of coloured glass in a variety of forms to take advantage of the fashionably new electric light. At the beginning of the 20th century several new varieties of glass were introduced by Frederick Carder and the Steuben Glass Company.

150

GLASS, PAINTED

Hand-painted glass, the colours applied by a process patented in 1851 by a Miss Wallace, became a vogue in the 1850s, when it was regarded as a genteelly suitable way for girls and women to earn a living. A guild was established to help them to do so by marketing their work. Since many young ladies of the time were reasonably skilled amateur artists some of the decoration is excellent in quality.

See *Independent decoration of pottery and porcelain*

GLASS, SWEDISH

In the 18th century the work of the Swedish glasshouses was often indistinguishable from the glass of Germany and Bohemia. The industry was not revived until 1898, when the Ørrefors* Glass Works* was established to make domestic glassware. After 1918 the designers Simon Gate and Edward Hald of Ørrefors developed a kind of flashed glass*, owing something to Gallé*, which was called *Graalglas*. Cut-glass, and glass engraved with abstract *motifs* and figure-subjects, became widely known, and a school of glass-engraving was founded. The designers Edvin Ohrstrom, Sven Palmqvist, Nils Landberg and Ingeborg Leindin, produced work especially for the Paris Exposition of 1937.

GLAZES

The covering of pottery and porcelain is usually either powdered glass or fusible feldspathic rock suspended in water which is then applied in a way which covers the surface with particles of the material. They are fused by firing in the kiln, at a low temperature for the glass-like glazes, or at a high temperature for feldspathic glazes. Colours are applied either before glazing (underglaze colours) or afterwards (enamel or overglaze colouring). Glazes are also coloured by the addition of metallic oxides of one kind or another.

The French distinguish between three kinds of glaze—*émail, vernis* and *couverte*. *Émail* is glaze opacified with tin oxide employed in the manufacture of *faïence, delft* or *maiolica* (different names for basically the same thing). *Vernis* is the transparent glaze of creamware* (*faïence-fine**) or earthenware*. *Couverte* is the high temperature glaze of porcelain. This nomenclature has led to a certain amount of confusion in the past. A good deal of the literature on the subject in the 19th century was in French, often translated by men unacquainted with the technicalities of the craft, who rendered '*émail*' by the English 'enamel', when 'glaze' would have been appropriate. In some cases this French usage even began to creep into English. Chaffers, for instance, sometimes refers to 'enamelled' when he obviously means 'glazed'. In English 'enamelling' should be reserved for decoration applied to the surface of an existing glaze. See also *Faïence* and *Maiolica* for other confusing examples of the 19th-century use of technical terms.

Another type of glaze, used on stoneware by potters like Doulton* and the makers of reproductions of

Rhineland stoneware*, is that in which salt is added to the kiln at maximum temperature. Salt is sodium chloride. The heat of the kiln separates the constituents. Sodium combines with the silica on the surface of the vessel to form a thin glaze usually pitted slightly, like the skin of an orange. The released gas chlorine passes out of the kiln chimney.

GOBELINS, NATIONAL MANUFACTORY OF (Paris)

At mid-century Gobelins had a London branch in George Street, Hanover Square, which they shared with the National Porcelain Manufactory of Sèvres*. At this time they were making high-warp velveted tapestries in the manner of the Savonnerie types of the 17th and 18th centuries, as well as a small number of fine quality carpets.

GODWIN, EDWARD WILLIAM (1833-1886)

Architect and designer, friend of Whistler*. Godwin designed a great deal of furniture in the so-called Anglo-Japanese* style, which also shows a good deal of Chinese influence, especially those examples which are symmetrical and made of polished wood, both features of Chinese furniture. (The Japanese rarely made large furniture, they employed asymmetrical shelving rather than closed cupboards, and the polished wood customary in China was replaced by lacquer.)

Godwin, however, succeeded in setting a fashion for furniture based on that of the Far East, and the short-lived Art Furnishers Alliance founded in 1880 by Christopher Dresser* might have produced more

GODWIN, E. W. Sideboard of ebonized wood with silver-plated fittings and panels covered with Japanese embossed leather paper, in the so-called Anglo-Japanese* style. Made about 1867 by William Watt to a design by Godwin*. Watt made Godwin's Anglo-Japanese furniture and issued a catalogue of it in 1877. *Victoria & Albert Museum, London*

acceptable designs had it survived, since Dresser had actually visited Japan. Manufacturers produced furniture in a kind of pseudo-Japanese style by grafting imitation bamboo and similar Oriental *motifs* on to European commercial designs.

GOEBBEL, WILHELM, (Oeslau, Bavaria)

Makers of hard-paste porcelain since 1879. Goebbel are especially noted for figures of children, well-modelled but sentimental, designed by a nun, the late Bertha Hummel, and usually referred to as 'Hummel figures'. These are especially popular in the United States. Recently the firm have produced large circular plaques in limited editions painted with figures after those designed by Bertha Hummel.

GOLDSCHEIDER (Vienna)

Manufacturers of *faïence* and porcelain founded in 1886 by Friedrich Goldscheider (1845–1897). After his death it was run by his widow with the aid of his brother, Alois, and from 1920 it came under the control of his sons, Walter and Marcel. The latter retired in 1927 to establish the Vereinigte Ateliers für Kunst und Keramik.

At the turn of the century, Goldscheider made vases in the *art nouveau* style, and figures always formed part of the production. A number of marks were employed, most of them consisting, in part, of the name. In one case the Imperial eagle is used in conjunction with the initials *FG*.

GONON, HONORÉ and EUGÈNE (PÈRE ET FILS) (Paris)

Bronze-founders, who cast many of Barye's* sculptures by the *cire perdue* method.

GOOD, J. WILLIS (fl. 1870–1880)

English *Animalier* sculptor specializing in horses— racehorses and jockeys, hunting groups etc.—in bronze or terracotta*. His bronzes, usually in pairs, were cast by Elkington* of Birmingham, and bear their stamp. Good exhibited at the Royal Academy from 1870 to 1878.

GOODE & CO. LTD, THOMAS (South Audley Street, London, W.)

Noted firm of china dealers founded in 1827. They have occupied their present address since 1844. Thomas Goode retired in 1867. His son, William James, became a partner in 1857. He was, in addition to being an excellent man of business, a talented designer and a collector. He painted *maiolica* plates, and devised a method of etching on porcelain which was praised at the Paris Exposition of 1878. He also designed several State services which were made by Minton's*, with whom Goode's were closely associated. W. J. Goode collected old Sèvres porcelain, and commissioned Minton to make copies, including the *vaisseau à mât*. The collection was displayed in a special room in the firm's South Audley Street premises until the death of W. J. Goode in 1892, when it was sold. The firm retain an extensive collection of *pâte-sur-pâte* by Solon and others, many examples of which were first exhibited in the Paris Expositions of 1878 and 1889.

GOODWIN, JOHN EDWARD (1867–1949)
English ceramic designer. Art-director for Wedgwood from 1902 to 1935. Goodwin designed new 'Queensware' shapes, some in the 18th-century tradition. Among his designs was the Edmé pattern of 1908, still in use, and the White House service of 1912 for Theodore Roosevelt.

GORHAM CORPORATION (Gorham Manufacturing Company)
American manufacturing silversmiths founded in Providence, R.I., in 1815 by Jabez Gorham. The business expanded rapidly, and by 1850 machine-finish was being employed, which is an indication of the size of the production. The manufacture of electro-plate dates from about 1861, when a New York showroom was opened. The firm became a corporate body in 1868.

They employed the sterling silver* standard from about 1868, and borrowed the lion and the anchor from the English hall-mark, to which they added the letter G. They later employed mass-production techniques, and in the 1890s made silver in the *art nouveau* style. To silverware they added the production of small *bronzes d'ameublement* at a foundry at Providence—human and animal figures stamped with the name of the artist and the initials of the Corporation. They also produced *art nouveau* furniture of ebony variously inlaid.

Gorham's greatest period of prosperity lies between 1870 and 1915 when branches were opened in many of the major cities of the United States. William Halbrook, president of the Corporation from 1887, brought over in 1891 William J. Codman from England, and he designed much of the silver which gained international awards for Gorham's at exhibitions. Codman also devised a type of *art nouveau* silver with decoration of hammer-marks known as *Martelé*.

GOSS'S ARMORIAL CHINA
William Henry Goss F.G.S. (1833–1906) worked for W. T. Copeland* as a modeller and designer before starting on his own account in 1858. He moved to the Falcon Pottery, Stoke-on-Trent, in 1870. He made Parian* ware of excellent quality from the first, and portrait busts were among his early productions. He devised a method of insetting 'jewels' into the porcelain body in a technique which somewhat resembled *champlevé* enamelling*. He specialized in small pieces—trinkets and ceramic jewellery—which were extremely successful.

The armorial china for which he is chiefly remembered today began about 1892 when he made small pieces of good quality porcelain bearing the crest of various seaside resorts for sale to tourists as souvenirs. These were in various shapes, but many were in the form of well-known vessels of antiquity, such as Roman bronze buckets etc. They were little regarded at the time and were sold cheaply, but they have since become collectors' items, and they have also been the subject of inferior copies. The usual marks are *W. H. Goss*, or a falcon with *W. H. Goss* beneath. In 1934 the factory became the Goss China Co. Ltd., when it was taken over by Cauldon Potteries. It closed in 1944.

GOTHA (Thuringia)
The town had been the site of a porcelain factory since the 1760s, and by the end of the 18th century production was on a considerable scale. The 18th-century mark had been the letter *R*, but this was changed to a cursive *G* or *GOTHA* impressed in 1805. Thereafter a number of factories existed in the town—Egidius Henneberg from about 1802 who used the word *Gotha* and the impressed letters *HPM* (Hennebergsche Porzellan Manufaktur), Morgenroth & Co. from 1860 whose mark includes the word *Gotha* and the letter *M*, Fr. Pfeffer from 1892 who used the monogram *FPG* intertwined, and Gebr. Simson from 1883 whose mark was *Gotha* or the letter *S* within a shield.

These factories produced relatively large quantities of decorative hard-paste porcelain*, some of it inspired by Meissen*. The style of the early decades of the 19th century was a version of Empire popular among the Bohemian factories. Later they produced well-modelled figures of animals. Henneberg's factory produced lithophanes*. The cursive *G* was also the mark of the Gera factory in Thuringia.

GOTHIC REVIVAL, THE
Perhaps the greatest single influence on the art of design in the 19th century was the revival of the Gothic style which had predominated in England from the 12th to the 16th century, after which it was increasingly replaced by Renaissance classicism.

Towards the middle of the 18th century there was a revival of the Gothic style in new forms. This revival started with the landscape gardeners who were strongly influenced from the end of the 17th century by the romantic aspects of Chinese gardening, which led to the employment of artificial ruins as garden ornaments—sometimes ruins of classical derivation, but more often those based on ruined abbeys that Henry VIII had left to decay after he had dispossessed the monasteries. This, perhaps, was not surprising, since there were no genuine classical ruins in England, these being largely confined to Southern Europe. The pointed arch, which is one of the key features of the Gothic style, castellations taken from the military architecture of the same period and, in the interior, medieval ornament such as fan-traceries, derived from the interiors of Gothic cathedrals, were adapted by Horace Walpole (1717–1797) and others to domestic architecture. Walpole's house at Strawberry Hill, Twickenham, is the finest surviving example of mid-18th-century revived Gothic. These houses were not intended to be taken seriously, and Walpole in particular stated on several occasions that classical architecture was the only conceivable style for important houses and public buildings.

The enormous popularity of the neo-classical* style in the last quarter of the 18th century brought a temporary eclipse to revived Gothic, although the attitude of mind by which it had briefly flourished continued to pervade the literary scene. The mists and ivy-clad ruins of the Germanic and Anglo-Saxon north, where the classical style had never secured so firm a foothold as it had in the South, found expression in the work of the Graveyard Poets (represented by Gray and his *Elegy in a Country Churchyard*), and in Walpole's *Castle of Otranto,* the first of the 'Gothick' novels, a *genre* based on an atmosphere of vague terror, anxious suspense and supernatural intervention. 'Monk' Lewis (1775–1818) enjoyed great popularity with *The Monk* and other sensational novels of the supernatural. Mrs Radcliffe's *Mysteries of Udolpho* excelled in the description of scenes of mystery and

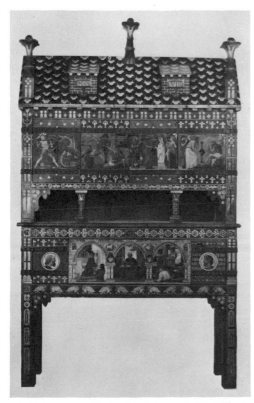

GOTHIC REVIVAL. Cabinet and gilded wood in the medieval style, the form reminiscent of the bronze *chassé.* Shown in the London Exhibition of 1862, it was designed by William Burges*, made by Harland & Fisher, and painted by E. J. Poynter. c. 1858. *Victoria & Albert Museum, London*

terror often set in gloomy romantic landscapes which caused her to be called 'the Salvator Rosa of British Novelists'. A considerable influence on the romantic imagination of the period was the epic poetry of a medieval, and perhaps mythical, bard named Ossian, whose works were reconstructed, and largely invented, by James McPherson (1736–1796) and based on folk-tales. Thought to be genuinely a translation from Ossian, this enjoyed European celebrity at the time. The strongest and most persistent of literary influences on style in the decorative arts was the poet and novelist Sir Walter Scott (1771–1832), whose house near Melrose, Abbotsford, gave its name to a version of the medieval style.

An important foreign influence on the revived Gothic style and the taste for medieval ornament, was German. From 1715 English sovereigns had been Electors of Hanover. In 1837, since a woman could not be an Elector, the title passed to the Duke of Cumberland, Ernst August, who was also King of Hanover. Queen Victoria married a German Prince, Albert of Saxe-Coburg-Gotha, and to the end of his life Edward VII retained the German accent of his youth. This influence more or less disappeared after the Great Exhibition of 1851, to be replaced by that of France, but Gothic ornament continued to be popular until the 1870s, and even afterwards, gradually merging into *art nouveau*.

At the end of the 18th century revived Gothic architecture received a new impetus from the building of Fonthill Abbey in Wiltshire for William Beckford* between 1796 and 1807. The architect was James Wyatt (1746–1813) whose reputation had accrued from his many buildings in the neo-classical style of the Adam Brothers. He based the design of Fonthill on Salisbury Cathedral where he had worked as a restorer. Due to lack of supervision on Wyatt's part, and a dishonest contractor, the 275-ft tower collapsed in 1825, and nothing now remains. The Abbey survives in a notable series of engravings by Rutter, the *Delineation of Fonthill.* Beckford, who had been left an enormous fortune derived from West Indian plantations, was a celebrated art-collector of his day and an arbiter of taste in the early decades of the century

By the beginning of the 19th century the Gothic style had been once more established in popular favour, but it was not the version which became popular a little later. Until the 1830s revived Gothic was just another style at the disposal of the designer and the decorator. The man who gave it the dominant position it acquired, and to some extent still holds as the architectural style especially favoured by the Christian religion, was A. W. N. Pugin*, who called it 'the pointed Christian style' and wrote a book—*Contrasts*—published in 1836 which was an impassioned appeal for a return to the style in ecclesiastical architecture. Many attempts have been made to explain the origin of Gothic architecture, one late 18th-century theory being that the pointed arch had been suggested by the overarching boughs of groves of trees sacred to the Druids. The true origin in the pointed arches of Islam, which predate those of the Christians by several centuries, was perhaps recognized by some authorities but avoided as unpalatable.

A good deal of church building was going on in the rapidly expanding towns and cities of the time and large numbers of second- and third-rate neo-Gothic edifices reared their steeples among the terraced streets of lower middle-class domestic architecture. The working-classes made shift with the cheaply erected Nonconformist chapels which were usually wooden, with window frames pointed at the top in the approved manner. Gothic was also extensively employed for provincial town halls and this aspect has been isolated by Osbert Lancaster as a separate category under the name of 'Municipal Gothic'.

The later development of revived Gothic was due to a variety of factors, including the necessity for providing a setting for stained glass windows, the latter craft being revived during the 19th century by William Morris*, among others.

Classical and Gothic architecture were poles asunder, and this mirrored vast intellectual differences between the proponents of each style. The temporary ascendancy of medieval and revived Gothic coloured not only the decorative arts, but the ethos of the middle decades of the 19th century. It was a fertile soil for the growth of romanticism, it facilitated the linkage of art with morality and religion and it led to a great deal of undisciplined designing in architecture and in the arts generally, since Gothic architecture was, from the first, essentially an undisciplined style. The system of proportion which governed the classical style did not always prevent monotonous architecture, but it did ensure that very little was wholly bad. The cast-iron urinal in the Gothic style was an occasional feature of Victorian streets: the classical urinal is something no one has yet seen. The Gothic railway station is a joke; the classical facade of Euston Station had a dignity of its own.

Pugin's designs had been based fairly strictly on medieval architecture and decorative art; the designs include furniture, metalwork, porcelain, and even stage scenery, and his design-books were used by others. The revived Gothic style, however, was employed much more loosely by some manufacturers; for instance, Minton* produced a vase of classical form on a pedestal moulded with a Gothic arcade and the 1860s saw the beginning of a short-lived furniture style which has been termed Japanese-Gothic*.

The Great Exhibition of 1851 was remarkable for the number of exhibits which were basically neo-Gothic in style, but by the Exhibition of 1862 it was already beginning to disappear in favour of a revived classical style. Neo-Gothic was represented there not by furniture carved with traceries and pointed arches, such as that designed by Pugin, but by medieval cabinets decorated with paintings like the one designed by William Burges* in 1858 and obviously based on the medieval bronze *chasse*.

GOULD, ST. JOHN (1793–1840)
Cabinet-maker of New Ipswich, New England, specimens of whose work have been identified from his label.

GOUPY, MARCEL (b. 1886)
French designer of glass and ceramics who worked in the *art nouveau** and *art déco** styles. In ceramics he designed mainly for Haviland* & Co. and Boch Frères*, services designed for the latter being produced under the *Keramis* trade-mark. In glass Goupy worked for Saint-Louis-Muntzthal, Lorraine, a branch of the Cristalleries de Saint-Louis*. He usually signed his work.

GOUTHIÈRE, PIERRE (1732–1813)
Fondeur-*ciseleur* who worked for the Court of Louis XVI and introduced a combination of matt and burnished gilding employed in the 19th century by, among others, his pupil Pierre-Phillipe Thomire*.

See *Acid gilding*

GRAALGLAS   See *Ørrefors Glasbruk*

GRAINGER, THOMAS (d. 1839)
Founder of a small porcelain factory at Worcester in 1801 which was taken over by the Worcester Royal Porcelain Company* in 1889. The factory did not close until 1902. After Thomas Grainger's death the firm became George Grainger & Co.

Grainger began by copying the wares of both Chamberlain* and Flight & Barr (see *Worcester*). They were skilled potters, producing ornamental wares of excellent quality. Some rare and well-modelled arbour groups were a continuation of a traditional 18th-century Staffordshire type. These were in the form of an overarching bower of flowers with a small figure or figures beneath. Both Grainger and Chamberlain also made pierced porcelain, usually in the form of pierced ledges to plates in the manner of the German factories in the 18th century. Until about 1850 they produced old Japan patterns (similar to those of Derby* and Chamberlain) which were poor in quality. After 1850 they introduced Parian* porcelain, and in the 1880s a kind of *pâte-sur-pâte** decoration. The early mark, from 1801 to 1860, was 'Grainger Lee & Co. Worcester.' The mark from 1889 to 1902 was a shield, inside which were the words *Royal China Works* surrounding the initials *G. & Co.*

GRAINING
The process of painting furniture and woodwork generally to imitate the grain and figure of more costly woods. First used in England in the 16th century, the practice was popular at times in the 19th, especially in the 1870s.

GRAND RAPIDS FURNITURE

Generic term for mass-produced furniture made at Grand Rapids, Michigan, from the mid-19th century onwards. This was not only widely sold in the United States, but extensively exported. Every fashionable style from American Colonial to *art nouveau** was adapted to quantity manufacture, which necessarily required considerable modifications in some cases. For this reason the most important furniture of the period was still made by small firms elsewhere by relatively traditional methods. Furniture from the Grand Rapids area was shown at the Philadelphia Centennial Exhibition of 1876.

'GRANDFATHER' AND 'GRANDMOTHER' CLOCKS See *Clocks, American; Clocks, English*

GRANITE WARE

A hard, durable and cheap white earthenware, or stoneware, made in the middle decades of the 19th century in Staffordshire largely for export to America. It was also made by a number of American factories, for example, the Etruria factory of Trenton, N.J. Josiah Wedgwood made a white earthenware with a greyish mottled glaze imitating the appearance of granite which is quite distinct from the above.

GRASSET, EUGÈNE (1841–1914)

Architect, writer, and designer, of Swiss origin, who came to Paris in 1871. At first attracted by the Gothic of Viollet-le-Duc*, and then by Japanese art, his influence on the *art nouveau** style in France was very considerable. The designer, Paul Follot*, was one of his pupils.

GRAY & CO., A. E. (Stoke-on-Trent, Staffordshire)

Pottery decorating studio founded in 1912 to decorate wares bought 'in white'. Susie Cooper* worked here before starting her own pottery. Gray produced hand-painted wares, including resist lustre*, and used the mark of a full-rigged sailing ship lithographed in colours.

GREATBACH, DANIEL (fl. mid-19th century)

English potter from Harby, Staffordshire, who emigrated to the United States in 1839 and was employed at the Jersey City potteries and then, from 1852, at Bennington, Vt., where he was the originator of many new models including the hound-handled pitcher (also a Staffordshire model).

GREEK SLAVE, THE

A marble nude by the American sculptor, Hiram Powers, of a Greek girl exposed for sale in a Turkish slave-market. It was a popular sensation of the Great Exhibition of 1851, and the subject of much high-minded comment on the morals of Turkish slave-merchants. Minton* reproduced it in Parian* porcelain.

GREEK SLAVE, THE. A Parian figure by Minton's after the marble statue by Hiram Powers exhibited at the Great Exhibition of 1851. The Minton version is a testimony to the popularity of the statue. Made c. 1851. *Minton Museum, Royal Doulton Tableware*

GREEN, STEPHEN (Imperial Pottery, Lambeth, London)

Maker of salt-glazed stoneware* who specialized in such things as pistol-shaped spirit flasks, and other wares of the same kind. Their mark was STEPHEN GREEN LAMBETH impressed. The factory, the Imperial Pottery, was sold in 1858 and closed in 1869. See *Gin-flasks*

GREEN GLAZED WARES

Plates and dishes, usually circular but sometimes leaf-shaped, and comports decorated with floral and foliate ornament in low relief, which are covered with a translucent copper-green glaze. They were popular in the 1840s but were very fashionable from the late 1850s onwards. The most sought are those of Wedgwood*, which bear an impressed mark and three letters which signify the month and year of manufacture. Similar wares were made by Copeland*, Minton*, and others in Staffordshire.

GREENAWAY, KATHERINE (KATE) (1846–1901)

English book-illustrator and designer of Christmas cards etc. She specialized in coloured drawings of children, especially girls in pseudo-Regency bonnets and frilly dresses and ribbons, the boys in frilled shirts and pantaloons. Her work was exceedingly popular at the time, and she was much praised by Ruskin*. She set new fashions for girls' dresses, especially in the 1880s, and sentimental lithographs* after her drawings were disseminated in large quantities. Her children occur as pottery figures, and as the decoration of nursery china. She also designed figures for the Worcester Royal Porcelain Company*. She had a number of imitators who worked in her style. Books illustrated by her are now sought.

GREENER & COMPANY, HENRY (Sunderland, Co. Durham)

English manufacturers specializing in press-moulded glass* and slag glass* especially American lacy glass* and vine-leaf patterns. Since 1920 the firm has been known as James A. Jobling & Co. James Jobling bought the company in 1885. The mark is a lion rampant holding an axe.

See *Sowerby & Co.*

GREENPOINT POTTERY (Long Island, N.Y.)

Factory established by Charles Cartlidge & Co. in 1848 for the manufacture of table-china, as well as portrait busts in biscuit porcelain*. Production was excellent in quality, but the factory closed about 1856.

GREENWOOD ART POTTERY COMPANY (Trenton, N.J.)

Pottery established in 1861 by an immigrant Staffordshire potter, Stephen Tams, which specialized in semi-porcelain for hotels, and also made a fine translucent porcelain inspired by the products of the Royal Worcester Company*.

GRÈS (French)

Pottery term meaning stoneware* which has been mistranslated as 'sandstone'.

GRIVOISERIES (French)

Obscene, indecent or pornographic scenes or writings. These have been produced at all periods from the beginning of history, but probably in greater quantity during the 19th century than ever before. The carefully cultivated aura of respectability which characterizes the period was superficial and very tenuous. It was a time during which high-class prostitutes, sometimes termed *grandes horizontales* in France and 'horse-breakers' in England, enjoyed large fortunes and considerable influence. In these days *grivoiseries* from the 19th century are comparatively rare, but Mayhew (*London Labour and London Poor*, 1851) records that snuff-boxes and cigar-cases* thus decorated were offered by street-hawkers to likely customers for 2s 6d upwards. Mayhew was told that these were imported from France, which may have been because France was, most unjustifiably, supposed to have a monopoly of the trade.

It seems probable that most of these objects were destroyed by heirs or executors as reflecting on the deceased person's character, but the British Museum possesses a notable collection of 19th-century pornographic writing in a section to which the public is not easily allowed access. A number of private collections also exist of objects of *vertu*, notable among them one which belonged to the late King Farouk of Egypt.

GROSSHERZOGLICHE EDELSGLASMANU-FAKTUR (Darmstadt)

The Grand Ducal Fine Glass Factory founded in 1907 by the Grand Duke Ernst Ludwig of Hesse-Darmstadt. The director was Josef Schneckendorf (1865–1949), a designer in the *Jugendstil**, who produced ornamental wares in iridescent glass*. Marks: *EL* (for Ernst Ludwig) under a coronet; sometimes *SCHNE* or *JESCH* as a monogram.

GROSSHERZOGLICHE KERAMISCHE MAN-UFAKTUR (Darmstadt)

The Grand Ducal Ceramic Factory which produced figures and vases after designs provided by artists from the Matildenhöhe, an artists' colony at Darmstadt. The factory, which was founded by the Grand Duke Ernst Ludwig, was directed by J. Scharvogel from 1906 to 1913. Scharvogel had worked for Villeroy & Boch* at Mettlach before establishing his own workshop at Munich about 1900. Marks: EL (for Ernst Ludwig) beneath a coronet; *HD* (for Hesse-Darmstadt) also under a coronet, impressed.

GROTESQUES

Italian *groteschi*. Type of decoration discovered about 1509 during excavations on the site of Nero's Golden House in Rome. The subterranean position of these excavations caused them to be regarded as being grottoes, or caves; for this reason the decorations were termed *grotesques,* i.e. belonging to a cave. These *motifs* had been forgotten for 1,500 years, but they soon became very popular. Raphael employed them in the decoration of the *loggie* of the Vatican, and they were commonly employed in the painting of the *maiolica** of Urbino and Faenza, as well as providing a subject for small bronzes. Grotesques were employed almost until the end of the 19th century as a form of pottery decorations, and even today they have been used by Wedgwood* and Worcester* in revived Renaissance patterns.

The commonest element of the grotesque type of decoration is the nude human torso, usually female, with arms and legs in the form of acanthus* foliage.

Women sometimes end in twin fish tails instead of foliage. Mingled with these figures are fauns and sphinxes, birds, insects, foliage, and masks based on the ancient theatrical mask.

In the 19th century grotesques often occur as part of the decoration of objects in the revived Renaissance style* especially from about 1850 to 1870. They are also to be found as the subject of ivory inlays on ebonized furniture made in Rome during the 19th century. They are sometimes inaccurately called arabesques*.

GROULT, ANDRÉ (b. 1884)
French interior decorator and furniture designer. Many of his furniture designs were inspired by 18th-century styles, and his work is noted for luxurious upholstery. He exhibited at the 1925 Paris Exposition.

GROUND-LAYING
A method of applying coloured grounds to porcelain especially. The area to be coloured is covered with a thin layer of oil spread evenly with a silk pad. The pigment in powder form is then dusted on. The oil burns away in the kiln. Until the invention of the aerograph* underglaze ground colours were often sponged on, a technique employed in the 18th century which yields a very effective, slightly uneven, ground. Sponged decoration on earthenware of the cheaper kinds is usually crude.

GRUEBY FAÏENCE COMPANY (Boston, Mass.)
Factory organized in 1897 by William H. Grueby (1867–1925). Grueby had formerly been employed at the Art Tile Works of J. & J. G. Low*. He experimented with glazes, for which the factory became widely known, and he produced imitations of Hispano-Moresque* tiles and Della Robbia* plaques. Wheel-thrown vases in matt tin-enamel glazes attracted attention both at home and abroad, some of

GUILD OF HANDICRAFTS. Silver cup and cover made by the Guild of Handicrafts*. Maker's mark. London. 1912. *Sotheby & Co*

which recall the work of August Delaherche*. The factory ran into financial difficulties and production of vases had more or less ceased by 1908, although the manufacture of tiles, including those decorated by hand, continued until about 1919. A paperweight* in the form of a scarab was a Grueby production.

The mark employed was GRUEBY POTTERY.

GUEYTON, A. (fl. mid 19th century)
Jeweller and silversmith in Paris whose work was much commended in 1851. His contribution to the

GUEYTON, A. Casket of oxidized silver set with jewels and surmounted by the figure of a woman at her toilet, by A. Gueyton* of Paris. Shown at the Great Exhibition of 1851. *Victoria & Albert Museum, London*

GUIMARD, HECTOR. Single chair of carved wood in the *art nouveau* style by Hector Guimard. c. 1908. *Cooper-Hewitt Museum of Decorative Art and Design, Smithsonian Institute*

Exhibition included silver figures and ornamental boxes in what was described, at the time, as a mixed Gothic and medieval style. His presentation swords, hunting-knives and silver knives were much admired and he also displayed silver snuff-boxes and *bonbonnières*.

GUEYTON, CHARLES (fl. 1890s)

Parisian silversmith who worked in the *art nouveau** style, decorating his work with asymmetrical floral *motifs* in relief.

GUILD OF HANDICRAFTS

Guild of artist-craftsmen founded by C. R. Ashbee* in 1888 on the lines of the medieval craft guilds. It had a workshop where craftsmen could work in association in Mile End Road, East London. A retail store was opened in Mayfair, West London, in 1890. In 1902 the workshops were removed to Chipping Campden, Gloucestershire, where they remained until the Guild went into voluntary liquidation in 1908. From 1898 it was a limited company.

The Guild made furniture, silver, jewellery and leatherwork to designs by C. R. Ashbee*, Lewis Day* and others, and when William Morris* died in 1896 they bought the presses and type of the Kelmscott Press and started a limited amount of book-production. Their silver did not always bear the maker's mark, which was *CRA*, until 1898. *G of H Ltd* was also used after 1898.

GUIMARD, HECTOR (1867–1942)

French architect, *art nouveau** designer from 1896 onwards who inspired furniture and architectural woodwork in mahogany and pearwood. He was also responsible for the *art nouveau* entrances of some of the Paris Métro stations which are among the key examples of the style. These date from 1900, the year of the Paris Exposition.

H

HACKWOOD, WILLIAM & SON (Shelton, Staffs)
Manufacturers of earthenware from 1818 to 1853.
Ornamental wares included figures decorated with
gilding, and enamelled table services. They employed
a transfer-printed mark with the name of the pattern
within an ornamental frame and the initials *W. H.
& S.* immediately below.

HADLEY, JAMES (1837–1903)
Modeller for the Worcester Royal Porcelain Company* from 1870 to 1896. In the latter year he
established his own small factory which was taken
over by the main factory in 1905. Beginning in 1870
Hadley was employed by the Worcester factory to
model figures of all kinds, including those in the 'Kate
Greenaway'* series. He also modelled some of the
more elaborate wares in the new Japanese style
introduced by R. W. Binns*. For this an ivory-toned
porcelain decorated with bronzing and gold of
different colours was used. His figures include such
diverse subjects as the 'Grecian' series, a group of a
cat and kittens and political caricature depicting
Joseph Chamberlain and the Boer leader, Paul
Kruger. His *chef d'oeuvre* was a pair of highly
modelled vases depicting potters at work. From about

HADLEY, JAMES. *Cat playing with her kittens*. Biscuit
porcelain* group modelled by James Hadley*. c. 1880.
Worcester Royal Porcelain Company

1875 much of Hadley's work for the factory was done
as a free-lance, a common arrangement in the
industry, and Hadley's inventive genius was of great
value to the factory. When Hadley founded his own
factory in 1895 it was extremely up-to-date and even
included an electric polishing lathe. When Hadley
died in 1903 his sons attempted to carry on, but the
difficulties proved too great. The undertaking was
absorbed by the main factory but Hadley's sons
continued to make the type of wares with which they
had been associated.

HAIRCLOTH
Cloth woven from horsehair used in the middle of the
19th century for upholstery. Horsehair was also used
for padding in cheap furniture.

HAIRWORK PICTURES
Pictures dating from the beginning to the middle of
the 19th century which were composed of strands of
human hair arranged in the manner of pencil lines by
needlework techniques. Subjects are usually landscapes with buildings, and the framing was commonly
of maplewood. The hair picture was strictly an
amateur product.

HADLEY, JAMES. *The Water-carriers*. A
pair of ivory porcelain* figures by
James Hadley* for the Worcester Royal
Porcelain Company*. c. 1880. *Private
collection*

HALL, JOHN AND RALPH (Burslem and Tunstall,
Staffordshire)
Manufacturers of earthenware, especially wares
transfer-printed* in blue, as well as figures which
sometimes bear the impressed mark, *HALL*. The
partnership was in existence soon after 1800 and

continued until 1822, when it was dissolved. Ralph Hall continued at Tunstall and in 1846 the firm became Hall and Holland. He produced a series of 'English Views', 'Italian Views', and 'Picturesque Scenery' in a dark blue much favoured in America. John Hall at Burslem took his sons into partnership, and the firm became bankrupt in 1853.

HALL STAND
Piece of furniture introduced in Victorian times in England comprising a mirror, coat and hat pegs, a drawer for gloves, an umbrella stand and (usually) a shelf underneath for a potted plant, or an arrangement of dried foliage. Usually in oak or walnut, small versions in cast iron were made by the Coalbrookdale Ironworks*.

HANCOCK, JOHN (d. 1842)
Staffordshire potter reputed to have invented copper lustre. He emigrated to the United States in 1828, and worked successively at South Amboy, N.J., Louisville, Kentucky, and East Liverpool, Ohio.

HANCOCK, SAMPSON (d. 1898)
Sampson Hancock eventually took over the porcelain factory started at King Street, Derby, by William Locker*. Hancock had worked at the original Derby factory, and continued at King Street until his death, at first as manager under Stevenson, Sharp & Company, then as partner with Stevenson, in Stevenson & Hancock, and finally as owner. The factory, distinct from the Royal Crown Derby factory*, was later absorbed by them.

Much of the King Street factory's output was based on, or inspired by, the work of the old Duesbury Derby* factory, but despite the occasional use of a crown and crossed batons (the Duesbury mark) without further additions, there is usually little difficulty in distinguishing between early models and later repetitions.

Sampson Hancock normally employed the mark of a crown over the Meissen* crossed swords instead of batons, flanked by the letters S and H. Sometimes D was added underneath. Stevenson & Hancock employed a similar mark to the old Duesbury mark flanked by the letters S & H.

'HAND AND CUP' VASES
Small flower-vase of English biscuit* or Parian porcelain* clasped by a naturally-modelled hand, made by various factories in the 1850s and 1860s. There is little doubt that the popularity of ornamental hands was due to the contemporary cult of spiritualism*.

HAND-COOLERS
Glass spheres or ovoids for holding in the hands to cool them in summer, made in France, England, and America. The best French hand-coolers were made by the factories specializing in fine paperweights*— Baccarat*, Saint-Louis*, and Clichy*. The more

'HAND AND CUP' VASES. Vase in the form of a cornucopia of bluish-mauve glass terminating in an *ormolu* hand resting on a white marble base. c. 1860. *Constance Chiswell*

prosaic hand-coolers—egg-shaped, of coloured glass—also did duty as darners. Apart from glass, decorative stones were employed for this purpose, including marble, onyx, agate, and alabaster.

HANKE, REINHOLD (Hohr)
Factory in the Westerwald producing stoneware* decorated with *flambé* glazes designed by Henri van der Velde* in the early years of the 20th century. Mark: incised signature *Hanke*.

HARDMAN & CO., JOHN (Birmingham, Warwickshire)
Ecclesiastical furniture manufacturers established in 1838 by John Hardman and A. W. N. Pugin*, the latter being the chief designer. They specialized in metalwork of all kinds. They also made jewellery designed by Pugin. Hardman exhibited at the Great Exhibition of 1851 and the International Exhibition of 1862.

HARD-PASTE PORCELAIN
More correctly, true porcelain, i.e. porcelain made in the Chinese manner from china clay and a fusible rock, usually feldspar, but sometimes soaprock. The Chinese refer to clay as the 'bones' of porcelain and the feldspar (*petuntse*) as the 'flesh'. Porcelain is a kind of natural glass, the fusible element (feldspar) fusing at a much lower temperature (1450°C) than the clay (1650°C). Clay, therefore, not only provides the plastic element of the mixture which enables the object to be shaped by normal ceramic means, but it is refractory in the kiln, and holds its shape at the normal firing temperature of 1450°C, while the feldspathic rock (which has been ground to a fine powder and mixed with the clay) fuses to a natural translucent glass. This type of porcelain was made in England at Plymouth, Bristol, and New Hall in the 18th century, but Worcester, Caughley, and Liverpool made a porcelain with soaprock, in which the principle was the same.

True porcelain, apart from being the only type of

porcelain made in China and Japan, was also the standard Continental type from the beginning of the 18th century to the present day. The same type has always been widely favoured in America. English bone-china (see *Porcelain*) is a modification of true porcelain devised about 1800 by Josiah Spode*. It is a true porcelain with up to about 40 per cent of calcined oxbones added. Bone-china has been the standard English body for about a century and a half, both for the home-market and for export, but in recent years one or two of the larger English manufacturers, such as the Worcester Royal Porcelain Company, have begun to employ true porcelain for ornamental wares.

HASELER & CO., W. H. (Birmingham, Worcestershire)

Manufacturers of silver and other kinds of decorative metalwork and jewellery, established in 1870. In partnership with Liberty & Co.* from 1899 to 1926 in the manufacture of 'Cymric'* silver. They also made 'Tudric'* pewter from 1903. Their maker's mark is *WHH*. Liberty's trade name usually occurs in addition where appropriate.

HAUSMALEREI

Literally, home painting; German studio enamel painting on glass, porcelain, and *faïence**. The *Hausmaler* functioned principally in the 17th and 18th centuries, but the practice continued throughout the 19th century, although after about 1850 it rarely assumes much importance. The *Hausmaler* worked at home and fired their work in a small enamelling or muffle kiln, employing glass or porcelain bought in an undecorated state from one of the factories. An example of important *Hausmalerei* is the glass painting of Kothgasser*. The Viennese term for painters of this kind was *Winckelmann*, the French, *chambrelan*, and in England they are usually called independent decorators*.

HAVILAND, CHARLES FIELD (b. 1814)

Charles Field Haviland married into the porcelain-making family of Alluaud of Limoges and eventually inherited their factory. He also founded a factory of his own and opened a design studio at Auteuil, just outside Paris, which was under the direction of Felix Bracquemond*. The studio was moved into Paris in 1882, where it came under the direction of Ernest Chaplet*.

HAVILAND, DAVID (1814–1879)

David Haviland began life as a New York importer of porcelain from England. In 1842 he established his own decorating studio in Limoges* to produce wares for the American market, and followed this by undertaking actual manufacture of the white ware. These table-services were highly successful in the United States, and included many decorated with American subjects.

HAVILAND, THEODORE (b. 1842)

Son of David Haviland*. He established his own factory in 1892 and exhibited table-ware designed by Jean Dufy and Suzanne Lalique at the Paris Exposition of 1925.

HEAL, SIR AMBROSE (1872–1959)

English furniture designer, apprenticed as a cabinet-maker in 1890 before joining the family firm. He was a member of the Art Workers' Guild*, and his early designs especially reveal the influence of William Morris* and the Arts and Crafts Movement*, as well as that of Ernest Gimson*. He was among the first to use fumed oak* for simply-designed bedroom furniture. He also employed painted decoration and inlays

HEAL, SIR AMBROSE. Cabinet of cupboards and drawers of macassar ebony and ivory, designed by Sir Ambrose Heal*. Heal & Son Ltd. c. 1920. *Victoria & Albert Museum, London*

of ebony and pewter. In the 1930s he experimented with steel and aluminium*. Although Heal is principally noted for simple, well-constructed oak furniture, he also designed elaborate pieces for exhibition purposes, the firm displaying their products at the Paris Exposition of 1900.

HEAL & SON LTD (London)

Furniture manufacturers and interior decorators. One of the few commercial firms to adopt successfully the principles of the Arts and Crafts Movement*. This largely began in 1897 with designs by William Lethaby* (1857–1931), who was also associated with Kenton & Co.* Heal exhibited bedroom furniture of oak or ash (plain or stained) at the Paris Exposition of 1900.

HEATHCOTE & CO. LTD, C. (Longton, Staffordshire)

Manufacturers of earthenware (especially wares

transfer-printed* in blue) in the early years of the 19th century. They appear to have made use of some of Turner's engraved plates since identical examples bearing the marks of Heathcote and Turner occur in the Hanley Museum. Heathcote's mark was the name impressed.

HÉBRARD, A. A. (fl. 1900–1925)
Paris *fondeur** who cast the work of Dalou*, Bugatti*, and Degas*.

HECKERT, FRITZ (Petersdorf, Bohemia)
Glass factory founded in 1866. Heckert specialized in enamelled glassware, notably reproductions of 16th- and 17th-century German and Bohemian enamelled glass, especially types like the *Humpen* (cylindrical beakers) and the *Stangengläser* (pole glasses). They also imitated early *Waldglas* and some Rhineland glasses, such as the *römer*.

Heckert produced two art glasses* towards the end of the century—chameleon glass* and Cyprus glass*.

HEMPHILL, JOSEPH (1770–1842)
Partner with William Ellis Tucker* in the successful production of porcelain in Philadelphia. He operated the factory after the death of Tucker in 1832 until 1838.

HENNEMAN, WILLIAM C. (1769–1856)
Boston brassworker who had been apprenticed to Paul Revere. He made domestic utensils of all kinds, including candlesticks, kettles, warming pans and irons, as well as brass movements for the clocks of Simon Willard*.

HENRI DEUX WARE
Otherwise known as Saint-Porchaire faïence. A ware made at Saint-Porchaire (Deux-Sèvres) between about 1525 and 1560. The body is almost white, and the walls of vessels very thin. The piece is covered with a transparent lead glaze, and the ware is very soft, the result of a low temperature firing, perhaps for some technical reason connected with the method of decoration. This was to impress or incise ornament into the unfired clay with the aid of bookbinder's stamps or roulettes, the incision and depressions being filled with black, brown or reddish clay, a technique unique in Europe, but well known in the Far East, which was imitated during the 19th century by Charles Toft at Minton's in a mixture of painting and inlaying. Specimens are marked *C. Toft Mintons*, with sometimes the date.

About 65 pieces of Saint-Porchaire ware were known to exist in 1861, when C. Delange published his book *Recueil de toutes les pieces de la faïence française dite Henri II*. This illustrated all known examples, and Colin Minton Campbell and Minton's art-director, Léon Arnoux, were subscribers. The first Minton examples were made by Arnoux himself in 1858. The Minton copies are harder than the originals which, in any case, few people are ever likely to have an opportunity to handle.

Copies of Henri Deux ware were also made on the Continent, notably by Avisseau of Tours, and a few forgeries also exist.

HENS ON NESTS
Covered dishes or tureens in the form of hens on nests were made in earthenware in Staffordshire in the middle of the 19th century. They were also made in pressed glass* in both England and America.

HERCULANEUM (Liverpool, Lancashire)
A pottery founded in 1793 which passed through a number of hands before it closed finally in 1841. Its wares included creamware* (usually transfer-printed*), blue-printed earthenware, earthenware figures, and drab and basaltes* stonewares. Herculaneum made a number of excellent portrait-busts, and recently recognized as coming from this factory are some large creamware jugs painted with flowers in the Billingsley* style. A good deal of the production was unmarked, some bear the word *Herculaneum*, and some a scroll on which the Liver bird is depicted.

HEREND (Hungary)
A factory was established here for the manufacture of porcelain in 1839 by Moritz Fischer, who enjoyed the patronage of the Emperor Franz Joseph. The factory became noted for clever and deceptive copies of 18th-century Chinese porcelain, especially *famille verte.** These copies were rarely marked. They also reproduced 18th-century European porcelain, especially that of Sèvres*, but generally these wares are less deceptive. Their ordinary porcelain, of excellent quality, bears a variety of marks, usually *HEREND* impressed, the Austrian arms, or, much more rarely, the monogram, *MF*. Moritz Fischer, who died in 1876, exhibited in London in 1851. After his death the factory passed from his family to new owners.

HERRENCHIEMSEE, SCHLOSS (near Munich, Bavaria)
Herrenchiemsee, which was never completed, was built for Ludwig II* of Bavaria in the 1880s. It was intended to be a close imitation of Versailles. It has a *Salon de l'Oeil de Boeuf* containing an equestrian statue of Louis XIV, a *Galerie des Glaces* 245 feet long, with a *Salon de la Paix* at one end and a *Salon de la Guerre* at the other, and a copy of Louis XIV's bedchamber built at a cost of 120,000 gold pounds (say £7 million in 1978). Herrenchiemsee is an extreme example of the historicism* of the 19th century. It is open to the public.

HILL POTTERY (Burslem, Staffordshire)   See *Alcock, Samuel & Co.*

HINGRE, LOUIS-THÉOPHILE
French *Animalier** sculptor who exhibited at the *Salon*

of 1881, and was still working in the early years of the 20th century.

HISPANO-MORESQUE ORNAMENT
Ornament principally derived from Spanish sources executed during the Moorish occupation. Sometimes called Moresques, this kind of ornament is often virtually indistinguishable from the variety called arabesques, in turn derived from the Romans by the Saracens. Ornament of this type was employed in England and France from about 1840 onwards under the influence of such books as Murphy's *Alhambra* and Owen Jones's* *Plans, Sections, Elevations and Details of the Alhambra* of 1842.

HISTORICAL WARE
Transfer-printed* earthenware principally made in Staffordshire or Liverpool for export to America from late in the 18th century until the middle of the 19th century. The subjects are American Views*, portraits of statesmen and military and naval heroes, and notable events (i.e. the visit of Lafayette in 1824, the opening of the Erie Canal, etc.). Much of this ware, which is now greatly sought, was unmarked, but the makers include Enoch Wood*, Ridgway*, Clews*, Meyer and Stubbs*, among many others. Transfer-printing in colours other than blue was done after 1830; jugs with portraits and marine subjects printed in black overglaze came from Liverpool. Reproductions of these and other transfer-printed subjects have appeared on the market in recent years, some from the original copper-plates.
See *Herculaneum*

HISTORICISM
The practice of relying on the art of the historic past in contemporary designing, especially where the art of former periods has been closely imitated, such as at the Schloss Herrenchiemsee*, or the copy of the *bureau du roi* by Dasson* in the Wallace Collection, London. It has much in common with, but is not the same as, eclecticism*, where the historic styles of several periods are usually combined. These two terms can be applied to most of the decorative art of the first three quarters of the 19th century.

HITCHCOCK, LAMBERT (1795–1852)
American chairmaker who gave his name to a popular type of chair said first to have been manufactured by him (see below). His factory, erected in 1826, was located in a town named in his honour, Hitchcockville (now Riverton), and his chairs were decorated with stencilling, usually on a black ground. His first factory failed owing to competition, and he started the Unionville Chair Company in 1843 which also failed.

HITCHCOCK CHAIRS
Open-back type of American chair originally made by Lambert Hitchcock*, and others, beginning about 1826. Hitchcock's chairs were usually of birch or maple, with cane or rush seats and painted decoration stencilled on a black ground. Some early examples have Hitchcock's name on the back of the seat.

HOADLEY, SILAS
A leading Connecticut clock-maker who was apprenticed to Eli Terry* in 1809. He continued in business until 1849, when he retired with a fortune. His clocks were excellent in quality, but are now rare.

HOADLEY, LUTHER AND SAMUEL (fl. 1807–1813)
Clock-makers of Winsted, Conn., who made wooden movements.

HOBBS, BROCKUNIER & CO. (Wheeling, W. Va.)
Glass-makers founded about 1845 by James Barnes. William Leighton, who developed lime glass* in 1864, worked here. The factory was noted for coloured glass of all kinds, cased glass*, threaded* glass, several varieties of art glass* (including their own version of Peachblow*), spangled glass* and cut-glass* in great variety.

HOCHSCHNITT (German)
Term used to describe glass-engraving in high relief or cameo-cutting of the type formerly employed for decorating rock-crystal. Literally 'high-cutting'.

HOETZENDORF, COUNT (fl. 1878–1888)
Painter of figures and landscapes at the Crown Derby factory (see *Royal Crown Derby Porcelain Company*). He appears to have been a Saxon nobleman, and was at Osmaston Road from 1878 to 1888. He initialled his work *GH*. Specimens are rare, and sought by collectors.

HOFFMANN, JOSEF (1870–1936)
Architect, designer, and founder-member of the Vienna *Sezession* (1897), and among the founders of the Wiener Werkstätte* (1903), where he was one of the principal metalwork designers. His furniture designs for Thonet* are strongly rectilinear. Hoffmann designed pottery for the Wiener Keramik*, porcelain for Augarten*, and glass for Lobmeyr*. He also contributed considerably to the design of the Palais Stoclet, Brussels (1904–1911). Rare mark is the monogram *JH*.

HOLLAND & SONS (London)
London cabinet-makers since the 18th century extensively patronized by Queen Victoria who entrusted them with the furnishing of Osborne (Isle of Wight), Balmoral (Aberdeenshire) and Sandringham (Norfolk). Designers who worked for them include, among others equally eminent, Gottfried Semper*, Bruce Talbert*, and G. E. Street. Holland & Sons were noted both for satinwood furniture, and for pieces in the style of Chippendale, Adam, Hepplewhite, and Sheraton during the revival of 18th-century designs.

Some of these are, no doubt, among those 19th-century examples often mistaken for 18th-century work today. Some pieces are stamped *Holland and Sons*.

HONORÉ, E. D. (Paris)

Porcelain manufacturer, one of two brothers who, until 1820, were in partnership with P. L. Dagoty. The enterprise was originally founded in 1785 under the patronage of the Duchesse d'Angoulême. Hard-paste porcelain* of good quality was manufactured.

HONORÉ, E. D. Alhambresque* vase with pierced, impressed, applied and enamelled decoration. Mark: *E. D. HONORÉ BOULEVARD POISSONIERE No. 6, Paris.* Exhibited at the Industrial Arts Exposition, Paris, 1844. *Victoria & Albert Museum, London*

HOOK, WILLIAM (1777–1867)

Cabinet-maker who, starting in 1800, supplied many of the leading families in and around Salem, Mass., with high quality furniture.

HOOKED RUGS

A type of American rug made by hooking strips of cloth or wool through a canvas or burlap foundation. Essentially a kind of folk-art, the patterns are unsophisticated. Principally they are floral, but animals and birds and geometric *motifs* occur. Patterns could also be purchased by those who lacked imagination, which accounts for the close resemblance of some rugs to one another. Quality varies enormously, in workmanship, design and materials employed, but the best rugs are very good. Nearly all surviving hooked rugs have been made since 1800, and most of them between 1860 and 1890. They are still being made today. Most of the 19th-century examples seem to have come from New England.

Sometimes confused with the hooked rug is the much rarer shirred rug. Strips of material were shirred (i.e. gathered) and then *sewn* to the background instead of being hooked through it. From the upper surface of the rug there is little difference between the two techniques, but, of course, the appearance of the back is very different.

HOPE, THOMAS. Mahogany table in the Regency style inlaid with ebony and silver and supported on lion-paw feet. Designed by Thomas Hope*, and once in his possession. c. 1815. *Victoria & Albert Museum, London*

HOPE, THOMAS (1769–1839)

English architect. Hope travelled widely from 1786 to 1795, and then settled in London, acquiring a country house at Deepdene, Surrey, in 1807. He was an art-patron who took great interest in Greek and Roman antiquities. He was acquainted with Flaxman*, and was much influenced by the designs of Charles Percier who, with Fontaine, was the premier architect of the Empire style*. In 1807 Hope published his *Household Furniture and Interior Decoration* based principally on Greek and Roman *motifs*, but with Egyptian decorative features also, which had considerable influence on Regency* furniture and interior decoration. Some of his furniture designs were made to his order.

See *Smith, George*

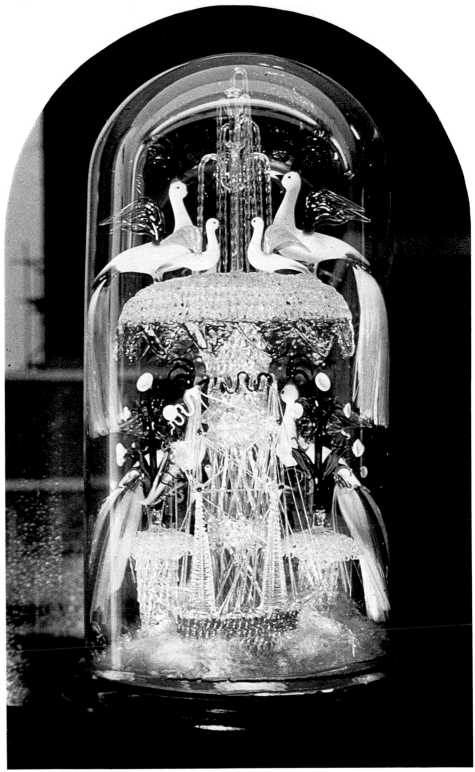

FRIGGERS. Group of birds made 'at the lamp' with tails of
spun glass under a domed glass shade. c. 1850. *Victoria &
Albert Museum*

SILVER. An early Victorian christening cup. Charles Fox.
1837. *Sotheby & Co*

MINTON. Bone-china vase in the Sèvres style painted with panels allegorical of the *Seasons* by Thomas Allen. Shown at the Great Exhibition, 1851. *Minton Museum, Royal Doulton Tableware Ltd*

1. CENTURY GUILD. The Angel with the Trumpet. Cretonne print designed for the Century Guild by Herbert Horne. c. 1884. *William Morris Gallery, Walthamstow*

3. MORRIS, WILLIAM. Blackthorne Wallpaper design. Morris & Co. 1892. *William Morris Gallery, Walthamstow*

2. MORRIS, WILLIAM. Trellis. The first wallpaper designed by William Morris, with birds by Philip Webb. 1862. Trimmed 3ft 4in. length 1ft 9in. width. *William Morris Gallery, Walthamstow*

HORN FURNITURE

Furniture made partially of horns and antlers (especially chairs) was very popular in the United States in the second half of the 19th century. A fall-front writing-desk by A. F. C. Rompendahl of Hamburg decorated with figures of stags and dogs, the handle of the fall-front in the form of a stag's head, and with full-sized antlers on top, was displayed in the London Exhibition of 1851.

HORNE, HERBERT (1864–1916)

Born in Chelsea, Horne was apprenticed to A. H. Mackmurdo* as an architect in 1883, and two years later became his partner. He helped Mackmurdo to design for the Century Guild, and retired to Florence in 1900.

HORSE BRASSES

These brass ornaments, attached to leather horse harness, were at first intended as amulets or charms against ill-fortune, and only recently have they been no more than decoration. Genuine old specimens are now extremely rare, and reproductions are common. From the collector's point of view it is important that the brasses were made for use, and actually used. Otherwise they are merely ornamental brassware of no great merit.

Horse brasses are usually circular, with an upper pierced rectangular part through which the strap was passed.

The number of subjects has been estimated as between 1,000 and 3,000, and some are of great antiquity, such as the crescent moon. Others, like the barrel, once belonged to a brewer's dray-horse. Possibly the steam-locomotive denotes a horse pulling a railway delivery van.

It is not easy to distinguish between the old and the new when the subject is traditional, but those accustomed to evaluating the age of metalwork can usually do so. Carters spent a good deal of time polishing harness, and old brasses ought to show signs of wear in the right places from this activity. It is a good, but not a certain guide.

HORSEHAIR See *Haircloth*

HORTA, VICTOR (1861–1947)

Belgian architect and designer, and one of the most notable pioneers of the *art nouveau** style. The Tassel Residence* in Brussels of 1892–3 is regarded as one of the key features of the style, and almost equally important is the house for the Baron van Eetvelde in the Avenue Palmerston, Brussels, erected in 1905. Horta also designed furniture to harmonize with his interiors, employing veneers to match wall-panelling, and wrought iron ornament with sinuous curves to repeat those of the balustrades, columns, etc. His designs for furniture and fittings for the *hôtel* (i.e. town house) Solvay in the Avenue Louise, Brussels, were executed between 1894 and 1900 in exotic materials of all kinds, especially woods from the Belgian Congo. His own house at 25 rue Americaine, Brussels, designed in 1898, is now the Musée Horta. He became head of the Belgian Academy in 1913.

HOUND-HANDLED PITCHERS

The use of a hound as the handle for a jug or pitcher began in Derbyshire, at Brampton, where greyhounds were employed for this purpose on jugs and mugs. With these examples the hound is attached at the top by its nose and at the bottom by the hind paws. The chief designer of hound-handled pitchers in the United States was Daniel Greatbach, a mould-maker from Staffordshire, who introduced them at the Jersey City Pottery and then took the idea to the United States Pottery at Bennington, Vt.*, where the best were made. The hound is attached by fore- and hind-paws, and the body of the pitcher is decorated with a deer hunt on one side and a boar hunt on the other. When the United States Pottery closed, Greatbach took his moulds elsewhere. A few jugs made by the Vance Faïence Company are properly marked. Fox-handled pitchers were made in the 19th century in Hungary.

HOWARD, EDWARD (b. 1813, ret. 1882)

Clock- and watch-maker of Roxbury, Mass., who founded the E. Howard Clock Company in 1861.

HOWELL & JAMES (London)

Retailers of 'art' products of all kinds, especially pottery and porcelain, established in 1820. To encourage amateur porcelain painting (then a fashionable pursuit) the firm organized exhibitions beginning in 1876. Before the rise to popularity of the typewriter, pottery and porcelain painting was thought to provide genteel employment for ladies. Howell & James had their own mark, which was added to wares ordered by them from the principal potters of the day, as well as from small 'art' potteries. Their stock included silver and jewellery, and a miscellany of artistic objects for interior decoration, many of them made in their own workshops. The firm exhibited at the Paris Exposition of 1878.

HUBBARD, ELBERT (1856–1915)

American furniture designer, manufacturer, and writer who promoted the Arts and Crafts Movement* in the United States. He settled in East Aurora, N.Y., and founded the Roycroft Shops* which sold the products of a number of artist-craftsmen. Hubbard visited William Morris* in 1894, and was so influenced that he bought a printing press. He also produced decorative pottery, including portrait busts of Morris and Walt Whitman, and promoted the Mission* style, and was very influential among the *avant-garde* circles of his time.

HUECK, EDWARD (Ludenscheid, Westphalia)

Firm of German metalworkers, founded in the late

18th century and still working in the 20th. They produced pewter in the style of the *Sezession**. Impressed mark.

HUGGINS, VERA (fl. 1932–1950)

Designer of stoneware* (usually vases) for Doulton* at Lambeth. She decorated her work with soft colours, and signed it in full.

HUKIN & HEATH (Birmingham, Warwickshire)

Silversmiths who specialized in such things as tea- and coffee-sets, cruet stands etc., in both silver and electro-plate. Christopher Dresser* was the art director from about 1880, when Japanese and Persian influence began to be perceptible. The firm produced *art déco** designs soon after 1930 and closed in 1953.

HUMMEL FIGURES See *Goebbel, William*

HUNT & ROSKELL (London)

Silversmiths and makers of electro-plate, who were also retailers. The firm was founded as John Mortimer & John S. Hunt, the latter a nephew of Paul Storr*, in 1841, but Mortimer retired in 1843, and the firm continued under the style above. Hunt & Roskell exhibited in the Great Exhibition of 1851, and they specialized in presentation plate, race-cups, etc., a field in which their principal competitors were Garrard & Co.* Among their racing trophies was the Royal Hunt Cup of 1849.

Makers' marks: IM over ISM, or ISH over crown.

HÜRTEN, CHARLES FERDINAND (1818–1897)

Of German origin, Hürten worked as a flower painter at Sèvres* from 1846 until 1859, when he came to England and was employed by Copeland* until his death. His work was shown at the Paris Exposition of 1855.

HYALITH

Trade name for a kind of opaque glass made at the Bohemian factory of Count von Buquoy. There were two varieties—sealing-wax red, imitating Wedgwood's* *rosso antico*, introduced in 1803, and black, imitating Wedgwood's basaltes* ware, from 1817.

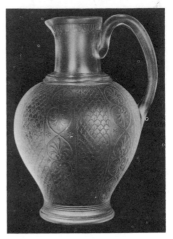

HYDROFLUORIC ACID. Glass jug decorated with an acid-etched pattern. Stourbridge. c. 1860. *Constance Chiswell*

HYDROFLUORIC ACID

The only acid which will attack glass and similar silica products, such as pottery and porcelain glazes. It was discovered by Scheele in 1771, but it was principally employed in the 19th century for decorating glass and for removing unwanted material in cameo cutting*.

See *Northwood, John*; *Cameo glass*; *Etched glass*

ICE GLASS

This type of glass was popular in the 19th century in both England and the United States, and was a revival of an old Venetian technique. The methods used were the same as those employed by the Muranese glass-makers. A vessel was partially blown, plunged into cold water, and then reheated and blown to its final shape. This gave a smooth outer surface and an interior network of cracks. The other method was to take the vessel when partially blown and roll it while still soft in glass fragments. The object was then reheated and blown to its final shape, incorporating the fragments into the surface. The second method was more effective, but specimens are rarer. Some work of this kind was done both in Bohemia and France, and in England it was introduced by Apsley Pellatt*.

Also called crackle glass.

See *Frosted glass*

IMAGE, SELWYN (1849–1930)

Designer associated with Mackmurdo* in the foundation of the Century Guild* in 1882. Image received his education from Marlborough and at New College Oxford, where he studied drawing under Ruskin*. He was ordained in 1871, but relinquished Orders in 1883. Image was Master of the Art Workers Guild* in 1900, and Slade Professor at Oxford from 1910 to 1916.

IMARI PATTERNS

Japanese porcelain decorations often based on brocades and made at Arita, Hizen Province, from the early years of the 18th century until the first decades of the 19th. The type was so called from the port of shipment at Imari, not far from the factory.

It was always popular, and versions of the Imari patterns were also made in China ('Chinese Imari'). In England these patterns were copied and adapted by Worcester*, Derby*, Spode*, Minton*, and Mason* among others. They found little favour among the major Continental factories, although a type of Imari pattern was made at Bayeux* by the Langlois factory in the 19th century. In England they were also termed 'Japan' patterns.

INCRUSTATIONS   See *Crystallo-ceramie*

INDEPENDENT DECORATION OF POTTERY AND PORCELAIN

This practice is known in Germany as *Hausmalerei**, and studios for the painting of porcelain especially were an important feature of the art in the 18th century. At the beginning of the 19th century the decoration of stocks of white porcelain which had accumulated at Sèvres* occupied studios in both Paris and London and attempts were made to decorate some of it deceptively. At this time factories such as Nantgarw* and Swansea* depended on supplying white porcelain to decorators for much of their trade. Before about 1815 Coalport* issued a price-list of white porcelain they were prepared to supply to London decorators like Robins & Randall*, Thomas Baxter*, and others. During the 19th century the tradition varied a little, but it continued. Minton* opened a London decorating studio, for example.

In France, England, and the United States a new kind of independent decorator made an appearance—

IMARI PATTERNS. An 18th-century Imari* dish from Arita (Hizen Province, Japan) which belongs to the group forming the prototype of later English 'Japan' patterns popular throughout the 19th century at Derby and elsewhere. *Victoria & Albert Museum, London*

women who pursued it as a hobby, or who, left without an income of their own, sought a genteel pursuit by which they could earn a living. Studios were opened where women of this kind could work, artists' colourmen produced the necessary materials and books were published giving the essential information. One of the most authoritative was G. Campbell Hancock's *Amateur Pottery and Glass Painter*, published under the aegis of the Department of Science and Art, South Kensington. The preface refers to the many exhibitions of amateur work, some under the patronage of royalty, which had been held in London.

A good deal of untypical porcelain especially may be traced to this source and the quality of some amateur painting is excellent.

INDIAN SPORTING VIEWS
A series of views of Indian sporting scenes which were the subject of blue transfer-printed* patterns used by Spode*. The subjects were derived from a publication of 1805 called *Oriental Field Sports*, most of the plates for which were engraved by Thomas Howitt. The name of the subject, e.g. *The Hog Deer At Bay*, is on the reverse. The subject was first used about 1810, and continued until after 1850. It was also sometimes used by J. & R. Clews*.

INFLATION
In a number of cases sale-room prices for objects sold before 1914 are quoted in this Dictionary. It must be remembered that these were in gold pounds, the purchasing power of which was at least 25 times as much as that of the £ in 1978. A price of £10,000, therefore, is approximately the equivalent of £250,000 today, which helps to put some of the current record sale-room prices into perspective. On this basis, many of today's prices will be seen to be *less* than those realized for the same or comparable objects in the 19th century.

Like precious metals and real property, the value of antiques advances as the value of money depreciates, a process which can be well seen if sale-room prices are compared with those of stocks and shares. At times when the latter have fallen, record prices in the sale-rooms for works of art have become positively common.

An examination of sale-room prices realized during the economic crisis of 1929–1930 shows that works of good quality retained much of their value, and sometimes even realized higher prices than before, despite the fact that shares in many cases were worth no more than the value of the paper on which they were printed. There is nothing new in this. Works of art as a form of investment first became established in France in the early decades of the 18th century with the inflation of John Law. During the French Revolution the Duc d'Orléans, Philippe Egalité, succeeded in preserving part of his fortune by exporting his grandfather's picture collection, even

though he was not so successful in preserving his head.

Since 1945 works of art and antiques generally have shown a steady appreciation which has outstripped the depreciation of money, and there is no reason to suppose that this process will alter in future, since new buyers are continually coming into the market to compete for a diminishing supply of objects.

INGRAHAM, ELIAS (1805–1885)
Clock-maker of Bristol, Conn., who originated the 'Sharp Gothic' design of case for shelf-clocks* which proved very popular and was widely copied.

INRŌ (Japanese)
Small, decorative, lacquer case, usually in two or three compartments fitting into each other, for the purpose of carrying seals and medicines. The *inrō* was suspended from a cord, which passed through the sash, at the opposite end of which was a *netsuké*. The best *inrō* were superbly decorated in a variety of techniques, including Shibayama*. They have been eagerly sought by Western collectors since the reopening of Japan in 1853.

INTERNATIONAL POTTERY COMPANY (Trenton, N.J.)
Pottery founded in 1878 the principal production of which was fine quality porcelain especially noted for a rich blue ground.

INTERNATIONAL STYLE   See *Functionalism*

IRIBE, PAUL (1883–1935)
French designer of furniture etc. whose work was strongly influenced by *art nouveau*. He designed furniture for the art-collector, Jacques Doucet, and from 1914 to 1930 he was in America with film-maker Cecil B. de Mille. His furniture is characterized by rich upholstery materials, and the curves of *art nouveau*.

IRIDESCENT GLASS
Glass which has been buried for a long period, particularly soda-glasses like those belonging to Rome and Persia, develops a surface appearance as the result of deterioration which is somewhat like that of oil spilled on a wet road. This is termed iridescence and various means were devised during the 19th century for imitating the effect as a kind of decoration. In England iridescence occurs as decoration on the 'Clutha' glass* designed by Christopher Dresser* and on certain decorative glasses made at Stourbridge, Worcestershire. Lötz* Witwe of the Klöstermühle factory, Bohemia, patented a method of iridizing glass in 1872 and they were exporting glass of this kind to North America in 1879. The same technique was adopted by other Bohemian factories. Gallé* in France experimented with the technique, and in the United States both Tiffany* ('Favrile'* glass) and

IRIDESCENT GLASS. Vase by L. C. T. Tiffany* with an iridescent surface, an effect originally suggested by excavated Roman glass. Early 20th century.
Pilkington Glass Museum

Frederick Carder* (Aurene glass*) employed it extensively and effectively.

IRISH GLASS   See *Cut-glass*

IRONBRIDGE   See *Coalbrookdale*

IRONSTONE CHINA
A type of earthenware resembling fine stoneware* or coarse opaque porcelain introduced early in the 19th century. A patent for a body of this kind was taken out by Charles James Mason* in 1813 which included ironstone slag in its specification, but, like so many patents of this kind, the specification was deliberately obscure to prevent its unauthorized use. Several other firms subsequently made an ironstone china and some used the name, but Mason's wares are the earliest and the most sought.

See *Mason, Miles and family*

IRONWORK
Iron is of two kinds—cast and wrought. Cast-iron takes its shape from being poured into moulds, usually those made of founder's sand, but occasionally of fireclay. Iron is specially treated in the blast furnace to make it suitable for casting, but articles of this metal are brittle, and are broken comparatively easily by a blow. The Coalbrookdale* factory specialized in furniture and works of art in cast-iron, as well as structural metalwork. They exhibited extensively at the Great Exhibition of 1851.

Wrought-iron, once employed for such superb examples of the craft as the gates at Hampton Court, is produced by a process which confers on it the qualities of malleability and tensile strength lacking in cast-iron. Instead of being cast, it is worked with

IRONWORK. Cast-iron umbrella stand decorated with pheasants. Coalbrookdale Ironworks*. c. 1860.
Antique Collectors' Club

a hammer on an anvil in a blacksmith's forge, and in recent years it has become popular for grates and hearth-furniture for country houses. During the 19th century it was not very popular, and although Coalbrookdale still employed it, by far the greater part of their production was the product of casting.

Wrought iron became very popular in the 1920s in Paris during the currency of the *art déco** style, when a good deal of furniture was made in this way, especially supports for tables of marble or glass. Chairs, fire-screens, decorative lamps and panels were also produced for interior decoration, but the fashion eventually declined with the introduction of tubular steel furniture, such as that designed by Marcel Breuer*.

ISLINGTON GLASS WORKS   See *Rice & Sons, Harris*

ISNIK POTTERY
Turkish pottery made at Isnik in Anatolia on the site of ancient Nicaea from the beginning of the 16th to the end of the 17th century. Designs are characteristic and almost always floral, although some 17th-century examples are painted with Mediterranean sailing-ships with lateen sails. Most of the polychrome painting is characterized by a deep red pigment raised slightly in relief from the surface. This pottery was imported into England in Elizabethan times, when it was usually mounted with silver.

In the 19th century the country of origin of this

ware had been lost to view, and on the strength of fragments found at Lindos, on the island of Rhodes, it was credited to the island, and sought by collectors under the misnomer of 'Rhodian'. Its styles inspired a number of English potters of the second half of the 19th century, especially William de Morgan*, and tiles from Isnik bought in the Near East were employed by Lord Leighton to decorate the Arab Hall*, together with matching tiles by de Morgan.

The somewhat similar types of ware from Damascus was also sometimes mistakenly referred to as 'Rhodian'.

ISOKON FURNITURE COMPANY
Formed in 1935 when former Bauhaus* designers arrived in England. Marcel Breuer* was among the Isokon designers.

ITALIAN SCENES
Blue printed views of Italy were employed to decorate earthenware by Spode* and others. At least one of Spode's Italian views has been in constant use from 1800 until the present day. Spode drew inspiration from Merigot's *Views of Rome and its Vicinity* (1797–1798). Italian views from various sources were also employed by several other potters, notably J. & R. Clews* of Cobridge, the Cambrian Pottery of Swansea, and the Don Pottery of Swinton (Yorkshire).

IVORY PORCELAIN. Jug of ivory porcelain decorated with lizards in high relief, the gilding, dark in colour, of excellent quality. Worcester Royal Porcelain Company*. c. 1880. *Private collection*

IVORY PORCELAIN
Porcelain body introduced at Worcester* in the 1860s principally for wares decorated in Japanese styles inspired by lacquer and ivory rather than porcelain, with gilding of different shades and bronzing. Forms were modelled by Callowhill*, and gilded by Béjot. The ivory body was praised by the *Art Journal* and specially commended at the Vienna Exposition of 1873.

JACK, GEORGE (1855–1932)

Architect and furniture designer of American origin, and Philip Webb's* chief assistant from 1880 to 1900, when he bought the practice. From 1890 Jack was chief furniture designer to Morris & Co.* and was responsible for their more important productions. He was a member both of the Art Workers' Guild* and the Arts and Crafts Exhibition Society*.

JACKSON & GRAHAM (London)

Manufacturers of ornate furniture in the French style; apparently the same as Mungo, Jackson & Graham who were Barbedienne's* London agents. The firm of Jackson & Graham was established in 1840, and they took advantage of the unrest on the Continent in 1848 to employ a number of immigrant French craftsmen, chief among whom was the designer Eugène Prignot. By 1855 they were employing 250 workmen and, by 1875, 600. They closed in 1880. Production was under the supervision of Peter Graham and among their commissions was the furnishing of the palace of the Khedive in Cairo.

Jackson & Graham made what was probably the most expensive piece of furniture produced during the 19th century in England—a cabinet for Earl Bective which cost £4,000 (about £100,000 in 1978). In the 1850s they installed a steam-engine to operate a machine for sawing wood, and in the 1860s they did a certain amount of wood-carving by machine. They specialized in large furniture—principally cabinets

decorated with metal inlays and mounts. They also employed ebony inlaid with ivory in the Italian style.

A number of their more important pieces have survived, and one of the most ornate—a cabinet exhibited in Paris in 1855—is now in the Victoria and Albert Museum, London. This was designed by Prignot in what was called the Louis XVI style, with caryatids by Carrier, and the rest of the modelled ornament by Protât* and Phénix. Thirty-five workmen, whose names have survived, were employed in the work of assembly. The bronze castings were by Cope & Collinson of Birmingham electro-gilded by Elkington's* process. The porcelain plaques were enamelled by Grey and fired by Minton*. The cabinet in question, highly praised and awarded a gold medal, is fairly typical of Jackson & Graham's style.

JACQUEMART, HENRI-ALFRED MARIE (1824–1896)

French *Animalier** sculptor who exhibited in the *Salon* from 1847 until 1879. Most of his subjects were wild animals, but he executed occasional small bronzes of domestic animals. He also supplied designs to Christoflé*, and executed some major animal sculptures decorating Paris fountains. He signed *AJ.* or *A. Jacquemart.*

JAHN, LOUIS (d. 1911)

Porcelain painter, born at Oberweisbachin, Thuringia, who learned his art in Vienna, and then emigrated

JACK, GEORGE. Mahogany dining-table with eight legs connected by Y-shaped stretchers, with inlaid decoration on the edge and top. Designed by George Jack*. c. 1900. *William Morris Gallery, Waltham Forest*

JACKSON & GRAHAM. Cabinet designed by Eugène Prignot*, with caryatids by Carrier-Belleuse*, modelled ornament by Hugues Protât* and Phénix, bronze-casting by Cope & Collinson, electro-gilding by Elkington's*, and porcelain plaques enamelled by Gray and fired at Minton's*. Reputedly assembled by 35 men, this cabinet was awarded a Gold Medal at the Paris Exposition of 1855. The style is a curious mixture of the Louis XIV and Louis XVI styles—referred to at the time as 'in the style of all the Louis's', but it has the merits of none of them. Jackson & Graham*. 1855. *Victoria & Albert Museum, London*

to Staffordshire in 1862 where he painted vases in the manner of Sèvres* for Minton*, specializing in cupids after Boucher. He joined Brownfield* in 1872 as art-director, and returned to Minton in the same capacity in 1895, remaining until 1900.

From 1900 until 1911 he was Curator of the Hanley Museum.

JAIPUR ENAMELS   See *Jeypore enamels*

'JAPAN' PATTERNS   See *Derby Porcelain Factory*; *Imari patterns*

JAPANESE FURNITURE

The Japanese in the 19th century used very little furniture in the interior of their homes. For example, they ate from low tables while seated on the floor. They did, however, employ comparatively small and light wooden shelving, arranged asymmetrically so that the shelves were at split levels. Part of the shelving was enclosed with a door to provide a cupboard. The wooden surface was lacquered, nearly always in black, and sometimes simply decorated, for instance dusted with gold powder. This type of shelving had some influence on Anglo-Japanese furniture but, to judge from its appearance, most

furniture of this kind was more strongly influenced by imports from China.

See *Godwin, E. W.*

JAPANESE-GOTHIC STYLE

A number of attempts to combine the elements of these two styles were made from the 1860s onwards, especially in pottery and furniture designs. The combination was perhaps not quite so incongruous as the earlier attempts of one or two English porcelain factories to combine the classical and Gothic styles. A notable example of Japanese-Gothic was the Peacock Room* for which Jeckyll* provided a Gothic ceiling with pendentives. A much more intimate blending of Japanese and Gothic occurs in some *art nouveau** designs, the synthesis being so skilful that it is not easy to recognize either at first glance, or without considerable knowledge of both styles.

JAPANESE INFLUENCE

The influence of Japanese art on the art of the West has been powerful but uneven in its effect. It first assumed importance in the second half of the 17th century, and continued to inspire the decorative arts until the return of classical styles to popularity (see *Neo-classicism*). During the 18th century, however, Japan was once more closed to foreign trade, and its art was more or less forgotten by all but some of the porcelain factories, who continued to make wares

JAPANESE INFLUENCE. Vase in the style of Japanese *cloisonné* enamel with bamboo handles, the base simulating a carved blackwood stand. Minton bone china. c. 1880. *Minton Museum, Royal Doulton Tableware*

inspired by earlier Imari* porcelain patterns. At this time, and sometimes later, the debt owed to Japan was not always realized because the untutored eye found it difficult to see the difference between Chinese and Japanese art, but the principle of asymmetry which forms a prominent feature of the rococo style in the 18th century, and of its revived 19th century form, was undoubtedly inspired by Japan.

In 1853 Commodore Perry of the U.S. Navy steamed into Nagasaki harbour and reopened Japan to foreign trade. This came at a period of turbulence and unrest in China, where the arts had greatly deteriorated in taste and quality, and the best things were now, for the most part, copies of 18th-century wares.

Japanese influence on the arts of 19th-century Europe began in France and the Japanese Government sent a magnificent and representative collection of Japanese art of all kinds to the Paris Exposition of 1867. This started a vogue, which could well be termed a craze, that had not been exhausted by the beginning of the First World War. After 1867 many collections of Japanese art of all kinds were made. Dealers like Samuel Bing* became increasingly knowledgeable, and Western scholars such as Ernest Fenellosa, devoted their energies to the study of both Japanese and Chinese art. In France the wood-block print influenced the painting of artists like Manet and Van Gogh. Whistler took Japanese influence from Paris to London. Studio-potters and the great porcelain factory at Sèvres* experimented with forms and glazes suggested by Japanese pottery, and although neither the Chinese nor the Japanese ever paid much attention to the art of glass, the glass-makers of France, especially Émile Gallé*, found ways of producing glass decorated in a manner inspired by Japan. In England, Godwin* designed Anglo-Japanese furniture*, and Christopher Dresser*, who travelled in Japan and wrote a book about his travels, produced designs which owed a good deal to this source.

English porcelain factories were also inspired by Japan in the 1870s. The Worcester* ivory-toned porcelain body, first introduced in 1856, was extensively used for wares in the Japanese style (mainly the work of James Hadley*), but the inspiration was not always Japanese porcelain, but a derivation from works in other materials. George Owen's* pierced porcelain, for instance, was often strongly influenced by ivory-carving.

In 1876 the Japanese government sent an important exhibit to the Philadelphia Centennial Exhibition. This contained a good deal of Tea Ceremony Ware, and pottery covered with the low-temperature *raku* glazes. The collection was later bought for the South Kensington Museum (now the Victoria and Albert Museum, London), and a handbook was produced by Sir A. W. Franks with the aid of Japanese experts. Work of this kind captured the imagination of French collectors rather than English, the latter preferring

objects which were more obviously the product of meticulous craftsmanship, but Japanese glazes of this kind later influenced English studio-potters such as Bernard Leach*.

More than any other material Japanese pottery introduced Europe to a new aesthetic which clashed violently with the factory-made precisely finished pottery to which Europeans had become accustomed. Japanese potters who had made a symmetrical bowl often pushed it out of shape in the hope of achieving something more interesting or significant. They experimented continuously with glazes, and valued accidental effects. The kind of bowl which might be valued by a Zen Tea Master would be stigmatized by most Staffordshire potters as a kiln-waster. The more perceptive Europeans pursued this new path, which was Zen Buddhist in inspiration, in the hope of illumination. Most pursued more conventional paths and collected naturalistically carved ivories, composite works of semi-precious materials like Shibayama* panels and small lacquer objects like *inrō** with their attendant *netsukés**. Decorative bronzework, especially vases, also became popular, but few of the kind valued in Japan were actually exported. The Japanese took up the art of enamelling on a large scale during the 19th century and vases in the *cloisonné* technique were widely exported to the West. They also introduced a type of *cloisonné* without wires to divide the colours one from the other, especially employed for large dishes, popular in the West as wall-decoration, which may still be found in the shops of provincial antique dealers. The same technique was imitated on porcelain vases. These imports from Japan influenced the revival of the craft of enamelling during the currency of the *art nouveau** style.

If the art of Japan influenced that of the West, it was itself influenced by the presence of Western customers who were learning, painfully, to discriminate in a strange field, and whose tastes appeared to be omnivorous. Some Japanese potters began to turn out large quantities of pottery vases and figures covered all over with garishly painted ornament, largely meaningless, which became known, quite incorrectly, as 'Satsuma'*. Walter Crane* commented on the catastrophic effect the export market was beginning to have on Japanese taste and 'Satsuma', and large quantities of miscellaneous and trivial *bric-à-brac*, eventually ended the fashionable craze. Japanese art was then largely neglected, except among specialists, until the 1960s.

JAPY FRÈRES

A factory for the making of clock movements and watches was established at Beaucourt (Belfort) as early as 1770 by Frédéric Japy. His three sons continued the business after his death in 1812, eventually manufacturing clock-movements on a large scale for Paris workshops to insert into cases. Japy Frères began to make complete clocks in the 1880s. Their products are usually marked *JAPY*.

JARVES, DEMING (1795–1869)
American glass-maker born in Boston, Mass. From 1818 to 1825 he was connected with the New England Glass Company* of Cambridge, Mass., and in the latter year he founded the Boston and Sandwich Glass Company* which he continued to direct until 1858, when he resigned to start the Cape Cod Glass Company*, also at Sandwich, Mass. This, however, proved unsuccessful. He also founded the Mount Washington Glass Works* in 1837 which established an important reputation later in the century for the manufacture of art glass*. Deming Jarves especially interested himself in the development of the pressed glass* industry, and took out a patent in 1828 for a machine for making glass in this way.

JASPER
A fine, close-grained, high-fired stoneware* capable of taking a high polish and of being worked with lapidary's tools. It could either be stained throughout with a metallic oxide ('solid' jasper) or coloured on the surface only ('dip' jasper). It is most commonly seen with a blue background decorated with white applied reliefs (usually figures) of the same material; but it was also made in black and a wide variety of colours, some of which (yellow especially) are extremely rare. Also rare are single pieces displaying several colours. Jasper was first developed in 1774 by Josiah Wedgwood* I, who referred to it as his biscuit porcelain*. However, very few 18th-century examples, and no later ones, exhibit even a slight translucency, a circumstance Wedgwood was careful to avoid for fear of infringing existing porcelain patents. The material is properly classified as a stoneware.

It has been almost continuously employed by Wedgwood since its inception for high-quality ornamental wares. It was also copied by a number of contemporary English makers and Continental factories (including Sèvres*, using biscuit porcelain). It has a wide number of uses—portrait medallions, jewellery, plaques for mounting in furniture, vases (including copies of the Portland Vase*), tea-ware (glazed inside) etc. It is much sought by collectors.

JEANNENEY, PAUL (1861–1921)
Artist-potter and collector of Oriental pottery and porcelain. He joined a colony of artist-potters at Saint-Amand-en-Puisnaye (Nièvre), in 1890. This colony was headed by Jean Carriés*, and here Jeanneney made stoneware* strongly influenced by Japanese taste. He also cast bronzes by Rodin* in stoneware. Mark: *Jeanneney*, incised.

JEANNERET, CHARLES-EDOUARD (1887–1965) See *Le Corbusier*

JEANNÈST, PIERRE ÉMILE (1813–1857)
Porcelain modeller who had studied with the sculptor Delaroche. Jeannest came to England about 1842 and became a modeller at the Minton* factory. From 1848 to 1852 he was instructor in modelling at the Potteries School of Design and in 1852 he was employed by Elkington* as a designer.

JECKYLL, THOMAS (1827–1881)
English architect and designer of furniture and metalwork. Jeckyll was influenced by Japanese art, and became associated with the Aesthetic Movement*. The Peacock Room* for Francis Leyland was, until altered by J. M. Whistler, in a kind of Japanese-Gothic taste. Many of his designs in a Japanese style were for Barnard, Bishop & Barnard of Norwich who exhibited at the Philadelphia Centennial Exhibition of 1876. He commonly employed the sunflower* *motif*. His furniture designs were also strongly influenced by Japanese art, even, in some instances, to the point of asymmetry.

JELIFF, JOHN (fl. 1836–1890)
Furniture-maker of Newark, N.J., who worked in the 18th-century tradition, refusing to employ machinery. He used the neo-Gothic*, revived rococo, 'Louis XIV', and neo-Renaissance styles.

JENNENS & BETTRIDGE
Manufacturers of *papier mâché* whose factory was situated in Birmingham, where they were successors to Henry Clay, the noted 18th-century maker. Jennens & Bettridge made *papier mâché* of all kinds including furniture. They introduced the use of mother-of-pearl in decoration. The *Day Dreamer* chair, successfully shown at the Great Exhibition of 1851, was made by them. Jennens died sometime after 1851, and the firm's display at the exhibition of 1862 was in the name of Bettridge & Co. A good deal of their production is marked with their name. They were also suppliers to Spiers & Son* of Oxford.

JASPER. Satinwood cabinet mounted with an oval jasper plaque by Wedgwood*, and inlays of purplewood and ebony. Attributed to William Johnson & Son. c. 1870. *Sotheby & Co*

JENNENS & BETTRIDGE. A *papier mâché* chair of about 1850 with mother-of-pearl inlay. Jennens & Bettridge, Birmingham. *Antique Collectors' Club*

JENSEN, GEORG (1866–1935)

Danish silversmith, sculptor, and potter who exhibited ceramics at the Paris Exposition of 1900. In the same year he won a scholarship which took him to France and Italy. On his return he attempted to establish a porcelain factory, without success, and he then started to specialize in silver.

In 1907 he began to collaborate with the painter Johann Rohde in the design of silverware. These early pieces are much sought. His handwrought coffee-pots and tea-ware received a gold medal at the Brussels International Exhibition of 1910 which secured for him an international reputation. Jensen began to employ both silversmiths and designers to cope with increasing business, and shops for the sale of his work were to be found in Paris, London, New York, and Stockholm. These shops displayed jewellery and silverware of fine quality and good design which had been made by mass-production methods. The mark employed was *Jensen*.

JEROME, CHAUNCEY (1793–1860)

American clock-maker who started in business at Bristol, Conn., in 1821. Here he began to use brass movements for shelf-clocks* which revolutionized the clock-making industry of his day. Wooden movements were soon discontinued by his competitors. Jerome built up a flourishing business as well as a large export trade to Europe. He wrote a history of the clock-making industry in America from 1800 onwards which was published in 1860. He is regarded as one of the most important figures in American clock-making.

JERSEY CITY POTTERY COMPANY

Founded in 1825 as the Jersey Porcelain & Earthenware Company, it later became the American Pottery Manufacturing Co., and this was changed again to the style of the heading above in 1853. They made earthenware in considerable variety, and were the first American manufacturers to use transfer-printing* as a method of decoration. Porcelain was also produced. The factory closed in 1892.

JET

Type of coal (i.e. fossilized wood) found in Britain principally near Whitby, Yorkshire. It is relatively hard and will take a high polish. It is usually carved, engraved or cut into single facets. Jet was immensely popular in Victorian England, principally for jewellery. Beginning in the 1820s, it was not only fashionable at intervals thereafter, but it was also in demand for the many periods of mourning which occurred in the average Victorian family. The death of the Prince Consort in 1861 gave it especial impetus and it was also popular during the 1880s when black was a fashionable colour.

JEWELLED PORCELAIN

Porcelain in the decoration of which jewels are simulated by small drops of enamel. The invention of Cotteau at Sèvres* in 1771, the technique was revived in the 19th century by Worcester*, Spode*, and Minton*.

JEWELLED PORCELAIN. Pair of vases in the Sèvres style painted with a continuous band of figures in landscape (left; the well-known Cherry Pickers, probably from an 18th-century print). Jewelled round top and bottom. Paris. c. 1890. *Antique Collectors' Club*

JEYPORE ENAMELS

Enamel work of fine quality was done in India during the 19th century, a noted centre being Jeypore (Jaipur).

Jeypore enamels came from the north-west of India, and the designs usually show fairly strong Persian influence. These enamels are probably the best of Indian workmanship, but enamels of variable quality, some extremely good, came from Delhi, Benares, Multan, Kashmir, Lahore, Hyderabad, Karachi, Lucknow, Cutch, Bahawalpore and many places in the Punjab where enamelling on copper in particular was practised. Jeypore, with Delhi and Benares, was noted for enamelling on gold.

Generally the Sikhs enjoyed the reputation of being the best craftsmen in enamel in the Indian continent. In the 19th century there were four families at Jeypore, working in their own houses, executing orders for jewellers on objects of gold or silver already prepared for them. The designs thus prepared were in either the *cloisonné* or the *champlevé* technique and taken from books of patterns, some of considerable age, from which the customer could choose.

The enamels employed were a form of glass paste coloured with metallic oxides and a wide range of colours was available for application to gold. The number of colours which could be employed on silver was more limited and on copper only black, white and pink are to be found. The latter sometimes failed to adhere properly.

The gold employed was always pure, usually not lower than 18 carats, because it is difficult to enamel successfully on gold of a lower standard. Little work was executed in silver because of the difficulty of fixing the enamel to the surface, probably because the metal employed was too pure. Fabergé employed a silver of lower than normal standard for enamelled work, due to the difficulty of securing firm adherence of enamels to official alloys. The traditional colours were excellent in quality, but enamels imported from Europe were employed on some of the later work, with injurious results. The enamellers of Jeypore were skilled in the application of a fine ruby red which was commended by the jurors of European international Exhibitions where their work was shown.

The processes were uncertain, and it was not unusual for a piece to be re-started two or three times when blemishes occurred at one stage or another. The maharajahs were always the most favoured customers. About a third of the output, not particularly large, was for European buyers.

Necklaces, bracelets, and handles of various kinds (sword, dagger, fly-whisk, umbrella, etc.) formed a considerable part of the manufacture. Horse, camel, and elephant trappings were enriched with gold, precious stones and enamel. Cups, small stands, bowls, decorative spoons, cardcases, match-boxes, scarf-rings and cuff-links were also made.

JONES, OWEN (1809–1874)
English architect and decorator. Jones travelled in Italy, Greece, Turkey, Egypt, and Spain, and on his return he achieved a modest success as a designer of several public buildings. Nevertheless, his speciality was interior decoration, and his influential work, *The Grammar of Ornament*, was published in 1856. He was associated with Sir Henry Cole* and Matthew Digby Wyatt* and became a superintendent of works for the Exhibition of 1851. When the Crystal Palace was removed to Sydenham he designed the Greek, Roman, Egyptian, and Alhambra Courts. In 1867 he published *Examples of Chinese Ornament*.

JUGENDSTIL, DER
The Youth Style, the German version of *art nouveau** which was also linked with the *Sezession** in Austria and Germany. The style took its name from that of the magazine *Jugend*, first published in Munich in 1896, with the slogan *Aufbruch der Jugend* (youth is on the march). It played a similar part to *The Studio* in England.

'JULIUS CAESAR' JUGS   See *Meigh & Son, Job*

'JULIUS CAESAR' JUGS. Jug decorated in low relief with a scene depicting the landing of Julius Caesar in 55 B.C., by Charles Meigh*. Second quarter of the 19th century. *Godden of Worthing Ltd*

K

KANDERN POTTERY (Baden)
Pottery under the artistic directorship of Max Laüger*
from 1895 to 1913. The principal manufactures were
tiles in the *art nouveau* style, vases, bowls, and wall-
plaques. Figures were made after models by the
sculptor B. Hoetger. Impressed mark incorporates
Laüger's monogram.

**KARLSRUHE GROSHERZOGLICHE MAJO-
LIKA-MANUFAKTUR** (Baden)
Factory founded in 1900 by H. Thoma and Wilhelm
Süs. It moved in 1916 to Hartwald. Figures were
modelled by J. Wackerle*, Franz Blazek, and Emil
Pottner, and Max Laüger produced vases decorated
with slips of contrasting colours in a style inspired by
South German peasant pottery. Thoma painted
faïence with nymphs and dragons. Carl Kornhas
(1857–1931), who had studied at the Kunstgewerbe-
schule at Nürnberg, made pottery painted in the style
of 15th-century *maiolica* which he had studied in
Italy. The art-director was Max Laüger. Mark: *GMK*
impressed or painted.

KAYSER, JEAN (Krefeld-Bochum)
Manufacturers of ornamental metalwork founded by
Jean Kayser (1840–1911) in 1885 near Düsseldorf.
From 1896 pewter in the *Jugendstil* was made
extensively with the mark *KAYZERZINN* (Kayzer
Pewter). Objects were principally ash-trays, dishes,
lamps, vases etc. decorated with floral *motifs* typical
of the style. Their products were sold in London by
Liberty & Co.*

KEENE GLASS WORKS (Keene, New Hampshire)
A factory for the making of green and amber bottles
and flasks was established here in 1816, although it
did not immediately achieve success. The 'Sunburst'
flask, and those with Masonic and Eagle decorations,
blown into two-piece moulds were made here.

KELLER & GUERIN (Lunéville, Meurthe-et-
Moselle)
Manufacturers of pottery who commissioned designs
from Edmond Lachenal*. Mark *KG* or *K&G,
Lunéville*.

KENDALL, T. H. (1837–1911)
Furniture designer and manufacturer of Warwick.
Both Kendall and his son were trained by J. M.
Willcox, a master-carver, and were skilled practitioners of the art. They became known for their
sideboards, but they also produced firescreens, tables,
chairs, etc. especially between 1850 and 1870.

They were commissioned by the County of Warwick to carve a sideboard for presentation to Queen
Victoria, which she refused.

KENT, WILLIAM (fl. 1878–1894)
At first in partnership as Kent & Parr in Burslem,
Staffordshire, making earthenware figures, many of
them from old moulds bought from discontinued
factories. Most of their productions were the so-called
'flat-backs'* of c. 1840 onwards, but some reproductions of models by Obadiah Sherratt* and others
probably come from here and may have been moulded
from existing models.

From 1894 the firm was William Kent, and from
just after the First World War it became a limited
company. Kent's reproductions can be detected from
differences in colouring. The factory also produced
large pairs of spaniels and hens on nests* for the
decorative pottery trade. It closed in 1962, but the
'flat-back' moulds still exist in Staffordshire. In the
1900s the firm also possessed the moulds of figures
inspired by Tallis's *Shakespearean Gallery* (published
in 1852) which they employed to produce new
examples.

See *Staffordshire portrait figures*

KENTON & CO.
Established 1890 in Bloomsbury, London, by a group
of architects as an offshoot of the Arts and Crafts
Movement* including W. & R. Lethaby*. They held
an exhibition at Barnard's Inn in 1891, but the
company was wound up for lack of capital in the
following year.

KEWBLAS
Trade name of a decorative glass produced by the
Union Glass Company*. It is a satin glass* with an

177

iridescent* surface similar to 'Favrile'*. The name is an anagram of W. S. Blake, the works manager at the time.

KEYS, EDWARD (1798–after 1853)
Porcelain modeller, son of Samuel Keys*, who was a Derby* gilder. Edward Keys worked for Derby* until 1826. Then he left for Staffordshire to work for Minton*, and in 1842 unsuccessfully tried to make porcelain on his own account. When this venture failed he worked for Wedgwood* at Etruria until 1853.

KEYS, SAMUEL (fl. 1830–1864)
Modeller at Derby* who moved to Staffordshire about 1830. Here he went into partnership with John Mountford as a maker of Parian* ware, producing wares of sufficiently good quality to warrant an Honourable Mention at the Great Exhibition of 1851. The firm became Keys & Briggs before 1862, in which year they sent 'majolica'* to the London International Exhibition.

KITSCH (German)
This is a term more easily understood than defined, and it is applied to the kind of object rarely, or never, seen before the middle of the 19th century, although it exists very commonly today.

Kitsch refers to objects in bad taste. Good taste has been aptly defined as a sense of what is appropriate. *Kitsch* could therefore be defined as an excessively vulgar inappropriateness in the design of an object. It also implies the commercial use of art to make rubbish for mass-consumption. One or two examples are, perhaps, the best way of defining the word. A realistically vulgar seaside postcard by someone like Donald MacGill is not kitsch, but a porcelain figure of Venus produced by a Thuringian manufacturer in the 19th century which had a small clock neatly centred in the middle of her belly most certainly is. So is a porcelain inkstand produced by a French maker in the form of a woman's breast the cover of which is a nipple. A 19th-century poster depicting the Pope seated on his throne, drinking from a cup marked 'Bovril', beneath the words 'Two Infallible Powers—the Pope and Bovril' is another excellent example, and can be dated fairly precisely to 1870 when the Vatican Council proclaimed the doctrine of papal infallibility.

A good deal of highly carved Victorian furniture falls within this category, especially when it is something strictly utilitarian, like a hat-stand. Most kitsch is notable for maudlin sentimentality, and the *Angel Cot* in brass, exhibited in 1851 by Winfield of Birmingham, is an excellent example of an attitude of mind which developed in England towards the end of the 18th century and was not entirely dead in the 1880s.

In the 20th century kitsch has been especially connected with the cinema, and with objects inspired by it, and more recently by television. It is very commonly to be met in advertising, and in objects made for the mass market.

KLABLENA, EDWARD (1881–1933)
Potter, who studied at the Vienna Kunstgewerbe-schule and in Germany. He modelled for the Berlin Porcelain Factory* in 1910 and 1911. In 1911 he acquired his own workshop in Langenzersdorf, where he continued to make figures. Painted mark includes the name *Langenzersdorf.*

KLASTERAC (Czechoslovakia)
Formerly Klosterle, Bohemia. A porcelain factory founded in 1793 by Ignaz Prosse in the grounds of a castle belonging to Count Thun. Prosse had the aid of the arcanist, Sontag. The earliest production was in the style of the contemporary Thuringian factories. After passing through several hands, and suffering numerous vicissitudes the factory's production began to increase in both quantity and quality around 1811, when it specialized in enamel painting. Both French and Viennese styles were copied. After 1840 transfer-printing* and lithography were employed in decoration, and the production of figures began about the same time.

About 1895 the factory was renamed the Thun'sche Porzellanfabrik.

KLÖSTERLE (Bohemia)   See *Klasterac*

KNOBS, GLASS
Knobs as drawer- and door-handles were usually made from pressed glass* in a variety of colours, but commonly of clear or amber glass. In America opal and light blue knobs were also common. Knobs of blown and cut-glass* were produced, and among the most sought today are the very rare knobs with *millefiori** decorations.

KNOWLES, TAYLOR & KNOWLES CO. (East Liverpool, Ohio)
Pottery and porcelain factory started by Isaac W. Knowles in 1854 to make Rockingham* and yellow ware. The manufacture of ironstone china (granite ware)* was started in 1872, and a type of bone-china was later employed for decorative work. A kind of porcelain inspired by Irish Belleek* was termed 'Lotus' ware. The factory enjoyed considerable success.

See *Porcelain*

KNOX, ARCHIBALD (1864–1931)
Designer responsible for 'Tudric'* and 'Cymric'* pewter and silver for Liberty & Co,* the manufacturer being W. H. Haseler. Knox was born in Douglas (Isle of Man) and came to London in 1897. As a designer he was one of the leaders of the Celtic* revival. He executed several hundred designs for Liberty's. In his

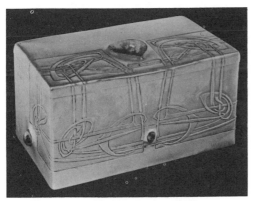

KNOX, ARCHIBALD. Casket of 'Cymric'* silver in the *art nouveau** style, designed by Archibald Knox and made by W. H. Haseler* for Liberty & Co*. The silver is applied over a wooden base. Mark: *L&Co.* Hall-mark for 1903–1904. *Victoria & Albert Museum, London*

later years he taught at the Kingston-on-Thames School of Art.

KNY, FRIEDRICH (fl. 1870–1920)
Bohemian glass engraver who had his own workshop in Stourbridge, Worcestershire, and also worked for Thomas Webb & Sons*. He was noted for cameo-glass* cutting and *Hochschnitt** engraving.

KOEPPING, KARL   See *Köpping, Karl*

KÖPPING, KARL (1848–1914)
German designer and glass-engraver who studied painting and engraving in Munich and Paris. By 1890 he was Professor of Etching and Engraving at the Berlin Academy and had begun to produce his tall, slender blown glass forms in iridescent metal. These important examples of *Jugendstil** glass design are notable for contorted stems arising from a flat base and terminating in multi-coloured bowls of leaf or flower form. His glasses, which are much sought, are signed *Koepping*.
   See *Zitzmann, Friedrich*

KOTHGASSER, ANTON (1769–1851)
Porcelain painter and gilder at the Vienna State factory, 1784–1840. Glass painter from about 1812 until at least 1830, probably as a *Hausmaler* (see *Hausmalerei**) and usually on the *Ranftbecher**. His subjects were varied and he excelled in floral paintings. He also executed minutely-detailed topographical studies of Vienna. Kothgasser's colours are brilliant, and he sometimes employed the yellow stain used for stained glass. Forgeries of his work, which is sought after, exist. Some of his glasses are inscribed in French and his work often bears his address

KNY, FRIEDRICH. The 'Elgin' claret-jug*, wheel-engraved by F. Kny* for Thomas Webb & Sons*. Executed for the Paris Exposition, 1878, the subject being taken from the Elgin marbles in the British Museum. Signed. *Victoria & Albert Museum, London*

(Spanischer Spitalberg, 227) in addition to his signature.

KRAMER, CHRISTIAN (1773–1858)
German glass-maker who emigrated to the United States in 1797 in which year he began to make domestic glass at New Geneva, Pa. About 1807, in company with other German glass-makers, he established a factory at Greenboro, Pa., where amber, green, cobalt and other coloured glasses of excellent design and quality were made until 1849. This glass is also sometimes called 'Kramer family' glass.

KRIEGER CO. (79, Faubourg St. Antoine, Paris)
Manufacturers of high-class furniture for drawing-rooms and dining-rooms. They specialized in richly-decorated cabinets and sideboards, and exhibited a large bookcase surmounted by cupids and festoons of flowers, with panels carved with hunting and fishing trophies, in London in 1851 which was described as being 'in admirable taste'.

179

CABINET. Cabinet designed by A. H. Mackmurdo and made
by E. Goodall & Co. Probably for Pownhall Hall,
Manchester. c. 1886. The inscription reads: Nor heed nor
see/What things they be/But of these create he can/Forms
more real than living man. (Shelley.) *William Morris
Gallery, Walthamstow*

OWEN, GEORGE. Vase of ivory porcelain decorated with elaborately pierced panels and moulded ornament. The style exhibits some Near-Eastern influence. George Owen for the Worcester Royal Porcelain Company. c. 1890. *Private Collection*

HENRI DEUX WARE. Earthenware ewer modelled and inlaid in the manner of the 16th-century Henri Deux (Saint-Porchaire) ware by Charles Toft. c. 1865. *Minton Museum, Royal Doulton Tableware Ltd*

L

LACEWORK IN PORCELAIN

The imitation of lace in porcelain is achieved by dipping actual lace into porcelain body diluted with water, followed by draping it round the figure. During firing the cotton burns away, leaving a copy of its mesh in porcelain. The introduction of this kind of decoration took place during the last quarter of the 18th century at Meissen* (some say Meissen was anticipated by Strasbourg), but at this time lacework additions were comparatively slight. Elaborately flounced lace skirts belong to the 19th and even the 20th centuries. Meissen have done some work of this kind.

In England both Derby* and some Staffordshire factories made limited use of lacework in the early decades of the 19th century. Charles Toft* also applied the principle to the decoration of pottery.

LACHENAL, EDMOND (1855–1930)

French studio-potter, who worked for Théodore Deck* in 1870, and started his own studio in Paris in 1880. He moved to Chatillon-sur-Bagneux in 1887. His stoneware and porcelain were often decorated in relief with foliage in the *art nouveau** style, the glaze surface sometimes modified by the use of hydrofluoric acid*. Lachenal also made *faïence* with painted decoration, and supplied designs to Keller & Guerin* of Luneville. His son, Raoul, made stoneware from 1904, using coloured glazes contained within raised clay outlines (a kind of *cloisonné* technique). Mark: *LACHENAL*, painted.

LACQUER DECORATION ON FURNITURE

Decoration in a pseudo-Chinese or Japanese style on furniture of many kinds became popular in the 1920s. It was executed either in bright colours, or in gold on black. Excellent reproductions of lacquer decoration on furniture are still being produced in East Anglia.

LACY GLASS

Pressed glass* with a stippled background between the elements of the pattern with an effect not unlike that of old lace. It was extensively manufactured in America by the Boston and Sandwich Glass Company*, whose cup-plates* in this style are especially sought.

LALIQUE, RENÉ (1860–1945)

French jewellery designer, and designer and manufacturer of decorative glass. He studied at the École des Arts Décoratifs, Paris, and served an apprenticeship with a goldsmith named Aucac. From 1878 to 1880 he studied at Sydenham College, London, and then started to design jewellery for Cartier and

LALIQUE, RENÉ. Honey-pot by Lalique* in the *art déco* style. France. 1927–1929. *Pilkington Glass Museum*

LALIQUE, RENÉ. Two automobile mascots by René Lalique. Left: St Christopher. Right: A Red Indian head for fitting to a radiator cap. c. 1925. *Antique Collectors' Club*

Boucheron. When Lalique exhibited in the Paris *Salon* of 1894 he had already attracted the attention of Sarah Bernhardt, which led to his receiving the patronage of Robert de Montesquiou, a prominent leader of fashion.

A little later he came to the notice of Calouste Gulbenkian and there is a notable collection of Lalique jewellery at the Gulbenkian Museum, Lisbon. As a designer of jewellery Lalique broke new ground by employing materials not often used for the purpose at the time. His *art nouveau** subjects were for the most part based on plant and animal forms. The dragon-fly is an example. Lalique was also probably the first to use the female nude as the subject of a piece of jewellery.

No doubt his use of glass in the making of jewellery turned Lalique's attention to the making of decorative glass generally and in 1909 he acquired his own glass works at Combes-la-Ville, producing pieces each of which was unique. Soon after the outbreak of the First World War he turned his attention to the design of commercially produced glass and to a range of elegant scent-bottles for the *parfumier*, M. Coty. In 1921 he acquired new premises at Wingen-sur-Moder in Lorraine.

Lalique specialized in the making of opalescent glass and glass coloured to resemble semi-precious stones. His crystal glass is of exceptional clarity. His panels often depict the nude female figure, or animal, bird, or insect subjects. His mark is *LALIQUE* or *R. LALIQUE*, diamond-engraved on the best pieces, and etched on the commercial productions.

LAMPS. *Torchère* (one of a pair) of gilt wood and gilt metal. Late 19th century. *Sotheby & Co*

LAMPS

Lamp-bases and reservoirs were made by the New England Glass Company* and the Boston and Sandwich Glass Company* from about 1828. Usually the bases were of pressed glass* both clear and coloured, the chimneys and shades being of blown glass. The shades, sometimes of opaline* or cased glass*, were decorated with cutting, engraving and etchings. The early fuel was whale-oil, replaced by kerosene about 1860. These lamps, the best of them extremely decorative, were the main sources of home-lighting until the introduction of the electric lamp. Similar lamps were manufactured in Europe by the glass factories in the same general style. Lithophanes* of porcelain were occasionally employed instead of glass shades. These are rare and much sought.

LANCASTER GLASS WORKS (Lancaster, Pa.)

A cooperative glass works founded by a group of Pittsburgh glassworkers which survived until the 1880s. They made liquor bottles, flasks, and perfume-bottles. Attributed to them is the 'Success to the Railroad' flask and those with Masonic emblems.

LANDAIS, C. J. (1800–1883)

Potter of Tours, nephew of Avisseau*, who also reproduced the work of Palissy* which he exhibited at the Paris Exposition of 1855. There are specimens in the Bethnal Green Museum, London.

LANNUIER, CHARLES HONORÉ (1779–1819)

French *ébéniste**, born in Chantilly, who came to New York in 1790. From 1805 he was in business and was very highly regarded, being the chief competitor of Duncan Phyfe*; in fact some of his furniture may have been mistakenly attributed to Phyfe. After Lannuier's death his foreman, J. Gruez, continued the business for about five years.

LANDAIS, C. J. Dish based closely on a 16th-century prototype of the type usually called 'rustic ware'. Made by C. J. Landais. Tours. Mid 19th-century. *Victoria & Albert Museum, London*

LANTERI, EDOUARD (1848–1917)

French sculptor, born in Auxerre, who came to London in 1872. In 1874 he joined the staff of the Royal College of Art from which he retired in 1910. His work is represented in English public galleries, including the Victoria and Albert Museum, London.

LARCHÉ, RAOUL-FRANÇOIS (1860–1912)

Art nouveau* sculptor, pupil of J. F. Jouffroy and F. A. Falguière, who modelled decorative objects for metal and porcelain, and is especially noted for a series of figures of the American scarf dancer, Loïe

LARCHÉ, RAOUL-FRANÇOIS. Gilt-bronze table lamp* in the form of a figure of Loïe Fuller*, by Raoul-François Larché*. c. 1900. *Antique Collectors' Club*

Fuller*, some of which were adapted as electric table lamps. His mark was impressed, *RAOUL LARCHÉ*.

LATTICINIO (Italian)

The practice of decorating glass by embedding 'canes' of white opaque glass in clear or coloured glass. By manipulation of the glass while in a softened state these canes can be formed into a variety of intricate patterns. The technique was very popular in Venice in the 16th century, where the type of glass employed was particularly suitable for work of this kind.

LATTICINIO. Ruler with *latticinio** decoration. c. 1848. *Pilkington Glass Museum*

Attempts were made to revive it in Bohemia* in the 1830s, but these were not particularly successful. It was left to the Choisy-le-Roy*, Baccarat,* and Saint-Louis* factories of France to revive it on a considerable scale. In the 20th century the technique has been employed by Paolo Venini* of Venice.

LAÜGER, MAX (1864–1952)

German architect and sculptor who became an artist-potter at the end of the 19th century. He became art director of the Grosherzogliche Majolikamanufaktur (Karlsruhe*). His work, influenced by the *art nouveau** style, was principally in slip of contrasting colours. He also experimented with ceramic sculpture.

LAVA CAMEOS

Italian high-relief cameo carving executed in relatively soft lava, the substance emitted in a liquid state from the crater of volcanoes. Much of the lava employed for carving came from the region of Pompeii. The colouring is variable, usually biscuit or red, but sometimes grey, green, or black. Many of these cameos were mounted as jewellery of one kind or another, especially brooches, in either gilt-metal or pinchbeck*. Unlike shell cameos a gold mount is exceedingly rare. Value depends on the quality of the work and the attractiveness of the subject. Lava cameos are not uncommon.

See *Shells, cameo-carved*

LAVA GLASS

Glass made by the Mount Washington Glass Works* in the 1870s, the appearance of which imitated lava ware*. A type known as slag glass* in Britain.

LAVA WARE

In America, a solid agate ware produced at the Bennington, Vt. factory between 1853 and 1858. It was a mixture of grey and brown clays under a clear glaze. Also known as scroddled ware.

In England, a coarse stoneware* with a hard glaze used in the 19th century for making 'cottage china'. A similar ware was made in Germany.

LAZY SUSAN
A revolving circular tray on a tripod foot intended to be placed on the table-top and used to carry condiments.

LEACH, BERNARD (b. 1887)
English studio-potter, born in Hong Kong, who studied at the Slade School, London. He returned to the Far East in 1909, and in Tokyo studied the art of *raku** pottery and stoneware*. He spent some years in China and Korea before returning to England and settling at St Ives in Cornwall. In 1933 he set up a slipware pottery at Shinner's Bridge, Devon. In 1934 he returned to Japan and from 1937 devoted himself to stoneware.

The Leach pottery produces distinctive utility stonewares excellent in quality, and fine quality decorative wares. In form and ornament this is often influenced by Chinese stonewares of the Sung dynasty and the *raku* wares of the Japanese potters. Bernard Leach's pupils include Michael Cardew*, Katherine Pleydell-Bouverie, and David Leach. His mark is the monogram *BL*.

LEBEAU, CHRIS (1878–1945)
Dutch potter and glass designer, at first in the *art nouveau** style. He was employed by the Royal Dutch Glass Works* from 1922 to 1925, and helped to develop the *Serica* and *Unica* ranges of glass in association with A. D. Copier*. His work also includes crackle and cameo glass*.

LE BLOND—BAXTER PRINTS See *Baxter prints*

LEBOEUF, MILLET ET CIE
Manufacturers of porcelain and *faïence-fine* who united the Creil* and Montereau* factories in 1841. A notable service was designed for them by E. Rousseau* with decoration by Félix Bracquemond* in 1867. The table-service by Rousseau was marked: Modèle
      E. Rousseau
      À Paris.
Usual marks: CREIL
          L. M. et CIE
          MONTEREAU

LE CORBUSIER (Jeanneret, Charles Edouard, 1887–1965)
Swiss architect and designer who worked mainly in Paris and became a naturalized French citizen in 1930. As an architect Le Corbusier became widely known for his dictum that a house is a machine for living in. However, his houses have not, for the most part, aged well, because he overlooked the fact that most people do not like living in machines. Nevertheless, at the time, his designs, intended for mass-production with synthetic materials, had great influence on modern styles. His tables, chairs and cupboards (open and closed) were especially designed to fit into his 'machine-like' houses, and were reduced to bare essentials. Many of his chairs, designed to fit the curves of the human body, were made by Thonet*.

LEEDS POTTERY
The 18th-century factory of Hartley, Greens & Co. continued to flourish for the first 20 years or so of the 19th century, but it then declined, and in 1825 was sold to Samuel Wainwright. Subsequently it became the Leeds Pottery Co., then Warburton, Britton & Co., closing finally in 1878.

The later wares, often imitated from those made earlier, even, in some cases, to the use of old moulds, were often marked LEEDS POTTERY impressed, but the 19th-century mark is very clear and even, unlike earlier marks which were apt to be uneven and irregular. Creamware* was the most usual body employed and the old pattern-books provided most of the designs, as they did later in the century for other Leeds factories who copied the old wares.

LEEDS POTTERY. Creamware* cruet stand with pierced walls inspired by contemporary silver, surmounted by the figure of a boy. c. 1805. *Author*

The factory also produced a small quantity of Egyptian black* (in competition with Wedgwood's basaltes*) and lustre*-decorated ware. A body whiter than creamware, with a bluish glaze, corresponded to Wedgwood's pearlware*.

A factory at Hunslett Field, Leeds, belonging to Petty & Rainforth was in existence from about 1790 to 1880. It made blue printed earthenware and creamware, and some unmarked creamware made by them is sometimes mistaken for the work of the old factory. Slee's Modern Pottery founded in 1888 also made imitations of old wares using the old pattern books, and possibly the moulds also. The original mark was imitated. These later copies are generally lighter in weight than the old specimens and too precisely finished.

LE GAIGNEUR, LOUIS See *Boulle marquetry*

LEGRAS ET CIE (Pantin, Paris)
French glass-makers founded as the firm of Stumf, Touvier, Viollet et Cie about 1855. This became two factories c. 1900, one the Verreries et Cristalleries de Saint-Denis and the other, at Pantin, the Cristallerie de Pantin* (See also *De Varreux*). In 1900 both glasshouses were under the direction of Charles Legras, who was succeeded by François-Théodore Legras in 1909. From 1908 the firm made glass for Lalique*, and about 1920 the two enterprises were reunited under the name of the Verreries et Cristalleries de Saint-Denis et de Pantin Réunies. Marks: these include *LEGRAS*, and the trade-mark, *MONTJOYE*.

LEIGHTON, THOMAS (1786–1849)
Glassworker from Birmingham, Warwickshire, who emigrated to the United States in 1826. He worked for the New England Glass Company* at Cambridge, Mass., until his death as 'gaffer' (foreman). He was succeeded in this capacity by his son.

LEISTLER & SON, CARL (Vienna)
Furniture manufacturers who exhibited at the Great Exhibition of 1851 and were widely acclaimed for the luxury and quality of craftsmanship displayed. Michael Thonet* was employed by them before he set up his own factory. The most notable piece of furniture exhibited by Leistler was a vast bookcase decorated in a spiky Gothic style which was designed by the architect Bernardo de Bernardis. This was presented to Queen Victoria by the Emperor Franz Josef of Austria and is now in the Bethnal Green

LEISTLER & SON, CARL. Bookcase by Carl Leistler* in a revived Gothic* style exhibited in 1851 at the Great Exhibition, and later given to Queen Victoria by the maker. It is now in the Bethnal Green Museum, London. *Illustrated Exhibitor*

Museum, London. Also exhibited by Leistler was a bookcase in a revived Renaissance style* and a monstrous canopied bed in the same style, carved with angels, cupids, and much besides; included were porcelain plaques and massive fringes and hangings more elaborate than anything the 17th century could show. Chairs and a *canapé* in a grossly exaggerated rococo style bore little resemblance to Royal French furniture of the Louis XV period apart from asymmetricality. The back of the *canapé* rose to an elaborate cresting of C and S scrolls*, acanthus* foliage and a cupid, while in the angle, where the back joined the arms, a grotesque mask occurred. The chairs were also heavily decorated with fringes and tassels in a manner quite out of keeping with French rococo of the 18th century. A contemporary description suggested that this furniture was only for the very rich, and that ordinary people could only look on and admire. Apart from the bookcase I have been unable to trace the whereabouts of any of it now, but it did influence subsequent production in England for a few years after the Exhibition, although nothing quite so elaborately decorated was produced.

LENOBLE, ÉMILE (1876–1940)
French studio-potter who started his career with Ernest Chaplet*, and then made wheel-thrown stoneware inspired by Chinese wares of the Sung dynasty (960–1280) and those of Korea, to which he was introduced by a friend who was a well-known *amateur* with a collection of wares of the period. Some of his carved and *sgraffito* decoration were obviously inspired by Lung Ch'üan celadons* and Tz'u Chou stonewares. In the 1920s he turned to geometric decorations usually incised through slip.

LENOIR, ALEXANDRE (1761–1839)
French antiquary, nominated by the Convention as keeper of the Musée des Monuments Français. He collected medieval sculptures, statues, and monuments from churches, abbeys, and convents to save them from destruction by the more ardent of the revolutionaries, and about 25 years later the Musée provided inspiration for French neo-Gothic* designs which, in turn, inspired the Cathedral* and Troubadour* styles.

LENOX COMPANY (Trenton, N.J.)
Factory established in 1906 for the manufacture of porcelain by Walter Scott Lenox, who was apprenticed at Ott & Brewer* and had been a partner in the Ceramic Art Company*. The Lenox Company principally made a 'Belleek'* type of porcelain with a glaze somewhat less lustrous than that employed at the Irish factory. The factory also employed acid gilding* and transfer-printing*.

LÉONARD, AGATHON (b. 1841)
Sculptor and designer, who studied at the Lille Academy and worked in Paris. He modelled figures

for Sèvres* in porcelain about 1900, notably the series called *Le Jeu de l'Écharpe*, inspired by Loïe Fuller*, and exhibited at the Paris Exposition, 1900. His work was also reproduced in gilt-bronze. Incised signature: *A. Leonard* Sclp.

LEROY, DESIRÉ (fl. 1874–1907)

French porcelain painter, trained at Sèvres*, who arrived in England about 1874 and worked for Minton*. He was at Derby* between 1890 and 1907. His subjects included miniature arrangements of fruit, musical trophies, exotic birds (inspired by the 18th-century work of James Giles and the Sèvres painters Evans and Aloncle) and large bouquets of flowers, as well as gilding and design.

LEROY, DESIRÉ. *Jardinière* in an Oriental *cloisonné* enamel style decorated by Desiré Leroy. The stand is simulating one of carved wood. c. 1875. *Minton Museum, Royal Doulton Tableware*

LESSORE, ÉMILE (1805–1876)

French painter and ceramic artist. His father was a notary, but Émile, preferring art to the law, studied under Ingres, and exhibited his first painting in the Paris *Salon* in 1830, continuing to exhibit annually with considerable success until 1850. In 1851 he was persuaded to take up porcelain painting at Sèvres*, where he was very successful, a pair of vases from his hand selling in 1853 to the Emperor of Russia for 1,000 guineas. Nevertheless, there were those who found his influence at the factory undesirable, and rather than become the focus of quarrelling factions Lessore left Paris in 1858 and went to England, working for a short time for Minton*, and then transferring his services to Wedgwood*. Here his work, principally on creamware*, was highly successful. He was awarded medals at the London Exhibition of 1862, the Paris Exposition of 1867, and the Vienna Exhibition of 1873. He attracted a great deal of attention at the time and, although highly-priced for the work of a contemporary artist, it was nevertheless eagerly bought by the fashionable as an investment, according to the press of the time. In

LESSORE, ÉMILE. Portrait of the artist Émile Lessore* by his son. *Josiah Wedgwood & Sons Ltd*

LESSORE, ÉMILE. Plate of glazed earthenware* painted with a rustic scene by Lessore*. This plate may be compared with Lessore's work for Wedgwood*. French. c. 1865. *Victoria & Albert Museum, London*

LESSORE, ÉMILE. A group of *putti* in characteristic style painted on 'Queen's ware'* by Lessore*. c. 1863. *Josiah Wedgwood & Sons Ltd*

1863, finding the climate of Staffordshire affecting his health, he returned to France, living at Marlotte, near Fontainebleau, although he continued to paint cream-ware for Wedgwood. Here he died in 1876.

Lessore is noted for a very individual style of figure painting which is delicate and spontaneous. His colouring is sparing, with a great feeling for light and shade, reminiscent of some contemporary French landscape painting. Lessore usually signed his work *É. Lessore* or *Émile Lessore*. Watercolours signed by him also exist.

LETHABY, WILLIAM RICHARD (1857–1911)

English architect and designer. Lethaby was principal assistant to R. Norman Shaw* from 1881 to 1893, a founder member of the Art Workers' Guild*, and of the Arts and Crafts Exhibition Society*, Professor of Design at the Royal College of Art in 1890, and a member of the firm of Kenton & Co.* He designed furniture, metalwork, and pottery. His furniture was principally in oak, sometimes decorated with marquetry. Rare pieces of mahogany or rosewood were designed for Marsh, Jones & Cribb*.

LEVEILLÉ, EUGÈNE (fl. late 19th cent.)

Leveillé succeeded Eugène Rousseau* in 1885, producing glass in the manner of his predecessor. Like Rousseau, his glass is massive and often crackled and he sometimes employed cased glass*. He exhibited successfully at the Paris Exposition of 1900.

LE VERRE-FRANÇAIS   See *Schneider, C.*

LEYRER, C. (Munich)

Bronze-foundry which cast models by E. von Stuck* and other sculptors. Mark: founder's name, impressed.

LIBBEY GLASS COMPANY (Toledo, Ohio)

Glass works founded in 1888 by Edward Libbey (former agent of the New England Glass Company*) who had leased it in 1878. The company made Amberina*, but specialized in cut-glass* of excellent quality which became extremely fashionable towards the end of the century. The mark, LIBBEY, was sometimes used.

LIBERTY, SIR ARTHUR LASENBY (1843–1917)

The son of a Chesham draper, the eldest of eight children, Liberty was educated at Nottingham University School, and at 16 he was apprenticed to a draper in Baker Street, London. At this time he was interested in the arts and the theatre, and probably to further these interests, which received little stimulation from his work as a draper's apprentice, he joined the firm of Farmers & Rogers of Regent Street, where he was engaged in handling Oriental textiles. Later he became manager of their Oriental warehouse, where he met fashionable people like Whistler, some of the pre-Raphaelites, and collectors of Oriental *objets d'art*, particularly blue and white porcelain.

With the aid of a loan from his father-in-law, Liberty began his own business of Liberty & Co.*, also in Regent Street, in 1875, starting with Oriental silks, but soon adding many other things for which the firm achieved a high reputation. By 1890 Liberty had acquired a modest fortune, and a beard which sometimes caused him to be mistaken for the Prince of Wales. He was Master of the Glass Sellers' Company, contributed papers to the Society of Arts, and belonged to an exclusive literary society known as The Sette of Odde Volumes. He was knighted in 1913. See below.

LIBERTY & CO. (London)

The Regent Street store founded by Arthur Lasenby Liberty* in May, 1875. Liberty had started his career with Farmer & Rogers' Oriental warehouse. This firm he joined in 1862, the year of the International Exhibition, and when the Exhibition closed Farmer & Rogers bought the Japanese exhibit, which included manufactures new to the European market. Liberty became manager of this department, and ran it very successfully. Here he came into contact with Whistler and other collectors of the fashionable Oriental blue and white porcelain.

He decided to open his own store in Regent Street, and at first concentrated on Oriental goods, especially fine silks, for which he soon established a considerable reputation. He also sold Japanese *bric-à-brac* of all kinds, from images of the gods to swords and metalwork, and objects of lacquer, which were listed under the heading of 'curios'.

Soon after starting in business, Liberty began to deal in furniture. This, and woodwork for interior decoration, was made for the firm by workshops, often not far away, which applied their label. Furniture was also imported from Egypt, Morocco, India, China, and Japan. The first catalogue of Oriental goods published in 1880 also included chairs, stools, and wastepaper baskets made in Africa of rattan* cane, and bamboo* furniture—chairs, tables, and shelves of one kind or another—were described as 'Anglo-Oriental', and made to order in nearby Soho.

In 1883 a furnishing and decorating studio was opened under the direction of Leonard F. Wyburd*, who also functioned as a designer. The 'Thebes' chair was a design patented in 1884. It was suggested by stools found in Egyptian royal tombs, but was a common design in the ancient world generally. It was among the Liberty products sold by Samuel Bing* in his Maison de l'Art Nouveau in Paris. It was also one of the exports to Berlin and Vienna. Liberty's furniture was sold by Serrurier-Bovy of Liège, who were designers of furniture and interiors, and in Italy the firm became synonomous with the name of the style, and *art nouveau** was commonly known as the *stile liberté*. In 1900 the well-known chair designed by Richard Riemerschmid* reached London, and was to be found in Liberty's showrooms.

Silver and jewellery began to assume importance in 1899 with the introduction of the 'Cymric'* range of designs, made in Birmingham in close association with W. H. Haseler*. The object was to offer a well-designed ware at a lower price than traditionally-made silver. This was made possible because a large part was played in the manufacture by machine and machine-production methods. Nevertheless, to meet the demands of the time, pieces were given some of the qualities and appearance of handwork. As the name implies, many of the early designs in particular were based on Celtic metalwork, and were the work of Archibald Knox*, who seems at one time to have worked in the studio of Christopher Dresser*. Other designers include B. Cuzner, Rex Silver, and J. M. King. The maker's mark is either *L&Co.* or *WHH*, and the word 'Cymric' usually occurs in addition. 'Tudric'* pewter was the result of the increasing demand for this alloy at the end of the century, when pewter of contemporary design, excellent in quality, was imported by Liberty's from Germany, made by Jean Kayser*. The 'Tudric' range was introduced at the end of 1901, and, like 'Cymric' silver, Celtic inspiration predominated. Designs were by Archibald Knox and Rex Silver, and the maker was W. H. Haseler. Manufacturing arrangements with Haseler ended in 1926, but 'Tudric' remained in production until 1939.

In the realm of pottery, porcelain, and glass, Liberty began by importing Japanese and Chinese ceramics, but by 1890 they were stocking a large variety of pottery from several European countries. Among their more important suppliers may be noted Max Laüger* of Karlsruhe, Arabia Osakeyhtio*, Cantagalli*, and Zsolnay of Hungary. Glass came from Lötz*, Ørrefors*, Leveillé*, and Venini*. Potteries in England supplying Liberty's, apart from such large firms as Wedgwood* and Doulton*, include the Bretby Art Pottery*, the Della Robbia Pottery*, Burmantofts*, and William Moorcroft*. Glass included the 'Clutha'* range, and the products of James Powell & Sons*. Some of these firms produced Liberty designs which are marked with their name.

The firm, which still flourishes and continues to uphold its traditions, celebrated its centenary in 1975 with an exhibition at the Victoria & Albert Museum. It played a very important part in the dissemination of the *art nouveau** style. After the First World War it reverted to more traditional styles to a considerable extent, and during the 1930s it tended to concentrate on textiles. The end of the Second World War, however, saw the adoption of a policy of encouraging fine quality craft work which still continues.

LIGHTER   See *Briquet*

LIME GLASS
A substitute for lead glass discovered in 1864 by William Leighton, a chemist employed by a glass works at Wheeling, W. Va. It was cheaper to make

than lead glass, it cooled more rapidly and it was lighter in weight, even though its appearance was inferior. At first employed for glass of domestic utility, it later became much more widely employed.

LIMED OAK
Oak treated with lime wash which, when dry, was brushed off the surface, leaving traces of lime in the grain. The wood itself is greyish in colour. It has enjoyed varying popularity in England since about 1900.

See *Fumed oak*

LIMOGES ENAMEL
The earliest enamels from Limoges (Haute-Vienne), were of the *champlevé** type. From the beginning of the 16th century to the end of the 17th, painted enamels predominated and these were revived in the 1820s when early examples were popular among collectors. They remained more or less popular until the First World War, and prices for good specimens have shown a considerable up-turn during recent years. Among the 19th-century collectors of antique

LIMOGES ENAMEL. Standing cup in a revived Renaissance style, the decoration based on that of earlier Limoges enamels, consisting of baroqu strapwork with grotesques, masks, flowers and acanthus foliage. Bone china painted by Stephen Lawton. c. 1858. *Minton Museum, Royal Doulton Tableware*

enamels was the Prince Consort, who suggested to the Worcester* factory that they could form a suitable inspiration for porcelain. The work was undertaken by Thomas Bott* who painted in thick white enamel on a dark blue ground. Similar work was done on porcelain at Sèvres* during the 1840s and at Rörstrand, Sweden, on earthenware in the 1880s. The technique was applied to *pâte-sur-pâte**. The revival of enamelling on copper during the 19th century included work from France and Austria which was strongly influenced by Limoges.

LIMOGES PORCELAIN (Haute-Vienne)

The discovery of kaolin, the clay essential to the manufacture of the true porcelain bodies used on the Continent, was made at Saint-Yrieix-la-Perche a little before 1770. Manufacture was undertaken in 1770 at nearby Limoges, in a factory which was bought by the king in 1784. This factory, in addition to its own wares, also produced white porcelain which was sent to Sèvres* for decoration. Jacob Petit* had some of his porcelain made 'in white' at Limoges for decoration in Paris.

By the end of the 18th century there were several factories in the district. Étienne Baignol produced table-services in the Empire style* and decorative, well-modelled figures in the popular biscuit porcelain*. A large part in the growth of the industry was played by François Alluaud who opened his factory in 1816. One of his innovations was a gold decoration on a black ground, and he also made some very large vases in the Empire style. Pierre Tharaud's factory, founded in 1817, was patronized by Charles X and produced decorative porcelain of fine quality, and the Monnerie factory, owned by Jean-Baptist Ruand, was the first to install a steam engine in 1845. In the same year the first experiments in firing with coal-gas were made in Limoges.

At this time vase forms were based on classical Greek and Italian vases and decorated with mythological subjects. Coloured grounds were popular, especially green and maroon, and limited use was made of a kind of transfer-printing* referred to as *l'impression*. The flower painting of the period is usually excellent in quality.

The Troubadour style* (the French version of neo-Gothic*, also called the Cathedral style*) made its appearance in the 1820s during the reign of Charles X, and is to be seen in some rare *veilleuses** in the form, suitably enough, of cathedrals.

By 1840 there were 30 factories in and around Limoges; by 1880 there were 42. A large export trade with America had been built up by 1853, largely due to the efforts of David Haviland*, who established a decorating studio in 1842 which was later expanded to take in manufacture.

After 1870 production at the Limoges factories was limited mainly to table-ware of good quality. The marks generally employed vary with the factory but the inclusion of the word *Limoges* is almost *invariable*.

'LINCRUSTA'

Trade name for a popular material for lining walls and ceilings during the 19th and early 20th centuries. Made, apparently, of coarse pulped paper, it was decorated with embossed floral ornament and painted or whitewashed *in situ*. When employed for wall decoration it usually covered only the lower half of the wall and was often painted dark brown. It was long-wearing and resistant to damage, but artistically unpleasing.

LINDNER, DORIS. A mountain pony made in a limited edition of 500 copies from the original model by Doris Lindner*. This spirited model is an excellent example of the high quality of modern Worcester* figure production. 1966. *Worcester Royal Porcelain Company*

LINDNER, DORIS (c. 1896)

Sculptor, porcelain designer and modeller, studied at Calderon's Animal School and St. Martin's School, London, and afterwards in Rome.

Doris Lindner was originally employed by Worcester Royal Porcelain Company to produce models of animals of all kinds, but has enjoyed widespread success with models in limited editions of horses and cattle. Her equestrian portrait of the Queen has been widely sought, and the model of the steeplechaser, Arkle, is also among her best-known works.

LINOSSIER, CLAUDIUS (1893–1953)

French metalworker noted for brass and copper vases in the *art déco** style. A vase of hammered copper

LINTHORPE POTTERY. Coffee-pot designed by Christopher Dresser*. Mark: *Linthorpe H.T. Sotheby & Co*

with inlaid silver decoration is in the Victoria and Albert Museum, London.

LINTHORPE POTTERY (Middlesbrough, Yorkshire)

Pottery established by John Harrison in 1879. Christopher Dresser* was art-director until 1882. Early wares were decorated with rich coloured glazes. Later decoration employed painting in slip or underglaze colours, *sgraffito**, and *pâte-sur-pâte**. Inspiration for some of its work was derived from Japanese and Chinese stonewares. The mark employed was LINTHORPE, sometimes with the name *Chr. Dresser* added when appropriate.

LISTON, JOHN (1776–1846)

A very popular comedian of his time. A large number of earthenware figures were made of Liston in his many roles from 1825 until his retirement in 1837. Perhaps the most frequent were Liston as Sam Swipes, from Hook's play *Exchange No Robbery*, and the name part from Poole's *Paul Pry*. Figures of Liston were also made in porcelain by the Derby* factory.

LITHOGRAPHIC DECORATION ON CERAMICS

Now the most widely employed method of decorating inexpensive pottery and porcelain, it was first used experimentally in Staffordshire in the 1840s in conjunction with engraving, but it was not until 1863

LISTON, JOHN. The actor John Liston in the role of Sam Swipes. c. 1830. *Author*

that Wedgwood* first attempted to use crude lithotransfers. By the 1890s several firms were working to develop the process, but it did not come into general use until relatively modern times. Photo-lithographic processes are also fairly modern, although the first attempts to use photography in the decoration of ceramic glazes started in the 1860s.

Lithographs for ceramic printing were made with a backing of special paper, using pigments capable of being fired on. The glaze was coated with a varnish and when this became tacky the picture was pressed on to it so that it adhered to the surface. The backing-paper was then stripped off.

See *Chromolithography; Currier & Ives; Decalcomania; Lithography; Transfer-printing*

LITHOGRAPHY

Printing process invented by an Austrian printer, Aloys Senefelder, towards the end of the 18th century. It became popular in France, England, and the United States. Lithographs are executed on a calcareous stone. The picture in monochrome is drawn on the surface in a greasy crayon or an oily ink. The area unmarked is then treated with dilute nitric acid. The prepared surface is used for printing by first wetting it with water and then passing an inked roller over it. The ink adheres only to the greasy surface and is repelled by the moist, nitric-acid treated areas, and the stone is then ready for printing.

Later developments include the substitution of metal plates for the stone, since these can be wrapped round rollers, and the use of rubber rollers for the final printing, a process which has both cheapened and vastly improved the quality of modern colour printing. In the case of photo-lithography a zinc or aluminium plate is given a light-sensitized coating. It is then exposed and must be developed and fixed before it is ready for use.

The principles here set out apply to lithographic printing of all kinds and the process enjoyed great popularity during the 19th century, being perhaps the cheapest and most efficient kind of colour printing using several stones, one for each colour, for a variety of purposes, including the multiplication of cheap prints for home decoration.

The process of decorating pottery and porcelain lithographically, introduced in the late 1840s, follows this sequence of operations, but the print is pressed on to the glazed surface while still wet, as in ordinary transfer-printing*. Patents for a process of this kind were taken out by Pierre-August Ducoté in 1839.

LITHOPHANE

A thin porcelain plaque with a design in *intaglio* intended to be viewed by transmitted light. Lithophanes were very commonly made into lampshades, where they are seen to best advantage. But they have a variety of ornamental uses, including the bottoms of beer-mugs, where the design can be seen when the mug is drained. The process appears to have originated as a novelty at Meissen*, and lithophanes were also made at Berlin—hence the term 'Berlin transparencies'. They were patented in France in 1827, and the rights were acquired in England by Robert Griffith Jones in 1828. He licensed several English factories to make a type of lithophane where the *intaglio* design was cast from a low-relief model instead of by the Continental method, where the original model was a wax *intaglio* used to take a low-relief working mould. The superiority of the Continental practice was due to the fact that the wax model was cut while light was passing through it so that the operator could see the picture forming as he worked and could therefore make continuous necessary modifications of thickness to produce the requisite variation of light and shade.

LITHYALIN. Waisted beaker of Lithyalin* glass by Friedrich Egermann* of Blottendorf-bei-Haida, Bohemia. c. 1830. *Pilkington Glass Museum*

LITHYALIN. Lithyalin* goblet in moulded blue and green glass. Friedrich Egermann*, Blottendorf-bei-Haida. Bohemia. c. 1840. *Sotheby & Co*

A mark often found on Lithophanes is '*AdT*', which has been associated with the Baron du Tremblay, thought to have invented the related *émail ombrant** process, but this is uncertain. Although usually unglazed and uncoloured, some lithophanes are glazed, made in a coloured body, or coloured on the surface. They are still made in Germany (sometimes from old moulds) and by the factory of Herend* in Hungary. In England known makers of lithophanes include Wedgwood*, Minton*, Copeland*, and Grainger* of Worcester.

LITHYALIN
Trade name for an opaque glass of variable colour imitating semi-precious stones invented by Egermann* of Blottendorf.

LLOYD, WILLIAM (1779–1845)
Cabinet-maker of Springfield, Mass. His work was excellent in quality and several pieces with his label are known.

LOBMEYR, J. & L. (Vienna)
Important makers of fine quality glass from about 1860 onwards. They specialized in cut and engraved work, and also devised techniques of iridizing the surface. The factory produced a great deal of *art nouveau** glass of distinction. Marked examples bear the monogram *JLB*.

See *Iridescent glass*

LOCKE, EDWARD (1829–1909)
Porcelain painter who worked at Grainger's* factory. In 1895 he established a small porcelain factory at Shrub Hill, Worcester, making wares which were principally copied from Grainger's, or from Royal Worcester*. Birds and animals in landscapes were

LOBMEYR, J. & L. *Ranftbecher* enamelled with musicians in an early 17th-century style, with 18th-century *Laub und Bandelwerk*. J. & L. Lobmeyr*, Vienna. Late 19th century. *Sotheby & Co*

LOBMEYR, J. & L. Large iridescent glass*
vase of classical form on pedestal,
decorated with a kind of *Laub- und
Bandelwerk* in enamels and gilt. J. & L.
Lobmeyr*, Vienna. Exhibited at the
Paris Exposition of 1878. *Victoria &
Albert Museum, London*

common objects. In 1902 the Worcester Royal
Porcelain Company obtained an injunction to prevent
Locke from using their mark. All the factory's
products are derivative.

LOCKER, WILLIAM (d. 1859)
Locker was clerk at the Old Derby* factory who,
when it closed in 1848, started another factory in
King Street, Derby, with the aid of some of the
original workmen (including Sampson Hancock)*
and some of the old moulds. Their output, limited in

amount, was very much in the old Derby style. After
Locker's death the firm was taken over by Stevenson,
Sharp & Company. The marks employed were *Locker
& Co. late Bloor*, and sometimes the old factory mark.

LOETZ (WITWE), J.   See *Lötz (Witwe), J.*

LONGWY (Meurthe-et-Moselle)
Factories for the manufacture of *faïence-fine** were
established here at the end of the 18th century. The
émaux de Longwy (Longwy enamels) were introduced about 1875. The designs owed some of their inspiration to the Near East, and the technique employed a
manganese outline which helped to confine variously
coloured enamels. Specimens of Longwy *faïence* are
in the Musée de Sèvres and the Bethnal Green
Museum, London. The mark is LONGWY
impressed.

LONHUDA POTTERY (Steubenville, Ohio)
Founded in 1892 by William A. Long, later of
Owens'* Pottery, Zanesville, the Denver China &
Pottery Company* of Colorado, and the Clifton Art
Pottery* at Newark, New Jersey. At Steubenville,
Long was in partnership with W. A. Hunter and
Alfred Day producing *faïence* decorated somewhat in
the manner of the Rookwood Pottery*. They were
assisted by Laura Gray, who had formerly worked at
Rookwood. Wares based on American Indian pottery
were made and exhibited at the Chicago World's
Fair, 1893. The pottery was bought by Samuel
Weller* in 1894, and moved to Zanesville. Mark:
LONHUDA impressed.

LOO TABLE
A circular table of medium size on a central pedestal
carried on a base with quadruple supports. The
support is usually well-carved, and the best quality
examples are either of walnut or rosewood.* The
central pillar and base which form the support are
distinct from one another in early examples, but in
the 1850s these elements were fused into an integral
design. The oval loo table made its appearance about
1860, the top sometimes with inlaid ornament, and a
'cage' of four pillars between the top and the stem of
the support (similar to that provided on some 18th-
century tip-up tables) may be found on certain
specimens.

The loo table, which is now in demand as a dining-
table, was originally intended for a card game of this
name.

LORENZL (SIGNATURE)   See *Art déco figures*

LOSANTI WARE
A hard-paste porcelain* made at Cincinnati by Mary
MacLaughlin (1847–1939) from 1898 to 1906. About
1901 painted decoration was replaced by carved floral
and foliate designs in an *art nouveau** style, and
pierced work was also employed. The ware was
exhibited at the Pan-American Exposition, Buffalo,
New York, in 1901. Marks: *LOSANTI* and *LMcL.*

LOTUS WARE   See 'Belleek' porcelain, American

LÖTZ (WITWE), J. (Klöstermuhle, Bohemia)
Johann Lötz acquired an existing glasshouse at Klöstermuhle in 1840 which was, as the name suggests, carried on by his widow after his death in 1848. The director in 1879 was his grandson, Max Ritter von Spaun*, who enlarged and modernized the factory, and specialized in glass imitating such semi-precious stones as agate. He also developed an iridescent glass with a surface similar to that of Tiffany's* 'Favrile'* glass. Lötz patented a technique of iridizing glass in 1873, and the firm was exporting iridized glass to North America by 1880. An analogous effect on porcelain glazes, which proved to be popular, had been achieved by Brianchon* in Paris 20 years before. Von Spaun's designs were numerous, and range from forms showing the influence of fourth century claw-beakers to those popular during the currency of the *art nouveau** style. Von Spaun died in 1908, but the firm continued until the Second World War.

LÖTZ (WITWE), J. Vase decorated with vertical feathering in pale mauve and gold iridescence. Engraved signature: LÖTZ. Vienna. c. 1900. *Sotheby & Co*

LOUDON, J. C. (1783–1843)
Author of the very influential *Encyclopaedia of Cottage, Farm, and Villa Architecture and Furniture* first published in 1833. There were three subsequent editions, the last of which was published in 1859.

LOUIS-PHILIPPE STYLE
Style current during the reign of Louis-Philippe (1830–1848). Generally it is notable for a continuation of Restoration styles with modifications. There was a pervasively sober air, the furniture being heavy and comfortable. Designs were also influenced by former styles, especially Gothic, Renaissance, and rococo, but new kinds of furniture became fashionable, notably the round table on a centre pedestal, new

varieties of occasional tables, the *fauteuil Voltaire*, and the *fauteuil crapaud* (a type of low armchair). Quantity production was started and chairs were well-stuffed and buttoned. Many kinds of wood were employed, stained in a variety of colours. Turning was employed for chair legs especially. The decorative *motifs* were those commonly employed in the rococo,

LOUIS-PHILIPPE STYLE. *Bonheur-du-jour* (a writing-desk for a lady's *boudoir*) decorated with porcelain plaques in the Sèvres style. c. 1830. *Phillips, Son & Neale*

LOUIS-PHILIPPE STYLE. Chair of fruitwood with caned seat and back and turned front legs. The design is typical of the change which overtook French styles with the accession of the *bourgeois* King Louis-Philippe. c. 1835. *Private collection*

neo-Gothic*, and neo-Renaissance* styles. It would not be unreasonable to call the style 'French Bierdermeier'.

LOW ART TILE COMPANY (Chelsea, Mass.)

A factory for the manufacture of tiles was established at Chelsea, Mass., in 1877 by John Low, who had studied art in Paris. The products of this company were noted for originality, both in America and abroad. For instance some were decorated with casts from moulds of such natural objects as flowers and leaves. Plaques with painted portraits, or portraits moulded by the chief modeller, Arthur Osborne, were among their more important products. William Grueby (who later founded the Grueby Faience Co.*) was trained here. The usual mark is *J & J. G. LOW. PATENT ART TILE WORKS.*

LÖWENICH, PETER (fl. second half of 19th cent.)

Maker of very deceptive copies of 16th-century Siegburg white stoneware* in the 19th century. These are usually ewers with a bridge spout ornamented in relief, or the tall, tapering tankards known as Schnellen. On one or two specimens examined the semi-circular ridges to be found under the base of genuine examples have been missing.

See *Rhineland stoneware*

LUCAS, DANIEL (d. 1867)

Landscape painter on porcelain at Derby*, who later worked in Staffordshire for Copeland* and several other factories. His painting, very much in the style of contemporary oil-painting, was in a romantic, topographical style which is not difficult to recognize. His sons—John, William, and Daniel—were apprenticed under him while he was still at Derby.

LUCAS, RICHARD COCKLE (1800–1883)

English sculptor, and maker of architectural models, who entered the Academy Schools in 1826, and won a Silver Medal in that year. Later he became well known for wax portraits and ivory carvings. He achieved notoriety because of the suggestion that he was responsible for a wax bust of *Flora* purchased by Dr Wilhelm Bode, director of the Kaiser Friedrich Museum of Berlin, as the work of Leonardo da Vinci. It is similar to a painting of *Flora* at one time attributed to Leonardo and now regarded as a schoolpiece. After Lucas's death a Southampton auctioneer stated that he remembered the bust being made in 1846 by Lucas, who had been lent the painting to copy. In this statement he was supported by Lucas's son, Albert Dürer Lucas, who said he remembered his father working on it. There was, however, another side to the story. The bust, according to the opposing parties, had belonged to Lord Palmerston and while in his possession it had been seriously damaged. Palmerston gave it to Lucas to restore, and told him if it proved beyond repair he

could keep it. The whole matter became bedevilled by the fact that German left-wing political journals seized on the matter as an excuse for an attack on the Establishment, represented by Bode, who was a scholar as well as being influential in Prussian government circles. Although it is not considered absolutely impossible as the work of Leonardo, it has never been satisfactorily decided whether or not it is contemporary work or a later forgery by Lucas. To judge by the latter's known work Lucas's authorship is somewhat doubtful. The battle raged hotly until 1914, when Dr Bode was awarded a title of nobility, becoming Wilhelm von Bode.

LUDWIG II (1845–1886)

King of Bavaria; friend and patron of Wagner; famous for his extravagant copies of earlier royal palaces. Ludwig may deservedly be called the last of the palace builders. His castle of Neuschwanstein* in the medieval style is built on a peak in the Allgau, the architects being Von Dollman, Riedl, and Hoffmann. Work was started in 1869 and completed in 1886. Mainly in a revived Romanesque style, it was an attempt to recreate the world of Tannhäuser and Lohengrin. From 1875 to 1878 Ludwig occupied himself with the Linderhof, based on the *Trianon* pavilion at Versailles. This possesses a *Salon* hung with Gobelins* tapestry. The palace of Herrenchiemsee*, situated on an island in the Chiemsee, was started in 1878. Work was stopped when Ludwig died in mysterious circumstances in 1886 and the building is incomplete. It contains a copy of the *Galerie des Glaces* of Versailles which is 245 feet long and cost about six million pounds in the currency of 1978. At the time of his death Ludwig was planning to build a copy of the Peking Summer Palace, and there was a rumour current in Munich that he was about to build a full-scale model of Vesuvius in eruption. His palaces were a very severe strain on the finances of Bavaria at the time, but they have since become a considerable tourist attraction.

LUKENS, ISAIAH (1779–1846)

A highly-skilled clock-maker of Philadelphia whose rare clocks are much sought today.

LUSTRE, NACREOUS

A process patented in 1857 in France and England by Jules Brianchon, which imparted a rich lustrous appearance to the glaze of porcelain, due to the action of bismuth. The inventor termed it 'Décor de couleurs nacrées', referring to a resemblance to the reflections of mother-of-pearl. Ware of this kind was made by M. Brianchon in the rue de Lafayette, Paris, and on the expiry of the English patent it was made by Belleek* and Worcester*. Similar glazes were also employed by Meissen*.

LUSTRE PIGMENTS
The technique of decorating pottery by depositing a thin metallic film on the surface of the glaze. The use of lustre in the 19th century may be divided into two classes: 1) lustre decoration on earthenware during the early part of the century, principally in Staffordshire and Sunderland, which owed little or nothing to the earlier employment of this technique: 2) the revival of the lustre-decorated Italian *maiolica** styles of the 16th century, and the still earlier styles of Islam and Moorish Spain (Hispano-Moresque), by William de Morgan*, Maw & Co.*, and Pilkington*, and a number of Continental factories, which took place towards the end of the 19th century and in the early years of the 20th.

The metals commonly used were gold, platinum, copper, and silver. Gold yields a red of varying shades, platinum a silver colour, copper its natural colour, and silver a pale yellow. Lustre pigments were often employed as complete covering. When this was silver derived from platinum the product was often called 'poor man's silver'. 'Resist' lustre required a paper pattern or stencil which was attached to the surface of the glaze, followed by the application of the lustre. During firing the paper burned away leaving a replica of its pattern underneath, the metallic film covering the remainder. By another method the part required to 'resist' the application of the lustre was covered with varnish.

Gold lustre, ranging in colour from pink to purplish-red, was painted or sponged on to jugs and mugs with transfer-printed* decoration. These were made for the most part in Sunderland.

Later in the century the very popular copper lustre jugs, sometimes with flowers raised in relief and picked out with opaque enamel colours, were made in large quantities and have continued to be made almost ever since.

The lustred wares made towards the end of the 19th century were of much higher quality than many of the earlier examples, but they were almost entirely derivative. The models were Hispano-Moresque* pottery, Isnik pottery* (then miscalled 'Rhodian' ware), and 16th-century Italian *maiolica*, principally from Deruta and Gubbio. Isnik pottery itself is never lustred, but some of its late 17th-century subjects were employed as inspiration for lustre decoration by de Morgan and others. The lustres were coppery red in colour, sometimes inclining to a very distinct red, when the ruby lustre of Gubbio was being imitated.

Some very close reproductions of 16th-century lustred Italian *maiolica* were made, including those of Gubbio with passages of ruby lustre, by Carocci, Fabbri & Co. Vases and dishes fairly closely imitated from Hispano-Moresque wares were also made by Cantagalli* of Florence and others, but in a copper-coloured lustre distinct from the lighter, almost straw-coloured lustres of Spanish wares of the Islamic period.

Among modern decorators to use lustre may be numbered Alfred and Louise Powell* and Daisy Makeig-Jones* for Wedgwood*, and Susie Cooper*.

See *Fairyland lustre*; *Moonlight lustre*; *Sunderland lustreware*

LUSTRES
Vases hung with prismatically cut glass drops are reputed to have been first shown in England at the Great Exhibition, 1851, by Count Harrach of the Riesengebirge, Bohemia. They became known as lustres and were widely popular in the middle decades of the century. Those of the finest quality were of cased glass*, with the upper layer partially cut

LUSTRES. Pair of table-lustres flashed with ruby glass, gilded, engraved and hung with prismatically cut drops of crystal glass. Bohemia. c. 1840. *Sotheby & Co*

through, often with enamelling and relatively profuse gilding. These were usually made in pairs, although larger garnitures are not unknown. The cheaper varieties were of coloured glass (usually pale pink, green or blue) with some mercuric gilding and these have not infrequently survived. The term 'prism vases' is sometimes applied to lustres of this kind.

LUTZ GLASS
A thin transparent glass striped with coloured twists in the Venetian *latticinio** style, introduced at the Boston and Sandwich Glass Works* by Nicholas Lutz* and also made elsewhere. The type is also sometimes referred to as 'candy stripe' glass. See below.

LUTZ, NICHOLAS (fl. 1869–1888)
French glassworker who was apprenticed at Saint-Louis* and worked at Murano, Venice. He went to the Boston and Sandwich Glass Company* in 1869, remaining until the factory closed. He specialized in *latticinio**, and introduced 'striped' glass* to America. His paperweights* are noted for miniature bouquets of flowers and fruits against a *latticinio* background. After 1888 he worked at the Mount Washington Glass Works* and the Union Glass Company*.

LYON & COMPANY, JAMES B. (Pittsburgh, Pa.)
The Company acquired the O'Hara Glass Works in 1852 and achieved a reputation for producing fine quality pressed glass* for which it received many awards. Some glass from this source has been regarded as deceptively close to cut-glass*. The works closed in 1886.

LYRE
Motif employed in the decoration of chair-backs and for the supports of some sofa-tables in the 19th century. In England the lyre principally occurs on Sheraton furniture, and in America it was employed by Duncan Phyfe*.

LYRE CLOCKS   See *Banjo clocks*

M

McGILL, DONALD (1875–1962)
Scottish comic artist who began as an architect's draughtsman, but turned to making drawings for coloured postcards of the kind sold at seaside resorts. McGill possessed an inexhaustible fund of vulgar humour of a kind calculated to embarrass the genteel and his work enjoyed a very wide circulation. The drawing is often witty, but his people are inclined to be stereotypes. His colours are flat and simple. His low-life subjects are best described as Rabelaisian and are certainly not pornographic. Since his death his work, especially some of his early cards, has been collected, and some of his original drawings were sold at Sotheby's late in the 1960s, bringing prices up to £60 apiece. McGill was the subject of an essay by George Orwell, and a biography, *Wish you were here,* by Arthur Calder Marshall. Some of his cards are still in print.

See *Postcards, picture*

MACHIN, ARNOLD, O.B.E., R.A. (fl. 20th century)
Ceramic designer, modeller and decorator who studied at Stoke-on-Trent and South Kensington. As a sculptor he is represented in the Tate Gallery, London, by two fine terracottas. In the 1930s he was connected with Minton* and Derby*, and in the 1940s began to model for Wedgwood*, where he has become especially well known for his creamware*

figures of bulls. A bust of Franklin Delano Roosevelt was executed in 1946. He has also produced sparsely coloured figures and groups inspired by Victorian 'flat-backs'*. He began to teach at the Royal College of Art in the 1950s. In the 1960s he became a Royal Academician and in 1968 modelled a series of figures allegorical of the *Four Seasons* for the Worcester Royal Porcelain Company* in hard-paste porcelain* in a limited edition of 150 sets.

MACHIN, WILLIAM (fl.1875–1912)
Owner of a factory at Hanley for making 'flat-back'* Staffordshire figures.

MACKINTOSH, CHARLES RENNIE (1868–1928)
Scottish architect and designer. The leader of a group of artists at the Glasgow School of Art who made important contributions to the *art nouveau** style. He belonged to a small group known irreverently as the 'Four Macs', which included the architect Herbert McNair and the two Macdonald sisters. Also at the centre of the group were Mrs Mackintosh and Mrs McNair, the wives of the two architects.

As an architect Mackintosh designed Glasgow School of Art (1899) and the Willow tea-rooms (1897–1898) for Miss Kate Cranston in Buchanan Street, the plans for which had been published in *The Studio**

MACHIN, ARNOLD. *The Seasons.* A limited edition of 150 sets in ormolu-mounted porcelain by Arnold Machin*. *Worcester Royal Porcelain Company*

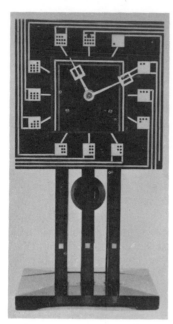

MACKINTOSH, CHARLES RENNIE. The
Domino Clock, veneered with ebony
and inlaid with ivory, designed by
Charles Rennie Mackintosh*, the case
made by German prisoners of war.
French movement. c. 1917. *Sotheby &
Co*

MACKINTOSH, CHARLES RENNIE.
Smoker's cabinet designed by Charles
Rennie Mackintosh*. 1916. *Victoria &
Albert Museum, London*

in 1897. The Art School and the tea rooms are key
works of the *art nouveau* style, although the appearance of the latter at the time they were opened is now
known largely from photographs.

By 1898 the influence of Mackintosh was apparent
in the interior designs of the Vienna *Sezession**. In
1900 he participated in the Paris Exposition and in
the same year the *Sezession* invited him to Vienna.
Apart from a local reputation in Glasgow, Mackintosh remained almost unknown in Britain, but his
reputation on the Continent was very high, especially
in Germany and Austria.

His furniture designs owe something to both
Godwin* and Philip Webb*, and some of his chairs
especially are not unlike Chinese domestic furniture.
His furniture designs date from 1890, and an early
cabinet with asymmetrical shelves in the lower part
is distinctly Japanese in style, the deliberate use of
asymmetry* being a Japanese characteristic. Both of
these influences may have come to him by way of
Godwin and the Anglo-Japanese* school. Mackintosh's furniture, often painted white, is much closer
to the *art nouveau* style properly understood than that
of most English furniture designers, and when he
exhibited with the London Arts and Crafts Society in
1896 he attracted a great deal of adverse criticism.

Nevertheless he received the enthusiastic support
of *The Studio*, the art magazine which began
publication in 1893, and was extremely influential in
promoting *art nouveau* internationally. As a furniture
designer Mackintosh was primarily an interior deco-

rator, and much of his furniture is not as effective
when divorced from its setting.

His career ends more or less with the First World
War and, although he lived for ten years afterwards,
it was in obscurity, a sufferer from ill-health and
financial stringency. Outside his native city, Germany
and Austria, his particular genius went largely
unrecognized until recent years.

MACKMURDO, ARTHUR HEYGATE (1857–1942)

English architect and designer, born in London,
educated at Felstead School, Essex, and Lambeth
School of Art. In 1869 he was apprenticed to T.
Chatfield Clarke of London, and in 1873 attended
Ruskin's* School of Drawing at Oxford. In 1874 he
made his first visit to Italy, and in the following year
established himself in practice as an architect in
London. Until 1880 he continued to visit Italy. He
met William Morris* in 1877 and Whistler* in 1880
and in 1882 he was elected an associate of the Royal
Society of British Architects. In 1882, he founded the
Century Guild*. He had craft workshops in Enfield,
and organized an Arts and Crafts Exhibition there
(see *Arts and Crafts Exhibition Society*). In 1902 he
married Eliza D'Oyly Carte, and his career after that
is unremarkable.

Mackmurdo designed furniture, wallpaper, metalwork and textiles, but his most important work was
as a book designer. Mackmurdo's *Wren's City
Churches* of 1883, which he wrote as an active member
of the Society for the Preservation of Ancient
Buildings which he joined in 1877, was the earliest
example of the style soon to emerge as *art nouveau**.
The title page of this book is a key work.

MAFRA (Caldas da Rainha, Portugal)

Mafra, since the early decades of the 19th century,
have specialized in reproductions of and derivatives

MACKMURDO, A. H. Small writing desk designed in 1886 by A. H. Mackmurdo for the Century Guild. Width 2ft 3in. *William Morris Gallery, Waltham Forest*

from coloured glaze wares, especially those of Bernard Palissy* and Whieldon. Copies of Whieldon tortoiseshell glazes come from here.

MAIOLICA (Italian)

Earthenware covered with glaze opacified with tin oxide. Wares of this type were first made in the Near East and were being produced in Italy by the 15th century. The secret of this glaze spread widely in Europe. It was termed *faïence* in France and Germany,

and *delft* in Holland and England. During the 19th century it was employed by Cantagalli* and the Ginori factory at Doccia*, among others, for reproductions of early wares, especially those of the 16th century.

MAISON MODERNE, LA (Paris)

A retail establishment under the management of the German art-critic Julius Meier-Graefe, who began it in 1897 to compete with Samuel Bing*. It commissioned designs from leading artists in the early years of the 20th century, including Henry van der Velde*, whose work caused considerable controversy, and in 1900 exhibited with the *Sezession** in Vienna. A printed mark was employed on the shop's wares giving the name and address.

'MAJOLICA'

A trade-name given to a type of pottery decorated with coloured glazes first shown at the Great Exhibition of 1851. Strictly, pottery of this kind is not *maiolica** in the correct sense of the word. This was a tin-enamelled ware with painted ornament produced in Italy during the 15th, 16th, and 17th centuries which, in its later versions, is often termed *faïence**. 'Majolica' seems to have been inspired originally by the coloured-glaze ware of the 16th-century French potter, Bernard Palissy*. It was introduced at Minton* by J-L-F. Arnoux*, the French art-director of that company. Palissy, who spent many years searching for the Italian secret, called his coloured-glaze ware '*maiolica*', which may account for the origin of the term. The Minton glazes were brilliant and varied in colour and the 1851 Exhibition displayed a vase of very large size designed by the sculptor, Baron Marochetti, which was highly commended by the Jury. A large amount of domestic ornamental ware was produced, as well as such architectural pottery as tiles and tile-panels and chimney-pieces.

MACKMURDO, A. H. Settee, or 'love seat', designed by A. H. Mackmurdo* and made by Collinson & Lock* for Morris & Co*. The upholstery is 'Tulip' pattern chintz designed by Morris & Co. c. 1890. *William Morris Gallery, Waltham Forest*

199

About 1860 Minton began to cover Parian* porcelain with the 'Majolica' glazes, which produced an ornamental ware of superior quality, at the same time as Wedgwood* began to use similar colours on

'MAJOLICA.' Pedestal decorated in variously coloured glazes, with lion-masks, busts, and vine-leaves in relief, and a vase *en suite* with handles in the form of female figures. Josiah Wedgwood & Sons Ltd*. Impressed mark. c. 1860. *Antique Collectors' Club*

a fine, white pearlware*. Others followed Minton in this development of Parian, notably George Jones of the Trent Pottery, Stoke-on-Trent, John Adams of Hanley and Thomas Bennington. This new development was in evidence at the London Exhibition of

1862. 'Majolica' remained fashionable until the end of the century. Much of the service-ware is in the form of overlapping leaves, and a revived Renaissance style* characterizes much of the ornamental ware. A few examples in the Japanese manner have been noted.

'MAJOLIKA' (German)

The German version of 'Majolica'* made at a number of factories from about 1860 onwards.

MAJORELLE, LOUIS (1859–1926)

One of the most prolific designers of *art nouveau** furniture. He was born at Toul, the son of an *ébéniste* who removed to Nancy while his son was still very young. Louis Majorelle eventually established a factory at Nancy where he made extensive use of woodworking machinery without sacrificing quality of either design or construction. This was a new departure since, until this time, machinery in France had been employed only for cheap mass-production

MAJORELLE, LOUIS. Chair from a small carved mahogany drawing-room suite by Louis Majorelle, Nancy, France. 1900. *Brighton Art Gallery & Museum*

furniture. Majorelle started to reproduce 18th-century styles, but came into touch with Émile Gallé*, also of Nancy, in the 1880s at a time when Gallé was also designing furniture. By 1890 Majorelle's furniture was markedly in the *art nouveau* style. His exhibits at the Paris Exposition of 1900 enjoyed great success and consolidated his reputation.

The factory at Nancy also had a department which produced metal mounts for furniture and metal table-lamps*, as well as a metal framework for containing decorative glass bowls and vases made by the brothers Daum*. The factory was closed when the German Army invaded Lorraine in the First World War, but was reopened in 1918, when the style of manufacture gradually turned to *art déco**. After Majorelle's death in 1926 the firm was continued by the former works manager, Alfred Levy.

MAKEIG-JONES, DAISY (1881-1945)
English ceramic designer, born the daughter of a doctor near Rotherham (Lancs). Her family moved to Torquay in 1899, where Daisy studied at the Torbay School of Art. She was given an introduction to Cecil Wedgwood, managing director of the great pottery firm, in 1909, and he agreed to her becoming an apprentice in the painting department. By 1914 she had exhibited such talent that she was on the designing staff, and Fairyland lustre* was first produced in October of the same year. Cecil Wedgwood was killed during the First World War, and although Daisy Makeig-Jones continued her work thereafter, she did not find it easy to work with his successors. In 1931, in consequence of a disagreement with Josiah Wedgwood (universally known as 'Mr Josiah') she retired to Torquay. There is little doubt that Mr Josiah recognized that the difficult times made Fairyland inappropriate, and sales were probably dropping. It began to return to fashion among collectors thirty years or so later, to start with in America.

MALACHITE
Malachite is copper carbonate, one of the ores of copper, a translucent mineral of light and dark copper greens with veining which will take a high polish. Russia has always been the principal source of supply, and blocks of very large size have been mined. Columns of malachite are to be found in the former royal palace of the Hermitage in Leningrad. Extremely large vases carved from this stone were displayed at the Great Exhibition, 1851, by Demidoff* of St Petersburg, who also displayed a small suite of malachite furniture, a large chimney-piece in the revived rococo* style with ormolu enrichments, and a pair of doors 14 feet high veneered with malachite. A small group of peasant figures in silver and malachite were similar in style to peasant figures from the Moscow porcelain factories and anticipated those in multi-coloured hardstones by Fabergé* later in the century. Fabergé employed malachite extensively for a wide variety of purposes.

Large objects in this stone are rare outside Russia, but small objects are not uncommon, although they are usually highly valued.

MARBLING
The painting of furniture to imitate marble. Used occasionally to a very limited extent during the Regency* period, it became a craze in England for a few years around mid-century. The painting of slabs of slate to imitate marble also belongs to the same period. The technique was sometimes referred to as 'Vitrilapis' or 'Vitrum Marmoratum'.

MARC, ANDRÉ (1887–1932)
Furniture designer; co-founder of the Compagnie des Arts Français with Louis Suë.

See *Suë et Marc*

MARINOT, MAURICE (1882–1960)
Originally a Fauvist painter who abandoned painting in 1912 to work in glass at Bar-sur-Seine. He became the master of many techniques, but all his glasses

MARINOT, MAURICE. Bowl of characteristically bubbled glass by Maurice Marinot*. France, Troyes, c. 1930. *Victoria & Albert Museum, London*

MARINOT, MAURICE. Heavy colourless glass vase with an induced crackle, showing the qualities at which Marinot aimed. c. 1925. *Victoria & Albert Museum, London*

were individually made and are rare. Marinot specialized in massive vases of bubbled glass with abstract, etched, or engraved decoration.

MARKS, HENRY STACY, R.A. (1829–1898)
English painter, especially of Shakespearean subjects, and designer of ceramics for Minton*. Plaques painted at Minton's Art Pottery Studio*, signed *H. S. Marks*, were shown at the Vienna Exposition of 1873.

MAROCHETTI, BARON CARLO (1805–1868)
Italian sculptor, born in Turin, studied in Rome and Paris, he settled in the last-named city until the

political disturbances of 1848, when he left for London. Here the Baron became well known, and he displayed some of his sculpture at the Great Exhibition of 1851. His statue of Richard, Coeur de Lion, was much praised, and a vase designed for Minton was highly commended. He died in Paris.

MARQUETRIE DE VERRE (French)
A type of glass introduced by Émile Gallé*, in which pieces of coloured glass softened by heating were pressed into the soft glass body of a vase. When the piece had cooled the surface was carved into a variety of ornamental motifs, usually floral. The technique was first employed in 1897.

MARREL FRÈRES (Paris)
Silversmiths and jewellers who flourished in the 1850s and enjoyed a notable reputation for work of fine quality. They seem principally to have worked in the revived Renaissance style*, contributing what they called a 'Cellini'* cup to the Great Exhibition. This was a large standing cup surmounted by a figure of Apollo with a lyre.

MARSH, JAMES R. (fl. 1845–1865)
Celebrated modeller in terracotta who exhibited a wine-cooler at the Great Exhibition of 1851. He worked as a modeller and designer for Davenport* for many years, and later functioned independently.

MARSH, JONES & CRIBB (London and Leeds, Yorkshire)
Cabinet-makers founded in 1850. Their early furniture was in the medieval style. Designers for the firm include Charles Bevan, Bruce Talbert*, and W. R. Lethaby*.

MARSHALL, PETER PAUL
A sanitary engineer from Tottenham who was a member of the firm of Morris, Marshall, Faulkner & Co. from 1861 to 1875. Marshall seems to have been one of those who suggested the firm, but his part in it otherwise appears to have been slight. Despite this he sided with Ford Madox Brown and D. G. Rossetti in the eventual break up of the partnership.

MARTIN, JOHN (1789–1854)
Newcastle painter of heraldic designs who later became noted for large fantastic paintings of the supernatural and the destruction of doomed cities. Soon after his arrival in London in 1806 he worked for the porcelain enameller Charles Muss*. It was said of Martin that he sometimes spent a whole day on a cup or vase.

MARTIN BROTHERS (Fulham and Southall, London)
English studio-potters (1873–1914) whose products are often termed 'Martinware'.

MARTIN BROTHERS. Covered vase of stoneware* in the form of a grotesque bird, designed by R. W. Martin, and a jug in the form of a fish with incised details. Martin Bros*, London & Southall. c. 1889. *William Morris Gallery, Waltham Forest*

The pottery was operated by four brothers, Robert Wallace, Walter, Edwin and Charles. The elder brother was trained as a sculptor, and had worked on some of the neo-Gothic* mouldings for the new Houses of Parliament. He studied at the Lambeth School of Art with George Tinworth* and did some modelling for Doulton* between 1870 and 1873. In the latter year he founded his own pottery in the

MARTIN BROTHERS. Stoneware clockcase in the neo-Gothic style. Martin Brothers, Southall. *Collection: Southall Public Library. Photo: Leonard Taylor*

MARTIN BROTHERS. Stoneware* vase
with floral decoration. Incised mark:
*MARTIN BROS. LONDON AND
SOUTHALL 1891. Constance Chiswell*

King's Road, Fulham, in association with his brother,
Charles. They were joined soon afterwards by Walter
and Edwin. In 1877 they established themselves at
Southall, Middlesex, a few miles away, where all the
operations appropriate to a pottery could be carried
on, and they opened a London showroom.

R. W. (Wallace) Martin was the leading spirit who
ran the firm's business affairs and modelled the
grotesque birds and figures for which the pottery is
noted; Walter prepared clay, threw vases on the
wheel and was responsible for incised decoration.
Although the grotesque animals and birds are now
the most widely known and sought of the Martin
products, their wares were extremely diverse in form
and decoration. They employed a grey stoneware*.
Decoration was incised or in relief, at first with
passages of cobalt blue and later with a more extended
range of colours. They usually made mask-jugs, mugs,
vases of all kinds, dishes, tobacco-jars (often in the
form of grotesque birds with detachable heads),
candlesticks and clock cases. The neo-Gothic* style
is apparent in the form and decoration of many
examples, and others exhibit Japanese influence.
Much of the important work was done by the brothers
themselves, but in the early years they employed the
young Mark Marshall, who left for Doulton's in 1876,
and W. E. Willey, who was a decorator in the 1890s.

Martinware seems invariably to have been marked.
R. W. Martin, R. W. Martin, London refers to the
Fulham period, *R. W. Martin, Southall* in script or
print, to the period after the removal. The opening of
the London showroom expanded the mark *R. W.
Martin London & Southall.* Also the form *R. W. Martin
& Brothers* occurs on many wares, or the simple
Martin Bros. All these marks were incised into the
unfired clay. The pottery closed in 1914.

MARTINUZZI, NAPOLEONE (fl. 1920s)
Italian sculptor, who started to cooperate with the
Muranese glass-maker Paolo Venini* in 1929, designing plant forms and figures, sometimes over a metal
framework in a bubbled glass known as *vetro pulagoso.*

A vase in the form of a plant is in the Brighton
Museum, Sussex.

'MARY GREGORY' GLASS
Glass painted with figures of children, so called after
Mary Gregory, who is said to have executed decora-
tion of this kind for the Boston and Sandwich Glass
Company*. The type originated in Bohemia, where

'MARY GREGORY' GLASS. Green glass
claret jug* painted with figure subject
in white enamel in the so-called 'Mary
Gregory'* style. c. 1870. *Constance
Chiswell*

'MARY GREGORY' GLASS. Fine quality dish enamelled in the
so-called 'Mary Gregory' style*. Last quarter of the 19th
century. *Sotheby & Co*

203

it was made in large quantities, and exported to the U.S.A.

MASON, MILES (1752–1822), AND FAMILY

Miles Mason, a London china dealer and glass seller, after some years of experience as a manufacturer in Liverpool and Fenton, started to make porcelain on his own account at Fenton in 1800. To judge from his advertisement he seems to have started by specializing in matching parts of existing Oriental services. He moved to new premises in Fenton in 1807, where he was in partnership with his son, William Mason, in the making of bone china (see *Porcelain*). Miles Mason retired in 1813, and his eldest son, William, took over another factory, leaving the first factory to the direction of the other sons, George Miles Mason and Charles James Mason. G. M. Mason withdrew in 1829. C. J. Mason invented and patented Mason's Ironstone China*, and became bankrupt in 1848. He opened a new factory at Longton in 1851 and

MASON, MILES, AND FAMILY. One of a pair of ironstone vases by C. J. Mason, of hexagonal Japanese shape decorated with subjects in an Oriental style. c. 1820. *Antique Collectors' Club*

MASON, C. J. Ironstone jug of typical form decorated with a 'Japan' pattern predominantly in underglaze blue and overglaze iron-red. C. J. Mason and George Miles Mason. c. 1820. V*ictoria & Albert Museum, London*

MASON, C. J. Bust of the Duke of Wellington in biscuit (unglazed) porcelain*, to be distinguished from the later introduction of Parian* or statuary porcelain. C. J. Mason. c. 1820. *Author*

exhibited at the Great Exhibition, but ceased business in 1854.

The early wares of Miles Mason included earthenware*, bone china, and a type of hard porcelain* which was both heavy and only slightly translucent. Oriental decoration is the rule, and a pseudo-Chinese seal (or square) mark was adopted, sometimes with the name *Miles Mason* in addition. Blue printed earthenware was also a popular manufacture.

G. M. and C. J. Mason were more ambitious and ironstone china lent itself to the making of very large pieces, including vases five feet in height and chimney-pieces made in sections. Ironstone services were frequently decorated in Oriental style. Blue printed earthenware continued to be popular, and the factory made a few rare biscuit figures, notably a portrait bust* of Wellington, of which an example is marked *C. J. Mason & Co.* Quality, generally, was mediocre, which may have been one reason for Mason's failure in 1848, when the moulds and engravings were bought by Francis Morley*. The latter formed a partnership with Taylor Ashworth in 1857, and when Morley retired in 1862, the enterprise was taken over by George L. Ashworth*.

The firm of George L. Ashworth & Brothers maintains a Works Collection of Mason's Ironstone China and they have reproduced some of the earlier wares.

Marks include the word MASON'S above a crown, with PATENT IRONSTONE CHINA beneath, and a factory building surmounting an ornamental border within which are the words FENTON STONE WORKS C. J. M. and outside GRANITE CHINA and STAFFORDSHIRE POTTERIES. Very similar marks were used by Morley, but with the name changed from Mason to Morley.

See *Ridgway & Sons, Job*

MASSIER, CLÉMENT (fl. late 19th–early 20th cent.)

Studio-potter at Golfe-Juan (Alpes-Maritimes), who had a showroom in the rue de Rivoli in Paris. He specialized in earthenware decorated with lustre on a brown glaze with floral and foliate *motifs*. He marked his ware *CLÉMENT-MASSIER, GOLFE-JUAN, A.M.* He is represented in the Brighton Museum, Sussex.

MASSIER, CLÉMENT. Earthenware bowl with lustre* decoration by Clément Massier*. Mark: *CM. Golfe-Juan. AM.* c. 1890. *Victoria & Albert Museum, London*

MATCH-HOLDERS AND CASES

Matches were not invented until 1826, when they appeared on the market under the name of 'Friction lights'. They were followed by Lucifers about 1829, and the waxed Vesta during the 1830s. The latter were the first to contain phosphorus as the igniting agent. It was soon discovered, however, that phosphorus matches, usually made in Germany, ignited very easily and accidents were numerous, so metal containers, often japanned, were introduced, and continued to be popular until the 1870s, by which time the match had become reasonably safe. The most practical of these early boxes were, of course, steel or brass, and are little more than curiosities although, in keeping with the spirit of the time, all of them were ornamental in one way or another. Boxes to be stood on the table for containing matches have a roughened surface, usually on the bottom, for

MATCH-HOLDERS. Cast-iron match-box holder in the form of a donkey with provision for striking Vestas. Provenance unknown. Last quarter of the 19th century. *Constance Chiswell*

striking them. Those of wood were commonly of *lignum vitae*, with a screw top, and those of Tunbridge ware*, Mauchline ware*, or *bois durci** may be found occasionally. The best ceramic boxes are those made by Wedgwood* in either basaltes* or jasper*, but other materials were often used, to be identified from the striking surface where there is doubt otherwise. Porcelain match-holders were often well decorated. Table match-holders of cast-iron, notably those in the form of road-sweepers, flower-sellers and other characters of the streets, were made by Zimmermann of Hanau, Germany.

During the 1850s small boxes, usually of silver, were first made to contain wax Vestas for the lighting of cigars and were kept either in the waistcoat pocket or hung from the watch-chain; the usual form was thin and rectangular and hinged at the side, with a roughened surface on the bottom on which the match could be struck. The type of match used was the 'strike anywhere' variety which survives today as 'Swan' Vestas, which are also a suitable size for many old match-cases.

Silver match-cases were decorated with chasing, engraving and enamelling for the best qualities. Many were embossed in low relief by die-stamping. Some of the more unusual and sought-after types are in such shapes as a woman's leg (a survival of the 18th-century porcelain *étui* in this form), the owl, the violin, champagne bottles, etc., while the Boer War saw boxes decorated with photographs of royalty and successful generals. Boxes in the form of champagne bottles, and of other things lending themselves to manufacture in miniature form, were often forms of advertisement for the products they represented. Dual-purpose match-cases which had a compartment for holding a sovereign in the days of real money, or stamps, or with a cigar-cutter, can all be found. Apart from silver, brass and white metal were both extensively employed. Silver is hall-marked. Boxes in other metals sometimes carry the diamond-shaped registry mark* if the design was registered before 1883, and after this date, a registration number.

The introduction of the safety-match with the striking composition on the side of the box brought the wearing or carrying of match cases to an end, since there was no way of providing a permanent striking composition, and few were made after the 1920s. The First World War also saw the rise to popularity of the cigarette lighter (French—*briquet**) which was increasingly made in a portable version, instead of the earlier table-lighters which had existed since the 1830s. These, too, are now collected.

MATIFAT, CHARLES STANISLAS (Paris)

Manufacturer of decorative metalwork during the middle decades of the 19th century, especially clock cases, chandeliers, vases, mirror-frames, figures and furniture mounts. Matifat also produced some important and decorative examples of cast and chiselled silver. He exhibited in London in 1851 at the Great Exhibition.

MAUCHLINE WARE
Small objects of light coloured sycamore wood, decorated with pen and ink drawings in the early period, or with painted ornament. From 1832, when the business had greatly expanded, black transfer-prints (nearly always topographical) were increasingly employed instead. The enterprise was started by W. & A. Smith of Mauchline, Ayrshire, Scotland, about 1821, who made snuff-boxes and razor-strops. They soon diversified in favour of many other objects of decorative utility and by 1829 had opened a warehouse and showroom in Birmingham, Warwickshire. By 1843 they had agents in London and Paris. A little later they opened a factory in Birmingham for assembly and decoration.

The partnership between Andrew and William Smith was dissolved in 1843, each continuing in business on his own account. William died in 1847, and Andrew, by taking his son William into partnership, revived the old name of W. & A. Smith. This firm continued in business until 1904. In the 1840s the Smiths had considerable success with tartan wares (see *Tartan ornament*). At first the patterns were painted directly on to the wood, but manufacture was speeded up by printing them on paper which was glued to the wood. The Birmingham Museum (Pinto Collection) has a tartan calendar intended for the French market. The transfer-printed* wares were largely intended as souvenirs, and were decorated with views of fashionable resorts, spas, watering places and so forth. They cover the British Isles, the United States and Continental countries. The views of France included most of the places popular with British tourists.

MAUCHLINE WARE. A Mauchline ware* holder for a travelling-glass decorated with a view of William Shakespeare's house at Stratford-on-Avon. Second half of the 19th century. *Constance Chiswell*

Although the Smiths were the principal makers of Mauchline ware, similar work, mainly snuff-boxes, was produced by other Scottish makers, but they did not long survive the waning of the fashion for snuff-taking.

MAW & CO. (Worcester and Jackfield)
Potters, originally established at Worcester, who made vases and decorative earthenware, and were among the pioneers of tile-manufacture in the 19th century. They removed their factory to the site of an old ironworks at Jackfield, near Broseley and Iron-bridge, in Shropshire, where they used Severn Gorge clays. A factory (known as the Benthall Works) was erected at Jackfield early in 1883, where the manufacture remained until removed to Stoke-on-Trent in 1970.

Tiles became fashionable for the decoration of walls and floors with the Gothic revival* and Maw began by producing tiles in the medieval style, followed by those with relief ornament and tiles decorated with coloured glazes. About 1860 they started to make *tesserae* for mosaics in the form of cubes of pottery. The general styles of ornament followed those fashionable at the time, including Near Eastern *motifs*. The production of art-pottery dates from about 1875, and Walter Crane* provided some of the designs. The factory designer from 1889 to 1906 was Charles Temple, who was responsible for many of the exhibits sent to the Chicago World's Fair of 1893. Maw & Co. were probably the largest manufacturers of tiles in England during the 19th century, and they supplied the tiles for some of London's Underground stations at the turn of the century. After their removal to Stoke, the Ironbridge Museum inherited a large collection of sample tiles and plaster moulds, representing the work of a century. The mark usually employed was MAW, and occasionally FLOREAT MAW SALOPIA.

MAZEPPA, JAN (1645–1700)
A hetman (chief) of the Cossacks who was in the service of the King of Poland, Mazeppa was surprised by a Polish nobleman while making love to his wife. Seized, stripped, and bound to his horse, Mazeppa was turned loose into the forest. Nevertheless he survived the journey to be made Prince of the Ukraine by Peter the Great. His adventures have been the subject of a poem by Byron, a novel by Bulganin, and of paintings by Horace Vernet. A play based on his amorous adventure in Poland, with Ada Isaacs Menken as Mazeppa, provided the subject of Staffordshire pottery figures, in which the half-naked actress, bound to the back of a galloping horse, is depicted with wolves running alongside.

MEAKIN, J. & S. (Hanley, Shropshire)
Manufacturers of earthenware founded by James Meakin in 1845 and still operating. The firm has always exported extensively to the American market,

and has principally made wares of domestic utility. The mark used is the name of the firm.

MEASHAM WARE
A name sometimes given to barge ware* made at several centres in Derbyshire because it was sold on the canal at Measham, Leicestershire.

MEDIEVAL COURT, THE
A section of the Great Exhibition of 1851 principally decorated by A. W. N. Pugin*, assisted by Hardman & Company* of Birmingham, J. G. Crace*, the interior decorator of Wigmore Street, and the porcelain manufacturer Thomas Minton*. The furniture (including pianofortes), stained glass, carpets, and brass ecclesiastical decoration were all in Pugin's revived Gothic and Minton supplied a tiled stove to his designs which looked more like a medieval tomb than a piece of heating apparatus. Much of the brasswork, made by Hardman, consisted of lecterns, alms dishes and altar rails. At this time Pugin was at the height of his influence on contemporary decoration, but he died in the following year, and revived Gothic began to follow new paths under the guidance of other hands.

See *Gothic Revival, The*

MEEKS & SONS, JOSEPH (New York)
Furniture-makers from 1794 to 1868. Much of their furniture was based on French styles of the 1820s, principally revived rococo and neo-Renaissance. The firm opened a branch in New Orleans in 1835.

MEHWALDT POTTERY (Bergholtz, near Niagara Falls)
Pottery founded by Charles Mehwaldt in 1851, who made a red-brown lead glazed ware which somewhat resembles that of Bennington* except that the glaze does not have the metallic appearance of the latter. The pottery closed in 1887.

MEIGH, CHARLES   See *Meigh & Son, Job*

MEIGH & SON, JOB (Hanley, Staffordshire)
Job Meigh founded the Old Hall Pottery about 1805, and took his son into partnership in 1812. The style of the firm was not immediately altered after Job Meigh's death in 1817, and only became Charles Meigh in 1835. They made a large quantity of printed wares, including a series known as *Zoological Sketches*. They produced large quantities of stone china and became noted for stoneware* jugs moulded with an arcaded Gothic decoration (probably suggested by old Rhineland stoneware*) with figures in niches. These jugs, popular in America, were widely copied there. Figures, groups and busts of Parian* ware were usually white, but there is a Parian jug decorated with a moulded portrait of Prince Albert against a blue background. The 'Julius Caesar' jugs*, moulded with elaborate scenes representing the invasion of Caesar's Legions in 55 B.C., were produced by Charles Meigh in the 1840s. The marks include the initials J. M. & S. or C. M. & S.

MEISSEN PORCELAIN MANUFACTORY (Saxony)
This world-famous royal factory, founded in 1710, had, by 1800, reached a disastrous period in its history, principally due to the devastations of the Napoleonic Wars, the collapse of the market at home for fine quality porcelain and the virtual impossibility of exporting its products to its traditional markets abroad. In addition, what demand still existed in the home market was largely being supplied by factories making creamware* in the manner of Wedgwood*. In 1814 the Russian government appointed a commission under Count Repnin to reorganize the administration of Saxony, and Counsellor of Mines von Oppel was placed in charge of the factory. Von

MEISSEN PORCELAIN. Shepherd and shepherdess in 18th-century costume, the girl with an open birdcage, the boy holding a dove—an allegory of Liberty and Matrimony. Meissen*. Late 19th century. *Sotheby & Co*

MEISSEN PORCELAIN. Plate with a *bleu-de-roi* ground finely painted with a subject after Caspar Netscher. Meissen. Mid-19th century. *Sotheby & Co*

MEISSEN PORCELAIN. *Tête-à-tête* in a revived rococo* style painted with harbour scenes, a popular subject of the 1720s and 1730s. Meissen. Cancelled mark, probably denoting decoration outside the factory. Late 19th century. *Sotheby & Co*

MEISSEN PORCELAIN. Large figure of a monkey based on a figure of about 1730 by Kirchner or Kändler. Meissen. Second half of the 19th century. *Sotheby & Co*

MEISSEN PORCELAIN. *Bolognese Hound*, after a model by Johann Joachim Kändler of about 1735, probably from the original moulds. Mid-19th century. Meissen. *Sotheby & Co*

Oppel immediately discontinued painting in underglaze blue (an expensive type of decoration) except to special order, and ordered ornaments in the classical style from Wedgwood and Etruria to act as an inspiration. Underglaze blue painting was again started in 1819. Porcelain in the manner of Wedgwood's jasper* (*Wedgwoodarbeit*) mainly belongs to this period. Heinrich Kühn was appointed technical director.

The factory was soon put on a more profitable basis, and antiquated techniques and business methods were constantly improved. The first sign of the new dispensation was the reduction of prices at the Leipzig Fair. Slightly defective wares which had been stored 'in white' were sold off to independent decorators (*Hausmaler*), and from 1822 a poorer quality porcelain was employed for the making of utilitarian wares. Kühn introduced a type of mercuric gilding which was a good deal cheaper than the method formerly employed, although inferior in appearance. Another attempt to cheapen production involved the employment of pressed glass* vessels from which moulds were made, but the quality of wares made in this way was obviously inferior, and the experiment was discontinued.

The glass-painter Schubert introduced transfer-printing* as a method of decoration, a technique which had been little used on the Continent, apart from the wares of the French creamware factory at Creil*. Transfer-printing was employed at the factory for border patterns, landscapes, figures, animals and portraits, and it was continued from about 1824 until the 1870s. In 1827 Carl Gottlieb Böttger devised a method of using lithography (see *Chromolithography*) in the gilding of porcelain, and also succeeded in transfer-printing underglaze. The introduction of chrome green, used underglaze, dates from 1817.

The neo-classical style, which Meissen adopted in the last quarter of the 18th century, favoured figures of white biscuit porcelain*, and these were extremely popular with Continental factories. They continued to be fashionable well into the 19th century as part of

MEISSEN PORCELAIN. Pair of flower-encrusted pot-pourri vases. Vases pierced on the shoulders or in the cover are always intended for pot-pourri. Meissen. Mark: crossed swords. c. 1840. *Sotheby & Co*

MEISSEN PORCELAIN. A pair of Grecian dancers in porcelain. Meissen. Mid-19th century. *Sotheby & Co*

MEISSEN PORCELAIN. Dessert-plate from the Meissen Saxon Service decorated with a view of Apsley House (Number One, London) as it was originally designed by Robert Adam. c. 1818. *Apsley House, London*

the Empire style*. At Meissen in the period under review, the chief modeller was Schöne, and the factory with a certain impartiality produced busts of Napoleon and pipe-bowls in the same form, as well as Saxon royal portraits, religious figures, mythological figures and plaques modelled in relief.

At the beginning of this period painting had deteriorated to a very marked extent, and only four painters were capable of producing work of good quality. Two of them—Schaufuss and Arnoldt—were also teachers of apprentices. Schaufuss, in particular, was regarded as a painter of exceptional ability. Arnoldt painted landscapes. Of the other two, Wollmann painted figures, and Richter, flowers. In 1818 Georg Friedrich Kersting, from the Academy at Dresden, was brought to Meissen to oversee the painting department. It is not very clear what influence Kersting was able to exert, but he supervised the design and painting of a service decorated with battle-scenes which the factory presented to the Duke of Wellington. Another landscape painter, Carl Scheinert, later became drawing master. Schubert died in 1826 and Arnoldt two years later. Their place was taken by Ludwig Richter in 1828.

Until 1831 the factory had been royal property; in this year its ownership was transferred to the State. Two years later von Oppel died, and his place as director was taken by Heinrich Gottlob Kühn, and the years between 1833 and 1870 are often termed the 'Kühn period'. Many new developments took place under his direction—the modification of kiln-design, the substitution of coal for wood as fuel, the introduction of chrome colours etc. The modelling department was directed by Ernst August Leuteritz from 1849 to 1886—a most successful appointment. Painting was directed by Kersting until 1847, by Scheinert (also known as a glass-painter) from 1848 to 1860 and by Carl August Müller from 1860 to 1880. The principal aim of the period was to reduce the cost of decoration by using mercuric gilding and simplified printing, although some popular work of a more elaborate and detailed kind consisted of copies of paintings in the Dresden Art Gallery done as exhibition pieces. In 1852 Kühn introduced iridescent glazes containing bismuth which later became popular at other factories, including those of Paris.

In general, in spite of a few scarcely successful essays into neo-Gothic*, the Empire style remained popular, especially for figures, although by this time the rococo revival was already apparent. This, under Leuteritz, was soon the principal production and models based on 18th-century work, like the relief *Ozier* borders, tureens reminiscent of the great services of the 1740s, figures after Eberlein, pierced baskets encrusted with flowers, painted Watteau scenes, and many other subjects from the period between 1740 and 1755, the beginning of the Seven Years' War, continued to proliferate. Some of the most distinguished figures were modelled by Leuteritz, who also turned occasionally to the Academic

Period for inspiration, and based some of his work on that of Acier.

Revived rococo enormously increased the factory's sales, and once more widely extended its influence. Members of the administration and the Academy of Art, however, regarded the style as slightly vulgar and in any case certain to be ephemeral. A commission was set up to supervise and criticize the work which included two professors of fine art from the Academy. The factory sent a varied collection of wares to the London Exhibition of 1862 which included vases specially made and decorated as show-pieces by Hübner, Nicolai and Braunsdorf. A candelabrum nearly two metres high was designed by Wiedermann and a collection of no fewer than 69 different models of animals was sent to the Exhibition. Afterwards the factory held an inquiry into what had been learned and formed the conclusion that while it could more than hold its own with French and German factories, its English competitors had been making truly giant strides. It was decided to purchase a number of models for the Meissen design department. The commission also noted that the public was now beginning to turn away from biscuit figures and was demanding coloured ones. Also noted were the *pâte-sur-pâte** enamelling (*sic*) of Sèvres* and the porcelain painting in the manner of Limoges enamels* at Worcester*. The latter was being imitated by 1865, the *pâte-sur-pâte* technique had to wait for a few years before it could be successfully employed.

With the death of Kühn in 1870 the factory entered upon its modern period. Trade flourished, especially after 1870, and became extremely profitable. By 1876 the beginning of what was to become a large export

MEISSEN PORCELAIN. Figure of a wild-fowler in 18th-century style. Kuhn period, Meissen. c. 1840. *Private collection*

trade with the United States had been established. Auction sales, which had hitherto always formed part of the factory's outlet for its wares, were discontinued, except for sub-standard and defective pieces sold 'in white' to independent decorators.

The factory had moved from its original premises in the Albrechtsburg in 1860–1864 to the Triebischtal. Buildings soon had to be increased in number and kilns multiplied. Figures and plastic work generally were the most important side of the factory's production and in 1870 the most popular styles were still revived rococo and one which the factory described as 'Renaissance'. The latter included a figure of Dürer from a statue by Rauch reduced in size and portraits of Raphael and Michelangelo. Many of the sculptors of the time contributed designs—men like Schwanthaler* of Munich, who contributed an *Omphale* and a *Lorelei*. Professor Hirt, also of Munich, provided, among other models, a *Gretchen* and a *Cinderella*, and König of Vienna designed a cupid and a water-sprite. Ludwig II* of Bavaria invited the participation of Meissen in the decoration of his castles of Herrenchiemsee* and Linderhof. A group representing *Lohengrin* was made for Ludwig in 1866, and ten years later a figure of Marie-Antoinette. Between 1866 and 1885 the factory made services, table-candlesticks, chandeliers, mirror-frames, an occasional table, and porcelain plaques for the decoration of doors, the designs for which were sent from Munich.

Leuteritz retired as director of modelling in 1886, and his place as *Modellmeister* was taken by Emmerich Andressen, who executed a portrait bust of Johann Friedrich Böttger, one of the founders of the factory in the 18th century. Andressen was a sculptor of considerable ability who, as a modeller for porcelain, was fond of allegory and subjects from classical and Norwegian mythology, but it is perhaps a legitimate criticism that most of his models look as though they were reductions from large works rather than designs for the miniature size of porcelain. For the Munich Exhibition of 1888 he designed a chimney-piece and overmantel mirror in a mixed baroque and rococo style. He also designed massive clock cases and mirror-frames.

Belonging to the period beginning in 1870 are figure subjects taken from real life and ranging from a bathing-girl in what must have been a daring costume for the time, to the soldiers of 1870, some with the *pickelhaube*, of which a wounded Prussian, a Bavarian artillerymen, a group called '*Heroic death*' and Saxon grenadiers, are examples. A revival of a popular 18th-century subject towards the end of the 19th century was the creation of 12 Italian Comedy figures by Andressen's son, Romanus. About the same time an interesting series of figures in national costume was modelled by Spieler of Dresden.

A Meissen speciality with which they had great success was a long series of animal figures, the best by two Dresden modellers, Pilz and Fritz. These figures inspired similar models elsewhere, notably Gotha*, Thuringia, which made animals excellent in quality. So successful was the factory with these models that they began to send modellers abroad to zoological gardens and other sources of information, to ensure the necessary verisimilitude.

Meissen made special efforts to provide a noteworthy exhibit for the Paris Exposition of 1900. Generally, little notice had been taken of the various contemporary movements in art. The factory had flourished without concessions of this kind and was reluctant to disturb a profitable business unnecessarily. Moreover, Dresden was a long way from Paris and London, where most of these movements were taking place and they hardly disturbed the even tenor of thinking about art at the Dresden Academy and the factory's drawing-school. Much of the porcelain sent to Paris was based on the baroque and rococo models of the 18th century which were popular among antique collectors and realizing high prices in the auction-rooms, but efforts to adapt old forms were hardly successful, and the resulting product was controversial. Chandeliers by Kändler, for instance, were not easily adapted to electric light.

By the 1880s pâte-sur-pâte had been mastered, and the watercolourist Braunsdorf had succeeded in the art of painting naturalistic flowers in enamel colours on porcelain. He communicated his style to other flower painters in the department. Technically there was a great increase in the number of underglaze colours, which accentuates the departures from tradition. A feature of this period was a considerable number of commemorative plates, usually dated, and those with named topographical views (usually of Dresden) which were made in varying quantities according to the nature of the event commemorated. Plates impressed in very light relief with topographical subjects and painted in underglaze blue by Barth include views of Dresden, Moritzburg, Freiberg, Pillnitz, Chemnitz, Plaue-an-der-Havel etc. These were very popular. Plates relating to military and naval establishments are now unusual and seem to have been made for the officers' messes by Meissen and other German factories. Owing to the present interest in militaria, unmarked reproductions have recently made an appearance in Germany.

New men, with up-to-date ideas, were appointed, but the old forms were not neglected. Instead the factory turned to closer and more accurate reproductions. In the years following 1900 not only were the old moulds, where they existed, used to produce new models, but, whenever possible, an 18th-century example was used as a standard, the painting also following 18th-century practice as closely as possible, although an exact reproduction of the appearance of 18th-century enamelling was hardly possible. A well-known London dealer in antique porcelain in the early years of this century recorded that, to his own knowledge, a fellow-dealer having a valuable antique figure for repair from a customer ordered a duplicate

from Meissen, damaged it in the same way as the old figure, had it repaired, and returned it to his customer, keeping the genuinely old figure for himself. It is unlikely that this happened very often, but it is important to recognize that it could happen at all. Old moulds from Nymphenburg* and Frankenthal are being used today to make reproductions of figures by Bustelli and others by the Bavarian Staatliche Porzellan Manufaktur, but these are not only specially marked, but the forms of the bases have been altered, so the distinction is clear.

Among the designers of service-ware in the early years of the 20th century may be numbered Henri Van de Velde*, but, like so many artists who have turned to porcelain late in their careers, he was not entirely successful, failing fully to appreciate the difficulties of the medium. Porcelain, as a material, was not particularly suited to the art nouveau* style; no designer ever succeeded in adapting art nouveau motifs to porcelain in a credible manner. This is as easily observed at Sèvres* or Worcester* as at Meissen. The most successful art nouveau porcelain to come from Sèvres were the series of biscuit dancing figures by Agathon Léonard which look much more effective in gilt bronze.

Andressen died in 1903 and Erich Hösel was appointed Modellmeister. Under Hösel figure production increased. Many of these were what the factory termed 'the modern style' at the time, but this term meant little more than non-traditional subject-matter and treatment, and included such subjects as skaters, ladies in riding-habits, ballet-dancers etc. In the painting department Ludwig Sturm held the position of Obermaler from 1880 to 1906. He had been educated at the Munich and Dresden Academies and as a young man had earned his living as a portrait painter. He took over at a time when the painting department had been overshadowed by the plastic department since the days of Marcolini at the end of the 18th century. Nevertheless, Sturm still favoured the meticulous copying of oil-paintings from the Dresden Gallery as a form of decoration. Work of this kind, however, was expensive and soon abandoned. Sturm also introduced the practice of painting flat plaques to be used in the decoration of furniture, or for insetting into doors and walls.

After the First World War, Adolf Pfeiffer was appointed director, and he assembled a small but brilliant team of modellers, notably Paul Scheurich, Max Esser, Paul Börner and August Saul. Scheurich modelled chinoiserie and exotic figures, theatrical and everyday types and classical models. His colouring is slight, and limited, for the most part, to recently introduced colours. Max Esser continued the tradition of modelling animals, but in a more stylized fashion instead of the earlier naturalism. Börner was extremely versatile, but specialized in relief-work. August Saul was also a modeller of animals.

Throughout the period from 1800 to 1914 the factory enjoyed a large export trade, principally with

America and England. For the most part exports to these countries were figures, dessert-baskets and centrepieces, mirror frames and so forth in the revived rococo style. These are fairly common; most of the other Meissen productions are scarce. The mark throughout has been the crossed swords from the Electoral arms of Saxony. Only the swords were employed, but imitators employed marks deliberately designed to look like the crossed swords without being an exact copy. The crossed hayforks of Rudolstadt are a case in point. Other 19th-century factories, despite efforts to stop them, pirated the crossed swords mark, but added letters or figures (or both) near them. The factory's principal difficulty was the lack of any legal protection for trade-marks in Germany until 1874, and this was followed by a number of legal actions.

See *Wolfsohn, Helena*; *Thieme, Carl*

MELI, GIOVANNI (fl. mid-19th-cent.)
An Italian modeller and designer who emigrated to Staffordshire about 1850 and worked for Copeland* and Robinson & Leadbeater* as a modeller in the Parian* body. Later he set up on his own account, and displayed some large figures in Parian at the London Exhibition of 1862. He emigrated to America soon after 1865.

MÊNE, PIERRE-JULES (1810–1859)
French *Animalier* sculptor who established his own foundry in 1838 and first exhibited in the *Salon* in the same year. In 1861 he was awarded the Cross of the Legion of Honour. Mêne's work was very popular in both France and England. His daughter married A. N. Cain* in 1857, and from this time the two men appear to have worked to some degree in collaboration, sharing the foundry and issuing a joint catalogue. Mêne's choice of subject was very wide—deer, race-horses, goats, rabbits, and many more. To the influence of Landseer may perhaps be attributed some groups of Scottish huntsmen with hounds. Casts

MÊNE, PIERRE-JULES. *Stag brought down by hounds*, bronze by Pierre-Jules Mêne. Mid-19th century. *Antique Collectors' Club*

212

done during Mêne's lifetime bear his signature incised and the foundry stamp. After his death models were re-issued by his son-in-law, A. N. Cain, and Susse Frères*. Bronze casts were made at the Coalbrookdale Ironworks* in England and marked COALBROOKDALE. Some poor quality pirated editions appeared on the market about 70 years ago, and such casts should be regarded with suspicion.

MENU-HOLDERS
The first ceramic menu-holders date from about 1860. They sometimes bear a registry mark*. Silver examples date from about the same time. Menu-holders are often well-decorated.

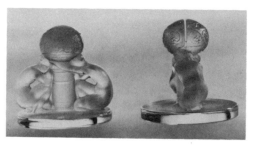
MENU-HOLDERS. Glass menu-holders* by Lalique*. c. 1925. *Victoria & Albert Museum, London*

MENUISIER (French)
The *menuisier* (carpenter) made ordinary plain furniture, chair-frames for painting and gilding, and supports for marble table-tops, most of which were decorated by the carver.

MERKELBACH & WICK (Grenzhausen, Germany)
A factory was established at Grenzhausen in 1873 by Reinhold Merkelbach. They made reproductions of old Westerwald stoneware, and wares influenced by the earlier techniques with modern design and decoration by Riemerschmid*.

METAL BOXES, PRINTED
These minor examples of social history are now collected, and collectable examples of reasonably good quality were made from about 1860 until the First World War. They were made to contain a variety of products, chiefly biscuits, and the largest 19th-century makers were located at Reading and Carlisle, near the biscuit factories. Generally the decorations were landscapes or figure subjects of one kind or another. Until about 1875, when offset-lithography was invented, the decoration was transfer-printed* on to sheets of paper stuck on the box and varnished, but the offset process enabled it to be printed directly on to the metal surface. The boxes themselves were made of tinned light-gauge sheet-iron, assembled in parts and soldered together by the tin-smith. They always needed a good deal of hand work. Tins for special purposes, such as gift-caskets,

Above:
JAPANESE INFLUENCE. Cloiseonne enamel clock garniture in the Japanese manner. The enamelled clock case, surmounted by a pair of gilt-metal dragons, is flanked by a pair of four-light candelabra. Signed *Cristofle* and dated 1874. *Sotheby & Co*

Below:
JAPANESE INFLUENCE. Three-piece teaset of 'Japanese' design, parcel-gilt by Elkington & Co., Birmingham, 1875, with two Worcester porcelain cups and saucers *en suite*.

Above:
HARRY DAVIS. Finely painted Scottish landscape on an oval china plaque by Harry Davis. Worcester Royal Porcelain Company.

Below:
SUNDERLAND POTTERY. Plaque, transfer-printed and partially coloured, the moulding framing the print coloured with pink and copper lustre. First half of the 19th century.
Constance Chiswell

were often made in quite complicated shapes, the quality good enough to make the box worth keeping for decorative purposes when emptied of its original contents. These were especially popular for the Christmas trade. The name of the maker of the product was not, in the case of early specimens, given undue prominence, and sometimes appears only impressed on to the box. Subjects of decoration are varied and while none of them can be regarded as great art, a good deal of competent commercial work was done in this medium, some of which was specially commissioned. One box particularly sought by collectors is flat, rectangular, and bears a portrait of Queen Victoria, the royal monogram, and the words *South Africa 1900*. This was a New Year gift to the troops fighting the Boer War and contained half a pound of chocolate.

METHEY, ANDRÉ (1871 1921)
French studio-potter who began life as a stonemason and, after completing his military service, took up pottery. He exhibited his work in 1901. Especially notable is a series of plates, dishes and vases painted by artists belonging to the École de Paris* (Bonnard, Denis, Redon, Rouault, van Dongen, and Vlaminck), signed and marked with the initials *AM*, which was shown in the Salon d'Automne in 1909. His own style was influenced by Near Eastern and Hispano-Moresque* wares then in demand among collectors of antiques. He employed geometrical forms, stylized plants, and human and animal figures. Mark: signature or initials, incised.

MEUNIER, CONSTANTIN (1831–1905)
A Belgian painter and poster artist who took up sculpture in the 1880s. He was especially attracted to the Social Realist school, with the miners of Le Borinage as a subject. These were published as small bronzes in limited editions. Meunier exhibited in London in 1899 at the Grafton Galleries, and at Samuel Bing's* exhibition of art nouveau in 1900.

MICHEL, EUGÈNE (fl. 1900)
Glass-engraver who worked for E. Rousseau* and E. Leveillé*. He began to work independently c. 1900, and his productions include designs inspired by Chinese glass, and coloured ice glass, cameo-cut in the *art nouveau** style. Mark in script, *E. MICHEL,* incised.

MIDDLE LANE POTTERY (East Hampton, Long Island)
Studio pottery started by E. W. Brouwer* in 1893; the mark adopted was the letter *M* inside an arch formed of the two jawbones of a whale which were on either side of the workshop gate. Specimens are scarce.

MIES VAN DER ROHE, LUDWIG (1886–1969)
German architect and furniture designer. Vice-president of the Deutscher Werkbund, 1926, and a director of the Bauhaus* from 1930 until its closure by the Nazis in 1933. Mies was in charge of the German Pavilion at the Barcelona World's Fair in 1929. Apart from his architecture he is probably most widely known for his 'Barcelona' chair comprising a curved steel frame with suspended leather-covered seat and back which is manufactured by Knoll Associates.

MILITARY CHEST
A chest of drawers in two parts with recessed brass drawer-handles and carrying handles, intended for the use of senior officers in temporary or tented accommodation (see *Military desk*). The many campaigns of the 19th century have made such chests a not uncommon survival. The earliest date back to the period of Waterloo, and they continued to be made until about 1875.

MILITARY DESK
Sometimes called a campaign desk. Portable kneehole desk in three parts, the top resting on two flanking pedestals. The drawer-handles are recessed and the feet were made to unscrew. The construction, usually of mahogany, cedar or camphor wood (the latter woods employed for their relative immunity from the attacks of tropical insects), was intended to make stacking and transport easy.

MILDNER, JOHANN JACOB (1763–1808)
Glass-maker of Gutenbrunn, Austria, who specialized in a kind of *Zwischengoldgläser,* that is, glass made in two separate parts and accurately fitted together with a layer of silver or gold foil between them, decorated by painting or engraving. Mildner

MILDNER, JOHANN JACOB. Beaker decorated with an inset medallion covering a monogram on gold leaf by J. J. Mildner, Gutenbrunn, Austria c. 1800. *Pilkington Glass Museum*

usually ground an oval recess into the thickness of his glasses, the interior of which was covered with metal foil. Any required decoration was executed, after which the recess was sealed with a medallion of glass, which formed the second layer. The rest of the glass was decorated with wheel-engraving or diamond-point engraving. Mildner's technique, and variations of it, were used later in the 19th century, but specimens are rare.

See also *Verre doublé*

MILK GLASS (MILCHGLAS)

English and American glass made white and opaque by the addition of tin oxide, a type first made by the Venetians in the 16th century, probably suggested originally by the *maiolica** glaze. It was popular in Bohemia and the German States in the 17th and 18th centuries, where it was known as *milchglas*. The type is closely related to opaline, but it was often employed for plates and similar objects customarily made by the porcelain factories. Colouring oxides were sometimes added to glass of this type and much of it was pressed (see *Pressed glass*).

MILLEFIORI (Italian)

Literally 'a thousand flowers'; French, *millefleurs*. A very ancient technique used in the 19th century principally for the making of paperweights*. Rods of glass of several colours were placed side by side and fused together. The mass was then reheated and drawn out into a long, thin cane. Several of these canes of different patterns were then cut into sections, put together side by side, and covered with clear glass, thus forming a typical *millefiori* paperweight (see illustration under paperweight). The colouring and disposition of the pieces of glass before they were fused and drawn out into canes were responsible for the shape of the miniature pattern eventually formed, usually a stylized florette.

The technique was probably revived in Bohemia in the 1830s and in Venice at about the same time. The first production of paperweights on any considerable scale, however, undoubtedly belongs to Baccarat*, Saint-Louis*, and Clichy*. The earliest dated *millefiori* weight from Baccarat was made in 1846. The English glass factories at Stourbridge were probably experimenting with the technique about the same time, perhaps with the aid of French craftsmen.

Millefiori was not limited as a form of decoration to paperweights; inkwells, rulers, door-knobs, knife-rests, seals, and many other small decorative items were ornamented in this way. Bontemps* devoted his attention to *millefiori* glass in 1844, and was no doubt responsible for many of the more spectacular developments of this and allied techniques.

MILLEFLEURS DECORATION ON PORCELAIN

A decorative technique, first employed on porcelain vases at Meissen* during the 1740s, by which the surface was completely encrusted with applied simple, single, flowers. The process was sometimes employed during the 1830s and 1840s by English porcelain factories inspired by Meissen* but with more elaborate flowers. Specimens in good condition are now comparatively rare.

MINAUDIÈRE (French)

Term of uncertain derivation applied to a kind of metal box with compartments for cigarettes, cosmetics, money, etc. which became a fashionable substitute for an evening bag about 1935. Usually in lacquer, or in engine-turned gold or silver, some examples in chromium plate were produced. The *minaudière* was first introduced by the Paris jewellers, Van Cleef and Arpels, and it was obtainable from Cartier in Paris and Asprey's in London.

MINTON LTD (Stoke-on-Trent, Staffordshire)

Thomas Minton*, who worked as an engraver for Thomas Turner of Caughley* and for Spode*, founded the firm in 1793 with the aid of William Pownall (who provided the capital), Joseph Poulson (master-potter), and Samuel Poulson (modeller and mould-maker). The new factory was also greatly assisted by Thomas Minton's brother, who acted as the London agent. In 1808 Minton became responsible for the running of the business, taking his son into partnership in 1817.

During this period the business was at first mainly concerned with the manufacture of blue printed earthenware and the development of bone china (see *Porcelain*). Even in the early period Minton made highly translucent porcelain of exceptional quality. Its appearance when held up to the light has been likened to sodden snow.

When Thomas Minton died in 1836 the firm was then taken over by his son, Herbert Minton*, who was in partnership with John Boyle* until 1841. The relationship proved to be very unsatisfactory, and Boyle appears to have been responsible for difficulties with the firm's employees. In 1845 Boyle was superseded by Michael Daintry Hollins, whose appointment proved much more successful, and who took charge of the manufacture of tiles. At this time the firm was divided between the main factory carried on under the style of Minton & Co., and an enterprise for the making of tiles known as Minton, Hollins & Co., or Minton & Hollins. In most respects artists etc. seem to have been interchangeable. When Herbert Minton died in 1858 his place was taken by his nephew, Colin Minton Campbell, and in 1883 the style of the firm changed from Minton & Co. to Minton Ltd.

Under Herbert Minton's direction the firm continually increased in reputation, and it began to attract artists from other factories. The most successful appointment was that of the French art-director J-L-F. Arnoux*, in 1848. His 'Majolica'* was one of the successes of the Great Exhibition of 1851. Arnoux's

MINTON. Earthenware bottle apparently derived from a damaged Persian bottle in the Victoria & Albert Museum with some differences in the detail and disposition of the decoration. A somewhat similar bottle taken from the same source was made in porcelain in Paris by Edme Samson & Cie. c. 1870. *Minton Museum, Royal Doulton Tableware*

MINTON. Two porcelain figures, *Persia* and *Arabia*, as water-carriers. c. 1840. *Minton Museum, Royal Doulton Tableware*

services proved valuable in another direction. Already well known on the Continent, a man of considerable reputation as a potter and an artist, his presence at Stoke enabled Minton's to attract other artists of importance. It will be noticed that most of the French artists who came to England did so for political reasons, the two largest influences taking place in 1848 (the July Revolution which unseated Louis-Phillipe) and 1870 (the Franco-Prussian War). Marc-Louis Solon*, Minton's second most important acquisition from France, arrived in 1870.

The invention of Parian* ware in the 1840s was taken up successfully by Minton, whose products in this medium were of exceptional quality. The sculptor John Bell* modelled for them, as did the American, Hiram Powers, whose *Greek Slave* was one of the sensations of the Great Exhibition. Carrier-Belleuse*, the French sculptor, worked for Minton about this time, and the factory achieved a considerable reputation for figure-work, both in Parian* and in glazed porcelain. Figures formed part of some services, such as the baskets supported by cupids belonging to dessert-services which distantly owe their inspiration to mid-18th-century Meissen*. The production of porcelain in the 18th-century style of Sèvres* began in the 1840s before Arnoux arrived. This was probably undertaken in competition with Coalport*, where the copying of Sèvres had advanced almost to the point of forgery. Before 1836 Minton had begun to employ a mark consisting of two opposed curving lines with the letter M between them, which might very easily be mistaken by the unitiated for the opposed L monogram of Sèvres, which usually has a date-letter added, of which M is one.

The very successful 'Majolica' of Arnoux was inspired not by the Renaissance painted wares of Italy, but by the pottery of Bernard Palissy*, and the firm also produced a ware copying an almost contemporary French pottery—Henri Deux ware*. These were both an antiquarian taste, the second in particular hardly likely to have come to the attention of the public without the mediation of the antique collector. When Minton started to make their version in the 1860s fewer than 90 pieces of this 16th-century ware, which was elaborately inlaid in coloured clays and covered with a thin, varnish-like glaze, remained in existence, and were being eagerly sought. The Minton copies were made by Charles Toft*, who came originally from Worcester*, and who also modelled figures in Parian and glazed porcelain. (His son, Albert, became a well-known sculptor, and the author of one of the few books on the technical aspects of his craft.)

Before the Great Exhibition of 1851 the factory had already begun to specialize in fine quality dinner- and dessert-services. These were characterized by rich borders, fine-quality painting in enamel colours and elaborately moulded tureens, dessert-baskets, and centre-pieces, which were a continuation of the fashions set by the royal factories of the 18th century. One such service from Minton, made in 1850, had a Royal designer: the plates have pierced borders, the decoration features the Balmoral Tartan and the intertwined monogram of Victoria and Albert, and the design was by Prince Albert. The art of making the sumptuous service has not been lost. In modern times the factory has executed an order for a foreign customer which cost £500 a plate.

In 1870 Marc-Louis Solon arrived at Minton, bringing with him the art of *pâte-sur-pâte*—painted decoration underglaze using slip instead of pigment. This technique, introduced at Sèvres some 20 years earlier and derived by them from the decoration of some late Chinese porcelain celadons*, was greatly developed by Solon. Most such wares are vases which began as coloured Parian over which Solon built up the decoration by painting on layers of white slip, building up the subject in very low relief. This task took several weeks, since each layer had to become firm enough to support the application of the next. Finally, small details were added with a steel tool, and the finished work glazed and fired. One of the most complex vases took a total of seven months to complete. Excellent work in this style was done by Solon's pupil, Alboin Birks*, who was at the factory from 1876 until 1937, the kind of long-service record one sometimes finds in the industry.

Minton specialized in painted decoration and found it difficult to staff its painting shop with artists of sufficient skill to keep pace with the demand. Pay and working conditions were good enough to bring many competent artists from the Continent, but in an endeavour to train painters of their own the factory set up the Minton's Art Pottery Studio* in Kensington Gore, London, in 1871. This was under the direction of W. S. Coleman (1829–1904), who had formerly been employed by Copeland*, and who joined Minton in 1869. The studio was destroyed by fire in 1873 and it was not replaced. Coleman was also responsible for some of the designs in the Japanese style.

Notable designers who provided Minton's with material during the 19th century include Sir Henry Cole* (Summerly's* Art Manufactures), A. W. N. Pugin*, Alfred Stevens*, Walter Crane*, Henry Stacey Marks*, J. Moyr Smith* and, of course, Prince Albert. Pugin and Minton were associated in the decoration of the Medieval Court* at the Great Exhibition (1851). Modellers of distinction include Carrier-Belleuse*, Paul Comolera*, the *Animalier* sculptor, Hugues Protât*, and Charles Toft. Comolera's most important work was a life-size pheasant, of which five copies were made.

During the 20th century Minton's have preserved their reputation for fine porcelain and have continued to produce services worthy of their 19th-century traditions. Throughout their existence they have used a wide variety of marks. Basically, the mark has either been crossed opposing serpentine lines (imitating the Sèvres monogram) with *M* between them, or the name MINTON. The addition of 'England' denotes manufacture after 1891. On transfer-printed* wares the name of the pattern surrounded by an elaborate framework has *M & Co* underneath. From about 1824 impressed marks were added to record the date of manufacture. These are found on porcelain, and sometimes on earthenware. Some artists signed their work or added initials, but this practice was not widespread.

MINTON'S ART POTTERY STUDIO

Studio established in 1870 in Kensington Gore, London, with W. S. Coleman from Stoke-on-Trent as art-director, for the purpose of training students in design and painting on earthenware. Students from National Schools of Art from various parts of London also found employment here. Artists who worked

MINTON'S ART POTTERY STUDIO. Large plaque, white on a blue ground. Impressed mark. Minton's Art Pottery Studio*. 1873. *Mrs F. H. Stubbley*

here include Hannah Barlow*, later at Doulton*, and Edward Reuter, who, when the studio was burned down in 1875, went on to Minton at the Stoke-on-Trent factory. The mark is MINTON'S ART POTTERY STUDIO in circular form, as well as MINTONS and the date cypher impressed.

MINTON, HERBERT (1793–1858)

Son and successor of Thomas Minton* to whom the great expansion of the factory was largely due. He engaged Pugin* as a designer and the products of their collaboration appeared in the Medieval Court* of the Great Exhibition of 1851, to which he lent powerful support. Minton was responsible for the introduction of 'Majolica'*, Parian* and the decorative wares based on the 18th-century work of the Sèvres* factory. He was responsible for bringing a number of French artists and craftsmen to Staffordshire, and was foremost in supporting a school of design in the Potteries. When he died the factory was giving employment to about 1500 work people.

MINTON, THOMAS   See *Minton Ltd*

MISSION FURNITURE

Furniture the design of which was based on that of the old Spanish Missions of the south-west United States. Construction was comparatively plain and ornament sparse. Chair-seats and backs were of slung leather held in position with large-headed copper nails. Mission furniture became popular just before 1900, and continued to be fashionable for many years, especially in conjunction with polished wood floors and Navajo rugs. Later furniture of this type, however, was sometimes badly made and of poor quality.

See *Roycroft Shops*

MITCHELL & RAMMELSBERG (Cincinnati, Ohio)

Furniture manufacturers founded in 1844 whose work was in the historic styles popular during the period. Some of their furniture was inspired by the designs of Bruce Talbert*.

MOCHA

Ware, usually mugs and jugs, decorated with coloured bands and moss-like or dendritic effects said to be the result of applying a pigment made from tobacco juice, stale urine and turpentine to the unfired body. This decoration was used on a creamware*, drab ware, or pearlware body, and its name is derived from a

MOCHA. A mug, and a rarer jug, of mocha* ware. Staffordshire. c. 1840. *Constance Chiswell*

resemblance to the Arabian mocha stone, a quartz with dendritic markings. The principal source of these wares was Staffordshire, and they were made from about 1780 to the beginning of the First World War.

MOHN, SAMUEL (1762–1815)

Glass-painter of Meseburg who began his career as an independent porcelain painter. He rediscovered the 17th-century transparent colours and started a workshop in association with his son, Gottlob Samuel Mohn (1789–1825). They enjoyed the patronage of Frederick William III of Prussia and Queen Louise, for whom Gottlob painted and dedicated a number of glasses. They established workshops in Neubrandenburg and Leipzig and then, in 1812, in Dresden. Gottlob went to Vienna in 1811 to execute commissions for stained glass, and there met Anton Kothgasser*.

The style of the two Mohns is often very similar. Their topographical glasses usually depict Leipzig, Dresden or Vienna. The elder Mohn also painted flowers and butterflies with considerable skill. Other *Hausmaler** of the time employed transparent colours.

MOIGNIEZ, JULES (1835–1894)

Moigniez studied in Paris under the sculptor Paul Comolera*. He first exhibited at the Paris Exposition of 1855, and in the Salon from 1859 to 1892. He specialized in birds of all kinds, many of their subjects

MOHN, GOTTLOB SAMUEL. Glass beaker painted in enamel colours by Gottlob Samuel Mohn of Dresden. c. 1812. *Victoria & Albert Museum, London*

MOIGNIEZ, JULES. *Golden Pheasant*, bronze by Jules Moigniez*. Third quarter of the 19th century. *Antique Collectors' Club*

based on Dutch 17th-century bird-painting, and a light golden-brown patination is characteristic. He also produced models of dogs, but these generally have not the same quality. The casts are excellent, and most were done under the supervision of his father, who started a foundry in 1857 especially to undertake the work. Moigniez's bronzes enjoyed considerable popularity in England and America, as well as in France.

MONART GLASS   See *Moncrieff's Glass Works*

MONCLOA, LA (Florida, near Madrid)

A porcelain factory founded by Ferdinand VII in 1817 which worked largely in the French style. Until 1829 the director was Bartolomé Sureda, formerly director of Buen Retiro, and white ware from the latter factory was decorated at La Moncloa. The enterprise closed in 1850. It used the impressed mark of *La Moncloa* beneath a crown.

MONCRIEFF'S GLASS WORKS (Perth, Scotland)
Glass works founded about 1864 for the manufacture of utility glass by John Moncrieff, and known as the North British Glass Works. In 1922 the factory began to make decorative glass. About this time they first employed a Spanish glassworker, Salvador Ysart (1877–1955) who came from Barcelona. Most glass of this type produced—Monart glass, paperweights* and other ornamental categories—was probably made under his influence. Monart glass is a heavy clear glass, usually in the form of vases or bowls, heavily streaked with opaque or translucent colours, including scarlet and black, in the *art déco** style. Paperweights made by Salvador's son, Paul Ysart, are sometimes marked with the initials *PY*.

MONKEY BAND
Series of figures of monkeys modelled in porcelain playing on musical instruments. The series was first modelled by J. J. Kändler at Meissen* about 1750, and proved to be very popular. During the 19th century several porcelain factories made Monkey Bands of this kind, not necessarily exact imitations, and the series was repeated by Meissen. It also gave rise to other bands inspired by the general idea, such as Frog Orchestras. Sets of these figures of a 19th-century date are now rare and sought after.

MONROE, THE DEATH OF
Lieutenant Hector Monroe of the Bengal Lancers was killed and partially eaten by a tiger near Calcutta in December 1792. Some rare 19th-century Staffordshire groups depict the event, with Monroe prone and the tiger gnawing his head.

MONTEREAU (Seine-et-Marne)
A factory making *faïence-fine** was founded here in 1774 by English potters. The enterprise at first enjoyed royal support and it became extremely prosperous, uniting with Creil* early in the 19th century.

MONTGOLFIER BACK   See *Balloon-back*

MONTI, RAFAELLE (1818–1881)
Designer and sculptor of Milan. Monti studied under his father, Gaetano Monti, and at the Imperial Academy, where he gained a gold medal. He was in Vienna in 1838, returned to Milan in 1842, and paid his first visit to England in 1846. He took part in the hostilities of 1848 as an officer of the National Guard and was compelled to flee to England, which he made his home until his death in 1881.

Monti's successful career as a sculptor in England began with his contribution of several works to the Great Exhibition of 1851, and in 1862 he displayed a much-admired work, *The Sleep of Sorrow and the Dream of Joy,* an allegory of the Risorgimento, at the Exhibition, which is now in the Victoria and Albert Museum, London. Monti specialized in female nudes of marble partially draped with transparent veils, a kind of *trompe l'oeil* which accentuated the nakedness of his subject and enormously appealed to the mid-century Victorian public, with whom the nude in chains was already a firm favourite (see *Greek Slave, The*). In this Monti was no doubt influenced by the 18th-century sculptor Antonio Corradini, and the influence of Bernini is also often more than merely perceptible. Monti produced many veiled female busts noted more for technical facility than artistic importance. During the 1850s he supplied Copeland* with maquettes for Parian* figures and he also designed bronze figures for Elkington*. He appears to have abandoned marble-carving after 1862, but until his death he was designing silver vases and race-cups for the royal silversmith C. F. Hancock.

MOONLIGHT LUSTRE
A type of lustre decoration introduced by Wedgwood* early in the 19th century, and also employed by Turners of Lane End. It was difficult to use and was soon discontinued. This lustre gave a marbled effect by producing gold, grey, pink, and other colours over the surface of the glaze. Much of the ware was made in the form of nautilus and pecten shells. Examples, especially of service ware, are rare.

MOONSTONE GLAZE
A type of matt white glaze introduced by Wedgwood* in the mid-1920s, possibly inspired by earlier Chinese wares. It was used for figures and reliefs of animals commissioned from John Skeaping*, and for some designs by Keith Murray*.

MOORCROFT, WILLIAM (Cobridge, Staffordshire)
Moorcroft, born in 1872, received his training at the Wedgwood Institute, Burslem, from 1886 to 1895. In 1898 he became designer of art-pottery to MacIntyre's of Cobridge. Between 1898 and 1904 he produced several types of ware, notably *Aurelian* and *Florian*, both decorated with floral motifs. *Flammarion* ware, from 1905, was decorated with coloured glazes and flowers in trailed slip. Much of Moorcroft's work for this firm bears his signature. MacIntyres closed their art department in 1913, and Moorcroft opened his own factory, employing some of MacIntyre's former employees. Monochrome glazes were produced until about 1920, and the *flambé* glaze* began to be popular about this time. Moorcroft died in 1946.

The mark appearing on his post-1913 work is usually MOORCROFT BURSLEM impressed and the facsimile signature *W. Moorcroft*. His products, exported at the time, are now collected.

MOORE, ALBERT JOSEPH (1841–1913)
Painter, friend of Whistler, who was much influenced by the classical style. Moore occasionally painted furniture for William Burges* and his classically draped figures influenced fashion in the 1880s. He is represented in the Tate Gallery, London.

MOORE, BERNARD (1853–1935)

Potter of Stoke-on-Trent and Longton, Staffordshire. Moore began as a member of the family firm of Moore Brothers at Stoke, but established himself as an independent potter and designer in 1905. He achieved an important reputation from his imitations of the Chinese *sang-de-boeuf** glaze (using copper oxide fired in a reducing kiln as a colouring agent) since he was the first European potter to discover the Chinese secret. He exhibited successfully at the Turin International Exhibition of 1911. His work was marked with the monogram *BM* and some specimens bear the signature in full.

MORAVIAN WORK

The term is applied principally to pictures on silk or satin embroidered by Moravian emigrants to Pennsylvania in the late 18th and early 19th centuries.

MORESQUES See *Arabesques*

MORGAN, WILLIAM FREND DE (1839–1917)

Potter and designer. William de Morgan was educated at University College, London, and entered the Academy Schools in 1859 as a painter. He gave this up two years later to work on stained glass window design. In 1863 he met William Morris* and Burne-Jones*, and began to contribute designs for tiles and painted cabinets to Morris, Marshall, Faulkner & Co.* when the firm was established in 1865. His interest in the decoration of pottery began in 1869, and his experiments with lustre pigments* soon afterwards. At first he decorated earthenware bought 'in white' from manufacturers such as Wedgwood*, an undoubted de Morgan decoration occurring on a dish with the impressed Wedgwood mark.

In 1872 he established himself in Chelsea and began to make his own tiles. The venture was successful, and the premises were soon enlarged to include showrooms. By this time de Morgan was able to employ a number of assistants. After the dissolution of Morris's partnership in 1875 de Morgan continued to supply tiles to Morris & Co.*, and in 1879 he was commissioned to supply tile pictures for the yacht of the Czar of Russia, as well as tiles for Leighton's Arab Hall* to supplement those brought from the Near East. In 1880 Morris moved his workshops to Merton Abbey, Surrey. Two years later de Morgan followed him and set up a pottery on land nearby. Four years later he opened showrooms at 45 Great Marlborough Street, London, and in 1887 he married Evelyn Pickering. In the year following he left Merton Abbey and opened the Sands End Pottery, Fulham, in partnership with the architect Halsey Ricardo. In 1892 he was awarded the silver medal of the Society of Arts for a paper on lustre, and in 1893 he visited Egypt at the request of the Egyptian Government to report on pottery. In 1895–1896 he was absent for a prolonged period in Florence, where he came into contact with the firm of Cantagalli*, then making excellent reproductions of old Italian *maiolica**.

De Morgan's absence in Italy and a contract with the P. & O. Line for tile decoration in six of their vessels led to disagreements with Halsey Ricardo. In 1897 Reginald Blunt was appointed manager of the Sands End Pottery, and in 1898 the partnership with Ricardo was finally dissolved. De Morgan entered a new partnership with Charles and Fred Passenger, and Frank Iles, the kiln master. In 1906 de Morgan published his first novel, *Joseph Vance*, which was an immediate success. The following year, 1907, the Sands End Pottery was closed, although manufacture and decorating was continued until 1911 by Iles and the two Passengers. De Morgan continued to write novels until his death in 1917.

William de Morgan was the most notable of 19th-century artist-potters. At the outset of his career he was attracted to the metallic pigments classified under the general heading of 'lustre'* which decorated a great deal of early Islamic pottery, as well as the *maiolica* of Gubbio and Faenza in the 16th century. This process involved depositing a film of pure metal on the surface of the glaze while it was in a softened state. Throughout his subsequent career as a potter de Morgan continually returned to the use of lustre in decoration. The origin of lustre in the Near East, as well as the contemporary interest in Near Eastern decorative art, led him to derive inspiration from this source, although many of the designs which are often described as 'Persian' are actually far more closely related to the 16th-century pottery of Isnik*, Anatolia, at this time erroneously described as 'Rhodian'. Some of de Morgan's bottle-shaped vases resemble Chinese porcelain, but the inspiration is still Near Eastern, the forms having been derived from Persian and Turkish copies of Chinese ware.

Birds, fish and floral and foliate subjects were commonly employed to decorate dishes, vases and tiles, the peacock* and the sunflower* being *motifs* especially popular during the 1880s. An interesting and rare group of wares are those decorated with human figures in the manner of 16th-century Urbino *maiolica*, which were designed by de Morgan, painted by A. Faini, and produced in the factory of Cantagalli* in Florence.

Marks include the initials D.M., WILLIAM DE MORGAN & CO., SANDS END POTTERY, FULHAM, and W. DE MERTON ABBEY above the sketch of an abbey.

MORLEY, FRANCIS (fl. 1840–1865)
Francis Morley, son of one of the founders of J. & R. Morley, the hosiery manufacturers, married Emma Ridgway, and became a partner in the firm of Ridgway, Morley, Wear & Co. He took over the firm in 1845. It became Morley & Co. in 1850, and Morley & Ashworth from 1858 to 1862 when he retired. Morley bought the moulds and engravings of C. J. Mason, and used a similar mark, having bought the right to use the Mason back-stamp.

See *Ashworth & Brothers, George L.*; *Ridgway & Sons, Job*

MORRIS & CO. (London)
Successors to Morris, Marshall, Faulkner & Co.* in 1875, the sole proprietor being William Morris*. The showrooms were removed to 449 Oxford Street in 1877. They began by specializing in textiles and stained glass, the latter designed by Burne-Jones*, and pottery from William de Morgan*. They supplied simply-designed, soundly-constructed furniture and, by 1890, were selling more elaborately decorated cabinet work of good quality, often with veneering and marquetry. George Jack* and Philip Webb* were among the designers who worked for Morris & Co. at this time. The firm survived until 1940. From c. 1890 furniture was stamped *Morris and Company*.

'MORRIS' CHAIR
An armchair of ebonized beechwood, with a rush seat, turned legs and arm-supports and a straight back. It was based on a traditional Sussex chair adapted by Philip Webb about 1865, and made in large numbers by Morris, Marshall, Faulkner & Co*, and later by Morris & Co*.

MORRIS, MARSHALL, FAULKNER & CO. (London)
Firm specializing in interior decoration and fine art work founded in 1861 by William Morris*, Ford Madox Brown, Philip Webb*, D. G. Rossetti*, E. Burne-Jones*, Peter Paul Marshall and Charles Faulkner*. They specialized in furniture in the neo-Gothic* and medieval styles designed by Philip Webb and painted by Burne-Jones, Morris, or Rossetti. For work of this kind the firm obtained major awards at the International Exhibition of 1862. They set out ambitiously to change public taste, which provoked opposition from established manufacturers who, in the higher-priced furniture range, were perhaps being

MORRIS & CO. Sussex rush-seated armchair of turned wood by Morris & Co*, made from 1870 onwards. *William Morris Gallery, Waltham Forest*

influenced rather more by the Second Empire* styles of France. After the Exhibition the firm went on to design simpler kinds of furniture capable of wider sale, especially the 'Morris' chair*, which was very popular and widely copied. The firm produced designs in a wide variety of materials, including ceramics, textiles, wallpaper, stained glass and metalwork. It was reorganized as Morris & Co.* in 1875, all the partners except Morris withdrawing.

MORRIS WALLPAPERS
During his lifetime more than 100 different wallpapers were designed by Morris and his associates. These were originally printed by Jeffrey & Co. The blocks are now the property of Arthur Sanderson & Sons Ltd., and many of the Morris patterns are available commercially.

MORRIS, WILLIAM (1834–1896)
Craftsman, designer, poet and socialist, William Morris was born in Walthamstow and educated at Marlborough College and Exeter College, Oxford. At Oxford he met Burne-Jones*, who became a close friend, and amused himself by writing tales of medieval chivalry. He had already occupied himself with drawing Gothic details and making brass-rubbings when he read Ruskin's* chapter on the nature of Gothic in the *Stones of Venice*, and ultimately he abandoned ideas of taking orders for architecture. In 1855 he inherited £900 a year, which gave him a certain freedom of choice, and he entered the Oxford office of the architect George Edmond Street, while Burne-Jones, who had also intended taking orders, turned to painting. Within a year Morris had given up architecture for painting, and had begun to design furniture. He formed a friendship

MORRIS, WILLIAM. Cabinet designed and painted by William Morris*. c. 1865. *Victoria & Albert Museum, London*

with Street's senior assistant, Philip Webb*, and had also become a patron of the arts, buying Rossetti's *Hayfield* for £40. In 1857 he met Jane Borden and with Burne-Jones rented rooms at Red Lion Square, London, where they stayed until 1859, when Morris married Miss Borden. From 1860 to 1865 he lived at the Red House, Bexleyheath, Kent, designed for him by Philip Webb, and in 1861 he became the principal founding member of the firm of Morris, Marshall, Faulkner & Co.*, with premises at Red Lion Square, to design and produce wallpaper, furniture, embroideries, stained glass, metalwork etc. The other members were Webb, Burne-Jones, Rossetti, Ford Madox Brown, Marshall and Faulkner*. The object of the firm, as set out in the prospectus, was to cooperate in the decorative arts generally. The original partnership was dissolved in 1875, but the firm survived as Morris & Co.* until 1940, its most influential products being furniture and wallpapers, textiles and tapestries designed by Morris. A year after it was founded the new firm successfully showed its products at the Exhibition of 1862.

Morris left the Red House for London in 1865 and lived at the firm's premises at 26 Queen Square, Bloomsbury. With Rossetti he acquired Kelmscott Manor, Oxfordshire, in 1871. Later he was to acquire an old Georgian house in Hammersmith which was renamed Kelmscott House, and this, in 1891, gave its name to the Kelmscott Press. In 1877 he founded the Society for the Preservation of Ancient Buildings, with the object of protecting them against excessive restoration. Morris now began to take an interest in politics and became a Liberal, abandoning the party

in favour of Socialism in 1882. For some years he joined a variety of groups and contributed heavily to their funds, but he was a failure as a public speaker, and towards the end of his life he abandoned politics for causes with which he was more in sympathy.

In 1881 the firm's workshops were moved to Merton Abbey, Surrey, and William de Morgan*, with whom he had been associated since the early days of Morris, Marshall, Faulkner & Co., followed him to a nearby site in 1882 which, largely due to ill-health, de Morgan gave up in 1888. In 1883 Morris joined the Democratic League, and, in the following year he founded the Art Workers' Guild*. Some of the most distinguished craftsmen of the day became members and a group of architects was headed by Norman Shaw*. In 1885 he founded the Socialist League. The Arts and Crafts Exhibition Society*, which he established in 1888, exerted tremendous influence on middle-class taste at the time. The Kelmscott Press, founded in 1891, with Morris as its principal designer, was an extremely important factor in modern English book-production. He died in 1896, largely because for years he had been grossly overworking. Morris was a man of amazing versatility as an artist, craftsman and designer, but it is in the field of designing that his most important work was done. He was much influenced by Ruskin, the Gothic revival* and the pre-Raphaelites*.

Morris was among the first to recognize the damaging effect of industrialization and mechanization on the contemporary arts and proposed a return to hand-craftsmanship. He did succeed in producing designs by these means which proved a useful corrective to much of the bad taste observable at the Great Exhibition of 1851. He helped to prepare the ground for *art nouveau** and the modern movement. His political ideas were naive, and prompted more by his sympathy with the poor than by any deep understanding of economics.

MORTIMER & HUNT   See *Hunt & Roskell*

MORTLOCK, JOHN (London)

China-seller and merchant who bought white porcelain from factories such as Coalport*, Swansea* and Nantgarw* which was painted to his order by decorating studios like Robins & Randall (see *Randall, Thomas Martin*). Mortlock bought a variety of decorated or finished wares, such as 'Cadogan' teapots from several factories, including Wedgwood* and Rockingham*, all of which were marked with the Mortlock back-stamp. His transfer-printed* mark added to a marked Wedgwood commemorative jug of 1881 is in the form of a globe with radiating lines on which are the words: JOHN MORTLOCK, OXFORD ST, LONDON. W. From a point a little west of the north pole projects a flagstaff, and a flag with the figures, 1748. Underneath are the words TRADE MARK REGISTERED. The figures, 1748, may have been the year of the founding of the business. To judge by the number of 19th-century services which bear his name, Mortlock's business was very great.

MOSCOW PORCELAIN

There were a number of factories in and around Moscow in the 18th and 19th centuries, and pre-Revolutionary specimens are sometimes to be found. Porcelain made after 1917 is apt to be very unusual in the west, and is often decorated with Communist sentiments in a Social-Realist style. The first factory, situated at nearby Verbilki, was started by an Englishman named Francis Gardner and a German named Hattenberg in 1765.

The factory remained in the hands of the Gardner family until 1891, when it passed to the Kusnetsoffs. Much 19th-century production is in the Empire style and excellent in quality. The factory is noted for a bright blue with a matt surface, to be found on figures of peasants and others. The usual mark is *Gardner* in Cyrillic characters (Гарднеръ) impressed, or printed in red in oval form. Meissen and Sèvres marks in conjunction with stars are said to have been used by this factory.

The factory of Popoff at Gorbunovo, near Moscow, was founded about 1806 by an Englishman, Charles Miely. Like Gardner, the factory made excellent peasant figures and porcelain in the Empire style. It closed in 1872. Its mark was the monogram ПТ.

Among the other numerous small factories existing early in the 19th century, probably the only other one of whose work a specimen might be found in the West is that of Kozloff, who made figures and porcelain in the Empire style from about 1820 to 1836. They used the monogram ГК incised.

MOSER, KOLOMAN (1868–1918)

Austrian artist and designer who studied painting under Otto Wagner; he was a founder member of the *Sezession** and of the Wiener Werkstätte* in 1903 with Fritz Warndörfer and Josef Hoffmann*. Moser was not only noted as a graphic and poster artist, but he designed furniture, glassware, ceramics, textiles, metalwork and many other things mainly in the *Jugendstil**. He taught at the School of Applied Art in Vienna from 1899.

MOSER UND SÖHNE, LUDWIG (Karlsbad, Bohemia)

Glasshouse founded in 1857 by Ludwig Moser (1833–1916), a glass-engraver of Karlsbad who was also a glass-merchant. In the 19th century they made a good deal of fine-quality engraved glass and glass with a gilded frieze, for tourists, some of which were signed

MOSER, LUDWIG. Bowl of dark purple glass by Ludwig Moser*, decorated with a gilded frieze of figures in low relief. Signed in script: *Moser, Karlsbad*. The type was repeated after the First World War with the addition of the words 'Czechoslovakia', which Bohemia became. Bohemia, end of the 19th century. *Private collection*

Moser, Karlsbad. Later, around 1900, they made coloured iridescent glass* inspired by Tiffany*. After the First World War production continued, and included some earlier types, the mark having *Czechoslovakia* added.

MOTTO WARE

An ornamental type of earthenware principally made in the west of England from terracotta* clay covered with coloured slips and further decorated with a proverb, maxim, folk-saying etc. incised through the slip, e.g. a marmalade jar, inscribed 'AISY ON THE MARMALADE'. These wares have all been made during the past hundred years or so in a large variety of forms, and are now collected. Some specimens are comparatively recent.

MOULDED AND MOULD-BLOWN GLASS

Glass formed by being blown or pressed into a metal mould made in two, three or more sections hinged together. The act of forming glass by blowing it into

MOTTO WARE. Motto ware* teapot stand and sugar-caster typically decorated. England, Devonshire. c. 1920. *John Darby*

MOULDED GLASS. Vase of clear moulded glass with ornament in the revived rococo* style. French. c. 1830. *Victoria & Albert Museum, London*

a mould with a blow-pipe is very ancient and preceded free-blowing. The process was revived in the early years of the 19th century as a method of making glass vessels easily and of exactly similar form quickly. The pattern was cut in *intaglio* on the interior surface of the mould and a 'gather' of molten glass blown into it with the pipe, forcing the glass into its interstices. Hinged moulds of iron were in two parts or, much more commonly, three, these specimens being known as 'three-mold glass'. 'Three-mold glass' was made before 1850, principally in America. A type of moulded glass peculiar to America was blown into a mould smaller than the size of the intended object. It was then taken out of the mould, reheated and reblown to a larger size. This had the effect of expanding the pattern taken up from the original mould.

In the case of pressed* or pattern glass*, which belongs to the period after about 1830, most of it being considerably later than this, molten glass was placed into the mould and a plunger then formed the interior of the vessel, forcing the glass into the interstices of the mould as it descended. Vessels made in this way always have a smooth interior surface, while mould-blown glass has an undulating interior surface which follows to a lesser degree the depressions and prominences of the pattern. Since the mould is in sections, which need to be taken apart to remove the finished object, seams will be noticed where the mould-sections joined. These are more prominent in a worn mould. Generally, the surface of a mould-blown object is more highly polished than a pressed glass specimen, but the surface polishing of pressed glass, and the removal of seams, was sometimes practised when trying to imitate cut-glass*. The patterns are sometimes sharpened on the engraver's wheel in addition if the specimen is intended to be seriously deceptive.

In the second half of the 19th century both mould-blown and pressed glass techniques were adapted in America to automatic production, the former process being limited to plain or lightly-patterned bottles.

MOUNT WASHINGTON GLASS WORKS (New Bedford, Mass.)

Founded by Deming Jarves* for his son, George. In its early years it made both pressed* and cut-glass*. In its later years the enterprise specialized in art glass*, including Burmese, 'Coralene'*, Rose Amberina*, Royal Flemish*, and a version of Peachblow*. Burmese glass was made in England under licence by T. Webb & Sons*, and there called 'Queen's Burmese'. A type of cameo glass* with classical designs, the unwanted glass mainly removed with hydrofluoric acid*, was also made here. The firm was taken over in 1894 by the Pairpoint Manufacturing Company.

MOUSSELINE GLASS

A very thin blown glass made by A. Jenkinson of Edinburgh. It was shown at the Paris Exposition of 1878, but had been made for some considerable time before this.

MOUSTACHE CUP

A cup with a perforated guard just below the rim to protect the moustache while drinking. The type was introduced by Harvey, Adams & Co. of Longton, Staffordshire, in the 19th century.

MUCHA, ALPHONSE (1860–1931)

Artist born in Bohemia (now Czechoslovakia) who specialized in posters*, but also designed jewellery, furniture, lace, etc. in a very personal *art nouveau* style. His best posters are theatrical, but he produced effective advertisements for other products, such as cigarettes. Mucha spent many years in Paris and most of his work belongs to the period between 1890 and 1903. In the latter year he went to the United States, where he remained until 1909.

223

MUCKLEY, WILLIAM

Glass-engraver and designer who executed a ruby glass goblet for John Richardson* of Wordsley which was included in the Great Exhibition of 1851. The glass is now in the Stourbridge Municipal Collections. Muckley later became Principal of Manchester School of Art.

MÜLLER, FERDINAND See *Royal Bronze Foundry*

MÜLLER FRÈRES

Henri and Desiré Müller were pupils of Émile Gallé who became independent about 1900, and took over a glasshouse at Croismare, near Nancy. Subsequently they opened a design and decorating studio at Lunéville, Meurthe-et-Moselle. Their products were largely derivative. They produced cameo glass*, moulded glass* and a considerable variety of coloured decorative glass. The mark, which includes the name, *MULLER FRÈRES*, can be engraved, incised, etched, in relief or painted.

MUNGO, JACKSON & GRAHAM See *Jackson & Graham*

MURRAY, KEITH (b. 1893)

New Zealand architect and designer, resident in England from 1935. Designed silver and pottery and, from 1913, provided glass designs for the Whitefriars Glass Works*, and later for Stevens & Williams*. His pottery designs were executed for Wedgwood* and are often lathe-turned.

MURRAY, WILLIAM STAITE (1881–1962)

English artist-potter, studied at Camberwell Art School, taught in the Royal College of Art from 1925 to 1940, and in the latter year went to Southern Rhodesia. Staite Murray was much influenced both by Japanese pottery and Chinese stonewares of the Sung dynasty (960-1280), and he had many pupils. With Bernard Leach* he was one of the artist-potters principally concerned in making these styles fashionable between the Wars. Examples of his work are in the Victoria and Albert Museum, London.

MUSÉE CÉRAMIQUE DE SÈVRES

An important collection of the ceramic art founded in 1805 by Alexandre Brongniart, director of the Sèvres Porcelain Factory*. He began by asking all the European manufactories of his day for specimens of their production. These were acquired between 1805 and 1812. M. Riocreux, *conservateur* of the Musée for many years, was largely responsible for arranging and classifying the collection as it was formed during his term of office, contributing with Brongniart to the *Catalogue du Musée Céramique de Sèvres*. The collection is now very extensive and includes important 19th-century wares from Sèvres as well as those made elsewhere. The Musée is attached to the factory and

MUSICAL BOXES. Miniature cylinder musical box, the movement by Albert et fils, the top well painted with a shipping scene. Third quarter of the 19th century. *Antique Collectors' Club*

is on the further side of the Pont-de-Sèvres from Paris.

MUSICAL BOXES

The musical box enjoyed a tremendous popularity throughout much of the 19th century, the movements being made either in Switzerland or France. The general principle on which they operated was a simple one. A steel comb, each tooth of which was tuned to a different note, was placed in a fixed position in relation to a cylinder, rotated by clockwork, which was covered with short steel pins. These pins struck and vibrated the teeth of the comb in a succession determined by their position on the cylinder. The same cylinder could be used to play a number of different tunes with the aid of a device which simply

MUSICAL BOXES. A typical musical box playing eight airs. Swiss movement. Last quarter of the 19th century. *Antique Collectors' Club*

shifted it slightly sideways, thus bringing a fresh set of pins into contact with the comb, the pins not in use passing through the gaps between the teeth. As time passed, especially after 1850, all kinds of refinements were added. A damping mechanism prevented the teeth from continuing to vibrate and causing a sustained sound, which would give rise to discordant interference with notes struck later. The damper was also essential to enable a note to be struck twice in rapid succession with clear definition. Chords, at first simulated by *arpeggios*, were introduced soon after 1850. This required exceptional accuracy in the positioning of the pins, since a number of teeth had to be plucked at precisely the same instant. A drum or bell accompaniment was introduced after 1850, as well as a way of controlling the passage of air through reeds, utilizing the mouth-organ principle. Nicole Frères of Geneva, one of the best makers, introduced a second comb by which the intensity of the sound could be varied, and eventually as many as five combs were employed for special effects. The more elaborate of these instruments needed a cylinder almost two feet long to actuate them.

The earliest appearance of the rotating cylinder was towards the end of the 18th century, when they were fitted to a few clocks, either long-case or bracket, in conjunction with a chime of bells, the pins actuating hammers. The more elaborate clock mechanisms were able to play a number of tunes, usually selected with the aid of a pointer on the dial. Miniature mechanisms to actuate watch chimes or snuff-boxes with musical movements were made in Geneva and Paris, where the finest watches were made.

From Switzerland came the singing-bird musical box, known in France as a *Serinette**. This also dates from late in the 18th century. In most examples, when the box is set going a small oval lid opens to allow a bird to rise up, flap its wings, turn back and forth, and then, when its song is ended, sink back into the box, the lid closing after it. Some of the best, also dating from the late 18th century, were placed in handsomely decorated small cages, but these are rare. The song is produced by air blown through a reed. The air comes from a small spring-driven bellows, and the mechanism also moves a piston which varies the pitch of the notes. It is from origins such as these that the later musical box sprang. The standard type already described appeared in a small, simple version by 1820 and developed rapidly.

Cases were not necessarily made by the makers of the movements. Snuff-boxes, for instance, were made by silversmiths and fitted with movements made elsewhere. Cases of this sort, as with those in the form of cages for the *serinette*, are usually small works of art in themselves. Some good quality small movements of the cylinder and comb type were fitted into cases of tortoiseshell, or *tôle** decorated with transfer-printing* on a coloured ground by the manufacturers. The later large musical boxes were also often fitted into cases made elsewhere. These were of polished wood, decorated in a variety of ways, including veneering and inlay, and the finest cases were usually employed for the best movements.

By 1885 a new type of musical box utilizing a card disc had been developed in Leipzig. This was called the *Symphonion*. It was developed into the *Polyphone* before 1890, the card discs being replaced by those of metal. These were considerable improvements on the earlier types of musical box, although they had the disadvantage of large size. They survived for only a short time, because first the phonograph and then the gramophone became fashionable and took their place.

MUSIC STOOLS
The popularity of the pianoforte in the typical drawing-room of the early 19th century led to the introduction of a special stool with a seat the height of which could be adjusted to suit the player's convenience and also enable him to swing round to face his audience. These date from about 1810 and still continue in use, the late Vladimir Pachmann making the adjustment of his stool an indispensable part of his performance. The stem and foot of the stool vary in style with the date, although reproductions of earlier styles are not uncommon. The rectangular stool of fixed height with a cupboard for the storage of music was a later development for the drawing-room rather than the concert platform.

MUSKINGHAM COUNTY POTTERIES (Ohio)
A number of potteries were located in the region in the first half of the 19th century. They were principally operated by immigrant Staffordshire potters, and they made yellow, brown and red earthenware for domestic use in familiar Staffordshire forms.

MUSS, CHARLES (1779–1824)
London independent porcelain and glass-enameller, formerly a painter at Caughley*. Muss employed John Martin* (painter of the well-known *Fall of Babylon*) who painted *Paradise Lost* on Worcester* porcelain which is now in the Victoria and Albert Museum, London.

MUYBRIDGE, EADWEARD   See *Fine Arts*

NAILSEA (Gloucestershire)

Glasshouse near Bristol established towards the end of the 18th century which produced novelties in considerable variety in a kind of coarse, dark brown or greenish glass, which was less highly taxed under the Glass Excise Act than lead glass. The wares most typically Nailsea were made by blowing and manipulation while hot, and were usually decorated with surface blobs or spatters of differently coloured glass (see *Spatter glass*).

A class of wares mostly coming into the category of friggers*, were more sophisticated. These include such objects as pipes, bells, walking-canes, shoes, rolling-pins, ships, figures of animals etc. sometimes with *latticinio** or combed decoration. Rolling-pins especially often bear gilt inscriptions. These wares are sometimes thought to have been the work of French glassmakers who had settled near Nailsea.

The word 'Nailsea' has become a generic term among collectors and dealers for glass in this and related styles made at Stourbridge, Worcestershire, Wrockwardine, Shropshire, and Bristol. The Nailsea glasshouses closed about 1878.

NAILSEA. Jug from Wrockwardine Wood, Shropshire. A type often confused with the products of Nailsea*. c. 1810. *Pilkington Glass Museum*

NAMED VIEWS

Topographical subjects on pottery, porcelain and glass the location of which is inscribed either under the scene itself or under the base. The practice was particularly in vogue during the first 30 years or so of the 19th century, especially in England and Germany. Some fine quality enamelled glass of this kind comes from Bohemia*. Towards the end of the century Meissen* produced porcelain plates with views of German cities. This fashion later inspired a good deal of souvenir china of poor quality with views of watering-places and spas, which was either made in England or imported from Thuringia*.

NANTGARW (Glamorgan, Wales)

Porcelain factory founded in 1813 by William Billingsley* in partnership with his son-in-law, Samuel Walker. A third person, William Weston Young*, advanced some of the capital and eventually joined the partnership. Unfortunately, the available capital proved to be insufficient and the porcelain body used, although of superb quality, was very unstable, with an estimated kiln-wastage of nine-tenths. The partners appealed to the Board of Trade for assistance, and the Government asked Lewis

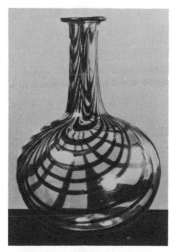

NAILSEA. Clear glass bottle with blue glass striations. Nailsea, Gloucestershire. Early 19th century.

NAILSEA. A rare fox-hunt in glass formed 'at the lamp'. First half of the 19th century. *Antique Collectors' Club*

Weston Dillwyn, proprietor of the Cambrian Pottery, to report on their prospects. As a result the undertaking was transferred to Swansea* to the Cambrian Pottery. By 1816 Billingsley had returned to Nantgarw. Walker returned in 1817 and fresh capital was raised by Young and others. In this way the factory was able to continue until 1820. Young took over the plant, moulds and stock of porcelain, both white and decorated. The plant and moulds, and possibly some of the white ware, were bought in 1821 by John Rose of Coalport*. A good deal of white ware was also painted independently by Thomas Pardoe*.

The factory undoubtedly failed because of the uneconomic nature of the porcelain body employed, which closely resembled a mid-18th-century glassy artificial porcelain. There is, indeed, reason to think that Billingsley was actually experimenting with a porcelain formula acquired from Zachariah Boreman, a fellow-painter at Derby* who had worked at Chelsea* during the gold anchor period (1758–1765). Nantgarw porcelain, therefore, was an anachronism which owed its popularity to its resemblance to '*vieux Sèvres*'* soft-paste porcelain and to its appearance on the market at a time when the stocks of soft-paste white porcelain bought from Sèvres* for decoration after the post-Revolutionary reorganization were exhausted. A great deal of Nantgarw production was bought by London dealers 'in white' and painted in such independent studios as those of Robins & Randall*. Simple flower painting was done at Nantgarw by Billingsley, Pardoe, and others.

Most of the production was of tea-, dessert- and dinner-services and plates are by far the commonest survival. These are either plain, or with a low-relief moulded decoration on the ledge. Pot-pourri vases, taper-sticks, and finely painted cabinet cups and saucers were also made, but are relatively infrequent. The mark is NANTGARW, NANT GARW or NANT GARW C.W. Specimens are much sought.

NAST, JEAN-NEPOMUC-HERMAN (1754–1817)

Nast, of German origin, and his sons were manufacturers of porcelain at the rue Amandiers-Popincourt,

Paris. The factory was founded in 1782, and by the end of the century was one of the most prosperous in Paris. It was continued by Nast's sons until 1835 and was afterwards operated by other proprietors. It sent an exhibit to the London Exhibition of 1851 under the name of H. J. Nast. The factory specialized in service-ware decorated with well-painted flowers. They also produced biscuit porcelain* decorated in relief, and also wares with relief against a coloured background in the style of Wedgwood's jasper*. Portrait busts* in white biscuit porcelain are known but are rare. One of Napoleon probably dates from the beginning of the century. The usual mark is NAST À PARIS or N . . . . . à Paris.

NATURALISTIC STYLE

Style of ornament, especially floral and foliate, in which the subjects are represented as exactly as possible to their natural appearance. It was especially popular during the middle decades of the 19th century. Naturalism in this sense may be used in conjunction with a Romantic or Realist treatment of the subject.

See *Realism*; *Romanticism*

NAUTILUS SHELLS

The nautilus shell, engraved on the exterior with a variety of decorative *motifs* and handsomely mounted in gold or silver, was a speciality of the German goldsmiths of the 16th and 17th centuries. These were copied in porcelain during the 19th-century fashion for Renaissance *objets d'art*, especially by the Worcester Royal Porcelain Company*.

NAVARRE, HENRI (b. 1889)

French glass craftsman who worked somewhat in the manner of Marinot*. His work, mainly vases with textured surfaces, belongs to the *art déco** style. The mark is usually *H. Navarre* diamond-engraved into the base.

NAZARENER (German)

A group of German painters who, at the beginning of the 19th century, founded a movement with a quasi-

STEVENGRAPHS. Book-mark woven in silk with the Arms of
the Ancient Order of Foresters, by Stevens of Coventry.
Last quarter of the 19th century. *Constance Chiswell*

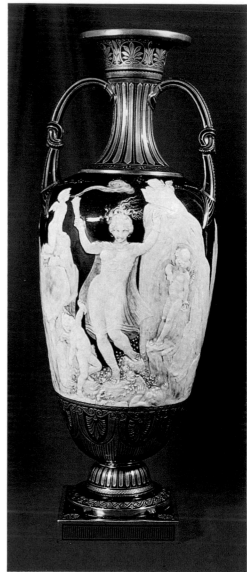

PARGETER, PHILLIP. The Milton Vase. Designed by Philip
Pargeter showing the Archangel Michael. The subject taken
from Milton's *Paradise Lost* and executed by John
Northwood. 1878. *Sotheby & Co.*

SOLON, MARC-LOUIS. A tinted Parian vase by Minton with
pâte-sur-pâte decoration by Solon. c. 1890. *Minton Museum,
Royal Doulton Tableware*

DOULTON. A jug decorated with an early motoring scene.
c. 1900. Royal Doulton. *Private Collection*

SUNFLOWER. A Majolica plate in the form of this favourite
motif of the Aesthetic movement, c. 1880, and a jug in the
form of overlapping vine leaves appropriately coloured. c.
1860. Josiah Wedgwood & Sons, Etruria. *Trustees of the
Wedgwood Museum*

ART NOUVEAU. Display cabinet in mahogany with floral
inlay in various woods. *Art nouveau* style. English. c. 1900.
Brighton Art Gallery & Museum

religious basis inspired by Dürer and early Renaissance artists. They established a cooperative workshop on the old monastic lines in 1820. The movement was derided at the time by Goethe and others, 'Nazarener' being one of the epithets applied to them. The group of English painters known as the Pre-Raphaelites* had some affinities with the Nazarener.

NEALE & COMPANY (Hanley, Staffordshire)
Earthenware potters, the proprietor, James Neale, having taken over the enterprise from Humphrey Palmer in 1778. The firm imitated Wedgwood*, including basaltes* (Egyptian black) and jasper*. Cream-coloured ware was also manufactured in large quantities, and much use was made of Wedgwood's designs. Most sought today are the well-modelled figures decorated with good enamel colours produced by Neale in the early years of the 19th century. Marked examples occur not infrequently. The usual mark is the name impressed.

NEEDLES, JOHN (fl. 1812–1853)
Furniture-maker of Baltimore, Maryland, who worked in traditional ways.

NEO-CLASSICISM
Term applied to the revival of classical styles which was inspired by the discovery and excavations of Pompeii and Herculaneum in the 1750s. The movement gained impetus in France, where the style was cultivated principally by financial and intellectual circles in opposition to the king and the aristocracy who clung for most of the 1760s to the earlier rococo style.

In England neo-classicism became fashionable as the Adam style, inspired to some extent by the vogue in France, but also by the visit of Robert Adam to the Roman province of Dalmatia and his studies of Diocletian's palace at Spalato (Split, in modern Yugoslavia). The journey of 'Athenian' Stuart to Athens and his studies of Greek architecture helped to bring Greek influence into English neo-classicism at the turn of the century, to be followed by the Empire style* of Napoleon I which, in English hands, became the Regency style*, a period conveniently extended until 1830 and even later. Neo-classicism was one of the principal styles of the 19th century in various guises, and it eventually emerged victor in Edwardian times in the 'Battle of the Styles', as it came to be called, with medievalism ultimately discredited.

On the Continent medievalism never gained the kind of hold which it did in England under the influence of Pugin* and Walter Scott. In France little neo-Gothic* building was done. The taste for medievalism was satisfied to a considerable extent by the extensive restorations of Viollet-le-Duc* to places like the fortifications of Carcassonne. In Germany, also, the predominant 18th-century style was classical, merging into Empire*, and followed by Biedermeier* which, itself, was a variant of Empire styles. At mid-century, especially in Austria, a particularly complicated kind of neo-Gothic was employed for furniture by Leistler* and others. Ludwig II* furnished his Byzantine palace of Neuschwanstein with a Gothic

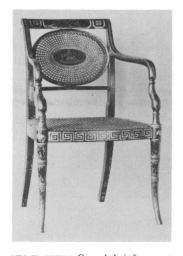

NEO-CLASSICISM. Carved chair from a set of neo-classical* beechwood dining-chairs japanned in black and decorated in gold, the oval medallion in the centre of the caned back painted *en grisaille*. c. 1805. *Victoria & Albert Museum, London*

NÉO-GREC STYLE. Oxidized silver-plated incense-burner in the néo-Grec* style. Exhibited at the London International Exhibition, 1862. Ferdinand Barbedienne*, Paris. *Victoria & Albert Museum, London*

bedroom, but his other palaces at Herrenchiemsee* and Linderhof are classically based. In Germany, also, medievalism took the form of restorations and additions to existing Gothic buildings. It is noteworthy that German scholars continued the 18th-century tradition of classical studies begun by Winckelmann.

NEO-GOTHIC   See *Gothic revival*

NÉO-GREC STYLE (French)
Style popular in France during the Second Empire. Despite its name, objects in this style often had a much closer affinity with the Near East than with Greece. Barbedienne* exhibited an example at the Paris Exposition of 1855. The style is allied to the revived Egyptian style* current in America during the 19th century and the two are sometimes confused.

NEO-VENETIAN STYLE
Style in glass-making and designing, approved by Ruskin*, which first appears just before the Great Exhibition, but which was particularly evident at the Paris Exposition of 1867, at which the comparatively recent Compania Venezia-Murano successfully exhibited. The technique of Neo-Venetian glass was primarily manipulative, and included such processes as *millefiori**, *latticinio**, ice glass* and fairly close copies of early Venetian glasses, and those reminiscent of the old *façon-de-Venise*. Apsley Pellatt* was among the earliest exponents of the style in England.

NETSUKÉ (Japanese)
Pronounced *netski*. The *netsuké* was a small, carved toggle which was at the opposite end of the cord which attached the *inrō** to the sash. They are carved from ivory, bone, or wood, and occasionally may be found in lacquer and other materials. Two holes are pierced through which the cord could be passed. If these are not present the object is not a *netsuké*, and may be spurious. The subjects of the carvings are innumerable, and are usually taken from mythology or folklore. The best are now very highly valued. Modern copies exist.

NEUSCHWANSTEIN, SCHLOSS (near Munich, Bavaria)
Started in 1869, this castle was built in the Romanesque style for Ludwig II*, King of Bavaria, by the architects von Dollman, Riedel, and Hoffman. This is probably the largest of Ludwig's palaces and it is sited on the top of a precipitous rock. The throne-room is in the Byzantine style, with a mosaic floor; the minstrels' hall is 90 feet long and decorated with mural paintings of scenes from *Parsifal*. A dressing-room is decorated with scenes from the lives of Walther von der Vogelweide and Hans Sachs, and the walls of the Gothic bedroom illustrate the story of *Tristan und Isolde*. The king's study has scenes from *Tannhäuser*, and the sitting-room illustrates the legend of *Lohengrin*, all *motifs* appropriate to Wagner's chief patron.

Between them, the palaces of Neuschwanstein, Linderhof, and Herrenchiemsee* represent the three predominating historical styles which were inspiring designers of the period. Ludwig was the last of the great palace-builders, and his expenditure almost bankrupted the small state of Bavaria. When he was drowned in mysterious circumstances in the Chiemsee, rumours were going round Munich that he intended to build a replica of Vesuvius in eruption. While this was probably malicious, he had certainly been thinking aloud about a proposition to build a replica of the Summer Palace at Peking—the Yüan-Ming-Yüan.
See *Herrenchiemsee, Schloss*

NEWCOMBE POTTERY, NEW ORLEANS, La.
Pottery founded in New Orleans, Louisiana, in 1897, and associated with the Sophie Newcombe Memorial College for Women. It was under the direction of Miss Sheener. Decoration was carved or incised by pupils of the department, who often signed their work.

Subjects employed were of Southern derivation such as rice, magnolia, etc., and work was often signed by the artist. The wares were popular throughout the South.

NEW ENGLAND GLASS BOTTLE COMPANY (Cambridge, Mass.)
A factory existing from 1826 to 1845 and closely connected with the New England Glass Company*. It made bottles of green and black glass, some of them types now sought by collectors.

NEW ENGLAND GLASS COMPANY (Cambridge, Mass.)
The company was founded in 1818 by Edward H. Monroe, and by 1850 it seems to have been the largest glass manufactory in the world. Until 1825 its manager was Deming Jarves*, and from 1878 the works were leased by Edward Libbey, who transferred them to Toledo, Ohio, in 1888 where supplies of natural gas were available as fuel. For about 60 years almost every kind of glass was manufactured—blown, moulded, pressed, cut, and engraved. The pressed glass* process was introduced either here or at the Boston and Sandwich Glass Company*. Several early varieties of art glass* were developed here, including Agata*, Amberina*, Pomona* and Wild Rose Peachblow*. The factory also produced paperweights*, especially those decorated with a single large fruit. For most of its life the factory made a type of lead glass, but in the 1870s it suffered increasingly from the competition of lime glass* and the high cost of fuel.
See *Libbey Glass Company*

NEW ENGLAND POTTERY COMPANY (Cambridge, Mass.)

This factory was founded in 1834 to make Rockingham* glazed ware and yellow ware. After 1875 it also made creamware* and granite ware. Later it added porcelain to its products, especially an old ivory body, and wares with a mazarine blue ground.

NEW HALL (Shelton, Staffordshire)

An 18th-century factory making true porcelain which continued its activities into the 19th century. Soon after 1804, when many of the original founders had dropped out, Peter Warburton* became a partner. In 1810 he took out a patent for printing in gold and silver. Warburton was also a manufacturer of creamware* on his own account and specimens occur printed in gold marked 'WARBURTON'S PATENT'. The New Hall factory closed finally in 1835.

About 1810 the original hard-paste porcelain*, made in accordance with Richard Champion's patent, was abandoned in favour of a bone china body. An earthenware was also produced. The factory concentrated largely on the production of services—tea- and dessert-services especially. Although adopting a new body the factory remained faithful to many of the old silver shapes, but they also introduced new styles and shapes influenced by those in current use in Staffordshire. *Chinoiseries* were a popular form of decoration, sometimes with fairly lavish gilding, and painted landscapes were crudely washed with colour. Output was large, but wares were only rarely marked and are not always certainly identifiable. A pattern number is usual, those containing four figures occurring on specimens in bone china. The mark, when it exists, is the words 'New Hall' in script within a double circle.

NIBELUNGENLIED, DIE (German)

A 12th-century German epic poem which relates how Siegfried won his wife, Gudrun, how Siegfried's murder was encompassed by Brünhild with the loss of his treasure, the fate of Kriemhild (who married Attila, the fifth-century Hun chieftain), and how she was, herself, slain. The subject was especially popular in Germany as a source of inspiration for decorative themes in the 19th century, and it sometimes occurs as relief decoration on carved ivory tankards, especially those from Bavaria.

'NORMAN CONQUEST' VASES

Pair of Worcester* vases of Sèvres* form decorated with scenes from the Norman Conquest of 1066 by Thomas Bott*, after designs by Daniel Maclise. Executed in 1868, they were Bott's last major work.

NORTHWOOD, JOHN (1837–1902)

Northwood was a glass-engraver who revived the ancient Roman craft of the *diatretarius*, the cameo-carver, using cased glass* for the purpose. His methods followed those of the Romans to a certain extent, the detailed work being done with hardened steel or diamond-pointed chisels struck with a light mallet. Unlike the Romans, however, Northwood had the advantage of hydrofluoric acid* to clear away unwanted glass. A commission to engrave a clear glass vase, known from its subject as the Elgin vase, took him eight years. The experience gained, however, enabled him to complete his copy of the Portland Vase*, with which he won Benjamin Richardson's £1,000 prize, in three years. With his son, John Northwood Junior (who had assimilated the elder man's techniques), he founded a school of cameo-carving on glass, one member of which, George Woodall (1850–1925), did some distinguished work. Joshua Hodgett (1858–1933) executed floral subjects with the engraver's wheel.

NORTON, JOHN

John Norton was a captain in the Revolutionary Army who founded a pottery for the manufacture of red earthenware in 1793 at Bennington*, Vt. Norton retired in 1823, leaving his sons, Lyman and John, to continue the business, which eventually became the United States Pottery Company under the management of Christopher Webber Fenton*.

NORTON STONEWARE COMPANY See *Bennington Pottery*

NUDE, THE

The Puritan ethic to which the Victorians were outwardly addicted was in most cases very much a surface gloss. From the end of the Regency period the female nude was a favourite subject with artists and craftsmen alike. It was especially popular during the Great Exhibition of 1851, not only in such statuary as *The Greek Slave* of Hiram Powers, but as part of the decoration of porcelain dessert-services (for example, the painting of Thomas Bott* on Worcester* porce-

NUDE, THE. Porcelain plaque painted with a nude in characteristic mid-19th century style. French or German. c. 1860. *Sotheby & Co*

lain), and later in some examples of cameo glass*, in metalwork and in many other forms. It was no less popular as a subject in the Exhibition of 1862, when John Gibson's* *Tinted Venus** drew large crowds, and towards the end of the century the nude became one of the principal *motifs* of the *art nouveau** style.

NYMPHENBURG (Bavaria)

Porcelain factory located opposite the Schloss Nymphenburg on the outskirts of Munich. It is now the Staatliche Porzellanmanufaktur. Until 1764 Nymphenburg possessed one of the finest modellers of porcelain figures ever to practise the art—Franz Anton Bustelli. They still have many of the moulds, and repetitions of Bustelli's figures are being produced, properly marked to distinguish them from 18th-century work. When the Frankenthal factory closed at the end of the 18th century the moulds were removed to Nymphenburg, and copies of these old figures and groups are produced today. In 1880 the factory purchased the Höchst moulds from Damm*, and these also have been used. The models selected are chiefly those of J. P. Melchior, who became *Modellmeister* at Nymphenburg in 1799 after the closure of Frankenthal.

In the early years of the 19th century Nymphenburg produced figures in white biscuit* in the Empire style*. Later in the century some well-modelled animal and peasant figures were made. At the beginning of the present century the factory introduced new underglaze colours and revived some of the 18th-century services of Auliczek. Excellent services of modern design were also produced, as well as figures by Josef Wackerle and Resl Lechner. The latter succeeded in adapting 18th-century styles to 20th-century purposes. Wackerle was art-director from 1906 to 1909, and designed figures decorated in underglaze colours. At the present time the factory makes high quality porcelain, and much of the service-ware is hand-painted.

NYMPHENBURG. Figure in Bavarian costume by Resl Lechner. *Staatliche Porzellanmanufaktur, Nymphenburg*

NYMPHENBURG. Tureen, cover and stand of porcelain in a revived rococo* style handsomely painted with flowers. Nymphenburg Porzellanmanufaktur, Bavaria. Mid-19th century. *Sotheby & Co*

NYMPHENBURG. Porcelain plate finely painted with a nude. Nymphenburg Porzellanmanufaktur. c. 1860. *Sotheby & Co*

'OFF-HAND' GLASS

The term in America includes such domestic glassware as pitchers, mugs, bowls, salts etc. made by workmen for their own use at factories principally making window-glass and bottles.

See *Friggers*

'OLD ENGLISH' STYLE

Term given especially to a furniture style current in the last quarter of the 19th century, but often used loosely. The principal difference between 'Old English' represented by Pugin* and the neo-Gothic* style is that the latter was ultimately based on medieval and early Renaissance styles, while the former derived its repertory of ornament from Gothic architecture.

OLDFIELD & CO.   See *Brampton*

OMEGA WORKSHOPS

Enterprise founded in 1913 by Roger Fry in Fitzroy Square, London, and at Poole, Dorset, to revive 'joy in craftsmanship'. The Workshops produced furniture, pottery, and textiles of one kind or another made by artists and designers, few of whom had received any practical training in the crafts. Designs were of a post-Impressionist type, midway between *art nouveau** and *art déco**, but quality of construction and finish was poor and the workshops never achieved any kind of real success.

The pottery was covered by a tin glaze, a technique which had then fallen into disuse in England, and decorators included Roger Fry, Vanessa Bell and Duncan Grant. The mark employed was the Greek letter *Omega* inside a rectangle.

OPALINE (OPAL) GLASS

Translucent glass partially opacified by the addition of tin oxide or bone-ash (calcined cattle bones). The latter was known in Germany as *Beinglas* (bone-glass). Opaline glass was a revival of the old Venetian white opaque glass which was often enamelled in the late 18th century in the manner of contemporary porcelain. Its forms were also based on those produced by the porcelain factories. The term *'opalin'* was coined for this type of glass by the Baccarat* glass

works about 1823 and it was in fairly general use by 1838. 'Opaline' first came into general use in the early years of the 20th century.

The opacifying agent only made the glass white. White opaline first appeared about 1810. Before 1820 colouring oxides were being added in France and some delicate colours were being produced. Much

OPALINE (OPAL) GLASS. Vase of opaline* glass, its general form reminiscent of Chinese porcelain, enamelled with flowers. Glass vases, usually decorated with enamel painting, closely based on porcelain vases, especially those from Derby*, were made at Stourbridge from about 1850 onwards. *The Corporation of Dudley*

OPALINE (OPAL) GLASS. Pressed glass bowl of yellow opaline, probably coloured with uranium oxide. The edge exhibits the colour very strongly. Last quarter of the 19th century. English. *Constance Chiswell*

OPALINE (OPAL) GLASS. A faceted and enamelled jug and two beakers. Bohemian. c. 1840. *Antique Collectors' Club*

sought is the *gorge de pigeon* (pigeon's throat) which is faintly tinged with mauve. The *boulles de savon* was a combination of several pale, misty colours suggesting the soap bubble. The very rare yellow opaline dates from about 1810, turquoise (also a comparatively rare colour) from about the same year and violet from 1828. A black opaline was made about 1820, and a marbled version about five years later, influenced by Bohemian work. Greens and blues were the most popular, especially sky-blue, which became plentiful after 1835.

Vases formed the greater part of the output, the earliest in the Empire style*, although carafes*, candlesticks and other useful objects were also made. The best vases in the early period were sometimes mounted in ormolu or gilt-bronze. Painted decoration done before 1835 was usually in 'cold' colour (i.e. unfired pigment), and in enamel colours thereafter. Gilding employed in conjunction with 'cold' painting was usually done with gold-leaf. A few examples are in a revived Gothic* style, and these belong to the period between 1825 and 1848.

'Opaline' glass in England was usually termed 'opal'. It was made in Birmingham by George Bacchus & Sons* and at Stourbridge, Worcestershire. A limited amount was also made in Bohemia.

OPAQUE GLASS
Glass which is only slightly translucent or completely opaque, dependent on its thickness. When white it is

termed milk glass* (German *milchglas*), but this variety usually retains a well-marked translucency. Other opaque varieties are Hyalith*, Lithyalin*, Haematin, Purpurine* (employed by Fabergé*), Aventurine* and glasses imitating such natural stones as malachite*, lapis lazuli, jasper* and porphyry. These were made principally in Bohemia, by von Buquoy, Egermann* and others between 1835 and 1855.

See *Bohemian and Austrian glass*

OPPITZ, PAUL (fl. 1870–1880)
Glass engraver of Bohemian extraction who worked in England, possibly for Thomas Webb* of Stourbridge. He engraved a vase commissioned by W. T. Copeland* & Sons of London. This was subsequently shown at the Vienna Universal Exhibition of 1873, where Oppitz was awarded a prize medal. It was later bought by Sir Richard Wallace.

ORMOLU
An alloy, for the most part made in England, which is principally copper and zinc, the proportions varying between 60%–63% of copper and 34%–30% of zinc, with possibly a little lead to give fluidity. Ormolu is, in fact, a kind of brass, light yellow in colour, which does not need gilding, although it is normally covered with a clear lacquer. It is employed for similar purposes to gilded bronze (a superior metal) in France, although some 19th-century French bronze alloys contain so much zinc that they could well be

ORMOLU. Pair of ormolu vases in the style of Sèvres porcelain*. French. c. 1840. *Antique Collectors' Club*

regarded as brass instead of bronze. 'Ormolu' is derived from the French *dorure d'or moulu* (i.e. gilding with milled or powdered gold, which actually refers to gilding with an amalgam of powdered gold and mercury) and the word has been used in England since about 1770. Wedgwood, in a letter of this period, refers to clock cases of 'D'Or Moulu' which he had seen at Matthew Boulton's factory.

ØRREFORS GLASBRUK. Glass vase by Victor Lindstrand decorated with an engraved male swimmer. Mark: *ØRREFORS* engraved. 1928–1941. *Sotheby & Co*

ØRREFORS GLASBRUK (Småland, Sweden)

A factory for the production of decorative and table-glass was founded at Ørrefors in 1915. In its initial stages it was far from successful, and it was decided to appoint two advisers, Simon Gate and Edvard Hald. Their designs were mainly figure subjects for engraving in the earlier German baroque and rococo styles, which were traditional in Sweden. Ørrefors developed a glass 'flashed'* with coloured stains on the exterior which was called 'Graalglas', and it also founded a school of glass-cutting and engraving. Notable engravers have been Viktor Linstrand, Edvin Öhrstrom and Sven Palmqvist. The factory gained an international reputation in the 1920s, and achieved a notable success at the Paris Exposition of 1937. In the case of individually decorated glass the artist has usually added his initials. The name *Ørrefors* is also engraved into the glass. A factory for the manufacture of table-services is operated at Sandvik.

OSLER, F. & C. (Birmingham, Warwickshire)

Glass-manufacturers who made painted opaline* vases about the time of the Great Exhibition of 1851. Their production included glasses with fine quality floral engraving and cast portrait busts* of contemporary notabilities. Osler made the cut-glass Crystal Fountain for the Great Exhibition which was 27 feet high and several tons in weight, as well as cut-glass candelabra on the same generous scale which were presented to the Queen.

OTT & BREWER   See *Etruria Pottery*

OTTOMAN

In the 18th century a kind of overstuffed bench without back or arms (see *Pouf*) to be placed in the centre of a room. In the 19th century a popular model was circular with a central back and seats on all four sides, also intended for the centre of a room. Other models were adapted for use in corners. They were particularly popular during the Second Empire* in France and at about the same time in England.

OVERLAY GLASS

Alternative term for cased glass*. Glass of one colour overlaid by a layer (usually opaque) of another colour, through which patterns and designs are cut to reveal the layer beneath. Sometimes further decorated by enamelling, especially in Bohemia*. Overlay glass was made principally in Bohemia, England (Birmingham and Stourbridge) and America. It should not be confused with cameo glass*, which is a type of overlay glass from which the necessary parts of the top layer are mainly removed by the methods of the Roman cameo-cutters—i.e. diamond or steel-pointed chisels and copper engraving wheels.

See also *Northwood, John*

OVERSTUFFED

Chairs, sofas etc. on which the padding has been carried over the back and arms. Furniture of this kind is also usually deep-buttoned to keep the padding in place. Overstuffing was fairly common after 1850, although early specimens in good condition are rare.

See *Buttoned upholstery*

OSLER, F. & C. The Crystal Fountain by F. & C. Osler*. Erected in the transept of the Crystal Palace for the Great Exhibition, 1851, this 27 ft high cut-glass fountain was sited at the focal point of the Exhibition. After the *Illustrated Builder*

OWEN, GEORGE (d. 1917)

Owen made porcelain vases and other decorative pieces for the Worcester Royal Porcelain Company*. They were elaborately pierced to a point where some were little more than a large number of holes held together by a slender porcelain network. Specimens of this kind, done at intervals between more normal work, carry the Worcester backstamp with Owen's signature incised. He also modelled flowers for attachment to small decorative pieces for presentation to his friends. The pierced work is usually referred to at the factory as 'Owen's pierced porcelain'.

OWENS, J. B. (Zanesville, Ohio)

Owens established a factory for the manufacture of utilitarian pottery in the 1880s, and moved to Zanesville in 1891. Here he produced 'Majolica'* *jardinières* and pedestals. In 1896 the potter W. A. Long produced a ware which was called 'Utopian', decorated with American Indians and animals painted in slip underglaze. Other varieties of art pottery were introduced, including autumn leaves painted under a matt glaze, and *motifs* derived from American Indian pottery. The mark employed was *Owens*.

P

PALISSY, BERNARD (1510–1590)

French potter, glassworker and glass-painter who, from 1540, devoted his energies to discovering the secret of Italian *maiolica**. He did not succeed in his purpose, but he produced a remarkable series of coloured glazes which he referred to as '*maiolica*'. No doubt for this reason when factories, which included Sèvres* and Minton*, developed a ware decorated with coloured glazes in the 19th century it was called '*majolica*'. Palissy's technique was continued after his death by the Avon Pottery, and the pottery of both was widely copied and adapted in the 19th century. Especially copied were Palissy's rustic wares—dishes decorated to represent a stream of water, with modelled fish, small reptiles, insects, shells and aquatic plants. These wares were copied by potters like Avisseau*, Georges Pull* and Mafra* at Caldas da Rainha.

PALISSY POTTERY (Longton, Staffordshire)

The work of Palissy Pottery Ltd from 1946 is thus called. Formerly A. E. Jones (Longton) Ltd., earthenware manufacturers from 1905.

PANTIN GLASS FACTORY (Paris)

A factory in the north-eastern district of Paris founded by E. Monot in 1855. It made coloured, decorative glass of excellent quality and among its specialities according to recent research, were some quite elaborate paperweights* especially those containing a lizard. The factory exhibited work of this kind at the Paris Exposition of 1878, where they were awarded a gold medal. There were several changes of name and ownership during the 19th century although the Monot family remained connected with it. In 1900 it was constituted the Cristallerie de Pantin, owned by Saint-Hilaire, Tourier de Varreux et Cie.

PAPERWEIGHTS, GLASS

Until the 19th century small bronzes or bronze-mounted porcelain were used as paperweights (*presse-papiers*). The decorative glass paperweight is a 19th-century innovation. The enclosure of a cameo of some refractory substance in a ball of glass (known as a sulphide*, incrustation, or crystallo-ceramic*),

developed at the beginning of the 19th century by Barthélémy Desprez* and patented in England by Apsley Pellatt*, was the first glass paperweight, but the most sought are the *millefiori** and *latticinio** types, or those with colourful enclosures, such as lizards, fruits and single flowers, the best of which were made in France between 1840 and 1850. The earliest Venetian paperweights of the *millefiori* type are those produced by Pierre Bigaglia before 1845. These were a revival of a much earlier Venetian type from which the Bohemian glasshouses derived the technique, but the French soon developed and improved it to a point which has never been surpassed.

The first dated Saint-Louis* weights were made in 1845, although the years 1847 and 1848 are more frequent. Baccarat* weights are dated from 1846 to 1849, with 1849 as the commonest year, and Clichy* weights are not dated at all, although the letter *C* is concealed in the decoration, and very occasionally *Clichy* in full. Manufacture, of course, was not confined to these years, but continued after 1850, although quality began to fall away, and the vogue was no longer at its height. The finest weights are those from Saint-Louis, the rarest come from Baccarat. The same technique of decoration was also applied to other small objects, such as inkwells, small vases, rules, perfume-bottles, drinking-glasses, door-knobs, *tazze*, seals, and decanters.

In England excellent paperweights of the *millefiori* type were made in Birmingham, and those made at the Whitefriars Glass Works*, London, are sometimes dated 1848. The first American weights were made after 1851 by the New England Glass Company*, and the earliest dated specimens belong to the year 1852. Weights were also made by the Boston and Sandwich Glass Company*, William Gillinder* and one or two other makers of decorative glass. The small manufacturers, far too numerous to be listed here, are discussed in detail in Paul Hollister's *Encyclopedia of Glass Paperweights*, essential to collectors.

Most of the best quality weights were decorated with *millefiori* patterns, or a combination of *millefiori* and *latticinio* designs covered by a hemispherical

PAPERWEIGHTS. Model showing stages in the manufacture of a *millefiori** paperweight. *Pilkington Glass Museum*

mound of glass of exceptional clarity. Some were dipped into opaque coloured glass which was ground away in places down to the crystal glass, so the interior decoration could be viewed as through a window. These are referred to as 'overlay' weights. Generally, decoration may be classified into several types:

An even distribution of flower canes (*millefiori*) over the whole ground.

A geometric pattern arranged from contrasting *millefiori* sections.

Isolated *millefiori* groups on a ground of a *latticinio* pattern, or some other background. These are usually termed 'carpet weights'.

Single flowers, two or three flowers, bouquets, animals, butterflies, reptiles, etc. formed in a mould. These were sometimes employed in conjunction with a *millefiori* or *latticinio* background.

The normal size of the paperweight is about three inches in diameter. A miniature version measures slightly less than two inches, and the large size, made in England, four inches. Paperweights are still being made today. Early French styles are being reproduced in America and Bohemia (Czechoslovakia) at a small fraction of the cost of an antique example.

Paperweights and other decorative glass objects of the *millefiori* type have been very popular among collectors during recent years, and high prices have been paid for French paperweights of the 1845–1850 period.

PAPIER MÂCHÉ (French)

Literally, pulped paper. The use of *papier mâché* dates from the late 17th century, and it was originally imported from Japan, where it was used as a foundation for lacquer. In Europe it was employed for decorative wares of many kinds which, in their surface appearance and style of decoration, usually exhibit the influence of Oriental lacquer-ware.

The early varieties of *papier mâché* were made from pulped paper mixed with chalk and gum mastic pressed in moulds. Commonly this was used for moulded ceiling decoration, and similar interior

work. It was easier to apply, and cheaper, than plaster moulding. These were still being made in the 19th century. The best known 19th-century type of *papier mâché*, however, was devised by Henry Clay of Birmingham in 1772, who laid pasted sheets of paper successively into a wooden mould, where they were pressed into shape. After the required thickness had been attained the object was removed, stoved, smoothed and japanned or varnished. The principal colour employed was black: crimson and green are much rarer. The tray was one of Clay's most popular manufactures, and his technique, which was very widely adopted, obviously lent itself to the making of such flat objects as panels and trays. These panels had considerable strength in certain directions, and could therefore be safely employed for such large furniture as beds, small tables, and cabinets, but structural supports, stems and pedestals of tables, for example, needed to be made of wood or metal.

The value of *papier mâché* in the making of panels lay in the ease with which they could be moulded into curves, their light weight and the suitability of the surface for decoration. During the 19th century, for instance, light-weight work-boxes and similar items could be made with moulded curves impossible in wood.

Furniture, which was especially popular from about 1840 to 1880, was made in France, England and America, the English production being the best and largest in quantity. The principal English centres were Wolverhampton and Birmingham, and the largest manufacturers were Jennens & Bettridge* of the latter city, who were prominent at the Great Exhibition of 1851 (see *Day Dreamer, The*). Among the products listed as being made by this firm were firescreens, chairs of all kinds, settees, small tables, cabinets, *secretaires* and clock cases, apart from the customary trays, small boxes, teapoys, and hand-screens. In America the Litchfield Manufacturing Company began to manufacture *papier mâché* in 1850. They specialized in clock cases, but also made boxes, screens, and small tables with the aid of craftsmen from England. On the whole, their products are not so well-finished as those of European manufacturers.

Generally techniques of decoration were adapted from those employed on Japanese lacquer of the earlier period, but the reopening of Japan to Western trade by Perry in 1853 came too late to have much influence. *Papier mâché* imitated lacquer, and the surface was finished by painting it with a pigment suspended in a varnish medium which was termed 'japan'. The Japanese practice of dusting the surface while tacky with gold and silver powder was imitated in England with bronze powder, beginning in 1802. Green bronze powder was employed for foliage, and graphite for shadowing. The use of stencils in conjunction with bronze powder for pictorial decoration came later, probably before 1843. The use of mother-of-pearl shell inlay was introduced in 1825 by Jennens & Bettridge. For the best work these inlays were wafer-thin slips of coloured nautilus shell cut to shape and glued to the surface, which was then built up to a level surface by successive coats of varnish. The shell was incorporated into the design (usually painted) in a variety of ways, for instance, it was often employed as flower-petals. Between 1830 and about 1845 this kind of decoration was exceedingly popular.

Also popular was decoration in gold leaf and powder, often Oriental landscapes and pavilions. The best work in the Oriental style is to be found in the painted decoration of Edwin Booth, done in Birmingham in the 1830s. Painting is variable in quality, but in general it is comparable with porcelain painting of the period. Birmingham enamel, fan, and *papier mâché* painters were often recruited by the porcelain factories in search of new talent. Edward Haselar and George Neville were well-known for the quality of their flower-painting and David Sargent painted ferns. Exceptional, and usually of fine quality, are romantic landscapes, sometimes with aluminium powder simulating moonlight, the best of which were executed on trays in the 1840s and the 1850s, and copies of paintings after such popular artists as Landseer. The best trays were probably those produced by the Wolverhampton firm of Frederick Walton & Company and notable painters include David Roberts, John Martland, and Alfred Dixon. A good deal of damaged *papier mâché* has been cleverly restored in recent years and it requires careful examination when being purchased from any but well-established sources.

See also *Stobwasser und Sohn*

PARDOE, THOMAS (1770–1823)
Painter of flowers, birds, animals and landscapes on Swansea earthenware and porcelain, employed by the factory until about 1819 and afterwards on his own account.

PARGETER, PHILIP (fl. 1869–1890)
English glass-maker, nephew of Benjamin Richardson*, patron of John Northwood I*. Pargeter was a partner with his uncle, and one of the Hodgett family, at the Red House, Wordsley. In 1869 the partnership was dissolved, and Pargeter continued alone as a manufacturer of 'Flint and Coloured Glass in great Variety'. At this time Northwood had been at work for some years on the 'Elgin' claret-jug*. Northwood's jug was intended for Sir Benjamin Stone, and in 1873, when it was finished, Pargeter judged that he was now proficient enough in the art of carving glass to undertake a copy of the Portland Vase*. With the co-operation of the British Museum, Pargeter commissioned Northwood to make his copy which he completed in three years, in 1876. Emulating his achievement Joseph Locke then produced a second copy for Richardson's. One of the initial difficulties which had to be surmounted was to supply Northwood with the necessary 'blank' for the carving of blue glass cased with white (see *cased glass*), and it was only after seven attempts that Pargeter succeeded.

The Portland Vase was followed by the 'Milton' vase with figures of Adam and Eve in the Garden of Eden and the Archangel Michael, and a series of three *tazze* allegorical of Literature, Science, and Art, with portrait heads of Shakespeare, Newton, and Flaxman*.

See *Kny, Friedrich*

PARIAN PORCELAIN
A type of biscuit porcelain* developed by Copeland* & Garrett about 1845 with the assistance of Thomas

PAPIER MÂCHÉ. A *papier mâché* chair (one of a pair) inlaid with mother-of-pearl, the panel painted with a view of St Ruth's Priory and Holy Island. English. c. 1850. *Sotheby & Co*

<hr />

239

PARIAN PORCELAIN. Wall-bracket in Parian body. c. 1860. *Minton Museum, Royal Doulton Tableware*

Battam*, the art-director. The object of the initial experiments was to provide a substitute for the biscuit porcelain of Sèvres* which was employed for some distinguished figure-modelling in the 18th century, and had been successfully copied from about 1774 by Derby*. Biscuit porcelain figures had to be of exceptional quality without blemishes. Those which were defective were glazed and painted and sold at a cheaper rate.

The source of the attribution of Parian porcelain to Copeland & Garrett is the Art Union*, which especially encouraged the new manufacture, but its invention has also been claimed by Minton* and T. & R. Boote*, while John Mountford stated that he discovered 'statuary porcelain' (by which name Parian was at first known) in 1845 and gave the formula to Stephen Garrett. Whoever discovered it, Parian was being produced commercially in 1846, and in large quantities by several firms by 1850. Wedgwood* called their version 'Carrara'*.

The earliest Parian was creamy white in colour, but by the 1870s tinted Parian had become popular. Lazulite was stained a copper-blue, malachite a copper-green, obsidian imitated the natural volcanic glass in colour and porphyry was stained red in a manner thought to resemble the stone. At first reserved for figures, the body proved suitable for the modelling of flowers, and was used for this purpose almost from the first. Jugs and similar wares made their appearance by the 1850s, usually decorated in relief and glazed inside. Later the relief decoration was provided with a tinted background, usually blue, influenced by Wedgwood's jasper*.

Manufacturers of Parian on a large scale were Robinson & Leadbeater* of Stoke-on-Trent who were working from 1885 to 1924 and used the mark R & L on the backs of their figures.

Parian made its appearance in America very soon after its emergence in England. It was made, for instance, at the United States Pottery and at Ott & Brewer's* factory. At the end of the 19th century some large standing figures in 18th-century costume

were made in Thuringia of a type of Parian or biscuit porcelain and painted with pastel colours with some gilding. They are allied in type and quality to large figures from the same source, and of the same period, which were glazed and painted.

Also allied to the fashion for Parian figures was the 19th-century revival of the biscuit body at Sèvres, sometimes used for reproductions of 18th-century figures. These bear a factory mark; no 18th-century biscuit figure was ever marked.

See *Léonard, Agathon*

PARIAN PORCELAIN, AMERICAN

Parian ware, an unglazed porcelain, was made in the United States from about 1847, and became extremely popular after the New York Exhibition of 1853. Introduced at Bennington, Vt., its manufacture later became widespread. In appearance it resembled contemporary English Parian as nearly as the difference in the available local materials permitted. Figures, vases, and pitchers were made, and also a number of items not manufactured in England, such as cow milk-jugs and toby jugs. Bennington may have introduced a pitcher with low-relief decoration in white against a pitted blue background which was probably inspired by Wedgwood's jasper*. Pitchers especially were glazed inside, and the exterior was sometimes given a 'smear' glaze by allowing a little glaze material to accumulate in the sagger. Among the sought-after examples of American Parian are hound-handled pitchers*.

PARIS DECORATING STUDIOS

A number of studios for the enamelling of porcelain flourished in Paris during the 19th century. The practice of outside decoration existed in the 18th century, but it was principally in the hands of factory painters, who purloined white ware to paint at home. When Brongniart* sold the existing stock of 'seconds' accumulated at Sèvres* soon after 1800 it was largely bought by three dealers, Perez, Ireland, and Jarman, who arranged for it to be enamelled in independent studios, often by former Sèvres painters. Many porcelain factories had stocks of second-grade white ware for sale from time to time during the 19th century, and some were prepared to supply it to order. Much ware decorated in this way was in the style of '*vieux Sèvres*'*, sometimes with deceptive marks.

PARIS EXPOSITION, 1925

This project was first discussed in 1907 towards the end of the currency of the *art nouveau** style, but little was done until 1913, when plans were made to mount the Exposition in 1916. War broke out before plans were far advanced, and the exhibition was first postponed in 1922 and then to 1925. It was this event which was the origin of the *art déco** style, since the exhibition was called, in full, Exposition Internationale des Arts Décoratifs et Industriels Modernes. It was planned on similar lines to the great 19th-century exhibitions, as a display of fine examples of art and craft. Although *art nouveau*, and the revival of historical styles were both firmly discouraged, much of the work displayed was traditional, and many of the *avant garde* disapproved. Le Corbusier* built a pavilion of protest at the edge of the exhibition, reminiscent of the *Salon des Refusés*. Futurism, Cubism*, Fauvism* and Expressionism* were perhaps the principal influences on the current style, but the excitement which had been caused by the discovery of Tutankhamun's tomb in 1922 had not yet died down, and the influence of both Egyptian and Mayan art were reflected in the design of objects of all kinds. Pervading the Exposition was an emphasis on geometric patterns. The style of some of the figures suggests that Karel Capek's play *RUR* (*Rustum's Universal Robots*) had not been without its influence. This had been produced with great success in 1913. Another important influence was Diaghilev's *Ballets Russes*, which opened at the Théâtre des Champs-Elysées, Paris, in 1909.

PASTILLE-BURNERS

Small models of houses, cottages, churches, etc. made for the purpose of burning pastilles for scenting the air. They were especially popular between 1820 and 1850, and were made in porcelain and earthenware by many factories.

The model is provided with a hole at the back for inserting the pastille and a hole in the roof (the chimney) for the smoke to emerge. Reproductions have appeared on the market recently with no outlet for the smoke, proving they were never made for a practical purpose. It is often possible to date these cottages by the architectural style, especially the occurrence of neo-Gothic* windows.

See *Cottages, pottery and porcelain*

PÂTE D'APPLICATION   See *Pâte-sur-pâte*

PÂTE-DE-CRISTAL   See *Pâte-de-verre*

PÂTE-DE-VERRE (French)

Literally, glass paste. Powdered glass mixed with an adhesive and formed in a mould. After firing the particles cohere to form a translucent glass with a slightly waxy surface. The technique seems to have been suggested by investigations during the 19th century into ancient Egyptian methods of making their so-called '*faïence*'. The *pâte-de-verre* process in the hands of Décorchement* and others was capable of yielding some very striking colour effects. *Pâte-de-cristal* is a variety of *pâte-de-verre* made with powdered lead glass. Specimens date from the end of the 19th century and are rare.

PÂTE-SUR-PÂTE (French)

Literally, paste on paste. Decoration thus called is built up in low relief, either white or tinted, by

PÂTE-SUR-PÂTE. Pilgrim-flask with *pâte-sur-pâte*. decoration. Minton*. c. 1890. *Victoria & Albert Museum, London*

painting on successive coats of clay slip, or, in some cases, by modelling. The process originated in China, some 18th-century celadons* being decorated with floral patterns in this way. The technique was developed at Sèvres*, and brought to England by Marc-Louis Solon* in 1870. The statement often made that the technique was introduced at Sèvres by Solon is inaccurate. It was suggested to Louis Robert, the chief painter, by Riocreux, *conservateur* of the Musée de Sèvres before 1855, and specimens were exhibited in the Paris Exposition of that year. The technique is generally termed *pâte d'application* in France.

PÂTE-TENDRE (French)

Soft-paste porcelain, a term commonly employed by French and English writers in the 19th century.
See '*Vieux Sèvres*'

PATTERN GLASS

American term for pressed glass*.

PAXTON, SIR JOSEPH (1801–1865)

Gardener and architect. Paxton superintended the gardens at Chatsworth from 1826, and became a friend of the Duke of Devonshire. He designed the building for the Great Exhibition of 1851 which was taken down and re-erected at Sydenham, London, in 1853–1854, in a district later known as the Crystal Palace. It was burned down in 1938.

PEACHBLOW GLASS

A partially opaque glass which is shaded from cream or blush-white to pink or violet-red, the latter colour being related to the Chinese *rose* enamel. Peachblow was made by the Mount Washington Glass Works* in New Bedford, and by the New England Glass Company* at Cambridge, Mass., where it was called 'Wild Rose'. Much of it has a satin surface. The name is said to have been derived from a resemblance to the peachbloom glaze, a variety of Chinese porcelain then very popular with collectors, but the similarity is slight. Specimens of Peachblow (which comes into the category of art glass*) are rare.

PEACOCK, THE

A fashionable *motif* during the Aesthetic Movement* of the 1880s, the peacock (*kujaku*) was also popular in Japanese art, although it was not introduced into that country from China much before 1600. No doubt the

PEACOCK, THE. Scent-bottle of ribbed glass with a stopper decorated with opposed peacocks. Formerly in the Handley-Read Collection. English or French, c. 1890. *Victoria & Albert Museum, London*

Japanese version inspired the employment of this *motif* in English decoration, of which the most notable example is the Peacock Room* (now in the Freer Gallery, Washington, D.C.). The fashion seems to have begun with Rossetti* in the 1860s. He kept peacocks in his Chelsea garden. Peacocks inspired Albert Moore*, Stacy Marks* and others who employed them as decoration, or used abstract designs based on Japanese sources which were derived from the markings on the tail-feathers.

PEACOCK ROOM, THE

The dining-room of 49 Prince's Gate, London, designed by Thomas Jeckyll* for Francis Leyland, the shipping magnate, in 1877. This room was an essay in the Japanese-Gothic style, and it is now part of the Freer Collection, Washington, D.C. No expense had been spared in the decoration of this room, which included covering the walls with leather hangings brought to England by Catherine of Braganza when she married Charles II. These cost Leyland £1,000. His collection of Chinese blue and white porcelain was arranged on shelves, and over the chimney-piece was Whistler's *Princesse du pays de la porcelaine*. Whistler, who had already contributed mural paintings to the decoration elsewhere in the house, complained to Leyland about the colouring

of the walls in the dining-room which, he claimed, clashed with that of his picture. Leyland gave him permission to make changes. Whistler shut himself up in the dining-room, kept his patron out, and proceeded to cover the expensive leather with peacocks in blue and gold leaf. Leyland was away and for a time knew nothing of what was going on, but even royalty visited work in progress to see Whistler's symphony in blue and gold. Jeckyll came to see what was happening to his masterpiece, and retired to die soon afterwards in a madhouse. Finally, Leyland returned. On the whole he took it very well. The room could no longer be used for his collection of porcelain because the blues clashed violently, his *suite* of leather hangings was now completely covered with blue and gold peacocks, his house had been turned into a *salon* in which Whistler received his friends, and he had received a good deal of undesirable publicity. Whistler asked 2,000 guineas for the work, and Leyland gave him £1,000, deducting the cost of the hangings. After Leyland's death the room was offered to Charles Lang Freer, the American collector of Oriental art, who had it taken down and re-erected in Washington D.C.

PEARLINE GLASS

A blue-shaded art glass* introduced by George Davidson* of Gateshead and patented about 1889. It varies from deep to pale opaline blue in the same piece. Other colours are sometimes employed in the same way.

PEARLWARE

A body devised by Josiah Wedgwood* in 1779. It is an earthenware containing a higher proportion of flint and white clay than creamware and it is both harder and whiter in appearance. Pearlware was made at a number of factories in the 19th century on a fairly extensive scale, since it was especially suitable for decoration in underglaze blue.

PECHE, DAGOBERT (1887–1923)

Austrian artist and designer who studied at the Vienna Akademie de Bildenen Kunst. He became a leading designer for glass, metalwork, etc. for the Wiener Werkstätte*. He designed porcelain for Josef Bock*, provided models for the Gmundner Keramik and the Wiener Keramik, and designed glass for Lötz*.

PEGG, WILLIAM 'QUAKER' (1775–1851)

Porcelain painter who appears to have been afflicted with religious melancholia as a result of being taken to hear a Calvinist preacher at the age of six. He became a Quaker in 1800. He started to paint pottery in 1788, and went to Derby* as a flower-painter in 1796. As a result of overmuch meditation on the Second Commandment he gave up porcelain painting in 1800 to work in a cotton stocking factory, but found his conscience troubled by the necessity for adding some ornamental detail, so procured his transfer to the manufacture of plain hose. In 1813 he returned to porcelain painting at Derby, but losing the sight of one eye in 1820 he gave it up permanently. His flowers are always large and in the nature of exact botanical specimens and pieces painted by him have little extra in the way of ornament. The name of the flower is usually on the reverse of the piece. His work is scarce and sought after.

PELETON GLASS
Bohemian art glass patented in 1880 by Wilhelm Kralik of Neuwelt. Objects were dipped while hot into glass threads of contrasting colours. The piece was then reheated to incorporate the additions and manipulated into the desired shape. Some specimens were given a satin finish. This glass was manufactured under licence in England and America.

See *Satin glass*

PELIKAN, FRANZ ANTON (1786–1858)
Father of a family of Bohemian glass engravers of Meistersdorf, Steinsschönau, consisting of four sons and four daughters. There was also another family of the same name in this town, one member of which (Josef) sometimes used a pelican in his landscapes. All of them engraved landscapes, hunting scenes, horses, etc. A number of signed examples have survived.

PELLATT, APSLEY (1791–1863)
English glass-maker, designer and technician who introduced the cristallo-ceramie* process from France, taking out his own patent in 1819. He was also a pioneer of pressed glass*, taking out patents in 1831 and 1845. He inherited the Falcon Glass Works in Southwark, from his father, and here he manufactured decorative glass of good quality, including *millefiori** types. He exhibited successfully at the Great Exhibition of 1851. In 1848 he published an important work entitled *Curiosities of Glassmaking*. Pellatt retired from active business in 1852 when he became a member of Parliament. The firm continued to manufacture glass until the 1890s, and then became a retail store only.

PENNSYLVANIA-GERMAN
American local style at one time known as Pennsylvania-Dutch, 'Dutch' being a corruption of 'Deutsch' (German). From about 1683 successive waves of immigrants from the Rhineland and Switzerland arrived in America and settled in Pennsylvania. Here the community was isolated to a great extent by its language, and its members tended to keep together. Naturally enough its handicrafts and styles were those of the part of Europe from which its members had come. The most commonly surviving piece of furniture is the chest, made from about 1700 until about 1850. These chests were painted in bright colours with traditional flowers, hearts, birds, angels, heraldic

PELLATT, APSLEY. Perfume-bottle of crystallo-ceramie* made by Apsley Pellatt* at Falcon Street, Southwark, London. *Pilkington Glass Museum*

motifs, stars, mermaids, and many more subjects of folk-art on a background of blue, green, brown, or black. Chests were often in tulipwood, but walnut, oak, and yellow pine were also employed, especially for dressers, cupboards, and wardrobes. The latter were given the German name for a cupboard—*Schrank*. Furniture in walnut, oak, and pine was left unpainted. Perhaps the most impressive was an enormous *schrank* with a large moulded cornice, two panelled doors, and great ball feet.

From the same region comes a tradition of pottery decorated with *sgraffito** designs of birds, flowers, and figures, a technique employed both in Silesia and Switzerland. The potters employed a red clay covered with yellow slip through which the designs were incised and covered with a transparent lead glaze. Around the 1800s somewhat crudely modelled figures of animals and birds were made by these potters.

See *Frakturschriften*; *Schimmel, William*

'PENNY PLAIN, TWOPENCE COLOURED'
Printed sheets of figures of actors and actresses intended to be cut out and used as players in toy theatres. Many of the figures were intended as portraits of contemporary actors and actresses in parts in which they had been successful. The theatres in which they played were miniature representations of the popular theatres of the time. The earliest of these sheets appear to be those published about 1808 by a man named Green under the name of Juvenile

243

Theatrical Sheets. This publisher died in 1860, when some of his plates were bought by another publisher, John Ledington, and reissued. Ledington's daughter married Benjamin Pollock, and the Pollocks took over the firm in 1876. Pollock himself survived until 1937, and in his later years the business was carried on by his daughters. The firm still exists as Pollock's Toy Museum, and publishes new editions of the old sheets. The familiar phrase 'Penny plain, twopence coloured', which records the original price of the sheets, was popularized in 1887 by R. L. Stevenson, who wrote an essay on the Toy Theatre with this title. The larger prints were sometimes decorated, principally by amateurs, with costumes of silk and velvet with the addition of tinsel.

See *Tinsel pictures*

PERCIER, CHARLES (1764–1838) and FONTAINE, PIERRE-FRANÇOIS-LÉONARD (1762–1853)

French architects to Napoleon I who were largely responsible for the Empire style. Their design-book, *Recueil des décorations intérieures*, of 1812 was the most influential of any to be published at the time. Fontaine was responsible for a great deal of Paris architecture during the reigns of Louis XVIII and Louis-Philippe.

PERFUME-BOTTLES

Decorative perfume and toilet-bottles have been made by the large glasshouses and porcelain factories since the 18th century, and a great deal of fine craftsmanship has been lavished on some of them. Since most perfume is expensive the bottles made to contain it, even when they have been purely commercial productions, have been well-designed and produced. Bottles in opaline* glass made by Lalique* for Coty, beginning in 1908, are typical examples of the *genre* in more recent times, but nearly a century earlier good examples in cased and flashed glasses were being made, especially in Bohemia. Some perfumes deteriorate with exposure to light, and bottles in coloured or opaque glass were usually employed for this purpose, including Lithyalin* bottles by Egermann at Haida, but bottles of crystal cut-glass, English or Irish, were made in the 1820s. Bottles of blue glass decorated with exotic birds in gold were made in the 18th century, and blue glass was again employed during the 19th. Cranberry glass* scent-bottles and toilet-bottles were made in Stourbridge in the second half of the 19th century, and decorated with enamels and gilding. Webb & Son produced bottles of cameo glass. *Millefiori* bottles also came from here.

Perfume is exceedingly volatile, and both perfume-bottles and toilet-bottles were given exceptionally well-fitting stoppers, tapering and ground to fit. Toilet-bottles were often part of a fitted dressing-case, and sometimes made *en suite* with a scent-bottle. Towards the end of the 19th century the perfume-bottle with a glass base, and an atomizer with a rubber bulb, made its appearance.

During the 19th century porcelain perfume-bottles are fairly plain in form, and decorated with enamelling and gilding, unlike those of the 18th century which are made in such forms as a figure, a flower-bouquet, or something similar. Gold, silver, and enamel bottles are unusual, and not often seen. The perfume-bottle should not be confused with the Chinese snuff-bottle, which looks something like it. The snuff-bottle has a stopper with a small spoon attached for extracting the contents.

PERSONNAGE (French)

A porcelain *veilleuse** made in the form of a figure, the lower part containing the *godet*, the upper part of the figure designed as a teapot, usually with one arm arranged to form the handle and the other one as a spout. The hat formed the cover. The *personnage*, well-modelled and painted, was a speciality of the Jacob Petit* factory. They were also made in Thuringia and Bohemia, although these are rare.

PETIT, JACOB & MARDOCHÉE (Fontainebleau)

Porcelain manufacturers at Fontainebleau from 1830, with a branch factory at Belleville from 1834 to which the Fontainebleau enterprise was eventually removed. The firm was noted for decorative porcelain in the revived rococo* style and for fine quality enamelling. Production included vases, clock cases, figures, and candlesticks, as well as service-ware. Some of their vases in particular were decorated with applied flowers. The factory also made excellent biscuit porcelain*. Among their specialities was the *veilleuse** in the form of the *personnage**. The factory was moved to Avon, Seine-et-Marne, in 1851. In 1862 this was sold and a new factory opened in the rue Paradis Poissonière, Paris, with showrooms in the rue de Bondy.

PETIT, JACOB & MARDOCHÉE. Coffee-pot by Jacob Petit* in the revived rococo* style. France. c. 1840. *Private collection*

Above:
ART DÉCO. Bowl of Monart glass. 1920s.

Below:
EARTHENWARE. Earthenware tureen, cover, stand, and ladle decorated with underglaze blue transfer-printing with a view of Lancaster. Rogers, Staffordshire. c. 1830. Marks: ROGERS impressed, and an American eagle in blue.
Constance Chiswell

Above:
RICHARDSON & SONS. Small jug of white opal glass threaded with a criss-cross pattern of pink glass. Richardson & Son Stourbridge. c. 1875. *Private Collection*

Below:
GALLÉ, ÉMILE. Faience tureen and stand in the form of a pigeon, by Émile Gallé. France, Nancy. c. 1880. Mark: Script G incised. *Private Collection*

Around 1860 the factory began to counterfeit old Meissen* porcelain, adding the crossed swords mark. These imitations were regarded as deceptive at the time. The factory mark was J.P. in blue.

PEWTER

An alloy of tin and lead used from early times for making articles of domestic utility, such as mugs, dishes, candlesticks, etc. During the first two-thirds or so of the 19th century pewter was unfashionable, although some wares were made, largely in traditional styles for cheaper markets, and especially mugs for public houses and bars. In the 1870s there was a revival of pewter as a fashionable metal by the Arts and Crafts Movement*, and later by *art nouveau** metalworkers. Pewter as a container for potable liquids was dangerous because of its high lead content, since this metal is soluble in liquids. By Act of Parliament in 1907 the maximum permitted content of lead in new pewter was limited to 10 per cent. Old pewter was collected in the 19th century, and while forgeries were not particularly common, fakes were more numerous. Pewter is a very soft and malleable metal, easily worked, and relatively common objects, with a little ingenuity and the occasional addition of handles and so forth, could be turned into something much rarer and more expensive. The rare ewer, for instance, could be made by adding a pouring lip to a large mug.

PHOENIXVILLE POTTERY (Phoenixville, Pa.)

Pottery founded in 1867 and operated by Griffen, Smith & Hall, who were noted for Etruscan Majolica*. Much ware of this kind consisted of relief decoration of plants and marine life covered with coloured glazes. The mark is *Etruscan Majolica* with or without the initials *GSH*.

PHOTOGRAPHIC DECORATION OF POTTERY. Porcelain plate decorated with a photographic portrait. Poland, Baranovka c. 1905. *Author*

PHOTOGRAPHIC DECORATION OF POTTERY

The use of photography for the decoration of ceramics started in the 1860s, when a method of applying photographs on prepared backing-paper to the surface of the glaze was devised. Soon afterwards Wedgwood* began to make limited use of photography in the decoration of pottery, and in 1896 W. E. Henry and H. S. Ward published a book entitled *Photo Ceramics* which dealt with the application of photographs to pottery glazes. During the 1870s several methods for applying photographs to wooden and enamel surfaces were patented. Limited use was made of the technique, but it had disappeared by about 1880.

See also *Canarsac, Lafon de*

PHRENOLOGY

A pseudo-science much in vogue during the early part of the 19th century, and especially popular between 1830 and 1860. Phrenology is based on the theory that the mental faculties originate in particular areas of the brain and that those which are particularly well-developed cause an elevation of the part of the cranial bone immediately above the area (the so-called 'bumps'). Phrenologists were men who claimed to be able to give character-readings by feeling the sitter's 'bumps', which are, in fact, only the normal irregularities of the skull, unrelated either to the brain underneath or to human faculties generally. Plaster skulls devoid of hair, but with lines delimiting the various areas, were cast and sold by casters like De Ville*, and some of these have survived.

PHYFE, DUNCAN (1768–1854)

Noted American cabinet-maker of Scottish extraction who emigrated to New York in 1784 and changed his name from Fife to Phyfe (sometimes spelt Phyffe). He was in business from 1795 until about 1845, although his best work was done before 1825. He excelled in carved ornament, and a good deal of furniture has survived and can reasonably be attributed to him. His designs, copied by others, were derived from imported Georgian and French furniture in the neo-classical* and Empire* or Regency styles*. He made much use of the lyre* in the design of his furniture, which was of excellent workmanship, and nearly always of mahogany.

See *Federal style*

PICTURE-MEDALS

A small bronze or copper box with a screw top, usually about an inch and a half in diameter, bearing the portrait of a famous man, the interior when unscrewed containing several miniatures. Thus, a picture-medal of the Prince Regent of 1811 contained the aquatint portraits of the kings of England; one of the Duke of Wellington of 1815 contained pictures of some of his battles. Picture-medals are very rare and seem to have been confined to the early decades of the 19th century, probably made in Birmingham.

PIERCED PORCELAIN   See *Owen, George*

PIERRET, VICTOR-ATHANASE (1806–1893)
French horologist who specialized in complex movements for clocks and watches. His skeleton clocks* were particularly popular at the Great Exhibition* of 1851.

PIETRA DURA
Sometimes called Florentine mosaic, *pietra dura* is a mosaic of coloured, polished stones shaped and disposed in such a way as to form a picture or pattern. At its best in Italy during the 17th and 18th centuries, *pietra dura* continued to be made during the 19th, although quality began to deteriorate. In England work of this kind was done in Derbyshire marble*.

PILKINGTON TILE & POTTERY CO. LTD
(Manchester, Lancashire)
Pottery founded at Clifton Junction in 1892 for the manufacture of tiles. The manufacture of decorative pottery started in 1897, the forms at first being slipcast or pressed into moulds and covered with flecked glazes, or those with crystalline effects. In 1903 the pottery chemist and historian William Burton developed scarlet and tangerine orange from uranium oxide*. Throwing on the potter's wheel seems to have dated from 1906, and Lewis Day* and Walter Crane* were employed as designers for pottery decorated with lustre. Gordon Forsyth (1879–1952) joined the firm in 1906 and left in 1919 when he was appointed Principal of the Stoke-on-Trent School of Art. Charles Cundall R.A. worked at the factory in his early years, and a number of other talented artists were employed, all of whom signed with a distinctive signature, monogram, or mark. Painting in lustre* ceased in 1927, and the making of decorative pottery was discontinued in 1938. The factory mark is the letter *P* within a square frame.

PILKINGTON TILE & POTTERY CO LTD. A vase of Royal Lancastrian pottery, a type introduced in 1903, noted for a variety of glaze effects. Pilkington Tile & Pottery Company, Manchester. c. 1910. *Constance Chiswell*

PIN-BOXES, PORCELAIN
The porcelain pin-boxes popular in the second half of the 19th century were, for the most part, made by the same German factory as the one which produced the small groups termed 'fairings'*, although occasional specimens may be regarded as earlier, and were possibly made by one of the Staffordshire factories. Pin-boxes were at their most popular between 1855 and 1870, and they are sometimes related in general style to porcelain match-boxes, except that the latter have a roughened surface for striking the matches. The earliest are probably the best, in both modelling and colouring. Over 400 different examples have been recorded. Nearly always the base has moulded ornament and the cover is surmounted by a small figure or group of figures. Although the modelling is similar in style, the use of the same subject for the decoration of both fairings and pin-boxes is comparatively rare. Examples of the same subject appearing on both are *The last in bed to put out the light* and *Shall we sleep first, or how*. Generally, pin-boxes are rarely titled, whereas fairings are titled commonly.
See *Pössneck*

PINCHBECK
An alloy principally of copper and zinc employed to imitate gold in the manufacture of cheap jewellery and objects of *vertu*. It is not ordinarily deceptive, but some better quality work was covered in one way or another with a thin layer of gold to improve the colour. The remedy is to look for the hall-mark in cases of doubt. Pinchbeck was so called after its 18th-century inventor, Christopher Pinchbeck.

PINDER, BOURNE & CO   See *Doulton*

PIRKENHAMMER   See *Březová*

PITTSBURGH (Pa.) GLASS WORKS
There were many glass works in and around Pittsburgh, most of them making window-glass, bottles and wares of domestic utility. The O'Hara Glass Works, eventually acquired by James B. Lyon & Company*, was the first to use coal for fuelling the furnaces. Bakewell, Pears & Company* made the first American crystal chandelier*.

PLASTER-MOULDS
Plaster-moulds (made from gypsum plaster or plaster of Paris) are extensively used in the making of works of art of all kinds, especially in the pottery industry. There are two principal kinds: waste-moulds, mainly used by sculptors for a single copy, and piece-moulds widely employed where a number of copies are required.
   A waste-mould begins with a clay model. Over this is formed a thin coat of blue plaster, which is oiled and covered with a thick white coat, often reinforced with iron rod for large work, after which the interior clay can be dug out. The interior surface of the mould

is then oiled, liquid plaster is poured in, swilled round, and poured out. This process is repeated until a fairly substantial layer is built up, which is thickened in weak places by hand. The outer mould is then cut away with a mallet and a chisel as far as the blue layer, and this is flaked away with small tools to reveal the cast.

Piece-moulds are built up of a large number of pieces which slot into one another, each of which will draw away from the surface of the cast without damaging or disturbing it. A thick case is cast over the pieces to hold them in position. This type of mould can be used to take plaster-casts, but in porcelain factories it is used to take slip-casts, i.e. casts in liquid clay. When this is poured into the mould the thick plaster walls take up water from the slip and leave a layer of firm clay adherent to them. Surplus slip is then poured off, and when the clay is firm enough, the mould is removed, dried, and reassembled. Most objects which are not circular in section (these are usually thrown on the wheel) are made in this way.

Plaster-moulds are used for the casting of metals such as bronze, when the plaster is heavily mixed with a refractory material such as brick-dust, and for electrotyping, when the mould surface is coated with plumbago (black-lead). Moulds for taking several casts are sometimes lined with gelatine which is strong enough for most purposes, and flexible enough to be eased away from the projections of a cast which is not too complicated. Gelatine moulds are cheaper and easier to make than piece-moulds, but they do not give such sharp casts as a piece-mould, and they need to be renewed more often. They can only be employed in conjunction with plaster which sets chemically and are useless for slip-casting since they do not absorb water.

PLATED GLASS
An American term equivalent to the European cased* or overlay glass*. The New England Glass Company* took out a patent for plating with Amberina* in 1886.

PLIQUE-À-JOUR ENAMEL
An enamelling technique in which wires similar to those employed for cloisonné enamel*, but not permanently attached to the background, are used to confine transparent and translucent colours which, after firing, have the background removed, leaving them unsupported except by the wires. The technique, which is rare, was employed for jewellery and small works towards the end of the 19th century in Paris. Carl Fabergé made a gold cigar-case for Kaiser Wilhelm II with the Brandenburg eagle inset in plique-à-jour.

See Baisse-taille; Champlevé enamelling

POINTING MACHINE
Apparatus in the form of a long rod pivoted on a stand to give one long and one short section, employed to transfer measurements from the salient points of a large piece of statuary to a small one as a method of making accurate reductions in size. The pointing-machine was used in the 19th century in the making of small furnishing bronzes from large statues. The size of the reduction could be controlled by adjusting the relative length of the arms. The same apparatus was also employed for copying reliefs.

POKER-WORK   See Pyrography

POLITO'S MENAGERIE
Staffordshire earthenware group by Obadiah Sherratt*. S. Polito claimed to own the largest travelling menagerie in Europe, which arrived in Staffordshire in 1808. Polito died in 1814. The same model was later used for Wombwell's Circus.

POLITO'S MENAGERIE. Polito's menagerie*, a rare group in Staffordshire earthenware, probably by Obadiah Sherratt*. The menagerie was in Staffordshire in 1808, and Sherratt died in 1814, so the probable date of this example is about 1810. City Museum & Art Gallery, Stoke-on-Trent

POMONA GLASS
Variety of art glass* patented by the New England Glass Company* in 1885, which was blown into a part-sized mould and then reheated and expanded. The surface was stippled by etching and stained yellow. Further ornament of applied flowers was sometimes added. Specimens are now very rare.

PONTYPOOL WARE
Term for a variety of objects, useful and ornamental, made of sheet-iron (tôle) at Pontypool, Wales, and later elsewhere. The Pontypool Japan Works were founded in 1730 by Edward Allgood. The commonest article of production was the tray in black, crimson, or chocolate-brown decorated with Oriental scenes in gold, Oriental lacquer being the most obvious source of inspiration. Another factory operated by members of the Allgood family was established at Usk, Monmouthshire, and both factories made similar wares.

Towards the end of the 18th century, and at the

beginning of the 19th, the quality of decoration improved considerably. A journeyman painter, Benjamin Barker, did sporting scenes, and his sons Thomas Barker (of Bath) and Benjamin, did landscapes. Production was extended to include such objects as tea and coffee urns and kettles, the forms based on contemporary Sheffield plate*, and all kinds of small items from snuff-boxes to candlesticks, tea-caddies, letter-racks, spill-vases, etc. were no doubt inspired to some extent by contemporary papier-mâché*. The Pontypool factory closed about 1820 and the one at Usk continued until about 1860.

Similar wares were made at Bilston (Staffordshire), Birmingham, and Wolverhampton (Staffordshire), a factory in the latter town being started by a former Pontypool workman. The wares made here were called 'Pontypool' which, by this time, had become a generic name for objects made from japanned sheet-iron. Wolverhampton became noted for trays, and about 1812 bronze powder was employed in their decoration, obviously inspired by papier mâché. Edwin Booth, who also worked on papier mâché, did some of his characteristic Oriental scenes on 'Pontypool' trays. About the same time, trays painted with figures were extensively exported to India. The block-printing of trays began about 1850, as well as transfer-printing* techniques similar to those employed by the pottery and porcelain factories. Stencils were increasingly used, principally for stylized floral decorations, and wares of this kind, often coal-scuttles and ewers, are still being made.

The wares produced at Bilston were generally poorer in quality than those of Pontypool, Wolverhampton, and Birmingham. Here they produced 'blanks' which were sold for painting elsewhere. Much of the ware was painted in crude colours (red, blue, and yellow), and a large export trade flourished with the United States, reaching its height in 1882. About this time the industry was established in America on the lines of the Wolverhampton enterprise. Pattern-books relating to the latter factory are preserved in the Wolverhampton Museum.

The quality of 'Pontypool' ware is to be judged mainly by its decoration. Some rare examples, usually trays, are exceptionally well painted. The more ordinary specimens of domestic utility are not uncommon and obviously new-looking specimens are what they seem to be.

POOLE (Dorset)
There have been a number of potteries at Poole. The firm of J. Carter & Co, established in 1873, made wall and floor tiles, and lustre* pottery in the art nouveau* style after 1890. The firm of Carter, Stabler & Adams, trading as the Poole Pottery, was founded in 1911. They make service and ornamental wares of excellent quality decoratively painted in colours. The same pottery also made architectural features in the Della Robbia* style.

PORCELAIN
A generic term for several different types of ceramic body characterized by great hardness and translucency when held to the light. The several types are listed hereunder:

True (or hard) porcelain
This is termed 'hard' because it is given a 'hard', or high-temperature, firing, in the region of 1,500°C. It is made from a white-burning clay, known as kaolin or china clay, and a fusible rock which is a kind of feldspar. The powdered ingredients are mixed together with water and a flux to assist fusion, and the plastic material thus obtained is shaped by the usual pottery methods. The clay is highly refractory and only fuses at temperatures of about 1,600°C. It therefore serves to hold the object in shape during firing, when the feldspar fuses into a kind of natural glass at about 1,450°C. When left unglazed it is termed biscuit porcelain*. The glaze normally employed is powdered feldspar distributed over the surface before firing. It was decorated in the 19th century with underglaze colours fired at the same time as the body and glaze, or with enamels fired on afterwards at a lower temperature. True porcelain is made in China and Japan, on the continent of Europe, and in the United States. In recent times the Worcester Royal Porcelain Company* have also begun to use this body for ornamental wares.

Artificial ('soft') porcelain
So called because it was given a 'soft', or low-temperature, firing at about 1,250°C. This type was widely manufactured during the 18th century, but firing was always attended by a large kiln-wastage. It hardly survived into the 19th century, although it was made at Nantgarw*, and its manufacture was revived at Sèvres* for wares in the 18th-century style. In principle it was a white-burning clay mixed with powdered glass, and the ingredients of glass, which replaced the feldspar of true porcelain, hence the term 'artificial'. It was glazed at a second firing with a lead glaze. Its principal advantage was that the glaze lent itself to fine quality enamel-painting and ground-laying*. In colour it was a softer, creamier white than the harder, often slightly bluish white of hard porcelain. A soft-paste body has been used occasionally since c. 1820 for special purposes, e.g. forgeries of some 18th-century porcelains.

Bone porcelain
Usually termed 'bone china' in the trade, this was a modification of true porcelain made by adding calcined cattle bones. The invention is usually attributed to Josiah Spode II* about 1800. Calcined bones had been added to 'soft' porcelain in the 18th century in an effort to overcome the problem of kiln-wastage. Bone china, which has been the preferred body in England since the beginning of the 19th century, is fired at a slightly lower temperature than true porcelain, and has many of the advantages of

both the 'soft' and 'hard' types and few of the disadvantages of either.

Soaprock porcelain

A type of porcelain in which soaprock replaces feldspathic rock. It was first employed at Bristol and Worcester in the middle of the 18th century, and continued to be used at Worcester until the 1820s. In its day it was highly successful, since it could bear boiling water without cracking, which was one of the hazards attending 'soft' porcelain.

Parian

Also termed 'statuary porcelain' when first developed, Parian is a biscuit porcelain usually with a waxy surface said to have been developed by Copeland* & Garrett by 1845. There are, however, a number of other claimants for whom the evidence is more or less persuasive. A similar type of body made by Wedgwood* was termed 'Carrara'.

Semi-porcelain

Also termed 'ironstone china'*, 'opaque china', 'stone-china'. 'Semi-porcelain' is a type of white porcellaneous stoneware, hard and compact. When fired at a higher temperature than usual, specimens may even be slightly translucent. At first employed for decorative purposes, it later became popular for hotel and restaurant ware, and was widely manufactured in England and the United States in the 19th century.

See *Biscuit porcelain*; *Creamware*; *Hard-paste porcelain*; *Parian porcelain*

PORCELAIN FIGURE-MAKING

There are several ways of making ceramic figures ranging from the 'flat-back'* method, where the clay is pressed into the front and back sections of a mould and after removal joined together and fired, to the much more complex and sophisticated technique of the assemblage of various parts by a highly-skilled operator known as a 'repairer' (see 'Repairing'). The former method was employed for cheap pottery figures, rarely for porcelain, the latter for good-quality porcelain figures of all kinds.

In the making of porcelain figures of fine quality the artist's original clay or wax model is carefully dissected into parts and each part is moulded. The parts are then duplicated from these moulds and passed to the 'repairer', who sits at his bench with a completed model in front of him as a standard. Using liquid clay slip as an adhesive he carefully puts the figure together according to the standard. During the firing process a point is reached where the figure will be virtually on the point of collapse, due to the vitrification of the fusible ingredient which is then taking place, so before firing the assembled figure goes to another workman who arranges an elaborate system of 'props' made of refractory clay under any part which might at this point sag out of shape, the points of contacts being dusted with powdered

aluminium to prevent adherence during firing. Porcelain flowers are made by squeezing porcelain clay into press-moulds to shape petals and leaves, followed by arranging each petal as it is shaped in a rest-mould in which the flower is built up. The flowers, also, are made to a standard. Completed flowers are given to the 'repairer' who attaches them before the figure is propped.

When the figure has been assembled and propped it is given its first firing. This is done nowadays in a tunnel-kiln. The assembled figures are loaded on to trolleys which move at a speed measured in feet per hour into a tunnel that, at its centre, is heated to about 1,200°C. Here the vitrification of the fusible ingredients takes place, the propping holding the various parts in position. Travelling on from this point, the atmosphere becomes progressively cooler, until the figure emerges at the other end as biscuit porcelain*.

At this point the biscuit figures are inspected and any which are imperfect are discarded. If the edition is limited and intended to be of high quality, defective specimens are smashed, but in the past (and today at small factories producing less expensive work) figures with slight defects were put on one side and sold as 'seconds' at a cheaper price. The Derby* factory in the early years of the 19th century specialized in biscuit figures, and perfect specimens coming from the type of kiln then in use were put on one side for sale in their unglazed state, those with slight defects being glazed and painted and sold more cheaply. Today the fashion is for glazed and painted figures, so the biscuit figures are next sprayed with a glaze coloured pink so that it can be seen instantly when any part has been missed. The pink burns out in the glazing (or glost) kiln, leaving a white figure with a glossy, smooth, impervious surface. From the glazing kiln the figure goes to the painting studios, where it is carefully coloured according to a standard provided. Not all colours develop at the same temperature, so those which need the highest temperature to develop properly go to the kiln first, those requiring lower temperatures being added later. Before completion a figure may require seven or eight separate firings, each with its attendant risk of damage. Finally the figure is inspected against a standard, and discarded if it fails to meet it.

High quality figures intended to be sold in limited editions at prices ranging upwards to several hundreds of pounds are, of course, those on which most care is lavished, and these are always original designs by designers of note, made by highly-skilled craftsmen. Also of exceptionally fine quality, are figures which have been cast in 18th-century moulds, such as the Italian Comedy figures of Bustelli made at Nymphenburg* by the Bavarian State factory, where the 18th-century originals can cost £10,000 or more. Other factories, particularly those of Germany, adapt 18th-century models by famous modellers, but unless the original moulds have been employed the price should be distinctly less. The greatest value is in original work by a recognized designer, such as Dorothy Doughty* at Worcester or Paul Scheurich at Meissen*. Work of this kind often makes few concessions to the necessity for reproducing models. For instance, one of the Doughty birds needed two years of experiment before the model could be successfully reproduced.

The process of figure-making described is an improvement upon the methods generally employed in the 18th and 19th centuries, but it does not depart from them in principle. In earlier times, however, when rigid adherence to standards was not insisted upon, much more hand-modelling of small parts was undertaken, and figures have a greater degree of individuality in both assembly and painting than is the case today. Nor were the factories so scrupulous, before 1850 at least, in rejecting minor imperfections. For this reason variations in quality between figures having the same subject and coming from the same factory are not uncommon. Until about 1850 figures were still produced principally as table or chimney-piece decoration, but after this date the influence of antique-collecting* increasingly inspired people to regard them as examples of fine craftsmanship to be kept in cabinets.

PORCELAIN IN THE 19TH CENTURY

After enjoying a period of great prosperity for most of the 18th century, the porcelain factories of Europe started the 19th century with their fortunes at a low ebb. In France the royal factory at Sèvres*, which had suffered very severely during the Revolution, had come under the patronage of Napoleon I and was now the Imperial factory, beginning its climb back to prosperity without occupying the monopoly position it had enjoyed during the reigns of Louis XV and Louis XVI. In Germany many of the factories had been closed by the Napoleonic Wars, or, like Meissen*, were struggling to survive. Their fortunes had been in decline before the end of the 18th century, largely due to imports of Wedgwood's* creamware* and pearlware* and the subsequent manufacture of these types of earthenware by German faïence* and porcelain factories under the name of Steingut*. Creamware was also made in France, notably at Creil*, under the name of faïence-fine* and in Italy, where it was called terraglia inglese. In the two last-named countries, however, the faïence (i.e. tin-enamel glazed ware) industry proved to be more resistant to this new development and not only did wares of this nature continue to be produced throughout the 19th century, but excellent reproductions of such early wares as 16th-century Italian maiolica* were made by factories like Doccia* and Cantagalli*.

Conditions of trade in England for the porcelain factories had differed considerably in the 18th century from those of the Continent, where factories had nearly always been extensively subsidized and protected by rulers and the State. English factories not

only had to make a profit to survive, receiving no financial assistance whatever, but they had to meet a vogue for wares of superior quality from Meissen, and to a lesser extent from Sèvres. In addition they were exposed to the cold wind of home competition from Wedgwood's creamware, pearlware and decorative stonewares*, jasper* and basaltes*. All the porcelain factories, English and Continental, found

PORCELAIN IN THE 19TH CENTURY. Typical 19th-century basic vase-shape made with many different styles of decoration. Registered by Samuel Alcock* in 1844. *Antique Collectors' Club*

it difficult to produce effective designs in the neoclassical* style. Wedgwood's bodies were much better suited to the new style.

It must be remembered that porcelain had always been a luxury material produced on the Continent without much regard for price. In England few attempts were made to produce the kind of ambitiously decorated wares that were made at Meissen and Sèvres. The competitive new creamware was decorated with transfer-printing* on simple shapes. For coloured wares an outline transfer-print was employed to act as a guide for semi-skilled painters. At the beginning of the 19th century, during the Regency period, Worcester*, which was then the principal porcelain factory, made wares of classical shape decorated with topographical painting, a popular subject at the time which also occurs on Bohemian glass of the same period.

The changes in fashion which are to be observed between 1810 and 1840 seem to be traceable to the vogue among collectors for 18th-century 'vieux Sèvres'* and the appearance on the market of the white ware released from this factory by Alexandre Brongniart*, the director appointed by Napoleon. The Sèvres styles of painting adopted were principally floral, to be seen on both Coalport* and Minton* copies. Figure-subjects are rarer, and most are termed 'Watteau' (see 'Watteau figures'), although it is usually impossible definitely to trace the origin of the painting to Watteau, Lancret, or any of their contemporaries. In the last quarter of the 19th century the Sèvres factory itself revived a type of soft-paste (like the old pâte-tendre*) which they decorated with a turquoise blue ground and Watteau subjects. English manufacturers imitating old Sèvres porcelain made considerable use of a ground colour which they termed rose du Barry*. But Mme du Barry, Louis XV's mistress who succeeded Mme de Pompadour, never had a ground colour associated with her in the 18th century, and there is no historical precedent for the name. Rose du Barry is a poor imitation of a delicate rose-pink ground introduced at Sèvres in 1757 and discontinued there in 1764 when Mme de Pompadour died. The factory called it rose Pompadour, and it was the most prized and sought of the ground colours among 19th-century collectors.

Undoubtedly the most influential of the 19th-century factories was that of Minton, who employed many French artists, including Arnoux, Carrier-Belleuse*, Rodin's employer, and Marc-Louis Solon* from Sèvres. There were two principal influxes of French workmen into England coinciding with the Revolution of 1848 which unseated Louis-Philippe, and the disastrous ending of the Franco-Prussian War of 1870 and the Paris insurrections which followed. Parian*, a type of porcelain especially suited to figure-modelling, was introduced about 1840–1845 by Copeland* & Garrett, successor to Josiah Spode, and was soon taken up by other factories, including Minton's and Worcester. Parian is usually thought of as distinctively 19th-century, but it is, in fact, a biscuit porcelain—a type first introduced for figures early in the 1750s by Bachelier at Sèvres, and varies only slightly in surface appearance from 18th-century biscuit, although its composition differs somewhat from the standard bodies used for service-ware. Mintons diversified their production in the 1850s and later with 'Majolica'*, which was a coloured glaze earthenware, and such novelties as Henri II* ware. Their most important introduction in porcelain during the last three decades of the century was the introduction of the pâte-sur-pâte* technique brought by Solon from Sèvres.

Worcester, which became the Worcester Royal Porcelain Company* in 1862, produced some interesting new departures, like the dessert-service based

PORCELAIN IN THE 19TH CENTURY. A dessert plate in the Alcock* manner. c. 1850. Antique Collectors' Club

on Shakespeare's Midsummer Night's Dream exhibited in Dublin in 1852 and the paintings in white on a deep blue ground by Thomas Bott*, which copied the colour-scheme of some late Limoges enamels*, it is said at the suggestion of the Prince Consort. Bott specialized in the seductive nudes very popular among the Victorians by whom the subject was regarded as high art. In the 1870s and 1880s Worcester introduced Japanese styles with considerable success, and these were more in sympathy with the current fashions of the time than most products of the other porcelain factories.

At the beginning of the 19th century the Worcester factory was still making porcelain with soaprock and in 1814 Billingsley* at Nantgarw* was making a porcelain which closely resembled the best of the 18th-century soft pastes. By the 1820s the bone china body had been universally adopted in England. Bone china is generally assumed to be the invention of Josiah Spode II* about 1800, by which he added a percentage of ground and calcined ox-bones to the true porcelain body consisting of china clay and feldspathic rock. This body had many advantages, not the least a greatly reduced kiln-wastage factor, and it is still the standard English body, although it is rarely employed elsewhere. The Continental and American porcelain body is basically the same as the Chinese, a combination of china clay and feldspathic rock. These ingredients are finely ground and diluted with water to form a plastic mixture from which the objects are made. They are then exposed to a kiln temperature of about 1,450°C which fuses the rock into a kind of natural glass, the relatively infusible clay serving to hold the object in shape.

The porcelain industry in England, and to some extent on the Continent, was adversely affected by the series of international exhibitions which began in 1851. They set themselves to provide showpieces,

PORCELAIN IN THE 19TH CENTURY. An ornate ormulu-mounted vase in the Sèvres* style of the 18th century, with cupid handles and finials, the figure painting on one side and the flower painting on the other, are both surrounded by foliate ornament in raised gilding. France. c. 1860. *Antique Collectors' Club*

large quantities, of which the best known today are the fairings* of Conta & Böhme of Pössneck*, now much sought. These had no 18th-century affiliations, except perhaps that they sometimes continued the occasional 18th-century practice of using book-illustrations or prints as a source of inspiration. New factories sprang up in and around Dresden itself which attempted to exploit the reputation of the Meissen factory. One of these was a decorating studio belonging to Helena Wolfsohn*, who adapted an 18th-century design of alternating white and coloured panels, the former with 'Watteau figures' and the latter with flowers. Much of her output consisted of cabinet cups and saucers, but pairs of vases are still to be found. She employed the monogram of Augustus the Strong, patron of the Meissen factory, as her mark, but this monogram, which rarely occurs on 18th-century wares, and then only on the finest especially made for the Elector, is never seen on the kind of designs from the late 1740s which Mme Wolfsohn was copying. Meissen took legal action and forced her to change her mark to a crown over the word 'Dresden', sometimes referred to as 'Crown Dresden'. Carl Thieme of Potschappel produced fairly close copies of Kändler's crinoline groups of the 1740s, some of which were sold to an English collector at the end of the 19th century as genuinely of the 18th century, and formed the subject of a *cause célèbre* in the Courts when Christie's refused to catalogue them as Meissen.

Meissen itself was haunted by its 18th-century achievements, and much of its 19th-century production in one way or another reflects the rococo and early neo-classical styles of the period betwen c. 1740 and 1775. There were, however, novelties introduced to help revive a flagging trade for fine porcelain with a public who had largely forgotten the meaning of quality. Mirrors encrusted with applied flowers were popular, dessert-services with comports decorated with figures of cupids and applied flowers, and large table-candelabra similarly decorated, were freely exported. In 1870, a period referred to as *die Neuzeit*, the factory made a series of contemporary figures of bathing girls, sportsmen, dancers, groups of lovers and, inspired by the Franco-Prussian War, a series of military figures, many with the familiar *pickelhaube*. The factory had retained many of the 18th-century moulds and towards the end of the 19th century they issued a catalogue (now extremely rare) which listed those figures they were able and willing to supply. Today the modern Nymphenburg factory at Munich possesses the 18th-century moulds of Bustelli's Italian Comedy figures and those which they inherited in 1790 from the Frankenthal factory. These figures are being reproduced for sale in properly marked versions.

In France the monopoly of Sèvres, greatly weakened by the patronage extended to small Paris porcelain factories towards the end of the 18th century by members of the royal family, was broken

often of immense size, which were badly conceived and tastelessly decorated.

The principal manufacturers of true porcelain in the 18th century had been German, but by 1800 many of these early factories had disappeared. Among the major surviving factories were Meissen, Nymphenburg, Berlin, and Vienna. Towards the end of the century many new factories sprang up in Bohemia, now Czechoslovakia, as a result of private enterprise, and these continued to increase in numbers throughout the 19th century. Quality, however, deteriorated, because these factories had to make a profit to survive and were operated on a strictly commercial basis. Much of their output was inspired by the 18th-century figures of Meissen suitably adapted to appeal to Victorian taste and for quantity production. What is meant in the literature of the time by references to 'Dresden* shepherdesses' is these adapted figures from the commercial Bohemian factories, many of them using marks which were easily mistaken by the novice for the old Electoral Crossed Swords. Some factories produced even cheaper wares for export in

by the Revolution. Henceforward, although it continued as a national factory, it had to meet competition from a variety of factories, such as those of Jacob Petit*, Nast*, and others, even though it enjoyed the support of Napoleon I, Louis-Philippe and Napoleon III. Napoleon's campaigns inspired the factory to produce services and table-decorations in the Egyptian style and imposing and lavishly gilded examples of classical Empire decoration. Brongniart introduced new colours, and the white porcelain surface tended to disappear under a spate of gold and colour. By 1830 porcelain plaques were being employed for meticulous copies of oil-paintings. Shortly after this the *pâte-sur-pâte** technique was introduced, and experiments were made with such novelties as the celadon glaze. Towards the end of the century the factory reintroduced a type of soft paste body distinguishable by the 19th-century idiom in drawing which, after a little experience, is never difficult to detect. About the same time the biscuit figure was also reintroduced, and commonly reproduced 18th-century models, when the factory employed biscuit porcelain for the creation of a miniature sculpture gallery. It is worth remembering that 18th-century biscuit figures from Sèvres are *never* marked. The factory also used the biscuit body for contemporary work such as the set of dancing figures based on Loïe Fuller's* scarf dance by Agathon Léonard* about 1893. Contemporary English sculptors also designed Parian figures in the 19th century. Many were distributed through the Art Union* and are so inscribed. The Sèvres factory was very influential throughout the 19th century, especially on such English firms as Coalport and Minton, and in America on Tucker* of Philadelphia who imported European workmen.

There were also numerous Continental factories and undertakings, such as Saint-Amand-les-Eaux*, or Edmé Samson et Cie* of Paris, who devoted some of their output to reproducing '*vieux Sèvres*'*, to a point where one authority early in the present century gave it as his opinion that much of what passed as '*vieux Sèvres*' in most private collections, and even in some museums, was spurious in one way or another. The writer recalls being asked to give an opinion on a collection of '*vieux Sèvres*' formed in the early years of the present century, and being unable to find one single piece of 18th-century manufacture or any imitations earlier than about 1840. Many of the specimens bore a convincing mark.

PORTLAND VASE, THE

Roman cameo glass* vase, now in the British Museum, originally produced in a limited edition in jasper* by Josiah Wedgwood* in 1786–1790. This copy is so accurate that when the Portland Vase itself was smashed by a drunken lunatic in 1845 a Wedgwood version was used to help in its restoration.

There were several editions in the 19th century. An edition of 1839 varies from the original in that the nude figures are draped. An edition of 25 copies issued between 1877 and 1880 was undercut and polished by John Northwood*, who had previously copied the Portland vase in cased glass*. This bears the initial *N* above the impressed *Wedgwood*. The Bellows edition of 1909 was made for an American firm. From 1880 several jasper editions have been issued. These have been made with backgrounds varying from almost black to lighter blue in colour, and in several sizes.

PORTRAIT JUGS AND FLASKS

Jugs and flasks, often modelled in the general form of the toby jug or the stoneware* gin-flask*, which are recognizable portraits of royalty, politicians or celebrities. The practice has continued almost to the present day. Lord Kitchener, Sir Austen Chamberlain and Sir Winston Churchill have all been portrayed in this way.

PORTRAITS ON SÈVRES PORCELAIN, ROYAL

A *déjeuner* service decorated with portraits of Louis XIV and members of his Court executed outside the factory on porcelain purchased at the sale of 'seconds' from Sèvres was presented to Louis XVIII in 1815 as genuine, but was later found to be spurious. It was placed in the Sèvres Museum, together with other spurious examples purporting to be '*vieux Sèvres*'*. This work appears to have been done by a former Sèvres painter named Soiron*. A cup and saucer signed by him with the date-letter for 1762 and decorated with portraits, is in the Victoria and Albert Museum, London. Porcelain decorated with royal portraits, and portraits of such famous persons as Mme de Pompadour or Mme du Barry, belong to the 19th century, whatever the mark and date-letter.

PORTUGUESE SERVICE, THE

An elaborate silver table-decoration made in Lisbon Arsenal to designs of Domingos Antonio da Sequeira, a painter turned silversmith who had a marked taste for allegory. The service was presented to the Duke of

PORTUGUESE SERVICE, THE. Soup-tureen of silver, parcel-gilt, from the Portuguese Service*. 1816. *Apsley House, London*

PORTUGUESE SERVICE, THE. Silver table-decoration from the Portuguese Service* designed by D. E. de Sequeira, made in the Lisbon Arsenal and presented to the Duke of Wellington by the Prince Regent of Portugal, afterwards John VI. London, Apsley House. 1812–1816. *Author*

Wellington in 1816, and is at present on view at Apsley House, Hyde Park Corner, London. Twenty-six feet long, the service runs the length of the table. The various figures and ornaments are allegorical of Wellington's campaigns and the centrepiece represents the Four Continents. It numbers more than 1,000 pieces.

PÖSSNECK (Saxony)
Factory founded in 1790 which, in the second half of the 19th century, produced the small groups known

as 'fairings' for the English market. The mark of a dagger held aloft by a mailed arm within a shield very closely resembles the Elbogen mark, and the two have often been confused.

POSTCARDS, PICTURE
The collecting of pictorial postal cards of one kind or another has become very popular during the last ten years or so and desirable specimens are continually increasing in value. The first plain postcards were issued by the Austro-Hungarian post office in 1869. One side, to be used for the address, bore an impressed stamp. The other side was intended for a brief message. A year later, in October 1870, the same facility was introduced into England, the pale buff card bearing an impressed halfpenny stamp. In England postcards used by commercial firms were often overprinted, frequently with the name and address of the sender, and sometimes with a small picture. Postcards sent by the Coalbrookdale Iron-works*, for example, bore a small picture of the famous Iron Bridge. Commercially produced picture cards were available on the Continent from the first, but their introduction was delayed for several years in England because only official cards with an impressed stamp were allowed to be used. Souvenir cards for tourists bearing coloured views of resorts were available on the Continent especially in Germany, France, Austria, and Switzerland by the 1880s and had become quite elaborate by the 1890s. These cards were widely sold and, before the days of cheap cameras, were bought and collected by travellers.

In 1894 the people of Britain were at last given a freedom long enjoyed by their Continental cousins. They were allowed to buy postcards other than those with the impressed stamp of the post office and to stick on an ordinary adhesive stamp unsupervised, but only on condition that one side should be used for the stamp and the address, and the other side for the message. In 1897 this rule was relaxed to allow a brief message to be written on the same side as the address, provided the address could be easily read and in 1899 a larger size of card, equivalent to those already in use on the Continent, was permitted.

From 1894 until the beginning of the First World War the picture postcard enjoyed enormous popularity, and in 1900 a monthly magazine, *The Picture Postcard*, addressed to collectors began publication. Subjects multiplied. So did the number of firms engaged in the production of cards. They began to be offered in series, and packaged in quantities of 6 and 12, illustrating such diverse subjects as *Our Generals* or *Feathered Songsters*. The postcard illustrating typical music-hall jokes, forerunners of Donald McGill*, also made their début. The theatre was a popular source from which subjects were drawn, and included portraits of celebrated actors, actresses and selected members of the *demi-monde*. These remained popular for many years. Even politicians were not neglected in an age when press photographs were poor and the electorate less sophisticated.

Museums, churches and cathedrals as custodians of works of art began to issue photographs of their possessions in postcard form, individually and in series. Generally, there was almost no subject capable of being represented on a postcard which was forgotten, while leading manufacturers maintained staffs of photographers who took bulky and complicated apparatus from place to place in search of new material.

The First World War produced large numbers of propaganda and patriotic postcards in all belligerent countries, as well as portraits of war leaders. Many of these subjects were drawn by artists instead of being reproductions of photographs, no doubt because it was thought that photographs might in some cases have shown details of assistance to an enemy. Humorous cards were often macabre in their sentiments. During the Second World War the postcard was no longer so popular, but played its part when the Admiralty appealed for postcards depicting French coastal resorts to help provide visual information useful to the invading armies.

Today's cards are rarely black and white, and developments in printing have greatly improved the quality of the coloured ones. Subjects are usually topographical, important buildings, or works of art, but the comic postcard survives, and the art of the late Donald McGill still has many devotees. Observing some new-style cards in a Southern French provincial town a year or two ago, which were reminiscent of *La Vie Parisienne* 40 years before, the writer inquired the reason for this new departure, and was told that they were intended for English visitors.

Cards of all kinds are now widely collected, and prices vary considerably according to age, quality, rarity and interest. Many of them form important social documents, especially now that many early photographs have either been destroyed or have degenerated to a point where they are hardly worth preserving. Dealers are now beginning to specialize in this field.

POSTERS

Reproductions of 19th-century posters are now much in vogue as decoration, although the originals have only rarely survived, and those by Toulouse-Lautrec, for example, realize very high prices. Posters first assumed the status of a minor art-form in the 1870s with Fred Walker's black-and-white poster for Wilkie Collin's *Woman in White*. A little later the art of chromolithography* was employed to produce coloured posters advertising improved versions of the bicycle. Jules Cheret in the 1880s designed posters for everything, from vermouth to music-halls, and he was the first to introduce the poster girl as a means of selling everything from laxatives to bicycles. The posters of Toulouse-Lautrec are the minor works of a major artist. He startled English critics of the medium by the faithfulness with which he depicted the life of the boulevards, but no one has ever designed better posters.

In England *Bubbles* became a popular advertisement for Pear's soap without the permission of Sir John Millais, the original painting having been purchased by Thomas Barratt, the soap king. W. P. Frith's *The New Frock* was turned into a poster advertising soap with the slogan 'So Clean' by Lord Leverhulme. Artists publicly expressed chagrin at this vulgarization of their work, but privately they did not despise the money that advertisers were willing to pay for their help, and some actively sought commissions. Walter Crane* made many designs for posters, so did Aubrey Beardsley*, while John Hassall and the Beggarstaff Brothers (*nom de plume* of William Nicholson and James Pryde) were among the first to add a touch of caricature. Alphonse Mucha* was a Bohemian artist who spent many years in Paris and devoted himself to posters in the *art nouveau** style. Most of his work belongs to the 1890s.

POTICHOMANIE (French)

Strictly, a *potiche* in French is a Chinese vase, but the word is sometimes applied, as in this case, more widely. The term *potichomanie* refers to covering the *inside* surface of glass vases with cut-out pictures similar to those appearing in scrap-books of the period. It was also possible to buy sheets of coloured figures in the manner of those painted on Meissen* and Sèvres porcelain. When these were applied to the interior and the intervening spaces filled with white oil-paint a tolerable imitation of porcelain could be produced. As may be deduced from the name, the fashion started in France, but had crossed to England by the 1850s. It may have been suggested originally by Chinese painting on the interior of glass snuff-bottles which seem to have arrived in Europe shortly after 1800.

POT-LIDS

Flat, circular lids intended to cover low, cylindrical pots, the receptacles of such toilet preparations as bear's grease, and later ointments, and meat pastes.

POT-LIDS. Two pot-lids* showing a view of Saint Paul's Cathedral, London, and the Chin Chew river, China. Staffordshire. Second half of the 19th century. *Antique Collectors' Club*

255

These lids, which have now become a much-sought collectors' item, are decorated in polychrome underglaze transfer-printing*, a technique which dates from the 1840s. The best lids were made by Felix Pratt*, employing a method said to have been developed by an employee, Jesse Austin. Charles Ford of Shelton patented a transfer-printing process in 1846, and in 1848 Collins and Reynolds took out a patent for decorating china in this way at a higher firing temperature. Earthenware lids were made by John Ridgway of Hanley, and the technique was employed by Brown, Westhead, Moore & Co.*

The variety of patterns is enormous—something in the region of 300 has been estimated—and most of them came from Pratt's factory. The objects are also diverse, and range from a bear (indicative of the contents) to topographical and religious themes, portraits and miscellaneous subjects. The greatest diversity occurs after 1850 and these lids were at the height of their popularity during the 1850s and 1860s.

In recent years reproductions have appeared on the market, although they are not deceptive to anyone acquainted with genuine examples. The method of printing adopted by Pratt was to add each colour in the design by means of a separate transfer, and these were accurately located by a dot or tiny white circle at the edge which is missing from some reproductions that have been decorated by a modern, less expensive process.

The application of the process of decalcomania* to pottery decoration dates from 1864. Pratt also employed coloured transfer-prints to decorate plates, small vases, and other objects of domestic utility.

POTTERY IN THE 19TH CENTURY

When the century opened industrial pottery in England of the kind made in Staffordshire and Liverpool by such firms as Wedgwood*, Adams and Enoch Wood* for the more sophisticated markets consisted mainly of creamware* and pearlware*. By this time tin-enamelled ware (or *delft**), popular in the 18th century, had been almost discontinued, unable to compete with the more efficient bodies first introduced by Josiah Wedgwood. The decorative stonewares—jasper* and basaltes*—also introduced by Wedgwood in the last 30 years of the 18th century, had become common property among the larger Staffordshire manufacturers, and some of the best of their products were comparable with those of Wedgwood. The best creamware was painted with enamel colours in the manner of porcelain, some exceptional pieces of this kind being produced by the Herculaneam* Pottery at Liverpool. The Leeds Pottery* continued to produce wares in the 18th-century tradition until about 1840, and some of the later of these wares so closely resemble those of the 18th century that they are sometimes passed off as belonging to that period.

Throughout the second half of the 18th century increasing use was made of transfer-printing* in the decoration of pottery and porcelain, both the type which resembles a line-engraving complete with hatching to represent shading and the outline print intended to be coloured by hand. Most of these prints had been overglaze and few underglaze blue prints had been produced after about 1765. In the early years of the 19th century, however, technical improvements enabled topographical prints in blue underglaze much more elaborate in style and execution than those of the 18th century to be produced. These became extremely popular and were exported to Europe and America in large quantities. Before 1800 relatively few colours apart from underglaze blue were used for this kind of printing, but as the century advanced several new underglaze colours became possible, and the firm of Felix Pratt* specialized in polychrome prints which they used to decorate potlids* and small plates which are now much sought. These they produced in time for the Great Exhibition of 1851.

Creamware was yielding in popularity to pearlware before 1800. This was a white or bluish-white variety of creamware, but both body and glaze were harder and more durable. It was only one of the many variants of the basic earthenware body produced during the 19th century which were especially employed for the popular transfer-printed wares. Another very important introduction was a body known as opaque china, ironstone china* or semiporcelain. An earthenware body hardened by the inclusion of china-stone was introduced by Josiah Spode II* in 1805, and an improved version called Ironstone China* was developed by Mason* in 1813. It was supposed to contain some of the vitreous residue of iron-smelting furnaces termed 'slag'. The Spode body was originally introduced for the purpose of imitating Chinese export porcelain of the period decorated in the *rose-verte* palette, and a good deal of the early production of this type of ware from Mason is decorated in Chinese styles.

Stoneware was widely produced. In the hands of Doulton* of Lambeth and the Martin Brothers* of Southall it became a notable art-form. There were also repetitions of 18th-century styles, such as tankards and beer-jugs decorated with applied reliefs. An amusing sidelight on popular attitudes to contemporary politics is provided by gin-flasks* which refer to such events as the Reform Bill and the trial of Queen Caroline.

Among the new techniques of decoration popular in the first quarter of the century was the use of metallic lustres*, the best applied over a canary yellow ground. Lustre, of course, had been known for many centuries to the potters of Islam, Spain, and Italy, but had fallen into disuse. Their introduction to England dates from about 1805 (see *Lustre pigments*).

Earthenware figures were made throughout the century, the earliest continuing the 18th-century tradition started by the porcelain manufacturers.

Enoch Wood* and Wood & Caldwell produced figures of excellent quality but a little uninspired during the first quarter of the 19th century. Enoch Wood himself was a very competent modeller whose self-portrait bust is in the British Museum, but his style was pedestrian, and it seems to have influenced the work of others. Much more amusing and lively were the figures of Obadiah Sherratt* of Burslem working in the 1820s. Later in the century figures sketchily finished at the back, and for this reason sometimes termed 'flat-backs'*, were produced in enormous quantities by Sampson Smith* of Longton and others. These are discussed under the heading of *Staffordshire portrait figures*, since most of them are portraits of one kind or another. They are much sought today and form a valuable social document. The series devoted to the theatre are of especial interest.

At mid-century we notice such special wares as Minton's 'Majolica'*—earthenware decorated with coloured glazes suggested by the antiquarian taste for the wares of Bernard Palissy*. The influx of French artists brought, in 1858, a pupil of Ingres, Émile Lessore*, who had worked at Sèvres*. His painting on Wedgwood creamware was impressionist in style, and it was adversely criticized in some quarters, but some people, perhaps the more perceptive, bought it at very high prices as an investment.

The School of Art at Lambeth inspired notable work towards the end of the century at Doulton's and by the Martin Brothers*. About this time the artist-potter working in his own studio began to emerge. William de Morgan* and the Martin Brothers, elsewhere discussed, both belong to this group. Bernard Moore* and William Burton, for instance, experimented with reduced copper glazes in imitation of the Chinese *flambé* or transmutation glaze, then much sought by collectors under the name of *sang-de-boeuf*.

At the opening of the 19th century the manufacture of tin-enamelled pottery (variously known as *faïence*, *delft*, or *maiolica* according to the place of manufacture) had gone from being a widespread and flourishing industry to one which had been almost abandoned for creamware in the manner of Wedgwood. A few of the larger centres continued to make a limited quantity of summarily decorated wares principally for sale in the local markets. Later in the century the technique was revived for reproductions of wares of interest to antique collectors, especially a limited number of close copies of Italian *maiolica* by Doccia*, Cantagalli* and others.

Creamware was extensively made in France under the name of *faïence-fine*, and in the early decades of the century a pottery at Creil*, near Paris, even decorated their wares with transfer-prints of English country houses, perhaps distantly inspired by the service which Wedgwood made for Catherine the Great in the 18th century. *Faïence-fine* became very popular later as a vehicle for excellent enamel decoration. In the 1840s, under the influence of the fashion for revived Renaissance styles*, the pottery of Bernard Palissy dating from the second half of the 16th century became very popular among collectors, and close imitations began to appear on the market made by Landais* of Tours and Georges Pull* of Paris. The most popular of Palissy's wares to be reproduced in this way were those decorated with highly-modelled reptiles, fish, and insects, repeated in a much cruder form by the Mafra* factory at Caldas in Portugal. The year 1845 saw the foundation of the Paris firm of Edmé Samson et Cie* to make replacements for broken parts of fine quality porcelain services, but the same firm soon extended its activities to reproductions of French *faïence*, especially the 18th-century wares of Strasbourg, and of early Dutch *delft*. These copies were accurate and deceptive. Many copies of old Dutch *delft* were made in Holland. Those with a tin-enamel glaze (comparatively rare) are deceptive, but vast quantities of wares decorated in the old styles in underglaze blue, were made of a type of pearlware, and these were merely intended as decoration. Towards the end of the century French artist-potters used *faïence-fine* for a variety of interesting decorative wares, including some in the *art nouveau** style.

In Germany the fashion for medievalism brought a return to popularity of the old stonewares* (*Steinzeug*) from Cologne, Raeren, and Siegburg which were popular during the 16th and early 17th centuries. Particularly popular were tankards and jugs, often with pewter mounts, in a greyish stoneware the relief decoration of which was picked out in cobalt blue and sometimes manganese purple. Most have a serial number stamped into the base, which is never found in the case of old wares. This type of stoneware is at present enjoying renewed popularity and is being manufactured today. A much smaller group of wares, mainly imitating the prized white stonewares of Siegburg, is reputed to have been made in the 1830s from the old beds of clay with the aid of the original moulds, but these are detectable from manufacturing idiosyncrasies. Many minor decorative wares, and those of domestic utility, were made from creamware and pearlware, termed *Steingut** in Germany, but in general German manufacturers tended to concentrate on porcelain for ornamental wares.

Artistic pottery of a very high standard was produced in America from 1880 onward by the Rookwood Pottery* of Cincinnati, Ohio, under the direction of Mrs Maria Longworth Stoner. Specially notable is a type of *faïence*, the glaze decorated with a variety of rich colours. Until 1910 pieces were individually designed, decorated and signed. The factory closed in 1941.

Generally, pottery exhibits much more variety and originality than porcelain during the 19th century. It was the preferred material of the studio-potter, since it was less costly and simpler to make than porcelain, which is essentially a factory operation.

POTTIER & STYMUS (New York)

Interior decorators and manufacturers of decorative furniture who were especially active during the 1870s and 1880s. They employed the revived rococo*, Louis XVI, revived Renaissance* and Egyptian styles*. They were responsible for designing and furnishing John D. Rockefeller's Moorish smoking-room (removed to the Brooklyn Museum) and exhibited successfully at the Philadelphia Centennial Exhibition of 1876. They also established their own workshop for the making of tapestries.

POUF (French)

A round or oval lavishly upholstered seat, low, and usually with no more than a narrow rail and four legs showing underneath the padding. They first appeared in France in 1845 as pieces of decorative drawing-room furniture, and were popular throughout the 19th century in France, England and the United States.

POWELL, ALFRED AND LOUISE (fl. 1905–1935)

Decorators who worked intermittently for Wedgwood* between the dates quoted. Louise, who married Alfred Powell, was a grand-daughter of Émile Lessore. Wares decorated with 'steel' or platinum lustre, such as the example illustrated, have been attributed to them by the Wedgwood Museum.

POWELL, ALFRED AND LOUISE. Vase with a light blue ground decorated with flowers and berries in platinum (steel) lustre. c. 1905. Wedgwood. *Mary Stubbley*

POWELL & SONS, JAMES (London)

Glass-makers who bought the Whitefriars Glass Works*, specializing in decorative glass. Powell's produced wares in the Anglo-Venetian style, using soda-glass for the purpose. A similar metal was employed for reproduction of ancient Roman glass. In 1859 they made table-glass for William Morris* to the design of Philip Webb*. Lead glass was employed for reproductions of appropriate early glass. Powell's were among the first to make double-walled silvered glass*. Towards the end of the century they began to make glass in the *art nouveau* style. Silver mounts were manufactured under the artistic direction of Harry J. Powell (1880–1914), and these were added to vessels of green glass in the Arts and Crafts* style. In recent times Powell's have provided glass for such engravers as Laurence Whistler*. Among the more unusual decorative items may be included *millefiori* paperweights*, and crystal chandeliers for Buckingham Palace.

POWOLNY, MICHAEL (1871–1954)

Austrian pottery decorator and teacher who started the ceramic department at the Vienna Kunstgewebeschule. He was a founder-member of the Vienna *Sezession*, 1897, and a co-founder with Berthold Löffler (1874–1960) of the Wiener Keramik. Powolny was noted for animal figures, and his pupils include the artist-potter, Lucy Rie.

POYNTER, SIR EDWARD JOHN (1836–1919)

President of the Royal Academy, 1896; Director of the National Gallery, 1881–1894; worked largely in the revived classical style, and painted one of the 19th-century's best-known paintings, *Faithful to the Last*, depicting a Roman legionary guarding one of the gates of Pompeii during the eruption of A.D. 79. Poynter painted furniture designed by W. Burges*, and executed designs for tiles for Minton's Art Pottery Studio* in London. Tiles designed by Poynter decorate the walls of the old grill-room in the Victoria and Albert Museum, London.

PRATT & SONS LTD, CHRISTOPHER (Bradford, Yorkshire)

Cabinet-makers, furniture retailers, and interior decorators. Established in 1840, Pratt's made furniture by hand until about 1874, when their workshops were largely mechanized, a gas-fired steam-engine supplying motive-power. Machines included those for cutting veneering, mouldings, frets, mortice and tenon joints, trenching, twisting, mitres, planing, a circular saw and a horizontal saw, which is fairly typical of workshops of the period. Pratt's made furniture in large quantities for public contracts, as well as for the retail trade. They enjoyed a wealthy middle-class clientele, especially among members of the wool trade, and bought widely from other suppliers for stock. Their label, therefore, can be found alike on their own furniture and that purchased from trade suppliers.

PRATT, FELIX (1780–1859)

Felix Pratt was the son of William Pratt of Lane Delph who owned a factory there from 1783 until his death in 1799. For a time the business was carried on by his widow and their sons, who eventually started business on their own account, F. & R. Pratt & Company from 1812, and John Pratt probably in 1815. F. & R. Pratt specialized in polychrome transfer-printing*, principally employed to decorate

PRATT, FELIX. Jug with a portrait of Admiral Lord Nelson in relief decorated with coloured glazes, by Felix Pratt*. c. 1805. *Author*

PRATT, FELIX. Classical vase in the form of a hydria with volute handles decorated in colours in the so-called Etruscan style by Felix Pratt. English, Staffordshire. c. 1845. *Private collection*

pot-lids*, but also table-ware. Much of the engraving was done by Jesse Austin (1806–1879) whose name or initials are to be found on some examples of his work.

Figures, jugs and plaques decorated in relief, painted with a distinctive underglazed palette which includes an ochre, olive green, brown and blue, are commonly attributed to F. & R. Pratt, and the name PRATT is to be found on some of them, but this type

was made elsewhere in Staffordshire, and in Sunderland. Examples marked PRATT were probably made by William Pratt.

F. & R. Pratt made red terracotta* decorated with enamel colours, also made by Wedgwood*, and a type of Etruscan ware. They used the transfer-printed mark *PRATT FENTON*.

PREIS, F. D.   See *Art déco figures*

PRE-RAPHAELITE BROTHERHOOD (P.R.B.)
The term, first applied to the Nazarener* (a group of early 19th-century German artists) was adopted by a group of English artists led by Rossetti*, Millais, and Holman Hunt shortly before 1850, since they shared many of the Nazarener ideas. Without knowing very much about early Italian art, and at a time when Italian Primitives were being bought by the National Gallery for derisory sums, they developed a style which was considered to antedate Raphael, in spirit if not in fact. Their paintings were meticulously detailed, brightly coloured, and painted with a realism which demanded the use of models. Holman Hunt went to Palestine to paint *The Scapegoat*, employing a tethered goat as a model.

At one time much criticized, the pre-Raphaelites were strongly supported by Ruskin*, then supreme arbiter of taste in England, and their success from this time was no longer in doubt. With the coming of success the movement began to break up, Rossetti and Ruskin joining with William Morris*, and moving towards ideas of a revival of handicraft and the arts of design which became profoundly influential in the decorative arts generally. Rossetti signed his early pictures with the initials 'P.R.B.', the meaning of which was not made public until 1860.

PRESSED GLASS
For a discussion of the technique see *Moulded glass*.

Pressed glass seems to have been developed by 1828 by Deming Jarves* at the Boston and Sandwich Glass Company*. By about 1835 it was being made in England (at Birmingham), France, Bohemia and Austria. At first it was largely employed for making cheap substitutes for cut-glass* which was especially popular in England and Ireland, and work of this kind done in France is sometimes virtually indistinguishable from wheel-cutting. Pressed glass copies, however, are usually detectable by a suspicious exactness in the disposition of the elements of the pattern, whereas patterns cut by hand have minor divergences where the elements do not exactly fit, although close examination is essential to see them. The introduction of pressed glass imitations of cut-glass did more to account for cut-glass becoming unfashionable in England than Ruskin's* criticism.

In America, hitherto largely dependent on England and Ireland for table-glass, the introduction of the pressed glass process put the glass industry on its feet. By 1860 about 75 per cent of all glass made in the

PRESSED GLASS. Miniature pressed glass coal-truck, design registered in 1880 by W. H. Heppoll & Co., Newcastle, Northumberland. *Victoria & Albert Museum, London*

PRESSED GLASS. Creamer decorated with floral, foliate and abstract *motifs*, pressed in one piece. Fort Pitt Glass Works, Pittsburgh. c. 1830. *Corning Museum of Glass, Corning, N.Y.*

PRESSED GLASS. A covered butter dish of pressed glass imitating cut-glass. The blunt edges of the facets can be seen quite plainly, and should be compared with the illustration under *Cut-glass. Author*

United States was being produced in this way, although, after 1864, quality began to deteriorate due to the substitution of the newly developed lime glass* for the original lead glass.

Although the earliest pressed glass patterns were largely based on cut-glass, in America especially new kinds of decoration were speedily devised, and today several hundred patterns have been recorded. Manufacturers also began to produce glass in matching sets, emulating the pottery and porcelain factories, and adding many new items hitherto rarely or never made in glass.

PRIE-DIEU (French)

19th-century chair, apparently of French origin, with an upholstered low seat and a back surmounted by a narrow padded ledge for resting the arms. The type appeared in France during the currency of the Troubadour style*. In Victorian England, where it was frequently covered with Berlin woolwork*, it is rarely Gothic in style, but sometimes has cabriole legs*. It was generally used for family prayers, of which the Victorians were exceedingly fond, and it is sometimes termed a vesper or devotional chair. It belongs principally to the 1830s in France and to the following decades in England.

PRIMAVERA

Name of a retail department of the Paris store, Au Printemps, which sold studio-pottery incised with the retailer's name. Primavera glass was an extremely fragile mottled variety made in Venice by E. Barovier* during the 1920s.

PRIMROSE GLASS

Pale yellow moulded art glass* patented in the 1890s by George Davidson & Company*. Specimens are sometimes decorated with simulated simple cutting.

PRISONER OF WAR WORK

Between 1797 and 1815 Britain housed thousands of French prisoners of war, many of them seamen, but also conscripted soldiers whose ranks contained craftsmen of all kinds, such as ivory-workers from Dieppe, jewellers from Paris, or jet-carvers from Brittany. Prisoners were allowed to make all kinds of articles for sale outside the prison, a trade from which some of them accumulated considerable sums of money by the time their captivity ended.

Since they were not provided with materials, they were compelled to improvise; most of their work is made from wood; bone from the kitchens; straw, dyed and used to weave straw-pictures; and other, miscellaneous material.

A few extremely elaborate models have survived, but most work of this kind is relatively small, and includes rolled paper work, bone-carvings such as chessmen, and so on, which were sold by the guards on the prisoners' behalf. Boxes decorated with inlaid patterns have survived fairly commonly, and were obviously popular. The more elaborate models, such as houses and ships of war were, no doubt, ordered specially by private patrons. Of these, ships of war are, perhaps, the most numerous of rare survivals and are the most sought.

Work of this kind was done at prisoner of war camps all over Britain, but one at Norman Cross, in barracks there, no doubt accounts for an excellent collection in the Peterborough Museum. The superficial resemblance of some work of this kind to Tunbridge ware* has occasionally led to confusion.

Recently forgeries of ships of war of this kind have appeared on the market.

PRISONER OF WAR WORK. Model ship in bone made by French prisoners of war. c. 1810. *Antique Collectors' Club*

PROTÂT, HUGUES (fl. 1843–1875)

French sculptor; exhibited in the Paris Salon 1843–1850; assisted in the decoration of a large cabinet by Jackson & Graham* shown at the Paris Exposition of 1855, and now in the Victoria and Albert Museum, London; modelled Parian* figures for S. Alcock & Co.* of Burslem; modelling instructor at Hanley School of Design, 1850–1864; modeller and designer to Wedgwood and Minton*. His work for Wedgwood included the so-called Protât Vase, modelled about 1871, for which he received £25.

PROUVÉ, JEAN   See *Prouvé, Victor*

PROUVÉ, VICTOR (1858–1943)

French painter, sculptor and designer in the *art nouveau** style. One of Émile Gallé's* friends, he managed the Nancy workshop after Gallé's death. His son, Jean Prouvé, was an interior decorator in the Bauhaus* style.

PRUSSIAN IRON FOUNDRY, ROYAL (Berlin)

Berlin foundries generally achieved a very high reputation for decorative metalwork during the 19th century and the Royal Prussian Iron Foundry was particularly noted for fine quality iron castings which were often both intricate and delicate. A high degree of fluidity in the molten metal must have been essential to results of this kind and contemporary comment believed the technique of working to be a well-kept secret. The foundry contributed some important examples of their skill to the Great Exhibition of 1851.

PRUTSCHER, OTTO (1880–1949)

Architect, designer and poster artist who worked for the Wiener Werkstätte* designing furniture, metalwork and ceramics.

PUGIN, AUGUSTUS WELLBY NORTHWOOD (1812–1852)

Architect, ecclesiologist, and designer, son of Auguste Charles, Comte de Pugin, who fled from France during the Revolution and obtained employment with John Nash, architect of Buckingham Palace and Regent Street, of whom it was said that 'he found London of brick and left it of *stucco*'. Nash disliked Gothic, but at the time there was a certain demand for the style, so Nash gave his assistant, the Comte de Pugin, the task of studying it. The Comte did so to such good effect that he became an authority on the subject, and he passed his taste and knowledge on to

PUGIN, A. W. N. Chalice of silver, parcel-gilt, set with semi-precious stones, designed by A. W. N. Pugin* and made by John Hardman & Co.* c. 1851. *Victoria & Albert Museum, London*

PUGIN, A. W. N. Gothic revival* cabinet of carved and painted oak with panels of wrought brass designed by A. W. N. Pugin*, made by J. G. Crace* in 1851, and shown in the Medieval Court of the Great Exhibition, 1851. *Victoria & Albert Museum, London*

his son, A. W. N. Pugin, who was educated at Christ's Hospital, London, and showed a considerable talent for drawing.

At fifteen he was employed by a goldsmith to make designs for plate, and not long afterwards was commissioned to design Gothic furniture for Windsor Castle. His design book, *Gothic Furniture*, was published with the patronage of the Earl of Shrewsbury in 1835. During a period as designer of scenery at Covent Garden he produced stage-sets for an opera based on Scott's *Kenilworth*. In 1833 he built himself a Gothic house near Salisbury, and he received many commissions for churches, colleges, and houses in the Gothic style. In 1837 he became Professor of Architecture at the Roman Catholic College at Oscott, and about the same time he began to assist Sir Charles Barry, architect of the new Houses of Parliament. There has since been a great deal of controversy about the respective parts played by the two men, but it seems fairly well established that Barry was responsible for the design of the main structure and Pugin for the ornament, which accounts for Gothic ornament on a building predominantly classical.

In 1849 Pugin began to design for Minton*, and in this year, at the Birmingham Exhibition, they showed 'Pugin's bread plate' and 'Pugin's garden seat'.

He helped to design the Medieval Court at the Great Exhibition of 1851, which contained tiles and porcelain designed for Minton by Pugin. He wrote to the factory, 'I think my patterns and your workmanship are ahead of everything'. In 1851 he became insane, it was said from overwork, and after a period of confinement in an asylum, he died in Ramsgate, calling, it has been said, for a Gothic pudding.

To Pugin Gothic was known as the 'pointed Christian style', and the style, and the religion, were inextricably confused in his mind. Until recently Gothic was the only conceivable style for church building and equipment, which was largely the product of Pugin's influence.

PUIFORÇAT, JEAN (1879–1945)
French silversmith and sculptor who studied in London at the Central School of Arts and Crafts, and then under the sculptor Louis Lejeune. He is regarded as one of the principal founders of the modern style in silver design. He used restrained forms in conjunction with a variety of materials like wood, lapis lazuli,

PUIFORÇAT, JEAN. Four-piece tea-set of the 1920s. Stamp: *M. Horowitz, Alexandre. Sotheby & Co*

ivory and jade. Puiforçat exhibited at the 1925 Exhibition and became a member of the Union des Artistes Modernes.

PULL, GEORGES (fl. 1850–1860)
Paris naturalist and potter who began to make close imitations of the rustic dishes of Bernard Palissy* in 1856. Pull marked his work, but at least one instance is known of a dish by him being sold as 16th century with the mark covered by a collector's label.

PURDONIUM
A closed coal-scuttle with a separate interior container for coal, invented in the 19th century by Mr Purdon.

PURPURINE
A substance simulating a hardstone employed by Fabergé* for carving small animals, such as the rabbit and the squirrel. It often forms part of figures made from several hardstones joined together, where it provides a brilliant red. It is somewhat like the *sang-de-boeuf* * porcelain glaze in colour, but the shade is variable. A kind of glass, purpurine was devised at the Imperial Glass Factory at St Petersburg by a workman named Petouchkoff. It is reputed to have gold in its composition, and this seems likely, since the colour is not dissimilar from the purple of Cassius (the pigment of the Chinese *famille rose* and the Sèvres* ground-colour known as *rose Pompadour*) which owe their colour to gold chloride.

PUZZLE JUG
Jug with perforated neck and several small tubular spouts at intervals round the rim. The puzzle was to drink from it without spilling the liquid through the perforations in the neck. The solution was to suck it through one of the spouts, but to do this the others had to be closed with the fingers. There was also a small concealed hole, usually on the underside of the handle, to trap the unwary. First made in the 17th century in tin-enamelled ware, puzzle jugs became a favourite with Victorian stoneware* potters.

PYRAMIDS
Small gold wire frames of pyramidal shape from the apex of which were suspended small figures of porcelain or enamel. They usually rested on a plush-covered base under a glass shade.

PYROGRAPHY
The art of making pictures on light coloured wood, such as sycamore, holly, lime, or chestnut, by charring and scorching the surface with hot irons. Pyrography as an art antedated the 19th century by hundreds of years—there are 17th-century chests with pictorial panels executed in this way—but the most ambitious and intricate specimens belong to the 19th century, and were principally done by gifted amateurs. A wood of close grain was selected and the surface

burned to varying depths ranging from light scorching to charring, giving a range of colour varying from light brown to black. The tools employed were of steel, the ends being of various shapes best suited to the nature of the work. Some later pictures of this kind were executed with the additional use of a blowpipe, which enabled an effect comparable to the wash of a watercolour to be achieved. Occasionally additional effects were obtained by burning the surface with sulphuric acid which yielded brown or black. The technique is still employed today, and among modern technical aids are electrically heated pokers, the heat of which can be readily adjusted.

Since they were the work of amateurs, pyrographic pictures vary considerably in quality. Some pyrographers took their subjects from the work of well-known painters. Little is known of the artists, in many cases not even their names. The pictures are difficult to date closely, although in some cases costume may be an indication.

QUAINT STYLE, THE
A contemporary name in England for *art nouveau**.

'QUEEN'S BURMESE' See *Burmese glass*; *Webb & Sons, Thomas*

'QUEENSWARE' OR 'QUEENS WARE' See *Creamware*; *Wedgwood*

QUERVILLE, ANTHONY (fl. 1835–1849)
Furniture-maker of Philadelphia, who was born in France and trained as an *ébéniste*. His furniture was of high quality, mainly in the neo-classical* style, and noted for matched mahogany veneers.

QUEZAL GLASS
An iridescent semi-opaque imitation of Tiffany's* 'Favrile'* glass which is sometimes moulded. It bears the mark *Quezal*. It was made in Brooklyn about 1917.

'QUEEN'S BURMESE'. A night light of Queen's Burmese glass, yellow at the bottom, shading to deep pink at the top. A rare type of glass made by Thomas Webb & Sons*, Stourbridge under licence from the Mount Washington Glass Company*, New Bedford, Mass. c. 1890. *The Corporation of Dudley*

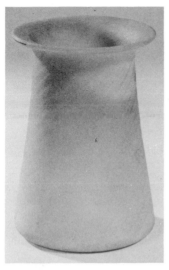

'QUEEN'S BURMESE'. Small flower-vase of yellow glass at the bottom shading to deep pink at the top. Thomas Webb & Sons, Stourbridge. c. 1890. *The Corporation of Dudley*

QUILTING
The quilted bedcover is a favourite item among American collectors. The best known is the patchwork quilt, and of this type there are two kinds—pieced and appliqué. In the pieced quilt the small pieces of material of which the design was composed were sewn together along the edges and provided with a lining. In the case of the appliqué quilt, small pieces of material of the required shape were applied to a foundation and sewn on. The work was done on a quilting frame, the lining or foundation being of cotton, with a layer of cotton wadding or wool between the lining and the pieced top. Geometric patterns seem to have been the most popular, especially in New England, probably because they were easier to set out. The more naturalistic patterns

'QUEENS WARE'. A group of 19th-century domestic Queens Ware notable for a design which is almost modern in its simplicity. *Josiah Wedgwood & Sons Ltd*

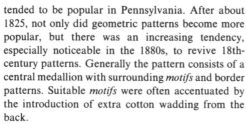

'QUEENS WARE'. A very rare jelly-mould of Queens Ware*. Early 19th century. *Josiah Wedgwood & Sons Ltd*

tended to be popular in Pennsylvania. After about 1825, not only did geometric patterns become more popular, but there was an increasing tendency, especially noticeable in the 1880s, to revive 18th-century patterns. Generally the pattern consists of a central medallion with surrounding *motifs* and border patterns. Suitable *motifs* were often accentuated by the introduction of extra cotton wadding from the back.

'Crazy' quilts, made from oddments of silk and velvet, trimmed and sometimes painted, usually belong to the 1880s. 'Autograph' quilts, each section sewn and signed by a different friend of the recipient, belong to the 1840s and 1850s. Individually signed quilts also exist. 'Autograph' quilts, also known as 'Bride', 'Friendship', or 'Album' quilts, were usually intended for a bride, but were often given to a minister popular among the young ladies. All-white quilts are rare, and usually of exceptional workmanship.

QUIMPER (Finisterre, Brittany)
There were a number of factories making *faïence** in Quimper. Of these, one started in 1782 by Antoine de la Hubaudière made stoneware* and *faïence*, including *faïences révolutionnaires*, and imitations of early Rouen wares. The factory of Fougeray, started in 1872, imitated 18th-century *faïence* generally.

R

RAILWAY MUGS

Mugs (more rarely plates and other wares) transfer-printed* with early railway engines and rolling-stock. They date from the 1830s until the 1850s. The earliest examples are the rarest and they are comparatively easy to date for anyone with a knowledge of railway history. For instance, among the earliest passenger carriages were flat trucks on which the traveller's carriage, minus horses, was conveyed. Rarities include a train with two locomotives (known as a 'double-heading') or a train without a locomotive at all. The transfer-prints are usually black, coloured by hand, and the same print is often used twice to encircle a mug. Earthenware decorated in this way is sought by collectors and it was made by several firms. Some bear a maker's name or initials.

RANDALL, THOMAS MARTIN (1786–1859)

Independent decorator of English porcelain who, in partnership with Richard Robins, did much work for London dealers, specializing in the style of Sèvres*. Some of his painting was executed on genuine but slightly defective *pâte-tendre** from Sèvres which had been accumulating since 1760, and was sold to Baldock, Perez, Ireland, and other dealers by Alexandre Brongniart*. He is also reputed to have removed sparse decoration from old Sèvres porcelain with hydrofluoric acid* in order to redecorate it in more sumptuous and expensive styles. When supplies of old Sèvres were exhausted Randall turned to the soft-paste porcelain of Nantgarw* and Swansea* and he later started a factory of his own which made a kind of soft-paste at Madeley, Shropshire, because he was unable to procure suitable ware from other sources. His reputation as an imitator of 'vieux Sèvres'* porcelain stood very high among the dealers of the day. When he died one dealer remarked that had Randall's conscience as a Quaker not forbidden him to use the 'vieux Sèvres' mark his work could have been passed off as genuine. This is an interesting reflection on the commercial ethics of the time. Randall's religious persuasion did not prevent him from making copies which he must have known were, in some cases, sold as Sèvres, but it forbade him to take the final step and mark them.

RANFTBECHER. *Ranftbecher* painted by Anton Kothgasser*. Vienna. 1823. *Pilkington Glass Museum*

RANFTBECHER (German)

A tumbler with slightly incurving sides, and a heavy, slightly protruding, fluted base. It was an especial favourite with the enameller, Anton Kothgasser*.

RAPHAELESQUE

A term employed in the 19th century with several meanings. It usually signifies some kind of connection with the early 16th-century painter, although this is often very tenuous. A kind of porcelain introduced by Worcester* in 1862 with a very rich glaze was termed Raphaelesque and according to Jewitt it bore a resemblance to the early porcelain of Capo-di-Monte*, although this is not particularly obvious.

The term was also applied to *grotesques** which were originally popularized by Raphael. Certain types of 16th-century Urbino *maiolica** decorated with grotesques had been termed Raphael (or Raffaele) ware in the 18th century and the name survived into the 19th century.

A Raphaelesque vase is a reproduction of an Urbino vase of about 1590 decorated with grotesques, more properly known as the Pisa vase. It is amphora-shaped, on a pedestal foot, with entwined serpent handles rising from two masks on the shoulders. The

267

19th-century examples are about 18 inches or more in height and the quality is variable.

RATEAU, ARMAND-ALBERT (1882–1938)
French interior decorator in the *art déco** style, who exhibited in the 1925 Exposition. His furniture designs were often inspired by oriental or ancient examples such as Minoan Crete. He preferred expensive materials, ornamenting furniture not only with patinated bronze, but with gold and silver. He designed furniture and interior decorations for the Paris apartment of the couturière, Jeanne Lanvin, in 1922.

RATTAN FURNITURE
The pliable stems of an East Indian climbing plant (*calamus rotang*) were woven into furniture, principally for outdoor use, which was popular from about 1850. A great deal of rattan was used in the eastern United States to make furniture in which it was woven round a wooden framework.

REALISM
The representation of things as they seem to be, and not in some ideal form. It had its origin in the painting of Gustave Courbet in the 1840s. Social Realism depicts some aspects of social life in painting or sculpture, and it is often critical or even satirical. The style may be noted in some rare bronzes by Daumier, or more frequently in some of Dalou's* peasant figures in bronze or terracotta*.

'REFORM' WARE
Jugs, gin-flasks*, and punch-bowls made before and during the passage of the Reform Bill in 1832. 'Reform' ware occurs in earthenware made in Staffordshire, or in stoneware made in London or at Denby. Inscriptions refer to the Bill, and gin-flasks are sometimes marked 'Reform Cordial'. Lord Brougham is frequently represented, and others include William IV and Queen Adelaide, Lord Althorpe, and Lord John Russell, all champions of Parliamentary reform.

REGENCY STYLE
The regency of the Prince of Wales lasted from 1811 until 1820 and in the latter year he became George IV consequent on the death of his father. By common consent, however, the Regency style is a term loosely applied to neo-classical* objects made from about 1805 until 1830.

The Prince of Wales was extremely fond of French furniture although, especially after the accession of Napoleon I, good specimens were not easy to import. The Regency style itself was largely based on the French Empire style*, although there are some basic

REGENCY STYLE. Small Carlton House desk, a type first made about 1815. Although the desk was named after Carlton House, the residence of the Prince Regent, no existing examples are known to come from there. Late 19th century. *Sotheby & Co*

REGENCY STYLE. Regency furniture in the Royal Apartments. Royal Pavilion, Brighton, Sussex. *Author*

REGENCY STYLE. Folding card-table on a central pillar support, with a circular base on four lion-paw feet. c. 1820. *Antique Collectors' Club*

REGENCY STYLE. Interior showing furniture and accessories from the accession of George IV to the early years of Victoria (1820–1840). During these two decades styles developed from English Empire to English Biedermeier. *Victoria & Albert Museum, London*

REGENCY STYLE. Interior showing turn-of-the-century and Regency furniture, especially a circular dining-table on a massive carved central stem and a tripod support with lion-paw feet. Dining-chairs customarily had straight front legs and leather seats. London, Sir John Soane's House, Lincoln's Inn. *Author*

variations, as well as *motifs* of decoration not present in the French version, particularly such marine *motifs* as the anchor. This dates from Nelson's victory at Trafalgar in 1805, which the French, naturally enough, were not anxious to commemorate.

The first, and probably the most influential, of Regency designers was Thomas Hope*, whose *Household Furniture*, with designs based on a variety of classical and Egyptian sources, was published in 1807. A year later George Smith published his *Collection of Designs* in which the ornament was much more elaborate.

Regency furniture made considerable use of dark coloured well-figured woods such as rosewood*. Brass stringing was commonly employed. Ormolu mounts, while simpler and less elaborate than those decorating French furniture, nevertheless occur quite often. Typical is the lion-mask with a ring in its mouth used for drawer handles, the winged Greek sphinx often in

bronze as a paperweight*, and other mythological figures. The marble top in the French style was employed for certain pieces of furniture, and a feature of Regency decoration is the use of simulated materials. Furniture is sometimes painted; plaster mouldings are replaced by *papier mâché**, and so forth. Large chandeliers* hung with faceted drops of glass were a favourite with the Prince Regent. Porcelain vases were handsomely painted, especially with topographical scenes.

The popularity of classical ornament at this period was due to the universality of classical learning. Most people were at least as well acquainted with classical mythology as they were with the Christian iconography. Sonorous Latin quotations from Cicero or Seneca were bandied between parliamentary benches and many people were better acquainted with Greek and Roman authors than with those writing in their native tongue. Although both the revived rococo* and

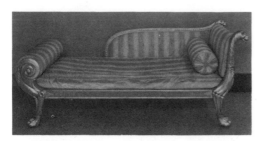

REGENCY STYLE. Settee of carved and gilt beechwood in the Regency style* with scroll end and lion-paw feet. The striped covering-material was fashionable at the time. c. 1810. *Victoria & Albert Museum, London*

REGENCY STYLE. Convex mirror of good quality and typical Regency-style form in a carved gilt-wood frame. *Harrods Ltd*

revived Gothic* styles existed to a minor extent during the currency of the Regency style, they were by no means popular. Revived rococo, to be found occasionally in silver and porcelain, was employed to decorate the drawing room in what was then an antiquarian taste, and Gothic appealed to the romantic few whose taste ran to medievalism. The struggle between classical and Gothic for pre-eminence came later in the century, when Gothic began to be identified with Christianity.

The final eclipse of the Regency style came with the accession of Queen Victoria, the growth of the *bourgeoisie*, and the elevation of domestic virtue to hitherto unknown heights.

REGISTRY MARKS

The Registry of Designs housed a drawing and description of every registered article from 1842 onwards. Provided objects are stamped with the diamond-shaped registry mark (see Appendix II), or bear a registered design number, it is possible to trace the original design in the Public Records Office, Chancery Lane, London WC2. The symbols in the diamond-shaped mark give the following informa-

tion—category and year, month and day of manufacture. The figure at the bottom of the diamond is the bundle or parcel number by which a manufacturer may be identified from the records. The categories are I, metal; II, wood; III, glass; IV, earthenware. After 1868 the system was altered slightly, the principal variation being the position of the symbols. The system was discontinued in 1883 and that of registered numbers (Rd. No.) began in 1884 and continued until 1909.

REMINGTON, FREDERICK (1861–1909)

American artist born at Ogdensburg, New York, and educated at Yale University. He went West as a young man, and spent four years working as a cowboy, prospector and saloon proprietor. He returned to New York and became an illustrator of the scenes he knew so well, and later a painter and sculptor. More than a hundred of his Western paintings were reproduced as colour prints, and bronze sculptures of his characteristic subjects also exist and are much sought. They are also imitated.

RENAISSANCE STYLE

The word *renaissance* means, literally, rebirth, and in this sense it refers to the rebirth of the classical styles of Greece and Rome and the ending of the Gothic style. In the 19th century a pseudo-Renaissance style was based largely on Italian and French styles current between about 1450 and 1700—a period normally covered by the High Renaissance and the Baroque. The 19th-century version, current in Europe from about 1850 to 1870, and in the United States perhaps from 1860 almost to the end of the century, is best described as pseudo-Renaissance because little attempt was ordinarily made at historical accuracy, and most examples of furniture especially consist of ornamental elements of several periods.

The style in the 19th century is especially to be seen in large profusely decorated cabinets. These were also popular in the 16th and 17th centuries, when vast sums were lavished on the finest specimens. The Great Exhibition of 1851, and the one following in 1862, both contained a number of cabinets decorated in this style. The arched pediment top, and sometimes the broken arched pediment, is a type derived from Renaissance architecture which had appeared by 1851, but most 'Renaissance' cabinets of fine quality belong to the Second Empire* of Napoleon III. As late as the 1880s in London Gillow's* were producing an occasional large Renaissance-style cabinet inlaid with mother of pearl. Allied to the cabinets were lavishly decorated *buffets* in similar styles, and reproductions, sometimes fairly exact, of Italian 16th-century seat-furniture and coffers (*cassone*) belong to this period.

Some of the fashion for Renaissance styles was the product of antique collecting* which, in the 19th century, was beginning to take its present form. From time to time this relatively new pastime not only

RENAISSANCE STYLE. Cabinet made by A. Hayball of Sheffield for the Great Exhibition*, 1851. *Illustrated Exhibitor*

RENAISSANCE STYLE. A wine-cooler decorated in 'Majolica' glazes and painting in the style of Limoges enamel, the cover surmounted by a satyr with grapes. Modelled by Hamlet Bourne. Probably from Renaissance metalwork or an engraved design from this source. c. 1860. *Minton Museum, Royal Doulton Tableware*

influenced the production of fairly exact reproductions or forgeries for sale to collectors, but also the decoration of objects for the general public. The pottery of Bernard Palissy*, not always strictly Renaissance in style but undoubtedly of the period, was extensively copied in both France and England with varying degrees of persuasiveness, and it led to the introduction of 'Majolica' by Minton* and others. The French 16th-century inlaid pottery known as Henri Deux ware* was also copied by Minton and in France. This too was a fashion led by the antique collectors. Belonging to the same category was the silver and metalwork connected with Benvenuto Cellini*, the swashbuckling Renaissance sculptor and goldsmith. So little remains of Cellini's work in gold and silver that it is hard to see on what basis

RENAISSANCE STYLE. A highly carved *buffet* in a revived Renaissance style*. Mid-19th century. *Antique Collectors' Club*

19th-century designers associated their work with his name, but it has to be remembered that many contemporary attributions to Cellini have not stood the test of later scholarship.

True Renaissance ornament, of course, is of classical derivation, and one very popular type, the grotesque* had been lost to sight for 1,500 years, until rediscovered in the ruins of Nero's Golden House, excavated soon after 1500. Raphael (1481–1520) adopted it for the decoration of the *loggie* of the Vatican. In the 19th century its origin went unremembered and it was regarded as an invention of Raphael's, and called Raphaelesque*. Similarly, the mid-16th-century *maiolica* ware from Urbino painted with pictorial subjects after Raphael were also more closely associated with him in the 19th century than their origin by way of engravings of Raphael's work by Marcantonio Raimondi warranted. Copies of Urbino *maiolica* were made at various Italian factories in the 19th century.

The Renaissance style had largely come to an end in Europe by the 1880s, although it persisted somewhat longer in America under the influence of the American millionaire antique collectors who were, at the time, especially drawn to the period. Throughout the century the Renaissance style was confined almost entirely to luxury objects for wealthy conservative buyers.

RENOIR, PIERRE-AUGUSTE (1841–1919)
French Impressionist painter. Renoir turned to sculpture in 1913 at the suggestion of the dealer

RENOIR, PIERRE-AUGUSTE. Small bronze, *La Laveuse*, by
Pierre-Auguste Renoir*. c. 1917. *Sotheby & Co*

Vollard, making small models which he originally
intended to have cast in a larger size. In his final years
his hands were so crippled with arthritis that he was
compelled to work first through an Italian sculptor
named Guino and then with the help of Marcel-
Antoine Gimard. Renoir's small bronzes, characteristic in style and subject-matter, are rare and much
sought.

'REPAIRING'

The 'repairer' in a porcelain factory is a highly skilled
man whose job has nothing whatever to do with
mending broken china. The most elaborate figures
are slip-cast in sections, and the parts are put together
before firing to form a complete figure by the
'repairer', a term dating from the 18th century. In the
case of the finest work, such as the preparation for
firing of the porcelain birds of Dorothy Doughty* at
the Worcester Royal Porcelain Factory*, the 'repairer' works with a standard in front of him to which
his final version must conform. When porcelain
reaches the maximum firing temperature, the point
where the fusible ingredients are at fusion point,
many of the free-floating pieces would sag out of
shape if they were not supported. The 'repairer'
arranges a series of struts and supports, prevented
from adhering to the model itself during firing by a
dusting of alumina powder, which keeps them in the
correct position.

In the case of limited editions it is the practice to
destroy any models which diverge from the standard
during any of the manufacturing processes.

See *Porcelain*

REPRODUCTIONS AND COPIES

The greater part of the 19th century, from the end of
the Regency onwards, was noted for the making of
reproductions of earlier things. This was usually by
mechanical methods, or by those utilizing recently-
discovered technical processes which yielded products of inferior quality, and with far lower standards
of craftsmanship, than would formerly have been
tolerated. This is discussed at greater length under
the heading of *Factories and mass-production*, but
here it is appropriate to remind the reader of
Gresham's Law, that bad currency always drives out
good.

The 16th-century pottery of Bernard Palissy*, for
which collectors were paying high prices in gold
pounds in the 1850s, gradually fell out of favour,
principally as a result of the numerous copies by
Avisseau*, Georges Pull* and others. At first these
were of good quality, but gradually degenerated into
tawdry imitations with the 'rustic' dishes of Mafra*
of Caldas da Rainha, Portugal, in the 1880s. The
magnificent 18th-century soft-paste of Sèvres* largely
maintained its value until the First World War, but
the numerous copies and derivations made by
Coalport*, Spode*, Minton*, Saint-Amand-les-
Eaux* and others eventually led to a point where it
was no longer in serious demand among the wealthier
collectors, and prices fell in consequence. The
popularity of old cased glass* declined with the
introduction of the much cheaper flashed glass* and
so on. Even today specimens of Palissy's pottery and
'*vieux Sèvres*' porcelain are undervalued in comparison with the products of such 18th-century factories
as Meissen* and certain kinds of early pottery, like
*faïence** and *maiolica**, were undervalued for many
years although prices are now beginning to recover.
Maiolica was at one time realizing prices far below
its 19th-century peak, partly because of the spate of
forgeries* in that period, none of which would be
deceptive now. In 1974 one had to turn to early Ming
vases at £450,000 however to see prices comparable
with those realized in the 19th century for the best
18th-century Sèvres. The figure quoted is approximately equivalent to £30,000 gold pounds in the
1890s, and therefore is far from a record price for a
piece of porcelain in terms of purchasing power.

REVERE, PAUL (1735–1818)

Silversmith of Boston, Mass., who took over his
father's business in 1754. Although he was an
excellent craftsman, he is most famous for his political
activities. He took part in the Boston Tea Party in
1773. The midnight ride of Paul Revere, immortalized
in Longfellow's poem, took place in 1775. Apart from
his silver, Revere also started a brass and iron
foundry. Examples of his silver may be found in the
Metropolitan Museum, New York, and the Boston
Museum of Fine Arts. Wedgwood have produced two
copies of bowls based on engravings—*the Boston
Bowl* and the *Harvard Old Buildings Bowl*.

REVIVED ROCOCO See *Rococo, Revived*

RHEAD, CHARLOTTE (fl. 1930s)

English ceramic designer working for the most part in a kind of *art déco** style. Her decorations, principally floral, were also stylized to a variable extent. The elements of the design, outlined by an extremely thin line formed from trailed slip, was completed with bright underglaze and overglaze colours. She did a great deal of work for Crown Ducal potteries (A. C. Richardson & Co Ltd) and on Bursley ware (H. J. Wood Ltd, Burslem) where her mark, in script, is as follows:

> Bursley Ware
> Charlotte Rhead
> England

She also sometimes signed her work *C. Rhead* or *Charlotte Rhead*.

RHEAD, FREDERICK ALFRED (1856–1929)

Ceramic designer apprenticed to M.-L. Solon*. He studied at the Newcastle, Staffordshire School of Art, and modelled a vase in *pâte-sur-pâte** for Wedgwood* which was exhibited in the Paris Exposition of 1878. With Louis Jahn* and Alfred Brownfields he became concerned in the short-lived Brownfield's Pottery Guild, and was later art-director to Wileman & Co.* of Longton and Wood* & Sons of Burslem. With his brother, G. W. Rhead, he was joint author of *Staffordshire Pots and Potters*, 1906.

RHEAD, FREDERICK HURTEN (1880–1942)

Ceramic designer, born in England, who emigrated to America early in the 20th century. In 1902 he was working for Samuel Weller* in Zanesville, Ohio, and from 1904 to 1908 he was art-director of the Roseville Pottery*, designing a good deal of *Rozane* ware. Most of his designs made use of stylized versions of natural forms in underglaze colours, with incised decoration and applied reliefs. He was also a contributor to the magazine, *Keramic Studio*.

RHEINISCHES GLASHÜTTEN, KÖLN-EHRENFELD

This glasshouse, founded in 1864, specialized in reproductions of old glass, such as Roman glass, medieval and Renaissance glass, and German enamelled glass of the 17th century, especially collectors' prizes, like the *Reichsadlerhumpen* (Imperial eagle tankard) decorated with the Arms of the Holy Roman Empire and the Electors. *Waldglas*, a Rhineland traditional glass, was also reproduced. No doubt, as with the production of Fleischmann of Nürnberg and Heckert* of Petersdorf, some of these things were passed off at the time on unsuspecting tourists as genuinely old, but none of them is likely to deceive anyone knowing the characteristics of old German glass.

This glasshouse achieved an excellent reputation at the turn of the century for iridescent glass in the *art nouveau** style.

RHINELAND STONEWARE

German salt-glazed stoneware* made at several centres in the Rhineland in the 16th and 17th centuries. Deceptive reproductions of the white stoneware tankards and spouted jugs of Siegburg, in clay from the original source and probably, in some cases, formed in old moulds, were made early in the 19th century when these things enjoyed a limited demand among collectors of the time. By far the greatest number of copies, reproductions and wares inspired by 16th- and 17th-century work however, were based on the grey stonewares of Raeren and Westerwald, which were decorated in relief picked out in blue or, more rarely, manganese purple. Many of these wares were made by Merkelbach & Wick* of Grenzhausen and Villeroy & Boch* of Mettlach, but a factory mark is a distinct rarity, although most examples have a serial number impressed into the base. The later reproductions nearly always have a footring slightly recessed within, whereas the old pots have a flat base. These wares are still being made today for sale to tourists.

RHEINISCHES GLASHÜTTEN. A selection of 19th-century reproductions of 16th- and 17th-century German enamelled glass. Second from the left, a *Reichsadlerhumpen* (Imperial eagle tankard) purporting to be about 1590. Probably Rheinisches Glashütten, but similar reproductions came from Fleischmann of Nürnberg. Third quarter of the 19th century. *Sotheby & Co*

'RHODIAN' POTTERY   See *Isnik pottery*

RICE, HARRIS & SONS (Birmingham, Warwickshire)

Founders of an enterprise known as the Islington Glass Works in 1848. The factory specialized in the manufacture of decorative glass in great variety—pressed glass*, opaline glass*, glass in a number of colours, threaded* glass, *millefiori* paperweights*, and other popular types. Paperweights sometimes bear the initials *IGW* and were probably first made in 1849.

RICHARDSON & SONS, STOURBRIDGE (Worcestershire)

English glass-makers established in the 1840s who supplied glass decorated with enamelled flowers to Summerly's* Art Manufacture between 1847 and 1857. Thomas Bott* joined the firm in 1846 and perhaps worked on orders from 'Summerly'. Richardson's, who exhibited at the Great Exhibition in 1851, were among the first in England to make pressed glass*. They produced good quality opaline* and a certain amount of glass decorated by etching. In the 1860s they were responsible for a glass-threading machine, which enabled glass threads to be applied as decoration accurately and expeditiously. In the 1880s they manufactured a type of glass known as Rusticana*, first introduced in Birmingham, which was based on tree-trunks and branches and a variety of foliate forms. In the 1890s George Woodall made engraved and cameo glass*. The firm's founder was Benjamin Richardson, who offered a prize of £1,000

RICHARDSON & SONS, STOURBRIDGE. A pair of clear glass vases enamelled in the so-called Etruscan style, the firm of Henry Richardson & Sons at this time being styled Webb & Richardson. c. 1855. *Victoria & Albert Museum, London*

in 1860 for the best reproduction of the Portland Vase* in glass. The prize was won by John Northwood* in 1876.

RIDGWAY & SONS, JOB (Shelton and Hanley, Staffordshire)

Job Ridgway built the Cauldon Place Works, Shelton, in 1802. It manufactured pottery, porcelain, and stone china and produced some very successful blue printed earthenware. From 1814 to 1830 the factory was in the hands of Job Ridgway's two sons, John and William, but in 1830 John took Cauldon Place and William removed to a factory at Bell Bank, Hanley. Cauldon Place porcelain was of very good quality, well painted, often with coloured grounds, and gilding. Table-services were a speciality, and some were executed for members of the Royal family. Stone china was made in large quantities, and the factory also made a kind of basaltes* and jasper*, the latter being particularly successful. Ridgway's also interested themselves in photolithographic processes of decoration.

Ridgway's were taken over in 1839 by Brown, Westhead, Moore & Co.* and the business continued to expand.

See *Lithographic decoration on ceramics*

RIEMERSCHMID, RICHARD (1868–1957)

Talented German architect and designer, born in Munich and a student at the Academy there. He helped to found the Vereinigte Werkstätte in 1897, and designed the Salle Riemerschmid at the Paris Exposition of 1900. He was Director of the Munich School of Applied Art in 1912, and Director of the Cologne Werkschule in 1926.

His early work was in the *Jugendstil**, but later designs are more remarkable for geometric and linear emphasis. For the Deutscher Werkstätten he designed furniture for machine production. Silver ware in a functional* style is in the Landesgewerbe Museum, Stuttgart. He designed stoneware for Merkelbach & Wick* and porcelain for Meissen*.

RICHARDSON & SONS, STOURBRIDGE. Goblet enamelled with flowers from Richardson & Sons*, Worcestershire. 1845–50. *Pilkington Glass Museum*

RISCHGITZ, EDWARD. Tazza painted with a wolf disguised as a shepherd, in a style influenced by that of Lessore*. Minton*. c. 1865. *Victoria & Albert Museum, London*

ROBINSON, GERRARD. Pair of knights in 16th-century armour, carved in oak by Gerrard Robinson*. Newcastle-on-Tyne, Northumberland. c. 1860

RISCHGITZ, EDWARD (1828–1909)
French ceramic painter who worked at Minton* (c. 1864–1870) and painted in the style of Lessore*. Some of his work was signed. His subjects were principally figures and landscapes, and he worked on porcelain and earthenware.

RISTORI, TITO (Marzy, near Nevers)
Ristori, an Italian from Pisa, established a pottery at Marzy, where he made tin-enamelled wares inspired by the 16th-century *faïence** of the region. He exhibited work of this kind at the Paris Exposition of 1855.

ROASTING-JACKS   See *Clock-jacks*

ROBERTSON, HUGH CORNWALL (1844–1908)
Pottery chemist at the Chelsea Keramic Art Works*, where he developed the *sang-de-boeuf** glaze, and also experimented with the crackled glaze later used at the Dedham Pottery*. Mark: *HCR* in the form of a monogram.

ROBINS & RANDALL   See *Randall T. M.*

ROBINSON, GERRARD (1834–1891)
The son of a blacksmith of Newcastle-upon-Tyne, Northumberland, who, at his death, was termed foremost among English woodcarvers of his day. Although this may have been an exaggeration, it was not excessively so. Robinson's skill as a craftsman far outran his talent as an artist and he is remembered today for a series of highly-carved sideboards with pictorial themes which told a story, in line with the contemporary vogue in painting and sculpture.

The *Chevy Chase* sideboard, 12 feet wide, was finished in 1863, and now reposes in an hotel in Shaftesbury, Dorset. It is carved in minute detail illustrating the medieval border ballad of the Chevy Chase, which is concerned with episodes from the history of the Percy family, the Dukes of Northumberland. Robinson successfully exhibited in London

in 1862. One of his carvings was of Robinson Crusoe, a theme he again took up in 1872 when he completed the *Robinson Crusoe* sideboard which is now in the Victoria and Albert Museum, London. A sideboard carved with scenes from Shakespeare was also exhibited in 1862, and he again returned to this theme in 1890, just before his death, when he carved a large dining-table with Shakespearian figures. Robinson's output was prolific, and his work includes panels, lecterns, chimney-pieces and a variety of similar objects.

ROBINSON, GERRARD. Oak sideboard designed and carved by Gerrard Robinson* in a pseudo-Renaissance style, the doors carved with trophies, the grotesque figures at the angles reminiscent of bronze figures by Peter Visscher on the tomb of Saint Sebaldus at Nürnberg. c. 1870. *Victoria & Albert Museum, London*

ROBINSON & LEADBETTER, Stoke-on-Trent, Staffordshire

Pottery at Glebe Street operated from 1856 by James Robinson and Edward James Leadbetter, who also acquired the Wharf Street Works in 1870. Although they produced tableware, vases, centrepieces, etc. in large quantities, they were especially noted for fine quality Parian* figures, usually with the impressed mark *R & L* on the back. Their Parian figures include mythological and religious subjects, and portrait busts of well-known personalities of the day. The firm closed in 1924.

ROCAILLE (French)

Usual French term for the style known in England as rococo*.

ROCHE, PIERRE (1855–1922)

French sculptor and potter, a pupil of Jules Dalou*, awarded a silver medal at the Paris Universal Exhibition of 1900. He executed figures of Loïe Fuller*, the American scarf dancer, in bronze.

ROCK-CRYSTAL ENGRAVING

Term sometimes applied to glass engraving in the *Hochschnitt** or high-relief style in imitation of Renaissance rock-crystal carving. The best known exponents in England were the Bohemian engravers Friedrich Kny* and Wilhelm Fritsche*.

ROCKINGHAM (Swinton, Yorkshire)

This earthenware and porcelain factory was first established about 1750. In the early years of the 19th century it was connected with the Leeds Pottery*, and its wares cannot be distinguished with certainty. In 1806, however, the factory was acquired by William Brameld and when he died in 1813 it passed to his three sons. They made earthenware of all kinds, but especially wares covered with the so-called Rockingham glaze*, a thick lustrous brown glaze coloured with manganese, which was often used to cover the Cadogan teapot*, then newly introduced. Other earthenware included creamware* in the manner of Leeds, and marbled and tortoiseshell glazes—survivals from the 18th century and stonewares* such as black basaltes*. Rockingham first began to make bone china in 1820, but in 1826 they were in financial difficulties and became bankrupt. They appealed to Earl Fitzwilliam, who gave them financial assistance, and the right to use his crest, the griffin *passant*, as a mark. This occurs in conjunction with the words: Rockingham Works, Brameld. The mark, Brameld, alone is also found.

Rockingham porcelain is noted for extremely skilled workmanship, and many small pieces are decorated with delicately modelled applied flowers. Gilding is usually lavish in accordance with the taste of the time, and the painting is sometimes reminiscent of Derby*, no doubt because some Derby artists were employed. Subjects include landscapes, figures, fruit, flowers and butterflies. An important service of 1832 made for William IV was decorated with views of castles and country seats.

Ground colours are usually pale, and one or two are more or less peculiar to the factory. Rockingham made a small number of biscuit* figures, sometimes on glazed and painted bases. It is very hard to believe that a factory capable of producing the decorative porcelain services customarily connected with it could also produce anything so hideous as the huge, grossly overdecorated 'Rhinoceros' vase in the Victoria and Albert Museum, London, so called from the figure of a rhinoceros surmounting the cover.

The factory undoubtedly produced a large quantity of well-decorated china, principally in the revived rococo style which has been sought by collectors for the best part of a century. A great deal of unmarked porcelain similar in style, but probably made at Coalport*, was once sold as Rockingham, and a saying in the trade ran, 'When you buy it, it's Coalport; when you sell it, it's Rockingham'. Many collectors today refuse to accept as Rockingham any but marked pieces, which is the best way of being certain but likely to lead to much smaller collections.

ROCKINGHAM GLAZE (American)

Ware made from buff coloured clay covered with a thick, dark brown, often mottled glaze, which has manganese oxide as the principal colouring agent. It was first made at an East Liverpool, Ohio, pottery in 1839 by an immigrant English potter, James Bennett*. Notable ware of this kind was produced at the Bennington Pottery, and it was later made at many other factories.

ROCKINGHAM GLAZE (English)

A thick purplish-brown lead glaze, coloured with manganese oxide, made at the Rockingham* factory at Swinton, Yorkshire, and in Staffordshire by Thomas Sharpe* and others.

ROCOCO, EDWARDIAN

There was a second revival of the rococo* style at the end of the 19th century which was associated with King Edward VII, and lasted until the First World War. The most famous example of decoration in this style is to be found in London's Ritz Hotel, the interior of which is largely in a very attractive revived rococo style, while the impressive exterior is based on the arcades of the rue de Rivoli in Paris. The Ritz was built in the early years of the present century and has now been carefully restored.

Gilt screens with carved crestings of C & S scrolls* made their appearance, and furniture based on the Louis XV period in France was manufactured. Except in attempts to reproduce the interiors of former times, often undertaken when surroundings of unusual luxury are required for such buildings as embassies, the rococo style largely disappeared with the First World War but copies and derivations are still fashionable.

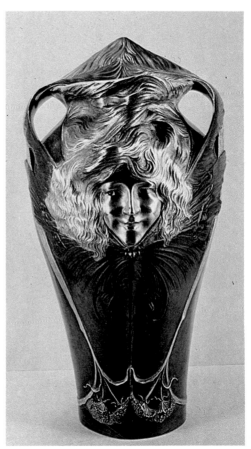

WEBB, THOMAS & SONS. Vase of crystal glass decorated with *champlevé* enamels, that is, enamels contained within recesses indented into the surface. Thomas Webb & Sons Ltd., Stourbridge, Mid-1970s. *Private Collection*

ART NOUVEAU. Vase in bronze, parcel-gilt, by P. P. Berthou, French. c. 1900. *Brighton Art Gallery & Museum*

Above:
SLAG GLASS. A selection of slag-glass, most of it bearing Sowerby's peacock mark, showing the principal colours available. Gateshead, Co. Durham. Last quarter of the 19th century. *Mary Stubbley*

Below:
LES ANIMALIERS. Figure of a dog cast in bronze by the Coalbrookdale Foundry. c. 1850. *Ironbridge Gorge Museum Trust*

ROCOCO, REVIVED. Continental silver snuff-box which clearly shows the type of asymmetrical scrollwork associated with the 19th-century version of the rococo style. *Constance Chiswell*

ROCOCO, REVIVED

The rococo style was current in France from about 1725 to the death of Louis XV in 1774. It was especially associated with the King and Mme de Pompadour, and it is often called the style Louis Quinze or the style Pompadour in that country. One of its most characteristic features is asymmetricality, and this is hardly to be seen before the death of Louis XIV in 1715, because symmetry was one of the guiding passions of his life. Other features of rococo are C and S scrolls*, so arranged as to be asymmetrical; a profusion of flowers; water, and subjects connected with it, such as shells, crayfish, corals, and water-weed; cabriole legs in furniture; wood-panelling (*boiseries*) in rooms with mouldings which rise higher at one side of a rectangular panel than the other; and asymmetrically-designed gilt-bronze mounts on furniture. In England the style was relatively short-lived. It was represented by the early porcelain of Chelsea, Bow, and Derby, the silver of such makers as Paul de Lamerie and Nicholas Sprimont, and the furniture, the mirrors especially, of Thomas Chippendale. By 1770 it had become unfashionable, although isolated objects made later in the century (some of Wedgwood's creamware vases based on Sèvres porcelain prototypes, for instance) could properly be classified as rococo.

Soon after 1820 a revival of the style took place. It began a little earlier than this in silver, represented mainly by occasional examples from Rundell, Bridge & Rundell, who had carried on a very profitable trade in French rococo silver with *emigrés* during the Revolution. About the same time it was taken up again by the porcelain factories, with whom it had always been popular, and who disliked the neo-classical style. It had little effect on furniture until the accession of Victoria in 1837, when drawing-room chairs with cabriole legs and balloon backs were popular. The style was fairly well represented at the Great Exhibition of 1851, when Leistler* of Vienna, among others, exhibited highly-carved Gothic and rococo furniture, and thenceforward it was variably popular throughout the century. For a brief period it returned to favour in England during the reign of Edward VII in a version often known as Edwardian rococo*. Decorative mirrors in asymmetrical gilt-wood frames, draught-screens, and easels for pictures

ROCOCO, REVIVED. Folding card-table in an early version of revived rococo*. c. 1840. *Antique Collectors' Club*

and photographs of the same material, belong to this period, and one of the most notable examples of the use of the style for interior decoration is to be found in the Ritz Hotel, Piccadilly, W. London.

In America, where the style was also popular during the 19th century, rococo furniture was produced by men like C. Baudoine* and John Belter*. It is often known as the French modern style, but in some of its aspects it borrowed freely from Louis XIV and Louis XVI, which gave rise to the boast of one maker that his furniture was in the style of 'all the

ROCOCO, REVIVED. *Papier mâché* sofa in the French style* painted with flowers and inlaid with mother-of-pearl. English. c. 1845. *Victoria & Albert Museum, London*

Louis's'. One version became popular in the Deep South, and is often called New Orleans rococo. Like Gothic, it was employed in the decoration of the plushier saloons of Mississippi steamboats in their hey-day, before the Civil War.

RODIN, AUGUSTE (1840–1917)

French sculptor who studied under Barye*. Rodin began by working in a plasterer's workshop cleaning up casts, and he then took employment in a commercial sculptor's studio operated by Carrier-Belleuse*, through whom he came to supply models

RODIN, AUGUSTE. *Study for the head of Balzac*, a bronze by Auguste Rodin. c. 1891. *Victoria & Albert Museum, London*

RODIN, AUGUSTE. *Cupid and Psyche*. Marble carving by Auguste Rodin*. c. 1908. *Victoria & Albert Museum, London*

RODIN, AUGUSTE. *Despair* in plaster, by Auguste Rodin*. Inscribed to M. Phillips, in 'amitié et homage'. c. 1890. *Victoria & Albert Museum, London*

for the Sèvres* porcelain factory. Edmond Tarquet, Under-Secretary of State for the Fine Arts, enabled Rodin to devote himself to sculpture by commissioning a bronze door for the École des Arts Décoratifs. This had as its subject the Gate of Hell, intended as the antithesis of Ghiberti's Gate of Paradise, and it was based on Dante's *Inferno*. Many of the subjects from this door, like *The Thinker*, *Le Baiser*, *La Belle Heaumière* (helmet-maker), etc., subsequently became independent works.

ROGERS, JOHN AND GEORGE (Dale Hall, near Burslem, Staffordshire)

Makers of creamware* and blue transfer-printed* ware, much of the latter for the American trade. The brothers continued in partnership until the death of George Rogers in 1815, when the firm became John Rogers & Son. John Rogers died in 1816, but the son continued the firm until 1842.

Although the factory was established in 1780, the making of blue printed ware, the variety most sought, did not start until about 1810, and it was on a very large scale, with a wide range of patterns and shapes. There is space only briefly to refer to some of the principal patterns. The Boston State House, of course, was especially for export to the United States. Popular topographical prints include a Country House series and other views; contemporary fashion was catered for by a Gothic pattern and one of Abbey ruins, while romantic ruins in the classical style were the subject of the Tivoli and Athens patterns. A series of animal patterns included those containing a zebra, an elephant, and a camel, and the Drama Series illustrated scenes from popular plays. They also produced such sentimental subjects as *The Adopted Child*. The usual mark was ROGERS impressed.

ROGERS GROUPS

American plaster groups of figures to designs patented by John Rogers and very popular between 1859 and 1893. The subjects were usually drawn from the Civil War, domestic life and popular legend. Large numbers of these parlour ornaments are preserved by the New York Historical Society.

ROMANESQUE STYLE

1) Architectural style, characterized by the use of the round-headed arch, which preceded the introduction of Gothic late in the 11th century.

2) Name given to a furniture style of the 1880s developed by the American designer H. H. Richardson, and made in New England. The term is a misnomer. The style was a kind of medieval English decorated with one or two carved *motifs* of classical derivation, such as the acanthus*.

ROMANTICISM

Romanticism is the opposite of classicism. Romantic art is art charged with emotion, classical art is restrained by rule and precept. The romantic artist is largely driven by his moods, the classical artist is governed by reason. The romantic is guided by his feelings about his subject, the classicist works within a framework of accepted rules. These two ways of thinking about art have always existed to a variable degree which has depended largely on the social factors of the time, but classicism has been the mainstream of European art and culture for at least 2,500 years, and the romantic attitude has made its appearance sporadically. For instance, both Hellenistic and Gothic art are romantic styles. The second played a considerable part in 18th- and 19th-century romanticism.

It might be argued that the rococo style of Louis XV and the neo-classicism* of Louis XVI were to some extent romantic styles. Rococo diverged from the classical style by neglecting the age-old principle of symmetry and neo-classicism was accompanied by many romantic undertones. Stylistically a porcelain group might be impeccably classical, but its subject, 'Charlotte weeping at the tomb of Werther', vapidly romantic. The neo-classical style was a revival of earlier classicism inspired by excavations at Pompeii and Herculaneum, and without these discoveries it is a little difficult to envisage what direction European styles might have taken.

Another and important aspect of 18th-century art, which was a direct cause of an increasingly romantic outlook, was the extensive import of Chinese art, and its influence on the decorative arts of the day. Perhaps the most important aspect of this influence was its effect on gardening. The old geometrically shaped and formally laid-out beds and walks of André le Nôtre, who created the grounds at Versailles, were exchanged during the 18th century for winding walks amid specially planted trees and coppices, summer houses masquerading as Greek temples, Roman ruins, Chinese pagodas, and Gothic ruins, artificial lakes and waterfalls, and all the appurtenances of the romantic garden. With few exceptions, features of this kind had formed part of Chinese gardening for centuries.

Equally significant is the popularity of painting by Claude Lorraine and Salvator Rosa in England during the 18th century. Landscaped gardens were laid out in the manner of paintings in their styles and were referred to as 'picturesque'. The word did not eventually acquire its present meaning of a landscape worthy to be painted until the early years of the 19th century.

Horace Walpole adapted a light-hearted version of the Gothic style for his house in Strawberry Hill, Twickenham. It was here that he wrote a romantic novel full of gloom and supernatural happenings, *The Castle of Otranto*, published in 1768. This began a fashion for similar novels by authors like Mrs Radcliffe and 'Monk' Lewis which went on into the early decades of the 19th century, gradually turning from supernatural horror to crime.

The poet Gray, who was a friend of Walpole, wrote the *Elegy in a Country Churchyard*. Death and churchyards exerted a peculiar fascination for a group which became known to a later, more irreverent, generation as the 'Graveyard Poets'. All this was going on at a time when Adam was designing his neo-classical houses and interiors, Wedgwood* was producing wares based on Greek pottery, and Matthew Boulton was making silver and Sheffield plate* which was similar in style.

In France there was no hint of the Gothic style. Not until 1825 did the Troubador style* emerge, probably inspired by the popularity of the novels of Sir Walter Scott. This never became really fashionable in the same way as neo-Gothic* style in England because it was never linked with religion and morality in the same way. Romanticism emerged in France in the 1770s with the paintings of Greuze, the sentimental approach of some of the Sèvres biscuit porcelain groups, and the preoccupation with ruins of such painters as Hubert Robert. The classical tradition was too strong for it to become very noticeable before the Revolution. Afterwards the victories and disasters of Napoleon and the preoccupation with military glory, paved the way for romantic history painting, but generally the Romantic school was far stronger in England and the States of Germany.

The classical vogue in Germany lasted until well into the 19th century, although its hold progressively diminished. German kings and princes had followed French fashions since the days of Louis XIV, and French remained the Court language until the fall of Napoleon. In the 1770s Meissen* produced some sentimental porcelain groups largely inspired by Sèvres* and executed by a French modeller, Michel-Victor Acier. In the 19th century, however, earlier and unsentimental figures were sentimentalized by minor alterations into the Dresden* shepherdesses of the Victorian mantelshelf. Goethe's best-selling novel, *The Sorrows of Young Werther*, was published in 1774 and translated into several European languages almost immediately. This exerted enormous influence on both the emerging Romantic movement and its readers to a point where men committed suicide with an open copy of the book beside them.

The decay of the Empire style* in Germany and the strong medieval tradition fostered the Romantic style in a country where, before the Second World War, almost every town could show good examples of Gothic architecture and 15th-century timber-framed houses. Today, even though museums like the Römisch-Germanisches Museum in Cologne have superb collections of classical antiquities found in the Rhineland, some of the most important of German museums, like the Germanisches Museum at Nuremberg, are fantastically rich in medieval works of art, while at Hildesheim the candlesticks of Bishop Bernward, which would be given pride of place in a national museum in any other country, are still used for their original purpose as altar-candlesticks.

The Romantic movement in Europe was largely responsible for the growth of interest in medieval works of art and the Gothic revival*, at its height between 1840 and 1860, but it took other paths when the public wearied of the 14th and 15th centuries. The vogue for things Japanese was Romantic in origin, and *art nouveau** for the most part has its roots in Japanese and Gothic art, even though these sources are not always easy to detect. The classical tradition, which had sustained and nourished art in Europe for over 2,000 years, and gained a firm hold in the United States during the 18th and part of the 19th centuries, became just another style. Its framework of rules which, without imposing any severe restraint on the artist's imagination, had prevented much bad art from seeing the light of day, was discredited. Henceforth there was to be no restraining influence. Anything might be regarded as art if its author could persuade others to think of it in that light.

Perhaps art suffered most in England from the development of photography. The English as art critics and patrons were handicapped by a Puritan heritage which had always regarded art and artists as, at best, slightly immoral. Photography was something which could be understood without much effort, and it was considered that painting especially was the more competent the more nearly it approached photographic verisimilitude. Under the influence of Pugin*, William Morris*, Ruskin* and others of similar views, Puritan ethical idealism led to an insistence that art, to be acceptable, must tell a story with a moral. To this austere doctrine the Victorians paid lip-service while indulging themselves clandestinely. This, perhaps, is the greatest social difference between England and its Continental neighbours. It explains the difference in the paths taken by the arts, and why England's only artistic contribution to the late 19th century was started by a Scotsman, A. H. Mackmurdo*, more or less ignored in England after the first year or two, and developed in France, Belgium, Austria and Germany. Only one further contribution of note to *art nouveau* came from the British isles, from Glasgow's Charles Rennie Mackintosh*, and his influence was almost entirely exerted in Europe.

ROOKWOOD POTTERY (Cincinnati, Ohio)
An important art-pottery established in 1880 by Mrs Marion Longworth (Nichols) Storer which began by producing good quality white and yellow domestic ware, as well as ware for sale to independent decorators. The principal product, art-pottery, was developed during the 1880s. It has points of resemblance with both stoneware* and semi-porcelain*, and was glazed and decorated in a variety of ways.

Laura Anne Fry (1857–1943) of the Women's Pottery Club (whose early incised decorations somewhat resemble the work of Hannah Barlow*) introduced the application of underglaze grounds with the aid of an atomizer, a forerunner of the aerograph*. She blended a number of colours, in conjunction with 'paintings' in coloured slip termed *barbotine**, a technique first introduced to the American public from France at the Philadelphia Centennial Exhibition of 1876. To this ware was presently added the use of tinted glazes and bodies. When the factory moved to new and larger premises in 1892 it employed new artists and greatly added to its decorative repertory. Its manager, William Watts Taylor, who became proprietor in 1900, was an astute salesman, and he introduced the practice of allowing only one retail outlet in each of the major cities.

The reputation of Rookwood products has increased with the passing of time and few museums possessing representative collections of ceramics are now without a specimen.
See *Cincinnati Pottery Club*

RÖRSTRAND (Stockholm)
Factory established in 1727 for the manufacture of *faïence**. For much of the 19th century it manufactured earthenware in the English style, the Rörstrand *flintporslin* being an imitation of Wedgwood's creamware*. It also made English bone china from the 1850s, often decorated in the Sèvres style, as well as imitations of Palissy* ware, ironstone china* and other popular 19th-century wares. In the 1870s the introduction of hard-paste porcelain* brought Rörstrand into line with other Continental factories. At the end of the century wares in the *art nouveau** style included modelled flowers painted in underglaze colours. Between the Wars the factory became noted for table-services in advanced, functionalist* designs.

Mark: Three crowns and the word, Rörstrand.
See *Arabia Osakeyhtio*

ROSE AMBERINA
Type of art glass* made by the Mount Washington Glass Works*. The colour is rose from gold chloride shading to amber.

ROSE DU BARRY
Ground colour on 19th-century porcelain, recalling the *rose Pompadour* of Sèvres invented in 1757 and

discontinued in 1764. The *rose du Barry* ground is pink in colour, but the 18th-century *rose Pompadour* was greatly superior to it in quality. No colour was connected with the name of Mme du Barry in the 18th century.

ROSE, JOHN (c. 1772–1841)
Brother of Thomas Rose* and founder of the Coalport Porcelain Factory*. Rose purchased the Caughley* factory in 1799, and his brother's factory in 1814. In 1822 he acquired the remaining stocks and moulds of Nantgarw* and Swansea. In 1820 he was awarded the 'Isis' gold medal of the Society of Arts for a leadless glaze, an improvement which had been sought in Staffordshire since the 1770s. Coalport commemorated this success with a special back-stamp.

Rose died in 1841, and the factory was continued by his nephew, William F. Rose, until his own death in 1864.

ROSE, THOMAS (fl. 1800–1814)
Brother of John Rose*, founder of the Coalport Porcelain Factory. Thomas Rose was a partner with William Reynolds and William Horton in the found-ing of a separate porcelain factory at Coalport in 1800. This made wares of excellent quality, especially the popular 'Japan' patterns. Reynolds died in 1803, and was replaced by Robert Anstice and in 1814 John Rose bought the factory and amalgamated the two undertakings.

ROSENTHAL & CO., PHILIP (Selb, Bavaria)
Porcelain factory founded in 1879 by Philip Rosenthal. It has since become noted for porcelain services of high quality, and it worked in both the *art nouveau** and *art déco** styles. Figures in the latter style are sometimes signed by the artist. The factory also owns a glass factory designed by Walther Gropius at Amberg, Bavaria (see *Bauhaus*).

Marks: a crown over two stylized roses with the signature, *Rosenthal*, beneath, or a crown over crossed batons and the letters *R* and *C*.

ROSEVILLE POTTERY (Zanesville, Ohio)
American pottery established at Roseville in 1892, and later removed to Zanesville. From about 1900 they made large quantities of art-pottery, especially a slip-painted, brilliantly glazed ware called 'Rozane'. Much of their work had a matt glaze over relief decorations and they also produced imitations of Rookwood Pottery*. The factory closed in 1954. Another factory owned by J. B. Owens*, and established at Roseville at a somewhat earlier date, also moved to Zanesville about 1891.

ROSEWOOD
Wood from trees of the species *Dalbergia* from India, Brazil, and the West Indies. This wood is coarse-grained and dark purplish-brown in colour, often with a well-marked figure. One variety has black veining and is termed blackwood. This was much used for furniture-making by the Chinese. In France rosewood is termed *pallisandre*, but one variety from Brazil was termed *bois violet* (violet wood), and early in the 19th century it became kingwood or *bois du roi*. The term 'kingwood' seems to have been English in origin.

The popularity of rosewood as a furniture wood began towards the end of the 18th century, but its greatest vogue was between 1837 and 1870, when it was used both in solid form and as a veneer. In America it was employed by John Belter* in lami-nated form for rococo ornament, and more recently for objects in the *art déco** style.

ROSSETTI, DANTE GABRIEL (1828–1882)
Poet and painter born in London of Italian origin. From 1842 to 1848 he studied at the Royal Academy Schools, and with Holman Hunt, Millais, Madox Brown and others, he formed the pre-Raphaelite Brotherhood*. In 1861 he became a founder-member of Morris, Marshall, Faulkner & Co.*, designing stained glass and tiles. He withdrew from the company in 1874 and ended his life as a recluse and an invalid.

ROSSO ANTICO (Latin)
Literally, ancient red. Name given to a brick-red stoneware* introduced by Josiah Wedgwood*, and used for the manufacture of wares of classical form often decorated with black relief work. The type was developed from the early 18th-century red-ware of the Elers brothers. During the 19th century it was sometimes decorated with opaque enamel colours.

ROUCHOMOWSKY, ISAAC (fl. 1900–1905)
Russian goldsmith working in Odessa. Maker of the tiara of Saitaphernes, a gold crown purporting to

ROSSO ANTICO. Small beaker in rosso antico painted in opaque enamels with flowers in the Chinese style. Impressed mark: Josiah Wedgwood & Sons, Etruria. First quarter of the 19th century. *Constance Chiswell*

have belonged to the Scythian Kings. It was offered to the Louvre with the spurious history of having been excavated at Olbia on the Black Sea coast, and purported to belong to the third–second century BC. Its purchase by the Louvre in 1903 led to violent controversy, and when the truth became known Rouchomowsky journeyed to Paris, where he was at first hailed as the greatest goldsmith since Cellini*, and then stigmatized as a forger and a criminal. He returned to Russia and disappeared into obscurity.

ROUSE, JAMES (1802–1888)
Porcelain painter, who was apprenticed at the Derby* factory, and then went on to Coalport* where his work included porcelain plaques. A signed plaque from Davenport* has also been identified. In the 1860s he was working for Ridgway* at Cauldon Place, and returned to Derby in 1875.

ROUSSEAU, EUGÈNE (fl. c. 1875 onwards)
French glass-designer whose designs were executed by Appert Frères of Saint-Denis, Paris. Rousseau was one of the first glass-makers to be influenced by the fashion for Japanese art and his work was much praised at the Paris Exposition of 1878. He also made some rare pieces inspired by Renaissance pottery; for example, one in the form of a 16th-century Rhineland stoneware* jug. He was succeeded by E. Leveillé in 1885.

ROYAL BRONZE FOUNDRY (Munich)
This foundry, under the direction of Ferdinand Müller, was especially noted for its skill in casting large objects. The bronze doors of the Capitol, Washington, D.C., were cast here. The same foundry cast the colossal statue of *Bavaria* in Munich by the sculptor Ludwig Schwanthaler*, which is 98 feet in height, including the pedestal. Müller displayed bronze lions at the Great Exhibition which were nine feet high and 15 feet long. They were remarkable for the fact that they needed no work on them after casting. Statues of a King and Queen of Bohemia by Schwanthaler were also displayed, and the same exhibition showed, among porcelain from the Munich factory of Nymphenburg, small porcelain figures modelled by him.

ROYAL COPENHAGEN PORCELAIN FACTORY
Porcelain factory founded in 1775 under the patronage of the Royal family. The factory, its fortunes at low ebb, was bought by the Aluminia Faience Factory of Copenhagen in 1882, and moved to Aluminia works in 1884. Philip Schon (1838–1922), part-owner of Aluminia, was director, and Arnold Krog (1856–1931), architect and designer, became art-director from 1885. He specialized in painting underglaze, for which the factory received a Grand Prix at the Paris Exposition of 1889. He also painted in coloured slips, achieving an effect of low relief—a technique related

ROYAL COPENHAGEN PORCELAIN. Sauce-boat designed for Royal Copenhagen Porcelain factory* by O. H. B. Olrik, with violet ground and gilt borders. 1868. *Danish National Museum, Copenhagen*

ROYAL COPENHAGEN PORCELAIN. Vase decorated in underglaze blue by Arnold Krog, for the Royal Copenhagen Porcelain Factory*. 1886. *Danish Museum of Decorative Art, Copenhagen*

to *pâte-sur-pâte*. He designed a popular range of simply modelled figures which could be slip-cast without difficulty.

The factory began to develop glazes of an Oriental type in the 1890s, starting with *sang-de-boeuf** and celadon*. After the First World War glazes inspired by those of the Sung dynasty (960–1280) were produced successfully. Apparently methods similar to those employed by the Chinese were used, since the same 'brown mouth and iron foot' was achieved on some examples as characterize the original wares. The appearance of these glazes from Copenhagen coincided with the popularity of Sung dynasty stonewares among collectors.

In the 1920s the Danish sculptor Arons Malinowski

ROYAL COPENHAGEN PORCELAIN. Royal Copenhagen Porcelain plate, painted by A. J. F. Wolff in the French style. *Landsmuseum, Schleswig*

modelled biscuit figures for the factory. The Swedish sculptor Gerhard Henning, also provided models.

The usual factory mark is a series of three wavy lines, one above the other. Sometimes a crown is added, and the words *Royal Copenhagen* also occur.

ROYAL CROWN DERBY PORCELAIN COMPANY, THE (Osmaston Road, Derby)

The Crown Derby Porcelain Company was founded in 1875 by Edward Phillips and William Litherland, who had been connected with the incorporation of the Royal Worcester Company in 1863, and decided to leave Worcester for Derby. By 1877, 400 hands were being employed in the making of porcelain, Parian, and stoneware. In addition to services, figures, groups, and busts were being made in large quantities, and the factory were already specializing in decorative vases. Some of the figures were repetitions of the earlier work of the Derby* factory, such as the 18th-century Mansion House dwarfs and the early 19th-century Dr Syntax. No doubt this is an important reason why a connection between the two factories is often implied, but no such connection ever existed.

The factory began to produce lavishly decorated wares, replete with rich ground colours and raised gilding, the latter a speciality which, even in the 1880s, brought them many Transatlantic orders. Raised gilding was executed by building up the pattern or design by painting in a paste made from enamel powder, somewhat in the manner that slips were used in the *pâte-sur-pâte* process. The object was put into the enamelling kiln, and the hardened, raised, design then gilded over. About the same time they began to produce patterns based on 'Persian' and 'Rhodian' (Isnik) prototypes, in which they were encouraged by the South Kensington Museum who ordered reproductions of objects in their possession.

The prefix 'Royal' and the use of the Royal Arms, was granted by Queen Victoria in 1890. In the same year the painter, Désiré Leroy*, was engaged by the factory. He came from Sèvres, and his enamel painting on a cobalt blue ground was reminiscent of *pâte-sur-pâte*.

About this time, also, attention was concentrated on the manufacture of 'Japan' patterns, of which the best known and most sought is probably No. 1128. These patterns have been much imitated elsewhere, but those made at Derby always bear the factory mark. Decorated with Japan patterns, including 1128, are the miniature pieces made in a considerable variety of shapes and introduced in 1904. These are now much sought.

The firm had by this time recruited a team of painters of skill and talent able to produce work to appeal to the market for high quality wares. Nevertheless, the number of skilled painters was insufficient to fill all the orders in hand, and, like other factories at the time, resort was had to outline transfer-printing to enable less skilled labour to be used.

Derby continued to produce good quality figures. In the 1880s a popular series had been based on characters from the works of Dickens and other literary sources, both in glazed porcelain and Parian*, and many of these were reissued in the 1920s and 1930s, as well as new and original models by M. R. Locke and Tom Wilkinson. After the Second World War a Latvian modeller, Arnold Mikelson, modelled a popular series of birds and animals. Parian figures from Derby are very rare, and it seems that few were made.

Crown earthenware was produced from the factory's inception to the outbreak of the First World War. For the most part it was employed for dinner-services and decorated by transfer-printing. One or two rare plaques more elaborately decorated suggest that it may have had other uses.

In 1935 the factory bought the King Street enterprise of Sampson Hancock* thus linking it with the old Duesbury tradition.

The usual mark is a printed crown over a monogram formed from two opposed letter *D*'s (somewhat in the manner of the Sèvres monogram) with the addition, from 1890, of the words *Royal Crown Derby*, and, after 1891, *Made in England*. The impressed mark *Derby* also occurs. From 1890 to 1937 the year of manufacture is given by a variety of symbols, one for each year. From 1938 the year is indicated by Roman numerals, starting with I.

There is an excellent museum of Derby porcelain at Osmaston Road which is open to the public.

ROYAL DUTCH GLASS WORKS (Leerdam, Nr Rotterdam)

The Koninklijke Nederlandsche Glasfabrik. Dutch glasshouse founded in the middle of the 18th century which, during the 19th century, predominantly followed French and German fashions, including *art nouveau**. In the 1920s the factory made a good deal of well-designed *art déco** glass. The designers, C. Lebeau* and A. D. Copier*, introduced a very important range of glasses under the trade names of *Serica* and *Unica* which were especially produced, without much regard for cost, for wealthy collectors and museums.

Frank Lloyd Wright, the American architect, also contributed designs to the factory. The enterprise is now incorporated in the Verenidge Glasfabriken Holland. Its more important products are usually signed or initialled by the artist.

ROYAL DUX PORCELAIN See *Duxer Porzellanmanufaktur*

ROYAL FLEMISH GLASS
Type of art glass* made by the Mount Washington Glass Works* decorated with thin surface staining and raised gilding.

ROYAL PAVILION (Brighton, Sussex)
This remarkable early 19th-century essay in the Oriental taste (it is Indian outside and Chinese within) grew from the Marine pavilion designed for the Prince Regent by Henry Holland and finished in 1797, which forms part of the present building. The style was then neo-classical* which was favoured by Holland, and it is probable that the furniture was predominantly French—a type much to the taste of the Prince, whose purchases at post-Revolutionary sales formed the nucleus of the present Royal collections. During the Revolution many *emigrés* of distinction were entertained by the Prince at the Marine Pavilion.

The rise of Napoleon I, however, made it difficult for the Prince to indulge his taste for imported French decoration, and in 1802 a Chinese gallery was added. During the middle years of the 18th century ornament in the Chinese manner had been extremely popular, although a more exact term would be *chinoiserie* because very little of it had been exactly copied from

ROYAL PAVILION, BRIGHTON. Wall-painting in the Chinese manner from the Banqueting Room of the Royal Pavilion, Brighton. c. 1810. *Author*

its source. One designer of the period boasted that English Chinese ornament was 'of our own invention'. Like Walpole's neo-Gothic, the mid-18th-century 'Chinese' style became unfashionable with the advent of Adam's neo-classicism*, but at the end of the century the Prince had commissioned a Chinese Room at his London residence, Carlton House, and from 1802 onwards the Pavilion at Brighton was increasingly decorated in this style. The style employed for the Pavilion had little in common with the earlier 'Chinese' styles, and in many ways it was less fantastic and more faithful to its source of inspiration.

At the beginning of the 18th century a new influence, that of India, began to emerge. In 1785 William Daniell R.A., accompanied by his nephew,

ROYAL PAVILION, BRIGHTON. 'Indian outside, Chinese inside.' An exterior view of the Royal Pavilion*, Brighton. *Author*

William, went to India, and in the following ten years or so made numerous topographical drawings there. His work was drawn upon by the architect Samuel Pepys Cockerell, in the design of a house at Sezincote, Gloucestershire, in the Indian style for a retired East India Company official. William Porden, who succeeded Henry Holland as the Prince's architect, had worked with Cockerell, and his Royal stables were the beginning of the Pavilion's Indian phase. The alteration of the rest of the building, however, was delayed by lack of funds until 1815, when the work was entrusted to the Surveyor-General, John Nash. The Banqueting Room, the Music Room and new State Apartments date from 1818, and the interior decoration was finished probably in 1821.

There can be little doubt that the Pavilion is the most remarkable example of decoration in the Chinese taste in the Western World. The style of some of the ornament belongs to the Yuan and Manchu dynasties, rather than the 18th century, and some of the more splendid interior architectural features are reminiscent of Marco Polo's description of the palace of Kublai Khan. The Prince's taste for magnificent chandeliers* can be seen in all the Pavilion's important rooms. The great chandelier in the Banqueting Room, designed by Robert Jones,

ROYAL PAVILION, BRIGHTON. The Banqueting Room of the Royal Pavilion, Brighton, with appointments of the period. It is notable for its chandeliers, an ornamental feature of which the Prince Regent was extremely fond. *Author*

weighs nearly a ton and cost almost £6,000 (probably equivalent to £150,000 today). The chandeliers of the Music Room, also by Jones, were made by Perry of London, who also supplied the pendant lustres* to Buckingham Palace.

The Pavilion was purchased from the Crown by Brighton Corporation in 1850. Most of the furniture and fittings are original and in a number of cases where wall-paintings were subsequently covered up in one way or another, they have been restored as far as possible to the original condition. The Pavilion had a limited influence on the arts of its period, but this did not extend beyond the reign of William IV. Queen Victoria disliked the Pavilion and readily agreed to its sale. It failed to catch the imagination of its time. Hazlitt called it a collection of 'stone pumpkins and pepperpots'. After the completion of the Pavilion there were no more essays in the Chinese taste on any considerable scale, and the style was limited to the decoration of blue printed earthenware, *papier mâché* and Pontypool ware*.

ROYAL WORCESTER PORCELAIN See *Worcester Royal Porcelain Company*

ROYCROFT SHOPS

Outlets founded in 1895 for the work of craftsmen (known as Roycrofters) who were influenced by Elbert Hubbard* and the Arts and Crafts Movement* of which they were more or less the American equivalent. They made furniture, textiles, pottery, and metalwork. The handmade furniture included work in the Mission* style and an American version of the 'Morris' chair*.

ROZANE

A trade name employed by the Roseville Pottery Company, founded in Roseville in 1892 and transferred to Zanesville (Ohio) in 1900. Rozane pottery was decorated in light coloured slip over a dark ground, and was often marked *RP Co.*

ROZENBURG (The Hague, Holland)

Factory, established in 1885 by the Freiherr von Gudenberg, which specialized in an extremely thin, translucent ware, known as 'eggshell', which was painted with designs inspired by Javanese batik-printed textiles. Vase-shapes are unusual in being designed with partly flat and partly curved surfaces (i.e. circular section at the top, square section below). The floral decoration, generally, is markedly *art nouveau** in style. Later, styles became more conventional. The art-directors were T. Colenbrander (1885–1889) and J. Juriaan Kok (1894–1913). The latter designed many of the vases. J. Schellink was employed as a painter. The factory closed in 1914. An attempt to revive it as the Neuw Rosenburg in 1919 was unsuccessful, and the factory closed finally four years later. Painted mark: *ROZENBURG, DEN HAAG.*

RUBELLES. Flower-pot stand of earthenware* decorated in the *émail ombrant** technique with the subject of two men in a cellar. c. 1851. *Victoria & Albert Museum, London*

RUBELLES (Mélun, Seine-et-Marne)

Factory for the manufacture of *faïence-fine** founded by the Baron A. du Tremblay some time before 1844. In this year he invented the *émail ombrant** process which was later employed by other factories. The Rubelles factory made a speciality of small tureens in the form of globe artichokes, bundles of asparagus, melons, and so forth based on the rococo tureens popular at Meissen* and Chelsea in the 1750s. The Baron sold his interest in the factory in 1855, and wares made until this date were sometimes marked *ADT*. The factory closed finally in 1876.

RUDIER, ALEXIS (Paris)

Bronze-founder who cast figures for Jules Dalou*, Auguste Rodin*, Antoine Bourdelle, Aristide Maillol, etc. Impressed mark: *ALEXIS RUDIER, FONDEUR, PARIS.*

RUDOLPHI, F. J. (fl. mid-19th cent.)

Parisian maker of *objets d'art*, including jewellery, in silver, gold, precious and semi-precious stones and enamels. Rudolphi sent a very comprehensive selection of work to the Great Exhibition of 1851, and representative purchases of his work were made by the Department of Art in Paris in 1855. These are now displayed at the Bethnal Green Museum, London. In 1855 Rudolphi was a large exhibitor, principally of works in lapis lazuli and oxidized silver, turquoise, and ivory mounted in silver, and bloodstones and lapis in combination. A tankard of carved ivory encrusted with turquoise was purchased by the Kensington Department of Art.

RUHLMANN, JACQUES-ÉMILE (1879–1933)

French furniture designer. Ruhlmann was born in Paris, and started his career as a painter. He began to design furniture in 1901, and by 1910 was exhibiting

RUDOLPHI. Casket of oxidized silver decorated with foliage and arabesques. Made by Rudolphi*, Paris, and shown at the Great Exhibition of 1851. *Victoria & Albert Museum, London*

RUNDELL, BRIDGE & RUNDELL. The Trafalgar Vase of silver (London hallmark 1805–1806) designed by Flaxman, and made by Digby Scott and Benjamin Smith Sr. *Victoria & Albert Museum, London*

at the *Salon d'Automne*. At the end of the First World War he joined in partnership with M. Laurent as Établissements Ruhlmann & Laurent, and by 1925 their *atelier* producing interior decoration of all kinds was the most important in Paris. Their *ébénisterie* was well designed, soundly constructed and extremely expensive. The lines of this furniture were plain and simple and the woods of the rarest and most costly kinds. Colour schemes were restrained but luxurious, like silver and black or gold and black. In general, Ruhlmann's designs owe more to the Empire style* than to the 1920s, and he can, despite his undoubted contributions to the modern style, be regarded as probably the last of the traditionalists.

RUNDELL, BRIDGE & RUNDELL

Goldsmiths to George III and the Prince Regent. The firm was founded by Philip Rundell in 1785 when he bought out his previous partner. In 1788 he took John Bridge into partnership, when the firm became Rundell & Bridge, and in 1806 his nephew, E. W. Rundell, joined the firm, which then adopted the style of this heading. The firm bought a good deal of plate from French *emigrés*, which influenced them in the direction of a French style. They had two workshops, one directed by Benjamin Smith* (1802–1823) and the other by Paul Storr* (1807–1819). Designs were provided by W. Theed* (partner in 1808), John Flaxman*, E. H. Baily, and Thomas Stothard. They also commissioned designs from Pugin* in the neo-Gothic style.

The firm was plunged into financial difficulties by the deaths of Philip Rundell in 1827, and John Bridge five years later, closing in 1842. For the first quarter

of the 19th century it was the most influential arbiter of taste in silver in England, and it exported extensively, especially to France, Russia, and Austria, as well as to Turkey which was a traditional English market.

See *Rococo, revived*

RUSKIN, JOHN (1819–1900)

Critic and reformer. Ruskin was the son of a wine-merchant who was a man of taste and minor artistic talent. His mother was a woman of unremitting piety, whose ambition was to see her son enter the church. During his childhood Ruskin was forced to learn chapters from the Bible by heart and was denied contact with the outside world. At an early age he turned to books, producing *pastiches* of Alexander Pope by the age of nine. After 1833 his parents increasingly travelled abroad, but they persisted in protecting their son from the real world, and up to the age of 40 he continued to travel under their tutelage. Even when Ruskin entered Christ Church, Oxford, in 1837, his mother took lodgings nearby so that she could watch over him. He gained the Newdigate Prize in 1839, but due to ill health he did not graduate until 1842. In 1840 he made the acquaintance of Turner, and the first volume of *Modern Painters* appeared in 1846, the third and fourth in 1856, and the fifth in 1860. In the meantime he had published *The Seven Lamps of Architecture* (1849), *The Stones of Venice* (1851–1853) and *Lecture on Architecture and Painting* (1854). These works made him into an arbiter of taste of his time, but his views on religion and art, two subjects inextricably mixed in his mind, had undergone considerable modifications in the 17 years which had elapsed since the first volume of *Modern Painters*. By this time he was an atheist. He detested both classical and Renaissance art, and the persistence of the neo-Gothic* style after the death of Pugin* was largely due to Ruskin's influence. Much of the influence which he wielded over Victorian opinion was due to the facility with which he linked art and morality and his relationship with the pre-Raphaelite Brotherhood*.

RUSKIN POTTERY (Smethwick, Warwickshire)
Pottery established in 1898 by Edward Taylor and his son, W. Howson Taylor. Many of the forms adopted were influenced by 18th-century Chinese porcelain, especially the *flambé* varieties, and they made *flambé* wares in considerable varieties called by such names as *sang-de-boeuf* *, snake-green, peach bloom, etc. They also produced wares decorated with mottled coloured glazes, and made a variety of lustre* wares, notably lemon yellow and orange. The mark, where present, is a pair of scissors and the words RUSKIN POTTERY or RUSKIN. Their work, of excellent design and quality, is now sought.
  See *Moore, Bernard*

RUSTICANA
Decorative English glass of the 1880s made in Birmingham and Stourbridge. The glass was either designed in the form of tree-trunks or branches, or was given twig handles and feet shaped like roots. Decoration of this kind had been in vogue in pottery and furniture on several occasions since the 18th century. This was its first application to glass.

RUSTIC FURNITURE
Furniture such as chairs and tables made of, or simulating, tree-branches. Especially popular during the Gothic revival* of the 1750s, furniture of this kind enjoyed a limited vogue during the early decades of the 19th century, either for use in gardens and conservatories, or, in a more highly-finished style, in the house itself. Furniture of this kind was made in cast-iron about 1850 by the Coalbrookdale Ironworks*.

S

SAARINEN, EERO (1910–1960)
Finnish architect and furniture designer who worked mainly in the United States. His furniture, designed for Knoll Associates, includes the tulip chair, which has a fibre-glass seat on an aluminium stalk, and a broad flat, circular base. Saarinen was among the first to employ plastics in the design of furniture. Examples of his work are to be found in the American Embassy, Grosvenor Square, London.

SABRE LEG
Chair-leg commonly employed for Empire* and Regency* dining-chairs. Apparently so-called from the similarity of its curve to that of the cavalry sabre, its origins are to be sought in Greek and Roman furniture as depicted on vase-paintings. In England from the 1830s a curved leg of this type is found at the back of the chair in conjuction with turned front legs.

SADWARE
An American term used in discussing pewter*. It means flatware, which not only refers to dishes and chargers, but to everything, which can be made in one piece, such as spoons. Anything which has to be fabricated in two or more pieces and soldered together is called hollow-ware. The word sad means heavy in this context.

SAINT-AMAND-LES-EAUX (Nord, France)
Porcelain factory acquired by Maximilian de Dettignies in 1800 for making *pâte tendre** in the manner of '*vieux Sèvres'**, specimens of which were exhibited at the London Exhibition of 1862. Some clever reproductions of Chelsea porcelain probably come from the same place. The factory was one of the very few outside England to make a bone china.

SAINT-LOUIS, CRISTALLERIE DE (Munsthal, Lorraine)
This factory was founded in 1767 as the Verrerie Royale de Saint-Louis, and it began the production of crystal table-glass in 1782. In 1829 it became the Compagnie des Verreries et Cristalleries de Saint-Louis, and it was among the first to adopt the press-moulding* technique. Saint-Louis produced a good

deal of purely decorative glass, including coloured glass, opaline*, and some of the most sought paperweights* of the period. Like Baccarat*, with whom Saint-Louis shares a Paris showroom in the rue de Paradis, they have recently revived the art of the paperweight. In company with Baccarat they were the most important commercial producers of fine quality glass in France during the 19th century. Unfortunately the factory archives were partly destroyed during the Second World War, making it difficult to find information about early activities.

SALON DES REFUSÉS (French)
Literally, Salon of Rejects. Name given to a gallery set up in Paris by Napoleon III in 1863 as a result of the controversies resulting from the rejection of Manet and others from the official *Salon*. The exhibitors included Boudin, Manet, Cézanne, Fantin-Latour, Pissarro and Whistler. Manet's *Déjeuner sur l'herbe,* exhibited here, provoked a certain amount of shocked criticism among the *bourgeoisie*. This *Salon* is one of the key factors in the history of art in the 19th century.

SALT, RALPH (1782–1846)
Manufacturer of earthenware* figures in Staffordshire from 1828. These comprised individual figures, groups, and models of animals, usually with a bocage background somewhat in the manner of John Walton*. Salt started his career as an enameller, and his figures are always brightly coloured. His mark is *SALT* incised on the back of the base.

SALVIATI & CO., ANTONIO (Murano, Venice)
Glass-makers founded in 1864 by Antonio Salviati and Giulio Rode. The firm became the Compania Venezia Murano in 1866. It revived Renaissance styles* and techniques, including varieties of *latticinio** and *millefiori**, and some of their work was very close to the older Venetian production, even, in some cases, to the point of deception. Salviati exhibited *millefiori* vases in the Paris Exposition of 1878, but the company do not seem to have made paperweights*. In the 1880s they had a London showroom in Regent Street in association with Burke & Co.,

where they sold mirrors, chandeliers, vases, table-glass, and *tesserae* for mosaics.

SAMSON ET CIE, EDMÉ (Paris)

This firm was founded in 1845 and at first specialized in making replacements for the broken parts of Meissen* or Chinese export porcelain table-services, for which they achieved a considerable reputation. Later they extended their business by making close and fairly accurate copies of specimens of interest to collectors. In the case of Meissen these were marked with the crossed swords and the letter S, but the S was often later removed to enable the object to be passed off as genuine. Similarly Chinese porcelain bore a simulated seal-mark of which the letter S formed part. Samson continually extended his repertoire, taking in 'vieux Sèvres'*, and some of the more popular 18th-century English porcelain, such as that of Bow, Chelsea and Worcester*, specimens of which have deceived many a novice.

The firm began to produce French porcelain, such as Chantilly, and copies of 18th-century *faïence*, especially the expensive kinds, such as the wares of the Veuve Perrin of Marseille and of Strasbourg. Samson employed a very white hard-paste porcelain* slightly speckled with black where the base is

SAMSON ET CIE, EDMÉ. A 19th-century reproduction by Edme Samson* et Cie in hard-paste porcelain* of a soft-paste porcelain figure from Chelsea made about 1763. It is principally accused by inaccurate colouring, variations in the height and in the shape of the base, and by a very large gold anchor *under* the base. Genuine gold anchor marks are small (about ⅓ in high) and placed on the *back* of the figure. *Author*

unglazed. Many of the figure models were made from moulds taken from a genuine original; since porcelain shrinks by about one-sixth during firing, the Samson copy will be smaller than the original by this amount. The firm continued until after the Second World War, and closed only a few years ago.

SAMPLERS

The sampler is usually a rectangle of linen on which has been embroidered, in a variety of decorative stitches, the name and age of the executant (usually a small girl aged seven and upwards), two or three alphabets in lettering of different styles, the numerals from one to ten, and an inspiring text from the Bible or an uplifting message.

Samplers, a sample of the girl's skill in needlework, were being made in the 17th century, but survivals become much more numerous from the 18th century, when they assumed their now familiar aspect. They are fairly common with dates from 1800 to 1850, but after the latter date they become fewer, although some examples occur in Berlin woolwork with dates in the 1850s.

In America the first samplers date back to the end of the 17th century. Those of the 19th century are not so fine in quality as the earlier examples, and the making of them more or less died out after the 1830s. American samplers are inclined to be a little more pictorial than the English variety and often depict houses, trees and flowers, and animals and birds within decorative borders.

SAND-BLASTING

A method of cleaning metals, 'frosting' glass surfaces, etc. by directing against the surface a jet of sand at high speed. The process was invented in 1870. Decorative window-glass for public houses, etc. was made by protecting with a stencil the parts to be left plain so that the sand attacked only the unprotected parts.

SAND-PICTURES

These developed from late 18th-century use of sand for table decorations and were made in the 19th century until about 1850, although they become increasingly rare as this date is neared. The picture is formed of coloured sands from Alum Bay in the Isle of Wight glued to a suitable background. Some of the subjects were original; others were copied from contemporary paintings. Views of the Isle of Wight, dating from around 1830, are rarely of very good quality. The best examples executed earlier in the 19th century are sometimes signed by Benjamin Zobel, the most widely known professional practitioner of the art.

SANDERSON, ELIJAH (1751-1825)

Cabinet-maker of Salem, Mass., who was active for many years in company with his brother, Jacob, and Josiah Austin. They made furniture in great variety, some of which was sent speculatively for sale to the Southern States. In company with other Salem craftsmen, they also exported furniture abroad, the ship's captain acting as salesman at destination.

SANDERSON & SONS LTD, ARTHUR
(London)   See *Morris wallpapers*

SANDOZ, GERARD (fl. 1920–1935)
French *art déco** silversmith who produced tea-sets with ebony handles and angular forms. His designs were geometrical, with ornament practically eliminated, but his work nevertheless has a certain individuality.

'SANDSTONE'
In a recent popular book a studio-potter is described as making 'sandstone vases'. This is a mistranslation of the French term '*Grès*' which means 'stoneware'*.

SANDWICH GLASS   See *Boston and Sandwich Glass Company*

SANG-DE-BOEUF (French)
Literally, ox-blood. Originally a Chinese glaze, crimson in colour, derived from reduced copper, often with areas resembling the coagulation of blood occurring principally on the shoulders of vases or near the base. The secret of its manufacturer was discovered in Europe towards the end of the 19th century by Bernard Moore* and others, and for a short time it became very popular.

SARATOGA GLASS WORKS (Saratoga, N.Y.)
A factory was founded here in 1854 by Oscar Granger, formerly at Mount Vernon. Glass of excellent quality, green, amber and aquamarine, was made, and the factory's staple line was bottles. It has become known among American collectors, however, for interesting 'off-hand' glass* (friggers*) which included pitchers, mugs, bowls, etc. for domestic use.

'SATAN OVERTHROWN'
A figure executed by the sculptor, James Sherwood Westmacott (1823-1890), for Theophilus Barnard. Small bronze replicas were produced in large numbers by Elkington* in 1853.

SATIN GLASS
Term used for glass made after 1855 with a matt instead of a polished surface. The effect was achieved by exposing the glass to the vapour of hydrofluoric acid*. This type of surface finish occurs on glass decorated in a variety of ways, often in combinations of shaded colours. It is rarely seen unaccompanied by any other kind of decoration. It was made by both English and American glass works, and falls into the category of 'art glass'*.

SATINWOOD
An East Indian wood, varying in colour from yellow to light brown, employed in England during the 19th century principally for veneered drawing-room furniture. It was especially popular during the 1870s for furniture inspired by late 18th-century examples, and the practice of painting it was repeated at the same time. Painted satinwood furniture was also made during Edwardian times.

SATSUMA POTTERY
Japanese cream-coloured earthenware, the glaze of which is minutely crackled, that influenced some European pottery designs during the second half of the 19th century. Some of it, made before 1850, is exceedingly well-painted with landscapes, flowers, and figure-subjects in enamel colours, but examples of this quality are comparatively rare. Most of the so-called 'Satsuma' exported to Europe towards the end of the century, probably made and decorated in the suburbs of Kyoto, is usually termed 'brocaded'. It is noted for overcrowded designs, with enamel painting and gilding largely intended to appeal to the least discriminating of Western buyers. It was made in large quantities without any regard for quality. The worst of it is heavily potted and very crudely decorated in poor colours. Specimens of this kind are quite common today in small antique shops, where better quality examples may sometimes be found.

Wares of this kind did a good deal of harm to the reputation of Japanese workmanship. In an attempt to correct the damage an exhibition comprising many varieties of contemporary or near-contemporary pottery was sent by the Japanese government to the Philadelphia Exhibition of 1876. This collection was bought for the South Kensington Museum, and a handbook by Sir A. W. Franks, assisted by Japanese experts, was published in 1880.

SAXON SERVICE
A dessert-service of 134 pieces made at Meissen* about 1818 for presentation to the Duke of Wellington. It was ordered by Friedrich August IV of Saxony and painted under the direction of G. F. Kersting. The plates are painted with battle-scenes, but two are decorated with contemporary views of Apsley House, the Duke's London residence, where the service is now on view.

SCAGLIOLA (Italian)
Also sometimes termed *pietra dura**. Process employed for ornamenting furniture, etc during the first half of the 19th century. Coloured marbles and other stones were embedded in a cement matrix, designed in imitation of slabs of rare and expensive marbles, or arranged in patterns, either geometric, or representative.
See *Derbyshire marble work*; *Florentine mosaic*

SCENT-BOTTLES   See *Perfume-bottles*

SCHIFFER, Hubert (Raeren, Rhineland)
Pottery founded in 1880 by Hubert Schiffer who employed both brown and grey clay to make reproductions of 16th- and 17th-century Raeren stoneware. Schiffer's copies are deceptively close to the originals, and some of them need particularly close examination. The base is the principal point of difference. Genuinely early Rhineland jugs usually have a series of slight semi-circular ridges under the base.

See *Rhineland stoneware*

SCHIMMEL, WILLIAM (fl. 1865)
Woodcarver in the Pennsylvania-German* style. He produced large quantities of wooden eagles, carved in the round, as well as parrots, cockerels, owls, squirrels, and dogs.

SCHINKEL, KARL FRIEDRICH (1781-1841)
Prussian architect and designer. Schinkel studied at the Berlin Academy where he began to design buildings and furniture in the neo-classical* style. In 1803 he journeyed to Italy by way of Austria and returned through Paris in 1805. By 1815 he had been appointed to the Prussian Office of Works where in 1830 he became director, and much of his work was done either for the State or the Royal family. Architecturally, his principal works were designed in the Greek revival style, although he also made use of neo-Gothic* and even Romanesque. His furniture designs have elements of both Grecian and Gothic, but much of his work foreshadows the later Biedermeier style*, especially to be seen in a bed veneered with pearwood which he designed for Queen Louise as early as 1809. His elegant and comfortably upholstered sofas and easy chairs provided a style which remained popular in Germany for many years.

SCHLAGGENWALD (Bohemia)   See *Slavkov*

SCHMELZGLAS
A type of glass originally introduced in Bohemia in the early decades of the 19th century which imitates hardstones. The term, which actually means 'enamel', refers in this context to the partial fusion of glasses of two or more colours.

SCHNEIDER, CHARLES (1881–1962)
French maker of decorative glass who studied at Nancy and acted as a designer for Daum Frères. In 1913 he founded the Cristallerie Schneider at Épinay-sur-Seine, near Paris. One of his specialities was the production of pieces decorated with coloured flecks and streaks sandwiched between two layers of glass—a type known as *intercalaires*. Between 1920 and 1933 he produced a range of decorative glass under the name of Le Verre Français with stylized floral decoration in several bright colours. His work is signed *Schneider* or *Le Verre Français* incised.

SCHOOLS OF DESIGN
These, in England, began with a select committee set up in 1849 to inquire into ways of improving design in the industrial arts, a subject of great concern for some years (see '*Summerly, Felix*'). It was this concern which led eventually to the Great Exhibition of 1851, one of the objects of which was to raise the level of public taste, seen even at that time as deplorably low. Government schools of design were established with a view to training designers in accepted principles, and manufacturers were encouraged to employ them. Schools of this kind already existed on the Continent where, since the 18th century, they had been established adjunct to most industries related to the decorative arts.

SCHWANTHALER, LUDWIG (d. 1848)
Bavarian sculptor whose works included the colossal statue of Bavaria in Munich, and porcelain figures for the Nymphenburg* manufactory.

SCHWARZBURGER WERKSTÄTTEN FÜR PORZELLANKUNST
Porcelain factory founded in 1905 at Unterweissburg, Schwarzburg-Rudolstadt by Max Adolf Pfeiffer. It later amalgamated with the Volkstedter Porzellanfabrik. Pfeiffer produced glazed, undecorated figures after models by the sculptors Ernst Barlach, Gerhardt Marcks, Max Esser, and Paul Scheurich. In 1918, Pfeiffer was at the Meissen* factory, where he was responsible for the design of figures, and worked with Scheurich and Esser.

SCRAPBOOKS
Albums into which young ladies pasted pictures and prints derived from various sources—cut from magazines, prints, Christmas cards, Valentines*, etc. The pictures were sometimes interspersed with drawings and watercolours and autographed verses. When the craze had become well-established, sheets of coloured subjects for scrapbooks, and ready for cutting out, were published. These can occasionally be found uncut but are very rare. Generally, value depends on the quality and variety of the contents. Most scrapbooks date from the 1850s or 1860s, and in the following decade folding draught screens decorated in the same way as the scrapbooks made their appearance. This type of work, often termed scrapwork, is now comparatively scarce.

SCRAPWORK SCREENS   See *Scrapbooks*

SCRIMSHAW
American folk-art developed by the New England whalemen in the early decades of the 19th century. The term is used to describe both the object itself, and the process of engraving or carving on the ivory teeth of the right or sperm whale, whale-bone, walrus ivory, or shell. Most common were whale's teeth, and the most popular subjects were ships and whales, flags

TIFFANY & CO. Table lamp of coloured glass in the *art nouveau* style. The shade decorated with a dragonfly, the stem representing a tree-trunk. c. 1900. L. C. Tiffany New York. *Sotheby & Co*

LEGRAS, AUGUSTE J. F. Vase decorated with a landscape showing Japanese influence in the design. Signed Auguste Legras, France, Paris. c. 1900. *Private Collection*

SHELLEY PORCELAIN. Spill-vase decorated in gold and colours in conjunction with an iridescent glaze. Shelley Potteries, Ltd. c. 1925. *Private Collection*

ROYAL PAVILION, BRIGHTON. Interior in the Chinese style.
Photo : Author

ROYAL CROWN DERBY. Royal Crown Derby vase painted by
Désiré Leroy, signed. Campana shape 1000. Date 1901.
Royal Warrant mark. *Leather & Snook Collection*

and eagles, and figures of men and women. The engraving was done with knives and ship's tools. It was used by the sailors as a way of passing the time and relieving the tedium of the hours spent off-watch. The origin of the term is very obscure. Early whaleboat logs refer to it as 'Skrim shouting', and in *Moby Dick* Melville refers to 'Skrim shander' articles.

The two commonest scrimshaw products are a carved busk (or bodice stay) and a crimping wheel for decorating the edges of a pie. Among the other objects made in this way were work-boxes, yarn-winders, spool-holders, clothes-pins, rolling-pins, napkin-rings and cane-heads. Objects of scrimshaw were not generally made for sale, but as gifts for the family at home.

SCRODDLED WARE
American alternative for lava ware*.

'SEAWEED' GLASS
Type of art glass* made at Stourbridge about 1885–1890. It consisted of layers of white and clear glass with colours introduced between the layers.

SEAWEED PICTURES
These date back to about 1840 and testify to the popularity of the seaside holiday. An engraving of a local view is surrounded by an arrangement of seaweeds, springing from a basket, the whole surrounded by the inevitable maplewood frame. Allied to the seaweed picture is the seaweed album in which seaweeds were pressed in the same way as flowers and land plants. The art of using seaweeds was principally the preserve of amateurs, although some were executed professionally for sale as seaside souvenirs. The term often employed by the Victorians was *algology*.

SECESSIONIST WARE
A range of earthenware vases, and decorative and table ware, designed for Minton's* by Leon V. Solon and John Wadsworth, and introduced in 1902. The

designs were strongly influenced by *art nouveau**, and by the Vienna Secessionist movement, (see *Sezession*). Abstract floral *motifs* were outlined by mouldings, or trailed slip, and decorated with *maiolica* glazes. The ware was very popular.

SECOND EMPIRE
This is the name given to the reign of the Emperor Napoleon III (1808–1870) which began in 1851 and ended with the Franco-Prussian war of 1870, and the Communist revolt in Paris which followed.

It was the most brilliant period of the 19th century in France, and it was marked by a brief resurgence of 18th-century luxury in interior furnishings. Louis-Napoleon was nephew of Napoleon 1 who married the Spanish comtesse Eugenie de Montigo in 1853. During his reign relations between France and England were particularly good, and French influence on English decoration was strong from about 1850 onwards. These relations even survived the family loyalties of the English Crown to the Prussian invaders of 1870, and at this time a number of French designers and craftsmen crossed to England.

Many artists and writers whose work foreshadowed the modern movement, even though they swam against the contemporary current, belong to this period, but for the most part the Second Empire leaned heavily on styles of former times, especially those of the 18th century. Louis-Napoleon was noted for sexual promiscuity, and it was even found necessary to warn Queen Victoria, when she visited Paris in 1855, not to turn her back to him. This promiscuity set a style for the period, and much of the conspicuous spending was done by the *demi-monde*, those known as *les grandes horizontales*, prominent

SECOND EMPIRE. Cabinet decorated with marquetry in a variety of woods, porcelain plaques painted in the manner of Sèvres*, and ormolu* mounts, the design with a side-glance at the Louis Seize style. France. c. 1865. *Victoria & Albert Museum, London*

SECESSIONIST WARE. Minton. Earthenware vases with coloured glazes, designed by Leon Solon and John Wadsworth. c. 1910. *Minton Museum, Royal Doulton Tableware*

SECOND EMPIRE. Small French gilt-bronze mantel-clock in the Second Empire* style. A shepherd plays a flute beside a fountain, the stream simulated by a revolving glass rod. c. 1865. *Author*

among whom were Cora Pearl and the Marquise de Paiva. The latter built a house on the Champs-Elysées and furnished it regardless of cost, employing Pierre Mauguin as architect. Women like this were often influential arbiters of taste during the 19th century, and they moved more or less clandestinely among the highest social circles. Frequently they had vast sums of money at their command, lavished on them by numerous lovers who were men of great wealth and included European royalty.

From the Restoration of Louis XVIII to the end of the reign of Louis-Philippe in 1848, fashion in France was, for the most part, influenced by the *bourgeoisie*. The emphasis was on comfort, but designs and materials were comparatively plain and simple, with many of the characteristics of the *Biedermeier* style* in Germany. Second Empire revivals include case-furniture (*ébénisterie**) of Boulle* brass-and-tortoiseshell marquetry, elaborate cabinets which echoed those of Louis XIV, and furniture lacquered in a manner developed from the Vernis Martin of the 18th century. Especially numerous were *vitrines*, glazed cabinets for exhibiting *bibelots*, which were painted with scenes of gallantry after Watteau and Lancret. Antique collecting* in the modern sense had started in France during the reign of Louis-Philippe, although, except among the few, the most fashionable

objets d'art of this kind were noted for costliness of materials and workmanship rather than for their antiquarian interest, and glazed cabinets to display them were made in increasing quantities.

A new departure evident from the beginning of the period was the emphasis on well-padded comfort, and overstuffed* furniture made its appearance. New varieties of this type of furniture include the *borne** and the *confident**. Much of the old skill in the making of bronzes for interior decoration still survived, and the finest work rivals that of the 18th century for craftsmanship, if not in design. The Imperial porcelain factory of Sèvres*, which Napoleon III inherited from the former kings of France, produced wares which continued the 18th-century traditions of luxury and craftsmanship, and the Emperor extensively patronized the factory.

For much of the time Napoleon ruled as virtual dictator, during which the press was censored and the *bourgeoisie* overawed, although the lot of a good many of the artisan and peasant classes was ameliorated. Paris was completely remodelled under the direction of Baron Haussmann, who widened streets, laid out boulevards and parks, and built new bridges over the Seine. Napoleon also promoted International Exhibitions (1855 and 1867) and concluded a number of commercial treaties.

The 1867 Exhibition has rightly been called the spectacle of the epoch, where the exhibits ranged from a 50-ton siege gun made by Krupp of Essen to exquisite jewellery of a quality rare even in this opulent age. The Beaux-Arts gallery displayed principally official art—paintings by Ingrès, Corot, and Théodore Rousseau. Pissarro, Cézanne and Monet were rejected, and Courbet and Manet, with some difficulty, obtained permission to erect a private pavilion (see *Salon des Refusés*) outside the exhibition where Manet's *Déjeuner sur l'herbe* could be seen for 50 centimes. In the sky above the exhibition a balloon transported visitors to view the scene below, and boats which carried 100 or more passengers made their appearance on the Seine for the first time. Oriental influence, especially Japanese*, was strong in many of the exhibits. The theatrical sensation of the year was Offenbach's *La Grande Duchesse de Gérolstein*, which made fun of a minor German Court and its General, which Bismark seemed thoroughly to enjoy. No one, perhaps, expressed the quintessence of the spirit of the Second Empire so well as Offenbach, but the Exhibition really marked the end of the brilliant period which it represented. Perhaps it was best summed up by Théophile Gautier in the words: *C'était trop beau!*

SEDDON, JOHN POLLARD (1825-1906)
English architect and designer of furniture mainly in the neo-Gothic* and medieval styles. J. P. Seddon was a descendant of George Seddon who founded the large 18th-century firm of furniture manufacturers in 1750. His father, Thomas Seddon, operated retail

SEDDON, J. P. Cabinet of oak and various woods designed by J. P. Seddon* and painted by Ford Madox Brown, Burne-Jones*, Rossetti* and William Morris* with scenes from Scott's *Anna von Geierstein*. *Victoria & Albert Museum, London*

stores for which J. P. Seddon made designs. An architect's table in oak decorated with paintings by Morris*, Rossetti* and Burne-Jones* was displayed at the International Exhibition of 1862. He also designed tiles for Maw*.

SEIGNOURET, FRANÇOIS (fl. 1800–1853)

The leading cabinet-maker in the Southern States. Seignouret was born in Bordeaux, France, and arrived in New Orleans, Louisiana in 1800. He specialized in large pieces in the revived rococo* style using rosewood and mahogany. He also followed tradition in employing marble tops for some tables and *commodes*.

SEMPER, GOTTFRIED (1803–1879)

German architect and designer who came to England with Albert, the Prince Consort. An ebonized cabinet designed by him and decorated with Wedgwood* cameos is in the Victoria and Albert Museum, London. Made by Holland & Sons*, it was shown at the Paris Exposition of 1855. Commercial copies were also made.

SERINETTE (French)

A bird-organ.

See *Musical boxes*

SÈVRES PORCELAIN FACTORY

Factory originally established at Vincennes near Paris with the aid of a privilege from Louis XV, who later became a major shareholder. It was removed to Sèvres in 1756. Mme de Pompadour, the King's mistress, was an influential patron of the factory, and Boucher and Falconet were among the artists who designed for it. Sèvres became widely known for luxury products in a kind of soft-paste porcelain ('*vieux Sèvres*'* or *pâte-tendre**) which are among the finest examples of the art of porcelain ever to be made. The wares made between 1756 and the death of Louis XV in 1774 were a primary source of inspiration to many contemporary factories, both in England and on the Continent.

In the 19th century, these 18th-century products of the Sèvres factory were even more popular. Collectors paid high prices for them. George Salting once paid the present-day equivalent of £250,000 for a pair of vases now in the Victoria and Albert Museum, London. Porcelain factories, especially those like Minton* and Coalport* founded at the turn of the century, specialized in producing almost exact copies, near enough to pass the inspection of most people not closely acquainted with the old ware. This trade grew to a point where even Sèvres found it profitable to

SEMPER, GOTTFRIED. Cabinet designed by Gottfried Semper* and made by Holland & Sons* of ebony with gilt metal mounts. It is further ornamented with Wedgwood* jasper* plaques, and a large porcelain panel painted with a copy of Mulready's *Crossing the Brook*. Exhibited at the Paris Exposition Universelle, 1885. *Victoria & Albert Museum, London*

SÈVRES PORCELAIN. Coffee-pot in the form of an elephant's head, enamelled over a celadon glaze, parcel-gilt. Imperial Manufacture of Sèvres. From the London Exhibition, 1862. *Victoria & Albert Museum, London*

one of his denouncers, J. B. Chanou, who proceeded to embezzle what small funds remained.

In 1804 Napoleon I decided to take the former Royal factory under his protection, and Alexandre Brongniart* was appointed director. From 1793 to 1804 the monogram *RF* above the name Sèvres took the place of the old Royal monogram of the double *Ls*, *RF* representing *République Française*. The mark of the Consular period of 1803 and 1804 was *M Nle* (manufacture Nationale), and from 1804 to 1809 *M Imple de Sèvres*, i.e. Manufacture Imperiale. With the Restoration of Louis XVIII in 1814 the factory reverted to using the Royal monogram, now enclosing a *fleur de lys*.

During the Napoleonic period the Empire style* was employed for pieces as ornate in their own way as anything made in the 18th century. The style was severe, less elegant and decorated in heavier, darker colours, with lavish gilding, both burnished and matt. Some vases were of great size. This had been done as a *tour-de-force* during the reign of Louis XVI, and it was repeated in the middle of the 19th century expecially for pieces intended for the Exhibitions. The Empire Style was continued during the reign of Lous XVIII, but with gradual modifications, so that it largely disappeared by the accession of Louis-Philippe in 1830.

When Brongniart was appointed director of Sèvres in 1800 it was financially in very low water, and it was essential to raise money for future operations. During the 18th century the factory had instituted a very rigid quality control and a great many undecorated, or sparsely decorated, 'seconds' had been accumulated. These Brongniart proceeded to dispose of at a series of sales in the early years of the 19th century. These 'seconds' were bought by decorators both in France and England, who proceeded to decorate them in enamel colours, and in some cases to market them as '*vieux Sèvres*'*. In the case of slightly decorated pieces, the original decoration was removed, and the piece repainted and refired. Porcelain of this kind, when it purports to be genuinely '*vieux Sèvres*', is properly to be classified as faked, and it has only curiosity value. However, many of the dealers and decorators involved found the trade profitable, and when factory stocks came to an end supplies of comparable porcelain were sought. In England this was to some extent provided by the Nantgarw* factory.

reproduce some of its 18th-century wares, although with hardly greater exactitude than the English factories.

The factory's first art-director, J. J. Bachelier, introduced the manufacture of figures in white biscuit porcelain* early in the 1750s. It was so successful that it was enthusiastically copied by many other factories (Derby* in England) during the 18th and 19th centuries, and Parian* ware was undoubtedly inspired by this vogue.

From 1774 to 1789, the year of the Revolution, the factory not only progressively abandoned its *pâte-tendre* in favour of a hard-paste porcelain* (*pâte-dure*) but it introduced many novelties, especially clock cases in the form of urns—a type repeated at Sèvres and elsewhere in the 19th century.

The factory barely survived the Revolution, and for a time production virtually ceased. Many of the workpeople obtained employment at other *faïence** and porcelain factories more fortunately situated. The director was arrested, and his position given to

SÈVRES PORCELAIN. Table decoration in biscuit porcelain* showing a faun creeping up on a sleeping nymph. Modelled by Georges Boterel from an original model by Goumont. 1923. *Sotheby & Co*

SÈVRES PORCELAIN. Pair of large
military figures entitled *En Sentinel* and
Le Reveil. Mark: *Mre. Imperle de
Sèvres*. c. 1900. *Sotheby & Co*

Brongniart introduced several new colours, including chrome green, and the white porcelain disappeared under a spate of enamel painting. The factory had always specialized in high quality painting, but the superiority of 18th-century work was due to the artistic climate of the day. Whatever deterioration is observed in the 19th century it is that of the period generally. Also, the factory no longer had people of influence like Louis XV and Mme de Pompadour to help to guide its policies and destiny, and pay its debts, just as the work of Meissen* deteriorated in the 18th century when the Electoral influence was removed. By 1832 inspiration had so far deserted the factory that they began to use porcelain plaques to copy oil-paintings, and Louis-Philippe tried to encourage production by giving orders for dinner and dessert services of which he was very fond.

Factory production always makes it difficult for any undertaking to adopt an adventurous policy in artistic matters, and this is even more difficult when, as in the case of Sèvres, it is nationally-owned, since the director rarely has the same freedom to experiment

as his counterpart in a privately-owned factory. He is more or less compelled to follow public taste rather than to attempt to lead it.

Nevertheless, Sèvres succeeded in holding the balance fairly well. They introduced *pâte-sur-pâte** decoration to Europe, and this technique was later taken to England by one of their employees, Marc-Louis Solon*. Work in this technique was also done by Albert Dammouse* whose father was a modeller at the factory. It was developed at the suggestion of the factory's chemist, Robert, and inspired by decoration of this kind on 18th-century Chinese porcelain. A number of artists and craftsmen from Sèvres emigrated to England, tempted possibly by financial reward, but also by greater political stability, since some of them arrived during the French troubles of 1848 and 1870.

The Second Empire* brought a prosperous period to the factory. It enjoyed the patronage of Napoleon III, and it was able to reintroduce many of the more sumptuous styles of earlier times.

In France small potteries and individual potters had always been an important part of the industry, and in the 19th century these continued side by side with the larger enterprises. A number of these individual potters (who today would be called studio-potters) formed a kind of *avant garde*, experimenting especially with glazes, some inspired by the Orient. Several of them were at one time or another connected with Sèvres, and one of them, Théodore Deck*, eventually became its art-director. 'Majolica' decorated in relief under coloured glazes was introduced experimentally in 1852 and abandoned in 1876. Some

SÈVRES PORCELAIN. Vase from the Sèvres Egyptian Service*
given to the first Duke of Wellington by Louis XVIII.
c. 1811. *The Duke of Wellington, K.G.*

SÈVRES PORCELAIN. *Tête-à-tête* painted with the Royal
Châteaux, tooled gilt borders. Fitted case. Château de
Tuileries. Mark: *537*. 1844. *Sotheby & Co*

SÈVRES PORCELAIN. A pair of vases with claret-coloured ground and elaborate gilding. The vases are based on a type introduced at Sèvres during the reign of Louis Seize. Paris porcelain. Last quarter of the 19th century. *Antique Collectors' Club*

notable work in this medium was done by Jean Denis Larue (d. 1884) which first appeared at the Paris Exposition of 1855.

The influence of the Orient, especially China, is apparent after mid-century with porcelain based on the styles of the 18th-century Ch'ing dynasty emperors, Yung Ch'êng and Ch'ien Lung. The celadon* glaze was copied, as well as the *famille rose* palette and some *flambé* glazes. Towards 1870 Félix Bracquemond*, whose work was among the earliest to be influenced by the Japanese, was also for a short time at the factory.

The sculptor, Carrier de Belleuse*, who was chief modeller for Minton* in the 1860s, returned to Paris in the 1870s to become art-director at Sèvres, at a time when Rodin* was also supplying the factory with models.

In 1876 the factory was moved to new and more convenient buildings in the Saint-Cloud district of Paris. Here it maintains a very important museum of ceramics of all kinds, as well as a showroom of modern production. From the time of its occupation of the new premises Sèvres became increasingly adventurous, although it also repeated earlier styles, particularly porcelain decorated with turquoise blue grounds and 'Watteau figures'* in reserves.

Eléanore Escalier*, who had worked in Théodore Deck's studio in a style strongly influenced by Japanese art, designed and painted porcelain at Sèvres from 1874 onwards. Deck himself was appointed art-director in 1877, and held the post until his death in 1894. He introduced the use of new underglaze colours, and encouraged the development of glazed stoneware for architectural purposes, which was then becoming popular.

In the 1890s the *art nouveau** style was adopted both in painted decoration and modelling. Notable among the artists working in this style was Taxile

Doat* (at the factory from 1875 to 1905). About 1900, Agathon Léonard*, the sculptor, modelled a notable series of biscuit* figures as a table decoration called *Le Jeu de l'Écharpe*. These are of Greek dancers, and are sometimes called *La Cothurne*, but from the play of the scarf in the pose of some of the figures the source of inspiration in Loïe Fuller* is fairly obvious. The right to cast these figures in bronze was bought by Susse Frères* who adapted them to electric light.

There were many pieces in the style of Sèvres made in Paris and elsewhere marked with the Royal double *L* monogram. These usually enclose either the letter *A* or *S*. *A* would, on a genuine piece, be the date-letter for 1756, and *S* for 1771, and either of these two marks need care. Eighteenth-century examples are exceedingly rare; 19th-century specimens quite common. Nineteenth-century Sèvres is marked clearly, and the import of the components can be discovered from one of the books of marks recommended in the Bibliography. Louis XVIII, Charles X, Louis-Philippe, and Napoleon III were fond of ordering porcelain from the factory, and care must be taken with any examples purporting to have come from a royal château, and bearing one of the so-called 'château' marks. Frequently these marks are spurious. It is not difficult to fire on a mark at a low temperature to hard-paste porcelain* by adding flux to the enamel employed.

Sèvres remains one of the world's most important producers of fine porcelain. The Musée de Sèvres is reached by taking the Métro to its terminal at the Porte de Sèvres, and then crossing the Seine by the bridge outside. The factory is on the other bank to the right.

SEWING-TABLES   See *Bag-tables*

SÈVRES PORCELAIN. Octagonal stand painted with silhouette heads *en grisaille.* Empire style. Sèvres. France. c. 1810. *Antique Collectors' Club*

SEZESSION

Austrian movement in art representing a breakaway from traditional associations. The founders of the Vienna *Sezession* were all associated with the *Jugendstil**, the German version of *art nouveau**, and the architect Josef Maria Olbrich designed an exhibition building with an iron cupola consisting of a pattern of laurel leaves. The early adherents of the *Sezession* included Gustav Klimt, Koloman Moser*, Alfred Adler, Otto Wagner, Josef Olbrich, Josef Hoffmann*, Egon Schiele, Oskar Kokoschka and Herbert Bölck. An exhibition (the eighth) of the applied arts held in 1900 included Charles Rennie Mackintosh* among the exhibitors.

Austria was much later in developing industrially than either France or England, and little progress in this direction was made before 1848. The Vienna World Fair of 1873 was the first exhibition in which the progress of Austrian industry could be seen, but the same reliance on a *mélange* of historic styles as had earlier been seen elsewhere was evident, and even as late as 1890 no real change was apparent. The *Sezession* was a counter-movement. An exhibition of 1898 showed a complete room designed by Josef Hoffmann with the object of demonstrating the importance of applied art, and in a following exhibition Mackintosh*, Ashbee*, Van der Velde* and the Paris Maison Moderne* contributed a series of furnished rooms.

Hoffmann visited London, and conceived the idea of setting up workshops similar to those of C. R. Ashbee's in the East End. In June 1903, in association with Koloman Moser and Fritz Warndorfer, he founded workshops known as the Wiener Werkstätte*, with Warndorfer as commercial director. Objects of gold and silver metalwork, book-bindings, leatherwork and furniture were produced employing 100 workmen, of whom 37 were 'masters' who signed their work. The group centred around Klimt left the *Sezession* in 1905, and its effectiveness was greatly reduced. Until then Moser's geometric style predominated in the applied arts.

In 1939 the group's activity virtually ceased and the building was closed. It was restored, and exhibitions restarted in 1966, and the *Sezession* remains a centre of artistic life. Lynn Chadwick and Henry Moore are contemporary British members. The term is also employed to describe contemporary groups with similar aims in Munich, Berlin, and Hamburg who also organized exhibitions reacting against the academic and official art of the time. As in Vienna, where painters like Klimt played a leading role, painters were to the forefront elsewhere, Slevogt in Munich, and Liebermann in Berlin.

See *Art nouveau*; *Jugendstil*

SGRAFFITO (SGRAFFIATO) (Italian)

Literally, 'scratched'. Decoration incised or scratched, usually through a coating of slip or glaze of a contrasting colour to the body.

SHADES, GLASS

Glass covers, dome-shaped at the top, used as protective dust-covers for a variety of ornamental objects. They were especially popular in the middle of the 19th century and were mainly, but not entirely, confined to England. No doubt they were first used to protect the mechanisms of clocks which, as the 19th century advanced, became more delicate and therefore needed greater protection from dust. Their use was extended to protect groups of wax flowers and fruit, the delicate colouring of which also needed protection, and bouquets of flowers and leaves made from wool and cloth mounted on wire stems. Victorian young ladies spent many hours of ingenious labour, making flowers and grottoes from shells. These were usually placed under glass domes, and less often in glazed cases. A mid-century advertisement offers glass shades from the Wholesale and Retail Glass Shade Warehouse, which recommended their use for clocks, statuettes, wax-figures, alabaster and other ornaments, and articles of *vertu*.

Among the fragile objects thus preserved may be noted birds with spun-glass tails, and glass ships rigged with spun-glass. The latter could hardly have survived otherwise. Some of the more delicately constructed Victorian automata* owe their reasonably intact condition to glass shades. Shades could be had in a variety of shapes and sizes—cylindrical or oval, and all with the characteristic domed top. They were produced by firms who made window glass by the broad glass* method, but when window glass began to be manufactured mechanically production of the shades ceased.

SHAKERS

Originally known as The United Society of Believers in Christ's Second Appearing and later as the Shaking Quakers, this religious sect, founded in 1758 in Manchester, England, emigrated to America in 1774, and founded their first colony at Watervliet, near Albany, in 1776. By the 19th century there were 18 communities principally located in New England. The Shakers lived in isolated, semi-monastic communities; they believed that objects should be designed to serve their purpose as perfectly as possible. Their furniture was characterized by simple, slender lines without ornament or paint. Chairs were frequently slat-backed and of spindled construction. Much of the furniture was made between 1800 and the beginning of the Civil War, and has been regarded as one of the precursors of the modern style. It influenced several American furniture-designers at the end of the century. There is a museum of Shaker furniture at Monroe, New York, and Shaker villages are open to the public at Chatham, N.Y., and near Pittsfield, Mass.

SHAKESPEARE SERVICE, THE

A dessert-service based on the theme of *A Midsummer Night's Dream* made at Worcester* by Kerr & Binns

SHAKER FURNITURE. Shaker sister's visiting-room. The chest and table are of maple. *The Shaker Museum, Old Chatham, N.Y.*

SHAKER FURNITURE. Shaker chest of drawers surmounted by a cupboard in pine with a rose-red stain. From Watervliet, N.Y. c. 1840. *The Shaker Museum, Old Chatham, N.Y.*

in 1852. The dessert-baskets, etc. were modelled by W. B. Kirk, son of the Irish sculptor, for Parian porcelain*, and Thomas Bott* was responsible for some of the painting. As far as possible Irish materials were employed in the manufacture of this service, and it was exhibited in the Dublin Exhibition of 1853.

SHARPE BROTHERS & CO., THOMAS (Swadlincote, near Burton-on-Trent)
Earthenware manufacturers from 1820 who made blue printed wares, Rockingham* glazed wares (including the 'Snufftaker' Toby jug), and caneware*. The mark was impressed *T. Sharpe* or *THOMAS SHARPE*.

SHAW, RICHARD NORMAN (1831-1912)
English architect and designer. Succeeded Philip Webb* as chief assistant to G. E. Street in 1858. Shaw was in partnership with W. E. Nesfield (1835–1888) in 1862. The so-called 'Queen Anne Style' of London domestic architecture of the 1870s was largely the work of Shaw. As a designer of art furniture* he was assisted by W. H. Lethaby*, and he was also a partner in the firm of J. Aldam Heaton who made embroidery, carpets, wallpapers, embossed leatherwork and furniture designed by him.

SHEFFIELD PLATE
Substitute for silver, developed in the 1740s by Thomas Bolsover of Sheffield, which could be used for nearly all the purposes for which silver was employed. It remained popular until the 1840s, when Elkington's* invention of silver plating by electrical deposition made the older process both laborious and uneconomic.

The method of making Sheffield plate was to fuse a sheet of silver to a thicker rectangular ingot of copper alloy. This was a mixture of copper, zinc and lead, with almost the same expansion rate as silver, and the first step was to fuse the two together. This was followed by hot rolling until a sheet of the desired size and thickness was obtained. This sheet could then be shaped by most of the methods employed for silver. After 1765 silver was fused to both sides of the copper ingot (double plate) which makes the resemblance to silver much closer, but single plate continued to be used for the cheaper markets. The interiors of teapots, coffee pots, etc. were tinned to disguise the absence of silver.

The methods of making objects of Sheffield plate were, for the most part, those of the silversmith, using the shears and the soldering iron especially. In practice, since Sheffield plate was made in quantity, shears were rarely used, and the sections from which teapots, coffee pots, etc. were made were die-stamped. Certain operations, however, were impossible. En-

appropriate shape to pierce the holes, since the silver layer was picked up by the punch and dragged over the raw copper edge, effectively disguising it. Wine-labels had also been developed before 1800.

In the early days it was difficult to disguise the nature of Sheffield plate at the edges, particularly at the bottom. Careful inspection would reveal two thin layers of silver on either side of a thicker line of copper. This, however, had been overcome long before 1800, first by soldering wire over the revealing edge, and thereafter by a variety of devices. Silver used for the addition of ornament was often of hardly more than foil-like thickness, and was then backed with lead which protected it from damage. On some old pieces, where cleaning has worn through the silver, the lead will be seen underneath.

About 1840 German silver*, recognizable from its very pale yellow colour, was used as the middle of the sandwich, instead of copper, but examples are few, and most German silver was electrically plated.

Wear and cleaning over the years result in the upper silver layer of objects of Sheffield plate being gradually worn away, revealing the copper beneath. Since value, even of a fine specimen, depends principally on appearance, a great deal of Sheffield plate has been restored by electro-plating. The most obvious difference is the colour. The silver employed in the manufacture of Sheffield plate was alloyed with a little brass which gave it a slightly yellowish cast, and as a result of many years of wear and cleaning this has become unmistakable. Electroplated surfaces, on the other hand, are the product of depositing pure silver particle by particle, and the colour is uniformly white and characterless. The soldered seams, also, will have been covered with deposited

graving, for instance, would have cut through the silver layer into the copper, and essential engraving on Sheffield plate such as armorial devices had to be executed on a small silver plate and separately attached. Engraving of ornament was simulated by flat-chasing* in which the lines were indented by dotting with a punch. This does not entail removal of metal, but the lines are faintly repeated on the back, by which the technique may be recognized. Cast ornament, also, needed to be of white metal throughout. On the best examples it was of silver, and of lead on cheaper articles. Generally, cast ornament was reduced to a minimum. Such parts as the spouts of teapots, coffee pots, and so forth, which were cast on silver and electro-plated wares, had to be die-stamped and curved into shape with Sheffield plate. Like the body of the object, spouts made in this way will have a soldered seam.

Pierced work, popular for late 18th-century silver decoration, was possible by the use of a punch of

silver, and their examination provides an excellent test. Objects such as this have lost a great deal of their value, and are unwanted by serious collectors.

Good Sheffield plate is now scarce. Much of it was broken up towards the end of the 19th century for its silver content. Manufacture had largely ceased by 1850. About 50 years ago the market was flooded with Continental copies and electro-plated reproductions which should deceive no one acquainted with the former methods of manufacture. To make detection simpler, many of these reproductions are spun without seams, an impossibility with Sheffield plate.

Makers' marks on Sheffield plate during the 19th century are not deceptive. A useful one-volume pocket handbook is *British and Irish Silver Marks and Old Sheffield Plate Makers' Marks* by Frederick Bradbury.

SHELF-CLOCKS
American term for mantel-clocks. These were relatively large, the dial in the upper part, the pendulum bob visible below, the whole enclosed by a glass-fronted door. The earliest clocks of this type were made by Eli Terry* of Plymouth, Conn., who specialized in 30-hour movements of wood and brass. A case with flanking pillars and a scrollwork cresting is particularly associated with him. Manufacture was soon on a large scale, and cases in a neo-Gothic* style became popular. The best of these were designed by Elias Ingraham* of Bristol. Shelf-clocks not only enjoyed considerable popularity on the home-market, but were also extensively exported.

SHELLEY CHINA   See *Wileman & Co.*

SHELLS, CAMEO-CARVED
The practice of carving conch or helmet shells in the manner of ancient cameos, usually with mythological scenes. It started at the beginning of the 19th century and the industry still exists in Naples and Rome, although quality now is rarely as good. The fashion was originated by the Empress Josephine and persisted until the 1880s. For the most part the designs were ovals of varying sizes for mounting into brooches or jewellery.

The large carved conch and helmet shells seem originally to have been made as show-pieces for jewellers' window-displays. The conch shells are carved in relief in white on a rose-coloured background; the helmet shell usually exhibits a greater variety of colour in the layers, and these are much rarer.

Some carved cameos were made in France, but the industry there never assumed any very great importance.

SHELLWORK
This was a kind of amateur art which probably made its début towards the end of the 17th century as a suitable pastime for gentlewomen. The collecting of shells was a fashionable pursuit throughout the 18th century. Information on the contemporary scene may be sought in the correspondence of Mrs Delaney, and the Wedgwood* family were also ardent collectors.

The craft of shellwork had lost none of its popularity with the opening of the 19th century, when shells of suitable colour, or those especially coloured, were employed. Vases were encrusted with shells, boxes were completely covered with shells glued to the surface, flowers and fruit were made out of shells, or shells were arranged in a decorative pattern. Pictures were made from a combination of shells and seaweeds glued to a flat background, and miniature grottoes were contrived, usually with such additions as pottery figures, and placed in glass cases. (Shellwork was always fragile, and most of it was placed under glass shades*.) Well-decorated examples in good condition are rare today.

The work began to go out of fashion in the 1860s. Dating is usually difficult without some kind of independent record, but the inclusion of pottery figures or vases is usually helpful in fixing the earliest date at which a specimen could have been made.

SHERRATT, OBADIAH
Manufacturer of earthenware figures in Staffordshire now much sought by collectors from 1815. After his death the firm was carried on by his son and his widow and closed finally during the 1850s. Sherratt's figures are not marked, but a distinctive type has been attributed to him with confidence. These include *Polito's Menagerie*, *The Death of Monroe*, and a large bull-baiting group, all on pedestal bases with four or six feet and intended for standing on a table. Other models are attributed to Sherratt on the basis of analogy with these and one or two examples traditionally assigned to him. The modelling is always fairly crude, and the enamel colouring bright.

SHIBAYAMA
A kind of Japanese lacquer decoration consisting of ornament carved in various semi-precious materials (ivory, amethyst, malachite, soapstone, gold, silver, etc.) and applied to objects of lacquer.

The Shibayama school was founded late in the 18th century by Dosho Shibayama who at first made panels often employed for the construction of screens. About the middle of the 19th century work of this kind in miniature form was employed for the decoration of *inrō*. When Europe began to import Japanese art numerous inferior copies of the screens were made for export, and these have not infrequently survived. Fine early specimens are rare.

SHIPPŌ   See *Enamels, Japanese*

SHIPS IN BOTTLES
Although many recent reproductions exist these are poor in quality, and of no interest to the collector. In

the 19th century models of much better quality were made by sailors, and the details were carefully carved and painted. The ship was small enough to pass into the bottle through the neck with the masts lowered on the deck. The 'sea' was made from plaster of Paris. When completed the ship was pushed into position through the bottle-neck, on to the 'sea', and the masts were raised by a thread attached to them. The bottle was then corked and sealed.

SHOOLBRED & CO., JAMES (London)
Manufacturers and retailers of furniture from about 1870 onwards, noted for good quality work in the 'Old English'* and Anglo-Japanese* styles. Furniture was sometimes stamped and sometimes labelled.

SHORTHOSE & CO. (Hanley, Staffordshire)
Also Shorthose & Heath. Manufacturers of good quality transfer-printed* ware (sometimes with added enamel colours), creamware*, and black basaltes* ware. The Shorthose & Heath partnership seems to have continued until 1822. Both forms of the name are known impressed as a mark.

SILHOUETTE PORTRAITS
Usually a profile portrait of the sitter's head cut from black paper and affixed to a white background. More rarely, full- or half-length profiles are used in this way, and sometimes groups of figures. The colour of the background can also vary. In England the term 'shades' was sometimes employed instead of 'silhouettes'.

Silhouettes became extremely popular about the beginning of the 19th century, and continued in vogue

SILHOUETTE PORTRAITS. Bohemian* cut-glass* jar decorated with flowers enamelled in colour, and black silhouette portraits* of Lessing, Schiller and Goethe. c. 1825. *Private collection*

until the arrival of the portrait photograph before 1850. A mechanical device was invented soon after 1800 for tracing profiles. This had one long arm, and one short, and was pivoted at the junction of the two. The long arm carried a pointer, the short arm a pencil, and when the pointer was used to trace the outline of the sitter's face, the pencil transferred it to paper. The drawing thus obtained was cut out and blacked over. We have the evidence of Dickens for the fact that a profile could be completed in this way in two-and-a-quarter minutes.

There were a number of professionals who enjoyed considerable success, and many amateurs. The best-known practitioner of the art in England was a Frenchman, Auguste Edouart, who retired in 1849, but published a treatise on the subject in 1835. John and W. H. Field produced silhouettes in the early 1840s, and Frederick Frith and John Dempsey continued until after mid-century. A profilist named West specialized in miniature silhouettes for mounting in rings and brooches.

Rarely some elaborate scenes in silhouette occur, such as one depicting field sports done by Edouart in 1835. These have the detail drawn in, the figures being in silhouette. A dinner-service of porcelain made for the banker, John Julius Angerstein, about 1820 was decorated with groups of women with children in silhouette, and the same medium was used in Germany for book illustration.

The silhouette was very popular in America until the rise of photography, and William King and others employed a profile-taking machine. All the normal European techniques were employed in America, Charles Polk (1767–1822) using the very rare gold ground. Edouart spent about ten years in America, where a great deal of his work was done.

French silhouettes often have additional work to the profile portrait. Hair for instance was sometimes

SILHOUETTE PORTRAITS. Plate from the Angerstein service decorated with silhouettes*. Coalport* porcelain. c. 1820. *Sotheby & Co*

303

SILHOUETTE PORTRAITS. *Master James Ronnie Swinton and Donald.* Silhouette* on black paper by Auguste Edouart (1789–1861). 1830. *Victoria & Albert Museum, London*

developed quantity production methods in which the various parts were made separately and later assembled. Moreover, ornament was mostly of standard types, which helped to make easier the task of meeting a greatly increased demand. Forms were modified to meet new methods of production, the straight-sided teapot and tea-caddy replacing the early rounded and waisted forms of the rococo period, and the popular pierced silver baskets, which had originally been handsawn, were being made from stamped-out sheets before the end of the 18th century. To reduce the price thinner sheet was employed for many objects, which were strengthened by fluting and reeding.

These methods were essential because silversmiths were meeting a good deal of competition from the less expensive Sheffield plate*, which was employed to make most of the articles available in silver. With the beginning of the 19th century, silversmiths tended to leave the less expensive wares of domestic utility to the makers of Sheffield plate, and to make large and imposing services and centrepieces, massive winecoolers and tureens, vases and urns, and elaborately

painted a lighter shade with gold ornament. Painted portraits are usually of military or naval officers, who were often the subject of portrait miniatures during the Empire* period. A Paris profilist, A. Forberger (d. 1835), specialized in silhouettes against a background of gold-leaf.

Although silhouettes became unfashionable in the last quarter of the 19th century the art has enjoyed a minor revival in recent years.

SILVERED GLASS

There are two methods by which 'silvered' glass was made. By the first a vessel was 'silvered' over and then coated with a thin layer of glass. Alternatively, a double-walled vessel had the 'silvering' material poured through a hole in the bottom, which was then closed up. The glass liner of a Thermos flask is an excellent example of the second method. Other colours than silver were used occasionally. The silvered glass often to be seen in 19th-century fairgrounds (known as 'poor man's silver) was first made in England about 1845 by Stevens & Williams* and in America about 1855 by the New England Glass Company*. Apart from table and ornamental wares, door-knobs, bell-pulls and lamp-bases were made of 'silvered' glass. The basis of the colour appears to have been akin to the platinum lustre of the potter (see *Lustre pigments*).

SILVER, ENGLISH

The Adam style, which became popular around 1770, was received with a certain amount of enthusiasm both by the silversmith and the maker of Sheffield plate*. The new shapes were plain and simple and lent themselves to manufacture by the sheetmetal worker's craft. Matthew Boulton, who made silver in large quantities at his Soho, Birmingham, factory,

SILVERED GLASS. Glass goblet blown in two layers, like the glass liner of a Thermos flask. A silver deposit was introduced through the pontil hole which was then closed. This example decorated with foliate enamel painting. The type was made in England from about 1850 by J. Powell & Sons* and Stevens & Williams*, and in America by the New England Glass Company*. *Constance Chiswell*

SILVER, ENGLISH. Soup-tureen with the Arms of Wellesley decorated with Oriental *motifs*; part of the Deccan Service. Made by John Edwards. London hall-mark for 1806–1807. *Victoria & Albert Museum, London*

wrought candelabra in the Empire* or Regency* style. Massiveness was the keynote of the designs in Charles Heathcote Tatham's *Designs for Ornamental Plate,* published in 1806, where emphasis was laid on the quality of chased ornament.

One of the principal Regency silversmiths was Paul Storr*, who first registered his maker's mark with the Goldsmiths' Company in 1792. He joined Rundell and Bridge who became silversmiths to the King, as a partner, and here he was associated with the sculptor, William Theed*, who was also a designer. The firm became Rundell, Bridge & Rundell* in 1805, and were appointed goldsmiths to the Prince of Wales. From 1803 to 1819, Storr was largely concerned with the Prince's commissions. Also working for Rundell's were the silversmiths Digby Scott and Benjamin Smith*. Working in association, they were responsible for the Trafalgar vase, designed by John Flaxman, R.A.*, which was made to the order of Lloyds Patriotic Fund for presentation to the Admirals and Captains who were present at the Battle in 1805. This vase, with volute handles, was Greek in inspiration. A massive tureen made in 1819 by Paul Storr and now in the Victoria and Albert Museum, London, is decidedly rococo in style, and worthy of one of the great French silversmiths of the 18th century. Later, in the 1830s, rococo became a popular silver style, and even surviving plain Queen Anne silver was redecorated by having rococo moulding hammered into it.

An Elizabethan style occurs in silver of the 1830s and 1840s, but neo-Gothic* is distinctly rare except for ecclesiastical silver. Regency domestic silver took on new forms as plain as those of ceremonial silver were ostentatious. The shapes of teapots, creamers and milk-jugs were plain and squat. Teapots have a short spout and the lid is recessed by a gallery around the opening. The period is also noted for vinaigrettes* of good quality.

The rococo embossing of the 1830s in many cases

was executed either wholly or in part by mechanical means, and much use was made of cast work. A surfaced covered with embossed ornament to the untutored eye made the piece look much more valuable than one which was relatively plain or decorated less obtrusively with engraving. Form partially obscured by the decoration did not demand so much attention. Generally the silversmith began to lose his importance as an individual and started to assemble and finish prefabricated parts as part of a larger enterprise, although a few individual silversmiths still survived and their work is valued accordingly. Many of the smaller wares, such as vinaigrettes, card-cases, snuff-boxes, and so forth belong to this category, and some are decorated with engine-turning. From the 1830s until about 1880 some of the most intricate and skilful craftsmanship was lavished on prestige pieces of great weight, such as centrepieces with sculptured ornament of figures, human and animal, or trophies of the chase. These were usually undertaken for display at one or other of the exhibitions, beginning with the London Exhibition of 1851.

A name constantly invoked for comparison in the mid-century Exhibition Catalogues is that of Benvenuto Cellini (1500–1571)*, whose treatise on the art of the goldsmith was translated by C. R. Ashbee* towards the end of the century. Never were so many influenced by so little, and the conclusion can hardly be avoided that Cellini's contemporary reputation was largely the product of the popularity of his *Autobiography.* At the time the only certainly attributed example of his goldsmith's work existing was the salt he made for François I now in the Vienna

SILVER, ENGLISH. Silver gilt centrepiece made by Paul Storr* for presentation to Sir Arthur Wellesley. London hall-mark for 1810–1811. *Apsley House, London*

305

SILVER, ENGLISH. A characteristic Victorian tea-service with half-fluted body and gadrooned edges, Sheffield hall-mark for 1900, together with a pair of candlesticks in the revived Adam style, Sheffield hall-mark for 1899. *Antique Collectors' Club*

Kunsthistorisches Museum. His statuary was represented by a few well-known examples, such as the *Perseus* in the Loggie dei Lanzi in Florence, or the bronze overdoor done for Diane de Poitiers' château at Anet, now in the Louvre. The fashion for Cellini, however, even though there was little on which it could be based, brought pseudo-Renaissance designs to 19th-century silver. Caskets and inkstands were often either medieval in design or based on Renaissance strapwork. A good deal of work of this kind might fairly be termed 'testimonial' silver, presentation pieces engraved with the name and circumstances of the gift being a favourite kind of recognition of long or exceptional service.

At mid-century there was a fashion for naturalistic ornament, and for pieces made in the form of such natural objects as flowers or melons, for example. Generally, some attempt was made to relate ornament to use; wine coasters and claret jugs were decorated with vine leaves and grapes, and fruit-spoons embossed with fruit. Less specialized objects received a general decoration of high relief flowers, birds and even insects. This form of ornament was closely allied to the rococo style.

The 1850s and 1860s also saw some revival of Greek styles based on ancient pottery forms like the *oenechoe*, a trefoil-lipped jug, which was used for coffee jugs or hot-water jugs. In 1851 Owen Jones*, whose *Grammar of Ornament* was published in 1857, advocated the abandonment of embossed or cast ornament, and its replacement by engraving or chasing.

Whatever the abilities of the Victorian silversmith as a craftsman he was often compelled to work to the designs of those who had little practical knowledge of the craft, and critics of the taste displayed were both numerous and vocal. One of the bodies who attempted to improve popular taste in the 1840s was the Society of Arts, and Henry Cole*, who founded the short-lived Felix Summerly's* Art Manufactures, was among the foremost of those who made practical efforts to effect an improvement. Certainly no impression had been made by 1851, when the Great Exhibition marked the low-water mark of European taste. The period, also, marks the introduction of electrotyping and electro-plating, the latter process patented by Elkington's* of Birmingham in the 1840s. They used a base of German silver, known as nickel-silver, which was an alloy of copper, tin and nickel. The alloy itself had been known in Europe for about a century as a metal imported from China under the name of *paktong*. This was plated with silver by electro-deposition, and became known by the initials EPNS (electro-plated nickel silver) or EPGS (electro-plate on German silver)*. Usage started to be confusing: sterling* and Britannia* silver were often termed 'plate'; the silver substitute made from a rolled silver-copper sandwich was called 'Sheffield plate'*; Elkington's products were termed 'plated ware'; and a kind of pewter made in imitation of silver was termed 'British plate'*.

Electrotyping and electro-plating brought inexpensive substitutes for silver to a new and increasing public, and except to the expert eye, or to someone who looked for the hall-mark, these wares were virtually undetectable. In some cases the same moulds were employed for cast ornament as for works in silver. The relatively inflexible nature of the manufacturing processes of Sheffield plate led to its gradual abandonment as being too expensive and tedious to make in relation to the newer silver substitutes.

In the 1860s there were comparatively few works which could be regarded as original, even within the framework of the historicism* of the 19th century, but William Burges* designed a decanter of green glass for his own use in 1865 which was mounted in lavish medieval strapwork of silver ornamented with malachite, carved ivory, crystal, and coral, and studded with ancient coins.

The 1870s saw a fashion for neo-classical* silver in a mixed Adam and Regency style, lighter, with engraved ornament, characteristic rams' heads, festoons*, swags and husk ornament. This was followed by other revived styles, especially one termed 'Queen Anne' which approached the true Queen Anne style to a varying degree, a few examples being almost replicas. The revived 18th-century styles proved to be very popular among the greater number of buyers of silver, and they persisted until the end of the century.

The Arts and Crafts Movement* brought a new impetus to the craft of the silversmith. Foremost among the designers of the Movement were C. R. Ashbee and Christopher Dresser*. Of the two, Dresser's designs were plain, simple and functional. With good reason he is regarded as one of the forerunners of modern design. Some of his designs exhibit marked Japanese influence*, and Dresser travelled in Japan in 1868, making a collection of the silver of that country for Tiffany*. His designs were carried out by James Dixon & Sons*, Hukin & Heath*, and Elkington's, and were executed both in silver and electro-plate. Ashbee was not a practising silversmith, and his designs were made by his Guild of Handicrafts*. He disliked machines, and encouraged his workmen to leave visible hammer marks. Shapes were simple, usually bowls and dishes, with or without a cover. The decorative use of silver wire was his speciality. The maker's mark is either *CRA* or *G of H Ld*. Other designers of silver include Philip Webb*, and C. F. A. Voysey*. Influenced by Ashbee's designs was the 'Cymric'* range of silverware marketed by Liberty's* from 1899 which was hand-hammered, decorated in a style based on Celtic ornament, and sometimes inset with semi-precious stones. *Art nouveau** is notable for the quality and originality of its metalwork in forms often tall and tapering, and decorated with sinuous plant-forms, but metals like copper and even zinc were commonly employed for objects which might at one time have been made of silver or plated metal. By far the greater amount of silver produced for ordinary domestic use, however, continued to be modifications of historic styles, especially the oval and oblong Regency forms.

SILVER ONYX GLASS
Pressed opaline glass* decorated by staining parts of the pattern with platinum lustre.

SILVER TABLES
Tables, usually of mahogany or rosewood*, for the purpose of displaying small decorative objects of silver and *bric-à-brac* generally. A gallery prevented objects from being accidentally knocked on to the floor. After 1860 the silver table was increasingly replaced by the small glazed cabinet.

SIOT-DECAUVILLE (Paris)
Bronze-founder who cast figures for Raoul Larché* and others, as well as decorative metalwork generally, especially in the *art nouveau** style. Impressed mark: *SIOT, FONDEURS, PARIS*.

SITZENDORF (Thuringia)
There were two porcelain factories in this town. The factory of Alfred Voigt was established in 1850 to make hard-paste porcelain*, using the mark of the letter *S* below a crown in conjunction with three lines. The Sitzendorf Porzellan Manufaktur also employed this mark on decorative porcelain figures, candelabra and centrepieces which have not uncommonly survived. These were generally in the revived rococo style inspired by Meissen*. The archives were destroyed during the Second World War.

SKEAPING, JOHN (fl. 1926–1930)
English sculptor of animals, who modelled for Wedgwood* between 1926 and 1930. A *Reclining Duiker* and a *Sea-lion* of 1930, a *Gazelle*, a *Panther and Gazelle* and a *Seal on an Ice Floe* are all signed.

SKELETON CLOCKS
Clock made without a case, the exposed movement protected from dust by a glass shade*. The first skeleton clocks were made as a curiosity in 18th-century France, but they increased in general popularity after 1800, both in France and England. At the Great Exhibition of 1851 they were very fashionable, many being sold by those exhibiting there. After 1850 large numbers were made in England on a mass-production basis, especially by Smith & Sons of London, and clocks made in Paris by Pierret* were also sold extensively in England. These clocks vary considerably in quality. J. Page of Bury St Edmunds exhibited a specimen in 1851 that needed winding only once every three years. This required a high degree of precision in design and manufacture. Many of them incorporated ingenious developments and innovations. The fashion had more or less run its course by 1900, although such clocks have been produced to a limited extent in modern times.

SKELETON CLOCKS. A skeleton clock* in revived Gothic* style by Richardson* of Middlesbrough. The type is sometimes called a 'Cathedral' clock. Mid-19th century. *Antique Collectors' Club*

SITZENDORF. Chimney-piece garniture: porcelain clock and candelabra decorated with figures and encrustations of flowers. Second half of the 19th century. *Sotheby & Co*

SKIDMORE & SONS, FRANCIS (Birmingham, England)

Francis Skidmore, silversmith and metalworker, entered his maker's mark at the Birmingham assay office in 1845. Skidmore & Sons began to specialize in Church plate in the revived Gothic* style, examples of which they exhibited in the Great Exhibition of 1851. In 1861 the firm expanded and became Skidmore's Art Manufacturers Company, with Bruce Talbert* among its designers. They amalgamated with another Birmingham firm of metalworkers in the 1870s.

SLAG GLASS

Glass first produced in the 1840s in the north-east of England. The formula was said to include slag (fused furnace waste) from steel works, and the product was press-moulded* in a wide variety of forms, some of them in imitation of porcelain. Slag glass was made in a variety of bright colours, as well as black by Sowerby* & Co., Greener & Co.*, G. Davidson & Co.* and others. Many pieces bear the trade mark of one of these companies, and a patent office registry mark*.

SLAVKOV (Czechoslovakia)

Formerly Schlaggenwald (Bohemia). a porcelain factory founded in 1792 with the aid of a Thuringian workman. It had little success until the early years of the 19th century when, under the direction of Georg Lippert, it made a good quality porcelain, producing wares in the Empire style* somewhat in the manner of Meissen* and Vienna. Enamel painting was encouraged, and excellent work was done. In 1812 the factory was visited by Francis I and granted a privilege from the Government. The works specialized in decorative coffe-cups, vases, and similar ornamental items, and much use was made of engravings of Prague by Vincent Morstadt, as well as views of other Bohemian towns. From about 1825 a revived rococo* style replaced the earlier Empire style, and from about 1835 onwards figures of good quality were produced.

The factory is still operating.

SLIP-CASTS

Method of making some porcelain and earthenware figures and vessels in which thick-walled moulds of plaster of Paris were filled with slip (body diluted with water to the consistency of cream). The walls of the mould took up water from the slip leaving adherent a thin firm layer of the body. The surplus slip was then poured off and the mould set aside to allow the natural shrinkage of the drying body to separate it from the mould. The latter was then removed and dried for further use. Slip-casting was used for fine quality vases and service-ware which, because of their shape, could not be thrown on the wheel, or those which were ornamented in relief. A

SLAG GLASS. Small vase of slag glass* moulded in the form of a coal-scuttle. Unmarked. English, Gateshead-on-Tyne. c. 1830. *Mary Stubbley*

large number of the finest ornamental wares today are made in this way.

See '*Flat-backs*'; '*Repairing*'

SMITH Sr, BENJAMIN (d. 1823)

English silversmith who worked in his early years for Matthew Boulton at Birmingham, and came to London in 1802. He formed an association with Digby Scott, working for Rundell, Bridge & Rundell*. He left Rundells' in 1814, although he continued to execute commissions for them. He entered into partnership with his son, also Benjamin, in 1816, and the latter continued his father's work after his death in 1823. He did excellent work in the Adam and Regency styles*. There are several maker's marks used on pieces by Benjamin Smith in whole or part; from 1802 *DS* (Digby Scott) above *BS*; in 1807 *BS* alone; from 1816 *BS* above *BS*.

SMITH Jr, BENJAMIN (1791-1850)

Apprenticed to his father (see above) whose business he continued after 1823. Much of his own work as a

SMITH, JR, BENJAMIN. Centrepiece by Benjamin Smith Jr*. London hall-mark for 1848. *Antique Collectors' Club*

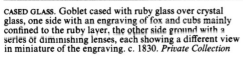

CASED GLASS. Goblet cased with ruby glass over crystal glass, one side with an engraving of fox and cubs mainly confined to the ruby layer, the other side ground with a series of diminishing lenses, each showing a different view in miniature of the engraving. c. 1830. *Private Collection*

Above:
MINTON. Earthenware plaque painted by William Wise, signed and dated 1877. *Minton Museum, Royal Doulton Tableware Ltd*

Below:
ALLEN, THOMAS. A pair of wall-plates painted with Mistress Ford and Sir John Falstaff from Shakespeare's *Merry Wives of Windsor*, by Thomas Allen. c. 1880. Josiah Wedgwood & Sons, Etruria. *Trustees of the Wedgwood Museum*

silversmith was based on a naturalistic representation of flowers and leaves popular during the 1840s and 1850s. He supplied Elkington's* with models for electrotyping, and seems to have directed their London workshop until 1849 without any great success.

SMITH, GEORGE (fl. 1800–1836)
London cabinet-maker and designer who was much influenced by Thomas Hope*. He worked mainly in the Regency style*, receiving commissions from George IV, but also made some Gothic* and Chinese designs. He established his workshop in Cavendish Square, London, but later removed to Brewer Street, Soho. He published three books of designs which were very influential.

SMITH, J. MOYR (fl. 1880s)
English designer of transfer-printed* tiles for Minton*, usually with illustrations from the Waverley novels of Scott, or the plays of Shakespeare. He also designed furniture for Collinson & Lock*.

SMITH, SAMPSON (1813–1878)
Especially noted as a manufacturer of 'flat-backs' at Longton, Staffordshire. Smith was probably the most prolific maker of figures of this kind. His output included not only figures of celebrities of the day, but also castles, cottages and the ever-popular large dogs, some of which bear his name under the base in relief. The figures of Sampson Smith were not the finest which were produced at the time in this *genre,* but they are the most common survivals today. The method of production (see '*Flat-backs*') made simple, uncomplicated modelling inevitable. The best were decorated with a rich blue and additional enamel colour, but some were very slightly painted with flesh tints, a little enamel colour elsewhere, and touches of gilding.

After Sampson Smith's death in 1878, the business was continued by his executors until 1888. From this date until 1912 the factory was operated by Adderley & Tams, and from 1912 by John Adderley and W. H. Davies. In 1918 the firm became Barker Brothers who discontinued the making of figures, and then revived it in 1948 when they began to be popular among serious collectors. At this time they had many of the original moulds. The factory is now Sampson Smith Ltd.

See *Staffordshire animal figures*; *Staffordshire portrait figures*

SMITH & CO., WILLIAM (Stockton-on-Tees, Yorkshire)
Earthenware* manufacturers founded by William Smith in 1822. They became notorious for imitations of Wedgwood* wares. In 1848 Wedgwood obtained an injunction against them restraining them from using a deceptive version of the name, *WEDGE-WOOD,* as a mark. They manufactured principally white and creamware*. Marks include *W S & CO'S WEDGEWOOD* and *W S. &. CO's QUEEN'S WARE, STOCKTON.*

SOAPROCK PORCELAIN See *Porcelain*

SOCCHI, GIOVANNI (fl. 1805–1815)
Italian cabinet-maker who worked for Napoleon's sister Pauline in the decoration of the Palazzo della Signoria, Lucca, and the Pitti Palace, Florence. The furniture made by Socchi is generally in the Empire style*, but he is noted principally for his work as an *ébéniste-mécanicien*, especially for writing desks, in the tradition of Oeben and Riesener, the makers of the *bureau du roi.*

SOCIAL REALISM See *Realism*

SOCIÉTÉ DES BRONZES DE FRANCE (Hamburg)
Bronze-foundry operated by Jean Kayser, where figures by French sculptors were cast for sale in Germany. Impressed mark.

SOFA-TABLE
A long, narrow table with drop-leaves at either end, and drawers in the frieze. It dates from the last half of the 18th century but was very popular during the first half of the 19th. Its name comes from its position in the drawing-room—along the back of the sofa.

SOIRON, FRANÇOIS (fl. 1800–1815)
Enameller from Geneva, working in Paris. He helped to revive a fashion for the art of enamelling* on copper during the First Empire and was noted for his portraits. In 1806 he executed an equestrian portrait of Napoleon I. Portraits of Napoleon and Josephine followed in 1808.

The art of enamelling on copper began to decline after the fall of the Emperor. Soiron had probably already turned his attention to porcelain, painting some of the white porcelain bought by the dealer Perez in 1804. He began to produce portraits of royalty from the *ancien régime* probably around 1814. His work appears on cabinet cups and saucers and vases, and his painter's mark has been identified with the letter *S* followed by points. It has been suggested that he also worked for Sèvres, but his name does not appear on the factory-list. In attributing unmarked portrait decoration of the period to Soiron, it is as well to remember that others also did this kind of work, but anything by him is likely to be exceptional in quality.

Specimens of Sèvres* porcelain bearing the mark associated with him are in the Victoria and Albert Museum, London.

SOLON, LOUIS-VICTOR (1872–1907)
Son of Marc-Louis Solon; ceramic designer in the *art nouveau** style who was much influenced by Alphonse

SOIRON, FRANÇOIS. Cup and saucer by François Soiron*, *bleu-de-roi* ground, jewelled decoration, painted with portraits of French royalty. Imitation Sèvres* porcelain. Mark: opposed Ls monogram containing the date-letter I. Signed *SOIRON*. First quarter of the 19th century. *Victoria & Albert Museum, London*

Mucha*; art-director at Minton* from 1900 to 1909, in which year he went to America and became an interior decorator.

SOLON, MARC-LOUIS (1835–1913)
French porcelain modeller and decorator, trained at Sèvres*, who came to England during the Franco-Prussian War of 1870. At Sèvres he had been engaged on the development of *pâte-sur-pâte*, and when he arrived in England he introduced the process at Minton*, continuing to work in this medium until 1904, when he retired. After his retirement he made occasional plaques with *pâte-sur-pâte* decoration. Solon wrote a number of books on French *faïence*, English pottery and porcelain, German stoneware, and the *pâte-sur-pâte* technique. He also formed a notable collection of English pottery which was dispersed, after his death, at a Stoke-on-Trent sale. He had two pupils, Alboin Birks* and F. A. Rhead*. Solon sometimes employed the pseudonym of 'Miles'.

SORRENTO (PROVINCE OF NAPLES) WARE
Small objects of wood decorated with wood-mosaic somewhat in the manner of Tunbridge ware*. Production began in the 19th century, about the same time as at Tunbridge, but there is greater use of dyed woods in the patterns. It has been thought that one of these places learned the craft from the other, although Pinto comments that such an idea could occur to two people widely separated at about the same time. It is, perhaps, also worth remembering that the technique is identical in principle with that employed for making *millefiori** glass—i.e. the placing of numerous 'canes' side by side followed by transverse slicing. At the time this process could conceivably have been known at least to Apsley Pellatt* in London, and to the glassworkers of Venice, although it had not been employed there for many years.

SOUTHERN PORCELAIN MANUFACTUR-ING CO (Kaolin, S. C.)
A factory was established here to make porcelain from the local clay in 1856. It also made Parian* and Rockingham* wares and white and cream-coloured earthenware. Its products were of good quality, but it closed in consequence of the Civil War. Another factory opened here after the War and operated for a few years, but little seems to be known of it. It was from this region that Wedgwood procured a supply of china clay (Indian, *unaker*) in the 18th century.

SOUVENIR WARE
Wares decorated and designed in such a way as to form a souvenir of visits to resorts, watering-places or places of interest were extremely popular throughout the 19th century. They were often of pottery or porcelain, usually decorated with a view of the town in question, and often with the inscription 'A present from . . .'. Goss* made a large range of small porcelain objects in a wide variety of forms decorated with the arms of cities and towns. Souvenir woodware was made at Tunbridge Wells, Kent, and Mauchline* in Scotland. Glass was not often employed for this purpose in England, but German and Bohemian spas sold glass engraved with local views, often executed in workshops attached to establishments selling glassware and fancy goods. *Papier-mâché** wares of this character were painted to order and sold by Spiers & Son* of Oxford.

Quality of souvenir ware varies considerably. Pottery and porcelain of this kind were usually intended to appeal to the cheapest market (especially when inscribed 'A present from . . .') and decorated with transfer prints*, although Royal Worcester* produced fine quality paintings of such subjects as Anne Hathaway's cottage. Tunbridge wood mosaic is of excellent quality, and German topographical glass-engraving is often extremely good. Much, of course, depended on the affluence of the clientele to whom these wares were intended to appeal.

SOWERBY'S ELLISON GLASS WORKS, GATESHEAD, CO. DURHAM
Founded by George Sowerby, this glasshouse has been known by various names, the above being the most recent. It has specialized in pressed glass, which it began to produce in the 1880s. Its output has included slag glass, opalescent glass, and an opaque

glass called vitro-porcelain used for imitating porcelain services. Sowerby's made much use of floral and foliate *motifs* and imitation basket-weaves in the decoration of glassware. Their mark was a peacock's head slightly raised from the surface.

SPA (Belgium)
A watering-place near Liège where, during the 19th century, small wooden souvenirs were made, some decorated in pen and ink in the manner of early Mauchline* ware.

SPANGLED GLASS
A decorative glass made by Hobbs, Brockunier & Co.* of Wheeling, W. Va. It was a cased glass*, the inner layer of which contained flakes of mica that sparkled when seen through the outer layer.

SPATTER GLASS
Type of opaque white or coloured glass in both England and America. The English colour version usually has a white lining. The exterior is mottled with large spots of differently coloured glass. Spatter glass, which was a development of a well-known Nailsea* type, was manufactured in America by Hobbs, Brockunier and Co*.

SPATTER WARE
A group of earthenwares made in Staffordshire between about 1820 and 1850 for the American market. It was decorated with crudely-painted designs and patches of sponged-on colours.

SPELTER   See *Zinc*

SPIERS & SON (Oxford, England)
Dealers in fancy goods, stationery, *papier mâché*, statuettes, bronzes, china and glass; founded in 1835. Spiers are mentioned in the mid-Victorian novel of Oxford undergraduate life, *Mr Verdant Green* by Cuthbert Bede. They were widely noted for remembrances of Oxford, particularly those of *papier mâché*, and they seem to have bought 'blanks' from the more prominent manufacturers of the day, like Jennens & Bettridge, and had them painted to their own order. Their stocks of *papier mâché* included tables, cabinets, desks, writing portfolios, envelope-cases, work-boxes, trays, fire-screens, hand-screens and panels for interior decoration painted with local views. They received Honourable Mention at the Great Exhibition of 1851, a Prize Medal in New York in 1853, and Honourable Mention in Paris in 1855.

SPILL-VASES
Usually cylindrical vases of pottery or porcelain, but occasionally of *papier mâché** and other materials. They varied in quality according to the room for which they were intended, those for the drawing-room being of porcelain, those for kitchen often of Pontypool ware*. Spills are thin strips of wood or folded paper employed to take fire from the grate to light candles, pipes and cigars.

SPINARIO, IL (Italian)
The Thorn. Subject of porcelain figure in the 19th century representing a boy seated extracting a thorn from his foot. It was taken from a Graeco-Roman statue in the Capitoline Museum, Rome.

SPINNING
Spinning was a 19th-century method, still continued, of forming bowls of soft metal (i.e. silver, pewter*, Britannia metal* etc.) on the lathe instead of by hammering. A circular disc of metal was brought into contact with a rapidly rotating former having the shape of the *inside* of the bowl, and by applying increasing pressure the metal disc gradually became bowl-shaped. Bowls made in this way are seamless, and show no hammer-marks, although, under a magnifying glass, minute concentric scratches are visible. Sheffield plate* could not be manufactured in this way, owing to its nature, and this was one reason for the abandonment of this type of metal.

SPIRITUALISM
The theory that the spirits of the dead survive and can communicate with the living through the agency of mediums. The movement originated in America in 1848 and soon extended its popularity to England and France. An example of the influence of spiritualism on the minor arts of the 19th century may be found in the vogue for hands made of pottery, porcelain, glass and ivory. Some rare hands of pottery cast from moulds taken from life have been observed, but these are distinctly uncommon.

SPODE, JOSIAH (Stoke-on-Trent, Staffordshire)
Manufacturers of earthenware* and porcelain*. The first Josiah Spode died in 1797, leaving a flourishing business to his son, Josiah Spode II, who, after his death in 1827, was succeeded by his son, the grandson of the first Josiah, who was Josiah Spode III. The latter survived for only two years, however, and in 1833 the firm passed to William Taylor Copeland*, already a partner in the business. From 1833 to 1847 he was in partnership with Thomas Garrett (d. 1867), after which the firm assumed the style of Copeland's, which it retained until recent times. The marks employed during this period are *Spode, Copeland & Garrett, Copeland, late Spode,* or *W. T. Copeland & Sons.* Spode wares are marked very consistently, and unmarked examples are rare.

Josiah Spode experimented with the manufacture of porcelain, basing his formula on Champion's patent, which called for the use of Cornish china clay and china stone. To these ingredients he added calcined cattle-bones to make bone china, later to become the standard Staffordshire porcelain body.

The earliest production under Josiah II from 1797 onwards was blue printed ware. Spode introduced many improvements in the technique of transfer-printing*, and these wares not only became popular, but have remained popular with collectors. Josiah II also developed the manufacture of bone china, some of which was decorated with improved forms of outline transfer-printing, the outlines subsequently serving as a guide to enamellers. This enabled the factory to reduce the cost of good quality porcelain services. The technique was not a new one. It had been employed by the Worcester* factory about 1760 for the Oriental-inspired wares, and the firm used it again towards the end of the 19th century. He also introduced the Spode, 'felspar' body and a type of stone china.

The rapidity with which Spode began to capture the fashionable market in the 19th century may be deduced from their appointment as Potters to the Prince of Wales in 1806. During Spode's lifetime they produced some copies of Meissen* and early Worcester from which the Spode mark has sometimes been removed. Painting based on that of James Giles on Chelsea porcelain also occurs.

Under W. T. Copeland* the firm began to specialize in lavishly decorated porcelain which was successfully exhibited at the Great Exhibition of 1851. Parian* figures were introduced in the 1840s. At this time general demand was for profuse and elaborate decoration and excessive gilding. This Copeland, late Spode, supplied, some wares being completely covered with gold. They also drew on Sèvres* for inspiration in common with most of the other porcelain factories. Generally the Spode factory was not in favour of its artists signing their work, so although some names are known it is difficult to identify their work with certainty.

Since 1970 the style of the firm has been Spode, Limited.

SPOOK SCHOOL, THE

Contemporary term derisively applied to some of the *art nouveau** designs of Charles Rennie Mackintosh* which were more than usually startling, particularly chairs with high, narrow backs.

SPOONWARMER. A plated spoonwarmer in the form of a shell on a base with Renaissance motifs. c. 1860. *Mrs F. H. Stubbley*

SPOONWARMERS

Receptacles of silver, plated metal, porcelain, or earthenware ('Majolica'*), made to contain hot water in which the bowls of spoons could be kept warm. Filled with iced water, they could be employed to serve a contrary purpose.

This decorative and supremely useless embellishment to the dining table was introduced in the 1860s. Minton* made one in 'Majolica'* in the form of a dolphin with an enlarged head and open mouth.

SPUN GLASS

Glass fibre made by drawing out molten glass into fine threads which can then, where desired, be spun like threads of silk. Although the technique had been known, and used, before the present era, it became popular during the 19th century for a variety of novelties, such as birds with tails of spun glass which curve downwards in a soft brush. Examples of this kind of work are in several museums, including the Victoria and Albert Museum, London. They seem to have been made around 1850 at Bristol, and can occasionally be found for sale. Considerably rarer are neckties of glass made both at Stourbridge and St Helens, Lancashire. Spun glass can also be found decorating other ornamental items, usually kept under glass shades*. Glass ships sometimes have rigging of woven glass fibre on the best specimens.

See also *Friggers*

SQUEEZE MOULDS   See '*Flat-backs*'

STAFFORDSHIRE ANIMAL FIGURES

Earthenware figures of animal and birds were an especial favourite among Staffordshire potters during the 19th century. Bull* and bear-baiting models (both very rare) belong to the early years of the century.

Deer are probably the most common of Staffordshire animals, and form part of spill-vases* as a rule. The inspiration was probably the enthusiasm of the Royal family for the Scottish moors, and the ever-popular Landseer who painted *The Monarch of the Glen* in 1852. Figures of horses include the animal by itself, or as part of equestrian portrait groups. Some of the Crimean War portraits, for instance, are mounted, and a well-known figure of Garibaldi* depicts him standing, leaning on his horse. Lions, tigers, and leopards are usually part of a circus or menagerie group, such as the lion-tamer, Van Ambergh, or Nellie Chapman the Lion Queen, and *Wombwell's* and Polito's Menagerie*—all very rare. A tiger forms part of the well-known *Death of Monroe**. Lion portraits include those of Nero and Wallace; their origin is uncertain, but Wombwell's menagerie or Astley's circus are probable sources. Jumbo, the elephant which the London Zoo sold to P. T. Barnum in 1882, was modelled, probably in that year. The giraffe* was first modelled in 1840, and two greyhounds named Macgrath and Pretender (belonging to Lord Lurgan and Mr Durchard respectively) distinguished themselves by winning the Waterloo Cup in 1871.

These models are now very rare. Models depicting dogs of all kinds, but usually the smaller breeds, are very numerous. The most common are spaniels of all kinds. Cats and rabbits are rare, although they were popular in the 18th century. Birds are fairly unusual. Eagles* were made for the American market. Peacocks, made around 1840, are unusual. Generally, animals form an excellent subject for the collector.

STAFFORDSHIRE PORTRAIT FIGURES

The use of earthenware and porcelain to make portrait figures was a well-established custom in the 18th century, and the practice was greatly extended in the 19th, especially in the second half of the century.

During the years which followed 1840 especially a large portrait gallery was built up of notabilities and notorieties ranging from the Royal family to popular preachers, and from well-known politicians and soldiers to the more widely publicized criminals of the day, who attracted the same kind of popular fascination as they do at present.

Beyond everything else, however, the theatre provided the principal attraction. Many of the untitled figures, if they are studied with this in mind, will be found to have a theatrical origin. The actual source of inspiration varied greatly. In these days, when many have been traced back to their source, it is possible to get a very good notion of the most popular sources, and music-covers seem to have been a particular favourite. Covers of popular ballads often bore a chromolithograph* portrait of the *artistes* who had made them so, and comparison of Staffordshire portrait figures with these covers usually reveals that they were faithfully copied. A particularly good example of this aspect is the portrait of the actress, Rebecca Isaacs (1829–1877), in costume as Mrs Bloomer* on the cover of a song entitled, 'I want to be a Bloomer'. The song itself came from *Follies of the Day,* presented at the Apollo Theatre, London, in 1851, the year of the Great Exhibition. This figure is a particularly faithful copy of the costume depicted on the music-cover, no doubt because the bloomers were an essential part of the costume. The *Illustrated London News* was another source of inspiration. A number of figures have been traced back to Baxter prints*, and several are versions of earlier porcelain figures, especially those of Derby*.

A large proportion of Staffordshire figures either bear the name of the subject, or have borne it in the past. Some of them were titled in gold which has worn off with washing and handling. It is reasonable to say that virtually every one of these figures, titled or not, represents someone who was at least fairly well known at the time even if they have by now been forgotten.

Dating is sometimes easy, sometimes difficult, depending on the evidence presented by the figure itself and its subject. In general, nearly all of them were inspired by the amount of publicity received by the person represented. This is not always the case, however. *The Death of Nelson,* for instance, was first made about 1850, as the style and decoration proves. On the whole the figures must usually have been put on sale within weeks or months of the person registering a popular success. In a few cases a figure of this kind would not enjoy a large sale for more than a year or two afterwards. An example of figures enjoying a fairly long life are those taken from Tallis's *Shakespeare Gallery* published in 1852–53 and therefore made after this date.

Most actors and actresses are in the costume worn in a particular play, so these can be dated fairly closely with a little research to find out when it was presented. A few *artistes* to which this does not apply, like the singer Jenny Lind, can be dated from the time of their successful appearances. Circuses were popular in the early decades of the century. To this period belong Polito's Menagerie, Van Ambergh the lion-tamer, Nellie Chapman the Lion Queen, and the lions, Nero and Wallace.

Early sporting figures include a group of the boxers Tom Sayers and John Heenan, and towards the end of the century the almost legendary cricketer, W. G. Grace, made an appearance. Figures of criminals, like James Rush of Potash Farm, can be dated by referring to the date of the trial.

Personages connected with the Crimean War, British and foreign, belong to the period of hostilities, and the earliest figures of Florence Nightingale belong to this period. Wounded soldiers may have been taken from illustrations in magazines, or even from patriotic theatrical presentations. Figures of Napoleon III were sometimes inspired by the Crimean War, but also, especially when in a less military guise and accompanied by the Empress Eugénie, by Queen Victoria's successful visit to Paris in 1855. In 1860, when it seemed, briefly, as though Napoleon might be contemplating the invasion of England the Staffordshire potters produced a caricature of a large lion seated on a small, recumbent Napoleon. The popular portraits of Garibaldi* belong to the occasion of his visit to England in 1864.

Figures of politicians date from some outstanding event in which they were involved, although it is not always certain exactly which event inspired some of them. Like those of preachers, they tended to have a longer life, and some were probably produced over a fairly long period. As might be expected from the religious and political leanings of the manufacturers, the preachers were usually Nonconformist and the politicians Liberals. Almost the only conservative politician represented is a rare figure of Disraeli, probably inspired by his astute purchase of the majority shareholding in the Suez Canal.

Staffordshire potters had always enjoyed an American market, and their portrait gallery included Washington, Franklin, Jefferson, and Lincoln. Other

STAFFORDSHIRE PORTRAIT FIGURES. Two cricketers, probably George Parr and Julius Caesar, members of the All-England XI of 1857. Examples of these rarely-surviving figures are unnamed, which suggests that they were especially well-known when they were made. *Antique Collectors' Club*

American subjects included the revivalists, Moody and Sankey, theatrical figures like the Cushman Sisters* (who spent several years in England, starting in 1845), folk heroes like John Brown, and fictional characters like Uncle Tom and Little Eva from *Uncle Tom's Cabin*. Portraits of English royalty are especially numerous, and vary from individual figures to family groups. The birth of early members of the Queen's numerous family usually prompted a new model.

Until 1840, the earthenware figures of Staffordshire were modelled 'in the round', even though they were often sketchily finished at the back. The best ones were prepared for firing in much the same way as the porcelain figure, although the cheapest had a certain amount of roughly hand-modelled detail, and some were completely hand-modelled. In the early decades of the 19th century Staffordshire figures by makers such as Enoch Wood* vied with those of the porcelain makers for quality. Some marked Wedgwood* figures seem to have been made to Wedgwood's order, possibly by Enoch Wood, or by another member of the family.

Most of the production of firms such as Pratt*, Sherratt* and Salt*, however, was decidedly less sophisticated. In the 1840s a new way of making these figures came into use which usually involved a two-piece mould of fireclay or plaster. The front mould was the deeper of the two, the back section being shallow. A bat of soft clay was pressed into each section and allowed to harden sufficiently to ensure safe removal. A base was made in the same way in a third mould. After removal the three sections were luted together with an adhesive of clay diluted with water. These were termed 'flat-backs'*, because the back section had very little modelling and the cast was almost flat. The details of the front section were made as simple as possible to facilitate extraction from the mould, and were represented by painting instead of moulding.

It is difficult to assign with certainty particular figures to a specific factory. Portrait figures generally were made at many factories, but a mere handful of specimens are marked. The name *Unwin* in relief probably relates to Poole & Unwin of Longton, but this is uncertain. A few very late figures by Lancaster & Sons of Hanley bear a mark. Some very rare flat-backs (principally dogs) bear the name of Sampson Smith* and the date, 1851, in relief, but the mark occurs more frequently on recent reissues for which the old moulds have been used.

Although the actual factories cannot, in many cases, be discovered, figures bearing a family resemblance to one another have been a way by which they can be identified. The products of the 'Alpha' factory, for instance, belong to the period from about 1845 to the early 1850s. These figures are designed 'in the round', are well-coloured, and the quality is superior to that of many of the later figures from elsewhere. The subjects belong to the contemporary scene or are historical personages.

The portraits of actors based on Tallis's *Shakespeare Gallery* (published in 1852) have been referred to as coming from the 'Tallis' factory. The master-moulds were later acquired by William Kent* Ltd, who used them to reissue some of the figures, but there is no certain record of their origin, and the moulds seem to have been acquired by them from an intervening source. Kent's ceased to make figures from these moulds in 1962, but the firm was still in existence a few years ago. According to the researches of Geoffrey Godden, Kent most probably acquired the moulds through their early connections with the Parr family, and they were almost certainly made originally by Thomas Parr between 1852 and 1870.

It is, of course, possible to take a mould from an existing figure, but clay always shrinks by a well-marked amount when fired, usually between one-sixth and one-seventh. Reproductions of this kind, therefore, can be detected from a comparison with a genuine original.

Up to 1865 much use was made of large areas of clear, bright underglaze blue in addition to enamel colours, but after this date there was an increasing tendency to leave the surface white, except for touches of enamel colour and gilding*. The earliest gilding was of the mercuric type, known as 'Best' gold. It tended to wear off. 'Bright' gold, a liquid gold, inferior in colour but easier to apply, was introduced early in the 1880s by Johnson Matthey, and is a useful way of dating.

New models were introduced up to 1900. Old models were reproduced probably from 1900, but those of which the collector should beware were made between 1944 and 1962, and perhaps later. The glaze of most old specimens is crazed; the glaze of later reproductions, however, is not, unless induced artificially. Glazes can be crazed artificially by reheating, pigment being rubbed into the cracks to simulate the dirt of ages. Some deceptive examples have appeared on the market with the network of crazing simulated by painting fine lines with a brush. These points are usually evident if the surface is examined under a ' × 5' magnifier. Only copies of rare and valuable items are likely to be treated in this way. These reproductions were made as forgeries, but they should never deceive anyone reasonably well acquainted with old specimens. One painter of faces seems always to have had difficulty with the mouth (the Achilles' heel of the bank-note forger) which is always recognizably 20th century.

It would be hazardous to guess how many different models made in the 19th century may still exist, but upwards of 600 would not be an unreasonable guess. Many of these can now be regarded as very desirable models for one reason or another, and some are excessively rare and highly valued. At the time these figures were made in enormous quantities and were sold very cheaply, often for only a few pence. For this reason the casualty rate was very high until they began to be the focus of the serious collector. By this time only the more common models had survived in quantity. Those of better quality, of course, were never made in large quantities in the first place.

STAITE MURRAY, WILLIAM See *Murray, William Staite*

STATUARY AND SCULPTURE IN THE HOME
Statuary of all kinds in marble, terracotta, Parian porcelain*, bronze, cast-iron and (for the cheaper market) bronzed zinc* (spelter) was very fashionable in the Victorian home, especially in the hall, the drawing-room and the conservatory. Queen Victoria, who much preferred sculpture to painting, led this fashion, which began in the 1840s and lasted almost until the end of the century. A good deal of decorative sculpture produced for the Victorian home took the form of accurate copies of well-known works, such as Canova's* *Eros and Psyche* in alabaster or Cellini's* *Perseus and the Medusa* in bronze in reduced size. A number of mechanical aids to accurate reproduction existed, and these enabled marble reductions to be made by any good stonemason. Bronzes, of course, were cast from moulds, and methods of making several moulds from a single original model had existed for centuries. Electrotyping was a new method of producing casts introduced in the 1840s and greatly improved in Berlin, where statues of heroic size could be cheaply reproduced by 1851. Also from Berlin, in the Great Exhibition of 1851, was a sculpture cast in zinc, which had first been used for the purpose a few years earlier.

At the same time Geiss* had devised a method of covering zinc with bronze, which was the beginning of an enormous trade, developed later on the Continent, in bronzed zinc casts as a substitute for the expensive bronze. Cast-iron became important as

STATUARY AND SCULPTURE IN THE HOME. *Cupid and Psyche*, a commercial reduction in alabaster of the well-known group by Canova*, on *verde antique* marble pedestal. A number of these were made, probably around the middle of the 19th century. *Leslie Curtis*

a material for decorative casts in the 1840s, especially at the Coalbrookdale* Ironworks. One of their masterpieces was a circular table resting on the backs of four life-size greyhounds, but they produced a vast amount of work, both small and large, including such evocations of the period as Bell's* *Eagle-Slayer* (now in the grounds of the Bethnal Green Museum, London) which was an attraction of the Great Exhibition. This, like so many more examples of contemporary sculpture, was reproduced for the Art Union*, either in bronze or in Parian porcelain.

Terracotta*, a popular statuary material, was easily reproduced with the aid of either piece-moulds in plaster, or gelatine moulds. Some terracotta busts and

STATUARY AND SCULPTURE IN THE HOME. *Les Bacchantes.* Painted plaster by Jules Dalou*. 1879. *Victoria & Albert Museum, London*

figures, however, are unique, and were fired as they left the sculptor's hand. Unique busts of this kind are hollowed out and freed from the sculptor's armature before firing.

Parian porcelain was, like the earlier biscuit porcelain*, especially devised for the reproduction of statuary in a reduced size for the decoration of the drawing-room and nearly all the larger models were taken from this source. Many of the originals were first shown at the Great Exhibition of 1851, where they had already become firm favourites with the public. This applied particularly to the female nude, and included Hiram Power's *Greek Slave*, Bell's *Andromeda,* and *Una seated on a lion.* The two former models were often placed on pedestals of Minton's* 'Majolica'* in either drawing-room or conservatory.

France had been a source of fine quality bronze-casting since the 16th century, when Cellini—and who more fitted to do so!—expressed admiration for the skill displayed. Throughout the 19th century France continued to produce bronzes for interior decoration. They were especially popular in England, which provided an eager market for the work of the *Animaliers** especially. The paintings of Landseer, popular in France as well as England, also provided inspiration for animal sculpture. Romantic figures of knights in armour, lute-players, figures in 17th-century Court attire, etc., were also popular from about 1840 to the 1860s. Knights may in some cases have been the product of the influence of the Eglinton Tournament* of 1839. Many of these things became unfashionable when cheap bronzed spelter copies began to be widely popular at low prices. Perhaps the most popular of these models are the pair known as *The Marly Horses.* These horses, held by a groom,

were originally carved in marble by Guillaume Coustou early in the 18th century for the gates of the riding-school of the King's château at Marly. They were removed in 1796, and placed on either side of the bridge at the end of the Champs-Elysées in Paris. Good quality bronze reductions are scarce. Poor quality spelter versions are very common.

During the 19th century copies of bronzes excavated at Herculaneum and Pompeii were made for decorative purposes, and patinated to imitate excavated specimens. These are not uncommon. Antique collectors specialized in Renaissance bronzes, and those by well-known sculptors like Riccio sold for large sums. Some very deceptive forgeries were made by the Viennese enameller, Solomon Weininger*. These remarks are concerned with 19th-century sculpture for interior decoration. Some important works of art from the studios of Rodin* and others belong to this period, for which appropriate works should be consulted.

STEELE, THOMAS (1772–1850)
Porcelain painter specializing in fruit. He worked first for Derby*, and then went on to the Rockingham* factory at Swinton, from thence to Davenport* and finally to Minton*, where he worked from 1825 to 1843. His work is meticulously detailed and highly coloured.

STEINGUT (German)
Creamware*; *faïence-fine**; lead-glazed. Cream-coloured earthenware, made in Germany from the last quarter of the 18th century.

STENCILS
The use of stencils to decorate furniture with painted polychrome designs began in America about 1815. Chairs, tables, clocks and trays in particular were ornamented in this way, and the addition of gold leaf was especially popular. Empire* ornament was often thus applied on cheaper furniture, as well as on neo-Gothic pieces. The fashion, however, had run its course by about 1860. Stencils were also employed for decorating other materials. Velvet with stencilled decoration, for instance, is now collected.
See *Hitchcock, Lambert*

STERLING SILVER
The word is derived from the Easterlings, a medieval German tribe noted for the purity of its silver. The sterling standard is actually 925 parts of pure silver to 75 parts of alloying metal, the latter being added to make the silver harder and easier to work. No system of hall-marking comparable to that of Europe was employed in America in colonial times, silversmiths being considered men of integrity who took a leading part in the community, and no instances of debasement appear to be known. In 1865, however, legislation laid down the sterling standard as a legal minimum for articles of silver, and enjoined the addition of the word 'sterling'.

The sterling standard is usual in England, but the Britannia standard, used occasionally, contains a higher percentage of pure silver. The English assay office refuses to permit the general sale of a lower standard than sterling, although it is difficult to cause enamel to adhere to silver as nearly pure as this.

STEUBEN GLASS WORKS. Bowl engraved with the signs of the Zodiac by Sidney Waugh. Steuben Glass Company*. c. 1935. *Victoria & Albert Museum, London*

STEUBEN GLASS WORKS (Corning, N.Y.)

This important American manufacture of decorative glass was founded by Frederick Carder* in 1903. Carder was born at Brierley, not far from Stourbridge, Worcestershire, in 1864, and entered his father's pottery factory, later becoming a designer of glass, and a salesman with the firm Stevens & Williams*. He founded the Steuben Works at Corning, New York State, in association with T. G. Hawkes, and imported workmen from England, France and Sweden. The factory suffered financially during the First World War and in 1918 it was bought by the Corning Glass Company. Carder remained as art-director until 1934, when he retired. He died in 1963.

From the first, Carder displayed enormous versatility both in designing and in technical ingenuity. He is best known for his iridescent glass* which he called Aurene*, and he does not seem to have been attracted by cutting and engraving as a decorative technique. Carder was the last of the glass designers to work in the tradition of such 19th-century designers as Gallé* and Tiffany*, and in the year before his retirement as art-director the decision was taken to concentrate on the manufacture of high quality crystal glass. Sculptor Sydney Waugh was engaged as a designer. His designs were carried out in wheel-engraving on blown glass, and the company gained a Gold Medal at the Paris Exposition of 1937. In 1940 Steuben commissioned designs from the English sculptor Eric Gill. Much success was also achieved with simple blown shapes which were left undecorated.

Since 1940 many well-known contemporary painters and sculptors have executed designs for glasses, including (after 1954) Frank Dobson, Jacob Epstein*, Laurence Whistler* (the glass-engraver), and Graham Sutherland. The Steuben Company has produced some of the most distinguished glass of the 20th century, rivalled only by that of the Swedish Ørrefors* Glass Works, and they were among the first to produce glass in what has since become the distinctive modern idiom.

STEVENGRAPHS

A trade name for silk pictures woven on a modified form of Jacquard loom by Thomas Stevens of Coventry. This loom was developed about 1835 for the weaving of elaborate patterns into silk ribbons, and its products were exhibited at the Great Exhibition of 1851. Stevens started a factory in 1854 for the manufacture of ribbons, bookmarks, and silk pictures, and he enjoyed great success almost immediately.

The number of subjects depicted is very large and diverse, and a list reveals a number of American subjects which are testimony to the popularity of the silk picture in that country. Manufacture continued at least until 1938. The factory was destroyed in the air-raid of 1940. Lady Godiva and Peeping Tom were obvious and favourite subjects with this Coventry firm. American Stevengraphs include the signing of the Declaration of Independence in 1776. Royalty; people in the public eye, including politicians like Gladstone; historical subjects, sporting scenes, including racing and hunting; bicycle races; boats and ships; mail-coaches, trains, and locomotives, and

STEVENGRAPHS. An early Stevengraph* specially woven for the York Exhibition of 1879. *Antique Collectors' Club*

many more were produced. Bookmarks were decorated with birthday or Christmas greetings, or a pious text.

The pictures were provided with cardboard mounts (at first green, and later of biscuit colour) which had the title of the subject on the front, together with Stevens' name. The name was repeated on the back. The lengthiest caption reads 'Woven in Silk by Thomas Stevens, inventor and manufacturer, Coventry and London (Registered).' 'Woven in silk' or 'Woven in pure silk', without the name, also occur. Some early pictorial ribbons of the 1850s bear the name of the manufacturer and that of the designer. A number of other Coventry firms later made silk pictures, the best known being W. H. Grant.

Stevengraphs have become an important collector's item in recent years, and two books devoted to the subject are noted in the Bibliography.

STEVENS, ALFRED GEORGE (1818–1875)
Born in Dorset, the son of a house painter, Stevens studied sculpture in Italy, at one time working under Thorwaldsen*. He was principal designer to the iron-founders, H. E. Hoole, and his work includes pewter and stoves. He also designed silver for Thomas Bradbury* of Sheffield in the 1850s, and furniture, and porcelain in a style strongly influenced by Renaissance models. His best-known work of sculpture is the Wellington Monument at St Paul's Cathedral.

STEVENS & WILLIAMS (Stourbridge, Worcestershire)
Although this glasshouse was operating from the 1830s, its most important work was probably done in the 1880s, when it made cameo glass* under the art-directorship of John Northwood*. John Hodgett, apprenticed to Northwood, did high-relief engraving. Northwood also developed 'Silvena', a type of glass in which silver foil was sandwiched between two layers of clear or coloured glass, and further decorated with trailings of coloured glass. Rusticana glass* (see *Richardson & Sons*) dates from the 1880s, and Alexandrite, a type of cased glass*, from the beginning of the present century. In the 1930s table-glass was made to the design of Keith Murray*. The mark *S&W* has been used on some examples.

STEVENSON, ANDREW (Cobridge, Staffordshire)
Potter making blue printed earthenware, mainly for export to the United States. The factory is said to have closed in 1819, but this is probably inaccurate. Some American Views* used by Stevenson were the work of an Irish artist, W. G. Wall*, who is reputed to have been in New York in 1818. Country houses in his *English Views Series* include one or two of importance which have since been destroyed, such as Wanstead House, Essex. The mark used was *A.*

STEVENS, A. G. Cabinet designed by Alfred Stevens*, the panel in the upper door painted at a later date by James Gamble, after Michelangelo. c. 1860. *Victoria & Albert Museum, London*

STEVENSON STAFFORDSHIRE WARRANTED around a crown.

STEVENSON & HANCOCK (Stevenson, Sharp & Company) See *Hancock, Sampson*; *Locker, William*

STEVENSON, RALPH (fl. 1815–1833)
Stevenson seems to have traded in partnership from the beginning of the century to 1815, when he continued alone until 1833. He made blue printed wares, much for export to America. Apart from American* and English Views he produced commemorative and portrait wares. His mark was *STEVENSON* and a three-masted ship. Andrew Stevenson* was his younger brother.

STICK-BACK
Chair with back made up of turned spindles.
　　See *Windsor chairs*; *'Morris' chair*

STILE LIBERTÉ
The name given to *art nouveau** in Italy, which testifies to the part played by the English firm of Liberty* in the promotion of the style. Apart from Carlo Bugatti*, Italy did not produce many *art nouveau* designers of consequence, and most decoration in this style was imported.

STINTON, JAMES (1856–1954)
Painter principally of Highland cattle (usually signed) at the Worcester* porcelain factory. His work is now much sought.

STOBWASSER UND SOHN (Germany)

The firm of Stobwasser, makers of japanned *papier mâché** and tin-ware (*tôle peinte**), was founded in the 1760s, and prospered throughout the rest of the 18th century. Stobwasser retired from business in 1810, and his son, Christian Friedrich, took over, and in 1832 moved from Brunswick to Berlin, where the manufacture of japanned ware was discontinued. Lacquered goods continued to be produced in Brunswick by Meyer und Ried, who found employment for 20 painters.

Although both Stobwasser's and Meyer und Ried's products were varied, ranging from trays and furniture decoration, to tea kettles, tobacco-jars, and snuffboxes; the last named are by far the most common today. They are usually circular and slim, well painted, with scenes or portraits on the lid, the landscapes often based on English topographical prints. The interior of the snuff box lid was sometimes decorated with a *grivoiserie** but specimens are rare. The name of Stobwasser often appears in red inside the lid or on the bottom.

Small decorative lacquer wares, usually with decoration transfer-printed*, or partially printed, continued to be popular from makers other than Stobwasser until the 1880s.

See *Pontypool ware*; *Papier mâché*; *Tôle-peinte*

STONEWARE

Stoneware is clay mixed with a fusible rock in powdered form and fired to a temperature high enough to fuse it. It is much harder than earthenware*, and in this respect it is similar to porcelain*. Unlike porcelain, however, it is opaque when held up to the light and is coarser in quality. It is impervious to liquid, even when unglazed. Stoneware varies in colour. Drab or brown is the colour of a good deal of Lambeth stoneware; white or off-white marks the finer qualities, such as those known as ironstone china*, opaque china, etc. In Germany stoneware is referred to as *Steinzeug* and during the 19th century many copies of 16th- and 17th-century Rhineland* ware were made. In France stoneware is referred to as *grès* but it was comparatively little used, the French preferring *faïence** and *faïence-fine**.

See *Basaltesware*; *'Dry' bodies*; *Jasper*

STORE, COQUEREL AND LEGROS D'ANISY (Paris)

Potters, 1807 to 1849, who patented the transfer-printing* process in France, and decorated Creil *faïence-fine** in this way during the early years of the 19th century.

STORR, PAUL (1771–1844)

English silversmith; apprenticed to Andrew Fogelberg in 1785; registered his mark with the Goldsmiths' Company in 1792. Storr's earliest work is in the Adam style of his master, but this later developed into a Regency style* in which the usual repertory of

STORR, PAUL. Centrepiece of silver, parcel-gilt, made by Paul Storr* for presentation to Lieutenant-General Sir Arthur Wellesley by the Field Officers of the British Army in Portugal. London hall-mark for 1811–1812. *Apsley House, London*

ornament was handled with superb skill. Somewhat later in his career he also proved himself a master of the rococo style in his treatment of occasional pieces in the French manner, but these are rare.

Until 1807 he had his workshop in Piccadilly. Then he began working with Rundell, Bridge and Rundell* the Royal Silversmiths, for whom he was principally engaged on commemorative and presentation plate. He became a partner in 1811. At this period he had a workshop in Dean Street, Soho, under the style of Storr & Co. His association with Rundell ended in 1819, when he removed to Harrison Street, Clerkenwell. In 1821 he entered into partnership with John Mortimer, as Storr & Mortimer, and retired in 1839. Apart from massive centrepieces, cups, and commemorative pieces, he made much domestic plate for royalty and the nobility. His maker's mark was *PS*.

STOURBRIDGE (Worcestershire)

Centre of English glass-making since the 17th century, and especially active during the 19th century. The most important firms are Richardson & Sons*, Stevens & Williams* of Brierley Hill and Thomas Webb & Sons*. Almost every variety of glass was made. In the early period, Bohemia was very influential, and pressed glass* was made from the 1830s. Richardson's introduced a glass threading machine, and John Northwood* founded a school of cameo engraving inspired by the Portland Vase*, which he successfully copied. Opaline glass of good quality was produced, often decorated with enamel painting, and the so-called rock-crystal engraving style, brought by such Bohemians as Fritsche* and Kny*, was the medium of some excellent work.

STOURBRIDGE. Crystal glass jug, acid etched with the subject of two monks enjoying a joke. Stourbridge. Monks and cardinals drinking, eating heartily, and telling humorous stories were a popular subject for paintings, which appealed to an unsophisticated market. Probably one such painting inspired this jug. c. 1860. *The Corporation of Dudley*

Paperweights*, and other forms of *millefiori* decorations, were made at Stourbridge from mid-century onwards. A number of glassworkers, such as Frederick Carder*, emigrated from here to the United States, where they became prominent in the industry.

STUBBS, JOSEPH (d. 1836)
Makers of blue transfer-printed* wares at Longport, Staffordshire. The firm was in existence by 1818. Between 1828 and 1830 its style was Stubbs & Kent. American Views* were made for export, as well as a series of English Scenes. The impressed mark, *STUBBS & KENT, LONGPORT,* has been recorded.

STUDIO, THE
English art journal first published in 1893 which did much to promote the *art nouveau** style in Britain and abroad. The articles in its early volumes are invaluable source material for the period. Special numbers were issued at irregular intervals, each devoted to a single topic, ranging from English watercolours to modern book-illustration and cottage architecture.

STUFFED BIRDS AND ANIMALS
The 19th century was not only a period when the amateur and professional taxidermist flourished, but great interest was taken in animals and birds as the subjects of works of art, especially to be seen in the work of the *Animaliers**. As in the case of the work of Landseer, there was a distinct tendency to endow animals with human emotions and sensibilities, a process which later in the century developed into a whimsical attempt by Lewis Carroll to turn them into miniature human beings by dressing them up in clothes, representing them as performing a variety of

actions normally associated with men and women. Although this phase is commonly to be seen in book-illustration, some late 19th-century *tableaux* of stuffed animals still survive, and music hall turns in which dogs and cats suitably trained and clothed were shown in a variety of human situations remained popular until the First World War.

Victorian taxidermy is rare today because most examples have been destroyed by moth, but in general it was an art which marked a new approach to animals hardly to be seen before the 19th century. A solitary exception, perhaps, was the Meissen* porcelain series known as the Monkey Band* modelled by Kändler in the 1740s, and repeated by several factories a century or so later. A 'Frog' orchestra in porcelain dates from the 19th century, and one or two *tableaux* of stuffed frogs still survive.

Towards the end of the century George Tinworth* made mouse chessmen and musicians, and frog cricketers in stoneware* for Doulton*.

STUFFED BIRDS AND ANIMALS. A rosewood* cabinet containing stuffed specimens of British birds and small mammals. *Sotheby & Co*

STYLE 25 See *Art déco*

SUË ET MARC
Louis Suë (b. 1875) and André Marc founded the Compagnie des Arts Français in 1919 to make furniture, textiles, etc. This undertaking was a development of L'Atelier Français founded by Suë in 1912. Marc and Suë formulated a theory which dealt with every aspect of interior decoration. Their furniture took some of its inspiration from the styles of Louis-Philippe. They exhibited at the 1925 Exposition.

SULPHIDES
Also called crystallo-ceramie* by Apsley Pellatt* who, in 1819, patented the process of incrusting an unglazed stoneware relief with glass. Paperweights*, inkwells, perfume-bottles*, decanters, etc. were decorated in this way. The usual subject for work of this kind was a profile portrait, and Pellatt was probably

inspired by the earlier work of James Tassie and by some portrait medallions by Josiah Wedgwood*.

Apsley Pellatt, in fact, developed a process first devised in France at the end of the 18th century, and manufacture was taken up by Baccarat* who made many portraits of contemporary notabilities, including Napoleon III and Queen Victoria, of this kind. Similar portrait subjects were made at Saint-Louis*, and both undertakings have revived manufacture in recent years with portraits which include Queen Elizabeth and Prince Philip, Sir Winston Churchill, President Kennedy, and others. Clichy* made portrait weights in the 19th century and the New England Glass Company* of America also produced portrait weights.

Apart from portraits, some quite elaborate subjects, such as the *Hunter and his Dog* from Baccarat, were made in this technique, as well as portraits representing historical and religious figures.

'SUMMERLY, FELIX'

Pseudonym of Henry Cole*, one of the organizers of the Great Exhibition of 1851 and first director of the South Kensington Museum (now the Victoria and Albert Museum, London). Felix Summerly's Art Manufacture was organized in 1847 by Henry Cole for the laudable purpose of improving public taste and educating artists, designers, and manufacturers. Summerly commissioned the design, usually with floral or foliate decoration in a naturalistic style*, and the manufacture in a variety of materials—pottery, porcelain, silver, and glass. Parian* figures were designed by John Bell*, and Cole himself designed glass to be made by Richardson* of Stourbridge. Examples of these productions are to be found in the 19th-century gallery of the Victoria and Albert

'SUMMERLY, FELIX'. Water carafe decorated with enamels and gilding designed by Richard Redgrave, R.A. for Henry Cole*, and made by J. F. Christy. Stangate Glass Works, Lambeth, London. Signed *R. Redgrave, A.R.A.* and *FS* (Felix Summerly). Shown at the Exhibition of Modern British Manufactures, Royal Society of Arts, 1850. *Victoria & Albert Museum, London*

Museum. Cole abandoned his interest in the project when he became involved in the organization of the Great Exhibition, but several of the designs continued to be made for some years afterwards.

SUNDERLAND LUSTREWARE

Earthenware jugs, mugs, wall-plaques, chamber pots, etc. decorated with a mauve-pink lustre in marbled* patterns and decorated with black transfer-prints* of a variety of popular subjects, including ships, agricultural implements, the famous Iron Bridge over the river Wear, and texts ('Prepare to meet thy God'; 'Thou God seest me', etc.). Nearly all Sunderland jugs, mugs, etc. were also printed with doggerel verse. Wares of this kind were made at several potteries. Among the best known are Dixon, Austin & Co.* of the Garrison Pottery, who made many of the Wear Bridge transfer-prints, with sentimental verses, and Samuel Moore & Co. of the Wear Pottery, Sunderland, who made popular subjects from about 1803. Mugs with modelled frogs and toads inside came from Sunderland potteries.

SUNFLOWER

A favourite decorative *motif* of the Aesthetic Movement* of the 1880s. It has been remarked that the

'SUMMERLY, FELIX'. Clorinda wounded by her lover, modelled by John Bell. Minton's, 1848. Parian figure made for Felix Summerley's Art Manufacture. *Antique Collectors' Club*

sunflower seems to have no connection with Japanese* art, which was especially influential at the time. It certainly occurs rarely or never as a Japanese *motif*, but in the stylized version of the sunflower often used during the 1880s there is a very strong resemblance to the Japanese stylized chrysanthemum, the *mon* or heraldic device of the Japanese emperor that is commonly used to decorate objects of all kinds.

The sunflower also occurs in a less stylized form, and it was a favourite with Thomas Jeckyll*. Sunflowers, for instance, decorated the Japanese-inspired wrought-iron pavilion designed by Jeckyll for Barnard, Bishop, and Barnard of Norwich for the Philadelphia Centennial Exhibition of 1876, also shown in Paris in 1878. Jeckyll's inclusion of the sunflower in a predominantly Japanese design suggests that he, at least, confused it with the *mon* referred to.

SUSSE FRÈRES (Paris)

Paris bronze-founders established in 1840 by J.-V. Susse and J.-B.-A. Susse. The firm did much to encourage the sale of small bronzes in limited editions, and they published (not 'edited' in the English sense as is sometimes stated) the work of *Animaliers** like Mêne* and Colomera*. Much of their work was exported to England and America. The casts were stamped *SUSSE*, and often bear the artist's signature in addition.

'SUSSEX' CHAIR   See *'Morris' chair*

SUTHERLAND TABLE

A type of mid-19th-century gate-leg table with two wide flaps. When the flaps were lowered the table became very narrow and took up little space against a wall. The legs were usually turned. The type was named after the Duchess of Sutherland, one of Queen Victoria's Mistresses of the Robes.

SWANSEA POTTERY AND PORCELAIN

The Cambrian Pottery, Swansea, was owned by Lewis Weston Dillwyn (1778–1855) from 1802. In 1817 the manager, Timothy Bevington and others, founded a company which leased the works from Dillwyn, trading as T. & J. Bevington & Co., but the works reverted to Dillwyn in 1824, and he continued in association with his son from 1831 until 1850. In this year the works were sold to David Evans, and they closed finally in 1870.

Most of the pottery produced—creamware, blue-printed ware, black basaltes, and wares decorated with enamel painting and lustre—closely resemble contemporary Staffordshire production. From 1814 Billingsley* and Walker were at Swansea attempting to improve on their Nantgarw* porcelain, but experiments seemed to prove that this could only be done at the expense of quality, and Billingsley returned to his kilns at Nantgarw. Dillwyn continued to experiment, and produced a kind of porcelain

which could be manufactured without excessive kiln-wastage, and was excellent in quality. This, the 'duck-egg' body, so-called because of its greenish translucency when held to the light, is now the most sought. A soaprock porcelain, the last to be made, is of poor quality, both in body and glaze.

Swansea porcelain owed much of its inspiration to current Paris production; well-painted flowers form the greater part of the factory's decoration, mostly on plates, the usual form of surviving Swansea porcelain. Tureens and vases are much rarer and are correspondingly expensive. The usual shape for vases is neo-classical.

The porcelain mark is *Swansea* with the occasional addition of a trident, or crossed tridents.

SYMBOLISTES, LES

Movement in the arts which crystallized in 1886 with the foundation of the magazine, *Le Symboliste*. Courbet had put forward the argument that painting was a concrete art which could only depict things that were real, and that the abstract did not belong to the realm of painting. According to Delaroche, *symbolisme* was intended to resolve the contradiction between the sensory and spiritual worlds—'to allude, to suggest, therein lies the dream'. Painters like Redon, Moreau and Carrière were more interested in poetic ideas than in form. The movement was principally limited to poetry (Verlaine, Mallarmé), to music (Wagner, Debussy), and painting, but the movement also inspired Gallé's* *verrerie parlante**.

SYNTAX DR

Dr Syntax was the chief character of *The Tours of Doctor Syntax in search of the Picturesque* first published separately in 1820. This, and two other works featuring Doctor Syntax, were by William Combe (1741–1828), and would probably have been forgotten had they not been illustrated by Rowlandson. These illustrations inspired transfer-printed

SYP TEAPOT. The SYP, Simple Yet Perfect teapot. c. 1910. *Josiah Wedgwood** *& Sons Ltd*

decoration on earthenware by James and Ralph Clewes.

Pottery figures of Dr Syntax of the Walton* type exist, and in porcelain the subject was used for painted decoration by Chamberlain's* factory at Worcester and for figures at Derby*. Combe intended, in these *Tours*, to satirize the notion of the picturesque put forward by Dr William Gilpin towards the end of the 18th century which contributed greatly to the development of English garden design and the art of romantic landscape.

SYP TEAPOT

The 'simple yet perfect' teapot introduced by Wedgwood* in 1893. It was divided into two parts in such a way as to drain the tea after infusion into a forward compartment from which the leaves were excluded, and from which it was poured.

TABERNACLE MIRRORS

Mirrors in the Empire style of the early decades of the 19th century originally based on a Sheraton design, made both in England and America. They are rectangular in shape, the height greater than the width. They are also in two sections, the upper section painted with a scene, or sometimes with a panel of stucco modelled in bas relief. The frame is usually gold, or gold and black, the sides in the form of pillars, and a number of gilt balls are found decorating the space under the cornice. Specimens also occur in plain mahogany.

TABLE LAMPS, ELECTRIC

Lighting by means of the clumsy and inefficient carbon arc was first employed in 1866, although it was unsuitable for interiors. The carbon filament lamp invented by Edison in the 1870s provided the first reliable source of domestic lighting, although power stations were few and far between and electricity was still regarded as something not far

TABLE LAMPS, ELECTRIC. Lamp on a base of clear glass, the shade flashed with panels of translucent blue glass and cut in diamonds. Probably French. c. 1900. *Sotheby & Co*

TABLE LAMPS, ELECTRIC. Table lamp* with a *millefiori* shade and base made from fused sections of colourful canes. Early 20th century. *Sotheby & Co*

TABLE LAMPS, ELECTRIC. Electric table lamp of gilt-metal and marbled glass, the shade divided into sections by gilt mouldings. American. c. 1909. *Brighton Art Gallery & Museum, Sussex*

removed from black magic. Electric lighting was the sensation of the Paris Exposition of 1878. Equally sensational were the electrically illuminated fountains of the Exposition of 1889. By 1900 electric lighting had become almost commonplace, and only something on the scale of the *Palais d'Electricité* could be really impressive. A little before 1900 electric table lamps in the *art nouveau** style began to appear, the fittings a little primitive in brass and porcelain. These were sufficiently novel to lead to a fashion for table lamps as a work of art, some of the best made in such forms as bronze statues of the American dancer, Loïe Fuller*, with shades of glass by such makers as Gallé* and Tiffany*. These are still among the most eagerly sought forms of *art nouveau* decoration. Electric lighting, however, made such rapid progress and became so universal that few important lamps were made after 1900.

See *Fairy lamps*

TABLE-LUSTRE   See *Girandole*; *Lustres*

TABLES, VICTORIAN

During the Victorian period English furniture-makers produced tables in great variety, most of which are a development from the 18th century. Today Victorian tables have not uncommonly survived. The breakfast-table with tip-up top, either oval or circular, on a central pillar, is among the most sought. These, later employed as dining-tables, were usually made in either solid wood or veneered in rosewood* or mahogany. The rosewood veneers in the best work are well-figured. Work of this kind is often further embellished with inlaid brass stringing, and ornament inherited and developed from Regency* times. Most of this ornament was classically based. The baluster-shaped pillar rested on a circular platform carrying three, or more usually four splayed legs. The later examples were more heavily carved than the earlier. Tables of this kind are complemented by matching furniture of all sorts—chairs, cabinets and bookcases.

TABLES, VICTORIAN. An occasional table of apparently unprecedented design, made for an unknown purpose, since the top is also carved. In its form and decoration it is characteristic of a good many objects especially made for exhibitions, especially that of 1851. *Leslie Curtis*

The earlier examples, from about 1830 to 1850, are more or less equivalent to contemporary German Biedermeier* furniture. Breakfast-tables are sometimes termed 'loo' tables when offered for sale, and undoubtedly there is no reason why they should not have been used for playing this card game, but they were not made especially for the purpose.

By mid-century the massive rectangular mahogany dining-table on turned legs began to replace the circular variety. These are not usually very attractive, and few have survived. Some dining-tables in the late 18th-century manner were made, comprising a number of sections each with its own pedestal, but these are rare. This type is also being reproduced to special order today, and it is often difficult to be certain of the date without close and detailed examination.

In the 1860s and 1870s the circular table began to return to favour with a variety handsomely veneered in walnut, and some specimens elaborately inlaid. These, expensive at the time, are sought today, and fine inlaid work may also be found on occasional and half-circular (*demi-lune*) side-tables of the 1870s, the latter veneered in satinwood*. The 1870s also saw the production of tables on neo-Gothic* supports, although these are rare.

Throughout the period small ornamental tables were popular. These tables had first become popular during the 18th century. As they had no fixed position in the room, but could be moved to suit the needs of the moment, they were called 'occasional tables in England and '*ambulantes*' (strolling tables) in France. The Victorians employed them as a repository for *bric-à-brac* of all kinds—pieces of china, glass, silver or photograph frames. The tops were almost infinite in their variety. Usually circular, the edge was often scalloped, indented, turned over in a curve (*papier*

TABLES, VICTORIAN. English oval tea-table in mahogany decorated with swags and arabesques, inlaid in hardwood and fruitwood. The upper part has a fitted tray. Late 19th century. *Sotheby & Co*

TABLES, VICTORIAN. A rosewood*
sewing-table on turned supports. Late
19th century. *Sotheby & Co*

TALBERT, BRUCE J. Jug designed by B. J.
Talbert and made by Skidmore & Co.,
Birmingham. Hall-mark for 1866.
Victoria & Albert Museum, London

mâché), or provided with a moulding (solid wood),
the surface of mosaic, Tunbridge ware*, inlays of
various kinds, veneering, and painting (with or
without mother-of-pearl inlay).

Most of the lighter tables were of the tip-up variety.
Those with heavy tops, such as tops of *scagliola**, or
marble or slate were unsuitable for this type of
support. *Papier mâché* tops however, much lighter in
weight, are nearly always of a tip-up variety. The
pedestal support is often a variation on the centre
baluster stem on splayed legs, but spiral or elaborate
ornamental stems sometimes replace the plain baluster. Some square or oblong tables, usually those of
plain veneered wood on four legs (one at each corner),
have ormolu mounts and galleries. These may be
either of French or English manufacture and in the
absence of specific evidence differentiation is sometimes difficult. Decorative Victorian tables are now
in demand and much sought.

See *Sutherland table*

TAHAN, ALEXANDRE (Paris) (fl. 1850–1865)
Manufacturer of small objects of luxury, such as
jewel-cases, dressing-cases, and small furniture. A
casket of lapis lazuli is exhibited at the Bethnal Green
Museum, London.

TALBERT, BRUCE JAMES (1838–1881)
Architect and furniture designer. Talbert began his
career as a wood-carver in Dundee. In 1862 he began
to design furniture for Doveston, Bird & Hull of
Manchester, and then in 1865, moved to London,
where he designed furniture for the eminent London
cabinet-makers, Holland & Sons*. Talbert favoured
a simplified neo-Gothic* style, and published his
Gothic forms applied to furniture in 1867. Most of his
furniture was large, with inlaid geometric *motifs*, low
relief carving and sometimes large strap hinges. He
introduced small enamel panels and tiles into some of
his designs. Talbert also enjoyed considerable success

as a designer of silver, and worked for a number of
London silversmiths. He later turned to designing
wallpapers and textiles which proved very popular,
his sunflower* designs being exhibited at the Paris
Exposition of 1878. His *Examples of Ancient and
Modern Furniture* was also extremely influential.

'TALLIS' FIGURES
Staffordshire earthenware portrait figures based on
illustrations in Tallis's *Shakespeare Gallery*, published
in 1852–1853. Although the moulds were later
acquired by William Kent, no certain record appears
to exist of the name of the original manufacturer, and
the type are generally referred to as 'Tallis' figures
faute de mieux.

See *Staffordshire portrait figures*

TANTALUS
A decorative polished case for holding cut-glass
decanters containing spirits, usually with glasses in
addition. The tantalus was so constructed that the
decanters could be seen, but neither lifted out nor
unstoppered unless the case was first unlocked. Its
purpose was to guard the contents against depredations of the servants, and it was named after Tantalus,
who was condemned to stand eternally up to his neck
in the river Styx without being able to drink.

See *Decanters*

TAPESTRY, AMERICAN
A tapestry loom was set up by a Frenchman in New
York in 1893, and other low-warp looms were later
set up and operated with the aid of foreign workmen.

The products were principally good copies of old tapestries for interior decoration.

TARTAN ORNAMENT
A tartan (or plaid) is a textile pattern in which different colours are woven side by side in both warp and weft, thus giving a checkered pattern. Tartans are much favoured in Scotland, where each clan wears a distinctive pattern, but the origin seems to

TARTAN WARE. A ruler and a spectacle case with tartan decoration. c. 1855. *Constance Chiswell*

have been Eastern Europe. Tartan patterns enjoyed a brief popularity soon after Queen Victoria's acquisition of Balmoral in 1852. The vogue extended to pottery, furniture (upholstered in tartan material), and small objects of all kinds. Most Staffordshire pottery figures* of Highlanders, or the royal family in Highland costume, date from this time. Tartan patterns also occur in Mauchline ware* as early as the 1840s, and appear to have been made until 1900.

TASSEL RESIDENCE (Brussels)
One of the key works of the *art nouveau** style, the *Maison Tassel* was designed by Victor Horta* and built in 1892–3. The ground floor was an open plan design from which partition walls were omitted, the upper floor being carried on columns ornamented at the top with long, curving strap-like forms which give the whole column a tree-like appearance. The design is markedly asymmetrical and the ornament is abstract but obviously based on plant-forms. Although neither influence is very obvious, indebtedness to both Japanese and Gothic art is perceptible.

TEETH-BOXES
Circular boxes made during the late 18th and 19th centuries of silver, pottery, porcelain, or *papier mâché**

in which artificial teeth could be placed when not in use. At table teeth were often so inefficient that they were removed and placed in the box if the food was soft enough. Teeth-boxes are difficult to separate from all the other circular boxes of the period in the absence of specific evidence as to their purpose. Size and shape must, in most cases, determine attribution.

TERRACOTTA (Italian)
A widely-distributed iron-bearing clay employed principally by sculptors for busts, reliefs, and architectural pottery, such as vases and urns. When fired the clay assumes a colour varying between brick-red and pinkish-buff. It is normally given a comparatively low temperature firing to minimize the risk of firecracks and warping. Terracottas may be either made individually, or cast in piece-moulds when several copies are wanted. Terracotta clay was sometimes employed in the 19th century by pottery factories for figures, vases, and decorative wares, when a glaze was sometimes added.

See *Bastianini, Giovanni*; *Clodion, Claude Michel*; *Plaster-moulds*; *Watcombe Terracotta Company*

TERRY, ELI (1772–1852)
An important American clock-maker of Plymouth, Conn., who began in the 18th century by making long-case clocks with wooden movements, and early in the 19th century introduced the shelf-clock* which remained popular for many years. He developed methods of quantity production, and many later Connecticut clock-makers served their apprenticeship with him.

THEATRICAL FIGURES
A favourite 19th-century subject with makers of pottery and porcelain, especially with the manufacturers of Staffordshire portrait figures*. Prints, music-covers, and illustrated journals were common sources, and research is continually identifying hitherto unattributed figures. Most unidentified figures probably have their origin in some kind of theatrical presentation.

THEBES CHAIR
A design registered by Liberty* in 1884. It is based on

THEATRICAL FIGURES. *Maria Foote*, the actress, in male attire. Staffordshire earthenware. c. 1840. *Constance Chiswell*

THEATRICAL FIGURES. *Dick Turpin*, a character from the popular 19th-century melodrama. Staffordshire earthenware. c. 1860. *Antique Collectors' Club*

THEATRICAL FIGURES. Porcelain figure of an unidentified actress. Minton*. c. 1845. *Constance Chiswell*

an Egyptian thong-seated chair to which a back has been added. A stool was made *en suite*. The design was by Leonard Wyburd, and the chair was sold by Samuel Bing* in his Paris shop.

THEED THE ELDER, WILLIAM (1764–1817)
English painter and sculptor, educated at the Academy Schools. Theed began to model for Wedgwood* from 1799 to 1804, and he then went to work for the Prince Regent's silversmiths, Rundell, Bridge & Rundell. Theed again worked for Wedgwood in 1811 and modelled a portrait of Tom Byerley.

THIEME, CARL (Potschappel)
Porcelain factory founded in 1875 specializing in the reproduction of early Meissen* figures and groups. These can sometimes be deceptive but are usually fairly obvious from well-marked differences in colouring. The most common mark is a diagonal cross, X, in conjunction with the letter 'T' the cross often being drawn superficially to resemble the Meissen crossed swords.

THIMBLES
The collecting of thimbles has become popular in recent years, and the rarest like those of Chelsea or Sèvres* porcelain or Bilston enamel, are highly valued. During the 19th century decorative thimbles were made from porcelain, silver, gold, tortoiseshell, wood banded with gold, and with tops of semi-precious stones like lapis lazuli and amethyst. The best are examples of fine craftsmanship, those of precious metals and stones being jewellers' work, and porcelain thimbles often exhibit excellent miniature

329

THEBES CHAIR. High-back thong-seated chair, based on a Roman or Egyptian stool with a back added. Trade-mark: *THEBES. Liberty & Co.* A stool *en suite* was also made. Designed by Wyburd*. c. 1890. *William Morris Gallery, Waltham Forest*

painting. Inscribed examples are rare in the 19th century, but thimbles commemorating such events as the Queen's Jubilee can be found occasionally.

THOMAS, SETH (1785–1859)
Connecticut clock-maker, briefly associated with Terry*, who started his own business in 1812 making shelf-clocks* with wooden movements. He organized the Seth Thomas Clock Company in 1853.

THOMIRE-DUTHERME ET CIE (Paris)
French *fondeurs-ciseleurs* founded by Pierre-Philippe Thomire (1751–1843). Before the Revolution Thomire cast sculpture for Houdon, Pajou, and others, and made bronze mounts for clocks, Sèvres* porcelain, and the principal Paris *ébénistes*. Surviving the Revolution he enjoyed the patronage of Napoleon I, and became an important exponent of the Empire style*. He retired in 1823. His work is often marked.

THONET, MICHAEL (1796–1871)
Thonet was the first to make well-designed, mass-produced furniture which was widely distributed and ultimately influenced the development of the modern movement in furniture design.

Thonet was born at Boppard-am-Rhein in 1796,

and by 1819 had established himself as a small independent manufacturer. In 1830 he was experimenting with furniture made from prefabricated parts, and ten years later he came to the attention of Prince Metternich. In the following year, in consequence of financial difficulties, he took his family to Vienna and began to work under Carl Leistler* on furniture for the Liechtenstein Palace. By 1849 he was once again independent, and was making chairs from laminated mahogany which became popular in cafés. In 1851 he exhibited at the Great Exhibition in London, where the products of Carl Leistler were regarded as the epitome of luxury, and Thonet's contribution was also much praised. He again exhibited successfully at the 1855 Paris Exposition and in this year first exported furniture to South America.

Soon afterwards Thonet began to employ production-line methods of making furniture and introduced new machinery for this purpose. The use of laminated wood was discontinued because it had proved unsuitable for humid climates, and methods of bending solid wood, usually beechwood, were adapted to new designs. His chair No. 14 was introduced in 1859. This is a type of chair with which most people are familiar, and there are few who have not sat on one, or one of its successors, at some time or another. The frame was of beechwood put together with screws, and one of its advantages was that it could be packed and transported in parts and assembled at its destination. In 1860 the first rocking chair was produced, and the new mass-produced furniture was successfully exhibited in London in 1862. By 1910, 50 million examples of chair No. 14 had been produced and sold, and with later modifications and improvements it continued to sell on a large scale throughout the world almost until modern times.

After Thonet's death in 1871, the enterprise continued to expand. New factories were opened in Poland and Germany with showrooms in many of the principal European cities, as well as New York and Chicago. Thonet designs were also widely manufactured under licence by others. Thonet chairs have been employed in interiors by such architects as Adolf Loos and Le Corbusier*. In modern times, the firm has manufactured furniture designed by Marcel Breuer* and Mies van der Rohe*. Products are usually stamped or labelled.

THOOFT & LABOUCHÈRE, JOOST (Delft, Holland)
Manufacturers of underglaze blue-painted earthenware, much of it in the old tin-glazed Delft manner. The factory was known as *De Porceleyne Fles* in 17th-century style, when potteries were established in disused breweries. In 1919 the factory was granted a Royal Privilege and became known as the Koninklijke Delftsche-Aardwerk Fabriek, 'De Porceleyne Fles'. The art-director from 1877 to 1919 was Adolphe Le Comte.

THORWALDSEN, BERTEL (1770–1844)

Danish neo-classical sculptor, resident in Rome from 1797 to 1838. Thorwaldsen spent his youth in Copenhagen, and was assisting his father, a wood-carver, at the age of 12. His training at the Academy ended in 1793 with the award of a gold medal, and for a time he returned to carving ships' figure-heads and mirror-frames for his father. His work at this time was in a kind of Louis XVI style, a mixture of rococo* and neo-classical*. In 1796 he was awarded the Academy's travelling scholarship, and arrived in Rome in 1797 on 8 March, which he later celebrated as his 'Roman Birthday'. From Georg Zoega, Danish Envoy to the Papal Court and an antiquarian, Thorwaldsen formed a sound knowledge of ancient classical art, and he began to approach the Graeco-Roman spirit more nearly than any other sculptor. He came to the notice of Canova, who helped him to establish his reputation, and a commission from Thomas Hope* gave him the means to stay in Rome when his scholarship expired. He now began to receive important commissions, and he was given honours. In 1819 he returned to Denmark and executed several commissions, but by the end of 1820 he was back in Rome, where his studio became one of the sights of the city. At this time he undertook a number of Christian subjects including the monument to Pope Pius VII in St Peter's.

In 1838 he returned to Copenhagen where his arrival became almost a national event, and he was given a studio in the grounds of the Christianborg Palace. He died in 1844.

THREADED DECORATION

Method of decorating glass by winding threads of different coloured glass around it, either in concentric circles, or in a variety of patterns. The practice is of great antiquity, but a machine for doing work of this kind was invented by Richardson's* of Stourbridge in the 1860s, and the technique became very popular during the latter half of the 19th century.

See *Latticinio*

TIFFANY & CO. Pepper-shaker and salt in traditional form, the surface decorated with floral *motifs*. Marked. Tiffany & Co. c. 1880. *Mrs F. H. Stubbley*

TICHBORNE CLAIMANT, THE

A *cause célèbre* of the Victorian period. A butcher from Wapping named Thomas Castro, alias Orton, put forward a bogus claim to the Tichborne estates in 1872, posing as Sir Roger Tichborne whose father had died ten years before. Castro answered all the questions put to him so convincingly, and with such astonishing knowledge, that at one point Lady Tichborne was prepared to accept him as her son. Eventually his claim was disproved, and he received a severe sentence for perjury. The participants are to be found in both pottery and porcelain, such as candle-extinguishers from Worcester*, and occur sporadically in other of the minor arts of the period.

TIEFSCHNITT (German)

Literally, deep-cutting. Term used in describing glass decoration: ornament not raised above the surface; *intaglio*.

TIFFANY & CO. (New York)

The world famous American firm of silversmiths and jewellers founded in 1834 which should not be confused with the firms established by Louis Comfort Tiffany, son of the founder, Charles Louis Tiffany (d.1902). L. C. Tiffany became art-director of Tiffany & Co. in the year of his father's death. Tiffany & Co. originally imported jewellery from Paris, but in 1848 began to make their own, employing Paris styles. The growth of enormous private fortunes in America during the 19th century enabled Tiffany to specialize in expensive precious-stone jewellery, and they also became noted for an immense collection of fine quality diamonds. They won an award for silver in the Paris Exposition of 1867 and Christopher Dresser* acquired Japanese silver on their behalf when he visited Japan in 1876. They were also the principal makers of commemorative and presentation pieces. Of these perhaps the most impressive is the vase made for the president of an oil company, Edward Dean Adams, in 1898. This is solid gold, ornamented with classical figures and has a cover of carved rock-crystal decorated with pearls, semi-precious stones and enamels. It has now found its

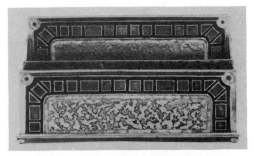

TIFFANY, LOUIS COMFORT. Gilt and enamel bronze letter-rack. Louis C. Tiffany Furnaces Inc. *Sotheby & Co*

way into the Metropolitan Museum, New York, as an example of what the 19th century could do when expense was no object.

In 1892 Tiffany set up a factory near Newark, N.J., for the manufacture of electro-plate.

TIFFANY GLASS See 'Favrile'

TIFFANY, LOUIS COMFORT (1848–1933)

Artist, designer, and manufacturer, born in New York, the son of Charles Louis Tiffany (1812–1902), a jeweller and silversmith (see *Tiffany & Co.*). Louis studied painting in Paris under Leon Bailly and travelled extensively in Europe. In the 1870s he turned to interior decoration and in 1879 established a firm called Louis C. Tiffany & Associates. In 1882 they were entrusted with the redecoration of the White House. Tiffany was interested in developing the decorative arts generally, but he became especially attracted to stained glass, then fashionable for windows, and in turn, to blown glass. In 1892 the Tiffany Glass & Decorating Company was formed and in 1896 it began to manufacture an art glass under the name of 'Favrile', noted for its blown *art nouveau** forms and an iridescent surface, which became widely sought and extremely influential. The name was changed to Tiffany Studios in 1900. A factory was established at Corona, Long Island, where Tiffany employed craftsmen from Europe, and in 1895 he began to ship glass to France for his friend Samuel Bing* to display in his Paris gallery, La Maison de L'Art Nouveau.

The use of bronze for decorative purposes, often combined with glass or hardstones, was started early in the 1890s. Tiffany Studios had, from its inception, taken a considerable interest in the decorative use of electric light, and in the 1890s designed table lamps with a bronze stem terminating in a mushroom-shaped shade of stained glass set in lead glazing bars. The shades were decorated in a variety of ways— with dragon-flies, wisteria and other popular *art nouveau* themes.

In 1902 L. C. Tiffany took over the position of art-director of his father's business, Tiffany & Co. He began to design jewellery in the *art nouveau** style. In 1905 pottery in the same style, first shown in the Saint Louis World's Fair the year before, was added to the repertoire. Vases covered with Oriental type glazes were among the most important decorative objects produced. The trade name 'Favrile' was also employed for pottery, which continued to be made until 1919.

Somewhat rare are copper panels, usually with embossing, and decorated with enamels, which Tiffany marketed in 1900, although he had been experimenting with various enamelling processes during the preceding few years. These panels were usually made up into boxes of one kind of another, or, occasionally, the enamels applied to glass as an additional embellishment.

Tiffany was usually to the forefront of the artistic movements of his day, except, perhaps, in furniture. The small quantity designed and made about 1880 for the decorating business had distinct affinities with some Louis XVI designs in lightness, elegance and a general classical air. Some of the furniture designs also had a distinctly Japanese flavour, especially in the carved floral decoration. He employed a kind of wood mosaic for surfaces such as table-tops, in which the pattern was made up of a large number of small square sections framed by thin metal strips flush with the surface—a new and time-consuming technique which was obviously expensive in its demands on skilled labour. Chair-backs were carved with restrained floral *motifs*, and glass balls in a brass four-pronged setting acted as casters.

Tiffany was one of the most important figures in the development of *art nouveau*, both in America and Europe, and his 'Favrile' glass especially greatly influenced a number of art glass manufactures of his time, including Frederick Carder* who founded the Steuben Glass Company*.

TIFFANY STUDIOS

Makers of art-pottery. L. C. Tiffany had experimented with pottery at Corona, New York, from 1898. It was first shown commercially at the Saint Louis World's Fair in 1904, and first marketed in 1905. The design was strongly influenced by *art nouveau**, much of the

TIFFANY STUDIOS. Bronze inkwell with rich verdigris patination. Stamped: *Tiffany Studio New York.* c. 1900–1910. *Sotheby & Co*

decoration (usually floral and foliate) was adapted from metalwork, and the glazes were principally moss-green and yellow in colour. Slip-casting was general, and wheel-thrown specimens unusual. Tiffany withdrew in 1919, and the incised monogram *LCT* belongs to a date earlier than this. The Tiffany trade-mark, *Favrile*, was also used.

TINSEL PICTURES

Pictures formed from glittering pieces of thin metallic foil in a variety of colours added to portrait engravings, particularly those depicting actors and actresses in costume. These were especially popular during the 1830s and 1840s, but the technique was revived in the 1920s by an artist named Carrington and others. Specimens are rare. Those by Carrington are signed. Tinsel pictures of the 19th century were based on the 'penny plain, twopence coloured'* portraits of theatrical personalities which were first marketed about 1808 and became increasingly popular in the following decades. The practice of 'dressing' portrait engravings in costume made up of small pieces of silk, satin, and coloured paper glued to the background dates from the last quarter of the 18th century, and probably inspired the tinsel portraits. The latter were rarely very elaborate till the 1820s, when the manufacturers of toy-theatres started to produce tinsel ornament already cut into a variety of shapes, not only stars, dots, and stripes, but helmets, crowns, plumes, daggers, boots and gauntlets which were added to engravings by amateurs of every degree of talent.

Professionally made pictures vary in quality with price and the purpose for which they were intended. Landscapes decorated with a few stars, and unsophisticated portraits of the young Queen Victoria, were made to be sold at fairs for a few pence. The best are usually portraits of actors in character, especially in such dramatic roles as Richard III. Actresses are not so often depicted, probably because their costumes were less effective as a foundation for tinsel additions. Most tinsel pictures can be dated with a little research, since they depict an actor (or actress) in a particular production for which they became well known. Some of the subjects may be found again in Staffordshire pottery theatrical portrait figures* for which the prints probably provided inspiration.

The best tinsel pictures are now much sought, especially those with an origin in the theatre.

See *Dressed prints*

TINTED VENUS
A marble statue by John Gibson*, R.A., which was shown in the London Exhibition of 1862. Nearly all Greek and Roman marble statuary had been recovered in an uncoloured state due to weathering. During the neo-classical period, starting in the middle of the 18th century, it was largely overlooked that in ancient times most statues, and a good deal of architectural marble, were painted and often partially gilded. André Malraux has described neo-classicism as a 'white world', but John Gibson reverted to the practice of earlier times, for which he had literary justification and the ocular proof of the mural paintings at Herculaneum. He painted some of his statues, to use his own words, 'in a manner never before seen in these times' (i.e. 1862). The *Tinted Venus*, nude except for a little partially-concealing drapery, was the most important example of his work in this style. He described the colouring as follows: 'The flesh is tinted warm ivory, the eyes are blue, the hair is blonde, an armlet and an apple in her hand are gold, and the drapery has a border of pink and blue'.

Two other statues from his hand in the Exhibition were also tinted. As might be expected, the *Tinted Venus*, outwardly received with some reservation, was extremely popular, rivalling the success of Hiram Powers's *Greek Slave*ic in 1851. It was included in 1962 at an exhibition at the Victoria & Albert Museum, London, commemorating the one of a century earlier. Reproductions in terracotta* were made by the Torquay Terracotta Company* in the 1880s. The *Tinted Venus* was sold by Christie's in 1890, realizing £1,837 (gold pounds), and it still exists in a private collection.

See *Nude, the*

TINWORTH, GEORGE (1847–1913)
Modeller at Doulton* who studied at the Lambeth School of Art and then at the Royal Academy Schools. He entered the employment of Doulton in 1866, and specialized in the modelling of terracotta plaques of

TINWORTH, GEORGE. Ebonized and giltwood cabinet designed by C. Bevan and made by Doulton* in 1872. The stoneware* plaques were modelled by George Tinworth* and depict the *Life of Christ*. Exhibited at the London International Exhibition, 1872. *Victoria & Albert Museum, London*

religious subjects in relief. An ebonized cabinet designed by C. Bevan and inset with stoneware plaques illustrating the life of Christ by Tinworth was exhibited in the London International Exhibition of 1872. It is now in the Victoria & Albert Museum, London. He also modelled small and amusing figures such as mice as musicians and chessmen, frogs as cricketers, and so forth, and designed vases with decorations incised and in relief. He signed his work with the monogram *GT* incised.

TITTENSOR, CHARLES (1764–after 1825)

Charles and John Tittensor were in business as earthenware figure-makers from 1803 until 1807. The firm then became Tittensor & Simpson until 1813, after which Charles Tittensor traded on his own account until at least 1823. His figures are much in the style of Walton*, and bear the name *Tittensor* impressed.

TOAD MUGS

Mugs in the bottom of which is placed a modelled toad, to be uncovered when the contents are drained. The use of the toad was inspired by the belief that this reptile was venomous. Most mugs of this kind were made during the early decades of the 19th century in the north of England. Chamber pots are found occasionally with a toad in the bottom.

TOFT, CHARLES

Figure modeller who worked first for Worcester* about 1855 and then for Elkington* in Birmingham. At Minton* in the 1860s he seems to have been largely responsible for copies of Henri Deux ware*, and later became a pupil of Marc-Louis Solon*, learning the *pâte-sur-pâte* technique. In 1872 he became chief figure modeller to Wedgwood*, and was responsible for a medallion portrait of Gladstone, the *War and Peace* vase exhibited in the Paris Exposition of 1878 and models after designs by Walter Crane*. He later opened a small factory making inferior wares decorated with slip.

TÔLE-PEINTE (French)

Japanned sheet-iron made into objects of domestic utility and usually decorated by painting. The range was very wide—from coffee-pots to *jardinières*—and the painted decoration was variable in quality. It dates from mid-18th-century until well into the 19th, the earlier specimens usually being the best.

See *Pontypool ware*

TÔLE WARE

Tôle is a French word meaning 'sheet-iron': *tôle-peinte** is ware made from sheet iron with painted decoration; *tôle-vernie* is japanned sheet-iron; *tôle-cuivre* is sheet-copper. The English equivalent of ware made from sheet iron is termed Pontypool ware*. Basically, English and French wares of this type are made with shears and rivets and a soldering iron. The essential shapes are cut (or in mass-production operation, stamped) from sheet metal, bent into shape and soldered. The method is the same as that of the silversmith making a coffee-pot, or the coppersmith making a kettle or a ewer. Generally tôle ware consists of jugs, trays, ewers, *jardinières* and vessels lending themselves to this method of manufacture. The surface was usually 'japanned', i.e. it was first covered with several coats of paint, then by layers of heat-resisting varnish. The ground colour was usually, but not invariably, black. The decoration was then painted on in coloured varnishes. Some of the best French work, dating from the early years of the 19th century, has painted decoration copied from that of Sèvres* porcelain. Some rare and interesting trays with a ground colour similar to that of a light-coloured wood were made about 1860 and decorated with coloured topographical engravings of France, varnished to preserve them from damage.

TOPOGRAPHICAL PAINTING. Porcelain mug with a view of the City of Worcester showing the Cathedral and the bridge over the river Severn. Worcester, Chamberlain's* factory. c. 1820. *Private collection*

TOPOGRAPHICAL PAINTING

Painting of a landscape with buildings, or of town-scenery, in such detail, and in so realistic a manner, that it can be recognized without difficulty. When titled, topographical paintings are usually termed 'Named Views'*.

TORQUAY TERRACOTTA COMPANY (Devon)

This pottery was founded in 1875 by Dr Gillow, who discovered a source of clay nearby. The body diverged from that of most Watcombe* pottery by being markedly lighter in colour. Occasional light-coloured examples of Watcombe pottery occur, but no dark Torquay pottery. The wares produced were varied. Small statues and figures based on the work of John Gibson* (including the *Tinted Venus**), and other sculptors of the time, and some original figures, vases, plaques and domestic wares were all excellent in quality, rivalling that of Watcombe. Much of the hollow-ware was turned. The marks employed give the name in full either impressed or printed in black, or the initials *TTC*. The factory closed in 1909.

TORTOISESHELL GLASS

Type of art glass* first produced by the Boston and Sandwich Glass Company* about 1880. It is amber in colour with dark brown patches, somewhat resembling tortoiseshell. It was widely imitated in the United States and in Europe.

TOURS (Indre et Loire) See *Avisseau, Charles C. J.*; *Landais,*

TOXOPHILITE, THE FAIR

Jugs and earthenware figures of a Pratt* type

representing a female archer. They record a society fashion for archery in the first half of the 19th century.

TRANSFER-PRINTING

A method of decorating pottery and porcelain by taking an impression on soft paper from an engraved plate. While the ink is still wet this is pressed on to the surface to be decorated. The ink used is a normal ceramic colour, but it is usually black overglaze or blue underglaze.

TRANSFER-PRINTING. Foot-basin by John Mere, Staffordshire, transfer-printed* in underglaze blue. c. 1820
Godden of Worthing

There are several ways of using this technique. Prints which resemble the normal black and white engraving are usually employed in monochrome, either under or overglaze. In the case of overglaze transfer-prints, colouring was sometimes added by hand, but this is comparatively rare and, on porcelain, often signifies painting done later in an independent studio. Simple outline prints, on the other hand, were intended for colouring by hand, and this enabled polychrome decoration to be produced overglaze on both pottery and porcelain by using semi-skilled labour. In the case of good quality porcelain careful examination is sometimes needed before it is possible to be sure whether or not outline prints have been used.

Another type of transfer-print introduced at the end of the 18th century is bat-printing, so-called because the medium of transfer was a 'bat' of soft glue instead of paper. Prints made in this way were built up from stipples in the same way as the Bartolozzi print, and the technique was not used for line-engraving.

Pratt* of Fenton developed a method of producing coloured stipple prints which were used for the decoration of pot-lids* and service ware. A small circle on either side, near the extreme edge of the pattern, was for the purpose of locating the colours in their correct positions. These are always present on a genuine specimen. Peter Warburton* invented transfer-printing in gold in 1810, and lithographic transfers came into use after 1851.

Relatively little use was made of transfer-printing on the Continent during the 18th century, but the practice became much commoner in France during the 19th century, especially on *faïence-fine* from

Creil*. Generally, Continental manufacturers have always been inclined to favour hand-work in decoration.

See *Decalcomania*

TRASK, ISRAEL (1786–1867)

Pewterer of Beverley, Mass., who specialized in whale-oil lamps, tea-pots, casters and tankards with chiselled ornament, a comparatively rare technique in the decoration of pewter.

TRAYS, METAL

Trays of Pontypool ware* or *tôle-peinte* are now sought when well decorated. Those of Pontypool ware were sometimes painted in polychrome with flowers and landscapes, or decorated with *chinoiserie* scenes in gold, influenced in some cases by the popular *papier mâché* trays. Decorative metal trays were also produced in France in the 1850s and 1860s. One type has a central oval flower bouquet surrounded by oval topographic transfer prints in polychrome against a light-coloured ground. These are much sought.

TROPHIES. Bronze clock case* surmounted by an equestrian figure; at the base, a trophy of arms. c. 1860.
Sotheby & Co

TROPHIES

In ancient times it was the custom to hang the arms of a beaten enemy on a tree, and this display was later carved or painted in formal decorative arrangements, termed trophies. Later, more peaceful implements – those of the artist, musician, or gardener, for instance – were similarly grouped and used for a variety of decorative purposes, retaining the name, trophy.

TROUBADOUR STYLE, THE

Néo-Gothique, the French version of the revived Gothic* style, current from about 1825 to 1848, and fashionable from 1830 to 1840. The Gothic style originated in the Île de France towards the end of the 12th century and was exported from there to England and the German States. South of the Loire the principal styles remained classical and Romanesque, and what Gothic buildings exist are usually Gothic ornament on a Romanesque framework. Purely Gothic buildings are more numerous in Northern France, but the style never achieved the dominant position it had in England. Louis XIV detested it and actively promoted the destruction of some Gothic survivals. In the 19th century the *néo-Gothique* style never became associated with religious evangelism. There was no reason why it should, since many, perhaps most, of the older French *basiliques* and cathedrals were Romanesque, and the people did not, in any case, suffer a period of religious enthusiasm comparable with that of England.

It is not surprising, therefore, that lacking a strong Gothic tradition, a Pugin* to link art and religion, and the ethical idealism so fatally attractive to the British character, the *néo-Gothique* of the French, sandwiched between the styles of the First and Second Empires*, should take a quite different course. It is possible that Pugin's father exerted influence on the style in France. Certain of his furniture designs for Ackermann's *Repository of the Arts* anticipate to some extent those of the 1830s. Inspiration certainly came from Lenoir's* Musée des Monuments Françaises that he began to form during the Revolution, which fostered the link between Romanticism* and the taste for medieval art. The pointed arch made its appearance in decorative chair-backs, and in the mouldings of doors to *armoires* and cabinets. Crockets and pendentives often occur as part of the decoration of chairs.

In general, French *néo-Gothique,* which extended to all objects of interior decoration during its currency, is much less serious in intent than its English counterpart, and it shared popular favour with a number of other revived styles, and those inspired from elsewhere, such as *néo-rocaille* (neo-rococo), néo-Renaissance, Persian, Chinese and Egyptian, to an extent which did not occur in England. A contemporary term for decoration of this kind was '*à la cathédrale*', hence, the style is occasionally termed 'Cathedral'.

TUCKER, WILLIAM ELLIS (1800–1832)

Maker of the first American porcelain on a commercial scale at a factory in Philadelphia which was started in 1825. After his death the business was continued by his partner, Joseph Hemphill, as the American China Manufactory.*

'TUDRIC'

Trade name of pewter with a silver content made for Liberty & Co*, London, from about 1900 onwards until the beginning of the Second World War. Until 1926 manufacture was carried out by W. H. Haseler & Co.* of Birmingham, a firm of silversmiths founded in 1870. Decoration was usually floral, and the style a kind of *art nouveau** based on Celtic *motifs,* the flowers having curving stalks or tendrils.

See '*Cymric*'

'TUDRIC'. 'Tudric'* pewter and enamel clock. Liberty & Co.* c. 1903. *Sotheby & Co*

'TUDRIC'. Pewter dish decorated in the *art nouveau** style with Celtic-inspired floral *motifs.* Designed and made for Liberty & Co.* and appropriately marked. c. 1905. *Constance Chiswell*

'TULIP' CHAIR   See *Saarinen, Eero*

TUNBRIDGE WARE

The wood inlays and mosaics commonly known as Tunbridge ware were first made in Tonbridge, Kent, during the early years of the 19th century, although novelties in both white wood and lignum vitae were being made, according to Celia Fiennes, for sale to visitors in the 17th century. In the 18th century the town, and nearby Tunbridge Wells which was a fashionable spa, was noted for decorative inlays or marquetries of excellent quality, and these were sold in London as well as in Tonbridge. The inlaid wares continued to be made in considerable variety until well into the 19th century. The conventional marquetry employed for this work was replaced to a large extent in the 1820s by a new process which was much quicker and less laborious, and therefore cheaper. Hardwood sticks of various colours and sections were glued together side by side to form a pattern which, in the case of the best specimens, was often very elaborate. When the block had become dry and solid it was sawn transversely into thin sections of about 1/16th of an inch in thickness. The mosaic picture thus obtained was glued to the surface of the object to be decorated, usually a box of some kind. About 150 different kinds of wood were employed in the making of the more elaborate of these pictures, some of which were dyed, and mosaic was often combined with marquetry. Examined closely the picture appears to be made up of many small pieces of wood put together like a miniature mosaic pavement. The glued blocks were also turned on the lathe with a variety of interesting effects. Most of these pictures were quite small, and suitable for the decoration of the ever-popular boxes which were made in great variety. One manufacturer of Tunbridge mosaic, however, exhibited a table at the Great Exhibition of 1851, the top of which was made up of more than a hundred thousand pieces of wood.

Designs are generally floral and foliate, the floral designs often based on the patterns of Berlin wool-work*. Topographical subjects are rarer, and views of Battle Abbey and of the Pantiles at Tunbridge Wells are impressive examples. Butterflies and birds are much sought and date from the late 1820s. Boxes are by far the most common—jewel-caskets, trinket-boxes, glove-boxes, handkerchief-boxes, tea-caddies, stamp-boxes, boxes for playing-cards, paint-boxes and cigarette-boxes are but a few dear to the Victorians, but objects of many other kinds were also manufactured, the most ambitious perhaps being the very rare tables and chairs. A folding games-table made in 1845 by Fenner & Co. for the Prince Consort is now in Kensington Palace.

Manufacturers of Tunbridge mosaic ware were numerous during the 19th century. Pinto records many of them in *Tonbridge and Scottish Souvenir Woodware* (London, 1970), and also draws attention to the manufacture of mosaic ware by James Medhurst of Weymouth, formerly of Tunbridge Wells, and Thomas Green who was making ware of this kind at Rye, Sussex, during the 1930s, and was the last of his trade. Small woodware with painted decoration was made in Tonbridge from 1790 to about 1830. There is an important collection in the Tunbridge Wells Museum.

See *Sorrento ware*

U

ULLMAN, FRANZ
Bohemian glass-engraver working for J. & L. Lob-meyr* at their Steinschönau glasshouse. His work was included in the Vienna Exhibition of 1871.

UNA AND THE LION See *Bell, John*

UNION GLASS COMPANY (Somerville, Mass.)
Company founded in 1854. They made a pressed glass* of good quality but of little originality, as well as silvered glass*. Their later work includes cut-glass*, ornamental vases, and an iridescent glass known as Kewblas* inspired by Tiffany's* 'Favrile' glass introduced in the 1880s. They were among the American producers of *art nouveau** styles. The factory closed in 1924.

UNION PORCELAIN WORKS (Greenpoint, Long Island, New York)
This factory was established in 1864 by Thomas C. Smith for the manufacture of a type of hard-paste porcelain* similar to that made at Meissen*, Sèvres* and other European factories. He seems to have been the first potter in the United States to overcome the difficulty of applying underglaze colour to porcelain of this type.

UNITED STATES POTTERY COMPANY See *Bennington Pottery*

UNIVERSITY CITY POTTERY
Founded at University City, Missouri, by Edward G. Lewis with the aid of Taxile Doat* from Sèvres*, E. Diffloth from Boch Frères*, F. H. Rhead* from Staffordshire, and Adelaide and Samuel Robinson, who, in 1899, founded a magazine for china decorators, the *Keramic Studio*. The pottery formed a department of the University where overglaze decoration and other technical aspects of the subject were taught. Porcelain of high quality was produced, and an exhibit at the Turin exposition of 1911 was awarded a gold medal. Production seems to have ceased finally when Doat left for France in 1915. The circular mark is printed, and incorporates Doat's monogram.

URANIUM OXIDE
Used early in the present century as a colouring agent for some rare lead glazes, either a brilliant tangerine-orange or a vermilion red. Pottery thus glazed was made by William Burton at Pilkington* in 1903 and by Minton* for their 'Solar' ware a little later. This glaze, which is very slightly radioactive, is not now in use.

Uranium oxide and iron oxide were also used to case opal glass in the making of amber onyx glass. The exterior being subjected to heat and gas fumes, then acquired a skin in transparent shades of amber. See *Cased glass*

PORCELAIN. A group of painted porcelain pipe-bowls with
early Victorian silver-gilt mounts. The bowls are probably
German and the mounts are by Rawlings & Summers, 1847.
The Arms are those of the Rev. Thomas Best, nephew of
the 1st Baron Whynford. *Sotheby & Co*

Above left:
SWANSEA PORCELAIN. Plate enamelled with flowers. Mark:
SWANSEA in red. *Private Collection*

Above right:
ROYAL CROWN DERBY. Plate decorated with Japan pattern
no. 1128. Current production. *Royal Crown Derby Porcelain
Company*

Below:
RENÉ LALIQUE. Table in clear and acid-etched glass on a
chromium-plated iron frame. Made in France, c. 1930, by
René Lalique. *Brighton Art Gallery & Museum*

VAISSEAU À MÂT (French)

An elaborate and decorative pot-pourri vase first made at Vincennes (later the Sèvres* factory) about 1755. It is made in two parts, the lower part boat-shaped on four feet, the pierced upper part representing the mast and rigging. A banner dependent from the mast-head is dotted with the *fleur-de-lys*. A single-masted vessel of this kind is part of the arms of Paris. An example in the Wallace Collection, London, is decorated with apple-green and *gros bleu* grounds, but most of the few known specimens show some variations in decoration.

The popularity of Sèvres porcelain during the 19th century inspired the making of a number of reproductions, by Minton* especially. Minton apparently copied an example in the collection of the Duke of Sutherland, who lent the factory some of his Sèvres porcelain for this purpose.

VALENTINES

Precisely how Saint Valentine, a bishop martyred by the Romans, became connected with the custom of sending greeting cards to sweethearts on February 14th (Saint Valentine's Day) is hardly a matter for conjecture. In the 18th century valentines were sent, but they were hand-painted and written; the first printed versions, produced lithographically, were not sold in England until the 1830s. By the 1840s the custom had become very popular, and by mid-century the card was elaborately gilded and coloured, with the addition of lacework imitated in pierced paper. Some were further ornamented with bows of ribbon and metal hearts. The 'flower-cage' type, originally French, was popular. By pulling a string set in a bunch of flowers on the front the valentine became a miniature paper cage.

Valentines are at their best from the collector's viewpoint between 1840 and the 1860s, after which they become increasingly vulgar, sometimes with indelicate (by Victorian standards) examples of anonymous humour. H. Dobbs, stationer to Queen Victoria, was noted for producing good quality valentines.

VAL SAINT-LAMBERT, CRISTALLERIE DU (Liège, Belgium)

Glasshouse founded in 1825. Throughout the 19th century it was one of the largest producers of domestic glassware in Europe, and towards the end of the century, under the direction of Georges Desprez, it began to produce iridescent glass and Gallé-inspired *art nouveau** cameo glass*. Philippe Wolfers* was associated with the factory from 1897 to 1903. They employed Charles Graffert as an engraver, and Henri van de Velde* as a designer. The Müller* brothers were employed here during 1906 and 1907. The etched marks are *Val St Lambert*, or the monogram *VSL*.

VALSUANI, C. (Paris)

Bronze-founder who cast work by Bonnard, Bourdelle, Braque, Picasso, Renoir, etc. Impressed mark: *C. VALSUANI, CIRE PERDUE*.

VALTON, CHARLES (1851–1918)

French *Animalier** sculptor who was a pupil of both Barye* and Fremiet*, and who exhibited for the first time in the *Salon* of 1868. He received medals at the Expositions Universelles of 1889 and 1900. His work includes mammals such as the lion, tiger and polar bear, and he is represented in a number of French museums, including the Natural History Museum and the Musée Galliera, Paris.

VALTON, CHARLES. *Pointing griffon*, bronze by Charles Valton*. Late 19th century. *Antique Collectors' Club*

VAN BRIGGLE, ARTUS (1869–1904)

American artist-potter, who studied painting at Cincinnati and pottery under Karl Langenbeck at the Avon Pottery. From 1887 he painted flowers in underglaze colours at the Rookwood Pottery* and in 1893 he gained a scholarship at the Académie Jullien, Paris, aided by Rookwood. He studied in Paris until 1896, and on his return, continued at Rookwood until 1899, when ill-health induced him to start his own pottery at Colorado Springs. This was continued after his death by his wife and is still in operation.

The Van Briggle Pottery Company dates from 1902. The principal production was vases in the *art nouveau** style usually moulded, with floral ornament and covered with glazes in soft colours. Human and animal figures sometimes form part of the design. After Van Briggle's death vases only partly covered with glaze which contrasted with the dark body were made.

Mark: *AA* monogram impressed.

VAN DE VELDE, HENRI (1863–1957)

Belgian painter, architect, and designer, who studied in Paris and Antwerp. In 1885 he joined the Belgian *avant-garde* group, *Les Vingt*, but from 1893 he devoted himself to the decorative arts, and became one of the earliest of the *art nouveau** designers, producing furniture for specific interiors. Samuel Bing* commissioned him to design four rooms for his new Paris gallery, La Maison de l'Art Nouveau, and in 1898 he established his own workshop at Ixelles, near Brussels. His reputation, however, was established by his contribution to the Exhibition of Applied Arts in Dresden in 1897, and he enjoyed so much success that he settled in Germany in the following year. In 1901 the Grand Duke of Saxe-Weimar-Eisenach requested Van de Velde to become his

VEILLEUSE. *Veilleuse-théière.* Mark: *FLAMEN FLEURY À PARIS, RUE DANBOURS, SAINT-DENIS.* Second quarter of the 19th century. *Victoria & Albert Museum, London*

artistic adviser, and he helped to found a school of arts and crafts in Weimar. In 1905 he was asked to design porcelain for Meissen*.

VAN SPANGEN (fl. 1800–1828)

A Dutchman who started a factory at Bow (E. London) for making terracotta* architectural ornament in 1800. The firm later became Van Spangen, Powell & Company, and it closed in 1828. It did similar work in terracotta to that of Coade & Sealy*.

See *Austin, Felix*

VASA MURRHINA

The name is a reference to the Murrhine vases of the ancient Romans, sometimes thought to have been of Alexandrian glass. The American art glass* thus named appears to be flecked with gold or silver, due to flakes of mica being suspended within a transparent coloured glass. Made by the Boston and Sandwich Glass Company*.

VASELINE GLASS

Decorative glass, probably originating in France and often known as yellow opaline*, which was produced in the second half of the 19th century in England and America. The best qualities are greenish-yellow in colour, with a fiery glow at the edges. Some quite large pieces (vases and decanters) were produced in this type of glass.

VEILLEUSE (French)

A type of food- or tea-warmer for use at night; German: *nachtlampe*. The *veilleuse* is a type of ceramic vessel introduced about the middle of the 18th century, but very popular during the 19th. Essentially it consists of a base with a cylinder fitted on to it. A lamp (*godet*) which gave about as much heat as a small candle, rested on the base inside and a small aperture in the side of the cylinder gave access to the lamp for lighting and refilling. A covered bowl, a teapot, or a coffee-pot fitted into the top of the cylinder. All these parts are separate.

The *veilleuse* was generally of porcelain and well painted on the exterior in enamel colours, the light from the lamp providing faint illumination by which the decoration could also be seen. On the Continent many were made of tin-enamelled earthenware, also with painted decoration, and Wedgwood* produced creamware* food-warmers usually undecorated. Minton* made a porcelain *veilleuse* in England, and there are a few rare blue printed earthenware examples from Staffordshire. Generally, apart from Wedgwood's version, they were not commonly made in England, but porcelain, *faïence*, and stoneware examples exist from most European factories as far east as Russia. French and Bohemian factories also specialized in a type which was known as the *personnage**.

The *veilleuse* has been widely collected on the Continent, especially in France and Italy, and for some years past reproductions of some of the more popular types have appeared on the market. These may be judged by normal criteria applicable to other wares.

The existence of *veilleuses* of opaque glass has been recorded in France, but no specimen could be traced at the time of writing.

VENETIAN GLASS

At the beginning of the 19th century the age-old Venetian glass industry was moribund, and the guild of glass-makers had been disbanded. Venice sent nothing to the Great Exhibition of 1851 and it was not until the middle of the century that the industry showed the first signs of revival. The Abbot Zaneth founded the Museo Vetrario and a school of design, and in 1864 Antonio Salviati* founded the enterprise which, two years later, became the Compania Venezia-Murano. A good deal of 19th-century Venetian glass was in the form of close copies of early work mainly for sale to tourists. Some of it is deceptive, although nothing will survive comparison with genuinely antique examples. In the present century Ercole Barovier* and Paolo Venini* have been responsible for distinguished work in the modern style.

In general, 19th-century Venetian glass also followed tradition in the type of glass employed. Due to the availability of suitable raw material the glass-makers of Murano had always made a soda-glass which tolerated a great deal of manipulation and reheating, and nearly everything was made with the aid of the blowpipe. Apart from a small amount of diamond-point engraving in the 16th century, hardly any cut or engraved glass was made, soda-glass being as unsuitable for this purpose as the lead glass of England and the potash glass of Bohemia was for manipulative techniques, a fact which reveals the fundamental absurdity of Ruskin's* attack on cut-glass*.

VENINI, PAOLO (1895–1959)

Italian glass manufacturer, also associated with Ercole Barovier* in the modern revival of the Venetian glass industry. He established the firm of Venini & Co. on the island of Murano in 1925 and among their productions are a bubbled clear glass known as *vetro-pulagoso* and *vetro corroso*, glass with a partially corroded surface, as well as new ideas in *latticinio* and *millefiori*. Venini's co-operation with the sculptor Martinuzzi* began in 1929. His glass is often marked, *Venini, Murano*.

VEREINIGTE WERKSTÄTTEN FÜR KUNST IM HANDWERK

Literally, the United Workshops for Art and Craftwork, founded in Munich in 1897 to act as a focus for designers and craftsmen of the *Jugendstil* movement, led by Richard Riemerschmid*, Peter Behrens and Theo Schmuz-Baudisz. The workshop produced ceramics, furniture and metalwork until 1907, when it

VENETIAN GLASS. Basket of blown glass fruit, probably by Salviati & Co. c. 1870. *Constance Chiswell*

was merged with the Deutsche Werkbund*. Bruno Paul (1874–1968), the architect and designer, worked here from 1893 to 1907, and designed furniture and glass for the Werkstätten.

Mark: a printed monogram *VW* joined together within a rectangle.

VERRE CANARI (French) See *Canary glass*

VERRE DOUBLÉ (French)

Glass in which the decoration is enclosed between two layers, which may be of contrasting colours. The technique was employed by Gallé* and others.

See *Mildner, J. J.*

VENINI PAOLO. A vase of plant form modelled in green glass over metal by Martinuzzi* for Paolo Venini*. Venice, 1928. *Brighton Art Gallery & Museum, Sussex*

VERRE EGLOMISÉ (French)

A term thought to be derived from the name of a French dealer, Jean-Baptiste Glomy (fl. c.1780). He ornamented the borders of glass in picture and mirror frames with engraved gold and silver ornament and occasional painted additions. However the technique, which was popular during the early years of the 19th century, often in an elaborate form, is much older than Glomy. It appears to have been suggested originally by the *Zwischengoldgläser* tumblers, one glass fitting inside the other, the interior surface of which was decorated in gold and painting.

VERRERIE PARLANTE (French)

A type of glass made by Émile Gallé* at Nancy.

VIENNA KERAMIK   See *Wiener Keramik*

VIENNA PORCELAIN FACTORY

The Vienna porcelain manufactory reached the final decades of the 18th century with an enviable reputation for fine painting. The styles of the period were much influenced by Sèvres*. At the turn of the century, enamelling had become so profuse that it almost covered the entire surface of the porcelain, and it was accompanied by lavish gilding. This continued into the 19th century. Biscuit* figures were produced about the same time, most of them in an Empire style*. Relief decoration in a classical style was largely inspired by Wedgwood's* jasper*. The fashionable topographical painting (which also occurs on some contemporary Bohemian glass*) belongs to the first two decades of the century. Well-painted cabinet cups and saucers belong to this period.

The factory's production declined steadily in quality throughout the 19th century until, in 1864, the State found its losses too great, and decided to close it. A large amount of white ware, both 'seconds' and ware awaiting decoration, remained in stock. This was bought by outside decorators, especially former factory employees, who decorated it for sale. Ludwig Riedl, who is among the best, specialized in earlier styles. To this period belong large dishes painted with classical subjects, somewhat in the manner of Angelica Kauffmann, which sometimes bear a spurious signature. When these stocks of white ware were exhausted other factories supplied the deficiency. By this time, however, quality was verging on the tawdry, and the old gilding was replaced by a coppery Dutch gold. Viennese outside decorators include Josef Böck (from 1820), Franz Dörlf (from 1880), and Josef Vater. The decorations of both Dörfl and Vater were often marked with the Vienna 'beehive'.

VIENNA WERKSTÄTTE   See *Wiener Werkstätte*

VIERTHALER, LUDWIG (1875–1967)

Sculptor and designer who taught at the Hanover Fachschule from 1921, and modelled figures for the

'VIEUX SÈVRES'. A Minton *jardinière* closely based on a Sèvres example of the *vase hollandais* of c. 1760, the centre panel painted with a fishing-scene somewhat in the style of Morin. This vase was also listed at Sèvres as a *jardinière éventail* from its fan-shaped outline. Minton. c. 1890. *Minton Museum, Royal Doulton Tableware*

Meissen* factory for reproduction in porcelain. Work signed.

'VIEUX SÈVRES'

A common 19th-century description of Sèvres* soft-paste porcelain made up to the time of the Revolution in 1789, and particularly before the introduction of hard-paste porcelain* in 1770. '*Vieux Sèvres*' sold for very high prices to collectors throughout the 19th century, and was the especial target of the forger. It was also reproduced by commercial factories such as Coalport* and Minton*, but these copies will not survive critical examination by anyone acquainted with early wares.

VILLEROY & BOCH (Mettlach)

Pottery for the manufacture of stoneware* (*Steinzeug*) and other wares formed in 1836 by the amalgamation of factories belonging to Villeroy & Boch. The firm subsequently operated several factories, using different marks–*Villeroy & Boch Mettlach, Villeroy & Boch, Schramberg, VBD*, for Villeroy & Boch, Dresden, and *Villeroy & Boch, Septfontaines* for their factory at Wallerfangen in the Saar. The factory made a good deal of stoneware in the 17th-century styles of the Rhineland*, much of which was exported to America. It also produced excellent creamware* (*Steingut**), and, at Mettlach, pottery decorated with inlays of coloured clays. The company is still operating.

VINAIGRETTES (French)

Aromatic or volatile vinegars as a prophylactic against a variety of pestilences and infections were being advertised in the 1750s, and the *vinaigrette* as a convenient means of carrying these around was popular in the 1770s, although the name for this small silver box only came into use towards the end of the century. From about 1800 onwards until the 1850s *vinaigrettes* were made in large quantities and in great variety, principally in Birmingham. They were the speciality of factories producing watch-cases.

They were made in the form of a small shallow box, about an inch and a half by one inch in size. When the lid was opened it revealed an inner pierced grid hinged at one end, beneath which reposed a small piece of sponge soaked in the aromatic liquid. These grids were decorated in a variety of ways on all but the cheapest specimens. Since the aromatics used contained acetic acid the interior of the box and the grid itself were gilded, heavily on the best qualities, to prevent corrosion. *Vinaigrettes* vary greatly in quality.

By the time they became popular many of the techniques of making small objects of silver by machine introduced by Matthew Boulton in the 18th century had been greatly improved, and the blanks were formed by machine and then decorated either by machine or, in the case of better quality examples, by hand. Most *vinaigrettes* are rectangular, more rarely square, but occasionally heart-shaped or circular, and those in the form of such objects as shells, fox masks, shoes, acorns etc, are seen occasionally. The decoration of good-quality early specimens was influenced by the contemporary gold box with engraving, chiselling and flat-chasing*. Engine-turning* also occurs on some early 19th-century specimens. Later, embossed lids, often of such architectural subjects as Kenilworth Castle, Windsor Castle, or St Paul's Cathedral, were mechanically pressed. Embossing of scrolls and flowers in the rococo style belongs to the 1830s and 1840s. Some of the best relief work was done by Nathaniel Mills, whose card-cases are also much sought.

Usually of silver, *vinaigrettes* are also known in gold, porcelain and glass. Most were made to be carried in the pocket, but a considerable proportion, especially those of heart—or locket—shape, are given a small ring by which they could be suspended from a chain. Larger specimens were intended to be passed round the table during a dinner-party in a hot crowded room. The *vinaigrette* was made until the end of the 19th century.

The term is French, but the English version, *vinegarette*, was occasionally employed at the time.

VINCENT, HIPPOLYTE (Marais, Paris)

Vincent had a London branch in Wigmore Street. He specialized in making repetitive plaster casts with the aid of gelatine moulds. A plaster case was formed over the original model in such a way as to leave a space between them. This was filled by a gelatine mixture which, after cooling, formed a fairly tough and elastic mould which could be used for taking a plaster cast. The gelatine was stretched and pulled to remove the cast and up to six good copies could be obtained before the mould became too worn for further use. This method made unnecessary the manufacture of piece-moulds, a process which was lengthier and needed considerably more skill. By 1851 the technique was being widely used in England for plaster casts for most purposes, as well as in France, and Vincent adapted it to electrotyping.

See *Plaster-moulds*

'VINEYARD' CLOCKS   See *Comtoise clocks*

VIOLIN-BOTTLES

Whisky bottles produced by the Ohio glass factories with an outline somewhat similar to that of a violin. They were made in many colours and sizes.

VIOLLET-LE-DUC, EUGÈNE EMMANUEL (1814–1879)

French architect and writer who, in some ways, exerted an influence in France similar to that of William Morris* in England. In 1840 he began his career as a restorer of churches and other medieval buildings, including the much-criticized work to the walls of Carcassonne (Aude), and to Notre-Dame in Paris (1845). Nevertheless, by 1855 he was widely acclaimed as the greatest living architect, and in 1863 he was appointed Professor at the École des Beaux-Arts. Viollet-le-Duc was a convinced medievalist and a strong opponent of eclecticism*. At the same time he somewhat inconsistently advocated the use of cast-iron as a support for masonry. In this he was probably inspired by the greenhouses in the *Jardin des Plantes* (Botanic Gardens) in Paris which were erected in 1833. The largest building of this type utilizing cast-iron and glass was Sir Joseph Paxton's Crystal Palace, built to house the Great Exhibition* of 1851. Viollet-le-Duc no doubt influenced Gustave Eiffel in the design of the Tower in Paris, and in the Viaduct of Garabit just south of Saint-Flour, Auvergne, which in 1880, when it was built, was the longest structure of its kind in the world. In his designs for buildings Viollet-le-Duc successfully caught the spirit of early Gothic, and, like William Morris, he strenuously advocated the repair of the breach between the fine and applied arts. He wrote many books, of which the most important was the *Dictionary of French Architecture* (1854–1868).

VISTA ALLEGRE (Oporto, Portugal)

Porcelain factory founded in 1824 by Jose Ferreira Pinto Basso and situated near Oporto, Portugal, in the town of Ilhavo. Apart from decorative vases and service-ware original in design, they have also made reproductions of old Meissen, Vienna, Paris, and English porcelains. In recent times they have exported fine porcelain to the United States. The usual mark is the initials *VA*.

VITRO-PORCELAIN

Type of slag glass* developed towards the end of the 19th century by Sowerby* & Co. It is a streaked opaque green with purple veining.

'VITRUM MARMORATUM' See *Marbling*

VITTOZ (Paris)
Manufacturer of ornamental metalwork, including furnishing bronzes, clocks, chandeliers, and silver vases. He was the *fondeur** of statues and groups by or after Coustou (Marly horses), Clodion*, Pradier, Feuché, Pascal, Houdon, Combercatt, Claymans etc. Vittoz exhibited at the Great Exhibition in London in 1851.

VLAMINCK, MAURICE (1876–1958)
Painter of the École de Paris* who decorated *faïence** made by the studio-potter André Methey*, with the painted signature, *Vlaminck*.

VOIGT, ALFRED See *Sitzendorf*

VOLKMAR, CHARLES (1841–1914)
American painter and artist-potter who studied in Baltimore and Paris and worked, in 1876, at a pottery at Montigny-sur-Loing, then at the studio of Théodore Deck*, and at the factory of Haviland* & Co. He returned to America in 1879, and established a pottery at Greenpoint, Long Island, forming the Volkmar Keramic Company in 1895. At Corona, New York, he produced work decorated in the *barbotine** (trailed slip) technique, and with plain matt glazes. In 1903 he set up the Volkmar Kilns at Metuchen, New Jersey, in association with his son, Léon (1879–1959). The son, some of whose work shows traces of Islamic influence, taught at the Pennsylvania Museum School of Industrial Art, and at the University of Ceramics, Cincinnati, Ohio. Mark: *V* or *VOLKMAR* incised.

VOLKSTEDT (Thuringia)
The site of porcelain factories since the 18th century when a mark imitating the Meissen* crossed swords consisting of crossed hayforks (from the arms of Schwarzburg) was employed. The hayforks mark was revived by Eckert, Richard & Co., makers of hard-paste porcelain* since 1895. Production includes table-services, vases, and figures of good quality, some in the manner of Meissen.

VOLPATO PORCELAIN FACTORY (Rome)
This factory was founded in 1785 by Giovanni Volpato, and made principally biscuit* figures of fine quality in the classical style, the designs usually derived from antique statuary in the Vatican and elsewhere, or from the work of Canova*. The factory was so successful that Volpato established another one for making wares of a similar style in a kind of white glazed earthenware. After Giovanni's death in 1803 the factory was continued by his son, Giuseppe, who died soon after his father, and then by Giuseppe's widow, who married Francesco Tinucci, the chief modeller. The pottery factory was operated by a grandson until 1857, when it was sold to Giuseppe Trocchi. The porcelain factory's closing date is uncertain, but it was probably 1831. The finest pieces bear an impressed mark, *G. Volpato, Roma*.

VON EIFF, WILHELM (1890–1943)
*Art déco** glass designer and engraver. He studied at the Stuttgart Art School, 1913, and directed teaching workshops for glass and gem-cutting at the Württembergische Metallwarenfabrik, 1921–1937, using a technique of chipping (*Schnitzen*). Mark: Initials *WvE*, engraved.

VON SPAUN, MAX RITTER (d. 1909)
Director of Lötz* Glassworks from 1879 to 1908, and grandson of the founder Johann Lötz. Von Spaun enlarged and modernized the factory which, under his direction, specialized in glass imitating such semi-precious stones as agate, and iridescent glass* in the Tiffany* style. Signature, painted, *SPAUN*.

VON STUCK, FRANZ (1863–1928)
German sculptor, architect, designer, painter and graphic artist who helped to found the Munich *Sezession** in 1893. He modelled figures for reproduction in both bronze and porcelain. Signature incised.

VOYSEY, CHARLES FRANCIS ANNESLEY (1857–1941)
Architect and furniture designer. Voysey was articled to J. P. Seddon in 1871, set up on his own account in 1882, and joined the Art Workers' Guild* in 1884. He first showed furniture with the Arts and Crafts Exhibition Society* in 1893. Before the end of the century he was regarded as one of England's leading furniture-designers, especially in the *art nouveau** styles. His cabinets were in oak, plain but noted for large decorative hinges and similar ornament which

VOYSEY, C. F. A. Writing-desk with characteristic copper hinges in the *art nouveau** style, designed by C. F. A. Voysey* and made by W. R. Tingey. 1896. *Victoria & Albert Museum, London*

had an Oriental derivation. In addition, he designed almost every kind of interior fitting—wallpapers, textiles, metalwork, pottery (including tiles for Pilkington*). Voysey designed the popular 'swan' chair, the front legs of which were curved in a manner based on the swan's neck, the uprights of the back terminating in carved swan's heads.

VULLIAMY, BENJAMIN LEWIS (fl. 1800–1850)
London clock-maker of Swiss descent. His father was clock-maker to George III, and Benjamin Lewis inherited the business and was appointed clock-maker to George IV. Vulliamy clocks are sought by collectors.

VYSE, CHARLES (d. 1968)
English studio-potter, trained at Hanley Art School. With his wife he started a studio pottery at Chelsea in 1919 where he produced good quality figures until 1963, which are now sought. These were exhibited at the time in Bond Street. Figures were either signed in full with the addition of the word 'CHELSEA', or with initials.

VULLIAMY, BENJAMIN LEWIS. Mantel-clock, the case in the revived rococo* style, the movement by Benjamin Vulliamy*. London. c. 1820. *Antique Collectors' Club*

WACKERLE, JOSEPH (b. 1880)
Sculptor and modeller of porcelain. He was art-director at Nymphenburg from 1906 to 1909, where he modelled figures decorated with underglaze colours. Wackerle taught in Berlin from 1909 to 1917, and also modelled figures for the Berlin Porcelain Factory*, of which the *Masked Lady* of 1911 is especially well known. He returned to Munich in 1917.

Mark: an incised signature.

WAHLISS, ERNST
Owner of the Alexander Porcelain Works, established about 1780, at Turn-Teplitz, Bohemia. Although mainly porcelain was produced, earthenware called Serapis-Fayence was made about 1910, marked *Serapis-Wahliss*.

WAIN, LOUIS (1860–1911)
English illustrator who was noted from about 1890 onwards for anthropomorphic studies of cats, very popular among the English young of the period. He designed postcards for Raphael Tuck. Earthenware figures of animals date from a year or two before his death.

WALL, WILLIAM GUY (1792–1864)
A gifted draughtsman, born in Dublin, who emigrated

WAHLISS, ERNST. Glazed pottery clock in the style of the Wiener Werkstätte*. Mark: *Serapis-Wahliss*. c. 1910. *Sotheby & Co*

to New York in 1818, and made many drawings of landscapes which were later employed by Staffordshire potters, such as Stevenson* and Clews* for the decoration of blue-and-white transfer-printed* plates and dishes.

WALTER, ALMÉRIC (1859–1942)
Glassworker and ceramist in the *art nouveau** and *art déco** styles, who studied at the École Nationale de la Manufacture de Sèvres, and began to work in *pâte-de-verre** about 1902. From 1908 to 1914 he worked for Daum Frères* making *pâte-de-verre* after H. Berger*. He established his own workshop at Nancy to make *pâte-de-verre*, principally heavy dishes, bowls, ash trays, etc in coloured glass (mostly green, turquoise, and yellow) decorated with flowers, insects, or a small reptile, like a chameleon.

Mark: *A. WALTER NANCY*, impressed.

WALTON, GEORGE (1867–1933)
Scottish architect and designer who studied at the Glasgow School of Art*, and founded a firm of designers and decorators, George Walton & Co. His work was in the modern idiom of his day, influenced by the manner of the Glasgow School (see *Mackintosh, C. R.*). Walton exhibited with the Arts and Crafts Exhibition Society* in 1890, and again in 1910. He designed furniture in the *art nouveau** style of Mackintosh for Liberty & Co.* and others, and decorative metalwork of all kinds. He also designed 'Clutha'* glass for James Couper & Sons* before he left for London in 1897.

WALTON, JOHN (fl. c. 1810–c. 1835)
Maker of earthenware figures at Burslem, Staffordshire. The name *WALTON* is impressed, usually within a scroll. His figures nearly always have a tree as a background, and a bright green enamel usually predominates. The moulds passed into the possession of the new owner of Walton's factory, George Hood, who probably used them to some extent.

WARBURTON, PETER (1773–1813)
Maker of creamware* and partner in the New Hall Joint Stock Porcelain Company*. In 1810 he patented a method of transfer-printing* in gold.

WARWICK SCHOOL OF WOODCARVING. *The Hare and the Pheasant*, carving in limewood by Thomas Henry Kendall* of Warwick. Kendall also made elaborately carved sideboards. *Warwick County Museum*

WATCOMBE TERRACOTTA COMPANY. A pair of terracotta busts of children, apparently symbolizing joy and sorrow, a subject employed in porcelain in the 18th century. Watcombe Pottery*, Torquay. c. 1890. *Constance Chiswell*

WARING & GILLOW (London)

Furniture-maker and retailer, the product of the amalgamation of S. J. Waring with Gillow's* in 1900. They specialized in good quality interior decoration, and Serge Chermayeff and Paul Follot were in charge of the department selling modern French furniture in 1929. Chermayeff was noted for modernist styles; Follot, a somewhat older man, was responsible for *art nouveau** designs at the beginning of his career, and later became one of the originators of *art déco**.

WARWICK SCHOOL OF WOODCARVING

During the 19th century Warwick became the centre of a notable school of furniture with pictorially carved ornament in the Gothic and Elizabethan styles. There were several firms in the town who employed some highly skilled carvers, notably W. Cooke* and T. H. Kendall*.

WATCHSTANDS

Ornamental stands intended to hold a watch were principally made of Staffordshire pottery for cottages whose inhabitants could not afford a mantel-clock, although some were made for bedside use. These stands were made in a variety of forms, all of them including a circular hole the size of the average pocket-watch. Here the watch was placed for the benefit of the household when not being used by the titular owner. For houses too poor even to possess a watch, specimens without the watch-recess, but with the figures and hands painted on a dial, are sometimes still to be found. Among the earliest watchstands are those in the form of a castle, usually with the aperture between twin towers or turrets. These date from early in the 19th century, and remained popular until about 1850. The long-case clock also occurs as a watchstand, usually in pottery of the Pratt* type, or made by Dixon, Austin* & Co. of Sunderland. These are usually flanked by figures, since they needed a somewhat larger base for safety than the long-case model provided.

One occasionally sees watchstands of materials other than pottery. Those of porcelain, rococo in style and made by Rockingham* or Copeland*, are of much better quality and beyond the reach of the cottager. These, no doubt, were made for bedside use, especially when the watch leans backwards at an angle when in position.

Wooden watchstands in the form of a long-case clock are not uncommon, but seem to have been amateur work for the most part. Ivory watchstands of European style were probably made in Dieppe, where there had been a flourishing school of ivory-carving from the 17th century. Some, Oriental in style, were probably made in India or the Far East for export.

WATCOMBE TERRACOTTA COMPANY (Devon)

This pottery was established in 1869 near Torquay, after the discovery of a bed of fine quality terracotta clay. The art-director was Charles Brook, formerly of Hanley, and the factory specialized in decorative wares such as vases, figures and busts which are now much sought. Vases are often ornamented with applied flowers, and are based on neo-classical forms. Tea services were glazed where necessary, the cups sometimes with an interior glaze of light blue. Sparse decoration with enamels and gold occurs on some wares and later wares were sometimes glazed and painted with flowers. The factory also produced architectural terracottas and garden furniture. The mark employed was *WATCOMBE, TORQUAY*. This pottery has a well-deserved reputation for wares of high quality and excellent design, but there were several other potteries in the neighbourhood using the same clay which made wares of cheaper quality for a wider market.

WATER-GILDING

The application of gold in the form of thin leaves to a surface prepared by painting it with gold size. The leaf on its backing of tissue is pressed into place, the tissue peeled away, and the exposed leaf gently pressed into firm contact with a rabbit's scut (tail). The process is generally applied to wood or gesso.

'WATTEAU FIGURES'

Figures in a landscape in 18th-century costume in the manner of Antoine Watteau (1684–1721), or the somewhat similar style of Nicolas Lancret (1690–1743). These were always referred to as 'Watteau scenes' in the 18th century and were current during the rococo period at Sèvres* and Meissen*. In the 19th century they occur on porcelain from Sèvres imitating the old wares, and porcelain made elsewhere in imitation of the wares of the French factory. Meissen Watteau scenes of the 1750s were copied by Wolfsohn* of Dresden on wares with alternate panels of flowers and marked *AR*. Scenes after Watteau also occur as the decoration of painted panels forming part of vitrines and similar pieces of furniture made in France during the second half of the 19th century in a technique similar to that of the *vernis Martin* of the 18th century. These opulent pieces of furniture, with *bombé* panels and gilt-bronze mounts, usually belong to the Second Empire* of Napoleon III. Many times removed from objects such as these are biscuit tins and other metal boxes, decorated with Watteau scenes, produced around the end of the century.

WEATHERVANES, AMERICAN

These have become a focus of interest among American collectors. They exist in the United States in great variety, not only the familiar cock, but the horse, the Indian aiming an arrow, the angel Gabriel blowing his horn, the mermaid, and regional devices like ships, whales, steers, and agricultural implements. Weathervanes were cut out of sheet-metal (iron or copper), or sawn out of wood and painted for protection against the weather. The silhouette type of vane is the commonest, but the best wooden examples are carved in low relief in a wide variety of subjects, some of them, like dragons and fish, unique to America. These preceded metal vanes in the same style. The more important examples were connected with a dial in the building below, indicating the direction of wind blowing.

When first made the best of these vanes were gilded with gold-leaf but this has now yielded to time in cases where the vane is of any considerable age. It is unusual for weathervanes to survive more than a century or so of exposure to the weather.

WEBB, PHILIP (1831–1915)

Architect and designer; principal assistant to G. E. Street at Oxford from 1852, where he met William Morris* in 1855. In 1856 Webb moved to London with Street and set up as an architect, designing the Red House, Bexley Heath, Kent, for Morris, which was completed in 1860. A year or so before he had designed his first furniture in association with Burne-Jones* and Morris, and in 1861 he became a founder member of Morris, Marshall, Faulkner & Co.* for whom he designed furniture, metalwork and glass. His furniture designs were neo-Gothic* in inspiration. A chest painted with scenes from the legend of Saint George by Morris is in the Victoria & Albert Museum collections, and Oxford's Ashmolean Museum has a wardrobe painted by Burne-Jones with scenes from Chaucer's 'Prioress's Tale', with additional floral paintings by Morris. The former was included in the London Exhibition of 1862. At this period Webb's settees and sideboards were given overhanging canopies in the medieval style. His glassware designs were made by J. Powell & Sons*, and he sought inspiration for his metalwork in early medieval times. From about 1880 his principal assistant was George Jack* who took over the practice when Webb retired in 1900.

WEBB, PHILIP. 'Morris'* armchair with an adjustable back in ebonized mahogany, the design developed by Philip Webb* from a traditional Sussex type. c. 1866, *William Morris Gallery, Waltham Forest*

'WATTEAU FIGURES'. Pair of Meissen* pot-pourri vases decorated with applied figures, encrusted with flowers, and painted with scenes in the manner of Watteau* or Lancret. Third quarter of the 19th century. *Antique Collectors' Club*

WEBB & SONS, THOMAS (Stourbridge, Worcestershire)

Makers of decorative glass who were especially known in the 19th century for *Hochschnitt** engraving by F. Kny* and W. Fritsche*, and for cameo-glass* by the Woodall Brothers (see *Northwood, John*). They also manufactured from about 1886 the 'Burmese'* glass of the Mount Washington Glass Works* of America under licence, renaming it 'Queen's Burmese'. 'Alexandrite' glass was made from the early years of the 20th century; as well as a certain amount of excellent quality enamelling on clear glass. Threaded glass*, for the making of which Richardson* had invented a machine in the 1860s, formed part of their production. A three-lipped decanter, one of their introductions, is still being made. The mark occasionally employed is the name, *Webb*.

WEDGWOOD, JOSIAH & SONS LTD (Staffordshire)

Josiah Wedgwood, founder of the firm died in 1795, leaving it to be continued by his son, Josiah Wedgwood II. The firm had achieved a world-wide reputation in the 18th century for successful experimentation and the factory started the 19th century with a number of well-established types of ware, especially jasper*, basaltes*, creamware*, caneware*, and pearlware*. These continued to be made throughout the period under review, although changes took place in forms and decoration. The first years of the new century were far from easy, due to the difficulties imposed by the Napoleonic Wars, but the factory continued to experiment, and produced some notable lustre* wares (see *Moonlight Lustre*).

During the last quarter of the 18th century, Josiah Wedgwood led the way in adapting the neo-classical style to ceramic design. The style had principally been employed in the manufacture of ornamental wares made from the jasper and basaltes bodies, and similar wares (often repetitions from existing moulds) continued to be made. New models made by modifying shapes or varying moulds were also produced; the classical forms of the 18th century often differed from

WEBB & SONS, THOMAS. Small vase of Queen's Burmese glass made by Thomas Webb & Sons* under licence from the Mount Washington Glass Company*, New England. c. 1890. *Victoria & Albert Museum, London*

those of the 19th, vases, for instance, tending to be slimmer and more elongated. Much 19th-century work of this character no longer has the quality of the earlier production. Jasper colouring became deeper, and the relief decoration was coarser due, no doubt, to the fact that it was too expensive in time and labour to finish it by hand in the 18th-century manner.

Although Josiah Wedgwood I had experimented with the manufacture of porcelain in the 18th century, he abandoned the pursuit because of the difficulty of producing it without infringing the then existing patent of Richard Champion. By 1812, however, the manufacture of bone-porcelain had become widespread, and Wedgwood began to produce it. The ware was competent in quality, and tea- and dessert-services were decorated with landscapes by John Cutts* (formerly of Pinxton), Arnold Steel (who was responsible for birds and Etruscan subjects), by a painter of fruit, and with coloured transfer-prints. Nevertheless, times were unpropitious, and after little more than ten years porcelain-making was given up. By 1828 business was extremely depressed. To raise money the stock was sold off cheaply, and some of the old models and moulds were also sold. The London showrooms were closed as a measure of economy.

The firm continued in the hands of the family, although persons from outside the family circle enjoyed temporary partnerships without leaving any very enduring mark of their presence. The firm made a characteristic contribution to the Great Exhibition of 1851, displaying ornamental wares in the neo-classical* style.

By the 1850s the firm was once more introducing or reintroducing more adventurous decorative wares. For instance, solid jasper (i.e. jasper with the body coloured throughout instead of only on the surface)

WEBB & SONS, THOMAS. Bowl of pinkish glass imitating a Chinese jade carving designed by Thomas Woodall and made by Francis Smith for Thomas Webb & Sons*, Stourbridge. c. 1890. *Victoria & Albert Museum, London*

WEDGWOOD, JOSIAH & SONS LTD. A group of wares decorated by Émile Lessore*. c. 1863. *Josiah Wedgwood & Sons Ltd*

was once more manufactured in 1856, and about this time the firm began again to make sets of chessmen after the designs of John Flaxman*. In 1860 'Majolica' decorated with coloured translucent glazes over a white body to give it an exceptional brilliance was introduced in competition with similar ware from Minton*. It was employed for a similar range of wares, including *jardinières* and umbrella-stands. Other new glazes included 'malachite', 'mottled', and agate. Green-glazed wares decorated with moulded floral and foliate patterns, the dishes usually of leaf-forms, were very popular. Some of the relief patterns were of Oriental derivation. The green glaze was also employed in the production of *émaux ombrants**. In the 1850s Wedgwood produced a limited number of lithophanes* and Parian* ware had been made since about 1849 under the name of 'Carrara'. Like procelain 'Carrara' is translucent, it is unglazed and its surface resembles a fine marble. Cream-coloured earthenware, Josiah Wedgwood's Queensware, was always a staple product, decorated in a variety of ways, and in the 18th century creamware tablets had provided supports for paintings by George Stubbs. A notable 19th-century artist to use creamware plates and dishes especially as a support for some excellent painting was Émile Lessore*, at the factory from 1858 to 1863.

In 1875 the firm once more reopened showrooms in London, and bone china was reintroduced in 1878, becoming one of the staple products. By 1880 'old Wedgwood' was attracting the attention of collectors, and the dealer, Phillips, held an exhibition. For this the firm produced an edition of 15 copies of the Portland Vase* from the moulds of the 1790 edition which they still retained, and, following the example of Josiah I, they had the white reliefs sharpened and undercut by the lapidary, John Northwood*, who had produced his copy in a glass a few years earlier.

The firm was as much to the forefront in experimenting with new processes in the 19th century as it

had been previously. In 1863 they began to employ lithography* as a method of decoration. Sets of transfer-printed* tiles with a variety of subjects (months, seasons, etc.) were made from about 1870. Somewhat rarer are tiles devoted to pious sentiments, and such elevating subjects as temperance. The practice of producing commemorative ware* began early in the 1880s. This has gone on ever since, and many such wares (mugs, dishes, etc.) were devoted to American subjects. Many were issued in limited editions. These are usually in Queensware, less often in bone china.

Wedgwood was alive to its traditions, and the value of its incomparable archives, especially the voluminous correspondence of the first Josiah on almost every subject under the sun. In 1906 the Wedgwood Museum was established, and can now be visited at Barlaston.

About the same time the factory succeeded in reproducing the Chinese powder-blue ground on bone china by sponging on the colour. This was extensively made in China in the first half of the 18th

WEDGWOOD, JOSIAH & SONS LTD. Large armorial meat-dish made for the Prince of Denmark. 1822. *Josiah Wedgwood & Sons Ltd*

353

WEDGWOOD, JOSIAH & SONS LTD. Popular 19th-century patterns for Wedgwood* table-ware. *Josiah Wedgwood & Sons Ltd*

WEDGWOOD, JOSIAH & SONS LTD. Tripod incense-burner of a type more familiar in 18th-century basaltes* stoneware*, here seen glazed and covered with lustre. A key piece for dating early examples of Wedgwood* lustre ware. 1805. *Victoria & Albert Museum, London*

century by blowing the colour on in powder form through a bamboo tube closed at one end by a silk screen. This technique played a part in the production of the Fairyland and Dragon lustre* by Daisy Makeig-Jones* produced until 1932. A variety of background colours had been employed for the white reliefs of jasper since the 18th century, and in 1925 a crimson jasper supplied a fashionable *art déco** colour.

Despite the weight of its traditions Wedgwood proved to be much more modern in its outlook during the years after the First World War than most of its rivals, and adopted a policy of employing talented designers and craftsmen in the modern idiom, such as Keith Murray* and the art-director from 1938, Victor Skellern. Especially during the 1930s the factory

produced both earthenware and bone china coloured throughout the body, a type then popular. Figures by sculptors such as John Skeaping* and Arnold Machin* were also among the most notable examples of ceramic plastic work of the period.

Since the Second World War the enterprise has expanded enormously. Societies for the study of the old wares have been founded in England and America. Since the days of the first Josiah, who supported the cause of the colonists during the American War of Independence, the firm has always enjoyed enormous popularity in America, and much of its output has been exported there. A highly successful exhibition of 18th-century portrait medallions was held in the National Portrait Gallery, London, in 1973. This kind of portraiture, very popular in the 18th century, was continued throughout the 19th with new portraits of eminent persons of the time. Reissues from old moulds were made in the

WEDGWOOD, JOSIAH & SONS LTD. A part tea- and coffee-service of bone china enamelled with landscapes by John Cutts*, formerly of Pinxton. c. 1812. *Josiah Wedgwood & Sons Ltd*

WEDGWOOD, JOSIAH & SONS LTD. The Wedgwood* 'Water Lily' pattern painted on a mug; on the plate, the 'Hibiscus' pattern, blue painted. First quarter of the 19th century. *Josiah Wedgwood & Sons Ltd*

1920s and again more recently, all bearing impressed identification marks.

The factory has employed the mark *WEDGWOOD* impressed since the 18th century, together with a large number of ancillary marks (see Appendix II). Since 1878 bone china has been marked with a replica of the Portland Vase. The words '*Made in England*' were added to the mark after 1891 to satisfy American tariff regulations. *Wedgwood & Co* is not a mark employed by Josiah Wedgwood & Sons, but by an independent company at Ferrybridge (Yorkshire) founded by Ralph Wedgwood, or of a company founded in Tunstall about 1842 by Enoch Wedgwood which manufactured earthenware. *WEDGEWOOD* (note the intrusive median 'e') is found on imitations of Wedgwood's wares made by William Smith & Co.,* Stockton-on-Tees (Yorkshire).

Wedgwood occupied their present model factory at Barlaston, near Stoke-on-Trent, in 1948. The Museum is open to the public who are also able to join conducted tours (particulars from the factory).

WEININGER, SOLOMON (fl. 1870)

Viennese enameller and metalworker, forger of enamels and Renaissance bronzes. Noted as a craftsman in his own right, Weininger also restored medieval enamels, and was suspected of copying them, returning the copy to the owner and keeping the original. His bronzes copying those of the Renaissance are exceedingly deceptive. Among the artists copied may be numbered Tiziano Aspetti.

WEININGER, SOLOMON. Two bronze figures of Minerva. One by Tiziano Aspetti (1565–1607) (right) and (left) a copy by Solomon Weininger*. c. 1875. *Ullstein*

Small Viennese ivory cabinets mounted with painted enamel plaques may, if of good quality, be by his hand.

WELLER, SAMUEL. A.

Potter of Zanesville (Ohio) who specialized in art-pottery from the closing years of the 19th century onwards. His innovations included Dickensware.*

WESTMINSTER CHIMES See *Clocks, English*

WHATNOT

A series of shelves, more or less square, supported by four turned corner-posts. It was used for the display of ornaments and *bibelots*, and for the storage of

WHATNOT. Three-tiered whatnot of thuya wood by Holland & Sons*. c. 1865. *Sotheby & Co*

books and music. The whatnot first occurs late in the 18th century, but the best specimens belong to the Regency* period. They continued to be popular until well after mid-century. Around 1860 whatnots occur in ornate varieties on three supports, intended to be stood in corners, and pieces of furniture of about the same date with long narrow open shelves, sometimes surmounted by a high back, are also included in this classification. Both are usually decorated with carving. English whatnots in a pronounced French style are termed *étagères*.

WHISTLER, LAURENCE (b. 1913)

English glass-engraver who employs both diamond-point and stipple techniques, the latter of 18th-century Dutch origin in which a diamond or steel point is lightly tapped with a mallet in such a way as to remove a small 'dot' of glass from the surface. The design is built up from the effect of the depth and spacing of the dots. Whistler's early work, some of which was executed on 18th-century glass, largely employed traditional *motifs*. His later work utilized glass provided by the Whitefriars Glass Works. His work is marked *LW* and dated.

WHITEFRIARS GLASS WORKS (London)

There was a glasshouse here from the days of Ravenscroft at the end of the 17th century until the early 1920s, when it moved to Wealdstone in Middlesex.

For the most part manufacture has been of good quality table-glass, and cut-glass* table-services were sent to the Great Exhibition of 1851. The works also revived some of the traditional decorative techniques, making excellent *millefiori** paperweights* and glass inspired by ancient Roman and Venetian types. During the fashion for stained glass which accompanied the Gothic revival it made glass designed by Burne-Jones*, Ford Madox Ford, and William Morris*. Towards the end of the century iridescent glass* was produced in the *art nouveau** style. In more recent times it has supplied glass for engraving to Laurence Whistler*.

WHITE GLASS WORKS (Zanesville, Ohio)

A factory started in 1815 for the manufacture of bottles, flasks, and domestic glassware. It made Masonic and Eagle flasks.

WICKER FURNITURE

Furniture, chairs, settees and tables made of woven wicker obtained from willow trees and introduced about 1870. Chairs etc. were usually supplied with a loose seat cushion, and occasionally with buttoned upholstery. Among the largest makers were W. T. Ellinmore & Sons Ltd of Leicester, who poineered this kind of furniture, and grew their own willows.

WIENER KERAMIK

Studio of artist-potters founded in Vienna in 1905 by M. Powolny* and B. Löffler. J. Hoffman* and

D. Peche* were included among the designers. It operated in conjunction with the Wiener Werkstätte*. Figures modelled by Powolny and Löffler, and black and white majolika designed by Hoffmann were among the productions Wiener Keramik contributed to the decoration of the Palais Stoclet, Brussels. It amalgamated in 1912 with the Gmundner Keramik, an art-pottery founded in 1909, to become the Vereinigte (United) Wiener und Gmundner Keramik.

WIENER WERKSTÄTTE (German)

Vienna Workshops. An association of Viennese artist-craftsmen founded in 1901, and organized on the lines of C. R. Ashbee's* Guild of Handicrafts*. The general director was the financier F. Warndörfer, and the art-directors were J. Hoffmann* and K. Moser*. The workshops produced furniture, metalwork and textiles, and (after 1905) ceramics in association with the Wiener Keramik*. The styles associated with the Workshops are simple and severe, beginning with the *Jugendstil** and gradually acquiring Cubist* elements. They were influenced by C. R. Mackintosh* and the Glasgow School. When Gustav Klimt broke away from the *Sezession** in 1905 the Werkstätte became the centre of Austrian decorative art, remaining in existence until 1932, when they

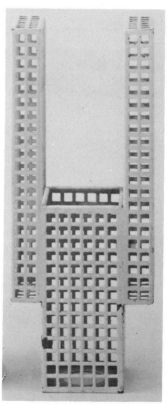

WIENER WEKSTÄTTE, Painted metal vase by J. Hoffman* or perhaps K. Moser*. c. 1905. *Sotheby & Co*

yielded to industrial competition. The usual mark is *WW* with the designer's monogram.

WILEMAN & CO. (Stoke-on-Trent, Staffordshire)
A factory was established by Henry Wileman in 1860 for the manufacture of earthenware and porcelain. It was called the Foley China Works*. After his death the business was continued by his sons, J. B. Shelley being taken into partnership about 1872. In 1925 the factory became Shelley Potteries Ltd., 'Shelley' being a trade name formerly used by Wileman & Co. The principal productions were decorative vases and service-ware. A decoration of gilding in conjunction with an iridescent glaze, produced about 1920, is reminiscent of Wedgwood's Fairyland lustre*.

WILKINSON, A. J. LTD (Burslem, Staffordshire)
Owners of the Royal Staffordshire Pottery, the art-director of which was Clarice Cliff*. The firm, in association with the Foley China Works*, provided tableware of distinctive contemporary forms and decoration for an exhibition in 1934 at Harrods. Among the contributing artists were Dame Laura Knight, R.A., Duncan Grant, Ben Nicholson, Paul Nash, Sir Frank Brangwyn, R.A.*, Graham Sutherland and Barbara Hepworth.

WILLARD, AARON (1757–1854)
Clock-maker of Roxbury, Mass.; brother of Benjamin and Simon Willard. Aaron was very prolific, but his clocks did not reach the high standard of Simon's work. He retired in 1823. His son, also Aaron (1783–1863), took over his father's business and retired in 1850. He was the originator of the lyre (banjo) clock.

WILLARD, SIMON (1753–1848)
The most important member of a distinguished clock-making family. He established himself as a maker of long-case clocks at Roxbury, Mass., in 1788, and he patented his banjo clocks in 1801, of which he made more than 5,000 in his lifetime. Willard lacked business acumen, however, and did not protect himself from infringements of his patent. In 1839 he was obliged to sell his business to Elnathan Taber, who had been his apprentice, and he retired from manufacture. Other members of this numerous family of clock-makers include his brother Aaron Willard*, whose shop was also at Roxbury, and his son, Willard, Jr*, who had premises at 9 Congress Street, Boston, Mass.

WILLARD, JR., SIMON (1795–1874)
Son of Simon Willard* of Roxbury, Mass., Simon Willard, Jr. had premises in Boston in 1828, and remained there until 1870. He specialized in watches and chronometers. Clocks bearing his name were made by another clock-maker to his orders.

WILLETTS POTTERY (Trenton, N.J.)
Factory started in 1853 by William Young & Sons for the manufacture of domestic white ware and Rock-ingham* glazed ware. Later they added decorated pottery and semi-porcelain, as well as a type of 'Belleek'* ware for which they were especially noted.

WILLOW PATTERN, THE
Probably the most popular and widely-used pattern ever to be transfer-printed* on to English earthenware, its origin must be sought in one or other of the numerous adaptions of Chinese blue-and-white *motifs* made in the middle years of the 18th century by Worcester* especially. Although the subject purports to be Chinese it has nothing whatever to do with any known Chinese decoration, nor is there a Chinese legend which it can be regarded as illustrating. The tale of the Willow pattern as related by Kai Lung, Ernest Bramah's market-place storyteller, is apocryphal. The elements of the design include willow trees, a pagoda, a bridge, usually three figures and a boat (or boats) on the river. The original pattern was engraved by Thomas Minton* for the Caughley* factory.

Numerous variants were produced elsewhere during the first half of the 19th century by Minton, Spode*, Adams, Davenport*, Turner, and others, and at Liverpool, Swansea, Sunderland, and elsewhere. It is the commonest survival today among blue-printed earthenware plates and dishes. Examples of its use on porcelain, apart from early Caughley specimens, are not numerous.

WILTSHAW & ROBINSON LTD (Carlton Works, Stoke-on-Trent)
Manufacturers of earthenware and porcelain established in 1897. Some of their ornamental porcelain especially, sold under the name of *Carlton Ware*, is now sought by collectors. Chinese influence is strong in the design of some of it. The earliest mark was *W & R Stoke-on-Trent*. Succeeding marks all have *Carlton Ware* or *Carlton China* as part of them.

WINDSOR CHAIRS
Stick-back armchairs with turned legs and a solid seat, usually of elm. Popular in both England and the United States, the English version was largely made in and around High Wycombe, Buckinghamshire. Windsor chairs have been made since the beginning of the 18th century and are still being made today. They were employed wherever seating of strength and durability was required—i.e. kitchens, inns, public buildings etc., and competed with Thonet's* mass-produced bentwood chairs.

WINFIELD, R. W. (Warwickshire)
English brass-founders who exhibited at the Great Exhibition* of 1851 and the London International Exhibition of 1862. They manufactured fittings for carpets and curtains, door-furniture, handles and escutcheon plates, gasoliers, chandeliers, ornamental lamps, and large brass furniture such as good-quality bedsteads, chairs, rocking-chairs, marble-topped

WINFIELD, R. W. Bedstead of a relatively plain design made of brass and exhibited by R. W. Winfield, Birmingham, in the 1851 Exhibition. After the *Illustrated Exhibitor*.

tables, etc. A four-poster bed in the Renaissance style was given Corinthian capitals topped by urns. The 'Angel' cot—a child's cot with a canopy supported by winged brass angels—was perhaps as revolting as anything in the 1851 Exhibition, and, as might be expected, it was extremely popular. Winfield was the most prominent of several manufacturers exhibiting brasswork of this kind, which had been made possible by the invention of drawn tubing. Later in the century, cheap bedsteads were made of iron rods covered with brass foil in imitation.

WOLFERS, PHILIPPE (1858–1929)
Sculptor, metalworker, and designer, who was apprenticed to the family firm of Wolfers Frères, Belgian Court Jewellers, after first studying sculpture in the Brussels Académie des Beaux-Arts. At the turn of the century he designed vases, bowls, etc in a naturalistic style. Bronze vases by him were made by E. Muller of Ivry, Seine, in stoneware in 1897. Wolfers also designed for ceramics. He usually employed his monogram impressed as a mark; occasionally an incised signature. His son, Marcel Wolfers, made sculptures in white *faïence* and stoneware about 1920.

WOLFSOHN, HELENA (Dresden)
Porcelain decorator who established a studio in Dresden in 1843 and started to paint wares such as vases and quatrefoil lobed cups and saucers decorated with alternating panels of turquoise, claret or yellow grounds overpainted with flowers and 'Watteau figures'* in reserves. To the annoyance of the Meissen* factory she marked her wares *AR*. These letters stood for Augustus Rex, the Meissen factory's patron in the early decades of the 18th century. They had originally been employed only on vases especially made to Royal order, usually for presentation, and

not in the least like the Wolfsohn products, which were derived from tea-ware of the late 1740s. Ultimately Meissen sought an injunction against her, and compelled her to stop using this mark. She then began to use a crown with a script letter D beneath it. These wares are sometimes described as 'Crown Dresden'. The early wares are of very good quality, but the later 'Crown Dresden' porcelain is usually coarser and less well painted.

WOMAN'S POTTERY CLUB See *Cincinnati Pottery Club*

WOOD, ENOCH (1759–1840)
Staffordshire potter, son of Aaron Wood, who was apprenticed to Humphrey Palmer at Hanley. Enoch Wood was a talented modeller, some of whose work survives. In 1784 he started an earthenware pottery in partnership with Ralph Wood. In 1790 he took James Caldwell into partnership, the firm becoming Wood & Caldwell until 1818. The style was then Enoch Wood & Sons until 1846, when it closed.

Enoch Wood himself modelled a number of portrait busts, including those of John Wesley, the preacher George Whitfield and the Emperor Alexander of Russia. He is also credited with the large figure of Demosthenes sometimes called 'St Paul preaching to the Athenians'. His self-portrait is in the British Museum, London. Many smaller works decorated with good enamel colours were made, and are among the best of the Staffordshire figures*. Much blue printed ware was made, a good deal of it for the American market. The popular subjects were English, American and French Views, and views of the country seats of English noblemen. A long series of sporting scenes, varying from duck-shooting to big-game hunting, was also popular. The firm also manufactured creamware*, jasper ware*, and basaltes* ware in the manner of Wedgwood.

Marks used include *E. WOOD* or *WOOD & CALDWELL,Wxxx.* and a circular mark in which the American eagle is surrounded by the words *Wood & Sons Burslem Warranted*.

WOOD MOSAIC See *Tunbridge ware*; *Sorrento ware*

WORCESTER ROYAL PORCELAIN COMPANY
Founded in 1751, the oldest Worcester factory, from which the Worcester Royal Porcelain factory dating from 1863 is derived, was based on an earlier factory in Bristol. During the 18th century, and until 1820, it made a highly successful porcelain using soaprock instead of china stone (feldspar). From 1783 the factory belonged to the Flight family, with Martin Barr in partnership from 1792. The style was then Flight & Barr. Later it became Barr, Flight & Barr (1807–1813), and Flight, Barr & Barr (1813–1840). In 1840 Chamberlain's* factory amalgamated with

WORCESTER PORCELAIN. Two-handled
vase decorated with Highland cattle by
James Stinton. Worcester Royal
Porcelain Company*. Signed and
dated, 1921. *Antique Collectors' Club*

WORCESTER PORCELAIN. A *petit déjeuner* service made in
1865 for the marriage of the Earl and Countess of Dudley
and presented to them by the City of Worcester. One
service is decorated with beading and jewelling by Samuel
Ranford and the heads in medallions were painted by T. S.
Callowhill*. *Worcester Royal Porcelain Company*

WORCESTER ROYAL PORCELAIN COMPANY. Plate designed by
the primitive painter Scottie Wilson, for Worcester
porcelain. c. 1965. *Worcester Royal Porcelain Company*

Flight, Barr & Barr, and in 1847 the enterprise was
moved to the site of Chamberlain's works nearby,
where the present factory stands. The concern in 1848
was owned by Walter Chamberlain and John Lilly,
who were joined in 1850 by W. H. Kerr. By 1852 it
was Kerr & Binns, and eleven years later it became
the Worcester Royal Porcelain Company.

The Worcester factory started by Thomas Grainger* in 1801 was taken over by Royal Worcester in
1889. The factory's modeller, James Hadley*, started
his own factory in 1896. This was also taken over in
1905, after his death. Royal Worcester today is one of
the principal manufacturers of fine porcelain with a
very important collection in the Dyson Perrins
Museum, adjacent to the factory which is open to the
public.

At the beginning of the 19th century the factory
employed a number of artists of note, including
William Billingsley* from Derby; Thomas Baxter,
landscape, figure, and flower painter from London,
who was master of apprentices; Robert Brewer, pupil
of Paul Sandby, said to have painted directly on the
glaze without preparation; and Moses Webster,
flower painter from Derby. At the time the factory
executed two important services—one for Lord
Nelson in 1802, and one for the Duke of Cumberland
in 1806.

But the competition from Chamberlain was becoming keener. They had already been appointed manufacturers to the Prince Regent (the Flights were

manufacturers to the King and Queen), and they
named their new and improved porcelain, the 'Regent'
body. In 1816 they produced a service in 'Regent'
porcelain for Princess Charlotte which cost £1,050,
and a service for the East Indian Company costing
£4,150. By the 1830s, however, economic conditions
were becoming very difficult, and the 'hungry forties'
were not far off. The porcelain factories, too, were
facing competition from the makers of stone china. In
common with other factories, the amalgamated
Worcester factory concentrated on utility wares in
order to survive. Their contribution to the Great
Exhibition of 1851 was comparatively modest, but in
1852 Kerr & Binns emerged as the leading spirits,
and both were men of taste and enterprise. The first
product was the Shakespeare* dessert-service, based
on *A Midsummer Night's Dream*, with figures modelled
in the Parian* body by the Irish sculptor, W. H.

359

WORCESTER PORCELAIN A porcelain inkstand consisting of combined pen-tray, inkwell, and pounce-pot, with carrying handle. Worcester. Mark of Flight, Barr & Barr (1815–1840). *Private collection*

WORCESTER PORCELAIN. Fine quality fruit-painting on Royal Worcester* porcelain. Last quarter of the 19th century. *Antique Collectors' Club*

Kirk, and painting by Thomas Bott*. This was exhibited in Dublin in 1853.

The Prince Consort, who took an interest in the factory, suggested his collection of Limoges enamel as a source of inspiration, and Thomas Bott developed the well-known series of wares painted in white on a deep blue ground. Somewhat similar work was done by his son, Thomas John Bott. Thomas Bott helped to decorate a tea-service made for the marriage of the Prince of Wales (later Edward VII) and Princess Alexandra. The old Sèvres* technique of 'jewelling' with drops of enamel, invented by Cotteau in 1781, was revived for the Countess of Dudley service in 1865, with gilding and jewelled work by Samuel Ranford, and heads painted in medallions by Thomas Callowhill*.

By the time R. W. Binns formed the Worcester Royal Porcelain Company the factory was concentrating on ornamental wares, and had achieved an enviable reputation for design, quality and craftsmanship.

In 1872 an ivory-toned porcelain body introduced some years earlier was employed for wares in the Japanese taste, in conjunction with gilding of different shades and bronzing. The shapes were derived from Japan and modelled by James Hadley*, decorated by Callowhill and gilded by Béjot. This ware won an award at the Vienna Exposition of 1873. In the Paris Exhibition of 1878 these wares not only achieved a gold medal for the factory but the Cross of the Legion of Honour for R. W. Binns.

Also undoubtedly Japanese-inspired was George Owen's* pierced porcelain which had its origin in Oriental ivory carving. From 1875 onwards fine quality modelling was being done by James Hadley, assisted by his three sons. Especially notable are his 'Grecian' figures. Hadley also modelled a notable pair of vases which depict potters at work. Two pairs exist, of which one is in the Worcester Museum and the other in the United States.

The factory entered the 20th century as a flourishing concern with a tradition of encouraging individual artists and craftsmen. One such artist was John

Stinton* (1854–1956) who specialized in Highland cattle. Harry Davis* who started with the factory in 1898 and retired in the 1960s continued the tradition as an artist who worked on almost every important project in one capacity or another. Perhaps his most historic work was a vase painted with an 18th-century view of Worcester Cathedral for presentation to Sir Winston Churchill. Since 1935 the factory has specialized in fine quality porcelain figures issued in limited editions. These began with the series of American Birds by Dorothy Doughty*, followed by her series of British Birds. Doris Lindner* specializes in horses and cattle, and her equestrian portrait of the Queen (then Princess Elizabeth) issued in 1948 is now much sought. A notable series of Victorian figures is by Ruth Van Ruyckevelt. Her husband, Ronald, models tropical fish studied from life.

The mark in 1783 was *Flight* in script, in 1789 a crown was added, and in 1792 it became *Flight & Barr*. From 1807 to 1813 the initials *BFB* were used, and from 1813 to 1840, *FBB*. From 1852 to 1862 a shield with the initials *K&B* was used, or a circular mark consisting of linked *W*s in script. The latter mark surmounted by a crown, usually with the words 'Royal Worcester' has been employed ever since on Worcester porcelain.

See also *Chamberlain, Robert*; *Grainger, Thomas*; *Hadley, James*

WRIGHT & MANSFIELD (London)
Cabinet-makers, fl. 1860 to 1880. Displayed furniture at the London Exhibition, 1862, including a satinwood* cabinet ornamented with marquetry, Wedgwood plaques, and ormolu mounts, acquired in 1867 by the Victoria and Albert Museum, London. Their copies of Adam satinwood furniture have often been mistaken for 18th-century work.

WROUGHT IRON See *Ironwork*

WYATT, MATTHEW COTES (1777–1862)
English sculptor, the youngest son of James Wyatt, architect of Fonthill*. His work was more or less controversial, perhaps the most criticized being the large equestrian statue of the Duke of Wellington, once on the top of Hyde Park Arch. Best known,

WRIGHT & MANSFIELD. Inlaid satinwood cabinet with gilt metal mounts and inset Wedgwood* jasper* plaques in the neo-classical* style. Exhibited and commended at the Paris Exposition Universelle, 1867. Wright & Mansfield*, London. *Victoria & Albert Museum, London*

WYATT, MATTHEW COTES. '*Bashaw, the faithful friend of man . . .*' a life-like portrait of Bashaw, a Newfoundland dog belonging to Earl Dudley, in marble and bronze by Matthew Cotes Wyatt. 1831. *Victoria & Albert Museum, London*

perhaps, is his carving of Lord Dudley's Newfoundland dog, Bashaw. This is a remarkable example of craftsmanship in white, grey, and black marbles which have been imperceptibly joined to simulate the animal's coat. Its eyes are of sardonyx and topaz, with a pupil of black lava. The top of the pedestal is a simulated cushion. The dog's right foot rests on the bronze head of a boa constrictor, the body of which rises to its belly and helps to support the weight of the marble, which would otherwise be poised on four relatively slender legs. The snake's eyes are rubies. The pedestal is of black marble decorated in a colourful Florentine mosaic of foliage, fruit, and flowers.

Lord Dudley died in 1834, Wyatt became involved in a quarrel with the executors over his bill of £5,000, and the sculpture was never delivered. It appeared, in 1851, in the Great Exhibition, where it was called, *The Faithful Friend of Man Trampling under foot his most Insidious Enemy*. There seems to be no reason, however, why the snake should be regarded as any more than a technical device included for the purpose of support.

WYATT, SIR MATTHEW DIGBY (1820–1877)

Architect and designer, articled to his brother T. H. Wyatt. In 1849 he reported to the Society of Arts on an industrial exhibition held in Paris and became, in 1851, secretary to the Executive Committee of the Great Exhibition. He designed the Byzantine, English, Gothic, Italian, Pompeian, and Renaissance Courts at the Crystal Palace which was re-erected at Sydenham in 1854. His many published works include *The Industrial Arts of the Nineteenth Century*, 1851–1853.

WYBURD, LEONARD F.

Son of the painter, Francis John Wyburd, Leonard Wyburd exhibited at the Royal Academy from 1888 until 1904. He became director of Liberty's* furnishing and decorating studio in 1883, and was responsible for furniture designs in a variety of styles, including 'quaint'*, 'artistic', 'Moresque', and Early English.

WYON, EDWARD WILLIAM (1811–1885)

English sculptor and designer, Wyon was educated at the Academy Schools, and exhibited a portrait bust of General Maitland in the Academy Exhibition of 1831. At the Great Exhibition of 1851 Wyon showed a *tazza* modelled from a Greek design executed for the Art Union* of London. Between 1852 and 1866 he modelled *Titania, Oberon, Hope*, a *Nubian water-carrier*, and a bust of Wellington for reproduction in Parian porcelain* by Wedgwood*. Also attributed to him are Wedgwood busts of Bunyan, Colin Campbell (the Palladian architect), Palmerston, George Stephenson, Tennyson, James Watt and Wesley.

XYLONITE

Celluloid, also known as Parkesine and pyroxylin plastic. This material was a substance invented by Parkes of Birmingham in 1856 and is an artificial celluloid prepared by the action of camphor on nitrocellulose. Hyatt of Newark, N.J., greatly improved the manufacture, and it became predominantly an American product. It could be coloured with mineral pigments including coal-tar dyes. It was much used as a substitute for ivory (for example, in the making of piano keys), and in imitation of horn and tortoiseshell. Imitation marble was made by pressing together differently coloured sheets. It was employed for making small boxes, picture-frames, brush-backs, and similar objects of utility. Its principal drawback was the fact that it was highly inflammable. Xylonite, the British name of the product, was the first true plastic in the modern sense of the work.

See *Bois durci*

YOUNG, WILLIAM WESTON (1776–1847)
Painter of porcelain at Swansea and Nantgarw*
mainly responsible for floral subjects and birds and
butterflies. He was one of those who invested money
in the Nantgarw factory.

YSART, SALVADOR (1877–1955) and PAUL
See *Moncrieff's Glass Works*

Z

ZIEGLER, JULES CLAUDE (1804–1856) See *Beauvais* (*Oise*)

ZINC

Zinc was not smelted commercially in Europe until the 1730s, when William Champion produced it in Bristol, principally for the manufacture of brass. In the 19th century it was very commonly employed for the making of decorative castings as a substitute for bronze, the white metal surface disguised by bronzing. Zinc melts at a much lower temperature than bronze, saving money on fuel, and the type of mould required. Even when bronzed, however, its appearance is inferior to bronze; it is softer and more easily damaged, and it does not make such sharp casts. Zinc was principally used to make decorative metalwork for large scale consumption, often by methods which could be well described as mass-production. Objects like clock cases were cast in parts and assembled afterwards with screws and nuts. The bronzing process was invented in Berlin in the 1840s, and a manufacturer named Geiss*, who may have been the inventor, specialized in work of this kind and exhibited in London in 1851. The Vielle Montagne Joint Stock Company of 19 rue Picher, Paris, directed by A. Guynemer, displayed objects of general utility, as well as statues, church ornaments, and vases. Their *pièce de resistance* was a zinc statue of Queen Victoria on her throne which was 18 feet in height. Bronzed zinc clock cases, like the *bronze d'ameublement* itself, became less fashionable towards the end of the century, and despite the popularity of decorative metalwork during the currency of the *art nouveau** style, comparatively little was made of zinc. The metal is also commonly termed spelter, especially in the antique trade.

ZITZMANN, FRIEDRICH (1840–1906)

German glass craftsman, a pupil of Karl Köpping, who specialized in decorative glass-blowing, and made glasses to Köpping's design partly at the lamp, i.e. the glass being shaped by manipulation after softening it in the flame of a Bunsen burner. Towards the end of the century Zitzmann designed glassware for the Ehrenfelder Glashütte*. His glasses were signed *F. Zitzmann*.

Appendix I

ENGLISH AND SCOTTISH SILVER MARKS

In these tables the date-letters in ordinary type are placed on the left, and opposite them the years to which they refer. The letter *A* of each cycle as it appears on the object is shown at the head of each column, and the remaining letters in the cycle will conform to this in the style of the type-face and the shape of the shield within which it is enclosed. Above the date letter is the device employed by the assay office—a leopard's head for London, an anchor for Birmingham, etc. Above the assay office punch is a mark which guarantees the standard, usually a lion *passant*. This is normally 925 parts of silver in 1,000 but the very rare Britannia standard of 975 parts of silver in 1,000 is designated by a punch bearing the figure of Britannia. The sovereign's head acknowledges payment of duty between the dates indicated. Makers' marks are much too numerous to be given here, but they may be sought in Sir Charles Jackson's monumental work, *English Goldsmiths and their Marks*. For misleading marks see *British Plate*.

London

	A	a	N	a	A	a	a	A
A	1796	1816	1836	1856	1876	1896	1916	1936
B	1797	1817	1837	1857	1877	1897	1917	1937
C	1798	1818	1838	1858	1878	1898	1918	1938
D	1799	1819	1839	1859	1879	1899	1919	1939
E	1800	1820	1840	1860	1880	1900	1920	1940
F	1801	1821[1]	1841	1861	1881	1901	1921	1941
G	1802	1822	1842	1862	1882	1902	1922	1942
H	1803	1823	1843	1863	1883	1903	1923	1943
I	1804	1824	1844	1864	1884	1904	1924	1944
K	1805	1825	1845	1865	1885	1905	1925	1945
L	1806	1826	1846	1866	1886	1906	1926	1946
M	1807	1827	1847	1867	1887	1907	1927	1947
N	1808	1828	1848	1868	1888	1908	1928	1948
O	1809	1829	1849	1869	1889	1909	1929	1949
P	1810	1830	1850	1870	1890[2]	1910	1930	1950
Q	1811	1831	1851	1871	1891	1911	1931	1951
R	1812	1832	1852	1872	1892	1912	1932	1952
S	1813	1833	1853	1873	1893	1913	1933	1953
T	1814	1834	1854	1874	1894	1914	1934	1954
U	1815	1835	1855	1875	1895	1915	1935	1955

The *Sovereign's Head* mark was added on 1 December 1784 to show the payment of duty and continued until 30 April 1890.

1. The *Leopard's Head* is no longer crowned after 1821.
2. The *Sovereign's Head* mark was not used after 1890.

Birmingham

The Assay Office was established at Birmingham in 1773, with the *Anchor* as its distinguishing punch. When the duty was doubled in 1797, the *King's Head* was duplicated for a short time. The sequences are of twenty-five, omitting *J* or *I*, or twenty-six letters.

A	1798	1824	1849	1875	1900	1925	1950
B	1799	1825	1850	1876	1901	1926	1951
C	1800	1826	1851	1877	1902	1927	1952
D	1801	1827	1852	1878	1903	1928	1953
E	1802	1828	1853	1879	1904	1929	1954
F	1803	1829	1854	1880	1905	1930	etc.
G	1804	1830	1855	1881	1906	1931	
H	1805	1831	1856	1882	1907	1932	
I	1806	1832	1857	1883	1908	——	
J	1807	——	1858	——	——	1933	
K	1808	1833	1859	1884	1909	1934	
L	1809	1834	1860	1885	1910	1935	
M	1810	1835	1861	1886	1911	1936	
N	1811	1836	1862	1887	1912	1937	
O	1812	1837	1863	1888	1913	1938	
P	1813	1838	1864	1889	1914	1939	
Q	1814	1839	1865	1890	1915	1940	
R	1815	1840	1866	1891	1916	1941	
S	1816	1841	1867	1892	1917	1942	
T	1817	1842	1868	1893	1918	1943	
U	1818	1843	1869	1894	1919	1944	
V	1819	1844	1870	1895	1920	1945	
W	1820	1845	1871	1896	1921	1946	
X	1821	1846	1872	1897	1922	1947	
Y	1822	1847	1873	1898	1923	1948	
Z	1823	1848	1874	1899	1924	1949	

The *Sovereign's Head* mark was added on 1 December 1784 to show the payment of duty and continued until 30 April 1890.

A	1797	1818	1839	1864	1884	1901	1926
B	1798	1819	1840	1865	1885	1902	1927
C	1799	1820	1841	1866	1886	1903	1928
D	1800	1821–2	1842	1867	1887	1904	1929
E	1801	1823	1843	1868	1888	1905	1930
F	1802	1824	1844	1869	1889	1906	1931
G	1803	1825	1845	1870	1890	1907	1932
H	1804	1826	1846	1871	1891	1908	1933
I	1805	1827	1847	1872	1892	1909	1934
K	1806	1828	1848	1873	1893	1910	1935
L	1807	1829	1849	1874	1894	1911	1936
M	1808	1830	1850	1875	1895	1912	1937
N	1809	1831	1851	1876	1896	1913	1938
O	1810	1832	1852	1877	1897	1914	1939
P	1811	1833	1853	1878	1898	1915	1940
Q	1812	1834	1854	1879	1899	1916	1941
R	1813	1835	1855	1880	1900	1917	1942
S	1814	1836	1856	1881	——	1918	1943
T	1815	1837	1857	1882	——	1919	1944
U	1816	1838	1858	1883	——	1920	1945
V	1817	——	1859	——	——	1921	1946
W	——	——	1860	——	——	1922	1947
X	——	——	1861	——	——	1923	1948
Y	——	——	1862	——	——	1924	1949
Z	——	——	1863	——	——	1925	1950

The *Sovereign's Head* mark was added on 1 December 1784 to show the payment of duty and continued until 30 April 1890.

Dublin

The figure of *Hibernia* was added in 1731; the duty stamp of the *King's Head* was not punched till 1807.

A	1797	1821	1846	1871	1896	1916	1942
B	1798	1822	1847	1872	1897	1917	1943
C	1799	1823	1848	1873	1898	1918	1944
D	1800	1824	1849	1874	1899	1919	1945
E	1801	1825	1850	1875	1900	1920	1946
F	1802	1826	1851	1876	1901	1921	1947
G	1803	1827	1852	1877	1902	1922	1948
H	1804	1828	1853	1878	1903	1923	1949
I	1805	1829	1854	1879	1904	1924	1950
K	1806	1830	1855	1880	1905	1925	1951
L	1807	1831	1856	1881	1906	1926	1952
M	1808	1832	1857	1882	1907	1927	1953
N	1809	1833	1858	1883	1908	1928	1954
O	1810	1834	1859	1884	1909	1929	etc.
P	1811	1835	1860	1885	1910	1930–1	
Q	1812	1836	1861	1886	1911	1932	
R	1813	1837	1862	1887	1912	1933	
S	1814	1838	1863	1888	1913	1934	
T	1815	1839	1864	1889	1914	1935	
U	1816	1840	1865	1890[1]	1915	1936	
V	——	1841	1866	1891	——	1937	
W	1817	1842	1867	1892	——	1938	
X	1818	1843	1868	1893	——	1939	
Y	1819	1844	1869	1894	——	1940	
Z	1820	1845	1870	1895	——	1941	

1. *Sovereign's Head* discontinued.

Edinburgh

	A	B/C/D/E	F/G/H	I/J	K/L/M	N/O	P/Q
A	1780	1806	1832	1857	1882	1906	1931
B	1781	1807	1833	1858	1883	1907	1932
C	1782	1808	1834	1859	1884	1908	1933
D	1783	1809	1835	1860	1885	1909	1934
E	1784	1810	1836	1861	1886	1910	1935
F	1785	1811	1837	1862	1887	1911	1936
G	1786–7	1812	1838	1863	1888	1912	1937
H	1788	1813	1839	1864	1889	1913	1938
I	1789	1814	1840	1865	1890	1914	1939
J	1789	1815	—				
K	1790	1816	1841	1866	1891	1915	1940
L	1791	1817	1842	1867	1892	1916	1941
M	1792	1818	1843	1868	1893	1917	1942
N	1793	1819	1844	1869	1894	1918	1943
O	1794	1820	1845	1870	1895	1919	1944
P	1795	1821	1846	1871	1896	1920	1945
Q	1796	1822	1847	1872	1897	1921	1946
R	1797	1823	1848	1873	1898	1922	1947
S	1798	1824	1849	1874	1899	1923	1948
T	1799	1825	1850	1875	1900	1924	1949
U	1800	1826	1851	1876	1901	1925	1950
V	1801	1827	1852	1877	1901	1926	1951
W	1802	1828	1853	1878	1902	1927	1952
X	1803	1829	1854	1879	1903	1928	1953
Y	1804	1830	1855	1880	1904	1929	1954
Z	1805	1831	1856	1881	1905	1930	1955

The *Sovereign's Head* mark was added on 1 December 1784 to show the payment of duty and continued until 30 April 1890.

Exeter

The amount of plate produced here declined in the 19th century and little was assayed after 1850. The office was closed in 1883.

A	1797	1817	1837	1857	1877
B	1798	1818	1838	1858	1878
C	1799	1819	1839	1859	1879
D	1800	1820	1840	1860	1880
E	1801	1821	1841	1861	1881
F	1802	1822	1842	1862	1882
G	1803	1823	1843	1863	
H	1804	1824	1844	1864	
I	1805	1825	1845	1865	
K	1806	1826	1846	1866	
L	1807	1827	1847	1867	
M	1808	1828	1848	1868	
N	1809	1829	1849	1869	
O	1810	1830	1850	1870	
P	1811	1831	1851	1871	
Q	1812	1832	1852	1872	
R	1813	1833	1853	1873	
S	1814	1834	1854	1874	
T	1815	1835	1855	1875	
U	1816	1836	1856	1876	
V	—				
W	—	—	—	—	
X	—	—	—	—	
Y	—	—	—	—	
Z	—	—	—	—	

The *Sovereign's Head* mark was added on 1 December 1784 to show the payment of duty and continued until 30 April 1890.

Glasgow

The Glasgow goldsmiths were incorporated with other metalworkers there as early as 1536, and a minute-book covering the period 1616–1717 survives. Although a cycle of date-letters has been tentatively traced from 1681 to 1705, when the *Fish, Tree, and Bell* mark (from the burgh arms) was used, it was not until as late as the Act of 1819 that the Glasgow Goldsmiths' Company was constituted a body corporate and the *Lion Rampant* mark (from the Royal Standard of Scotland) was introduced. A regular sequence of date-letters began in that year and the sixth cycle of twenty-six letters ended in 1974.

A	1819[1]	1845	1871	1897	1923	1949
B	1820	1846	1872	1898	1924	1950
C	1821	1847	1873	1899	1925	1951
D	1822	1848	1874	1900	1926	1952
E	1823	1849	1875	1901	1927	1953
F	1824	1850	1876	1902	1928	1954
G	1825	1851	1877	1903	1929	1955
H	1826	1852	1878	1904	1930	etc.
I	1827	1853	1879	1905	1931	
J	1828	1854	1880	1906	1932	
K	1829	1855	1881	1907	1933	
L	1830	1856	1882	1908	1934	
M	1831	1857	1883	1909	1935	
N	1832	1858	1884	1910	1936	
O	1833	1859	1885	1911	1937	
P	1834	1860	1886	1912	1938	
Q	1835	1861	1887	1913	1939	
R	1836	1862	1888	1914	1940	
S	1837	1863	1889	1915	1941	
T	1838	1864	1890[2]	1916	1942	
U	1839	1865	1891	1917	1943	
V	1840	1866	1892	1918	1944	
W	1841	1867	1893	1919	1945	
X	1842	1868	1894	1920	1946	
Y	1843	1869	1895	1921	1947	
Z	1844	1870	1896	1922	1948	

1. The *Sovereign's Head* indicates payment of duty.
2. The *Sovereign's Head* was discontinued in this year.

Newcastle

The Newcastle Assay Office was re-established in 1702, with an erratic cycle in gothic capitals, and closed in 1884.

A	1791	1815	1839	1864
B	1792	1816	1840	1865
C	1793	1817	1841	1866
D	1794	1818	1842	1867
E	1795	1819	1843	1868
F	1796	1820	1844	1869
G	1797	1821	1845	1870
H	1798	1822	1846	1871
I	1799	1823	1847	1872
J	———	———	1848	———
K	1800	1824	1849	1873
L	1801	1825	1850	1874
M	1802	1826	1851	1875
N	1803	1827	1852	1876
O	1804	1828	1853	1877
P	1805	1829	1854	1878
Q	1806	1830	1855	1879
R	1807	1831	1856	1880
S	1808	1832	1857	1881
T	1809	1833	1858	1882
U	1810	1834	1859	1883
W	1811	1835	1860	
X	1812	1836	1861	
Y	1813	1837	1862	
Z	1814	1838	1863	

The *Sovereign's Head* mark was added on 1 December 1784 to show the payment of duty and continued until 30 April 1890.

Sheffield

The assay office was instituted at the same time as that at Birmingham, with the *Crown* as its town mark. The first two cycles are complicated because the letters are jumbles and not in sequence.

A	1799	1806	1824	1844	1868	1893	1918	1943
B	1783	1805	1825	1845	1869	1894	1919	1944
C	1780	1811	1826	1846	1870	1895	1920	1945
D	1781	1812	1827	1847	1871	1896	1921	1946
E	1773	1799	1828	1848	1872	1897	1922	1947
F	1774	1803	1829	1849	1873	1898	1923	1948
G	1782	1804	1830	1850	1874	1899	1924	1949
H	1777	1801	1831	1851	1875	1900	1925	1950
I	1784	1818	——	1852	——	1901	1926	1951
J	——	——	——	——	1876	——	——	1952
K	1786	1809	1832	1853	1877	1902	1927	1953
L	1790	1810	1833	1854	1878	1903	1928	1954
M	1789–94	1802	1834	1855	1879	1904	1929	etc.
N	1775	1800	——	1856	1880	1905	1930	
O	1793	1815	——	1857	1881	1906	1931	
P	1791	1808	1835	1858	1882	1907	1932	
Q	1795	1820	1836	——	1883	1908	1933	
R	1776	1813	1837	1859	1884	1909	1934	
S	1778	1807	1838	1860	1885	1910	1935	
T	1787	1816	1839	1861	1886	1911	1936	
U	1792	1823	1840	1862	1887	1912	1937	
V	1798	1819	1841	1863	1888	1913	1938	
W	1788	1814	——	1864	1889	1914	1939	
X	1797	1817	1842	1865	1890	1915	1940	
Y	1785	1821	——	1866	1891	1916	1941	
Z	1796	1822	1843	1867	1892	1917	1942	

    The *Sovereign's Head* mark was added on 1 December 1784 to show the payment of duty and continued until 30 April 1890.

York

There are two cycles, each of twenty-five letters, omitting *J*, and part of a third which brought the series to an end when the office was closed in 1857.

A	1787	1812	1837
B	1788	1813	1838
C	1789	1814	1839
D	1790	1815	1840
E	1791	1816	1841
F	1792	1817	1842
G	1793	1818	1843
H	1794	1819	1844
I	1795	1820	1845
J			
K	1796	1821	1846
L	1797	1822	1847
M	1798	1823	1848
N	1799	1824	1849
O	1800	1825	1850
P	1801	1826	1851
Q	1802	1827	1852
R	1803	1828	1853
S	1804	1829	1854
T	1805	1830	1855
U	1806	1831	——
V	1807	1832	1856
W	1808	1833	
X	1809	1834	
Y	1810	1835	
Z	1811	1836	

Appendix II

BRITISH REGISTRY MARKS

The Registry mark, of which there are two forms, was used from 1842 to 1883. The first form was used from 1842 to 1867, and the second from 1868 to 1883. These marks indicate that the design was registered at the Patent Office; they also provide information about the year, month, and day of manufacture. The first registry mark was as follows

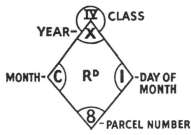

The key to this is, first, the roman numeral I in the circle at the top, which gives the classification of the object—I for metal, II for wood, III for glass, IV for earthenware. The letter in the upper angle of the diamond indicates the year of manufacture; in the angle to the left, the letter indicates the month, and in the angle to the right the figure is the day of the month of manufacture. At the bottom of the diamond the figure indicates the batch number, and hence the manufacturer.

The following lists give the key to the year and month.

X	1842	E	1855
H	1843	L	1856
C	1844	K	1857
A	1845	B	1858
I	1846	M	1859
F	1847	Z	1860
U	1848	R	1861
S	1849	O	1862
V	1850	G	1863
P	1851	N	1864
D	1852	W	1865
Y	1853	Q	1866
J	1854	T	1867

January	C	July	I
February	G	August	R
March	W	September	D
April	H	October	B
May	E	November	K
June	M	December	A

There are two errors. For September, 1857, the letter R (indicating August) was used. For December, 1860, the letter K (indicating November) was employed. The year is unaffected.

Where the name of the manufacturer is not given otherwise, it can be obtained from the Patent Office on payment of a fee.

A slight change took place in 1868, which consisted principally in rearranging the position of the symbols. The roman numerals indicating classification and the letters Rd. remained as before, but the letter indicating the year was now placed in the angle of the diamond to the *right*. At the top, directly under the circle, was the figure indicating the day of the month; the month letter was in the angle at the bottom. The figure in the angle to the left indicated the batch number. The year-letters used with the second mark are as follows:

X	1868	V	1876
H	1869	P	1877
C	1870	D	1878
A	1871	Y	1879
I	1872	J	1880
F	1873	E	1881
U	1874	L	1882
S	1875	K	1883

The same table of marks for the months as for the previous period was continued.

An error between March 1 and March 6, 1878, resulted in the letter W being employed *for the year*, instead of D. Since W was not otherwise used as a year-letter, however, this should not cause confusion. To ascertain whether a Registry mark belongs to the first or second group, look at the space at the top of the diamond immediately below the category mark (roman numeral). If it contains a *letter* the mark belongs to the first series: if a *figure*, to the second.

This system was replaced in 1884 by a simpler

system in which the registered number of a particular pattern or design was impressed, painted, or otherwise put on the object. This took the form of the letters Rd followed by a number. By the time the system ended in 1909 numbers exceeded half a million.

The table below shows the figure reached at the beginning of each year. From 1902, the starting figures are approximate only.

Rd. No.	1	1884
Rd. No.	19754	1885
Rd. No.	40480	1886
Rd. No.	64520	1887
Rd. No.	90483	1888
Rd. No.	116648	1889
Rd. No.	141275	1890
Rd. No.	163767	1891
Rd. No.	185713	1892

Rd. No.	205240	1893
Rd. No.	224720	1894
Rd. No.	246975	1895
Rd. No.	268392	1896
Rd. No.	291241	1897
Rd. No.	311658	1898
Rd. No.	331707	1899
Rd. No.	351202	1900
Rd. No.	368154	1901
Rd. No.	385500	1902
Rd. No.	402500	1903
Rd. No.	420000	1904
Rd. No.	447000	1905
Rd. No.	471000	1906
Rd. No.	494000	1907
Rd. No.	519500	1908
Rd. No.	550000	1909

ENGLISH PiANO # 19766
Allison & Sons
   Dundee & Perth

Appendix III

ART FORGERY IN THE 19TH CENTURY

The 19th century was a period in which the forger and faker of works of art and *vertu* flourished. Perhaps it is best to start a brief consideration of the subject with some definitions. A forgery is a copy of a work of art or craft made for fraudulent purposes. A pastiche is a work which has been constructed from selected parts taken from genuine works and combined together to make a new one which, if sold as genuine, is undoubtedly a forgery. Most picture forgeries are of this type; so was Rouchomowsky's* *Tiara of Saitaphernes*. A fake is a genuine work, usually of a minor character, which has been altered or added to for the purpose of enhancing its value. Reproductions are copies made for honest purposes which, of course, in some cases are used fraudulently. Replicas are contemporary copies, usually those made in the artist's studio, probably to fill an order. These are not uncommon in the history of art, and value depends on quality.

Art forgery is very ancient. The Phoenicians sold forgeries of Egyptian silver bowls in Italy. The Roman art market was notorious for forgeries. In 18th-century Italy, when young Englishmen were making the Grand Tour, the forging of painting and sculpture was a thriving industry. Forgers were also active in London, where they sold their work on the home-market which had been thus created. Even the greatest connoisseurs were deceived sometimes. A Leonardo in Sir Joshua Reynolds' sale fetched only two guineas. The 19th century saw by far the greatest number of forgeries produced not only by individuals, but sometimes even as a factory operation.

Until the Industrial Revolution, in which England led the way, there had been a shortage of actual cash, which kept prices low. The wealthiest men were those with large landed estates, cultivated, and grazed by sheep and cattle. There was, as a rule, a great house, one or two farmhouses, labourers' cottages, and barns. The great house usually contained its quota of works of art—paintings, porcelain, silver, etc.—but

the owner, more often than not, would have been hard put to it to find five hundred guineas in cash at short notice without recourse to a banker or money-lender. Pictures and *objets d'art* in the house were part of the interior decoration, and the porcelain and silver, which the 19th century locked up in glazed display cabinets, were in general use on the dining-table. The market for *objets d'art* was already expanding in the 1770s, when we find Josiah Wedgwood, writing to his partner, Bentley, discussing the necessity for making vases for the 'middling sort of people' because the aristocracy alone could not keep his factory sufficiently supplied with orders. By the beginning of the 19th century fortunes in cash were being accumulated, partly by manufacturers and factory owners and to a lesser extent from ventures abroad. Beckford*, for instance, derived some of his fortune from plantations in the West Indies, and others from the Oriental trade. It is at this point that we find prices beginning to rise.

Works of art regarded as an investment date at least from Roman times. Bankers were always connected with their sale. In Antwerp normal commercial business was carried on from the ground floor of the Bourse, and works of art were sold on the second floor. The banking houses of the Medicis and the Fuggers not only bought, commissioned and sold works of art but they accepted them as pledges for loans. The financiers of 18th-century France, reacting to the inflation of the notorious John Law (by no means the first of his breed and certainly not the last), bought works of art as an anti-inflation hedge, which turned out to be far more profitable, even at the time of the Revolution, than most other forms of investment, and the London National Gallery was founded on the private collection of John Julius Angerstein, the banker, who had bought some of his pictures from the Duc d'Orléans, Philippe-Égalité. Nor did the church neglect the opportunities offered. The great Cardinal Mazarin, in the 17th century, dealt in works of art and maintained a purchasing agent in Italy who reported on the quantity of forged paintings then being offered for sale in Rome. When Sir Robert Walpole needed money he sold his picture collection to Catherine the Great of Russia. This is so often ignored today in trendy discussions of the art-market that it seems that ignorance is more widespread than it ought to be, but this ignorance does not appear to extend outside certain limited circles, since we find staff pension funds investing in works of art, and bankers hanging Impressionists on their walls.

Before the 19th century buying works of art was more or less the prerogative of the aristocracy, the bankers and the wealthier merchants, the last two categories considerably influenced, until the middle of the 18th century, by the first. In the 19th century money was more widely spread. Towards the end of the century the millionaire and the multi-millionaire made their appearance on both sides of the Atlantic. Large numbers of people were able to buy what had formerly been within the reach of very few. The *bourgeoisie** made money from the speculation which marked the beginning of the Railway Age, and before mid-century relatively large sums were being paid for *objets d'art* of all kinds, although as yet very little was added for antique value itself. These things, however, were available in quantities too small to supply a growing market, and prices rose steadily. It is not surprising, therefore, that ways were found of supplying the demand.

Until the 19th century prices were guided by style and quality. Very little attention was paid to the concept of antiquity as a desirable quality, and old-fashioned furniture was relegated to the attic when fashions changed, and new furniture was bought. Silver and porcelain were bought new from various sources as they were needed for the dining-table.

During the French Revolution the possessions of the King and his Court were stolen by the mob. Some were auctioned at the time. Other things were either destroyed or found their way eventually to the shops of the *brocanteurs*, to be sought out in subsequent years by connoisseurs. In this way the old Roman custom of antique collecting was revived and became extremely popular.

The late Gerald Reitlinger documented in detail the rise of antique collecting in the 19th century, and the remarkable prices in gold pounds paid for some of the objects, in Volume II of the *Economics of Taste*. This took place in an atmosphere of almost universal ignorance, in which very few people had much idea of what a genuine object ought to look like, which circumstance was behind Hans Tietze's remark that a forgery seldom looks anything like the real thing. Some 19th-century forgeries, such as the 'Billies and Charlies'*, were so crude as to appear to be some kind of joke today, but they were taken quite seriously at the time by many.

The present-day collector beginning his career not only has numerous sources of expert information to consult but he is forewarned of the hazard of forgery, and is able to arm himself with knowledge against it. In addition there is the expertise of the great auction houses, and legislation directed towards consumer protection multiplies. The life of the forger, who now has to contend with an increasing amount of recondite scientific apparatus, from X-rays to lasers, becomes increasingly hard. A hundred years ago he had the field to himself in a century in which Barnum made his comment about 'one being born every minute'. It is not surprising therefore that forgeries multiplied and that many of the reproductions were made in full knowledge that they would probably be sold fraudulently. References to both forgeries and reproductions have been made throughout this Dictionary, but the subject is of such importance that it requires further discussions of particular aspects.

It is often difficult to detect a clever forgery made in one's own time. No doubt stylistic discrepancies exist which are due to the artistic idiom of the age, but this idiom is shared by the forger and the person examining his work. In fifty or a hundred years these discrepancies will be obvious to a new generation of connoisseurs, who will wonder at our stupidity in not being able to see them. For this reason many successful 19th-century forgeries are now obvious. There is rarely any difficulty about the dating of 'Watteau figures'*. The early, much valued, 18th-century versions can usually be separated without trouble from 19th-century copies, provided one is acquainted with both types. 20th-century 'Watteau figures' noticeably differ from either. Staffordshire figures are reproduced today from the old moulds, and examples are not uncommon in the shops of the smaller antique dealers. Since the mould is original, attention has to be directed towards the painting, and the weak point is usually the painting of the face, and particularly the mouth. A 20th-century mouth is quite different from one of the 19th century as comparison will show. The mouth is commonly the forger's weak point. It is the part of the Queen's portrait which is studied by bank clerks when examining bank-notes for forgeries. This is where any discrepancies can be noticed without difficulty during the course of normal counting by watching for slight changes in expression.

The 19th-century idiom in drawing, especially English drawing, is comparatively easy to recognize, and however deceptive they may have been at the time, forgeries of Italian *maiolica* with figure subjects are easily detected on this ground alone. Continental forgeries are more deceptive, but the period flavour is never missing. Bastianini's* sculpture was so deceptive at the time that his agent did not think it necessary to claim a *quattrocento* authorship for the work—he allowed the buyer (in one case, a famous museum) to do it. But even these have an obvious 19th-century air today. The same thing is true of 19th-century works copied in the 20th, and the surest way to become immune to most forgeries is to soak up the atmosphere of the period to a point where any discrepancies will affect the mind subconsciously. Then, even where the forgery goes unrecognized consciously, it will produce a feeling of unease which one rarely regrets listening to. It is not a rational method of making a decision, but if the subject is pursued subsequently it will often be found to be right.

The object, whatever it may be, has to be examined in the light of as much knowledge as possible. It has to be remembered that the original maker of a work of art worked in the pervasive spirit of his time. He knew what had passed; he worked within the framework of styles and ornamental *motifs* which were natural to him and his time. Of the future he knew nothing. The forger, working fifty or a hundred years later, is in the same position, but between him and the original artist or craftsman are many diverse styles, changes in materials and methods of working, and changes in attitudes of mind, and no matter how skilful he may be he cannot return to the intellectual position of the earlier man. 18th-century materials, for instance, contained many impurities which the technology of the time did not allow to be removed, and these affected the final result. The 19th-century forger could not obtain the same materials. In fact most of what he could buy was much purer and in some cases of a different composition which could not even have been made a century earlier. He therefore had to be content with reproducing the external appearance as closely as possible with other materials. It is, for instance, impossible to duplicate an 18th-century porcelain body in such a way that it would defy serious scientific analysis, and in most cases one or two minor tests are all that is required. None of the 19th-century reproductions of '*vieux Sèvres*'* are in the least deceptive to anyone acquainted with the genuine object. They could easily deceive someone who knew them only through the glass of a museum showcase or colour illustrations in books. In many cases, however, it is possible to list manufacturing idiosyncrasies which the collector can look for which will help to separate genuine from false.

Enthusiasm, wrote Giovanni Morelli, is not a method of judgement. Unfortunately, faced with an apparent bargain in the shop of a non-specialist, or second-hand dealer the aspiring collector too often relies on enthusiasm rather than knowledge, and this at a time when copies, not usually very good ones, are multiplying in shop windows to beckon in the unsuspecting. It is always worth remembering that these shops are regularly combed by experienced buyers in search of stock for their own shops, and if that glittering *millefiori* paperweight were 19th-century Baccarat and not 20th-century Czechoslovakia one of them would have bought it long before. For the buyer of old paperweights, shops are regularly visited by travelling salesmen with cases full of excellent copies of French paperweights made at the old Bohemian glass centres, which they offer for a few pounds. They are, if sold with a proper description, legitimate merchandise and good value, but with some scratches on the bottom to simulate signs of the wear of years, they could be sold as something more valuable. If the seller has made no claim for the piece he sells, then it cannot be returned as mis-described. The buyer should never make his own attribution unless he is also an expert in his own right.

One could draw a graph of the 19th-century market that would show two rising curves which would be almost parallel, one lagging slightly behind the other. One would mark the sale-room prices of genuine objects, and the other the quantity made and the popularity of reproductions. It would not, for obvious reasons, be possible to draw a third line showing the incidence of forgeries because these were a clandestine operation, but it is not assuming too much to say that the upward curve would follow the same path. The number of forgeries in circulation is largely regulated by demand, and therefore by the price of genuine objects. A forgery is often quite expensive to make, although if it can be sold successfully the profit is high, and the forger, therefore, does not move in on a particular object, or subject, until it is worth while. The buyer of popular collectors' items, therefore, has to become doubly vigilant when the price rises. No one copied fairings* until their value began to be reckoned in hundreds of pounds, but they have been copied within the last ten years or so. Staffordshire figures* were not copied until they had reached the status of a fairly important collectors' item, and the copies today are, for the most part, those objects awarded the highest value. Writing at a time when a piece of medieval enamel has reached a sale-room price of more than a million pounds, it is reasonable to speculate that somewhere or other a modern Solomon Weininger* is working on something of the same kind.

The authors of many deceptive copies cannot be identified, but a number have been identified in one way or another. Usually they are good craftsmen deficient in imagination, and therefore unable to produce anything worth while of their own. Van Meegeren, whose not very deceptive Vermeers nevertheless deceived a number of experts thirty years or so ago, gave as his reason for doing so that critics had ignored his own work and he was determined to show that he was the equal of the old Dutch masters. To anyone who has been able to examine his own work, the reason for the neglect is very clear. The only surprising aspect is that his forgeries should have been accepted in the face of so many indications otherwise.

The 19th-century was notorious for copies made by established factories, such as those of Henri Deux ware* and Palissy's* rustic dishes made by Avisseau* of Tours and Georges Pull* of Paris, for which the makers were sometimes awarded medals at Exhibitions. Pull, whose copies are really deceptive, always impressed his name into the back (or so he claimed),

Enamel portrait on copper of a late 17th-century subject by Samson* of Paris. Work of this quality occurs from time to time. *Sotheby & Co*

A figure of *Avocat* from the *Italian Comedy* after the Meissen figure by J. J. Kändler. Samson's mark has been removed and the depression filled with a paste which has been hardened in the enamelling kiln. *Sotheby & Co*

A Samson rabbit tureen after Chelsea of the red anchor period (1751–1756). It is one of the most sought of Chelsea pieces, with a very high value. This specimen is marked. *Sotheby & Co*

A large porcelain dish painted in Meissen style with *deutsche Blumen* (German flowers); *ozier* moulded border. Made by Carl Thieme*, Potschappel. Meissen original type, c. 1745; Thieme copy, c. 1890. Mark ✗. *Sotheby & Co*

A Samson ruby-backed *famille rose* dish of excellent quality. Although this dish is quite close to its Chinese original the decorator has been unable to make the faces convincingly Chinese. *Sotheby & Co*

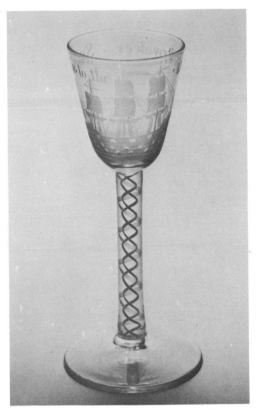

Copy of a Jacobite portrait glass which will meet virtually every test a collector is likely to apply. The portrait is Prince Charles Edward with the rose and thistle. Modern glass. *Sotheby & Co*

Copy of an English 'privateer' glass, a type always in demand, the bowl engraved with a full-rigged ship and an inscription. A genuine glass could be expected to realize at least £800. Modern glass. *Sotheby & Co*

Samson copy of a seated fruit-seller originally copied by Chelsea (c. 1755) from a Meissen model. The facial expression due to the painting is quite different from that of the Chelsea model, but it is otherwise an excellent copy. This is a much sought Chelsea figure. *Sotheby & Co*

A Bow parrot of c. 1756 after a Meissen model, imitated by a small modern pottery at Torquay within recent years. This was the source of a number of deceptive copies of 18th-century English porcelain which came on to the market about twenty years ago, starting with small 'Longton Hall' vases. *Sotheby & Co*

but this has sometimes been covered with a collector's label, and the writer found a Pull dish in the southern French shop of an *antiquaire* with the tell-tale name covered with a price ticket. The proprietor did not question an attribution to Pull, perhaps surprised that an Englishman should even know of Pull's existence, but would he have been so forthcoming had this rather expensive dish been accepted as a genuine Palissy specimen? Edmé Samson always claimed that every piece to come from his factory was marked. But obvious pieces of Samson manufacture are found without the mark, and only a slightly roughened spot on the base where it might have been. Samson's marks are removed with hydrofluoric acid* or fine emery cloth by people wishing to try to sell the object as something better at a higher price, and the profit margin on a successful operation could, in some cases, amount to more than a thousand per cent.

One occasionally sees dishes in an 18th-century Meissen style with a small patch bare of glaze in the middle of the footring, and no mark otherwise. The bare patch may have been the site of the mark of another factory, Carl Thieme*, for example, which has been removed in the hope that the dish can be passed off as the much more expensive Meissen. It was customary at the Meissen factory to score cuts in the glaze across the crossed swords mark to denote that the porcelain had been sold 'in white' to a decorator (*Hausmaler**), and the *Hausmaler*, after decorating a piece, could, and probably did in some cases, remove the original factory mark and the cancellation on the principle of better no mark than one which gives too much information.

A form of faking which started in the early years of the 19th century with the sale of Sèvres* white ware took a slightly different direction later when Cavallo* started to provide simply decorated Worcester* porcelain with opaque ground-colours and floral painting to make something superficially much more attractive to the collector on porcelain that was obviously old Worcester. A Worcester sale of white ware took place when Chamberlain's* and Barr, Flight & Barr merged in the 1840s, and at this time some blanks with scale-blue grounds and white reserved panels, some made by the old factory and some by Chamberlain's, were put on to the market. These could be utilized by enamel painters for coloured decoration in the 18th-century style as soon as the wares of the old Wall factory began to be sought seriously by collectors.

Glass did not suffer in quite the same way. Good pressed glass*, the facets sharpened to look like cut-glass*, was sold for a few years until the popularity of cut-glass waned, but there is no reason to suppose that vast profits were made by this small piece of chicanery. Generally, the technical aspects of glass-making in which advances were so rapid, and the appearance of decorative wares so diverse and colourful in comparison with the glass of earlier times, did not favour the making of forgeries, even though some remarkable reproductions were made, like John Northwood's* copy of the Portland Vase*.

Most forgeries of early English drinking-glasses belong to the 20th century, and such small decorative items from the 19th century as cranberry glass* have been copied to fill an increasing demand. Nevertheless, some glasses were reproduced in the 19th century in circumstances which were not a great deal short of forgery. 'Clutha' glass* was inspired by excavated Roman glass. The latter was collected, but good excavated specimens were very scarce. Fairly deceptive specimens which purported to be Roman glass were made in Italy. Probably most of them copied museum objects, and were museum inspired, but they bore no marks, and could be sold to an unsuspecting tourist as genuine. The writer has been shown a piece of it sold to a collector in England by an English dealer and described as Roman glass; apparently the blind leading the blind. Imitation Roman bronzes of the kind to be found in the Naples Museum, and artificially patinated to look like antiquities, are relatively common in England and are undoubtedly tourist souvenirs from the same kind of source. Whether they were bought originally as Roman or as decorative copies probably depended on the vendor's assessment of his customer's knowledge and gullibility.

The much-sought German enamelled glass of the 16th and 17th centuries, now extremely scarce, was in demand among antique collectors in the 19th century, especially the magnificent *Reichsadlerhumpen*. Very good reproductions were made by a number of German glasshouses which are accused by shapes too regular and a glass too green and free from blemishes. The green of some early glasses is due to impurities, mainly the presence of iron; in reproductions the colour has been added deliberately, and this is usually obvious. The enamelling of these glasses is excellent in quality, but they would only deceive anyone unaccustomed to handling genuine specimens. Much more deceptive are forgeries of late 17th-century *Hausmalerei*, much sought by collectors today. Forgeries of the later *Hausmaler*, such as Kothgasser*, almost certainly belong to the 20th century. The *Ranftbecher** is still made by Czechoslovak glass-houses and decorated in a variety of ways, but the glass is too free from blemishes to be accepted as any older than modern.

Silver was very commonly reproduced in inferior metal during the 19th century, and the process of electro-plating* was often used to increase the deceptive nature of the object. Sheffield plate, electro-plate and British plate* are all examples of silver substitutes; British plate probably comes nearest in its use of marks to being regarded as forgery in some cases. The system of hall-marking, added to stringent penalties for forging gold or silver of any kind, makes the problem much less acute in this area. The revived rococo* period of the 19th century saw a new kind of vandalism which induced silversmiths to emboss fine

Queen Anne plain silver with a mass of flowers and C and S scrolls*, which has ruined both appearance and value. Plain Queen Anne silver appears towards the end of the century as a fashionable style. A good deal of silver in antique styles was made during the 19th century, some legitimate enough as hall-marked reproductions, but others were given a 17th- or 18th-century hall-mark taken from scrap silver or a minor piece considered worth sacrificing. These marks were let in with varying degrees of persuasiveness. Usually the marks were taken from the bottom of an old mug too damaged to repair or sell, and transferred to a new coffee-pot in early 18th-century style.

The vigilance of the trade, led by the British Antique Dealers' Association and the Goldsmith's Company has done a great deal to remove faked silver from the market. The most audacious forgery in precious metal during the 19th century was Rouchomowsky's *Tiara of Saitaphernes*, sold to the Louvre, and other metalwork forgeries include Renaissance bronzes by men like Weininger* at a time when bronzes of this kind were much sought and were realizing high prices in the sale-room. The writer has had the opportunity to examine a large display dish with a deep border of *repoussé* flowers and fruit in the manner of the 17th-century Dutch silversmith, Van Vianen, with a central plaque in bas relief said by the vendor to be by Cellini*, but actually an electrotype after della Porta or Maderno, for which the sum of £15,000 was asked. This was undoubtedly the work of some 19th-century Continental silversmith, possibly in the 1850s, and the vendor was probably repeating an attribution to Cellini dating from that time.

Eighteenth-century furniture is sometimes the subject of forgery; more often it is faked. Plain and simple pieces in the hands of a skilled cabinet-maker can soon be converted into something much more expensive. An appendix as long as this one could be entirely devoted to forgeries of 18th-century Paris furniture without doing more than touch the fringes of the subject. Forgeries apart, as evidence of what could be done there are the splendid reproductions of Dasson* at mid-century, one of which does not look out of place in the Wallace Collection, and for which the buyer paid highly. Boulle marquetry* has continued to be copied since the days of André-Charles Boulle, but the best copies had been made by the time the 19th century was half over.

Eighteenth-century English furniture, especially the neo-classical* furniture of the last quarter of the century, returned to favour in the 1870s, and many specimens were more or less faithfully copied from the originals, and are now old enough to pass for 18th-century examples. They have sufficient of the signs of age to deceive most people, and only the furniture expert is able to say from variations in constructional details to which century a specimen belongs. Wright & Mansfield* made cabinets of this kind, and the craftsmanship is at least as good as that of the earlier makers. A great deal of pseudo 18th

century furniture, however, sought to improve on its models by mixing styles in a kind of *pastiche* and by varying proportions. These mixtures are sometimes referred to as being in the 'Chipplewhite style'* (a mixture of Chippendale and Hepplewhite), like the chair illustrated on page 69. Some pieces are even more incongruous. Ipswich, in Suffolk, is a centre of good reproduction furniture, as well as of some made for more dubious purposes, and the catalogues of local manufacturers are illuminating. It is not suggested that reproduction furniture, especially that which is accompanied by an illustrated catalogue, is made for any but honest purposes. Nor is it the business of the manufacturer to question what the purchaser intends to do with his acquisition. But some objects being made now will be quite difficult for anyone but an expert to separate from genuine antique pieces in fifty or a hundred years time. The reader may object that he is not in the least interested in possibilities a century away, but there is a process known in the trade as 'distressing', which can age a piece fifty years almost overnight. It takes somewhat longer to do this really deceptively, but it is possible to put on a couple of centuries in as many months. One German maker of small 'antique' tables used to lend them to the local sidewalk café for a few weeks to get the right sort of damage.

Collectors always associate damage with age, and forgeries are often deliberately damaged in places where no great harm is done and then carefully repaired. The vendor always calls attention to the repair; it is evidence of age. Chinese forgers break new 'T'ang' horses and repair them, simply because genuine horses are almost invariably excavated in a damaged condition and subsequently repaired. Those horses which are rebuilt from a pile of fragments are often very carefully restored to look like almost perfect figures, except for one obvious repair. The thinking is that if the buyer can see one repair which is obvious, and everything else is concealed sufficiently well to be invisible to normal sight, then he will assume that only this one repair is present, and, needless to say, this is always in an unimportant position.

Lacquer furniture has been popular for three hundred years or so. Craftsmen adept at imitating European lacquer are still working. Oriental lacquer is a different material, and only its external appearance can be imitated in Europe. An Italian forger known to the writer boasted that his lacquer furniture had deceived Italian museums, and in recent years the appearance of large scarlet lacquer cabinets on the market has suggested close examination of anything for which any great age is claimed. Much apparently antique lacquer is modern work, much of it not sold as antique, and it should not deceive anyone acquainted with genuine work. A quick test is to unscrew a lock-plate on an outer door, and look at the colour of the lacquer surface underneath. If it is the same as the rest, the piece is modern. Old pieces fade with exposure to light. Painted furniture in the Adam style is being produced today, as well as in the 1870s, and both varieties can be deceptive.

Good reproduction furniture, and most forgeries, are of excellent quality and craftsmanship. Most of them are a good deal better in materials and workmanship than most modern furniture, and at a reasonable price which takes into account time, materials, and quality, but not an antique value, they are probably much better investments than most 20th-century factory-made designs. A good many years ago, when prices were much lower, the writer asked a well-known restorer of metalwork to cost, on a time and materials basis, what he would charge to reproduce a long-case clock using Tompion's tools and methods, a task which he was quite capable of undertaking. He arrived at a figure which was almost exactly the same as similar genuine clocks were realizing in the London sale-room at the time. It is, of course, possible to produce a forged painting in a matter of hours and get a relatively large sum for it. A piece of furniture or a clock needs many hours of highly skilled work, and most forgers producing minor pieces which fetch little more on the market than a straightforward reproduction of the same thing could probably make more money by working honestly. Showpieces, of course, are a very different proposition, but it is difficult to market showpieces. They have to be provided with a history which will stand up to possibly rigorous investigation, and to provide a false history makes plain the vendor's criminal intent.

There are not many forgeries good enough to deceive someone of knowledge and experience who has a sceptical turn of mind. Most buyers of fakes and forgeries are put into a position where they can deceive themselves. It is not justified, in many cases, to regard a dealer who is occasionally deceived as necessarily culpable. Everyone makes mistakes, and most dealers handle a wide variety of merchandise. They cannot possibly be equally knowledgeable about everything, although they can apply general principles learned over the years which keep costly mistakes to a minimum. Even the major sale-rooms, where great efforts are made to describe everything accurately, occasionally make mistakes, and Sotheby's maintain a black museum of forgeries to assist them in their work, to which I am indebted for the illustrations to this Appendix.

The principal test of honesty of purpose is always the willingness to rectify mistakes if they are made, and a dealer who makes statements about the provenance of an object will not object to putting his attribution into writing in the form of an invoice, nor to adding an approximate date. Invoices, like auctioneers' catalogues, mean what they say, and they should be read carefully. 'In the style of Chippendale' is not the same as 'By Chippendale'. Unless a date is added, 'In the style of' can mean anything from mid-18th century to the present day. If a claim is being made in the Courts for which no invoice exists, an English judge will look at the price paid. If the price of a genuine antique has been charged, then it will be assumed that this is how it was described. In a case of this kind the dealer would also most probably be prosecuted under the Trade Descriptions Act, since the evidence of fraudulent intent is clear.

Most buyers are reasonably knowledgeable and able to buy on their own initiative without danger. If something is found which is known to be underpriced, this will probably be because the dealer either does not know what it is or what it is worth. It would, therefore, be unwise to raise the question of provenance. But here and there dealers will be found who will take advantage of someone who assumes that his knowledge is sounder than it is, to sell forgeries or reproductions by leaving him to make his own attribution. The writer was once consulted by one such buyer who said he had bought a Chelsea tea-service of the red anchor period (1751–1756) and wanted the attribution confirmed. The first piece he produced was an ordinary small bread-and-butter plate, not introduced into English tea-services until the 1820s. This had a large red anchor on the reverse. It was hard-paste porcelain, made in Paris in the 19th century, and, asked whether he had been given an invoice, he produced one for a 'red anchor tea-service', at a price which was four or five times what it was worth but a fraction of what it would have been worth had it been genuine. The dealer, by mentioning neither 'Chelsea' nor a date, could not be touched. Cases of this sort show how essential it is to remember the dictum of Emil Hannover—The surest way to get together a bad collection is to rely on marks.

Those who deal with reputable sources—old-established dealers with a reputation to lose, and members of a well-known trade or professional association—are not taking risks any greater than they would take in any other kind of commercial transaction with reputable people. Indeed, after many years spent in this field in one capacity or another, the writer has come to the conclusion that the standard of honesty shown is far higher than in many other trades and professions. Politics is an easy example. The dealer has to keep the confidence of his clients if he is to stay in legitimate business, and therefore he takes pains to see that they have a square deal. One soon becomes accustomed to judging shops and people.

In one sense the activities of the forger and the maker of reproductions lends spice to the pursuit of antiques, and has a salutary effect on the market. Their existence keeps the buyer on the alert and fosters the pursuit of knowledge which, ultimately, is the principal weapon against their machinations. The buyer of antiques who has served his apprenticeship will be much shrewder, and less likely to make mistakes in people, situations, or things, than one who has not enjoyed these advantages.

Bibliography

THE ART MARKET

Behrman, S. N.   DUVEEN, London, 1962.

Maas, Jeremy   GAMBART: PRINCE OF THE VICTORIAN ART WORLD, Barrie & Jenkins, London, 1975.

Reitlinger, Gerald   THE ECONOMICS OF TASTE, 3 vols, Barrie & Jenkins, London, 1961, 1964, 1966.

Saarinen, Aline   THE PROUD POSSESSORS, Random House, New York, 1958.

Savage, George   THE MARKET IN ART, Institute of Economic Affairs, London, 1969.

Schreiber, Lady Charlotte   JOURNALS, London, 1911.

Taylor, Francis H.   THE TASTE OF ANGELS, London, 1948.

CATALOGUES AND EXHIBITIONS

The Arts Council   THE AGE OF NEO-CLASSICISM, London, 1972.

Beard, C. R.   CATALOGUE OF THE COLLECTION OF MARTINWARE FORMED BY F. J. NETTLEFOLD, 1936

Camden Arts Club Exhibition   THE AESTHETIC MOVEMENT, 1869–1890, London and New York, 1972.

Musée Nationale de l'Art Moderne   LES SOURCES DU XXe SIÈCLE (Les Arts en Europe de 1884–1914 Exhibition catalogue), Paris, 1960

OFFICIAL DESCRIPTIVE CATALOGUE OF THE GREAT EXHIBITION, 3 vols, London, 1851.

Royal Academy of Arts   THE HANDLEY-READ COLLECTION OF VICTORIAN AND EDWARDIAN ART, 1972.

Sèvres Musée Nationale de Céramique   PORCELAINES DE PARIS, 1800–1850

William Morris Gallery, Walthamstow   A. H. MACKMURDO AND THE CENTURY GUILD COLLECTION, 1976.

William Morris Gallery, Walthamstow   THE MORRIS COLLECTION, 1969.

Worcester Royal Porcelain Company, London   ROYAL WORCESTER VICTORIAN PORCELAIN SUMMER EXHIBITION, 1961.

Victoria and Albert Museum, London   MARBLE HALLS: VICTORIAN SECULAR BUILDINGS, John Physick and Michael Darby, 1973.

CERAMICS, GENERAL

Cox, Warren E.   POTTERY AND PORCELAIN, Crown, New York, 1945.

Hannover, Emil   POTTERY AND PORCELAIN, Benn, London, 1925.

Leach, Bernard   A POTTER'S BOOK, London, 1940.

Moore, M. Hudson	THE OLD CHINA BOOK, New York, 1903.
Savage, George and Newman, Harold	A DICTIONARY OF CERAMICS, Thames & Hudson, London, 1974.

CERAMICS, AMERICAN

Barber, E. A.	POTTERY AND PORCELAIN IN THE UNITED STATES, G. P. Putnam & Sons, New York, 1893.
Barber, E. A.	MARKS OF AMERICAN POTTERS, Philadelphia, 1904.
Collard, Elizabeth	NINETEENTH CENTURY POTTERY AND PORCELAIN IN CANADA, McGill University Press, Montreal, 1967.
Elliott, Charles W.	POTTERY & PORCELAIN—THE PHILADELPHIA CENTENNIAL EXPOSITION OF 1876, D. Appleton Co., New York, 1878.
Hawes, Lloyd E.	THE DEDHAM POTTERY, Dedham, Mass., 1969.
Henzke, Lucile	AMERICAN ART POTTERY, Camden, N.J., 1970.
Peck, Herbert	THE BOOK OF ROOKWOOD POTTERY, New York, 1968.
Purviance, L. & E. and Schneider, N.	ZANESVILLE ART POTTERY IN COLOUR, Leon, Iowa, 1969.
Ramsey, John	AMERICAN POTTERY AND PORCELAIN, Hale, Cushman & Flint, New York, 1939.
Spargo, John	POTTERY AND POTTERS OF BENNINGTON, Houghton Mifflin, Boston, 1926.

CERAMICS, CONTINENTAL

Alfassa and Guérin	PORCELAINE FRANÇAISE, Paris, 1932.
Berling, K.	FESTSCHRIFT DER KÖNIGLICHE SÄCHSISCHE PORZELLANMANUFAKTUR MEISSEN, 1710–1910, Leipzig, 1910 (English translation: FESTIVE PUBLICATION COMMEMORATING THE 200TH JUBILEE OF THE OLDEST EUROPEAN PORCELAIN FACTORY, Meissen, 1911).
Dauterman, C. C.	SÈVRES, Studio Vista, London, 1971.
Ernould-Gandouet, Marielle	LA CÉRAMIQUE EN FRANCE EN XIXE SIÈCLE, Grund, Paris, 1969.
Giacometti, J.	FRENCH FAÏENCE, Fribourg, 1963 and Boston.
Graul, R. and Kurzwelly, A.	ALT-THÜRINGER PORZELLAN, Leipzig, 1900.
Lane, Arthur	ITALIAN PORCELAIN, Faber & Faber, London, 1951.
Meyer, H.	BÖHMISCHES PORZELLAN UND STEINGUT, Leipzig, 1927.
Pazaurek, G.	STEINGUT: FORMGEBUNG UND GESCHICHTE, Stuttgart, 1927.
Poche, Emmanuel	BOHEMIAN PORCELAIN, Artia, London.
Ross, Marvin C.	RUSSIAN PORCELAIN, University of Oklahoma Press, 1968.

| Stazzi, Francesco | ITALIAN PORCELAIN, Weidenfeld & Nicolson, London, 1967. |
| Verlet, Grandjean and Brunot | SÈVRES, Paris, 1953. |

CERAMICS, ENGLISH

Ball, A.	PRICE GUIDE TO POT LIDS AND OTHER UNDERGLAZE PRINTS ON POTTERY, The Antique Collectors' Club, Woodbridge.
Ball, R. C.	TYNESIDE POTTERY, Studio Vista, London, 1971.
Balston, Thomas	STAFFORDSHIRE PORTRAIT FIGURES, Faber & Faber, London, 1958.
Bemford, Joan	ROYAL WORCESTER MODELS OF RONALD VAN RUYCKEVELT, Worcester Royal Porcelain Co.
Barnard, Harry	CHATS ON WEDGWOOD WARE, London, 1934.
Barnard, Julian	VICTORIAN CERAMIC TILES, Studio Vista, London, 1972.
Barrett, F. A.	CAUGHLEY AND COALPORT PORCELAIN, London.
Bemrose, Geoffrey	NINETEENTH CENTURY POTTERY & PORCELAIN, Faber & Faber, London, 1952.
Binns, R. W.	A CENTURY OF POTTING IN THE CITY OF WORCESTER, Worcester, 1863.
Blacker, J. E.	THE ABC OF NINETEENTH CENTURY POTTERY AND PORCELAIN, Stanley Paul & Co., London, 1922.
Bristow, W. S.	VICTORIAN CHINA FAIRINGS, A. & C. Black, London, 1964.
Cannon, T. E.	OLD SPODE, London.
Clarke, H. G.	UNDERGLAZE COLOUR PICTURE PRINTS ON STAFFORDSHIRE POTTERY, London, 1955.
Coysh, A. W.	BLUE AND WHITE TRANSFER WARE 1780–1840, David & Charles, Newton Abbott, 1970.
Des Fontaines, J. K.	WEDGWOOD 1880 ILLUSTRATED BOOK OF SHAPES, Wedgwood Society, London, 1971.
Des Fontaines, Una	WEDGWOOD FAIRYLAND LUSTRE, Sotheby-Parke Bernet Publications, London and New York, 1976.
Digby, T. Wingfield	THE WORK OF THE MODERN POTTER IN ENGLAND, London, 1952.
Eyles, Desmond	ROYAL DOULTON 1805–1965, Hutchinson, London, 1965.
Fleming, J. A.	SCOTTISH POTTERY, Jackson & Co., Glasgow, 1923.
Godden, G. A.	VICTORIAN PORCELAIN, Herbert Jenkins, London, 1961.
Godden, G. A.	ENCYCLOPEDIA OF BRITISH POTTERY & PORCELAIN MARKS, 2 vols, Herbert Jenkins, London, 1964.
Godden, G. A.	MINTON POTTERY & PORCELAIN OF THE FIRST PERIOD, Barrie & Jenkins, London, and Praeger, New York, 1968.

Godden, G. A.	AN ILLUSTRATED ENCYCLOPEDIA OF BRITISH POTTERY AND PORCELAIN, Herbert Jenkins, London, 1968.
Godden, G. A.	COALPORT & COALBROOKDALE PORCELAIN, Barrie & Jenkins, London, and Praeger, New York, 1970.
Godden, G. A.	BRITISH POTTERY, Barrie & Jenkins, London, 1974.
Graham, John Meredith and Wedgwood, Hensleigh	WEDGWOOD, Brooklyn Museum, New York, 1948.
Grant, William and Clayton-Stamm, M. D. E.	WILLIAM DE MORGAN, Studio Vista, London, 1969.
Haggar, R. G.	STAFFORDSHIRE CHIMNEY ORNAMENTS, Phoenix House, London, 1955.
Haggar, R. G.	ENGLISH COUNTRY POTTERY, London, 1950.
Haggar, R. G. and Mankowitz, W.	CONCISE ENCYCLOPEDIA OF BRITISH POTTERY AND PORCELAIN, Deutsch, London, 1957.
Hall, John	STAFFORDSHIRE PORTRAIT FIGURES, Letts & Co., London, 1972.
Haslem, J.	THE OLD DERBY CHINA FACTORY, 1876.
Hayden, Arthur	SPODE AND HIS SUCCESSORS, London, 1925.
Hobson, R. L.	WORCESTER PORCELAIN, Quaritch, London, 1910.
Hughes, G. B.	VICTORIAN POTTERY AND PORCELAIN, Country Life, London, 1959.
Hurlbutt, Frank	OLD DERBY PORCELAIN AND ITS ARTIST-WORKMEN, London, 1925.
Jewitt, Llewellyn	CERAMIC ART OF GREAT BRITAIN, London, 1878.
John, W. D.	NANTGARW PORCELAIN, Newport, Mon., 1948.
John, W. D. and Baker, W.	OLD ENGLISH LUSTRE POTTERY, Ceramic Book Co., Newport, Mon., 1951.
Kelly, Alison	THE STORY OF WEDGWOOD, Faber & Faber, London, 1962.
Lewis, Griselda	A COLLECTOR'S HISTORY OF BRITISH POTTERY, 2 ed., Barrie & Jenkins, London, 1978.
Lockett, Terence A.	DAVENPORT POTTERY AND PORCELAIN 1784–1887, David & Charles, Newton Abbot, 1972.
Lomax, A.	ROYAL LANCASTRIAN POTTERY 1900–1938, Published by the author, 1957.
Meager, K. S.	SWANSEA AND NANTGARW POTTERIES, Swansea, 1948.
Messenger, Michael	SHROPSHIRE POTTERY AND PORCELAIN, Shrewsbury Museum, 1974.
Nance, E. Morton	THE POTTERY AND PORCELAIN OF SWANSEA AND NANTGARW, London, 1945.
Pugh, P. D. Gordon	STAFFORDSHIRE PORTRAIT FIGURES, Barrie & Jenkins, London, 1970.
Rhead, G. E. W.	THE EARTHENWARE COLLECTOR, London, 1920.

393

Rice, D.	THE ILLUSTRATED GUIDE TO ROCKINGHAM PORCELAIN, Barrie & Jenkins, London, and Praeger, New York, 1970.
Savage, George and Doughty, Dorothy	THE AMERICAN BIRDS OF DOROTHY DOUGHTY, Worcester Royal Porcelain Co., New York, 1965.
Savage, George	THE BRITISH BIRDS OF DOROTHY DOUGHTY, Worcester Royal Porcelain Co., Worcester, 1967.
Savage, George	THE STORY OF ROYAL WORCESTER AND THE DYSON PERRINS MUSEUM, Pitkin, London, 1968.
Shaw, J.	THE POTTERIES OF SUNDERLAND AND DISTRICT, Sunderland Library, 1961.
Shinn, Charles and David	THE ILLUSTRATED GUIDE TO VICTORIAN PARIAN CHINA, Barrie & Jenkins, London, 1971.
Twitchett, John and Bailey, Betty	ROYAL CROWN DERBY, Barrie & Jenkins, London, 1976.
Twitchett, John	DERBY PORCELAIN, Barrie & Jenkins, London [for publication 1979].
Wakefield, Hugh	VICTORIAN POTTERY, Herbert Jenkins, London, 1962.
Wentworth-Sheilds, Peter and Johnson, Kay	CLARICE CLIFF, L'Odéon, London, 1976.
Whiter, Leonard	SPODE: A HISTORY OF THE FAMILY, FACTORY, AND WARES, 1733 TO 1833, Barrie & Jenkins, London, and Praeger, New York, 1970.
Williams, S. B.	ANTIQUE BLUE AND WHITE SPODE, London, 1948.
Williams-Wood, C.	STAFFORDSHIRE POT-LIDS, Faber & Faber, London, 1972.

EXHIBITIONS

Ffrench, Yvonne	THE GREAT EXHIBITION, 1851, Harvill Press, London.
Gibbs Smith, G. H.	THE GREAT EXHIBITION, 1851, HMSO, London, 1950.
Hobhouse, C.	1851 AND THE CRYSTAL PALACE, London, 1937.

ILLUSTRATED EXHIBITOR, THE, London, 1851. Journal devoted to the Great Exhibition.

REPORT ON THE UNIVERSAL EXHIBITION, PARIS, 1855, London, 1855.

Wyatt, Digby M.	INDUSTRIAL ART OF THE 19TH CENTURY AT THE GREAT EXHIBITION, London, 1851–53.

CLOCKS, MUSICAL BOXES ETC.

Allix, P. and Bonnest, P.	CARRIAGE CLOCKS, Antique Collectors' Club, Woodbridge, 1974.
Clark, John E. T.	MUSICAL BOXES, Allen & Unwin, London, 1961.
Dreppard, Carl W.	AMERICAN CLOCKS AND CLOCKMAKERS, Branford, Mass., 1957.
Hawkins, J. B.	THOMAS COLE AND VICTORIAN CLOCKMAKERS, Antique Collectors' Club, Woodbridge, 1976.

Hume, A. J. W.	COLLECTING MUSICAL BOXES, Allen & Unwin, London, 1967.
Lloyd, H. Alan	THE COLLECTORS' DICTIONARY OF CLOCKS, Country Life, London, 1970.
Nutting, Wallace, Ord-Hume, A. W. J. G.	THE CLOCK BOOK, Framingham, Mass., 1924.
Ord-Hume, A. W. J. G.	CLOCKWORK MUSIC, Allen & Unwin, London, 1973.
Palmer, B.	BOOK OF AMERICAN CLOCKS, New York and London, 1950.
Palmer, B.	TREASURY OF AMERICAN CLOCKS, New York and London, 1967.
Rayner-Collard, F. H.	SKELETON CLOCKS, N. A. G. Press, London, 1969.
Roberts, Kenneth	ELI TERRY AND THE CONNECTICUT SHELF-CLOCK, Ken Roberts Publishing Co., Boston, 1973.
Webb, Graham	THE CYLINDER MUSICAL BOX HANDBOOK, London, 1968.
Willard, J. W.	SIMON WILLARD, INVENTOR AND CLOCKMAKER, E. O. Cockayne, Boston, 1911.

DESIGN

Ackerman. R.	REPOSITORY OF THE ARTS 1809–1829.
Hope, Thomas	HOUSEHOLD FURNITURE AND INTERIOR DECORATION, 1807.
Percier, Charles and Fontaine, G-F-L.	RECUEIL DE DECORATION INTÉRIEURE, Paris, 1811.
Pugin, A. W. N.	DESIGNS FOR IRON AND BRASS WORK, Ackerman & Co., London, 1836.
Robinson, J. C.	TREASURY OF ORNAMENTAL ART, London, 1857.

FURNITURE

Andrews, E. D. & F.	SHAKER FURNITURE, Macmillan, New York, 1937.
Aslin, Elizabeth	ENGLISH 19TH CENTURY FURNITURE, Faber & Faber, London.
Burroughs, P. H.	SOUTHERN ANTIQUES, Richmond, Va., 1937.
Butler, Joseph	AMERICAN ANTIQUES, 1800–1900, New York, 1965.
Cornelius, C. O.	FURNITURE MASTERPIECES OF DUNCAN PHYFE, Doubleday, Page & Co., New York, 1922.
De Voe, Shirley, S.	ENGLISH PAPIER MÂCHÉ, Barrie & Jenkins, London, 1971.
Down, Joseph	AMERICAN FURNITURE, New York, 1952.
Gloag, John	A SOCIAL HISTORY OF FURNITURE DESIGN, Cassell, London, 1966.
Harris, John	REGENCY FURNITURE DESIGN FROM CONTEMPORARY SOURCE-BOOKS, 1803–1821, London, 1961, and Levittown, N.Y.
Hayward, Helena	WORLD FURNITURE, Paul Hamlyn, London, 1965.

| Honour, Hugh | CABINET-MAKERS AND FURNITURE DESIGNERS, Weidenfeld & Nicolson, London, 1969. |

Honour, Hugh — CABINET-MAKERS AND FURNITURE DESIGNERS, Weidenfeld & Nicolson, London, 1969.

Hope, Thomas — HOUSEHOLD FURNITURE AND INTERIOR DESIGN, 1st ed. 1807. Reprint Tiranti, London, 1970.

Jervis, Simon — VICTORIAN FURNITURE, Ward Lock, London, 1968.

Jourdain, Margaret — REGENCY FURNITURE, London, 1935.

Moody, Ella — MODERN FURNITURE, Dutton Vista, 1966.

Otto, Colin Jackson — AMERICAN FURNITURE OF THE 19TH CENTURY, New York, 1965.

Symons, R. and Whineray, B. — VICTORIAN FURNITURE, Country Life, London, 1967.

GLASS

Amaya, Mario — TIFFANY GLASS, Studio Vista, London, 1968.

Barber, E. A. — AMERICAN GLASSWARE, OLD AND NEW, Patterson, White Co., Pa., 1900.

Bergstrom, E. — OLD GLASS PAPERWEIGHTS, London, 1947.

Chipman, F. W. — THE ROMANCE OF OLD SANDWICH GLASS, The Sandwich Publishing Co., Sandwich, Mass., 1937.

Cloak, Evelyn Campbell — GLASS PAPERWEIGHTS, Studio Vista, London, 1969.

Davis, Derek and Middlemas, Keith — COLOURED GLASS, Herbert Jenkins, London, 1968.

Elville, E. M. — THE COLLECTORS' DICTIONARY OF GLASS, Country Life, London, 1961.

Elvin, J. S. — AMERICAN GLASS PAPERWEIGHTS, New York, 1961.

Grover, R. & L. — EUROPEAN ART GLASS, Tuttle, Rutland, Vt., 1970.

Grover, R. & L. — ART GLASS, Tuttle, Rutland, Vt., 1967.

Guttery, D. R. — FROM BROAD GLASS TO CUT CRYSTAL (STOURBRIDGE), Leonard Hill, London, 1956.

Harro, Ernest — MODERNE GLÄSER, Darmstadt.

Haynes, D. E. — THE PORTLAND VASE, British Museum, London, 1964.

Hettes, Karel — GLASS IN CZECHOSLOVAKIA, Prague, 1958.

Hollister, Paul — ENCYCLOPEDIA OF GLASS PAPERWEIGHTS, Crown, New York, 1969.

Imbert, R. and Amic, Y. — LE PRESS-PAPIER FRANÇAIS, Paris, 1948.

Jackson, P. — ANTIQUE FRENCH PAPERWEIGHTS, New York, 1957.

Janneau, Guillaume — MODERN GLASS, Studio, London, 1931.

Larsen, A., Rismøller, P. and Schluter, M. — DANSK GLAS 1825–1925, Copenhagen, 1963.

Lee, Ruth Webb	EARLY AMERICAN PRESSED GLASS, New York, 1931.
Lee, Ruth Webb	NINETEENTH CENTURY ART GLASS, New York.
McKearin, H. & G. S.	AMERICAN GLASS, New York, 1941.
Moore, H. Hudson	OLD GLASS, EUROPEAN AND AMERICAN, Fredk. A. Stokes Inc., New York, 1924.
Northwood, John II	JOHN NORTHWOOD, Stourbridge, 1938.
O'Looney, Betty	VICTORIAN GLASS, Victoria and Albert Museum, London, 1972.
Pazaurek, Gustav	GLÄSER DER EMPIRE UND BIEDERMEIERZEIT, Leipzig, 1923.
Pellatt, Apsley	CURIOSITIES OF GLASS, London, 1897.
Plaut, J. S.	STEUBEN GLASS, New York, 1948.
Polak, Ada	MODERN GLASS, Faber & Faber, London, 1962.
Rabon, Josef	MODERN BOHEMIAN GLASS, London, 1964.
Revi, A. C.	NINETEENTH CENTURY GLASS: ITS GENESIS AND DEVELOPMENT, Nelson, New York, 1959.
Revi, A. C.	AMERICAN ART NOUVEAU GLASS, Camden, N. J., 1968.
Savage, George	GLASS, Weidenfeld & Nicolson, London, 1964.
Savage, George	GLASS & GLASSWARE, Octopus Books, London, 1973.
Schmidt, Robert	100 JAHRE ÖSTERREICHISCHER GLAS KUNST; LOBMEYR, 1823–1923, Vienna, 1923.
Steenberg, Elisa	MODERN SWEDISH GLASS, Lindqvist, Stockholm, 1949.
Van Rousselaer	EARLY AMERICAN BOTTLES & FLASKS, Transcript Printing Co., Peterboro, N.H., 1926.
Wakefield, Hugh	19TH CENTURY BRITISH GLASS, Faber & Faber, London, 1961.
Watkins, L. W.	AMERICAN GLASS AND GLASSMAKING, New York, 1950.
Watkins, L. W.	CAMBRIDGE GLASSWARE 1818–1878, Marshall Jones Co. Inc., Boston, 1930.
Weiss, Gustav	THE BOOK OF GLASS, Barrie & Jenkins, London, 1971.

WHISTLER, LAURENCE, THE ENGRAVED GLASS OF, London, 1952.

Wilson, K. H.	NEW ENGLAND GLASS AND GLASSMAKING, New York, 1972.

METALWORK

AMERICAN SILVER: A HISTORY OF STYLE, 1600–1900, Praeger, New York, 1971.

Bainbridge, Charles	PETER CARL FABERGÉ, Batsford, London, 1949.
Buhler, Kathryn C.	AMERICAN SILVER, New York, 1950.
Bury, Shirley	VICTORIAN ELECTROPLATE, Hamlyn, London, 1971.

Calder, C. K.	RHODE ISLAND PEWTERERS AND THEIR WORK, Johnson & Co., Providence, R.I., 1924.
Cellini, Benvenuto	TREATISE ON GOLDSMITHING (translated by C. R. Ashbee), London, 1898. Dover, New York, 1966.
Cooper, Jeremy	NINETEENTH CENTURY ROMANTIC BRONZES, David & Charles, Newton Abbot, 1974.
Ensko, S. S. C.	AMERICAN SILVERSMITHS AND THEIR MARKS, Privately printed, 1927, 1937, 1948.
Fouquet, Jean (redacteur)	BIJOUX ET ORFÈVRERIE, L'Art International d'Aujourdhui, Paris, 1929.
Freeman, L. G.	VICTORIAN SILVER, Century House, New York, 1967.
Goss, E. H.	THE LIFE OF COLONEL PAUL REVERE, Boston, 1892.
Harris, I.	PRICE-GUIDE TO VICTORIAN SILVER, Antique Collectors' Club, Woodbridge, 1971.
Haskins, J. B.	AUSTRALIAN SILVER, 1800–1900, Antique Collectors' Club, Woodbridge, 1971.
Hiatt, N. W. and L. F.	THE SILVERSMITHS OF KENTUCKY, 1785–1850, Louisville, Ky., 1954.
Honour, Hugh	GOLDSMITHS & SILVERSMITHS, Weidenfeld & Nicolson, London, 1971.
Hughes, Graham	MODERN SILVER THROUGHOUT THE WORLD, 1880–1963, Studio Vista, London, 1967.
Jacob, Lt. Col. S. S. and Handley, Surg. Maj. T.	JEYPORE ENAMELS, London, 1886.
Kerfoot, J. B.	AMERICAN PEWTER, Houghton Mifflin, Boston, 1925.
Laughlin, L. I.	PEWTER IN AMERICA, 2 vols, Boston, 1940.
Lindsay, J. Seymour	IRON & BRASS IMPLEMENTS IN THE ENGLISH AND AMERICAN HOME, The Medici Society of America, 1927.
Niclausse, J. J.	THOMIRE: FONDEUR-CISELEUR, Paris, 1947.
Peal, Christopher A.	BRITISH PEWTER AND BRITANNIA METAL, John Gifford, London, 1971.
Penzer, H. M.	PAUL STORR, Batsford, London, and Boston Books, Boston, 1954.
Peterson, Sigurd	MODERN SWEDISH SILVER, Stockholm, 1951.
Snowman, A. Kenneth	THE ART OF CARL FABERGÉ, Faber & Faber, London, 1953.
Turner, Noel D.	AMERICAN SILVER FLATWARE, 1837–1910, A. S. Barnes & Co., New York, 1971.
Wardle, Patricia	VICTORIAN SILVER AND SILVERPLATE, Herbert Jenkins, London, 1963.
Wills, Geoffrey	COLLECTING COPPER AND BRASS, Mayflower Handbooks, London, 1970.

MISCELLANEOUS

Ayres, James	AMERICAN ANTIQUES, Orbis Publishing Co., London.
Ayres, James	BRITISH FOLK ART, Barrie & Jenkins, London, 1977.

Entwistle, E. A.	A LITERARY HISTORY OF WALLPAPER, Batsford, London.
Howe, Bea	ANTIQUES FROM THE VICTORIAN HOME, Batsford, London, 1973.
King, Constance Eileen	THE PRICE GUIDE TO DOLLS: ANTIQUE AND MODERN, Antique Collectors' Club, Woodbridge, Suffolk, 1977.
Kuhn, Walt	TWENTY FIVE YEARS AFTER; *the story of the Armory Show*, New York, 1938.
Kock, Robert	LOUIS C. TIFFANY'S GLASS, BRONZES, AND LAMPS: A COLLECTORS' GUIDE, Crown, New York, 1971.
McClinton, K. M.	A HANDBOOK OF POPULAR ANTIQUES, New York, 1947.
Mayr-Ofen, F.	LUDWIG II OF BAVARIA, Cobden-Sanderson, London.
Müther, Richard	A HISTORY OF MODERN PAINTING, 4 vols, London and New York, 1907.
Norbury, John	THE WORLD OF VICTORIANA, Hamlyn, London, 1972.
Pinto, Edward & Eva	TUNBRIDGE AND SCOTTISH SOUVENIR WOOD WARE, Bell, London, 1970.
Pinto, Edward	TREEN AND OTHER WOODEN BYGONES, Bell, London, 1969.
Scott, A. & C.	TOBACCO AND THE COLLECTOR, London, 1966.
Tames, Richard	WILLIAM MORRIS (1834–1896), Shire Publications, Aylesbury, 1972.
Waring, Janet	EARLY AMERICAN STENCILLING, Dover Publications, New York.

SCULPTURE

Gunnis, Rupert	DICTIONARY OF BRITISH SCULPTORS—1650–1851, Abbey Library, London.
Horswell, Jane	THE BRONZE SCULPTURE OF LES ANIMALIERS, Antique Collectors' Club, Woodbridge, 1971.
Handley-Read, Charles	BRITISH SCULPTURE, 1850–1914, Fine Art Society, London, 1968.
Mackay, J.	LES ANIMALIERS, Ward Lock, London, 1971.
Saulnier, G.	ANTOINE-LOUIS BARYE, London, 1926.
Savage, George	CONCISE HISTORY OF BRONZES, Thames & Hudson, London, 1969.

STYLE

Amaya, Mario	ART NOUVEAU, Studio Vista, London, 1966.
	THE ARTS AND CRAFTS MOVEMENT IN AMERICA, 1896–1916, Princeton University and the Art Institute of Chicago, 1973.
Aslin, E.	THE AESTHETIC MOVEMENT, London, 1969.
Battersby, Martin	ART NOUVEAU, Hamlyn, London, 1969
Battersby, Martin	THE DECORATIVE TWENTIES, Studio Vista, London, 1971.

Battersby, Martin	THE DECORATIVE THIRTIES, Studio Vista, London, 1971
Battersby, Martin	THE WORLD OF ART NOUVEAU, Arlington, London, 1968.
Bliss, D. P.	CHARLES RENNIE MACKINTOSH AND THE GLASGOW SCHOOL OF ART, Glasgow School of Art, 1961.
Boe, A.	FROM GOTHIC REVIVAL TO FUNCTIONAL FORM, Oslo and Oxford, 1957 and New York, 1958.
Brunhammer, Yvonne	THE NINETEEN TWENTIES, Hamlyn, London, 1969.
Clark, Sir Kenneth	THE GOTHIC REVIVAL, Harmondsworth, and Baltimore, Md., 1964.
Crane, Walter	THE BASES OF DESIGN, Bell, London, 1898.
Deshairs, Louis	MODERN FRENCH DECORATIVE ART, Paris and London, 1929.
Dresser, Christopher	PRINCIPLES OF DESIGN, London, 1871.
Flaxman, John	LECTURES ON SCULPTURE, London (several editions).
Grant, Ian (ed.)	GREAT INTERIORS, Weidenfeld & Nicolson, London, and Dutton, New York, 1967.
Henderson, W. O.	THE INDUSTRIALIZATION OF EUROPE, 1780–1914, Thames & Hudson, London, 1969.
Hillier, Bevis	THE WORLD OF ART DECO, Studio Vista, London, 1971.
Hillier, Bevis	ART DECO, New York, 1969.
Kohle, Kathleen Morrison	MODERN FRENCH DECORATION, G. P. Putnam & Sons, New York, 1930.
Komody, P. G.	THE ART OF WALTER CRANE, London, 1902.
Lethaby, W. R.	PHILIP WEBB AND HIS WORK, London, 1935.
MacLeod, Robert	CHARLES RENNIE MACKINTOSH, Country Life, London, 1968.
Madsen, S. T.	SOURCES OF ART NOUVEAU, New York, 1952.
Madsen, S. T.	THE SOURCES OF ART NOUVEAU, London, 1967
Madsen S. T.	ART NOUVEAU, Weidenfeld & Nicolson, London, and McGraw Hill, New York, 1967.
Male, Emile	THE GOTHIC IMAGE, Collins, Fontana Library, London, 1961.
Maudell, R. B.	PARIS, 1900: THE GREAT WORLD'S FAIR, University of Toronto Press, 1967.
Mucha, Jan	ALPHONSE MUCHA, HIS LIFE AND WORK, Heinemann, London, 1966.
Naylor, Gillian	THE ARTS AND CRAFTS MOVEMENT, Studio Books, London, 1971.
Naylor, Gillian	THE BAUHAUS, Studio Vista, London, 1968
Novotny, F.	TOULOUSE-LAUTREC, Phaidon Press, London, 1969.
Overy, Paul	DE STIJL, Studio Vista, London, 1969.

Pevsner, Nikolaus   PIONEERS OF MODERN DESIGN, Harmondsworth, 1964.

Read, Brian   ART NOUVEAU AND ALPHONSE MUCHA, Victoria and Albert Museum, London, 1967.

Savage, George   A CONCISE HISTORY OF INTERIOR DECORATION, Thames & Hudson, London, 1966.

Scheidig, Walter   WEIMAR CRAFTS OF THE BAUHAUS, Studio Vista, London, 1968.

Schmutzler, Robert   ART NOUVEAU, Thames & Hudson, London, 1964.

Spencer, Robin   THE AESTHETIC MOVEMENT, Studio Vista, London, and Dutton, New York, 1972.

STYLES DE FRANCE (Furniture and Interiors from 1610 to 1920), Les Publications de France, Paris, 1969.

Tilbrook, A. J.   THE DESIGNS OF ARCHIBALD KNOX FOR LIBERTY & CO, Ornament Press, London, 1976.

Warren, Geoffrey   ART NOUVEAU, Octopus Books, London, 1972.

Waters & Harrison   BURNE-JONES, Barrie & Jenkins, London, 1971.

Watkinson, R.   WILLIAM MORRIS AS A DESIGNER, Studio Vista, London, 1967.